Defect

Detect

macOS
Core Dump Analysis
Accelerated

Version 3.0

Dmitry Vostokov
Software Diagnostics Services

Published by OpenTask, Republic of Ireland

OpenTask books and magazines are available through booksellers and distributors worldwide. For further information or comments, send requests to press@opentask.com.

A CIP catalog record for this book is available from the British Library.

ISBN-l3: 978-1-912636-75-4 (Paperback)

Revision 3.00 (December 2022)

Contents

About the Author

Dmitry Vostokov is an internationally recognized expert, speaker, educator, scientist, inventor, and author. He is the founder of the pattern-oriented software diagnostics, forensics, and prognostics discipline (Systematic Software Diagnostics), and Software Diagnostics Institute (DA+TA: DumpAnalysis.org + TraceAnalysis.org). Vostokov has also authored more than 50 books on software diagnostics, anomaly detection and analysis, software and memory forensics, root cause analysis and problem solving, memory dump analysis, debugging, software trace and log analysis, reverse engineering, and malware analysis. He has over 25 years of experience in software architecture, design, development, and maintenance in various industries, including leadership, technical, and people management roles. Dmitry also founded Syndromatix, Anolog.io, BriteTrace, DiaThings, Logtellect, OpenTask Iterative and Incremental Publishing (OpenTask.com), Software Diagnostics Technology and Services (former Memory Dump Analysis Services) PatternDiagnostics.com, and Software Prognostics. In his spare time, he presents various topics on Debugging.TV and explores Software Narratology, its further development as Narratology of Things and Diagnostics of Things (DoT), Software Pathology, and Quantum Software Diagnostics. His current interest areas are theoretical software diagnostics and its mathematical and computer science foundations, application of formal logic, artificial intelligence, machine learning and data mining to diagnostics and anomaly detection, software diagnostics engineering and diagnostics-driven development, diagnostics workflow and interaction. Recent interest areas also include cloud native computing, security, automation, functional programming, and applications of category theory to software development and big data.

Presentation Slides and Transcript

macOS
Core Dump Analysis
Accelerated

Version 3.0

Dmitry Vostokov
Software Diagnostics Services

Hello, everyone, my name is Dmitry Vostokov, and I teach this training course. The third edition of this course covers the M2 ARM64 platform and LLDB debugger. GDB debugger exercises were removed. If you are interested in GDB and ARM64 there's a Linux course available.

Prerequisites

Basic macOS troubleshooting

LLDB Commands

We use these boxes to introduce LLDB commands used in practice exercises

The prerequisites are hard to define. Some of you have software development experience and some do not. However, one thing is certain: to get most of this training you are expected to have basic troubleshooting experience. Another thing I expect you to be familiar with is hexadecimal notation and that you have seen or can read programming source code in some language, preferably in C. The ability to read assembly language has some advantages but for most parts not necessary for this training. I hope to provide all the necessary explanations in this edition. Windows or, better, Linux memory dump analysis experience may really help here and ease the transition but is not absolutely necessary. If you have attended training or read books Accelerated Windows Memory Dump Analysis or Accelerated Linux Core Dump Analysis, you would find a similar approach here.

Training Goals

- ◉ Review fundamentals

- ◉ Learn how to collect core dumps

- ◉ Learn how to analyze core dumps

Our primary goal is to learn core dump analysis in an accelerated fashion. So first we review absolutely essential fundamentals necessary for core dump analysis. Also, this training is about user process core dump analysis and not about kernel core dump analysis. An additional goal is to leverage Windows or Linux debugging and memory dump analysis experience you may have.

Training Principles

- Talk only about what I can show

- Lots of pictures

- Lots of examples

- Original content

For me, there were many training formats to consider, and I decided that the best way is to concentrate on hands-on exercises. Specifically, for this training, I developed 12 of them, and they utilize the same pattern-oriented approach I used in **Accelerated Windows Memory Dump Analysis** and **Accelerated Linux Core Dump Analysis** training courses.

Schedule Summary

- ⊙ **Day 1**

  - Analysis fundamentals (30 minutes)

  - Core dump collection methods (10 minutes)

  - Core dump analysis (1 hour 20 minutes)

- ⊙ **Day 2**

  - ARM64 disassembly (30 minutes)

  - Core dump analysis (1 hour 30 minutes)

This is a roughly planned schedule. This edition also includes ARM64 disassembly and I discuss it after we do some core dump analysis to have some context and possible "aha" moments.

Part 1: Fundamentals

Now I show you some pictures. We use 64-bit examples because all Mx Macs are 64-bit.

Memory/Kernel/User Space

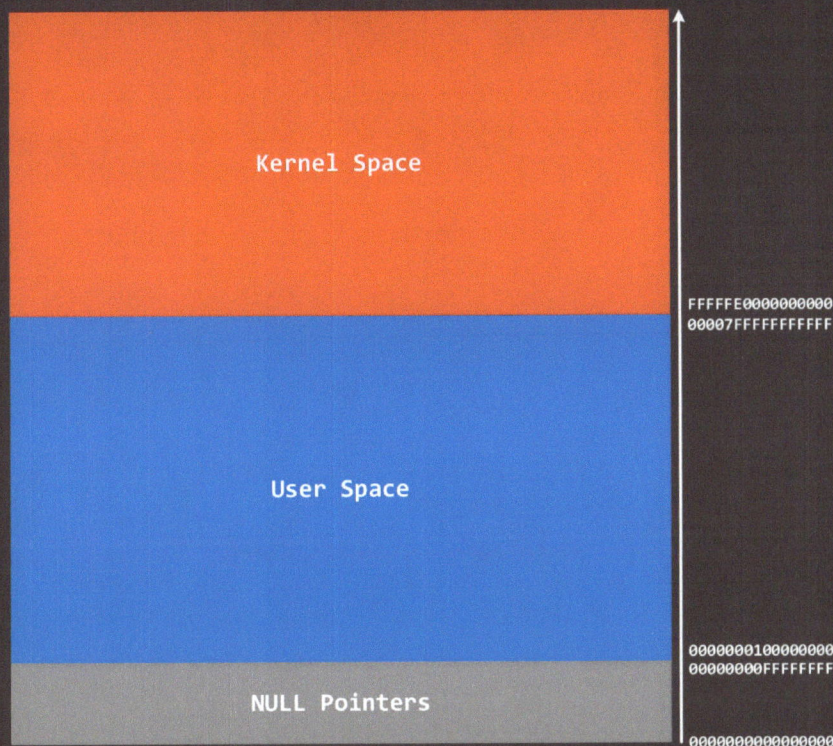

```
                                    FFFFFE0000000000
                                    00007FFFFFFFFFFF



                                    0000000100000000
                                    00000000FFFFFFFF

                                    0000000000000000
```

Kernel Space

User Space

NULL Pointers

© 2022 Software Diagnostics Services

If you are coming from Windows or Linux background, you find fundamentals almost the same. For every process, the macOS memory range is divided into kernel space part, user space part, and 4GB non-accessible part to catch null pointers. This non-accessible region is different from Windows where it is only a few Kb or Linux where it is 64KB on my Debian system. I follow the long tradition to use red color for the kernel and blue color for the user part. Please note that there is a difference between space and mode. Mode is the execution privilege attribute, for example, code running in kernel space has higher execution privilege than code running in user space. However, kernel code can access user space and access data there. We say that such code is running in kernel mode. On the contrary, the application code from user space is running in user mode and because of its lower privilege, it cannot access kernel space. This prevents accidental kernel modifications. Otherwise, you could easily crash your system. I put addresses on the right. This uniform memory space is called process virtual space because it is an abstraction that allows us to analyze core dumps without thinking about how it is all organized in physical memory. When we look at process dumps, we are concerned with virtual space only. In this training, we would only see user space. The picture is conceptually unchanged from Intel Macs and it is consistent with what we see in *spindump* and *vmmap* output.

App/Process/Library

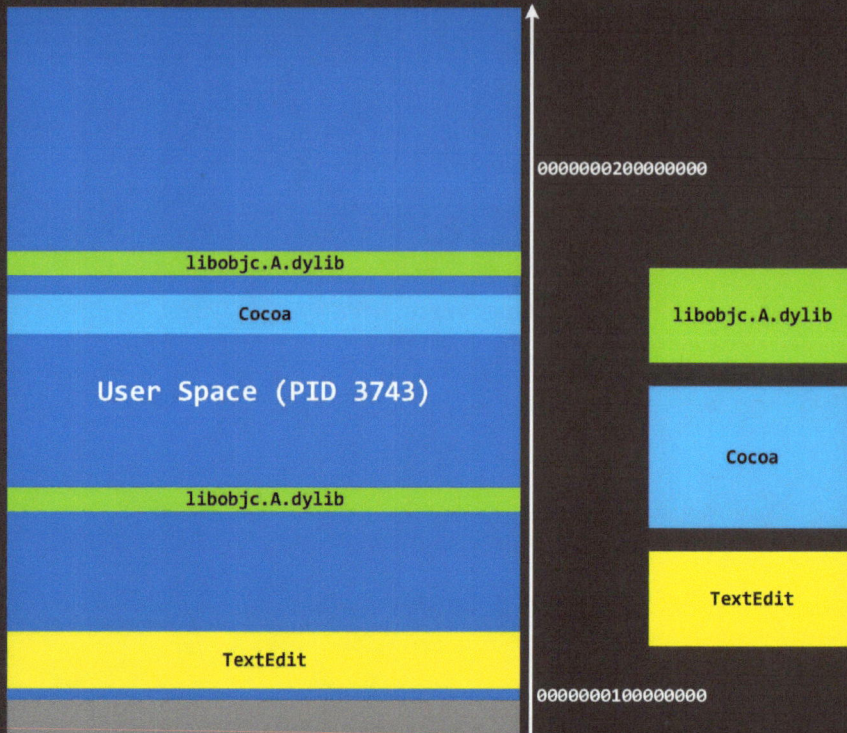

When an app is loaded all its referenced frameworks, and dynamic libraries are mapped to virtual memory space. Different sections of the same file (like code and data) may be mapped into a different portion of memory. In contrast, modules in Windows and shared libraries in Linux are organized sequentially in virtual memory space. A process then is setup for running, and a process ID is assigned to it. If you run another such app, it will have a different virtual memory space.

Process Memory Dump

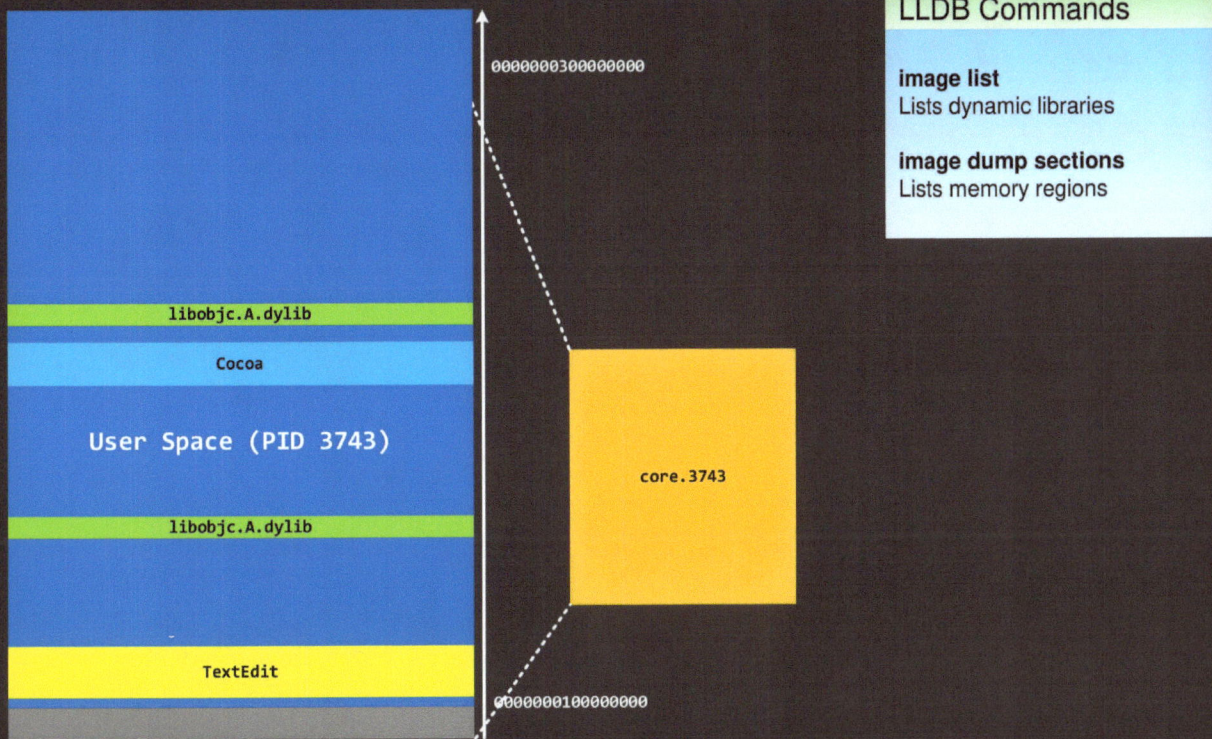

When we save a process core memory dump, a user space portion of the process space is saved without any kernel space stuff. However, we never see such large core dumps unless we have memory leaks. This is because process space has gaps unfilled with code and data. These unallocated parts are not saved in a core dump. However, if some parts were paged out and reside in a page file, they are usually brought back before saving a core dump. On the Mx platform, dumps are about 3GB.

Process Threads

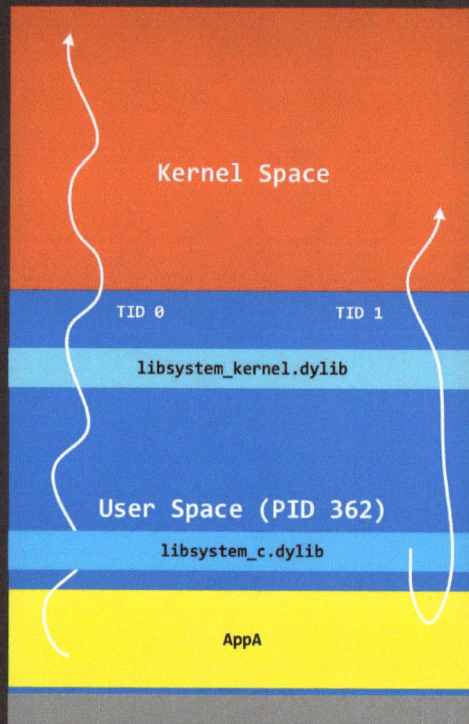

Kernel Space

TID 0   TID 1

libsystem_kernel.dylib

User Space (PID 362)

libsystem_c.dylib

AppA

LLDB Commands

thread list
Lists threads

thread select <n>
Switches between threads

thread backtrace all
Lists stack traces from all threads

© 2022 Software Diagnostics Services

Now we come to another important fundamental concept in macOS core dump analysis: thread. It is basically a unit of execution, and there can be many threads in a given process. Every thread just executes some code and performs various tasks. Every thread has its ID. In this training, we also learn how to navigate between process threads. Note that threads transition to kernel space via the *libsystem_kernel* dynamic library similar to *ntdll* in Windows or the *libc* in Linux. Threads additional to the main thread (POSIX Threads) originate from the *libsystem_c* dynamic library.

Thread Stack Raw Data

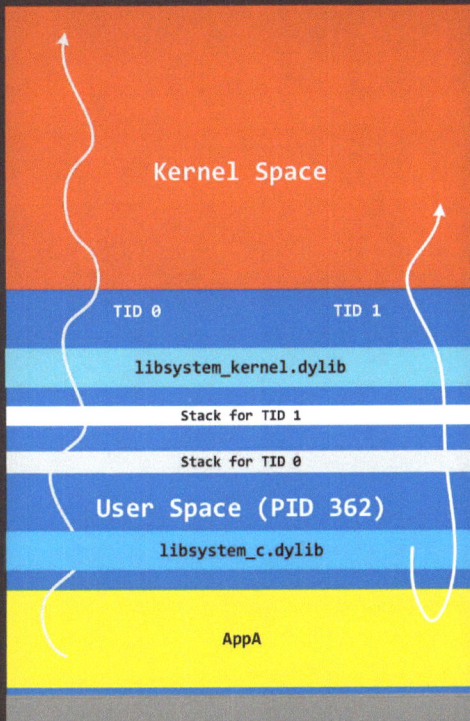

LLDB Commands

x/<n>a <address>
Prints n addresses with corresponding symbol mappings if any

Every thread needs a temporary memory region to store its execution history and temporary data. This region is called a thread stack. Please note that the stack region is just any other memory region, and you can use any LLDB data dumping commands there. We will also learn how to get thread stack region address range. Examining raw stack data can give some hints about the past app behavior: the so-called **Execution Residue** pattern.

Thread Stack Trace

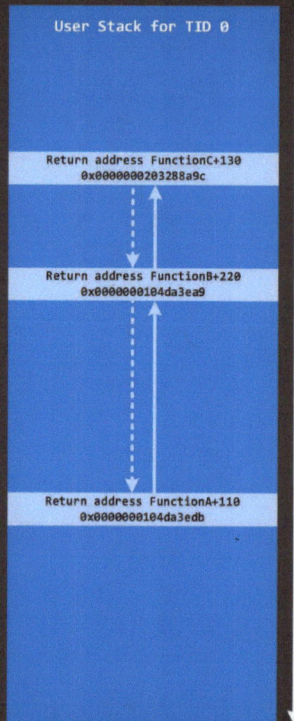

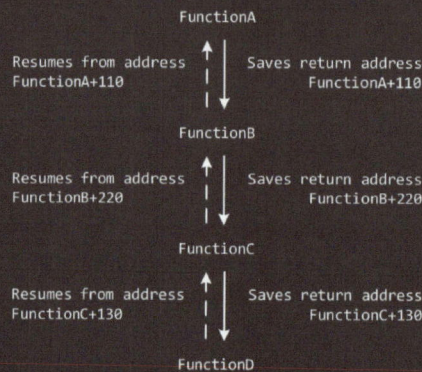

Now we explain thread stack traces. Suppose we have source code where *FunctionA* calls *FunctionB* at some point and *FunctionB* calls *FunctionC* and so on. This is a thread of execution. If *FunctionA* calls *FunctionB*, you expect the execution thread to return to the same place where it left and resume from there. This is achieved by saving a return address in the thread stack region. So every return address is saved and then restored during the course of a thread execution. Although the memory addresses grow from top to bottom in this picture, return addresses are saved from bottom to top. This might seem counter-intuitive to all previous pictures, but this is how you would see the output from LLDB commands. What LLDB does when you instruct it to dump a backtrace from a given thread is to analyze the thread raw stack data and figure out return addresses, map them to a symbolic form according to symbol files and show them from top to bottom. Note that *FunctionD* is not present in the raw stack data on the left because it is a currently executing function called from *FunctionC*. However, *FunctionC* called *FunctionD*, and the return address of *FunctionC* was saved. In the box on the right, we see the result of the LLDB command.

GDB and LLDB vs. WinDbg

GDB Commands

```
(gdb) bt
#0 0x000000020328982a in FunctionD ()
#1 0x0000000203288a9c in FunctionC ()
#2 0x0000000104da3ea9 in FunctionB ()
#3 0x0000000104da3edb in FunctionA ()
```

LLDB Commands

```
(lldb) bt
frame #0: 0x000000020328982a Module`FunctionD + offset
frame #1: 0x0000000203288a9c Module`FunctionC + 130
frame #2: 0x0000000104da3ea9 AppA`FunctionB + 220
frame #3: 0x0000000104da3edb AppA`FunctionA + 110
```

WinDbg Commands

```
0:000> kn
00 0000000203288a9c Module!FunctionD+offset
01 0000000104da3ea9 Module!FunctionC+130
02 0000000104da3edb AppA!FunctionB+220
03 0000000000000000 AppA!FunctionA+110
```

The difference from WinDbg here is that the return address is on the same line for the function to return (except for *FunctionD*, where the address is the next instruction to execute) whereas in WinDbg it is for the function on the next line. There's not difference from GDB except offsets.

Thread Stack Trace (no dSYM)

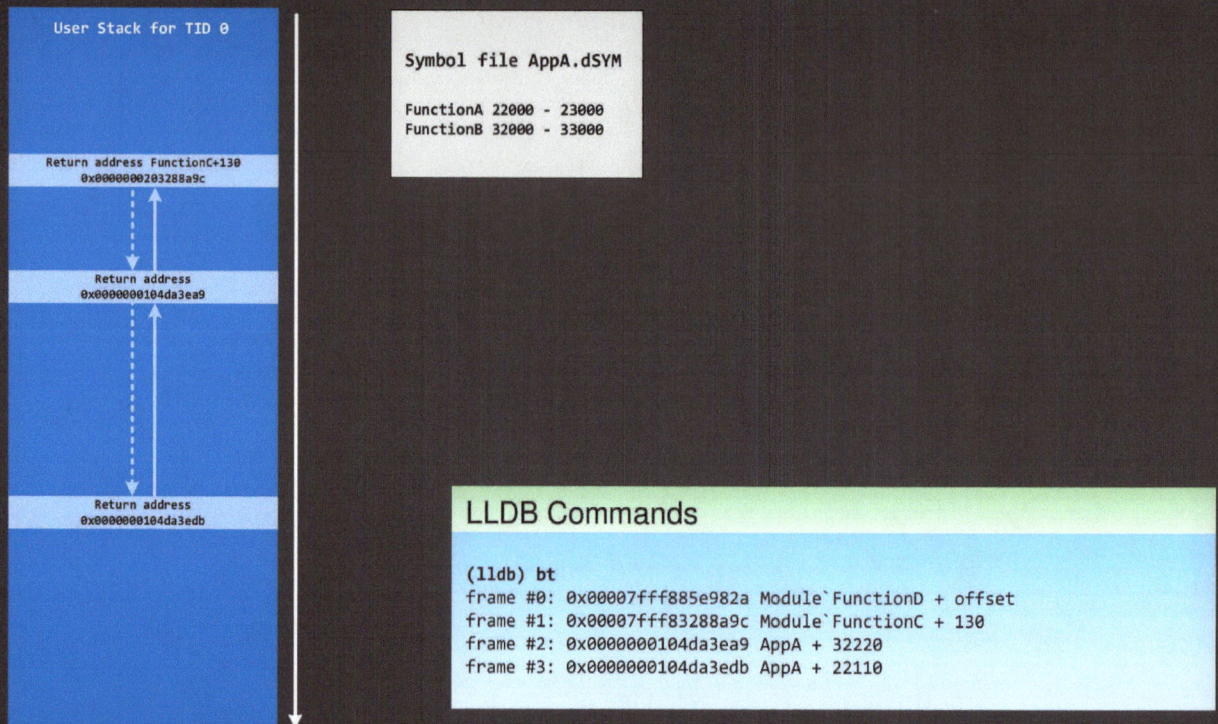

User Stack for TID 0

Return address FunctionC+130
0x0000000203288a9c

Return address
0x0000000104da3ea9

Return address
0x0000000104da3edb

Symbol file AppA.dSYM

FunctionA 22000 - 23000
FunctionB 32000 - 33000

LLDB Commands

```
(lldb) bt
frame #0: 0x00007fff885e982a Module`FunctionD + offset
frame #1: 0x00007fff83288a9c Module`FunctionC + 130
frame #2: 0x0000000104da3ea9 AppA + 32220
frame #3: 0x0000000104da3edb AppA + 22110
```

Here I'd like to show you why symbol files are important and what stack traces you get without them. Symbol files just provide mappings between memory address ranges and associated symbols like the table of contents in a book. So in the absence of symbols, we are left with bare addresses that are saved in a dump. For example, without *AppA* symbols, we have the output shown in the box on the right.

Exceptions (Access Violation)

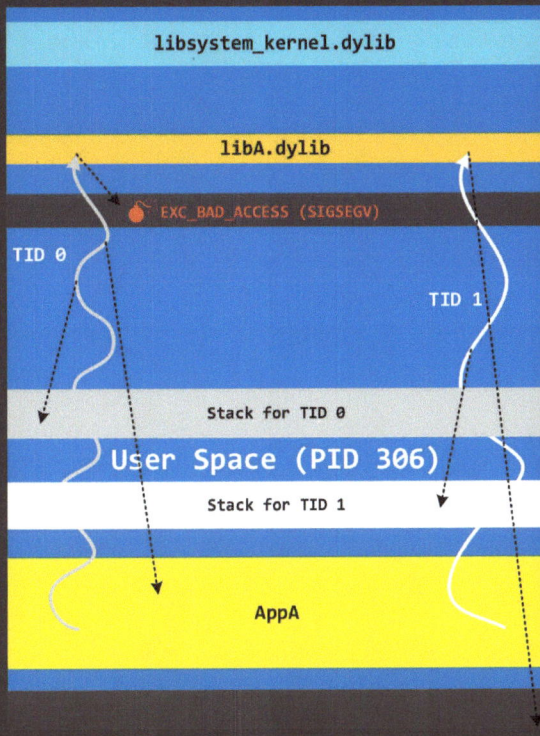

Now we talk about access violation exceptions. During the thread execution, it accesses various memory addresses doing reads and writes. Sometimes memory is not present due to gaps in virtual address space or different protection levels like read-only or no-execute memory regions. If a thread tries to violate that, we get an exception that is also translated to a traditional UNIX signal. Certain regions are forbidden to read and write such as the first 4GB. If we have such an access violation there, then it is called a NULL pointer access. Note that every thread can have an exception (a victim thread) and it often happens that there are multiple exceptions. It is also sometimes the case that code can catch these exceptions preventing a user from seeing error messages. Such exceptions can contribute to corruption, and we call then hidden.

Exceptions (Runtime)

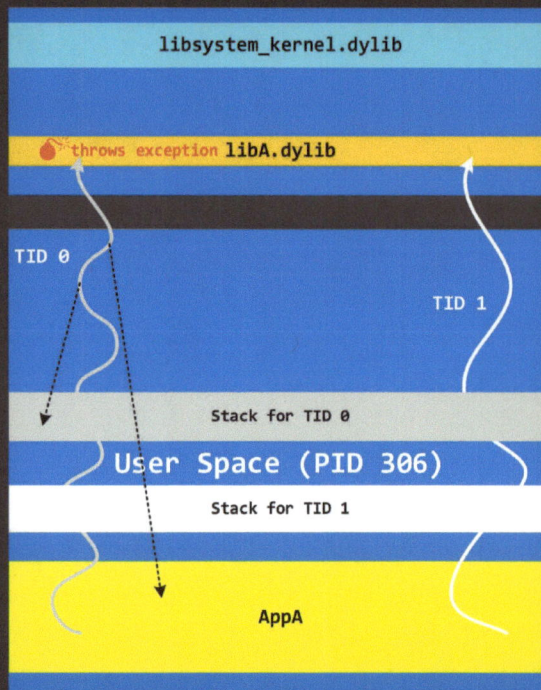

However, not all exceptions happen from invalid access. Many exceptions are generated by the code itself when it checks for some condition, and it is not satisfied, for example, when the code checks a buffer or an array to verify whether it is full before trying to add more data. If it finds it is already full, the code throws an exception translated to SIGABRT. We would see that in one of our practice examples when C++ code throws a C++ exception. Such exceptions are usually called runtime exceptions.

Pattern-Oriented Diagnostic Analysis

Diagnostic Pattern: a common recurrent identifiable problem together with a set of recommendations and possible solutions to apply in a specific context.

Diagnostic Problem: a set of indicators (symptoms, signs) describing a problem.

Diagnostic Analysis Pattern: a common recurrent analysis technique and method of diagnostic pattern identification in a specific context.

Diagnostics Pattern Language: common names of diagnostic and diagnostic analysis patterns. The same language for any operating system: macOS, Linux, Windows, ...

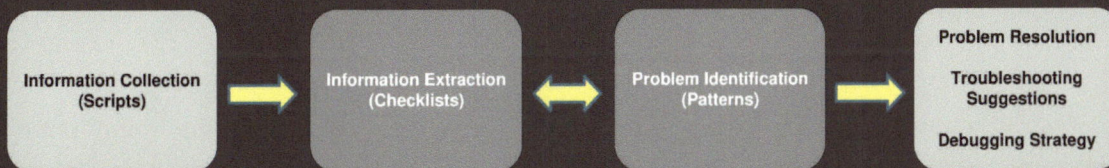

Information Collection (Scripts) → Information Extraction (Checklists) ↔ Problem Identification (Patterns) → Problem Resolution / Troubleshooting Suggestions / Debugging Strategy

A few words about logs, checklists, and patterns. Core memory dump analysis is usually an analysis of a text for the presence of diagnostic patterns. We run commands, they output text, and then we look at that textual output, and when we find suspicious diagnostic indicators, we execute more commands. Here pattern and command checklists can be very useful.

Core Dump Collection

Part 2: Core Dump Collection

Here I'd like to show you how to collect core dumps because by default this option is switched off on macOS and there are further complications compared to previous versions.

Enabling Collection

⊙ **Temporary for the current terminal session:**

```
% ulimit -c unlimited
```

⊙ **Add entitlements:**

```
% /usr/libexec/PlistBuddy -c "Add :com.apple.security.get-task-allow
bool true" tmp.entitlements
```

⊙ **Sign code:**

```
% codesign -s - -f --entitlements tmp.entitlements YourApp
```

⊙ **Set permissions**

```
% sudo chmod 1777 /cores
```

You should also have a directory **/cores** where all process core dumps are stored.

Generation Methods

◉ Command line:

```
% sudo gcore PID

% sudo kill -s SIGQUIT PID
% sudo kill -s SIGABRT PID
```

◉ GUI:

Utilities \ Activity Monitor
View \ Send Signal to Process...

ARM64 Disassembly

Part 3: ARM64 Disassembly

CPU Registers (ARM64)

- X0 – X28, W0 – W28

- Stack: **SP**, X29 (**FP**)

- Next instruction: **PC**

- Link register: X30 (**LR**)

- Zero register: XZR, WZR

- 128-bit **V0 – V31** (**Q0 – Q31**)

X 64-bit	W 32-bit

LLDB Commands
register read

There are 31 general registers from **X0** and **X30**, with some delegated to specific tasks such as addressing stack frames (Frame Pointer, **FP**, **X29**) and return addresses, the so-called Link Register (**LR**, **X30**). When you call a function the return address of a caller is saved in **LR**, not on the stack as in Intel/AMD x64. The return instruction in a callee will use the address in **LR** to assign it to **PC** and resume execution. But if a callee calls other functions the current **LR** needs to be manually saved somewhere, usually on the stack. There's Stack Pointer, **SP**, of course. To get zero values there's the so-called Zero Register, **XZR**. All **X** registers are 64-bit, and 32-bit lower parts are addressed via the **W** prefix. Additionally, when disassembly runtime functions you may see the usage of 128-bit SIMD registers(and also 64-bit floating point registers). These may be used to speed up some common operations such as zero-initializing structures. The References slide provides links to the ARM64 instruction set architecture. Next, we just briefly look at some aspects related to our exercises.

Instructions: registers (ARM64)

⦿ Opcode DST, SRC, SRC$_2$

⦿ Examples:

```
mov    x0, #0x10              ; X0 ← 0x10
mov    x29, sp               ; X29 ← SP
add    x1, x2, #0x10         ; X1 ← X2+0x10
mul    x1, x2, x3            ; X1 ← X2*X3
blr    x8                    ; X8 already contains
                            ;    the address of func (&func)
                            ; LR ← PC+4; PC ← &func
sub    sp, sp, #0x30         ; SP ← SP-0x30
                            ; make a room for local variables
```

This slide shows a few examples of CPU instructions that involve operations with registers, for example, moving a value and doing arithmetic. The direction of operands is the same as in Intel x64 disassembly flavor if you are accustomed to WinDbg and GDB on Windows and Linux platforms. It is equivalent to an assignment. **BLR** is a call to some function whose address is in the register. **BL** means Branch and Link.

Memory and Stack Addressing

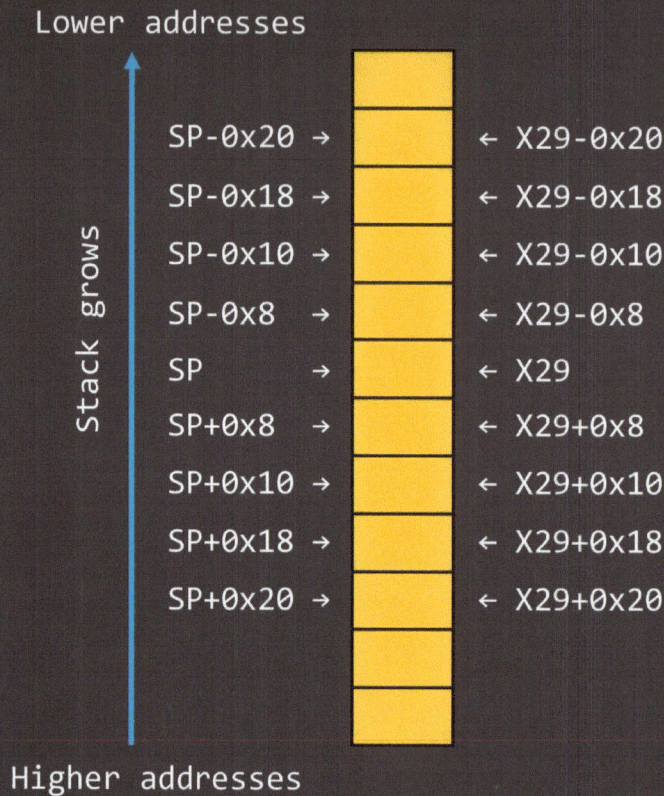

Lower addresses

SP-0x20 →		← X29-0x20
SP-0x18 →		← X29-0x18
SP-0x10 →		← X29-0x10
SP-0x8 →		← X29-0x8
SP →		← X29
SP+0x8 →		← X29+0x8
SP+0x10 →		← X29+0x10
SP+0x18 →		← X29+0x18
SP+0x20 →		← X29+0x20

Stack grows

Higher addresses

Before we look at operations with memory, let's look at a graphical representation of memory addressing. A thread stack is just any other memory region, so instead of **SP** and **X29 (FP)**, any other register can be used. Please note that the stack grows towards lower addresses so to access the previously pushed values you need to use positive offsets from **SP**.

Instructions: memory load (ARM64)

- Opcode DST, DST$_2$, [SRC, Offset]

- Opcode DST, DST$_2$, [SRC], Offset ; Postincrement

- Examples:

```
ldr    x0, [sp]                ; X0 ← value at address SP+0
ldr    x0, [x29, #-0x8]        ; X0 ← value at address X29-0x8
ldp    x29, x30, [sp, #0x20]   ; X29 ← value at address SP+0x20
                               ; X30 ← value at address SP+0x28
ldp    x29, x30, [sp], #0x10   ; X29 ← value at address SP+0
                               ; X30 ← value at address SP+0x8
                               ; SP ← SP+0x10
```

Constants are encoded in instructions but if we need arbitrary values, we must get them from memory. Square brackets are used to show memory access relative to an address stored in some register. There's also an option to adjust the value of the register after load, the so-called **Postincrement**, which can be negative. As we see later, loading pairs of registers can be useful.

Instructions: memory store (ARM64)

- Opcode SRC, SRC$_2$, [DST, Offset]

- Opcode SRC, SRC$_2$, [DST, Offset]! ; Preincrement

- Examples:

```
str   x0, [sp, #0x10]         ; x0 → value at address SP+0x10
str   x0, [x29, #-0x8]        ; x0 → value at address X29-0x8
stp   x29, x30, [sp, #0x20]   ; x29 → value at address SP+0x20
                              ; x30 → value at address SP+0x28
stp   x29, x30, [sp, #-0x10]! ; SP ← SP-0x10
                              ; x29 → set value at address SP
                              ; x30 → set value at address SP+0x8
```

Storing operand order goes in the other direction compared to other instructions. There's a possibility to **Preincrement** the destination register before storing values.

Instructions: flow (ARM64)

- ⊙ Opcode DST, SRC

- ⊙ Examples:

```
adrp  x0, 2                    ; x0 ← PC&0xFFFFFFFFFFFFF000 + 0x1000*2

b       0x10493fc1c            ; PC ← 0x10493fc1c
                               ; (goto 0x10493fc1c)

0x10493fc14:                   ; PC == 0x10493fc14
bl     0x10493ff74             ; LR ← PC+4 (0x10493fc18)
                               ; PC ← 0x10493ff74
                               ; (goto 0x10493ff74)
```

Because the size of every instruction is 4 bytes (32 bits) it is only possible to encode a part of a large 4GB address range, either as a relative offset to the current **PC** or via **ADRP** instruction. Goto (an unconditional branch) is implemented via the **B** instruction. Function calls are implemented via the **BL** (Branch and Link) instruction. For conditional branches please look at the official documentation provided on the References slide. We don't use these instructions in our exercises.

Function Call and Prolog

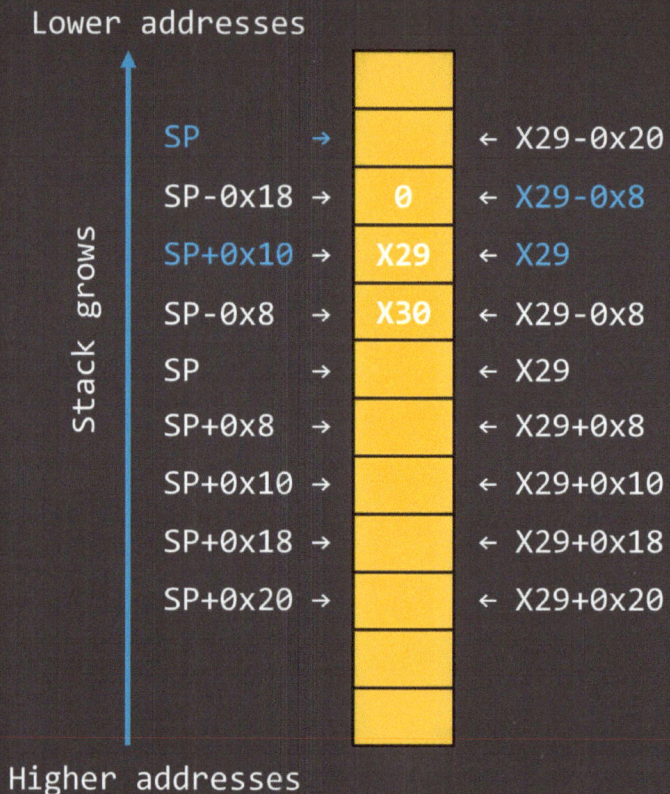

```
; void proc(int p1, long p2);
mov  w0, #0x1
mov  x1, #0x2
bl   proc


; void proc2();
; void proc(int p1, long p2) {
;    long local = 0;
;    proc2();
; }
proc:
sub  sp, sp, #0x20
stp  x29, x30, [sp, #0x10]
add  x29, sp, #0x10
str  zxr, [x29, #-0x8]
bl   proc2
...
```

Lower addresses

SP →		← X29-0x20
SP-0x18 →	0	← X29-0x8
SP+0x10 →	X29	← X29
SP-0x8 →	X30	← X29-0x8
SP →		← X29
SP+0x8 →		← X29+0x8
SP+0x10 →		← X29+0x10
SP+0x18 →		← X29+0x18
SP+0x20 →		← X29+0x20

Stack grows

Higher addresses

When a function is called from the caller, a callee needs to do certain operations to make a room for local variables on the thread stack and save **LR** if there are further calls in the function body. There are different ways to do that and the assembly language code on the left is one of them. I use a different color in the diagram on the right to highlight the updated **SP** and **X29** (**FP**) values before *proc2* is called. Please also note an example of zero register usage. For simplicity of illustration, I only use 64-bit values.

Stack Trace Reconstruction

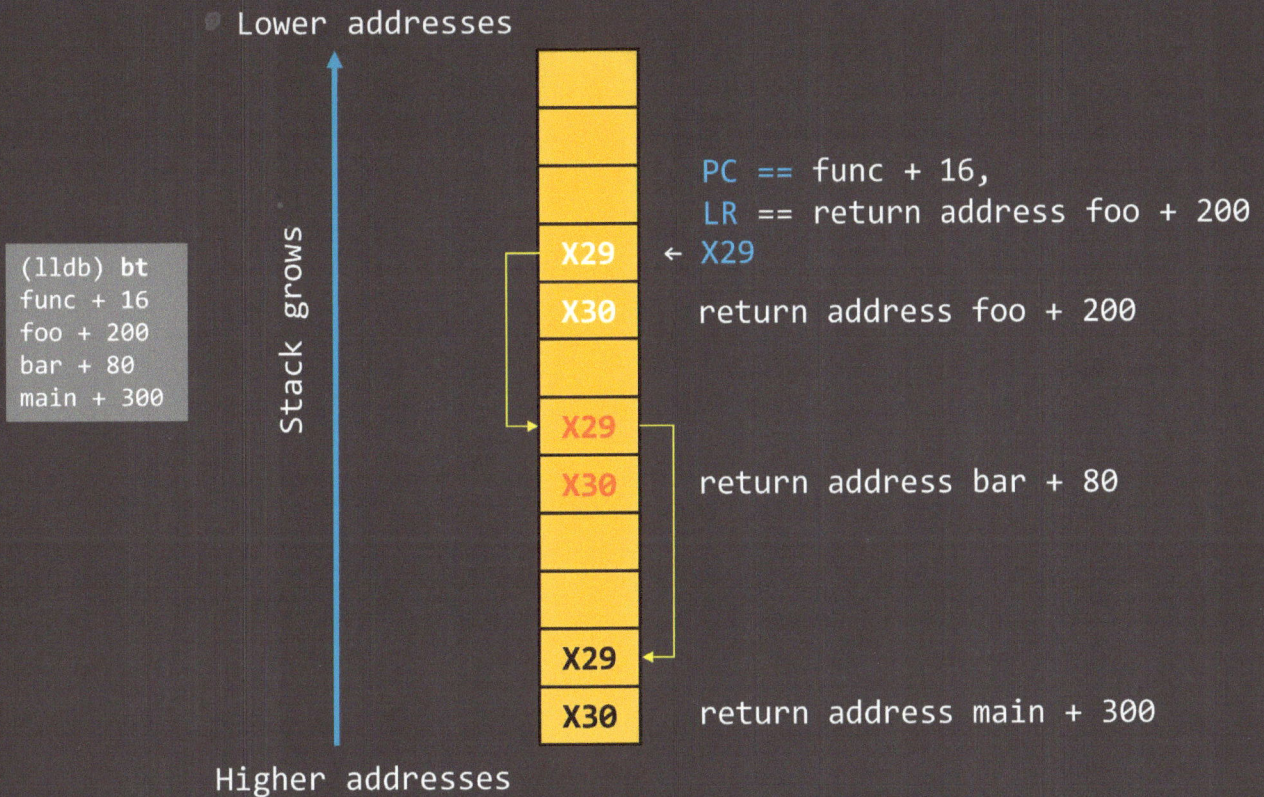

Lower addresses

Stack grows

```
(lldb) bt
func + 16
foo + 200
bar + 80
main + 300
```

X29	← X29

PC == func + 16,
LR == return address foo + 200

X30	return address foo + 200

X29	

X30	return address bar + 80

X29	

X30	return address main + 300

Higher addresses

You may have noticed on the previous diagram that the new **X29 (FP)** points to the **X29** of the caller and below the previous **X29** is the return address of the caller. So, if you know either the return address in **LR** or **X29** you can reconstruct the stack trace if the compiler follows the preceding function prolog convention.

Pointer Authentication

- ⊙ 0x823d80018ea0308c (0x000000018ea0308c) Module`func + 92

- ⊙ (lldb) x/a 0x823d80018ea0308c
     0x18ea0308c: 0x0b000269320107e8

Problem of reading real addresses:

- ⊙ (lldb) x/a 0x000060000a000000
     error: core file does not contain 0xa000000
     (lldb) x/a 0x000060a000000000
     error: core file does not contain 0x20000000

Solution via Typed Memory:

- ⊙ (lldb) p/x *(long *)0x000060000a000000
     (long) $1 = 0x0000000000000000
     (lldb) parray/x 10 (long *)0x000060000a000000

Another feature we encounter in our exercises is pointer authentication. The References slide contains the link to the PAC paper, so I only mention that some parts of a pointer value (higher bits) contain verification codes. Memory dumping commands automatically ignore these parts to show the real address value in order to provide a symbolic reference if any. However, these bits may be a part of the real virtual address (or considered such erroneously) as shown on this slide. In this case, you can use the so-called typed memory print in LLDB which doesn't remove these high bits.

Practice Exercises

Part 4: Practice Exercises

Now we come to practice. The goal is to show you important commands and how their output helps in recognizing patterns of abnormal software behavior.

Links

- Memory Dumps:

  Included in Exercise X0

- Exercise Transcripts:

  Included in this book

Exercise X0

- **Goal:** Install Xcode and check if LLDB loads a core dump correctly, compare the core dump backtrace with a diagnostic report

- **Patterns:** Stack Trace; Incorrect Stack Trace

- \AMCDA-Dumps\Exercise-X0.pdf

Exercise X0

Goal: Install Xcode and check if LLDB loads a core dump correctly, compare the core dump with a diagnostic report.

Patterns: Stack Trace; Incorrect Stack Trace.

1.   Download and install the latest version of Xcode from App Store.

2.   Download and unzip the following archives:

https://www.patterndiagnostics.com/Training/AMCDA/AMCDA-V3-Dumps-Part0.zip
https://www.patterndiagnostics.com/Training/AMCDA/AMCDA-V3-Dumps-Part1.zip
https://www.patterndiagnostics.com/Training/AMCDA/AMCDA-V3-Dumps-Part2.zip
https://www.patterndiagnostics.com/Training/AMCDA/AMCDA-V3-Dumps-Part3.zip
https://www.patterndiagnostics.com/Training/AMCDA/AMCDA-V3-Dumps-Part4.zip
https://www.patterndiagnostics.com/Training/AMCDA/AMCDA-V3-Dumps-Part5.zip
https://www.patterndiagnostics.com/Training/AMCDA/AMCDA-V3-Dumps-Part6.zip
https://www.patterndiagnostics.com/Training/AMCDA/AMCDA-V3-Dumps-Part7.zip
https://www.patterndiagnostics.com/Training/AMCDA/AMCDA-V3-Dumps-Part8.zip
https://www.patterndiagnostics.com/Training/AMCDA/AMCDA-V3-Dumps-Part9.zip
https://www.patterndiagnostics.com/Training/AMCDA/AMCDA-V3-Dumps-Part10.zip
https://www.patterndiagnostics.com/Training/AMCDA/AMCDA-V3-Dumps-Part11.zip
https://www.patterndiagnostics.com/Training/AMCDA/AMCDA-V3-Dumps-Symbols.zip

3.   Open a terminal window.

4.   Load a core dump *core.83932* and *App0* executable:

```
% lldb -c ~/AMCDA-Dumps/core.83932 -f ~/AMCDA-Dumps/Apps/App0/Build/Products/Release/App0
(lldb) target create "/Users/training/AMCDA-Dumps/Apps/App0/Build/Products/Release/App0" --
core "/Users/training/AMCDA-Dumps/core.83932"
Core file '/Users/training/AMCDA-Dumps/core.83932' (arm64) was loaded.
(lldb)
```

5.   Verify that the stack trace (backtrace) is shown correctly with symbols:

```
(lldb) bt
* thread #1
  * frame #0: 0x000000018e9d2d98 libsystem_kernel.dylib`__pthread_kill + 8
    frame #1: 0x000000018ea07ee0 libsystem_pthread.dylib`pthread_kill + 288
    frame #2: 0x000000018e942340 libsystem_c.dylib`abort + 168
    frame #3: 0x0000000100213f64 App0`bar + 12
    frame #4: 0x0000000100213f70 App0`foo + 12
    frame #5: 0x0000000100213f9c App0`main + 36
    frame #6: 0x000000010047508c dyld`start + 520
```

6.   The stack trace should correspond to the diagnostic report *App0-2022-11-24-014139.ips*:

```
-------------------------------------
Translated Report (Full Report Below)
-------------------------------------

Process:            App0 [83932]
Path:               /Users/USER/*/App0
Identifier:         App0
Version:            ???
Code Type:          ARM-64 (Native)
Parent Process:     zsh [73148]
```

```
Responsible:           Terminal [9503]
User ID:               501

Date/Time:             2022-11-24 01:41:39.4853 +0000
OS Version:            macOS 12.6 (21G115)
Report Version:        12
Anonymous UUID:        6F758133-2B79-4743-8B70-8B1D8C510718

Sleep/Wake UUID:       9C7E40B8-CD9F-4783-85B1-FEF3E5F4B82E

Time Awake Since Boot: 100000 seconds
Time Since Wake:       3049 seconds

System Integrity Protection: enabled

Crashed Thread:        0  Dispatch queue: com.apple.main-thread

Exception Type:        EXC_CRASH (SIGABRT)
Exception Codes:       0x0000000000000000, 0x0000000000000000
Exception Note:        EXC_CORPSE_NOTIFY

Application Specific Information:
abort() called

Thread 0 Crashed:: Dispatch queue: com.apple.main-thread
0   libsystem_kernel.dylib          0x18e9d2d98 __pthread_kill + 8
1   libsystem_pthread.dylib         0x18ea07ee0 pthread_kill + 288
2   libsystem_c.dylib               0x18e942340 abort + 168
3   App0                            0x100213f64 bar + 12 (main.c:12)
4   App0                            0x100213f70 foo + 12 (main.c:17)
5   App0                            0x100213f9c main + 36 (main.c:22)
6   dyld                            0x10047508c start + 520

Thread 0 crashed with ARM Thread State (64-bit):
    x0: 0x0000000000000000   x1: 0x0000000000000000   x2: 0x0000000000000000   x3: 0x0000000000000000
    x4: 0x0000000000000000   x5: 0x0000000000000000   x6: 0x0000000000000000   x7: 0x0000000000000000
    x8: 0x0e44af997a26394a   x9: 0x0e44af987a68bcca  x10: 0x0000000000000000  x11: 0x0000000000000002
   x12: 0x0000000000000002  x13: 0x0000000000000000  x14: 0x0000000000000008  x15: 0x0000000000000000
   x16: 0x0000000000000148  x17: 0x00000001e8b2b680  x18: 0x0000000000000000  x19: 0x0000000000000006
   x20: 0x00000001004e8580  x21: 0x0000000000000103  x22: 0x00000001004e8660  x23: 0x0000000000000000
   x24: 0x0000000000000000  x25: 0x0000000000000000  x26: 0x0000000000000000  x27: 0x0000000000000000
   x28: 0x0000000000000000   fp: 0x000000016fbef870   lr: 0x000000018ea07ee0
    sp: 0x000000016fbef850   pc: 0x000000018e9d2d98 cpsr: 0x40001000
   far: 0x00000001e8c5c170  esr: 0x56000080  Address size fault

Binary Images:
      0x18e9c9000 -        0x18ea00fff libsystem_kernel.dylib (*) <a9d87740-9c1d-3468-bf60-720a8d713cba>
/usr/lib/system/libsystem_kernel.dylib
      0x18ea01000 -        0x18ea0dfff libsystem_pthread.dylib (*) <63c4eef9-69a5-38b1-996e-8d31b66a051d>
/usr/lib/system/libsystem_pthread.dylib
      0x18e8c8000 -        0x18e949fff libsystem_c.dylib (*) <b25d2080-bb9e-38d6-8236-9cef4b2f11a3>
/usr/lib/system/libsystem_c.dylib
      0x100210000 -        0x100213fff App0 (*) <4e0eae20-fe4c-324f-b2d6-33f8851a0792> /Users/USER/*/App0
      0x100470000 -        0x1004cffff dyld (*) <38ee9fe9-b66d-3066-8c5c-6ddf0d6944c6> /usr/lib/dyld

External Modification Summary:
  Calls made by other processes targeting this process:
    task_for_pid: 0
    thread_create: 0
    thread_set_state: 0
  Calls made by this process:
    task_for_pid: 0
    thread_create: 0
    thread_set_state: 0
  Calls made by all processes on this machine:
    task_for_pid: 0
    thread_create: 0
    thread_set_state: 0

VM Region Summary:
ReadOnly portion of Libraries: Total=582.2M resident=0K(0%) swapped_out_or_unallocated=582.2M(100%)
Writable regions: Total=529.1M written=0K(0%) resident=0K(0%) swapped_out=0K(0%) unallocated=529.1M(100%)

                              VIRTUAL   REGION
REGION TYPE                      SIZE   COUNT (non-coalesced)
===========                   =======  =======
```

```
Kernel Alloc Once           32K        1
MALLOC                    137.3M       17
MALLOC_NANO (reserved)    384.0M        1       reserved VM address space (unallocated)
Stack                      8176K        1
Stack (reserved)           56.0M        1       reserved VM address space (unallocated)
__AUTH                       46K       11
__AUTH_CONST                 67K       38
__DATA                      173K       37
__DATA_CONST                258K       40
__DATA_DIRTY                 73K       21
__LINKEDIT                 577.6M       3
__OBJC_CONST                 10K        5
__OBJC_RO                  83.0M        1
__OBJC_RW                  3168K        1
__TEXT                     4708K       43
dyld private memory        1024K        1
shared memory                16K        1
===========               =======  =======
TOTAL                       1.2G      223
TOTAL, minus reserved VM space  815.2M  223
```

7.   To avoid possible confusion and glitches we recommend exiting LLDB after each exercise:

```
(lldb) q
%
```

Process Core Dumps

Exercises X1 – X12

All exercises were modeled on real-life examples using specially constructed applications. We will learn how to recognize more than 30 patterns.

Exercise X1

- **Goal:** Learn how to list stack traces, disassemble functions, follow function calls, check backtrace correctness, dump data, get environment

- **Patterns:** Manual Dump (Process); Stack Trace; Stack Trace Collection; Annotated Disassembly; Paratext; Not My Version; Environment Hint

- \AMCDA-Dumps\Exercise-X1.pdf

Exercise X1

Goal: Learn how to list stack traces, disassemble functions, follow function calls, check backtrace correctness, dump data, and get the environment.

Patterns: Manual Dump (Process); Stack Trace; Stack Trace Collection; Annotated Disassembly; Paratext; Not My Version; Environment Hint.

1.   Load a core dump *App1-84080-20221124T015838Z* and *App1* executable:

```
% lldb -c ~/AMCDA-Dumps/App1-84080-20221124T015838Z -f
~/AMCDA-Dumps/Apps/App1/Build/Products/Release/App1
((lldb) target create "/Users/training/AMCDA-Dumps/Apps/App1/Build/Products/Release/App1" --
core "/Users/training/AMCDA-Dumps/App1-84080-20221124T015838Z"
Core file '/Users/training/AMCDA-Dumps/App1-84080-20221124T015838Z' (arm64) was loaded.
(lldb)
```

2.   List all threads:

```
(lldb) thread list
Process 0 stopped
* thread #1: tid = 0x0000, 0x000000018e9ce06c libsystem_kernel.dylib`__semwait_signal + 8
  thread #2: tid = 0x0001, 0x000000018e9ce06c libsystem_kernel.dylib`__semwait_signal + 8
  thread #3: tid = 0x0002, 0x000000018e9ce06c libsystem_kernel.dylib`__semwait_signal + 8
  thread #4: tid = 0x0003, 0x000000018e9ce06c libsystem_kernel.dylib`__semwait_signal + 8
  thread #5: tid = 0x0004, 0x000000018e9ce06c libsystem_kernel.dylib`__semwait_signal + 8
  thread #6: tid = 0x0005, 0x000000018e9ce06c libsystem_kernel.dylib`__semwait_signal + 8
```

Note: We see LLDB listed 6 threads with their TIDs numbered from 0.

3.   Get all thread stack traces:

```
(lldb) thread backtrace all
* thread #1
  * frame #0: 0x000000018e9ce06c libsystem_kernel.dylib`__semwait_signal + 8
    frame #1: 0x000000018e8d6fc8 libsystem_c.dylib`nanosleep + 220
    frame #2: 0x000000018e8e1b78 libsystem_c.dylib`sleep + 52
    frame #3: 0x000000018e8e1b90 libsystem_c.dylib`sleep + 76
    frame #4: 0x0000000102603f90 App1`main + 164
    frame #5: 0x00000001028e108c dyld`start + 520
  thread #2
    frame #0: 0x000000018e9ce06c libsystem_kernel.dylib`__semwait_signal + 8
    frame #1: 0x000000018e8d6fc8 libsystem_c.dylib`nanosleep + 220
    frame #2: 0x000000018e8e1b78 libsystem_c.dylib`sleep + 52
    frame #3: 0x000000018e8e1b90 libsystem_c.dylib`sleep + 76
    frame #4: 0x0000000102603d6c App1`bar_one + 16
    frame #5: 0x0000000102603d80 App1`foo_one + 12
    frame #6: 0x0000000102603d9c App1`thread_one + 20
    frame #7: 0x000000018ea0826c libsystem_pthread.dylib`_pthread_start + 148
  thread #3
    frame #0: 0x000000018e9ce06c libsystem_kernel.dylib`__semwait_signal + 8
    frame #1: 0x000000018e8d6fc8 libsystem_c.dylib`nanosleep + 220
    frame #2: 0x000000018e8e1b78 libsystem_c.dylib`sleep + 52
    frame #3: 0x000000018e8e1b90 libsystem_c.dylib`sleep + 76
    frame #4: 0x0000000102603dbc App1`bar_two + 16
    frame #5: 0x0000000102603dd0 App1`foo_two + 12
```

```
    frame #6: 0x0000000102603dec App1`thread_two + 20
    frame #7: 0x000000018ea0826c libsystem_pthread.dylib`_pthread_start + 148
  thread #4
    frame #0: 0x000000018e9ce06c libsystem_kernel.dylib`__semwait_signal + 8
    frame #1: 0x000000018e8d6fc8 libsystem_c.dylib`nanosleep + 220
    frame #2: 0x000000018e8e1b78 libsystem_c.dylib`sleep + 52
    frame #3: 0x000000018e8e1b90 libsystem_c.dylib`sleep + 76
    frame #4: 0x0000000102603e0c App1`bar_three + 16
    frame #5: 0x0000000102603e20 App1`foo_three + 12
    frame #6: 0x0000000102603e3c App1`thread_three + 20
    frame #7: 0x000000018ea0826c libsystem_pthread.dylib`_pthread_start + 148
  thread #5
    frame #0: 0x000000018e9ce06c libsystem_kernel.dylib`__semwait_signal + 8
    frame #1: 0x000000018e8d6fc8 libsystem_c.dylib`nanosleep + 220
    frame #2: 0x000000018e8e1b78 libsystem_c.dylib`sleep + 52
    frame #3: 0x000000018e8e1b90 libsystem_c.dylib`sleep + 76
    frame #4: 0x0000000102603e5c App1`bar_four + 16
    frame #5: 0x0000000102603e70 App1`foo_four + 12
    frame #6: 0x0000000102603e8c App1`thread_four + 20
    frame #7: 0x000000018ea0826c libsystem_pthread.dylib`_pthread_start + 148
  thread #6
    frame #0: 0x000000018e9ce06c libsystem_kernel.dylib`__semwait_signal + 8
    frame #1: 0x000000018e8d6fc8 libsystem_c.dylib`nanosleep + 220
    frame #2: 0x000000018e8e1b78 libsystem_c.dylib`sleep + 52
    frame #3: 0x000000018e8e1b90 libsystem_c.dylib`sleep + 76
    frame #4: 0x0000000102603eac App1`bar_five + 16
    frame #5: 0x0000000102603ec0 App1`foo_five + 12
    frame #6: 0x0000000102603edc App1`thread_five + 20
    frame #7: 0x000000018ea0826c libsystem_pthread.dylib`_pthread_start + 148
```

4.   Switch to thread #3 and get its stack trace:

```
(lldb) thread select 3
* thread #3
    frame #0: 0x000000018e9ce06c libsystem_kernel.dylib`__semwait_signal + 8
libsystem_kernel.dylib`:
->  0x18e9ce06c <+8>:  b.lo    0x18e9ce08c                  ; <+40>
    0x18e9ce070 <+12>: pacibsp
    0x18e9ce074 <+16>: stp     x29, x30, [sp, #-0x10]!
    0x18e9ce078 <+20>: mov     x29, sp
```

Note: Also, we have code disassembly starting from the next instruction that was to be executed if the dump wasn't saved. The nice feature is annotated disassembly that shows symbolic names for branch and link destinations if we disassemble the function around the current address (**di** without an address can also be used, also, notice pointer authentication instructions for X30):

```
(lldb) di -a 0x18e9ce06c
libsystem_kernel.dylib`:
    0x18e9ce064 <+0>:  mov     x16, #0x14e
    0x18e9ce068 <+4>:  svc     #0x80
->  0x18e9ce06c <+8>:  b.lo    0x18e9ce08c                  ; <+40>
    0x18e9ce070 <+12>: pacibsp
    0x18e9ce074 <+16>: stp     x29, x30, [sp, #-0x10]!
    0x18e9ce078 <+20>: mov     x29, sp
    0x18e9ce07c <+24>: bl      0x18e9cc328                  ; cerror
    0x18e9ce080 <+28>: mov     sp, x29
    0x18e9ce084 <+32>: ldp     x29, x30, [sp], #0x10
    0x18e9ce088 <+36>: retab
    0x18e9ce08c <+40>: ret
```

Note: We can also list any thread stack trace without switching to it:

```
(lldb) thread backtrace 4
  thread #4
    frame #0: 0x000000018e9ce06c libsystem_kernel.dylib`__semwait_signal + 8
    frame #1: 0x000000018e8d6fc8 libsystem_c.dylib`nanosleep + 220
    frame #2: 0x000000018e8e1b78 libsystem_c.dylib`sleep + 52
    frame #3: 0x000000018e8e1b90 libsystem_c.dylib`sleep + 76
    frame #4: 0x0000000102603e0c App1`bar_three + 16
    frame #5: 0x0000000102603e20 App1`foo_three + 12
    frame #6: 0x0000000102603e3c App1`thread_three + 20
    frame #7: 0x000000018ea0826c libsystem_pthread.dylib`_pthread_start + 148
```

5.   Check that *bar_two* called the *sleep* function:

```
(lldb) bt
* thread #3
  * frame #0: 0x000000018e9ce06c libsystem_kernel.dylib`__semwait_signal + 8
    frame #1: 0x000000018e8d6fc8 libsystem_c.dylib`nanosleep + 220
    frame #2: 0x000000018e8e1b78 libsystem_c.dylib`sleep + 52
    frame #3: 0x000000018e8e1b90 libsystem_c.dylib`sleep + 76
    frame #4: 0x0000000102603dbc App1`bar_two + 16
    frame #5: 0x0000000102603dd0 App1`foo_two + 12
    frame #6: 0x0000000102603dec App1`thread_two + 20
    frame #7: 0x000000018ea0826c libsystem_pthread.dylib`_pthread_start + 148
```

```
(lldb) di -n bar_two
App1`bar_two:
    0x102603dac <+0>:   stp    x29, x30, [sp, #-0x10]!
    0x102603db0 <+4>:   mov    x29, sp
    0x102603db4 <+8>:   mov    w0, #-0x1
    0x102603db8 <+12>:  bl     0x102603fac               ; symbol stub for: sleep
    0x102603dbc <+16>:  ldp    x29, x30, [sp], #0x10
    0x102603dc0 <+20>:  ret
```

6.   Follow the *bar_two* function to the *sleep* function code:

```
(lldb) di -n bar_two
App1`bar_two:
    0x102603dac <+0>:   stp    x29, x30, [sp, #-0x10]!
    0x102603db0 <+4>:   mov    x29, sp
    0x102603db4 <+8>:   mov    w0, #-0x1
    0x102603db8 <+12>:  bl     0x102603fac               ; symbol stub for: sleep
    0x102603dbc <+16>:  ldp    x29, x30, [sp], #0x10
    0x102603dc0 <+20>:  ret
```

```
(lldb) di -a 0x102603fac
App1`sleep:
    0x102603fac <+0>:   adrp   x16, 1
    0x102603fb0 <+4>:   ldr    x16, [x16, #0x8]
    0x102603fb4 <+8>:   br     x16
```

Note: This short code fragment is an indirect call to the *sleep* library function. We can calculate it as follows:

```
(lldb) x/a 0x102603000+0x1000*1+0x8
0x102604008: 0x000000018e8e1b44 libsystem_c.dylib`sleep
```

7.   Disassemble the target address value:

```
(lldb) di -a 0x000000018e8e1b44
libsystem_c.dylib`sleep:
    0x18e8e1b44 <+0>:    pacibsp
    0x18e8e1b48 <+4>:    sub     sp, sp, #0x40
    0x18e8e1b4c <+8>:    stp     x20, x19, [sp, #0x20]
    0x18e8e1b50 <+12>:   stp     x29, x30, [sp, #0x30]
    0x18e8e1b54 <+16>:   add     x29, sp, #0x30
    0x18e8e1b58 <+20>:   mov     x19, x0
    0x18e8e1b5c <+24>:   stp     xzr, xzr, [sp]
    0x18e8e1b60 <+28>:   tbnz    w0, #0x1f, 0x18e8e1b88     ; <+68>
    0x18e8e1b64 <+32>:   mov     w8, w19
    0x18e8e1b68 <+36>:   stp     x8, xzr, [sp, #0x10]
    0x18e8e1b6c <+40>:   add     x0, sp, #0x10
    0x18e8e1b70 <+44>:   mov     x1, sp
    0x18e8e1b74 <+48>:   bl      0x18e8d6eec               ; nanosleep
    0x18e8e1b78 <+52>:   cmn     w0, #0x1
    0x18e8e1b7c <+56>:   b.eq    0x18e8e1ba0               ; <+92>
    0x18e8e1b80 <+60>:   mov     w19, #0x0
    0x18e8e1b84 <+64>:   b       0x18e8e1bc0               ; <+124>
    0x18e8e1b88 <+68>:   mov     w0, #0x7fffffff
    0x18e8e1b8c <+72>:   bl      0x18e8e1b44               ; <+0>
    0x18e8e1b90 <+76>:   mov     w8, #-0x7fffffff
    0x18e8e1b94 <+80>:   add     w9, w19, w0
    0x18e8e1b98 <+84>:   add     w19, w9, w8
    0x18e8e1b9c <+88>:   b       0x18e8e1bc0               ; <+124>
    0x18e8e1ba0 <+92>:   bl      0x18e942bb0               ; symbol stub for: __error
    0x18e8e1ba4 <+96>:   ldr     w8, [x0]
    0x18e8e1ba8 <+100>:  cmp     w8, #0x4
    0x18e8e1bac <+104>:  b.ne    0x18e8e1bc0               ; <+124>
    0x18e8e1bb0 <+108>:  ldr     w8, [sp]
    0x18e8e1bb4 <+112>:  ldr     x9, [sp, #0x8]
    0x18e8e1bb8 <+116>:  cmp     x9, #0x0
    0x18e8e1bbc <+120>:  cinc    w19, w8, ne
    0x18e8e1bc0 <+124>:  mov     x0, x19
    0x18e8e1bc4 <+128>:  ldp     x29, x30, [sp, #0x30]
    0x18e8e1bc8 <+132>:  ldp     x20, x19, [sp, #0x20]
    0x18e8e1bcc <+136>:  add     sp, sp, #0x40
    0x18e8e1bd0 <+140>:  retab
```

8.   Get the *App1* stack section from the output of *vmmap_84080.log*:

```
[...]

Virtual Memory Map of process 84080 (App1)
Output report format:  2.4  -- 64-bit process
VM page size:  16384 bytes

==== Non-writable regions for process 84080
REGION TYPE                START - END        [ VSIZE  RSDNT  DIRTY   SWAP] PRT/MAX SHRMOD PURGE   REGION DETAIL
__TEXT                     102600000-102604000  [   16K    16K     0K     0K] r-x/r-x SM=COW         /Users/USER/*/App1

[...]

==== Writable regions for process 84080
REGION TYPE                START - END        [ VSIZE  RSDNT  DIRTY   SWAP] PRT/MAX SHRMOD PURGE   REGION DETAIL
Kernel Alloc Once          102710000-102718000  [   32K     0K     0K    16K] rw-/rwx SM=COW
MALLOC metadata            102720000-102724000  [   16K    16K    16K     0K] rw-/rwx SM=COW
MALLOC metadata            102728000-102730000  [   32K    32K    32K     0K] rw-/rwx SM=COW
MALLOC metadata            102738000-102740000  [   32K    32K    32K     0K] rw-/rwx SM=PRV
MALLOC metadata            102748000-102750000  [   32K     0K     0K    32K] rw-/rwx SM=PRV
MALLOC metadata            10275c000-102760000  [   16K    16K    16K     0K] rw-/rwx SM=COW
__DATA                     102954000-102958000  [   16K    16K    16K     0K] rw-/rw- SM=COW         /usr/lib/dyld
MALLOC_TINY                12e600000-12e700000  [ 1024K    16K    16K    16K] rw-/rwx SM=PRV         MallocHelperZone_0x10271c000
MALLOC_SMALL               12e800000-12f000000  [ 8192K    16K    16K    16K] rw-/rwx SM=PRV         MallocHelperZone_0x10271c000
Stack                      16d004000-16d800000  [ 8176K    16K    16K    16K] rw-/rwx SM=COW         thread 0
Stack                      16d804000-16d88c000  [  544K     0K     0K    16K] rw-/rwx SM=COW         thread 1
Stack                      16d890000-16d918000  [  544K     0K     0K    16K] rw-/rwx SM=COW         thread 2
```

```
Stack                    16d91c000-16d9a4000  [  544K    0K    0K   16K] rw-/rwx SM=COW           thread 3
Stack                    16d9a8000-16da30000  [  544K    0K    0K   16K] rw-/rwx SM=COW           thread 4
Stack                    16da34000-16dabc000  [  544K    0K    0K   16K] rw-/rwx SM=COW           thread 5
```

[...]

Note: Page size on the Mx platform is 16KB.

9.   Compare with the section information in the core dump:

```
(lldb) image dump sections App1
Sections for '/Users/training/AMCDA-Dumps/Apps/App1/Build/Products/Release/App1' (arm64):
  SectID     Type             Load Address                                       Perm File Off.  File Size   Flags      Section Name
  ---------- ---------------- -------------------------------------------------  ---- ---------- ---------- ---------- ------------------------
  0x00000100 container        [0x0000000000000000-0x0000000100000000)*  ---  0x00000000 0x00000000 0x00000000 App1.__PAGEZERO
  0x00000200 container        [0x0000000102600000-0x0000000102604000)   r-x  0x00000000 0x00004000 0x00000000 App1.__TEXT
  0x00000001 code             [0x0000000102603d5c-0x0000000102603fa0)   r-x  0x00003d5c 0x00000244 0x80000400 App1.__TEXT.__text
  0x00000002 code             [0x0000000102603fa0-0x0000000102603fb8)   r-x  0x00003fa0 0x00000018 0x80000408 App1.__TEXT.__stubs
  0x00000003 compact-unwind   [0x0000000102603fb8-0x0000000102604000)   r-x  0x00003fb8 0x00000048 0x00000000 App1.__TEXT.__unwind_info
  0x00000300 container        [0x0000000102604000-0x0000000102608000)   rw-  0x00004000 0x00004000 0x00000010 App1.__DATA_CONST
  0x00000004 data-ptrs        [0x0000000102604000-0x0000000102604010)   rw-  0x00004000 0x00000010 0x00000006 App1.__DATA_CONST.__got
  0x00000400 container        [0x0000000102608000-0x0000000102610000)   r--  0x00008000 0x000052c0 0x00000000 App1.__LINKEDIT
```

Note: We don't see the __DATA section because it is possibly combined with thread 0 stack region since the address of the *environ* variable can be found at the top of that region:

```
(lldb) p/x environ
(void *) $0 = 0x000000016d7ffa88
```

10.   Dump the last 4KB of the stack region (512 8-byte values = 4096 or 0x1000 bytes) with possible symbolic information (we can find the *environ* variable address there too):

```
(lldb) x/512a 0x0000000016d800000-0x1000
error: Normally, 'memory read' will not read over 1024 bytes of data.
error: Please use --force to override this restriction just once.
error: or set target.max-memory-read-size if you will often need a larger limit.
```

```
(lldb) x/512a 0x0000000016d800000-0x1000 --force
0x16d7ff000: 0x0000000248e0ce34
0x16d7ff008: 0x0000000248e01bb4
0x16d7ff010: 0x0000000248e024fc
0x16d7ff018: 0x0000000248e020dc
0x16d7ff020: 0x0000000248e0cf0c
0x16d7ff028: 0x0000000248e0240c
0x16d7ff030: 0x000000016d7ff900
0x16d7ff038: 0x925b8001028e19c8 (0x00000001028e19c8) dyld`dyld4::prepare(dyld4::APIs&, dyld3::MachOAnalyzer const*) + 2124
0x16d7ff040: 0x0000000102610bf0
0x16d7ff048: 0x0000000248e0d5f4
0x16d7ff050: 0x0000000248e0d52c
0x16d7ff058: 0x0000000248e0cd04
0x16d7ff060: 0x0000000248e0d054
0x16d7ff068: 0x0000000248e0cf7c
0x16d7ff070: 0x0000000248e01d94
0x16d7ff078: 0x0000000248e01f94
0x16d7ff080: 0x0000000248e0276c
0x16d7ff088: 0x0000000248e0d38c
0x16d7ff090: 0x0000000248e0cb7c
0x16d7ff098: 0x0000000248e0b384
0x16d7ff0a0: 0x0000000248e0d2cc
0x16d7ff0a8: 0x0000000248e054ec
0x16d7ff0b0: 0x0000000248e01a6c
0x16d7ff0b8: 0x0000000248e022a4
0x16d7ff0c0: 0x0000000248e0d124
0x16d7ff0c8: 0x0000000248e09fd4
0x16d7ff0d0: 0x0000000248e08fb4
0x16d7ff0d8: 0x0000000248e0c364
0x16d7ff0e0: 0x0000000248e03f04
0x16d7ff0e8: 0x0000000248e0d44c
0x16d7ff0f0: 0x0000000248e021a4
0x16d7ff0f8: 0x0000000248e0295c
0x16d7ff100: 0x0000000248e0ca04
0x16d7ff108: 0x0000000248e01e94
0x16d7ff110: 0x0000000248e0521c
0x16d7ff118: 0x0000000248e044e4
0x16d7ff120: 0x0000000248e16574
```

```
0x16d7ff128: 0x0000000248e0a0bc
0x16d7ff130: 0x0000000248e0d1ec
0x16d7ff138: 0x0000000248e0258c
0x16d7ff140: 0x0000000248e0287c
0x16d7ff148: 0x0000000248e02664
0x16d7ff150: 0x0000000248e06d7c
0x16d7ff158: 0x0000000248e01c64
0x16d7ff160: 0x0000000248e0cde4
0x16d7ff168: 0x0000000248e01b64
0x16d7ff170: 0x0000000248e024ac
0x16d7ff178: 0x0000000248e0208c
0x16d7ff180: 0x000000016d7ff2d0
0x16d7ff188: 0x000000016d7ff1a0
0x16d7ff190: 0x000000016d7ff900
0x16d7ff198: 0x01568001028e1e94 (0x00000001028e1e94) dyld`dyld4::prepare(dyld4::APIs&, dyld3::MachOAnalyzer const*) + 3352
0x16d7ff1a0: 0x000000016d7ff2d0
0x16d7ff1a8: 0x0000000000000000
0x16d7ff1b0: 0x0000000000000000
0x16d7ff1b8: 0x000000016d7ff1a0
0x16d7ff1c0: 0x0000000000000000
0x16d7ff1c8: 0x0000000000000000
0x16d7ff1d0: 0x0000000000000000
0x16d7ff1d8: 0x0000000000000000
0x16d7ff1e0: 0x0000000000000000
0x16d7ff1e8: 0x0000000000000000
0x16d7ff1f0: 0x000000001f07000c
0x16d7ff1f8: 0x0000000000000000
0x16d7ff200: 0x0000000000000000
0x16d7ff208: 0x0000000000000000
0x16d7ff210: 0x0000000000000000
0x16d7ff218: 0x0000000000000000
0x16d7ff220: 0x0000000000000000
0x16d7ff228: 0x0000000000000000
0x16d7ff230: 0x0000000000000000
0x16d7ff238: 0x0000000000000000
0x16d7ff240: 0x0000000000000000
0x16d7ff248: 0x0000000000000000
0x16d7ff250: 0x0000000000000000
0x16d7ff258: 0x0000000000000000
0x16d7ff260: 0x000000016d7ff040
0x16d7ff268: 0x000000000000002a
0x16d7ff270: 0x0000000000000001
0x16d7ff278: 0x0000000000000000
0x16d7ff280: 0x0000000102954310 dyld`_NSConcreteStackBlock
0x16d7ff288: 0x0000000042000000
0x16d7ff290: 0x00000001028e2888 dyld`invocation function for block in dyld4::prepare(dyld4::APIs&, dyld3::MachOAnalyzer const*)
0x16d7ff298: 0x0000000010293c250 dyld`__block_descriptor_tmp.24
0x16d7ff2a0: 0x000000016d7ff2a8
0x16d7ff2a8: 0x0000000000000000
0x16d7ff2b0: 0x000000016d7ff2a8
0x16d7ff2b8: 0x0000004002000000
0x16d7ff2c0: 0x00000001028e286c dyld`__Block_byref_object_copy_.18
0x16d7ff2c8: 0x00000001028e2880 dyld`__Block_byref_object_dispose_.19
0x16d7ff2d0: 0x0000000000000000
0x16d7ff2d8: 0x0000000000000000
0x16d7ff2e0: 0x0000000000000000
0x16d7ff2e8: 0x0000000102954310 dyld`_NSConcreteStackBlock
0x16d7ff2f0: 0x0000000042000000
0x16d7ff2f8: 0x00000001028e26c0 dyld`invocation function for block in dyld4::prepare(dyld4::APIs&, dyld3::MachOAnalyzer const*)
0x16d7ff300: 0x0000000010293c220 dyld`__block_descriptor_tmp.17
0x16d7ff308: 0x000000016d7ff378
0x16d7ff310: 0x0000000102610060 -> 0x000000010293e400 dyld`vtable for dyld4::APIs + 16
0x16d7ff318: 0x0101000000000101
0x16d7ff320: 0x0000000101000000
0x16d7ff328: 0x000000016d7ff368
0x16d7ff330: 0x0000000000000000
0x16d7ff338: 0x0000000000000000
0x16d7ff340: 0x0100000000000101
0x16d7ff348: 0x0000000101000000
0x16d7ff350: 0x000000016d7ff368
0x16d7ff358: 0x0000000000000000
0x16d7ff360: 0x0000000000000000
0x16d7ff368: 0x0000000000000000
0x16d7ff370: 0x0000000102610bf0
0x16d7ff378: 0x0000000000000000
0x16d7ff380: 0x000000016d7ff378
0x16d7ff388: 0x0000005002000000
0x16d7ff390: 0x00000001028e25a0 dyld`__Block_byref_object_copy_.11
0x16d7ff398: 0x00000001028e25bc dyld`__Block_byref_object_dispose_.12
0x16d7ff3a0: 0x000000016d7ff3f0
0x16d7ff3a8: 0x0000000000000010
0x16d7ff3b0: 0x0000000000000001
0x16d7ff3b8: 0x0000000000000000
0x16d7ff3c0: 0x0000000000000000
0x16d7ff3c8: 0x0000000102610bf0
0x16d7ff3d0: 0x0000000000000000
0x16d7ff3d8: 0x0000000000000000
```

```
0x16d7ff3e0: 0x0000000000000000
0x16d7ff3e8: 0x000000010293c078 dyld`dyld4::sConfigBuffer + 8
0x16d7ff3f0: 0x0000000102610bf0
0x16d7ff3f8: 0x0000000016d7ffa68 -> 0x0000000102600000 App1`_mh_execute_header
0x16d7ff400: 0x0000001a01000012
0x16d7ff408: 0x0000000102954300 dyld`dyld4::sSyscallDelegate
0x16d7ff410: 0x000000016d7ff850 -> 0x0000000102603eec App1`main
0x16d7ff418: 0x45748001028e375c (0x00000001028e375c)
dyld`dyld4::ProcessConfig::Process::pathFromFileHexStrings(dyld4::SyscallDelegate&, char const*) + 124
0x16d7ff420: 0x000000016d7fff64
0x16d7ff428: 0x62696c2f7273752f
0x16d7ff430: 0x000000016d7ff5c8
0x16d7ff438: 0x000000016d7ff5a0 -> 0x0000000102954310 dyld`_NSConcreteStackBlock
0x16d7ff440: 0x000000018e887cc0
0x16d7ff448: 0x000000016d7ff54f
0x16d7ff450: 0x000000016d7ff500
0x16d7ff458: 0x5a52800102911ed8 (0x0000000102911ed8) dyld`invocation function for block in dyld3::MachOFile::forEachSection(void
(dyld3::MachOFile::SectionInfo const&, bool, bool&) block_pointer) const + 528
0x16d7ff460: 0x000000002e5d8000
0x16d7ff468: 0x0000000024151f49
0x16d7ff470: 0x0000000213db8000
0x16d7ff478: 0x00000001028dc000
0x16d7ff480: 0x66306db6e99fee38
0x16d7ff488: 0xc644690ddf6d5c8c
0x16d7ff490: 0x0000000000003eec
0x16d7ff498: 0x0000000000000000
0x16d7ff4a0: 0x000000000000002a
0x16d7ff4a8: 0x0000000000002330
0x16d7ff4b0: 0x000000018e887df8
0x16d7ff4b8: 0x0000000100000000
0x16d7ff4c0: 0x0000000000000006
0x16d7ff4c8: 0x0000000000000000
0x16d7ff4d0: 0x000000018e888128
0x16d7ff4d8: 0x000000018e887020
0x16d7ff4e0: 0x0000000000000017
0x16d7ff4e8: 0x000000016d7ff5a0 -> 0x0000000102954310 dyld`_NSConcreteStackBlock
0x16d7ff4f0: 0x000000018e887000
0x16d7ff4f8: 0x000000016d7ff608
0x16d7ff500: 0x000000016d7ff590
0x16d7ff508: 0x96238001028ddf98 (0x00000001028ddf98) dyld`dyld3::MachOFile::forEachLoadCommand(Diagnostics&, void (load_command const*,
bool&) block_pointer) const + 168
0x16d7ff510: 0x0000000000000000
0x16d7ff518: 0x000000016d7ff5d8
0x16d7ff520: 0x000000018e887000
0x16d7ff528: 0x000000016d7ff628
0x16d7ff530: 0x000000016d7ff5c0
0x16d7ff538: 0x54428001028ddf98 (0x00000001028ddf98) dyld`dyld3::MachOFile::forEachLoadCommand(Diagnostics&, void (load_command const*,
bool&) block_pointer) const + 168
0x16d7ff540: 0x0000000000000000
0x16d7ff548: 0x0000000000000000
0x16d7ff550: 0x0000000000000000
0x16d7ff558: 0x0000000000000000
0x16d7ff560: 0x000000016d7ff738
0x16d7ff568: 0x000000010293c0fc dyld`dyld4::sConfigBuffer + 140
0x16d7ff570: 0x000000010293c078 dyld`dyld4::sConfigBuffer + 8
0x16d7ff578: 0x000000010293c0f0 dyld`dyld4::sConfigBuffer + 128
0x16d7ff580: 0x000000018e887000
0x16d7ff588: 0x000000016d7ff658 -> 0x0000000102954310 dyld`_NSConcreteStackBlock
0x16d7ff590: 0x000000016d7ff640
0x16d7ff598: 0x6148800102911c9c (0x0000000102911c9c) dyld`dyld3::MachOFile::forEachSection(void (dyld3::MachOFile::SectionInfo const&,
bool, bool&) block_pointer) const + 220
0x16d7ff5a0: 0x0000000102954310 dyld`_NSConcreteStackBlock
0x16d7ff5a8: 0x0000000042000000
0x16d7ff5b0: 0x0000000102911cc8 dyld`invocation function for block in dyld3::MachOFile::forEachSection(void
(dyld3::MachOFile::SectionInfo const&, bool, bool&) block_pointer) const
0x16d7ff5b8: 0x000000010293efd8 dyld`__block_descriptor_tmp.87
0x16d7ff5c0: 0x000000016d7ff658 -> 0x0000000102954310 dyld`_NSConcreteStackBlock
0x16d7ff5c8: 0x000000016d7ff5e8
0x16d7ff5d0: 0x000000018e887000
0x16d7ff5d8: 0x000000016d7ff614
0x16d7ff5e0: 0x0000000042000000
0x16d7ff5e8: 0x0000000000000000
0x16d7ff5f0: 0x000000016d7ff5e8
0x16d7ff5f8: 0x0000002000000000
0x16d7ff600: 0x000000010000000a
0x16d7ff608: 0x0000000000000000
0x16d7ff610: 0x626f5f5f6d7ff608
0x16d7ff618: 0x6567616d695f636a
0x16d7ff620: 0x000000006f666e69
0x16d7ff628: 0x37f570e601fc0072
0x16d7ff630: 0x000000016d7ff688
0x16d7ff638: 0x000000018e887000
0x16d7ff640: 0x000000016d7ff6c0
0x16d7ff648: 0xdd5e00010290fd90 (0x000000010290fd90) dyld`DyldSharedCache::objcOpt() const + 216
0x16d7ff650: 0x000000016d7ff680
0x16d7ff658: 0x0000000102954310 dyld`_NSConcreteStackBlock
0x16d7ff660: 0x0000000042000000
```

```
0x16d7ff668: 0x000000010290fddc dyld`invocation function for block in DyldSharedCache::objcOpt() const
0x16d7ff670: 0x000000010293ebf8 dyld`__block_descriptor_tmp.41
0x16d7ff678: 0x000000016d7ff688
0x16d7ff680: 0x000000000e6dc000
0x16d7ff688: 0x0000000000000000
0x16d7ff690: 0x000000016d7ff688
0x16d7ff698: 0x0000002000000000
0x16d7ff6a0: 0x000000018e8babe0 libobjc.A.dylib`_objc_opt_data
0x16d7ff6a8: 0x000000060293c0f0
0x16d7ff6b0: 0x0000000102954300 dyld`dyld4::sSyscallDelegate
0x16d7ff6b8: 0x000000010293c110 dyld`dyld4::sConfigBuffer + 160
0x16d7ff6c0: 0x000000016d7ff8c0
0x16d7ff6c8: 0x5c1d0001028e4024 (0x00000001028e4024) dyld`dyld4::ProcessConfig::DyldCache::DyldCache(dyld4::ProcessConfig::Process&,
dyld4::ProcessConfig::Security const&, dyld4::ProcessConfig::Logging const&, dyld4::SyscallDelegate&) + 548
0x16d7ff6d0: 0x0000000102600000 App1`_mh_execute_header
0x16d7ff6d8: 0x000000016d7ff7d8
0x16d7ff6e0: 0x0000000000000000
0x16d7ff6e8: 0x0000000100000000
0x16d7ff6f0: 0x0000000000000001
0x16d7ff6f8: 0x0000000000000000
0x16d7ff700: 0x0000000000000000
0x16d7ff708: 0x0000000000000000
0x16d7ff710: 0x000000010293c0f0 dyld`dyld4::sConfigBuffer + 128
0x16d7ff718: 0x000000010293c078 dyld`dyld4::sConfigBuffer + 8
0x16d7ff720: 0x0000000102600000 App1`_mh_execute_header
0x16d7ff728: 0x000000016d7ff7f8
0x16d7ff730: 0x0000000000000000
0x16d7ff738: 0x0000000000000000
0x16d7ff740: 0x0000000000000000
0x16d7ff748: 0x0000000000000000
0x16d7ff750: 0x0000000000000000
0x16d7ff758: 0x0000000000000000
0x16d7ff760: 0x0000000000000000
0x16d7ff768: 0x000000010293c070 dyld`dyld4::sConfigBuffer
0x16d7ff770: 0x000000016d7ff840
0x16d7ff778: 0x000000016d7ff800
0x16d7ff780: 0x000000016d7ff7e0
0x16d7ff788: 0x791080018e9d02f8 (0x000000018e9d02f8) libsystem_kernel.dylib`clock_get_time + 100
0x16d7ff790: 0x000000000007c000
0x16d7ff798: 0x0000002c00001200
0x16d7ff7a0: 0x0000050700000000
0x16d7ff7a8: 0x0000044c00000000
0x16d7ff7b0: 0x0000000100000000
0x16d7ff7b8: 0x000190f500000000
0x16d7ff7c0: 0x000000001ad957d8
0x16d7ff7c8: 0x0000020300000008
0x16d7ff7d0: 0x000000016d7ff840
0x16d7ff7d8: 0x000000016d7ff830
0x16d7ff7e0: 0x000000016d7ff820
0x16d7ff7e8: 0x173400018e8d6f60 (0x000000018e8d6f60) libsystem_c.dylib`nanosleep + 116
0x16d7ff7f0: 0x000000018ea0cde8 libsystem_pthread.dylib`_pthread_attr_default
0x16d7ff7f8: 0x0000000000000000
0x16d7ff800: 0x1ad957d8000190f5
0x16d7ff808: 0x0000000000000000
0x16d7ff810: 0x0000000102603eec App1`main
0x16d7ff818: 0x000000007fffffff
0x16d7ff820: 0x000000016d7ff860
0x16d7ff828: 0x706400018e8e1b78 (0x000000018e8e1b78) libsystem_c.dylib`sleep + 52
0x16d7ff830: 0x0000000000000000
0x16d7ff838: 0x0000000000000000
0x16d7ff840: 0x000000007fffffff
0x16d7ff848: 0x0000000000000000
0x16d7ff850: 0x0000000102603eec App1`main
0x16d7ff858: 0x00000000ffffffff
0x16d7ff860: 0x000000016d7ff8a0
0x16d7ff868: 0x772700018e8e1b90 (0x000000018e8e1b90) libsystem_c.dylib`sleep + 76
0x16d7ff870: 0x0000000000000000
0x16d7ff878: 0x0000000000000000
0x16d7ff880: 0x0000000000000000
0x16d7ff888: 0x000000010293c070 dyld`dyld4::sConfigBuffer
0x16d7ff890: 0x0000000102603eec App1`main
0x16d7ff898: 0x0000000102610060 -> 0x000000010293e400 dyld`vtable for dyld4::APIs + 16
0x16d7ff8a0: 0x000000016d7ff900
0x16d7ff8a8: 0x1131800102603f90 (0x0000000102603f90) App1`main + 164
0x16d7ff8b0: 0x0000000000000000
0x16d7ff8b8: 0x0000000000000000
0x16d7ff8c0: 0x0000000000000000
0x16d7ff8c8: 0x000000016dab7000
0x16d7ff8d0: 0x000000016da2b000
0x16d7ff8d8: 0x000000016d99f000
0x16d7ff8e0: 0x000000016d913000
0x16d7ff8e8: 0x000000016d887000
0x16d7ff8f0: 0x000000016d7ffa78
0x16d7ff8f8: 0x0000000000000001
0x16d7ff900: 0x000000016d7ffa50
0x16d7ff908: 0x000000010228e108c dyld`start + 520
0x16d7ff910: 0x0000000000000000
```

```
0x16d7ff918: 0x0000000000000000
0x16d7ff920: 0x0000000000000000
0x16d7ff928: 0x0000000000000000
0x16d7ff930: 0x0000000000000000
0x16d7ff938: 0x0000000000000000
0x16d7ff940: 0x0000000102940138  dyld`_os_lock_type_unfair
0x16d7ff948: 0x0000000000000000
0x16d7ff950: 0x000000004d55545a
0x16d7ff958: 0x000020a000000000
0x16d7ff960: 0x4d55545a00000000
0x16d7ff968: 0x0000000000000000
0x16d7ff970: 0x0000000000000000
0x16d7ff978: 0xffffffffffffffff
0x16d7ff980: 0xfffffffe928006af
0x16d7ff988: 0x4d55545a4d55545a
0x16d7ff990: 0x0000000000000000
0x16d7ff998: 0x0000000000000000
0x16d7ff9a0: 0x0000000102954310  dyld`_NSConcreteStackBlock
0x16d7ff9a8: 0x0000000040000000
0x16d7ff9b0: 0x000000010028e1154  dyld`__start_block_invoke.3
0x16d7ff9b8: 0x000000010293c200  dyld`__block_descriptor_tmp.5
0x16d7ff9c0: 0x00000001028dc000
0x16d7ff9c8: 0x0000000102954310  dyld`_NSConcreteStackBlock
0x16d7ff9d0: 0x0000000042000000
0x16d7ff9d8: 0x000000010028e110c  dyld`__start_block_invoke
0x16d7ff9e0: 0x000000010293c1d0  dyld`__block_descriptor_tmp
0x16d7ff9e8: 0x000000016d7ffa00
0x16d7ff9f0: 0x00000001028dc000
0x16d7ff9f8: 0x00000001028dc000
0x16d7ffa00: 0x0000000000000000
0x16d7ffa08: 0x000000016d7ffa00
0x16d7ffa10: 0x0000003002000000
0x16d7ffa18: 0x00000001028e10f8  dyld`__Block_byref_object_copy_
0x16d7ffa20: 0x00000001028e1104  dyld`__Block_byref_object_dispose_
0x16d7ffa28: 0x0000000000000000
0x16d7ffa30: 0x0000000000000000
0x16d7ffa38: 0x0000000000000000
0x16d7ffa40: 0x0000000000000000
0x16d7ffa48: 0x0000000000000000
0x16d7ffa50: 0x0000000000000000
0x16d7ffa58: 0x6527800000000000
0x16d7ffa60: 0x0000000000000000
0x16d7ffa68: 0x0000000102600000  App1`_mh_execute_header
0x16d7ffa70: 0x0000000000000001
0x16d7ffa78: 0x000000016d7ffba8
0x16d7ffa80: 0x0000000000000000
0x16d7ffa88: 0x000000016d7ffbaf
0x16d7ffa90: 0x000000016d7ffbcb
0x16d7ffa98: 0x000000016d7ffbda
0x16d7ffaa0: 0x000000016d7ffbee
0x16d7ffaa8: 0x000000016d7ffc27
0x16d7ffab0: 0x000000016d7ffc40
0x16d7ffab8: 0x000000016d7ffc75
0x16d7ffac0: 0x000000016d7ffc83
0x16d7ffac8: 0x000000016d7ffcc5
0x16d7ffad0: 0x000000016d7ffd0e
0x16d7ffad8: 0x000000016d7ffd36
0x16d7ffae0: 0x000000016d7ffd77
0x16d7ffae8: 0x000000016d7ffd85
0x16d7ffaf0: 0x000000016d7ffd98
0x16d7ffaf8: 0x000000016d7ffda0
0x16d7ffb00: 0x000000016d7ffdb5
0x16d7ffb08: 0x000000016d7ffdc6
0x16d7ffb10: 0x000000016d7ffe02
0x16d7ffb18: 0x000000016d7ffe13
0x16d7ffb20: 0x0000000000000000
0x16d7ffb28: 0x000000016d7ffb90
0x16d7ffb30: 0x000000016d7ffe60
0x16d7ffb38: 0x000000016d7ffe70
0x16d7ffb40: 0x000000016d7ffe8f
0x16d7ffb48: 0x000000016d7ffec4
0x16d7ffb50: 0x000000016d7ffee0
0x16d7ffb58: 0x000000016d7fff16
0x16d7ffb60: 0x000000016d7fff3c
0x16d7ffb68: 0x000000016d7fff65
0x16d7ffb70: 0x000000016d7fffa0
0x16d7ffb78: 0x000000016d7fffdd
0x16d7ffb80: 0x000000016d7fffeb
0x16d7ffb88: 0x0000000000000000
0x16d7ffb90: 0x6261747563657865
0x16d7ffb98: 0x3d687461705f656c
0x16d7ffba0: 0x0000317070412f2e
0x16d7ffba8: 0x5400317070412f2e
0x16d7ffbb0: 0x474f52505f4d5245
0x16d7ffbb8: 0x6c7070413d4d4152
0x16d7ffbc0: 0x6e696d7265545f65
0x16d7ffbc8: 0x4c4c454853006c61
```

```
0x16d7ffbd0:  0x737a2f6e69622f3d
0x16d7ffbd8:  0x783d4d5245540068
0x16d7ffbe0:  0x3635322d6d726574
0x16d7ffbe8:  0x4d5400726f6c6f63
0x16d7ffbf0:  0x61762f3d52494450
0x16d7ffbf8:  0x7265646c6f662f72
0x16d7ffc00:  0x7672382f6c6e2f73
0x16d7ffc08:  0x7836306435746b72
0x16d7ffc10:  0x5f35626e6d387231
0x16d7ffc18:  0x3030306d5f32636c
0x16d7ffc20:  0x54002f542f6e6730
0x16d7ffc28:  0x474f52505f4d5245
0x16d7ffc30:  0x535245565f4d4152
0x16d7ffc38:  0x003534343d4e4f49
0x16d7ffc40:  0x5345535f4d524554
0x16d7ffc48:  0x3d44495f4e4f4953
0x16d7ffc50:  0x3534393231354330
0x16d7ffc58:  0x39342d413842442d
0x16d7ffc60:  0x2d453337422d3945
0x16d7ffc68:  0x3831383030353634
0x16d7ffc70:  0x4553550042354644
0x16d7ffc78:  0x696e696172743d52
0x16d7ffc80:  0x415f48535300676e
0x16d7ffc88:  0x4b434f535f485455
0x16d7ffc90:  0x7461766972702f3d
0x16d7ffc98:  0x6f632f706d742f65
0x16d7ffca0:  0x2e656c7070612e6d
0x16d7ffca8:  0x2e6468636e75616c
0x16d7ffcb0:  0x4a4b4b695a385a4d
0x16d7ffcb8:  0x657473694c2f6579
0x16d7ffcc0:  0x544150007372656e
0x16d7ffcc8:  0x6c2f7273752f3d48
0x16d7ffcd0:  0x6e69622f6c61636f
0x16d7ffcd8:  0x69622f7273752f3a
0x16d7ffce0:  0x2f3a6e69622f3a6e
0x16d7ffce8:  0x6e6962732f727375
0x16d7ffcf0:  0x2f3a6e6962732f3a
0x16d7ffcf8:  0x2f7972617262694c
0x16d7ffd00:  0x73752f656c707041
0x16d7ffd08:  0x5f5f006e69622f72
0x16d7ffd10:  0x656c646e75424643
0x16d7ffd18:  0x696669746e656449
0x16d7ffd20:  0x612e6d6f633d7265
0x16d7ffd28:  0x7265542e656c7070
0x16d7ffd30:  0x5750006c616e696d
0x16d7ffd38:  0x73726573552f3d44
0x16d7ffd40:  0x6e696e6916172742f
0x16d7ffd48:  0x2d4144434d412f67
0x16d7ffd50:  0x70412f73706d7544
0x16d7ffd58:  0x2f317070412f7370
0x16d7ffd60:  0x72502f646c697542
0x16d7ffd68:  0x522f73746375646f
0x16d7ffd70:  0x5800657361656c65
0x16d7ffd78:  0x5347414c465f4350
0x16d7ffd80:  0x435058003078303d
0x16d7ffd88:  0x454349565245535f
0x16d7ffd90:  0x00303d454d414e5f
0x16d7ffd98:  0x00313d4c564c4853
0x16d7ffda0:  0x73552f3d454d4f48
0x16d7ffda8:  0x696172742f737265
0x16d7ffdb0:  0x474f4c00676e696e
0x16d7ffdb8:  0x6172743d454d414e
0x16d7ffdc0:  0x4c4f00676e696e69
0x16d7ffdc8:  0x73552f3d44575044
0x16d7ffdd0:  0x696172742f737265
0x16d7ffdd8:  0x434d412f676e696e
0x16d7ffde0:  0x73706d7544d4144
0x16d7ffde8:  0x70412f737070412f
0x16d7ffdf0:  0x646c6975422f3170
0x16d7ffdf8:  0x746375646f72502f
0x16d7ffe00:  0x653d474e414c0073
0x16d7ffe08:  0x4654552e45495f6e
0x16d7ffe10:  0x73552f3d5f00382d
0x16d7ffe18:  0x696172742f737265
0x16d7ffe20:  0x434d412f676e696e
0x16d7ffe28:  0x73706d7544d4144
0x16d7ffe30:  0x70412f737070412f
0x16d7ffe38:  0x646c6975422f3170
0x16d7ffe40:  0x746375646f72502f
0x16d7ffe48:  0x7361656c65522f73
0x16d7ffe50:  0x317070412f2e2f65
0x16d7ffe58:  0x0000000000000000
0x16d7ffe60:  0x0000000000000000
0x16d7ffe68:  0x0000000000000000
0x16d7ffe70:  0x0000000000000000
0x16d7ffe78:  0x0000000000000000
0x16d7ffe80:  0x0000000000000000
```

```
0x16d7ffe88: 0x0000000000000000
0x16d7ffe90: 0x0000000000000000
0x16d7ffe98: 0x0000000000000000
0x16d7ffea0: 0x0000000000000000
0x16d7ffea8: 0x0000000000000000
0x16d7ffeb0: 0x0000000000000000
0x16d7ffeb8: 0x0000000000000000
0x16d7ffec0: 0x5f72747000000000
0x16d7ffec8: 0x00003d65676e756d
0x16d7ffed0: 0x0000000000000000
0x16d7ffed8: 0x0000000000000000
0x16d7ffee0: 0x6174735f6e69616d
0x16d7ffee8: 0x00000000003d6b63
0x16d7ffef0: 0x0000000000000000
0x16d7ffef8: 0x0000000000000000
0x16d7fff00: 0x0000000000000000
0x16d7fff08: 0x0000000000000000
0x16d7fff10: 0x7865500000000000
0x16d7fff18: 0x656c626261747563
0x16d7fff20: 0x78303d656c69665f
0x16d7fff28: 0x3030303031306131
0x16d7fff30: 0x64623178302c3231
0x16d7fff38: 0x646c796400313864
0x16d7fff40: 0x78303d656c69665f
0x16d7fff48: 0x3030303031306131
0x16d7fff50: 0x66666678302c3231
0x16d7fff58: 0x6430303066666666
0x16d7fff60: 0x6578650034393863
0x16d7fff68: 0x5f656c6261747563
0x16d7fff70: 0x373d687361686463
0x16d7fff78: 0x3063396235643761
0x16d7fff80: 0x3236386664643335
0x16d7fff88: 0x6461393065343935
0x16d7fff90: 0x6666333639636130
0x16d7fff98: 0x0030373063656532
0x16d7fffa0: 0x6261747563657865
0x16d7fffa8: 0x68746f6f625f656c
0x16d7fffb0: 0x373730643d687361
0x16d7fffb8: 0x3039646339313036
0x16d7fffc0: 0x3262323863313764
0x16d7fffc8: 0x3432656438346438
0x16d7fffd0: 0x6132663936306536
0x16d7fffd8: 0x6d72610064633832
0x16d7fffe0: 0x3d6962615f653436
0x16d7fffe8: 0x6f705f687400736f
0x16d7ffff0: 0x00000000003d7472
0x16d7ffff8: 0x0000000000000000
```

11.   Dump the contents of memory pointed to by *environ* variable in null-terminated string format:

```
(lldb) x/20s 0x000000016d7ffbaf
0x16d7ffbaf: "TERM_PROGRAM=Apple_Terminal"
0x16d7ffbcb: "SHELL=/bin/zsh"
0x16d7ffbda: "TERM=xterm-256color"
0x16d7ffbee: "TMPDIR=/var/folders/nl/8rvrkt5d06x1r8mnb5_lc2_m0000gn/T/"
0x16d7ffc27: "TERM_PROGRAM_VERSION=445"
0x16d7ffc40: "TERM_SESSION_ID=0C512945-DB8A-49E9-B73E-46500818DF5B"
0x16d7ffc75: "USER=training"
0x16d7ffc83: "SSH_AUTH_SOCK=/private/tmp/com.apple.launchd.MZ8ZiKKJye/Listeners"
0x16d7ffcc5: "PATH=/usr/local/bin:/usr/bin:/bin:/usr/sbin:/sbin:/Library/Apple/usr/bin"
0x16d7ffd0e: "__CFBundleIdentifier=com.apple.Terminal"
0x16d7ffd36: "PWD=/Users/training/AMCDA-Dumps/Apps/App1/Build/Products/Release"
0x16d7ffd77: "XPC_FLAGS=0x0"
0x16d7ffd85: "XPC_SERVICE_NAME=0"
0x16d7ffd98: "SHLVL=1"
0x16d7ffda0: "HOME=/Users/training"
0x16d7ffdb5: "LOGNAME=training"
0x16d7ffdc6: "OLDPWD=/Users/training/AMCDA-Dumps/Apps/App1/Build/Products"
0x16d7ffe02: "LANG=en_IE.UTF-8"
0x16d7ffe13: "_=/Users/training/AMCDA-Dumps/Apps/App1/Build/Products/Release/./App1"
0x16d7ffe59: ""
```

12.　Get the list of loaded modules:

```
(lldb) image list
[  0] 87587B20-46B7-331A-ABC0-F7ECB36E3DEB 0x0000000102600000 /Users/training/AMCDA-Dumps/Apps/App1/Build/Products/Release/App1
[  1] 38EE9FE9-B66D-3066-8C5C-6DDF0D6944C6 0x00000001028dc000 /usr/lib/dyld
[  2] 9232C168-6ECA-3B7D-B081-E7C46B379836 0x000000019956d000 /usr/lib/libSystem.B.dylib
[  3] 7E9E684F-57B6-3196-8AEC-908B46DEEBD4 0x0000000199567000 /usr/lib/system/libcache.dylib
[  4] FB7DF5AC-35DB-3B80-B2F6-BC69375390AE 0x0000000199525000 /usr/lib/system/libcommonCrypto.dylib
[  5] 68788078-BF1D-3CD1-91A7-4C59FD78FB75 0x000000019954e000 /usr/lib/system/libcompiler_rt.dylib
[  6] 654D0DA0-8277-361D-88DC-1430504B5436 0x0000000199545000 /usr/lib/system/libcopyfile.dylib
[  7] 2D00FEEC-7984-342B-9516-5D49C5D98204 0x000000018e78b000 /usr/lib/system/libcorecrypto.dylib
[  8] B3C7A004-1069-3171-B630-2C386A8B399C 0x000000018e840000 /usr/lib/system/libdispatch.dylib
[  9] F298A03D-5BC7-3BCA-8880-B956E52EAD01 0x000000018ea0e000 /usr/lib/system/libdyld.dylib
[ 10] 49D72074-0C58-317C-9B8B-762C13C0C084 0x000000019955d000 /usr/lib/system/libkeymgr.dylib
[ 11] ED4EE8AE-EA60-33B7-9676-E6119B7449E3 0x0000000199500000 /usr/lib/system/libmacho.dylib
[ 12] B887350E-B1C9-386C-B5EB-26F08C7C0152 0x000000198bf0000 /usr/lib/system/libquarantine.dylib
[ 13] 157C8E50-D4A5-3DFC-8E0B-756E03E2082B 0x000000019955a000 /usr/lib/system/libremovefile.dylib
[ 14] EC04DA81-C3B5-3AC5-9042-7F07DF48B42A 0x0000000193b86000 /usr/lib/system/libsystem_asl.dylib
[ 15] 96462BD5-6BB4-3B69-89C9-2C70FA8852E7 0x000000018e72d000 /usr/lib/system/libsystem_blocks.dylib
[ 16] B25D2080-BB9E-38D6-8236-9CEF4B2F11A3 0x000000018e8c8000 /usr/lib/system/libsystem_c.dylib
[ 17] 4928F3C4-D438-354F-BA1C-0BD79F6475F3 0x0000000199552000 /usr/lib/system/libsystem_collections.dylib
[ 18] 3977B29D-624D-3DEE-94EF-95D29FB25252 0x0000000198085000 /usr/lib/system/libsystem_configuration.dylib
[ 19] D38210EF-8F23-380B-8B43-BB06A7305F67 0x0000000001972de000 /usr/lib/system/libsystem_containermanager.dylib
[ 20] D5F19732-3AA0-3B93-9F25-318A27DE5AC5 0x000000019925d000 /usr/lib/system/libsystem_coreservices.dylib
[ 21] 5D456083-E21E-319D-9BA0-57702B3FB09B 0x000000019113f000 /usr/lib/system/libsystem_darwin.dylib
[ 22] 10A4374A-D15A-31C8-AC6F-2DCC10D06444 0x000000019955e000 /usr/lib/system/libsystem_dnssd.dylib
[ 23] 5B14B45B-A15B-31AD-93FB-BAC43C001A23 0x000000018e8c5000 /usr/lib/system/libsystem_featureflags.dylib
[ 24] 413C2A97-5D32-317D-8E32-4258B8E728CE 0x000000018ea23000 /usr/lib/system/libsystem_info.dylib
[ 25] 31A9DAE0-FB1F-3CB8-8AB6-CA5A1192DFD8 0x000000001994c8000 /usr/lib/system/libsystem_m.dylib
[ 26] 427675C6-C4BF-390A-AF93-B28DAC36876A 0x000000018e815000 /usr/lib/system/libsystem_malloc.dylib
[ 27] 4C9F32FA-D88C-3966-A2F0-7030841C8093 0x0000000193b14000 /usr/lib/system/libsystem_networkextension.dylib
[ 28] 12A2A8B6-80B4-36CA-8245-830EBEDEF1C4 0x0000000191598000 /usr/lib/system/libsystem_notify.dylib
[ 29] E49E2F05-0E01-352E-8CB7-276F8EF8E6D6 0x000000019f8c1000 /usr/lib/system/libsystem_product_info_filter.dylib
[ 30] 2A2EB0A4-9822-36D1-999B-181D1BB964B5 0x000000019808a000 /usr/lib/system/libsystem_sandbox.dylib
[ 31] 18F251D3-8C66-3B8B-817A-C124498478F4 0x0000000199557000 /usr/lib/system/libsystem_secinit.dylib
[ 32] A9D87740-9C1D-3468-BF60-720A8D713CBA 0x000000018e9c9000 /usr/lib/system/libsystem_kernel.dylib
[ 33] A57FE7FB-9FF8-30CE-97A2-625D6DA20D00 0x000000018ea1b000 /usr/lib/system/libsystem_platform.dylib
[ 34] 63C4EEF9-69A5-38B1-996E-8D31B66A051D 0x000000018ea01000 /usr/lib/system/libsystem_pthread.dylib
[ 35] 2906E453-3254-32EA-880E-14AEEF5D7ECD 0x00000001952ea000 /usr/lib/system/libsystem_symptoms.dylib
[ 36] B5524014-1A7F-3D07-8855-5E75A55E4A11 0x000000018e771000 /usr/lib/system/libsystem_trace.dylib
[ 37] D9CA1CE3-6B1A-3E2B-BBAD-9D9B1DB00F92 0x0000000199532000 /usr/lib/system/libunwind.dylib
[ 38] 21D05A8B-D782-3FA7-9A9D-55A45E6E6621 0x000000018e72f000 /usr/lib/system/libxpc.dylib
[ 39] EC96F0FA-6341-3E1D-BE54-49B544E17F7D 0x000000018e887000 /usr/lib/libobjc.A.dylib
[ 40] 4E8D8A11-4217-3D56-9D41-5426F7CF307C 0x000000018e9b1000 /usr/lib/libc++abi.dylib
[ 41] 7E53021F-FDCE-3EC9-8B4C-97AD3B21D02E 0x000000019953d000 /usr/lib/liboah.dylib
[ 42] 3D1E6031-901D-3DF1-9E9A-F85FF1C2E803 0x000000018e94a000 /usr/lib/libc++.1.dylib
```

Exercise X2

- **Goal:** Learn how to identify multiple exceptions, find problem CPU instructions

- **Patterns:** Multiple Exceptions (User Mode); NULL Pointer (Data); NULL Pointer (Code)

- \AMCDA-Dumps\Exercise-X2.pdf

Exercise X2

Goal: Learn how to identify multiple exceptions, and find problem CPU instructions.

Patterns: Multiple Exceptions (User Mode); NULL Pointer (Data); NULL Pointer (Code).

1.   Identify a crash in diagnostic report *App2-2022-11-24-193346.ips* (thread, module, function name):

```
-------------------------------------
Translated Report (Full Report Below)
-------------------------------------

Process:             App2 [86095]
Path:                /Users/USER/*/App2
Identifier:          App2
Version:             ???
Code Type:           ARM-64 (Native)
Parent Process:      zsh [73148]
Responsible:         Terminal [9503]
User ID:             501

Date/Time:           2022-11-24 19:33:46.4854 +0000
OS Version:          macOS 12.6 (21G115)
Report Version:      12
Anonymous UUID:      6F758133-2B79-4743-8B70-8B1D8C510718

Sleep/Wake UUID:     6434EB6A-65A3-4A64-A494-9721E051C188

Time Awake Since Boot: 120000 seconds
Time Since Wake:       26 seconds

System Integrity Protection: enabled

Crashed Thread:      2

Exception Type:      EXC_BAD_ACCESS (SIGSEGV)
Exception Codes:     KERN_INVALID_ADDRESS at 0x0000000000000000
Exception Codes:     0x0000000000000001, 0x0000000000000000
Exception Note:      EXC_CORPSE_NOTIFY

Termination Reason:  Namespace SIGNAL, Code 11 Segmentation fault: 11
Terminating Process: exc handler [86095]

VM Region Info: 0 is not in any region.  Bytes before following region: 4378263552
    REGION TYPE                 START - END         [ VSIZE] PRT/MAX SHRMOD  REGION DETAIL
    UNUSED SPACE AT START
--->
    __TEXT                   104f70000-104f74000    [   16K] r-x/r-x SM=COW  ...s/USER/*/App2

Thread 0::  Dispatch queue: com.apple.main-thread
0   libsystem_kernel.dylib              0x18e9ca8b0 mach_msg_trap + 8
1   libsystem_kernel.dylib              0x18e9cad20 mach_msg + 76
2   libsystem_kernel.dylib              0x18e9d02f8 clock_get_time + 100
3   libsystem_c.dylib                   0x18e8d6f60 nanosleep + 116
4   libsystem_c.dylib                   0x18e8e1b78 sleep + 52
5   App2                                0x104f73f88 main + 164
6   dyld                                0x10517508c start + 520

Thread 1:
0   libsystem_kernel.dylib              0x18e9ce06c __semwait_signal + 8
1   libsystem_c.dylib                   0x18e8d6fc8 nanosleep + 220
2   libsystem_c.dylib                   0x18e8e1b78 sleep + 52
3   libsystem_c.dylib                   0x18e8e1b90 sleep + 76
4   App2                                0x104f73d6c bar_one + 16
5   App2                                0x104f73d80 foo_one + 12
6   App2                                0x104f73d9c thread_one + 20
7   libsystem_pthread.dylib             0x18ea0826c _pthread_start + 148
8   libsystem_pthread.dylib             0x18ea0308c thread_start + 8

Thread 2 Crashed:
0   App2                                0x104f73d2c procA + 16
```

68

```
1   App2                              0x104f73db8 bar_two + 12
2   App2                              0x104f73dcc foo_two + 12
3   App2                              0x104f73de8 thread_two + 20
4   libsystem_pthread.dylib           0x18ea0826c _pthread_start + 148
5   libsystem_pthread.dylib           0x18ea0308c thread_start + 8

Thread 3:
0   libsystem_kernel.dylib            0x18e9ce06c __semwait_signal + 8
1   libsystem_c.dylib                 0x18e8d6fc8 nanosleep + 220
2   libsystem_c.dylib                 0x18e8e1b78 sleep + 52
3   libsystem_c.dylib                 0x18e8e1b90 sleep + 76
4   App2                              0x104f73e08 bar_three + 16
5   App2                              0x104f73e1c foo_three + 12
6   App2                              0x104f73e38 thread_three + 20
7   libsystem_pthread.dylib           0x18ea0826c _pthread_start + 148
8   libsystem_pthread.dylib           0x18ea0308c thread_start + 8

Thread 4:
0   ???                               0x0 ???
1   App2                              0x104f73e54 bar_four + 12
2   App2                              0x104f73e68 foo_four + 12
3   App2                              0x104f73e84 thread_four + 20
4   libsystem_pthread.dylib           0x18ea0826c _pthread_start + 148
5   libsystem_pthread.dylib           0x18ea0308c thread_start + 8

Thread 5:
0   libsystem_pthread.dylib           0x18ea03084 thread_start + 0


Thread 2 crashed with ARM Thread State (64-bit):
    x0: 0x0000000000000000   x1: 0x0000000000000000   x2: 0x0000000104f73dd4   x3: 0x0000000000000000
    x4: 0x000000016afa3000   x5: 0x00000000190008ff   x6: 0x0000000000000000   x7: 0x0000000000000000
    x8: 0x0000000000000001   x9: 0x0000000000000000  x10: 0x0000000000000000  x11: 0x0000000000000000
   x12: 0x0000000000000000  x13: 0x0000000000000000  x14: 0x0000000000000000  x15: 0x0000000000000000
   x16: 0x0000000000000174  x17: 0x00000001e8b2b6b0  x18: 0x0000000000000000  x19: 0x000000016afa3000
   x20: 0x0000000000000000  x21: 0x0000000000000000  x22: 0x0000000000000000  x23: 0x0000000000000000
   x24: 0x0000000000000000  x25: 0x0000000000000000  x26: 0x0000000000000000  x27: 0x0000000000000000
   x28: 0x0000000000000000   fp: 0x000000016afa2f90   lr: 0x0000000104f73db8
    sp: 0x000000016afa2f80   pc: 0x0000000104f73d2c cpsr: 0x20001000
   far: 0x0000000000000000  esr: 0x92000046 (Data Abort) byte write Translation fault

Binary Images:
       0x18e9c9000 -        0x18ea00fff libsystem_kernel.dylib (*) <a9d87740-9c1d-3468-bf60-720a8d713cba>
/usr/lib/system/libsystem_kernel.dylib
       0x18e8c8000 -        0x18e949fff libsystem_c.dylib (*) <b25d2080-bb9e-38d6-8236-9cef4b2f11a3>
/usr/lib/system/libsystem_c.dylib
       0x104f70000 -        0x104f73fff App2 (*) <89560f33-0b12-3446-8908-fd5d4f0a3b22> /Users/USER/*/App2
       0x105170000 -        0x1051cffff dyld (*) <38ee9fe9-b66d-3066-8c5c-6ddf0d6944c6> /usr/lib/dyld
       0x18ea01000 -        0x18ea0dfff libsystem_pthread.dylib (*) <63c4eef9-69a5-38b1-996e-8d31b66a051d>
/usr/lib/system/libsystem_pthread.dylib
               0x0 - 0xffffffffffffffff ??? (*) <00000000-0000-0000-0000-000000000000> ???

External Modification Summary:
  Calls made by other processes targeting this process:
    task_for_pid: 0
    thread_create: 0
    thread_set_state: 0
  Calls made by this process:
    task_for_pid: 0
    thread_create: 0
    thread_set_state: 0
  Calls made by all processes on this machine:
    task_for_pid: 0
    thread_create: 0
    thread_set_state: 0

VM Region Summary:
ReadOnly portion of Libraries: Total=582.2M resident=0K(0%) swapped_out_or_unallocated=582.2M(100%)
Writable regions: Total=531.8M written=0K(0%) resident=0K(0%) swapped_out=0K(0%) unallocated=531.8M(100%)

                            VIRTUAL   REGION
REGION TYPE                    SIZE    COUNT (non-coalesced)
===========                 =======  =======
Kernel Alloc Once               32K        1
MALLOC                       137.3M       17
MALLOC_NANO (reserved)       384.0M        1               reserved VM address space (unallocated)
```

69

```
Stack                          10.7M       11
Stack (reserved)               56.0M        1      reserved VM address space (unallocated)
__AUTH                           46K       11
__AUTH_CONST                     67K       38
__DATA                          173K       37
__DATA_CONST                    258K       40
__DATA_DIRTY                     73K       21
__LINKEDIT                     577.6M       3
__OBJC_CONST                     10K        5
__OBJC_RO                       83.0M       1
__OBJC_RW                       3168K       1
__TEXT                          4708K      43
dyld private memory             1024K       1
shared memory                    16K        1
===========                   =======  =======
TOTAL                           1.2G      233
TOTAL, minus reserved VM space 817.9M     233
```

2.   Load a core dump *core.86095* and *App2* executable:

```
% lldb -c ~/AMCDA-Dumps/core.86095 -f ~/AMCDA-Dumps/Apps/App2/Build/Products/Release/App2
(lldb) target create "/Users/training/AMCDA-Dumps/Apps/App2/Build/Products/Release/App2" --
core "/Users/training/AMCDA-Dumps/core.86095"
Core file '/Users/training/AMCDA-Dumps/core.86095' (arm64) was loaded.
```

3.   Switch to the problem thread identified in the diagnostic report (core thread 2, thread #3):

```
(lldb) thread select 3
* thread #3, stop reason = ESR_EC_DABORT_EL0 (fault address: 0x0)
    frame #0: 0x0000000104f73d2c App2`procA + 16
App2`procA:
->  0x104f73d2c <+16>: str    w8, [x9]
    0x104f73d30 <+20>: add    sp, sp, #0x10
    0x104f73d34 <+24>: ret

App2`procB:
    0x104f73d38 <+0>:  sub    sp, sp, #0x20
```

```
(lldb) bt
* thread #3, stop reason = ESR_EC_DABORT_EL0 (fault address: 0x0)
  * frame #0: 0x0000000104f73d2c App2`procA + 16
    frame #1: 0x0000000104f73db8 App2`bar_two + 12
    frame #2: 0x0000000104f73dcc App2`foo_two + 12
    frame #3: 0x0000000104f73de8 App2`thread_two + 20
    frame #4: 0x000000018ea0826c libsystem_pthread.dylib`_pthread_start + 148
```

4.   Disassemble the problem instruction and check CPU register(s) details (NULL Data Pointer):

```
(lldb) x/i 0x0000000104f73d2c
->  0x104f73d2c: 0xb9000128    str    w8, [x9]
```

```
(lldb) re r x9
     x9 = 0x0000000000000000
```

```
(lldb) x $x9
error: core file does not contain 0x0
```

5.   List all thread stack traces and identify other anomalies:

```
(lldb) thread backtrace all
  thread #1
    frame #0: 0x000000018e9ca8b0 libsystem_kernel.dylib`mach_msg_trap + 8
    frame #1: 0x000000018e9cad20 libsystem_kernel.dylib`mach_msg + 76
    frame #2: 0x000000018e9d02f8 libsystem_kernel.dylib`clock_get_time + 100
    frame #3: 0x000000018e8d6f60 libsystem_c.dylib`nanosleep + 116
    frame #4: 0x000000018e8e1b78 libsystem_c.dylib`sleep + 52
    frame #5: 0x0000000104f73f88 App2`main + 164
    frame #6: 0x000000010517508c dyld`start + 520
  thread #2
    frame #0: 0x000000018e9ce06c libsystem_kernel.dylib`__semwait_signal + 8
    frame #1: 0x000000018e8d6fc8 libsystem_c.dylib`nanosleep + 220
    frame #2: 0x000000018e8e1b78 libsystem_c.dylib`sleep + 52
    frame #3: 0x000000018e8e1b90 libsystem_c.dylib`sleep + 76
    frame #4: 0x0000000104f73d6c App2`bar_one + 16
    frame #5: 0x0000000104f73d80 App2`foo_one + 12
    frame #6: 0x0000000104f73d9c App2`thread_one + 20
    frame #7: 0x000000018ea0826c libsystem_pthread.dylib`_pthread_start + 148
* thread #3, stop reason = ESR_EC_DABORT_EL0 (fault address: 0x0)
  * frame #0: 0x0000000104f73d2c App2`procA + 16
    frame #1: 0x0000000104f73db8 App2`bar_two + 12
    frame #2: 0x0000000104f73dcc App2`foo_two + 12
    frame #3: 0x0000000104f73de8 App2`thread_two + 20
    frame #4: 0x000000018ea0826c libsystem_pthread.dylib`_pthread_start + 148
  thread #4
    frame #0: 0x000000018e9ce06c libsystem_kernel.dylib`__semwait_signal + 8
    frame #1: 0x000000018e8d6fc8 libsystem_c.dylib`nanosleep + 220
    frame #2: 0x000000018e8e1b78 libsystem_c.dylib`sleep + 52
    frame #3: 0x000000018e8e1b90 libsystem_c.dylib`sleep + 76
    frame #4: 0x0000000104f73e08 App2`bar_three + 16
    frame #5: 0x0000000104f73e1c App2`foo_three + 12
    frame #6: 0x0000000104f73e38 App2`thread_three + 20
    frame #7: 0x000000018ea0826c libsystem_pthread.dylib`_pthread_start + 148
  thread #5, stop reason = ESR_EC_IABORT_EL0 (fault address: 0x0)
    frame #0: 0x0000000000000000
    frame #1: 0x0000000104f73d50 App2`procB + 24
    frame #2: 0x0000000104f73e54 App2`bar_four + 12
    frame #3: 0x0000000104f73e68 App2`foo_four + 12
    frame #4: 0x0000000104f73e84 App2`thread_four + 20
    frame #5: 0x000000018ea0826c libsystem_pthread.dylib`_pthread_start + 148
  thread #6
    frame #0: 0x000000018ea03084 libsystem_pthread.dylib`thread_start
```

6.   Check the CPU instruction and the stack pointer for thread #6 (core thread 5) for any signs of stack overflow:

```
(lldb) thread select 6
* thread #6
    frame #0: 0x000000018ea03084 libsystem_pthread.dylib`thread_start
libsystem_pthread.dylib`thread_start:
->  0x18ea03084 <+0>: stp    xzr, xzr, [sp, #-0x10]!
    0x18ea03088 <+4>: bl     0x18ea081d8                ; _pthread_start
    0x18ea0308c <+8>: nop

libsystem_pthread.dylib`:
    0x18ea03090 <+0>: stp    x10, x11, [sp, #-0x10]

(lldb) x/gx $sp
0x16b147000: 0x2c41c5059bd95a05
```

```
(lldb) x/gx $sp-8
0x16b146ff8: 0x0000000000000000
```

```
(lldb) x/gx $sp-0x10
0x16b146ff0: 0x0000000000000000
```

Note: Memory is readable, so we don't expect a stack overflow here. Perhaps the thread was just caught during its start.

7.   Check the CPU instruction and a dereferenced pointer for thread #5 (core thread 4) for any signs of NULL pointers:

```
(lldb) thread select 5
* thread #5, stop reason = ESR_EC_IABORT_EL0 (fault address: 0x0)
    frame #0: 0x0000000000000000
error: core file does not contain 0x0
```

```
(lldb) bt
* thread #5, stop reason = ESR_EC_IABORT_EL0 (fault address: 0x0)
  * frame #0: 0x0000000000000000
    frame #1: 0x0000000104f73d50 App2`procB + 24
    frame #2: 0x0000000104f73e54 App2`bar_four + 12
    frame #3: 0x0000000104f73e68 App2`foo_four + 12
    frame #4: 0x0000000104f73e84 App2`thread_four + 20
    frame #5: 0x000000018ea0826c libsystem_pthread.dylib`_pthread_start + 148
```

```
(lldb) di -a 0x0000000104f73d50
App2`procB:
    0x104f73d38 <+0>:  sub    sp, sp, #0x20
    0x104f73d3c <+4>:  stp    x29, x30, [sp, #0x10]
    0x104f73d40 <+8>:  add    x29, sp, #0x10
    0x104f73d44 <+12>: str    xzr, [sp, #0x8]
    0x104f73d48 <+16>: ldr    x8, [sp, #0x8]
    0x104f73d4c <+20>: blr    x8
    0x104f73d50 <+24>: ldp    x29, x30, [sp, #0x10]
    0x104f73d54 <+28>: add    sp, sp, #0x20
    0x104f73d58 <+32>: ret
```

```
(lldb) x/gx $sp+0x8
0x16b0baf78: 0x0000000000000000
```

8.   Switch to thread #1 (core thread 0) and verify that the *main* function was engaged in thread creation prior to wait (this should correlate with thread #6 caught in being created, the numbering starts from the main thread):

```
(lldb) thread select 1
* thread #1
    frame #0: 0x000000018e9ca8b0 libsystem_kernel.dylib`mach_msg_trap + 8
libsystem_kernel.dylib`mach_msg_trap:
-> 0x18e9ca8b0 <+8>: ret

libsystem_kernel.dylib`mach_msg_overwrite_trap:
    0x18e9ca8b4 <+0>: mov    x16, #-0x20
    0x18e9ca8b8 <+4>: svc    #0x80
    0x18e9ca8bc <+8>: ret
```

```
(lldb) bt
* thread #1
  * frame #0: 0x000000018e9ca8b0 libsystem_kernel.dylib`mach_msg_trap + 8
    frame #1: 0x000000018e9cad20 libsystem_kernel.dylib`mach_msg + 76
    frame #2: 0x000000018e9d02f8 libsystem_kernel.dylib`clock_get_time + 100
    frame #3: 0x000000018e8d6f60 libsystem_c.dylib`nanosleep + 116
    frame #4: 0x000000018e8e1b78 libsystem_c.dylib`sleep + 52
    frame #5: 0x0000000104f73f88 App2`main + 164
    frame #6: 0x000000010517508c dyld`start + 520

(lldb) di -n main
App2`main:
    0x104f73ee4 <+0>:    sub     sp, sp, #0x60
    0x104f73ee8 <+4>:    stp     x29, x30, [sp, #0x50]
    0x104f73eec <+8>:    add     x29, sp, #0x50
    0x104f73ef0 <+12>:   mov     w8, #0x0
    0x104f73ef4 <+16>:   str     w8, [sp, #0x14]
    0x104f73ef8 <+20>:   stur    wzr, [x29, #-0x4]
    0x104f73efc <+24>:   stur    w0, [x29, #-0x8]
    0x104f73f00 <+28>:   stur    x1, [x29, #-0x10]
    0x104f73f04 <+32>:   sub     x0, x29, #0x18
    0x104f73f08 <+36>:   mov     x3, #0x0
    0x104f73f0c <+40>:   str     x3, [sp, #0x8]
    0x104f73f10 <+44>:   mov     x1, x3
    0x104f73f14 <+48>:   adrp    x2, 0
    0x104f73f18 <+52>:   add     x2, x2, #0xd88              ; thread_one
    0x104f73f1c <+56>:   bl      0x104f73f98                ; symbol stub for: pthread_create
    0x104f73f20 <+60>:   ldr     x3, [sp, #0x8]
    0x104f73f24 <+64>:   sub     x0, x29, #0x20
    0x104f73f28 <+68>:   mov     x1, x3
    0x104f73f2c <+72>:   adrp    x2, 0
    0x104f73f30 <+76>:   add     x2, x2, #0xdd4             ; thread_two
    0x104f73f34 <+80>:   bl      0x104f73f98                ; symbol stub for: pthread_create
    0x104f73f38 <+84>:   ldr     x3, [sp, #0x8]
    0x104f73f3c <+88>:   add     x0, sp, #0x28
    0x104f73f40 <+92>:   mov     x1, x3
    0x104f73f44 <+96>:   adrp    x2, 0
    0x104f73f48 <+100>:  add     x2, x2, #0xe24            ; thread_three
    0x104f73f4c <+104>:  bl      0x104f73f98                ; symbol stub for: pthread_create
    0x104f73f50 <+108>:  ldr     x3, [sp, #0x8]
    0x104f73f54 <+112>:  add     x0, sp, #0x20
    0x104f73f58 <+116>:  mov     x1, x3
    0x104f73f5c <+120>:  adrp    x2, 0
    0x104f73f60 <+124>:  add     x2, x2, #0xe70           ; thread_four
    0x104f73f64 <+128>:  bl      0x104f73f98                ; symbol stub for: pthread_create
    0x104f73f68 <+132>:  ldr     x3, [sp, #0x8]
    0x104f73f6c <+136>:  add     x0, sp, #0x18
    0x104f73f70 <+140>:  mov     x1, x3
    0x104f73f74 <+144>:  adrp    x2, 0
    0x104f73f78 <+148>:  add     x2, x2, #0xec0           ; thread_five
    0x104f73f7c <+152>:  bl      0x104f73f98                ; symbol stub for: pthread_create
    0x104f73f80 <+156>:  mov     w0, #0x3
    0x104f73f84 <+160>:  bl      0x104f73fa4                ; symbol stub for: sleep
    0x104f73f88 <+164>:  ldr     w0, [sp, #0x14]
    0x104f73f8c <+168>:  ldp     x29, x30, [sp, #0x50]
    0x104f73f90 <+172>:  add     sp, sp, #0x60
    0x104f73f94 <+176>:  ret
```

Exercise X3

- **Goal:** Learn how to identify spiking threads

- **Patterns:** Spiking Thread

- \AMCDA-Dumps\Exercise-X3.pdf

Exercise X3

Goal: Learn how to identify spiking threads.

Patterns: Spiking Thread.

1.   Load a core dump *App3-87311-20221125T213240Z* and *App3* executable:

```
% lldb -c ~/AMCDA-Dumps/App3-87311-20221125T213240Z -f
~/AMCDA-Dumps/Apps/App3/Build/Products/Release/App3
(lldb) target create "/Users/training/AMCDA-Dumps/Apps/App3/Build/Products/Release/App3" --
core "/Users/training/AMCDA-Dumps/App3-87311-20221125T213240Z"
Core file '/Users/training/AMCDA-Dumps/App3-87311-20221125T213240Z' (arm64) was loaded.
```

2.   Let's check all thread stack traces:

```
(lldb) thread backtrace all
* thread #1
  * frame #0: 0x000000018e9ce06c libsystem_kernel.dylib`__semwait_signal + 8
    frame #1: 0x000000018e8d6fc8 libsystem_c.dylib`nanosleep + 220
    frame #2: 0x000000018e8e1b78 libsystem_c.dylib`sleep + 52
    frame #3: 0x000000018e8e1b90 libsystem_c.dylib`sleep + 76
    frame #4: 0x0000000100947f78 App3`main + 164
    frame #5: 0x0000000100ab908c dyld`start + 520
  thread #2
    frame #0: 0x000000018e9ce06c libsystem_kernel.dylib`__semwait_signal + 8
    frame #1: 0x000000018e8d6fc8 libsystem_c.dylib`nanosleep + 220
    frame #2: 0x000000018e8e1b78 libsystem_c.dylib`sleep + 52
    frame #3: 0x000000018e8e1b90 libsystem_c.dylib`sleep + 76
    frame #4: 0x0000000100947d5c App3`bar_one + 16
    frame #5: 0x0000000100947d70 App3`foo_one + 12
    frame #6: 0x0000000100947d8c App3`thread_one + 20
    frame #7: 0x000000018ea0826c libsystem_pthread.dylib`_pthread_start + 148
  thread #3
    frame #0: 0x000000018e9ce06c libsystem_kernel.dylib`__semwait_signal + 8
    frame #1: 0x000000018e8d6fc8 libsystem_c.dylib`nanosleep + 220
    frame #2: 0x000000018e8e1b78 libsystem_c.dylib`sleep + 52
    frame #3: 0x000000018e8e1b90 libsystem_c.dylib`sleep + 76
    frame #4: 0x0000000100947dac App3`bar_two + 16
    frame #5: 0x0000000100947dc0 App3`foo_two + 12
    frame #6: 0x0000000100947ddc App3`thread_two + 20
    frame #7: 0x000000018ea0826c libsystem_pthread.dylib`_pthread_start + 148
  thread #4
    frame #0: 0x000000018e9ce06c libsystem_kernel.dylib`__semwait_signal + 8
    frame #1: 0x000000018e8d6fc8 libsystem_c.dylib`nanosleep + 220
    frame #2: 0x000000018e8e1b78 libsystem_c.dylib`sleep + 52
    frame #3: 0x0000000100947d24 App3`procA + 20
    frame #4: 0x0000000100947df8 App3`bar_three + 12
    frame #5: 0x0000000100947e0c App3`foo_three + 12
    frame #6: 0x0000000100947e28 App3`thread_three + 20
    frame #7: 0x000000018ea0826c libsystem_pthread.dylib`_pthread_start + 148
  thread #5
    frame #0: 0x000000018e9ce06c libsystem_kernel.dylib`__semwait_signal + 8
    frame #1: 0x000000018e8d6fc8 libsystem_c.dylib`nanosleep + 220
    frame #2: 0x000000018e8e1b78 libsystem_c.dylib`sleep + 52
    frame #3: 0x000000018e8e1b90 libsystem_c.dylib`sleep + 76
    frame #4: 0x0000000100947e48 App3`bar_four + 16
```

```
        frame #5: 0x0000000100947e5c App3`foo_four + 12
        frame #6: 0x0000000100947e78 App3`thread_four + 20
        frame #7: 0x000000018ea0826c libsystem_pthread.dylib`_pthread_start + 148
    thread #6
        frame #0: 0x0000000100947d3c App3`procB + 20
        frame #1: 0x0000000100947e94 App3`bar_five + 12
        frame #2: 0x0000000100947ea8 App3`foo_five + 12
        frame #3: 0x0000000100947ec4 App3`thread_five + 20
        frame #4: 0x000000018ea0826c libsystem_pthread.dylib`_pthread_start + 148
```

Note: App3 process was showing 100% CPU, so we look for non-waiting threads. We see that the thread was caught inside the *procB* function. It is not in some waiting state like other threads in the same process (*__semwait_signal*). Most likely it was a running thread.

3.   Switch to the identified problem thread #6:

```
(lldb) thread select 6
* thread #6
    frame #0: 0x0000000100947d3c App3`procB + 20
App3`procB:
->  0x100947d3c <+20>: ldr    d0, [sp, #0x8]
    0x100947d40 <+24>: fsqrt  d0, d0
    0x100947d44 <+28>: str    d0, [sp, #0x8]
    0x100947d48 <+32>: b      0x100947d3c                ; <+20>
```

```
(lldb) bt
* thread #6
  * frame #0: 0x0000000100947d3c App3`procB + 20
    frame #1: 0x0000000100947e94 App3`bar_five + 12
    frame #2: 0x0000000100947ea8 App3`foo_five + 12
    frame #3: 0x0000000100947ec4 App3`thread_five + 20
    frame #4: 0x000000018ea0826c libsystem_pthread.dylib`_pthread_start + 148
```

Note: From disassembly, we see an endless loop.

4.   Identify the problem thread in the sampling report *App3_sample.txt* (from Activity Monitor):

```
Sampling process 87311 for 3 seconds with 1 millisecond of run time between samples
Sampling completed, processing symbols...
Analysis of sampling App3 (pid 87311) every 1 millisecond
Process:         App3 [87311]
Path:            /Users/USER/*/App3
Load Address:    0x100944000
Identifier:      App3
Version:         0
Code Type:       ARM64
Platform:        macOS
Parent Process:  zsh [73148]

Date/Time:       2022-11-25 21:28:02.728 +0000
Launch Time:     2022-11-25 21:25:18.369 +0000
OS Version:      macOS 12.6 (21G115)
Report Version:  7
Analysis Tool:   /usr/bin/sample

Physical footprint:        1009K
Physical footprint (peak): 1009K
----

Call graph:
    2375 Thread_1898733   DispatchQueue_1: com.apple.main-thread  (serial)
    + 2375 start  (in dyld) + 520  [0x100ab908c]
    +   2375 main  (in App3) + 164  [0x100947f78]
    +     2375 sleep  (in libsystem_c.dylib) + 76  [0x18e8e1b90]
    +       2375 sleep  (in libsystem_c.dylib) + 52  [0x18e8e1b78]
    +         2375 nanosleep  (in libsystem_c.dylib) + 220  [0x18e8d6fc8]
    +           2375 __semwait_signal  (in libsystem_kernel.dylib) + 8  [0x18e9ce06c]
    2375 Thread_1898734
    + 2375 thread_start  (in libsystem_pthread.dylib) + 8  [0x18ea0308c]
    +   2375 _pthread_start  (in libsystem_pthread.dylib) + 148  [0x18ea0826c]
    +     2375 thread_one  (in App3) + 20  [0x100947d8c]
    +       2375 foo_one  (in App3) + 12  [0x100947d70]
    +         2375 bar_one  (in App3) + 16  [0x100947d5c]
    +           2375 sleep  (in libsystem_c.dylib) + 76  [0x18e8e1b90]
    +             2375 sleep  (in libsystem_c.dylib) + 52  [0x18e8e1b78]
```

```
  +                  2375 nanosleep  (in libsystem_c.dylib) + 220  [0x18e8d6fc8]
  +                    2375 __semwait_signal  (in libsystem_kernel.dylib) + 8  [0x18e9ce06c]
  2375 Thread_1898735
  + 2375 thread_start  (in libsystem_pthread.dylib) + 8  [0x18ea0308c]
  +   2375 _pthread_start  (in libsystem_pthread.dylib) + 148  [0x18ea0826c]
  +     2375 thread_two  (in App3) + 20  [0x100947ddc]
  +       2375 foo_two  (in App3) + 12  [0x100947dc0]
  +         2375 bar_two  (in App3) + 16  [0x100947dac]
  +           2375 sleep  (in libsystem_c.dylib) + 76  [0x18e8e1b90]
  +             2375 sleep  (in libsystem_c.dylib) + 52  [0x18e8e1b78]
  +               2375 nanosleep  (in libsystem_c.dylib) + 220  [0x18e8d6fc8]
  +                 2375 __semwait_signal  (in libsystem_kernel.dylib) + 8  [0x18e9ce06c]
  2375 Thread_1898736
  + 2375 thread_start  (in libsystem_pthread.dylib) + 8  [0x18ea0308c]
  +   2375 _pthread_start  (in libsystem_pthread.dylib) + 148  [0x18ea0826c]
  +     2375 thread_three  (in App3) + 20  [0x100947e28]
  +       2375 foo_three  (in App3) + 12  [0x100947e0c]
  +         2375 bar_three  (in App3) + 12  [0x100947df8]
  +           2375 procA  (in App3) + 20  [0x100947d24]
  +             2375 sleep  (in libsystem_c.dylib) + 52  [0x18e8e1b78]
  +               2375 nanosleep  (in libsystem_c.dylib) + 220  [0x18e8d6fc8]
  +                 2375 __semwait_signal  (in libsystem_kernel.dylib) + 8  [0x18e9ce06c]
  2375 Thread_1898737
  + 2375 thread_start  (in libsystem_pthread.dylib) + 8  [0x18ea0308c]
  +   2375 _pthread_start  (in libsystem_pthread.dylib) + 148  [0x18ea0826c]
  +     2375 thread_four  (in App3) + 20  [0x100947e78]
  +       2375 foo_four  (in App3) + 12  [0x100947e5c]
  +         2375 bar_four  (in App3) + 16  [0x100947e48]
  +           2375 sleep  (in libsystem_c.dylib) + 76  [0x18e8e1b90]
  +             2375 sleep  (in libsystem_c.dylib) + 52  [0x18e8e1b78]
  +               2375 nanosleep  (in libsystem_c.dylib) + 220  [0x18e8d6fc8]
  +                 2375 __semwait_signal  (in libsystem_kernel.dylib) + 8  [0x18e9ce06c]
  2375 Thread_1898738
    2375 thread_start  (in libsystem_pthread.dylib) + 8  [0x18ea0308c]
      2375 _pthread_start  (in libsystem_pthread.dylib) + 148  [0x18ea0826c]
        2375 thread_five  (in App3) + 20  [0x100947ec4]
          2375 foo_five  (in App3) + 12  [0x100947ea8]
            2375 bar_five  (in App3) + 12  [0x100947e94]
              2375 procB  (in App3) + 20,28  [0x100947d3c,0x100947d44]


Total number in stack (recursive counted multiple, when >=5):
        5       __semwait_signal  (in libsystem_kernel.dylib) + 0  [0x18e9ce064]
        5       _pthread_start  (in libsystem_pthread.dylib) + 148  [0x18ea0826c]
        5       nanosleep  (in libsystem_c.dylib) + 220  [0x18e8d6fc8]
        5       sleep  (in libsystem_c.dylib) + 52  [0x18e8e1b78]
        5       thread_start  (in libsystem_pthread.dylib) + 8  [0x18ea0308c]


Sort by top of stack, same collapsed (when >= 5):
        __semwait_signal  (in libsystem_kernel.dylib)        11875
        procB  (in App3)        2375


Binary Images:
       0x100944000 -        0x100947ffb +App3 (0) <873DDF0C-1326-32E5-8C25-4F45DD79CF3F> /Users/*/App3
       0x100ab4000 -        0x100b1174b  dyld (960) <38EE9FE9-B66D-3066-8C5C-6DDF0D6944C6> /usr/lib/dyld
       0x18e72d000 -        0x18e72effe  libsystem_blocks.dylib (79.1) <96462BD5-6BB4-3B69-89C9-2C70FA8852E7> /usr/lib/system/libsystem_blocks.dylib
       0x18e72f000 -        0x18e770ff3  libxpc.dylib (2236.140.2) <21D05A8B-D782-3FA7-9A9D-55A45E6E6621> /usr/lib/system/libxpc.dylib
       0x18e771000 -        0x18e78affe  libsystem_trace.dylib (1375.140.2) <B5524014-1A7F-3D07-8855-5E75A55E4A11> /usr/lib/system/libsystem_trace.dylib
       0x18e78b000 -        0x18e814fef  libcorecrypto.dylib (1218.120.10) <2D00FEEC-7984-342B-9516-5D49C5D98204> /usr/lib/system/libcorecrypto.dylib
       0x18e815000 -        0x18e83fffb  libsystem_malloc.dylib (374.120.1) <427675C6-C4BF-390A-AF93-B28DAC36876A> /usr/lib/system/libsystem_malloc.dylib
       0x18e840000 -        0x18e886ff7  libdispatch.dylib (1325.120.2) <B3C7A004-1069-3171-B630-2C386A8B399C> /usr/lib/system/libdispatch.dylib
       0x18e887000 -        0x18e8c4fee  libobjc.A.dylib (841.13) <EC96F0FA-6341-3E1D-BE54-49B544E17F7D> /usr/lib/libobjc.A.dylib
       0x18e8c5000 -        0x18e8c7fff  libsystem_featureflags.dylib (56) <5B14B45B-A15B-31AD-93FB-BAC43C001A23> /usr/lib/system/libsystem_featureflags.dylib
       0x18e8c8000 -        0x18e949fff  libsystem_c.dylib (1507.100.9) <B25D2080-BB9E-38D6-8236-9CEF4B2F11A3> /usr/lib/system/libsystem_c.dylib
       0x18e94a000 -        0x18e9b0ffb  libc++.1.dylib (1300.25) <3D1E6031-901D-3DF1-9E9A-F85FF1C2E803> /usr/lib/libc++.1.dylib
       0x18e9b1000 -        0x18e9c8ffb  libc++abi.dylib (1300.25) <4E8D8A11-4217-3D56-9D41-5426F7CF307C> /usr/lib/libc++abi.dylib
       0x18e9c9000 -        0x18ea00ffb  libsystem_kernel.dylib (8020.140.49) <A9D87740-9C1D-3468-BF60-720A8D713CBA> /usr/lib/system/libsystem_kernel.dylib
       0x18ea01000 -        0x18ea0dff3  libsystem_pthread.dylib (486.100.11) <63C4EEF9-69A5-38B1-996E-8D31B66A051D> /usr/lib/system/libsystem_pthread.dylib
       0x18ea0e000 -        0x18ea1afff  libdyld.dylib (960) <F298A03D-5BC7-3BCA-8880-B956E52EAD01> /usr/lib/system/libdyld.dylib
       0x18ea1b000 -        0x18ea22fea  libsystem_platform.dylib (273.100.5) <A57FE7FB-9FF8-30CE-97A2-625D6DA20D00> /usr/lib/system/libsystem_platform.dylib
       0x18ea23000 -        0x18ea4ffff  libsystem_info.dylib (554.120.2) <413C2A97-5D32-317D-8E32-4258B8E728CE> /usr/lib/system/libsystem_info.dylib
       0x19113f000 -        0x191149ff3  libsystem_darwin.dylib (1507.100.9) <5D456083-E21E-319D-9BA0-57702B3FB09B> /usr/lib/system/libsystem_darwin.dylib
       0x191598000 -        0x1915a7fff  libsystem_notify.dylib (301) <12A2A8B6-80B4-36CA-8245-830EBEDEF1C4> /usr/lib/system/libsystem_notify.dylib
       0x193b14000 -        0x193b2cff7  libsystem_networkextension.dylib (1471.141.2) <4C9F32FA-D88C-3966-A2F0-7030841C8093>
/usr/lib/system/libsystem_networkextension.dylib
       0x193b86000 -        0x193b9dff7  libsystem_asl.dylib (392.100.2) <EC04DA81-C3B5-3AC5-9042-7F07DF48B42A> /usr/lib/system/libsystem_asl.dylib
       0x1952ea000 -        0x1952f2fff  libsystem_symptoms.dylib (1617.140.3) <2906E453-3254-32EA-880E-14AEEF5D7ECD> /usr/lib/system/libsystem_symptoms.dylib
       0x1972de000 -        0x1972fcfff  libsystem_containermanager.dylib (383.120.2) <D38210EF-8F23-380B-8B43-BB06A7305F67>
/usr/lib/system/libsystem_containermanager.dylib
       0x198085000 -        0x198089fff  libsystem_configuration.dylib (1163.140.3) <3977B29D-624D-3DEE-94EF-95D29FB25252>
/usr/lib/system/libsystem_configuration.dylib
       0x1988a0000 -        0x19808efff  libsystem_sandbox.dylib (1657.140.5) <2A2EB0A4-9822-36D1-999B-181D1BB964B5> /usr/lib/system/libsystem_sandbox.dylib
       0x198bf0000 -        0x198bf2fff  libquarantine.dylib (133.120.2) <B887350E-B1C9-386C-B5EB-26F08C7C0152> /usr/lib/system/libquarantine.dylib
       0x19925d000 -        0x199262fff  libsystem_coreservices.dylib (133) <D5F19732-3AA0-3B93-9F25-318A27DE5AC5>
/usr/lib/system/libsystem_coreservices.dylib
       0x1994c8000 -        0x1994feffb  libsystem_m.dylib (3204.80.2) <31A9DAE0-FB1F-3CB8-8AB6-CA5A1192DFD8> /usr/lib/system/libsystem_m.dylib
       0x199500000 -        0x199508ff3  libmacho.dylib (994) <ED4EE8AE-EA60-33B7-9676-E6119B7449E3> /usr/lib/system/libmacho.dylib
       0x199525000 -        0x199531ffb  libcommonCrypto.dylib (60191.100.1) <FB7DF5AC-35DB-3B80-B2F6-BC69375390AE> /usr/lib/system/libcommonCrypto.dylib
       0x199532000 -        0x199953cfff  libunwind.dylib (202.2) <D9CA1CE3-6B1A-3E2B-BBAD-9D9B1DB00F92> /usr/lib/system/libunwind.dylib
       0x19953d000 -        0x199544ffb  liboah.dylib (254.25) <7E53021F-FDCE-3EC9-8B4C-97AD3B21D02E> /usr/lib/liboah.dylib
       0x199545000 -        0x19954dff7  libcopyfile.dylib (180.100.3) <654D0DA0-8277-361D-88DC-1430504B5436> /usr/lib/system/libcopyfile.dylib
       0x19954e000 -        0x199551ffb  libcompiler_rt.dylib (103.1) <68788078-BF1D-3CD1-91A7-4C59FD78FB75> /usr/lib/system/libcompiler_rt.dylib
       0x199552000 -        0x199556fff  libsystem_collections.dylib (1507.100.9) <4928F3C4-D438-354F-BA1C-0BD79F6475F3>
/usr/lib/system/libsystem_collections.dylib
       0x199557000 -        0x199559ffb  libsystem_secinit.dylib (107.100.5) <18F251D3-8C66-3B8B-817A-C124498478F4> /usr/lib/system/libsystem_secinit.dylib
       0x19955a000 -        0x19955cfff  libremovefile.dylib (60) <157C8E50-D4A5-3DFC-8E0B-756E03E2082B> /usr/lib/system/libremovefile.dylib
       0x19955d000 -        0x19955dfff  libkeymgr.dylib (31) <49D72074-0C58-317C-9B8B-762C13C0C084> /usr/lib/system/libkeymgr.dylib
       0x19955e000 -        0x199566fff  libsystem_dnssd.dylib (1557.140.5.0.1) <10A4374A-D15A-31C8-AC6F-2DCC10D06444> /usr/lib/system/libsystem_dnssd.dylib
       0x199567000 -        0x19956cff7  libcache.dylib (85) <7E9E684F-57B6-3196-8AEC-908B46DEEBD4> /usr/lib/system/libcache.dylib
       0x19956d000 -        0x19956efff  libSystem.B.dylib (1311.120.1) <9232C168-6ECA-3B7D-B081-E7C46B379836> /usr/lib/libSystem.B.dylib
       0x19f8c1000 -        0x19f8c1ff9  libsystem_product_info_filter.dylib (10) <E49E2F05-0E01-352E-8CB7-276F8EF8E6D6>
/usr/lib/system/libsystem_product_info_filter.dylib
Sample analysis of process 87311 written to file /dev/stdout
```

77

Exercise X4

- **Goal:** Learn how to identify heap regions and heap corruption

- **Patterns:** Dynamic Memory Corruption (Process Heap)

- \AMCDA-Dumps\Exercise-X4.pdf

Exercise X4

Goal: Learn how to identify heap regions and heap corruption, and compare core dumps with diagnostic reports.

Patterns: Dynamic Memory Corruption (Process Heap).

1.   Identify the problem thread and application-specific diagnostic from the diagnostic report *App4-2022-12-01-204725.ips*:

```
------------------------------------
Translated Report (Full Report Below)
------------------------------------

Process:            App4 [89676]
Path:               /Users/USER/*/App4
Identifier:         App4
Version:            ???
Code Type:          ARM-64 (Native)
Parent Process:     zsh [73148]
Responsible:        Terminal [9503]
User ID:            501

Date/Time:          2022-12-01 20:47:25.1420 +0000
OS Version:         macOS 12.6 (21G115)
Report Version:     12
Anonymous UUID:     6F758133-2B79-4743-8B70-8B1D8C510718

Sleep/Wake UUID:    7B919AF9-E753-43E4-B3C6-59C93539DBB1

Time Awake Since Boot: 140000 seconds
Time Since Wake:       79 seconds

System Integrity Protection: enabled

Crashed Thread:     3

Exception Type:     EXC_CRASH (SIGABRT)
Exception Codes:    0x0000000000000000, 0x0000000000000000
Exception Note:     EXC_CORPSE_NOTIFY

Application Specific Information:
abort() called


Thread 0::  Dispatch queue: com.apple.main-thread
0   libsystem_kernel.dylib          0x18e9ce06c __semwait_signal + 8
1   libsystem_c.dylib               0x18e8d6fc8 nanosleep + 220
2   libsystem_c.dylib               0x18e8e1b78 sleep + 52
3   libsystem_c.dylib               0x18e8e1b90 sleep + 76
4   App4                            0x104617f5c main + 164
5   dyld                            0x10472508c start + 520

Thread 1:
0   libsystem_kernel.dylib          0x18e9ce06c __semwait_signal + 8
1   libsystem_c.dylib               0x18e8d6fc8 nanosleep + 220
2   libsystem_c.dylib               0x18e8e1b78 sleep + 52
3   libsystem_c.dylib               0x18e8e1b90 sleep + 76
4   App4                            0x104617d3c bar_one + 16
5   App4                            0x104617d50 foo_one + 12
6   App4                            0x104617d6c thread_one + 20
7   libsystem_pthread.dylib         0x18ea0826c _pthread_start + 148
8   libsystem_pthread.dylib         0x18ea0308c thread_start + 8

Thread 2:
0   libsystem_kernel.dylib          0x18e9ce06c __semwait_signal + 8
1   libsystem_c.dylib               0x18e8d6fc8 nanosleep + 220
2   libsystem_c.dylib               0x18e8e1b78 sleep + 52
3   libsystem_c.dylib               0x18e8e1b90 sleep + 76
4   App4                            0x104617d8c bar_two + 16
5   App4                            0x104617da0 foo_two + 12
```

```
6   App4                                   0x104617dbc thread_two + 20
7   libsystem_pthread.dylib                0x18ea0826c _pthread_start + 148
8   libsystem_pthread.dylib                0x18ea0308c thread_start + 8

Thread 3 Crashed:
0   libsystem_kernel.dylib                 0x18e9d2d98 __pthread_kill + 8
1   libsystem_pthread.dylib                0x18ea07ee0 pthread_kill + 288
2   libsystem_c.dylib                      0x18e942340 abort + 168
3   libsystem_malloc.dylib                 0x18e8248c0 malloc_vreport + 552
4   libsystem_malloc.dylib                 0x18e839c84 malloc_zone_error + 100
5   libsystem_malloc.dylib                 0x18e82e4ac free_list_checksum_botch + 40
6   libsystem_malloc.dylib                 0x18e81d020 small_free_list_remove_ptr_no_clear + 1220
7   libsystem_malloc.dylib                 0x18e819fc0 free_small + 608
8   App4                                   0x104617cf8 proc + 288
9   App4                                   0x104617dd8 bar_three + 12
10  App4                                   0x104617dec foo_three + 12
11  App4                                   0x104617e08 thread_three + 20
12  libsystem_pthread.dylib                0x18ea0826c _pthread_start + 148
13  libsystem_pthread.dylib                0x18ea0308c thread_start + 8

Thread 4:
0   libsystem_kernel.dylib                 0x18e9ce06c __semwait_signal + 8
1   libsystem_c.dylib                      0x18e8d6fc8 nanosleep + 220
2   libsystem_c.dylib                      0x18e8e1b78 sleep + 52
3   libsystem_c.dylib                      0x18e8e1b90 sleep + 76
4   App4                                   0x104617e28 bar_four + 16
5   App4                                   0x104617e3c foo_four + 12
6   App4                                   0x104617e58 thread_four + 20
7   libsystem_pthread.dylib                0x18ea0826c _pthread_start + 148
8   libsystem_pthread.dylib                0x18ea0308c thread_start + 8

Thread 5:
0   libsystem_kernel.dylib                 0x18e9ce06c __semwait_signal + 8
1   libsystem_c.dylib                      0x18e8d6fc8 nanosleep + 220
2   libsystem_c.dylib                      0x18e8e1b78 sleep + 52
3   libsystem_c.dylib                      0x18e8e1b90 sleep + 76
4   App4                                   0x104617e78 bar_five + 16
5   App4                                   0x104617e8c foo_five + 12
6   App4                                   0x104617ea8 thread_five + 20
7   libsystem_pthread.dylib                0x18ea0826c _pthread_start + 148
8   libsystem_pthread.dylib                0x18ea0308c thread_start + 8


Thread 3 crashed with ARM Thread State (64-bit):
    x0: 0x0000000000000000   x1: 0x0000000000000000   x2: 0x0000000000000000   x3: 0x0000000000000000
    x4: 0x0000000000000000   x5: 0x0000000000000000   x6: 0x0000000000000001   x7: 0x0000000104674028
    x8: 0x9d071a11b63e2b68   x9: 0x9d071a10dda69b68  x10: 0xcccccccccccccccd  x11: 0x000000000000000a
   x12: 0x0000000000000000  x13: 0x0000000000000038  x14: 0x96b2ec9dab8dd888  x15: 0x000000005bdedc33
   x16: 0x0000000000000148  x17: 0x00000001e8b2b680  x18: 0x0000000000000000  x19: 0x0000000000000006
   x20: 0x000000016b98b000  x21: 0x0000000000000d03  x22: 0x000000016b98b0e0  x23: 0x0000000104674000
   x24: 0x0000000000000000  x25: 0x0000000000000000  x26: 0x0000000104784255  x27: 0x000000016b98b000
   x28: 0x000000000000000c   fp: 0x000000016b98ad70   lr: 0x0000000018ea07ee0
    sp: 0x000000016b98ad50   pc: 0x000000018e9d2d98 cpsr: 0x40001000
   far: 0x00000001e7968068  esr: 0x56000080  Address size fault

Binary Images:
       0x18e9c9000 -        0x18ea00fff libsystem_kernel.dylib (*) <a9d87740-9c1d-3468-bf60-720a8d713cba>
/usr/lib/system/libsystem_kernel.dylib
       0x18e8c8000 -        0x18e949fff libsystem_c.dylib (*) <b25d2080-bb9e-38d6-8236-9cef4b2f11a3>
/usr/lib/system/libsystem_c.dylib
       0x104614000 -        0x104617fff App4 (*) <6201e3ec-2401-3577-8912-6d464bfc1791> /Users/USER/*/App4
       0x104720000 -        0x10477ffff dyld (*) <38ee9fe9-b66d-3066-8c5c-6ddf0d6944c6> /usr/lib/dyld
       0x18ea01000 -        0x18ea0dfff libsystem_pthread.dylib (*) <63c4eef9-69a5-38b1-996e-8d31b66a051d>
/usr/lib/system/libsystem_pthread.dylib
       0x18e815000 -        0x18e83ffff libsystem_malloc.dylib (*) <427675c6-c4bf-390a-af93-b28dac36876a>
/usr/lib/system/libsystem_malloc.dylib

External Modification Summary:
  Calls made by other processes targeting this process:
    task_for_pid: 0
    thread_create: 0
    thread_set_state: 0
  Calls made by this process:
    task_for_pid: 0
    thread_create: 0
    thread_set_state: 0
```

```
  Calls made by all processes on this machine:
    task_for_pid: 0
    thread_create: 0
    thread_set_state: 0

VM Region Summary:
ReadOnly portion of Libraries: Total=582.2M resident=0K(0%) swapped_out_or_unallocated=582.2M(100%)
Writable regions: Total=540.8M written=0K(0%) resident=0K(0%) swapped_out=0K(0%) unallocated=540.8M(100%)

                          VIRTUAL   REGION
REGION TYPE                  SIZE    COUNT (non-coalesced)
===========               =======  =======
Kernel Alloc Once             32K        1
MALLOC                      530.3M       22
Stack                        10.7M       11
Stack (reserved)             56.0M        1         reserved VM address space (unallocated)
VM_ALLOCATE                   16K        1
__AUTH                        46K       11
__AUTH_CONST                  67K       38
__DATA                       173K       37
__DATA_CONST                 258K       40
__DATA_DIRTY                  73K       21
__LINKEDIT                  577.6M        3
__OBJC_CONST                  10K        5
__OBJC_RO                    83.0M        1
__OBJC_RW                    3168K        1
__TEXT                       4708K       43
dyld private memory          1024K        1
shared memory                 16K        1
===========               =======  =======
TOTAL                         1.2G      238
TOTAL, minus reserved VM space  1.2G    238
```

Note: The following console output was also reported:

```
% ./App4
App4(89676,0x16b98b000) malloc: Incorrect checksum for freed object 0x13e009600: probably
modified after being freed.
Corrupt value: 0x7243206f6c6c6548
App4(89676,0x16b98b000) malloc: *** set a breakpoint in malloc_error_break to debug
zsh: abort (core dumped)   ./App4
```

2.   Load a core dump *core.89676* and *App4* executable:

```
% lldb -c ~/AMCDA-Dumps/core.89676 -f ~/AMCDA-Dumps/Apps/App4/Build/Products/Release/App4
(lldb) target create "/Users/training/AMCDA-Dumps/Apps/App4/Build/Products/Release/App4" --
core "/Users/training/AMCDA-Dumps/core.89676"
Core file '/Users/training/AMCDA-Dumps/core.89676' (arm64) was loaded.
```

3.   Go to the identified problem core thread 3 (thread #4):

```
(lldb) thread select 4
* thread #4
    frame #0: 0x000000018e9d2d98 libsystem_kernel.dylib`__pthread_kill + 8
libsystem_kernel.dylib`:
-> 0x18e9d2d98 <+8>:  b.lo   0x18e9d2db8               ; <+40>
    0x18e9d2d9c <+12>: pacibsp
    0x18e9d2da0 <+16>: stp    x29, x30, [sp, #-0x10]!
    0x18e9d2da4 <+20>: mov    x29, sp
```

```
(lldb) bt
* thread #4
  * frame #0: 0x000000018e9d2d98 libsystem_kernel.dylib`__pthread_kill + 8
    frame #1: 0x000000018ea07ee0 libsystem_pthread.dylib`pthread_kill + 288
    frame #2: 0x000000018e942340 libsystem_c.dylib`abort + 168
    frame #3: 0x000000018e8248c0 libsystem_malloc.dylib`malloc_vreport + 552
    frame #4: 0x000000018e839c84 libsystem_malloc.dylib`malloc_zone_error + 100
    frame #5: 0x000000018e82e4ac libsystem_malloc.dylib`free_list_checksum_botch + 40
    frame #6: 0x000000018e81d020 libsystem_malloc.dylib`small_free_list_remove_ptr_no_clear +
1220
    frame #7: 0x000000018e819fc0 libsystem_malloc.dylib`free_small + 608
    frame #8: 0x0000000104617cf8 App4`proc + 288
    frame #9: 0x0000000104617dd8 App4`bar_three + 12
    frame #10: 0x0000000104617dec App4`foo_three + 12
    frame #11: 0x0000000104617e08 App4`thread_three + 20
    frame #12: 0x000000018ea0826c libsystem_pthread.dylib`_pthread_start + 148
```

4.   Check the corrupt heap entry address specified in the console report:

```
(lldb) x/s 0x13e009600
0x13e009600: "Hello Crash!"
```

5.   Switch to the stack frame 8 to check heap *free* functions and blocks they free:

```
(lldb) f 8
frame #8: 0x0000000104617cf8 App4`proc + 288
App4`proc:
->  0x104617cf8 <+288>: ldur   x0, [x29, #-0x20]
    0x104617cfc <+292>: bl     0x104617f78               ; symbol stub for: free
    0x104617d00 <+296>: ldur   x0, [x29, #-0x18]
    0x104617d04 <+300>: bl     0x104617f78               ; symbol stub for: free
```

```
(lldb) di -n proc
App4`proc:
    0x104617bd8 <+0>:    sub    sp, sp, #0x70
    0x104617bdc <+4>:    stp    x29, x30, [sp, #0x60]
    0x104617be0 <+8>:    add    x29, sp, #0x60
    0x104617be4 <+12>:   mov    x0, #0x400
    0x104617be8 <+16>:   str    x0, [sp, #0x18]
    0x104617bec <+20>:   bl     0x104617f84              ; symbol stub for: malloc
    0x104617bf0 <+24>:   mov    x8, x0
    0x104617bf4 <+28>:   ldr    x0, [sp, #0x18]
    0x104617bf8 <+32>:   stur   x8, [x29, #-0x8]
    0x104617bfc <+36>:   bl     0x104617f84              ; symbol stub for: malloc
    0x104617c00 <+40>:   mov    x8, x0
    0x104617c04 <+44>:   ldr    x0, [sp, #0x18]
    0x104617c08 <+48>:   stur   x8, [x29, #-0x10]
    0x104617c0c <+52>:   bl     0x104617f84              ; symbol stub for: malloc
    0x104617c10 <+56>:   mov    x8, x0
    0x104617c14 <+60>:   ldr    x0, [sp, #0x18]
    0x104617c18 <+64>:   stur   x8, [x29, #-0x18]
    0x104617c1c <+68>:   bl     0x104617f84              ; symbol stub for: malloc
    0x104617c20 <+72>:   mov    x8, x0
    0x104617c24 <+76>:   ldr    x0, [sp, #0x18]
    0x104617c28 <+80>:   stur   x8, [x29, #-0x20]
    0x104617c2c <+84>:   bl     0x104617f84              ; symbol stub for: malloc
    0x104617c30 <+88>:   mov    x8, x0
    0x104617c34 <+92>:   ldr    x0, [sp, #0x18]
    0x104617c38 <+96>:   stur   x8, [x29, #-0x28]
    0x104617c3c <+100>:  bl     0x104617f84              ; symbol stub for: malloc
```

```
0x104617c40 <+104>: mov    x8, x0
0x104617c44 <+108>: ldr    x0, [sp, #0x18]
0x104617c48 <+112>: str    x8, [sp, #0x30]
0x104617c4c <+116>: bl     0x104617f84             ; symbol stub for: malloc
0x104617c50 <+120>: str    x0, [sp, #0x28]
0x104617c54 <+124>: ldr    x0, [sp, #0x30]
0x104617c58 <+128>: bl     0x104617f78             ; symbol stub for: free
0x104617c5c <+132>: ldur   x0, [x29, #-0x20]
0x104617c60 <+136>: bl     0x104617f78             ; symbol stub for: free
0x104617c64 <+140>: ldur   x0, [x29, #-0x10]
0x104617c68 <+144>: bl     0x104617f78             ; symbol stub for: free
0x104617c6c <+148>: ldur   x0, [x29, #-0x10]
0x104617c70 <+152>: adrp   x1, 0
0x104617c74 <+156>: add    x1, x1, #0xfa8          ; "Hello Crash!"
0x104617c78 <+160>: str    x1, [sp, #0x8]
0x104617c7c <+164>: mov    x2, #-0x1
0x104617c80 <+168>: str    x2, [sp, #0x10]
0x104617c84 <+172>: bl     0x104617f6c             ; symbol stub for: __strcpy_chk
0x104617c88 <+176>: ldr    x1, [sp, #0x8]
0x104617c8c <+180>: ldr    x2, [sp, #0x10]
0x104617c90 <+184>: ldur   x0, [x29, #-0x20]
0x104617c94 <+188>: bl     0x104617f6c             ; symbol stub for: __strcpy_chk
0x104617c98 <+192>: ldr    x1, [sp, #0x8]
0x104617c9c <+196>: ldr    x2, [sp, #0x10]
0x104617ca0 <+200>: ldr    x0, [sp, #0x30]
0x104617ca4 <+204>: bl     0x104617f6c             ; symbol stub for: __strcpy_chk
0x104617ca8 <+208>: mov    x0, #0x200
0x104617cac <+212>: str    x0, [sp, #0x20]
0x104617cb0 <+216>: bl     0x104617f84             ; symbol stub for: malloc
0x104617cb4 <+220>: mov    x8, x0
0x104617cb8 <+224>: ldr    x0, [sp, #0x18]
0x104617cbc <+228>: stur   x8, [x29, #-0x10]
0x104617cc0 <+232>: bl     0x104617f84             ; symbol stub for: malloc
0x104617cc4 <+236>: mov    x8, x0
0x104617cc8 <+240>: ldr    x0, [sp, #0x20]
0x104617ccc <+244>: stur   x8, [x29, #-0x20]
0x104617cd0 <+248>: bl     0x104617f84             ; symbol stub for: malloc
0x104617cd4 <+252>: str    x0, [sp, #0x30]
0x104617cd8 <+256>: mov    w0, #0x12c
0x104617cdc <+260>: bl     0x104617f9c             ; symbol stub for: sleep
0x104617ce0 <+264>: ldr    x0, [sp, #0x28]
0x104617ce4 <+268>: bl     0x104617f78             ; symbol stub for: free
0x104617ce8 <+272>: ldr    x0, [sp, #0x30]
0x104617cec <+276>: bl     0x104617f78             ; symbol stub for: free
0x104617cf0 <+280>: ldur   x0, [x29, #-0x28]
0x104617cf4 <+284>: bl     0x104617f78             ; symbol stub for: free
-> 0x104617cf8 <+288>: ldur   x0, [x29, #-0x20]
0x104617cfc <+292>: bl     0x104617f78             ; symbol stub for: free
0x104617d00 <+296>: ldur   x0, [x29, #-0x18]
0x104617d04 <+300>: bl     0x104617f78             ; symbol stub for: free
0x104617d08 <+304>: ldur   x0, [x29, #-0x10]
0x104617d0c <+308>: bl     0x104617f78             ; symbol stub for: free
0x104617d10 <+312>: ldur   x0, [x29, #-0x8]
0x104617d14 <+316>: bl     0x104617f78             ; symbol stub for: free
0x104617d18 <+320>: mov    w0, #-0x1
0x104617d1c <+324>: bl     0x104617f9c             ; symbol stub for: sleep
0x104617d20 <+328>: ldp    x29, x30, [sp, #0x60]
0x104617d24 <+332>: add    sp, sp, #0x70
0x104617d28 <+336>: ret
```

```
(lldb) re r sp x29
      sp = 0x000000016b98af20
      fp = 0x000000016b98af80


(lldb) x/gx 0x000000016b98af20+0x28
0x16b98af48: 0x000000013e009a00


(lldb) x/s 0x000000013e009a00
0x13e009a00: ""


(lldb) x/gx 0x000000016b98af20+0x30
0x16b98af50: 0x000000013d704280


(lldb) x/s 0x000000013d704280
0x13d704280: ""


(lldb) x/gx 0x000000016b98af80-0x28
0x16b98af58: 0x000000013e009200


(lldb) x/s 0x000000013e009200
0x13e009200: ""


(lldb) x/gx 0x000000016b98af80-0x20
0x16b98af60: 0x000000013e008600


(lldb) x/s 0x000000013e008600
0x13e008600: "Hello Crash!"


(lldb) x/gx 0x000000016b98af80-0x18
0x16b98af68: 0x000000013e008a00


(lldb) x/gx 0x000000016b98af80-0x10
0x16b98af70: 0x000000013d704080


(lldb) x/gx 0x000000016b98af80-0x8
0x16b98af70: 0x000000013d704080
```

Note: We also wee use after free, highlighted in red in disassembly.

6. Notice different sections for heap metadata and heap block base addresses 0x000000013d700000 and 0x000000013e000000 and find them on the *vmmap* report *vmmap_89676.log*:

```
Process:         App4 [89676]
Path:            /Users/USER/*/App4
Load Address:    0x104614000
Identifier:      App4
Version:         ???
Code Type:       ARM64
Platform:        macOS
Parent Process:  zsh [73148]

Date/Time:       2022-12-01 20:42:01.218 +0000
Launch Time:     2022-12-01 20:40:37.973 +0000
OS Version:      macOS 12.6 (21G115)
Report Version:  7
Analysis Tool:   /Applications/Xcode.app/Contents/Developer/usr/bin/vmmap
Analysis Tool Version:  Xcode 14.0.1 (14A400)
----

Virtual Memory Map of process 89676 (App4)
Output report format:  2.4  -- 64-bit process
VM page size:  16384 bytes

==== Non-writable regions for process 89676
REGION TYPE           START - END        [ VSIZE  RSDNT  DIRTY   SWAP] PRT/MAX SHRMOD PURGE   REGION DETAIL
__TEXT                104614000-104618000 [  16K    16K     0K     0K] r-x/r-x SM=COW         /Users/USER/*/App4
__DATA_CONST          104618000-10461c000 [  16K    16K    16K     0K] r--/rw- SM=COW         /Users/USER/*/App4
__LINKEDIT            10461c000-104624000 [  32K    32K     0K     0K] r--/r-- SM=COW         /Users/USER/*/App4
shared memory         10462c000-104630000 [  16K    16K    16K     0K] r--/r-- SM=SHM
MALLOC metadata       104630000-104634000 [  16K    16K    16K     0K] r--/rwx SM=COW         MallocHelperZone_0x104630000 zone structure
MALLOC guard page     104638000-10463c000 [  16K     0K     0K     0K] ---/rwx SM=ZER
MALLOC guard page     104644000-104648000 [  16K     0K     0K     0K] ---/rwx SM=ZER
```

```
MALLOC guard page       104648000-10464c000   [  16K    0K    0K    0K] ---/rwx SM=NUL
MALLOC guard page       104654000-10465c000   [  32K    0K    0K    0K] ---/rwx SM=NUL
MALLOC guard page       104664000-104668000   [  16K    0K    0K    0K] ---/rwx SM=NUL
MALLOC metadata         104668000-10466c000   [  16K   16K   16K    0K] r--/rwx SM=PRV
MALLOC metadata         10466c000-104670000   [  16K   16K   16K    0K] r--/rwx SM=COW  DefaultMallocZone_0x10466c000 zone structure
__TEXT                  104720000-104780000   [ 384K  384K    0K    0K] r-x/r-x SM=COW  /usr/lib/dyld
__DATA_CONST            104780000-104798000   [  96K   32K   32K    0K] r--/rw- SM=COW  /usr/lib/dyld
__LINKEDIT              10479c000-1047d4000   [ 224K   80K    0K    0K] r--/r-- SM=COW  /usr/lib/dyld
dyld private memory     1047d4000-1048d4000   [1024K   16K   16K    0K] r--/rwx SM=PRV
STACK GUARD             1677ec000-16aff0000   [ 56.0M   0K    0K    0K] ---/rwx SM=NUL  stack guard for thread 0
STACK GUARD             16b7ec000-16b7f0000   [  16K    0K    0K    0K] ---/rwx SM=NUL  stack guard for thread 1
STACK GUARD             16b878000-16b87c000   [  16K    0K    0K    0K] ---/rwx SM=NUL  stack guard for thread 2
STACK GUARD             16b904000-16b908000   [  16K    0K    0K    0K] ---/rwx SM=NUL  stack guard for thread 3
STACK GUARD             16b990000-16b994000   [  16K    0K    0K    0K] ---/rwx SM=NUL  stack guard for thread 4
STACK GUARD             16ba1c000-16ba20000   [  16K    0K    0K    0K] ---/rwx SM=NUL  stack guard for thread 5
__TEXT                  18e72d000-18e72f000   [   8K    8K    0K    0K] r-x/r-x SM=COW  /usr/lib/system/libsystem_blocks.dylib
__TEXT                  18e72f000-18e771000   [ 264K  264K    0K    0K] r-x/r-x SM=COW  /usr/lib/system/libxpc.dylib
__TEXT                  18e771000-18e78b000   [ 104K  104K    0K    0K] r-x/r-x SM=COW  /usr/lib/system/libsystem_trace.dylib
__TEXT                  18e78b000-18e815000   [ 552K  536K    0K    0K] r-x/r-x SM=COW  /usr/lib/system/libcorecrypto.dylib
__TEXT                  18e815000-18e840000   [ 172K  172K    0K    0K] r-x/r-x SM=COW  /usr/lib/system/libsystem_malloc.dylib
__TEXT                  18e840000-18e887000   [ 284K  284K    0K    0K] r-x/r-x SM=COW  /usr/lib/system/libdispatch.dylib
__TEXT                  18e887000-18e8c5000   [ 248K  248K    0K    0K] r-x/r-x SM=COW  /usr/lib/libobjc.A.dylib
__TEXT                  18e8c5000-18e8c8000   [  12K   12K    0K    0K] r-x/r-x SM=COW  /usr/lib/system/libsystem_featureflags.dylib
__TEXT                  18e8c8000-18e94a000   [ 520K  472K    0K    0K] r-x/r-x SM=COW  /usr/lib/system/libsystem_c.dylib
__TEXT                  18e94a000-18e9b1000   [ 412K  380K    0K    0K] r-x/r-x SM=COW  /usr/lib/libc++.1.dylib
__TEXT                  18e9b1000-18e9c9000   [  96K   96K    0K    0K] r-x/r-x SM=COW  /usr/lib/libc++abi.dylib
__TEXT                  18e9c9000-18ea01000   [ 224K  208K    0K    0K] r-x/r-x SM=COW  /usr/lib/system/libsystem_kernel.dylib
__TEXT                  18ea01000-18ea0e000   [  52K   52K    0K    0K] r-x/r-x SM=COW  /usr/lib/system/libsystem_pthread.dylib
__TEXT                  18ea0e000-18ea1b000   [  52K   52K    0K    0K] r-x/r-x SM=COW  /usr/lib/system/libdyld.dylib
__TEXT                  18ea1b000-18ea23000   [  32K   32K    0K    0K] r-x/r-x SM=COW  /usr/lib/system/libsystem_platform.dylib
__TEXT                  18ea23000-18ea50000   [ 180K  164K    0K    0K] r-x/r-x SM=COW  /usr/lib/system/libsystem_info.dylib
__TEXT                  19113f000-19114a000   [  44K   44K    0K    0K] r-x/r-x SM=COW  /usr/lib/system/libsystem_darwin.dylib
__TEXT                  191598000-1915a8000   [  64K   64K    0K    0K] r-x/r-x SM=COW  /usr/lib/system/libsystem_notify.dylib
__TEXT                  193b14000-193b2d000   [ 100K  100K    0K    0K] r-x/r-x SM=COW  /usr/lib/system/libsystem_networkextension.dylib
__TEXT                  193b86000-193b9e000   [  96K   96K    0K    0K] r-x/r-x SM=COW  /usr/lib/system/libsystem_asl.dylib
__TEXT                  1952ea000-1952f3000   [  36K   36K    0K    0K] r-x/r-x SM=COW  /usr/lib/system/libsystem_symptoms.dylib
__TEXT                  1972de000-1972fd000   [ 124K  108K    0K    0K] r-x/r-x SM=COW  /usr/lib/system/libsystem_containermanager.dylib
__TEXT                  198085000-19808a000   [  20K   20K    0K    0K] r-x/r-x SM=COW  /usr/lib/system/libsystem_configuration.dylib
__TEXT                  19808a000-19808f000   [  20K   20K    0K    0K] r-x/r-x SM=COW  /usr/lib/system/libsystem_sandbox.dylib
__TEXT                  198bf0000-198bf3000   [  12K   12K    0K    0K] r-x/r-x SM=COW  /usr/lib/system/libquarantine.dylib
__TEXT                  19925d000-199263000   [  24K   24K    0K    0K] r-x/r-x SM=COW  /usr/lib/system/libsystem_coreservices.dylib
__TEXT                  1994c8000-1994ff000   [ 220K  156K    0K    0K] r-x/r-x SM=COW  /usr/lib/system/libsystem_m.dylib
__TEXT                  199500000-199509000   [  36K   36K    0K    0K] r-x/r-x SM=COW  /usr/lib/system/libmacho.dylib
__TEXT                  199525000-199532000   [  52K   52K    0K    0K] r-x/r-x SM=COW  /usr/lib/system/libcommonCrypto.dylib
__TEXT                  199532000-19953d000   [  44K   44K    0K    0K] r-x/r-x SM=COW  /usr/lib/system/libunwind.dylib
__TEXT                  19953d000-199545000   [  32K   32K    0K    0K] r-x/r-x SM=COW  /usr/lib/liboah.dylib
__TEXT                  199545000-19954e000   [  36K   36K    0K    0K] r-x/r-x SM=COW  /usr/lib/system/libcopyfile.dylib
__TEXT                  19954e000-199552000   [  16K   16K    0K    0K] r-x/r-x SM=COW  /usr/lib/system/libcompiler_rt.dylib
__TEXT                  199552000-199557000   [  20K   20K    0K    0K] r-x/r-x SM=COW  /usr/lib/system/libsystem_collections.dylib
__TEXT                  199557000-19955a000   [  12K   12K    0K    0K] r-x/r-x SM=COW  /usr/lib/system/libsystem_secinit.dylib
__TEXT                  19955a000-19955d000   [  12K   12K    0K    0K] r-x/r-x SM=COW  /usr/lib/system/libremovefile.dylib
__TEXT                  19955d000-19955e000   [   4K    4K    0K    0K] r-x/r-x SM=COW  /usr/lib/system/libkeymgr.dylib
__TEXT                  19955e000-199567000   [  36K   36K    0K    0K] r-x/r-x SM=COW  /usr/lib/system/libsystem_dnssd.dylib
__TEXT                  199567000-19956d000   [  24K   24K    0K    0K] r-x/r-x SM=COW  /usr/lib/system/libcache.dylib
__TEXT                  19956d000-19956f000   [   8K    8K    0K    0K] r-x/r-x SM=COW  /usr/lib/libSystem.B.dylib
__TEXT                  19f8c1000-19f8c2000   [   4K    4K    0K    0K] r-x/r-x SM=COW  /usr/lib/system/libsystem_product_info_filter.dylib
__OBJC_RO               1d89c2000-1ddcc4000   [ 83.0M 49.6M   0K    0K] r-x/r-x SM=COW  /usr/lib/libobjc.A.dylib
__DATA_CONST            1e0098000-1e0098130   [  304   304    0K    0K] r--/rw- SM=COW  /usr/lib/system/libsystem_blocks.dylib
__DATA_CONST            1e0098130-1e00987d0   [ 1696  1696    0K    0K] r--/rw- SM=COW  /usr/lib/system/libsystem_trace.dylib
__DATA_CONST            1e00987d0-1e0098ef0   [ 1824  1824    0K    0K] r--/rw- SM=COW  /usr/lib/system/libcorecrypto.dylib
__DATA_CONST            1e0098ef0-1e0098f48   [   88    88    0K    0K] r--/rw- SM=COW  /usr/lib/system/libsystem_malloc.dylib
__DATA_CONST            1e0098f50-1e0099b58   [ 3080  3080    0K    0K] r--/rw- SM=COW  /usr/lib/libobjc.A.dylib
__DATA_CONST            1e0099b58-1e0099b98   [   64    64    0K    0K] r--/rw- SM=COW  /usr/lib/system/libsystem_featureflags.dylib
__DATA_CONST            1e0099b98-1e009b370   [   6K    6K    0K    0K] r--/rw- SM=COW  /usr/lib/system/libsystem_c.dylib
__DATA_CONST            1e009b370-1e009bcd0   [ 2400  2400    0K    0K] r--/rw- SM=COW  /usr/lib/libc++.1.dylib
__DATA_CONST            1e009bcd0-1e009bda8   [  216   216    0K    0K] r--/rw- SM=COW  /usr/lib/libc++abi.dylib
__DATA_CONST            1e009bda8-1e009e060   [   9K    9K    0K    0K] r--/rw- SM=COW  /usr/lib/system/libsystem_kernel.dylib
__DATA_CONST            1e009e060-1e009e098   [   56    56    0K    0K] r--/rw- SM=COW  /usr/lib/system/libsystem_pthread.dylib
__DATA_CONST            1e009e098-1e009e258   [  448   448    0K    0K] r--/rw- SM=COW  /usr/lib/system/libdyld.dylib
__DATA_CONST            1e009e258-1e009e278   [   32    32    0K    0K] r--/rw- SM=COW  /usr/lib/system/libsystem_platform.dylib
__DATA_CONST            1e009e278-1e009e790   [ 1304  1304    0K    0K] r--/rw- SM=COW  /usr/lib/system/libsystem_info.dylib
__DATA_CONST            1e0127148-1e0129ac0   [  10K   10K    0K    0K] r--/rw- SM=COW  /usr/lib/system/libsystem_darwin.dylib
__DATA_CONST            1e0133dc0-1e0133f18   [  344   344    0K    0K] r--/rw- SM=COW  /usr/lib/system/libsystem_notify.dylib
__DATA_CONST            1e02c9868-1e02c9d60   [ 1272  1272    0K    0K] r--/rw- SM=COW  /usr/lib/system/libsystem_networkextension.dylib
__DATA_CONST            1e02cac70-1e02cb290   [ 1568  1568    0K    0K] r--/rw- SM=COW  /usr/lib/system/libsystem_asl.dylib
__DATA_CONST            1e032ea80-1e032ec30   [  432   432    0K    0K] r--/rw- SM=COW  /usr/lib/system/libsystem_symptoms.dylib
__DATA_CONST            1e05863b8-1e0586da0   [ 2536  2536    0K    0K] r--/rw- SM=COW  /usr/lib/system/libsystem_containermanager.dylib
__DATA_CONST            1e061d0e0-1e061d298   [  440   440    0K    0K] r--/rw- SM=COW  /usr/lib/system/libsystem_configuration.dylib
__DATA_CONST            1e061d298-1e061d308   [  112   112    0K    0K] r--/rw- SM=COW  /usr/lib/system/libsystem_sandbox.dylib
__DATA_CONST            1e064ac20-1e064ac70   [   80    80    0K    0K] r--/rw- SM=COW  /usr/lib/system/libquarantine.dylib
__DATA_CONST            1e06d5660-1e06d5dc8   [ 1896  1896    0K    0K] r--/rw- SM=COW  /usr/lib/system/libsystem_coreservices.dylib
__DATA_CONST            1e06fd5a8-1e06fdcf0   [ 1864  1864    0K    0K] r--/rw- SM=COW  /usr/lib/system/libmacho.dylib
__DATA_CONST            1e06fdd00-1e06fe4a0   [ 1952  1952    0K    0K] r--/rw- SM=COW  /usr/lib/system/libcommonCrypto.dylib
__DATA_CONST            1e06fe4a0-1e06fe7c0   [  800   800    0K    0K] r--/rw- SM=COW  /usr/lib/system/libunwind.dylib
__DATA_CONST            1e06fe7c0-1e06fe7d8   [   24    24    0K    0K] r--/rw- SM=COW  /usr/lib/liboah.dylib
__DATA_CONST            1e06fe7d8-1e06fea98   [  704   704    0K    0K] r--/rw- SM=COW  /usr/lib/system/libcopyfile.dylib
__DATA_CONST            1e06fea98-1e06feaa0   [    8     8    0K    0K] r--/rw- SM=COW  /usr/lib/system/libsystem_collections.dylib
__DATA_CONST            1e06feaa0-1e06feb10   [  112   112    0K    0K] r--/rw- SM=COW  /usr/lib/system/libsystem_secinit.dylib
__DATA_CONST            1e06feb10-1e06feb20   [   16    16    0K    0K] r--/rw- SM=COW  /usr/lib/system/libremovefile.dylib
__DATA_CONST            1e06feb20-1e06feb30   [   16    16    0K    0K] r--/rw- SM=COW  /usr/lib/system/libkeymgr.dylib
__DATA_CONST            1e06feb30-1e06feba8   [  120   120    0K    0K] r--/rw- SM=COW  /usr/lib/system/libsystem_dnssd.dylib
__DATA_CONST            1e06feba8-1e06fec08   [   96    96    0K    0K] r--/rw- SM=COW  /usr/lib/system/libcache.dylib
__DATA_CONST            1e06fec08-1e06fec18   [   16    16    0K    0K] r--/rw- SM=COW  /usr/lib/libSystem.B.dylib
__AUTH_CONST            1e8b08000-1e8b08030   [   48    48    0K    0K] r--/rw- SM=COW  /usr/lib/system/libsystem_blocks.dylib
__OBJC_CONST            1e8b08030-1e8b08390   [  864   864    0K    0K] r--/rw- SM=COW  /usr/lib/system/libsystem_blocks.dylib
__DATA_CONST            1e8b08390-1e8b0ce20   [  19K   19K    0K    0K] r--/rw- SM=COW  /usr/lib/system/libxpc.dylib
__OBJC_CONST            1e8b0ce20-1e8b0df90   [   4K    4K    0K    0K] r--/rw- SM=COW  /usr/lib/system/libxpc.dylib
__AUTH_CONST            1e8b0df90-1e8b0ec90   [ 3328  3328    0K    0K] r--/rw- SM=COW  /usr/lib/system/libsystem_trace.dylib
__OBJC_CONST            1e8b0ec90-1e8b0ee40   [  432   432    0K    0K] r--/rw- SM=COW  /usr/lib/system/libsystem_trace.dylib
__AUTH_CONST            1e8b0ee40-1e8b0ff10   [   4K    4K    0K    0K] r--/rw- SM=COW  /usr/lib/system/libcorecrypto.dylib
__AUTH_CONST            1e8b0ff10-1e8b104e8   [ 1496  1496    0K    0K] r--/rw- SM=COW  /usr/lib/system/libsystem_malloc.dylib
__DATA_CONST            1e8b10500-1e8b238e8   [  77K   45K    0K    0K] r--/rw- SM=COW  /usr/lib/system/libdispatch.dylib
```

```
__OBJC_CONST              1e8b238e8-1e8b24938    [   4K     4K     0K     0K] r--/rw- SM=COW         /usr/lib/system/libdispatch.dylib
__AUTH_CONST              1e8b24940-1e8b253c8    [ 2696   2696     0K     0K] r--/rw- SM=COW         /usr/lib/libobjc.A.dylib
__OBJC_CONST              1e8b253c8-1e8b25698    [  720    720     0K     0K] r--/rw- SM=COW         /usr/lib/libobjc.A.dylib
__AUTH_CONST              1e8b25698-1e8b25808    [  368    368     0K     0K] r--/rw- SM=COW         /usr/lib/system/libsystem_featureflags.dylib
__AUTH_CONST              1e8b25808-1e8b26168    [ 2400   2400     0K     0K] r--/rw- SM=COW         /usr/lib/system/libsystem_c.dylib
__AUTH_CONST              1e8b26168-1e8b282a8    [   8K     8K     0K     0K] r--/rw- SM=COW         /usr/lib/libc++.1.dylib
__AUTH_CONST              1e8b282a8-1e8b2b4b8    [  13K    13K     0K     0K] r--/rw- SM=COW         /usr/lib/libc++abi.dylib
__AUTH_CONST              1e8b2b4b8-1e8b2b5e0    [  296    296     0K     0K] r--/rw- SM=COW         /usr/lib/system/libsystem_kernel.dylib
__AUTH_CONST              1e8b2b5e0-1e8b2b810    [  560    560     0K     0K] r--/rw- SM=COW         /usr/lib/system/libsystem_pthread.dylib
__AUTH_CONST              1e8b2b810-1e8b2bfc8    [ 1976   1976     0K     0K] r--/rw- SM=COW         /usr/lib/system/libdyld.dylib
__AUTH_CONST              1e8b2bfc8-1e8b2c250    [  648    648     0K     0K] r--/rw- SM=COW         /usr/lib/system/libsystem_platform.dylib
__AUTH_CONST              1e8b2c250-1e8b2d3f0    [   4K     4K     0K     0K] r--/rw- SM=COW         /usr/lib/system/libsystem_info.dylib
__AUTH_CONST              1e8c5bd48-1e8c5c1c8    [ 1152   1152     0K     0K] r--/rw- SM=COW         /usr/lib/system/libsystem_darwin.dylib
__AUTH_CONST              1e8c77a80-1e8c77e00    [  896    896     0K     0K] r--/rw- SM=COW         /usr/lib/system/libsystem_notify.dylib
__AUTH_CONST              1e8dfea40-1e8dff608    [ 3016   3016     0K     0K] r--/rw- SM=COW         /usr/lib/system/libsystem_networkextension.dylib
__AUTH_CONST              1e8e4d718-1e8e4e160    [ 2632   2632     0K     0K] r--/rw- SM=COW         /usr/lib/system/libsystem_asl.dylib
__AUTH_CONST              1e8f17288-1e8f17560    [  728    728     0K     0K] r--/rw- SM=COW         /usr/lib/system/libsystem_symptoms.dylib
__AUTH_CONST              1e904e480-1e904f8c0    [   5K     5K     0K     0K] r--/rw- SM=COW         /usr/lib/system/libsystem_containermanager.dylib
__AUTH_CONST              1e915e250-1e915e560    [  784    784     0K     0K] r--/rw- SM=COW         /usr/lib/system/libsystem_configuration.dylib
__AUTH_CONST              1e915e560-1e915e768    [  520    520     0K     0K] r--/rw- SM=COW         /usr/lib/system/libsystem_sandbox.dylib
__AUTH_CONST              1e91a78b8-1e91a79c0    [  264    264     0K     0K] r--/rw- SM=COW         /usr/lib/system/libquarantine.dylib
__AUTH_CONST              1e922eac0-1e922ed50    [  656    656     0K     0K] r--/rw- SM=COW         /usr/lib/system/libsystem_coreservices.dylib
__AUTH_CONST              1e925ad88-1e925ada8    [   32     32     0K     0K] r--/rw- SM=COW         /usr/lib/system/libsystem_m.dylib
__AUTH_CONST              1e925ae28-1e925ae98    [  112    112     0K     0K] r--/rw- SM=COW         /usr/lib/system/libmacho.dylib
__AUTH_CONST              1e925afb0-1e925bd80    [ 3536   3536     0K     0K] r--/rw- SM=COW         /usr/lib/system/libcommonCrypto.dylib
__AUTH_CONST              1e925bd80-1e925be98    [  280    280     0K     0K] r--/rw- SM=COW         /usr/lib/system/libunwind.dylib
__AUTH_CONST              1e925be98-1e925c168    [  720    720     0K     0K] r--/rw- SM=COW         /usr/lib/liboah.dylib
__AUTH_CONST              1e925c168-1e925c5a0    [ 1080   1080     0K     0K] r--/rw- SM=COW         /usr/lib/system/libcopyfile.dylib
__AUTH_CONST              1e925c5a0-1e925c600    [   96     96     0K     0K] r--/rw- SM=COW         /usr/lib/system/libcompiler_rt.dylib
__AUTH_CONST              1e925c600-1e925c750    [  336    336     0K     0K] r--/rw- SM=COW         /usr/lib/system/libsystem_collections.dylib
__AUTH_CONST              1e925c750-1e925ca18    [  712    712     0K     0K] r--/rw- SM=COW         /usr/lib/system/libsystem_secinit.dylib
__AUTH_CONST              1e925ca18-1e925cb78    [  352    352     0K     0K] r--/rw- SM=COW         /usr/lib/system/libremovefile.dylib
__AUTH_CONST              1e925cb78-1e925cbf8    [  128    128     0K     0K] r--/rw- SM=COW         /usr/lib/system/libkeymgr.dylib
__AUTH_CONST              1e925cbf8-1e925cdb0    [  440    440     0K     0K] r--/rw- SM=COW         /usr/lib/system/libsystem_dnssd.dylib
__AUTH_CONST              1e925cdb0-1e925ce70    [  192    192     0K     0K] r--/rw- SM=COW         /usr/lib/system/libcache.dylib
__AUTH_CONST              1e925ce70-1e925d120    [  688    688     0K     0K] r--/rw- SM=COW         /usr/lib/libSystem.B.dylib
__LINKEDIT                222494000-2465e6000    [577.3M 11.8M     0K     0K] r--/r-- SM=COW         dyld shared cache combined __LINKEDIT

==== Writable regions for process 89676
REGION TYPE                   START - END        [ VSIZE  RSDNT  DIRTY   SWAP] PRT/MAX SHRMOD PURGE    REGION DETAIL
Kernel Alloc Once         104624000-10462c000    [  32K    16K    16K     0K] rw-/rwx SM=PRV
MALLOC metadata           104634000-104638000    [  16K    16K    16K     0K] rw-/rwx SM=COW
MALLOC metadata           10463c000-104644000    [  32K    32K    32K     0K] rw-/rwx SM=COW
MALLOC metadata           10464c000-104654000    [  32K    32K    32K     0K] rw-/rwx SM=PRV
MALLOC metadata           10465c000-104664000    [  32K    32K    32K     0K] rw-/rwx SM=PRV
MALLOC metadata           104670000-104674000    [  16K    16K    16K     0K] rw-/rwx SM=COW
__DATA                    104798000-10479c000    [  16K    16K    16K     0K] rw-/rw- SM=COW         /usr/lib/dyld
MALLOC_TINY               13d600000-13d700000    [ 1024K   32K    32K     0K] rw-/rwx SM=PRV         MallocHelperZone_0x104630000
MALLOC_TINY               13d700000-13d800000    [ 1024K   32K    32K     0K] rw-/rwx SM=PRV         MallocHelperZone_0x104630000
MALLOC_SMALL              13d800000-13e000000    [ 8192K   32K    32K     0K] rw-/rwx SM=PRV         MallocHelperZone_0x104630000
MALLOC_SMALL              13e000000-13e800000    [ 8192K   32K    32K     0K] rw-/rwx SM=PRV         MallocHelperZone_0x104630000
Stack                     16aff0000-16b7ec000    [ 8176K   32K    32K     0K] rw-/rwx SM=PRV         thread 0
Stack                     16b7f0000-16b878000    [ 544K    16K    16K     0K] rw-/rwx SM=PRV         thread 1
Stack                     16b87c000-16b904000    [ 544K    16K    16K     0K] rw-/rwx SM=PRV         thread 2
Stack                     16b908000-16b990000    [ 544K    16K    16K     0K] rw-/rwx SM=PRV         thread 3
Stack                     16b994000-16ba1c000    [ 544K    16K    16K     0K] rw-/rwx SM=PRV         thread 4
Stack                     16ba20000-16baa8000    [ 544K    16K    16K     0K] rw-/rwx SM=PRV         thread 5
__DATA                    1e4c04000-1e4c04060    [   96     96     96     0K] rw-/rw- SM=COW         /usr/lib/system/libsystem_blocks.dylib
__DATA                    1e4c04060-1e4c04d18    [ 3256   3256   3256     0K] rw-/rw- SM=COW         /usr/lib/system/libxpc.dylib
__DATA                    1e4c04d18-1e4c05050    [  824    824    824     0K] rw-/rw- SM=COW         /usr/lib/system/libsystem_trace.dylib
__DATA                    1e4c05050-1e4c0c788    [  30K    30K    14K     0K] rw-/rw- SM=COW         /usr/lib/system/libcorecrypto.dylib
__DATA                    1e4c0c788-1e4c0ea24    [   9K     9K     9K     0K] rw-/rw- SM=COW         /usr/lib/system/libsystem_malloc.dylib
unused __DATA             1e4c0ea24-1e4c0ea40    [   28     28     28     0K] rw-/rw- SM=COW         on dirty page  unused system shared lib __DATA
__DATA                    1e4c0ea40-1e4c120c0    [  14K    14K    14K     0K] rw-/rw- SM=COW         /usr/lib/libobjc.A.dylib
__DATA                    1e4c120c0-1e4c120f9    [   57     57     57     0K] rw-/rw- SM=COW         /usr/lib/system/libsystem_featureflags.dylib
unused __DATA             1e4c120f9-1e4c12100    [    7      7      7     0K] rw-/rw- SM=COW         on dirty page  unused system shared lib __DATA
__DATA                    1e4c12100-1e4c14270    [   8K     8K     8K     0K] rw-/rw- SM=COW         /usr/lib/system/libsystem_c.dylib
unused __DATA             1e4c14270-1e4c15000    [ 3472   3472   3472     0K] rw-/rw- SM=COW         on dirty page  unused system shared lib __DATA
__DATA                    1e4c15000-1e4c1b720    [  26K    26K    12K     0K] rw-/rw- SM=COW         /usr/lib/libc++.1.dylib
__DATA                    1e4c1b720-1e4c1ba68    [  840    840     0K     0K] rw-/rw- SM=COW         /usr/lib/libc++abi.dylib
__DATA                    1e4c1ba68-1e4c1bcd9    [  625    625     0K     0K] rw-/rw- SM=COW         /usr/lib/system/libsystem_kernel.dylib
__DATA                    1e4c1c000-1e4c24000    [  32K    32K     0K     0K] rw-/rw- SM=COW         /usr/lib/system/libsystem_pthread.dylib
__DATA                    1e4c24000-1e4c28000    [  16K    16K     0K     0K] rw-/rw- SM=COW         /usr/lib/system/libsystem_pthread.dylib
__DATA                    1e4c28000-1e4c28048    [   72     72     0K     0K] rw-/rw- SM=COW         /usr/lib/system/libsystem_pthread.dylib
__DATA                    1e4c28048-1e4c28050    [    8      8     0K     0K] rw-/rw- SM=COW         /usr/lib/system/libdyld.dylib
__DATA                    1e4c28050-1e4c28090    [   64     64     0K     0K] rw-/rw- SM=COW         /usr/lib/system/libsystem_platform.dylib
__DATA                    1e4c28090-1e4c28be0    [ 2896   2896     0K     0K] rw-/rw- SM=COW         /usr/lib/system/libsystem_info.dylib
__DATA                    1e4c96958-1e4c96968    [   16     16     0K     0K] rw-/rw- SM=COW         /usr/lib/system/libsystem_darwin.dylib
__DATA                    1e4c9de00-1e4c9de51    [   81     81     0K     0K] rw-/rw- SM=COW         /usr/lib/system/libsystem_notify.dylib
__DATA                    1e4d33600-1e4d33bd9    [ 1497   1497     0K     0K] rw-/rw- SM=COW         /usr/lib/system/libsystem_networkextension.dylib
__DATA                    1e4d343b8-1e4d344c8    [  272    272     0K     0K] rw-/rw- SM=COW         /usr/lib/system/libsystem_asl.dylib
__DATA                    1e4d6a118-1e4d6a158    [   64     64     0K     0K] rw-/rw- SM=COW         /usr/lib/system/libsystem_symptoms.dylib
__DATA                    1e4deca18-1e4decb40    [  296    296     0K     0K] rw-/rw- SM=COW         /usr/lib/system/libsystem_containermanager.dylib
__DATA                    1e4e2d090-1e4e2d159    [  201    201     0K     0K] rw-/rw- SM=COW         /usr/lib/system/libsystem_configuration.dylib
__DATA                    1e4e2d160-1e4e2d188    [   40     40     0K     0K] rw-/rw- SM=COW         /usr/lib/system/libsystem_sandbox.dylib
__DATA                    1e4e4f280-1e4e4f290    [   16     16     0K     0K] rw-/rw- SM=COW         /usr/lib/system/libquarantine.dylib
__DATA                    1e4e61bb0-1e4e61c88    [  216    216     0K     0K] rw-/rw- SM=COW         /usr/lib/system/libsystem_coreservices.dylib
__DATA                    1e4e71a20-1e4e71a24    [    4      4     0K     0K] rw-/rw- SM=COW         /usr/lib/system/libsystem_m.dylib
__DATA                    1e4e71ae8-1e4e723d9    [ 2289   2289     0K     0K] rw-/rw- SM=COW         /usr/lib/system/libunwind.dylib
__DATA                    1e4e723e0-1e4e723e8    [    8      8     0K     0K] rw-/rw- SM=COW         /usr/lib/liboah.dylib
__DATA                    1e4e723e8-1e4e723f8    [   16     16     0K     0K] rw-/rw- SM=COW         /usr/lib/system/libcopyfile.dylib
__DATA                    1e4e723f8-1e4e733f8    [   4K     4K     0K     0K] rw-/rw- SM=COW         /usr/lib/system/libcompiler_rt.dylib
__DATA                    1e4e733f8-1e4e73438    [   64     64     0K     0K] rw-/rw- SM=COW         /usr/lib/system/libsystem_secinit.dylib
__DATA                    1e4e73438-1e4e73468    [   48     48     0K     0K] rw-/rw- SM=COW         /usr/lib/system/libsystem_dnssd.dylib
__DATA                    1e4e73468-1e4e73470    [    8      8     0K     0K] rw-/rw- SM=COW         /usr/lib/libSystem.B.dylib
unused __DATA_DIRTY       1e7930000-1e7930120    [  288    288    288     0K] rw-/rw- SM=COW         on dirty page  unused /usr/lib/libMobileGestalt.dylib
unused __DATA_DIRTY       1e7930120-1e7930170    [   80     80     80     0K] rw-/rw- SM=COW         on dirty page  unused
/usr/lib/libUniversalAccess.dylib
unused __DATA_DIRTY       1e7930170-1e7930190    [   32     32     32     0K] rw-/rw- SM=COW         on dirty page  unused
/usr/lib/libapp_launch_measurement.dylib
unused __DATA_DIRTY       1e7930190-1e7931010    [ 3712   3712   3712     0K] rw-/rw- SM=COW         on dirty page  unused /usr/lib/libboringssl.dylib
__DATA_DIRTY              1e7931010-1e79321e0    [   4K     4K     4K     0K] rw-/rw- SM=COW         /usr/lib/libc++.1.dylib
```

```
__DATA_DIRTY               1e79321e0-1e7932208 [    40     40     40     0K] rw-/rw- SM=COW          /usr/lib/libc++abi.dylib
unused __DATA_DIRTY        1e7932208-1e7934000 [    7K     7K     7K     0K] rw-/rw- SM=COW          on dirty page  unused /usr/lib/libcoreroutine.dylib
unused __DATA_DIRTY        1e7938000-1e793a1c8 [    8K     8K     8K     0K] rw-/rw- SM=COW          on dirty page  unused /usr/lib/libnetwork.dylib
unused __DATA              1e793a1c8-1e793a200 [    56     56     56     0K] rw-/rw- SM=COW          on dirty page  unused system shared lib __DATA
__DATA_DIRTY               1e793a200-1e793d070 [    12K    12K    12K     0K] rw-/rw- SM=COW          /usr/lib/libobjc.A.dylib
unused __DATA_DIRTY        1e793d070-1e793d200 [    400    400    400     0K] rw-/rw- SM=COW          on dirty page  unused
/usr/lib/libpartition2_dynamic.dylib
unused __DATA_DIRTY        1e793d200-1e793d299 [    153    153    153     0K] rw-/rw- SM=COW          on dirty page  unused /usr/lib/libpmenergy.dylib
unused __DATA              1e793d299-1e793d2a0 [    7      7      7       0K] rw-/rw- SM=COW          on dirty page  unused system shared lib __DATA
unused __DATA_DIRTY        1e793d2a0-1e793d3e8 [    328    328    328     0K] rw-/rw- SM=COW          on dirty page  unused /usr/lib/libprequelite.dylib
unused __DATA_DIRTY        1e793d3e8-1e793d4f8 [    272    272    272     0K] rw-/rw- SM=COW          on dirty page  unused /usr/lib/libquic.dylib
unused __DATA_DIRTY        1e793d4f8-1e793d530 [    56     56     56      0K] rw-/rw- SM=COW          on dirty page  unused /usr/lib/libsandbox.1.dylib
unused __DATA              1e793d530-1e793d540 [    16     16     16      0K] rw-/rw- SM=COW          on dirty page  unused system shared lib __DATA
unused __DATA_DIRTY        1e793d540-1e7940000 [    11K    11K    11K     0K] rw-/rw- SM=COW          on dirty page  unused /usr/lib/libsqlite3.dylib
unused __DATA_DIRTY        1e795c000-1e795e610 [    10K    10K    10K     0K] rw-/rw- SM=COW          on dirty page  unused
/usr/lib/swift/libswiftFoundation.dylib
unused __DATA_DIRTY        1e795e610-1e795e7a0 [    400    400    400     0K] rw-/rw- SM=COW          on dirty page  unused
/usr/lib/swift/libswiftObjectiveC.dylib
unused __DATA_DIRTY        1e795e7a0-1e795e7b8 [    24     24     24      0K] rw-/rw- SM=COW          on dirty page  unused /usr/lib/swift/libswiftos.dylib
__DATA_DIRTY               1e795e7b8-1e795ef10 [    1880   1880   1880    0K] rw-/rw- SM=COW          /usr/lib/system/libcorecrypto.dylib
unused __DATA              1e795ef10-1e795ef40 [    48     48     48      0K] rw-/rw- SM=COW          on dirty page  unused system shared lib __DATA
__DATA_DIRTY               1e795ef40-1e79628e8 [    14K    14K    14K     0K] rw-/rw- SM=COW          /usr/lib/system/libdispatch.dylib
__DATA_DIRTY               1e79628e8-1e7962908 [    32     32     32      0K] rw-/rw- SM=COW          /usr/lib/system/libdyld.dylib
unused __DATA              1e7962908-1e8b08000 [    8      8      8       0K] rw-/rw- SM=COW          on dirty page  unused system shared lib __DATA
__DATA_DIRTY               1e7962910-1e7962a6c [    348    348    348     0K] rw-/rw- SM=COW          /usr/lib/system/libsystem_asl.dylib
unused __DATA              1e7962a6c-1e7962a70 [    4      4      4       0K] rw-/rw- SM=COW          on dirty page  unused system shared lib __DATA
__DATA_DIRTY               1e7962a70-1e7962c68 [    504    504    504     0K] rw-/rw- SM=COW          /usr/lib/system/libsystem_blocks.dylib
__DATA_DIRTY               1e7962c68-1e79657f0 [    11K    11K    11K     0K] rw-/rw- SM=COW          /usr/lib/system/libsystem_c.dylib
__DATA_DIRTY               1e79657f0-1e7965820 [    48     48     48      0K] rw-/rw- SM=COW          /usr/lib/system/libsystem_darwin.dylib
__DATA_DIRTY               1e7965820-1e7965830 [    16     16     16      0K] rw-/rw- SM=COW          /usr/lib/system/libsystem_featureflags.dylib
__DATA_DIRTY               1e7965830-1e7965ac0 [    656    656    656     0K] rw-/rw- SM=COW          /usr/lib/system/libsystem_info.dylib
__DATA_DIRTY               1e7965ac0-1e7966184 [    1732   1732   1732    0K] rw-/rw- SM=COW          /usr/lib/system/libsystem_kernel.dylib
unused __DATA              1e7966184-1e7966188 [    4      4      4       0K] rw-/rw- SM=COW          on dirty page  unused system shared lib __DATA
__DATA_DIRTY               1e7966188-1e79663a0 [    536    536    536     0K] rw-/rw- SM=COW          /usr/lib/system/libsystem_malloc.dylib
__DATA_DIRTY               1e79663a0-1e79663e1 [    65     65     65      0K] rw-/rw- SM=COW          /usr/lib/system/libsystem_networkextension.dylib
unused __DATA              1e79663e1-1e79663e8 [    7      7      7       0K] rw-/rw- SM=COW          on dirty page  unused system shared lib __DATA
__DATA_DIRTY               1e79663e8-1e79663f0 [    8      8      8       0K] rw-/rw- SM=COW          /usr/lib/system/libsystem_notify.dylib
__DATA_DIRTY               1e79663f0-1e7966404 [    20     20     20      0K] rw-/rw- SM=COW          /usr/lib/system/libsystem_platform.dylib
unused __DATA              1e7966404-1e7968000 [    7K     7K     7K      0K] rw-/rw- SM=COW          on dirty page  unused system shared lib __DATA
__DATA_DIRTY               1e7968000-1e796d838 [    22K    22K    22K     0K] rw-/rw- SM=COW          /usr/lib/system/libsystem_pthread.dylib
__DATA_DIRTY               1e796d838-1e796d848 [    16     16     16      0K] rw-/rw- SM=COW          /usr/lib/system/libsystem_symptoms.dylib
__DATA_DIRTY               1e796d848-1e796dcb8 [    1136   1136   1136    0K] rw-/rw- SM=COW          /usr/lib/system/libsystem_trace.dylib
__DATA_DIRTY               1e796dcb8-1e796e708 [    2640   2640   2640    0K] rw-/rw- SM=COW          /usr/lib/system/libxpc.dylib
unused __DATA              1e796e708-1e7970000 [    6K     6K     6K      0K] rw-/rw- SM=COW          on dirty page  unused system shared lib __DATA
__AUTH                     1e7970000-1e79701b8 [    440    440    0K      0K] rw-/rw- SM=COW          /usr/lib/system/libsystem_trace.dylib
__AUTH                     1e79701b8-1e7970218 [    96     96     0K      0K] rw-/rw- SM=COW          /usr/lib/system/libcorecrypto.dylib
__AUTH                     1e7974000-1e797c000 [    32K    32K    0K      0K] rw-/rw- SM=COW          /usr/lib/system/libsystem_malloc.dylib
__DATA                     1e797c000-1e797d400 [    5K     5K     0K      0K] rw-/rw- SM=COW          /usr/lib/system/libdispatch.dylib
__AUTH                     1e797d400-1e797d478 [    120    120    0K      0K] rw-/rw- SM=COW          /usr/lib/libobjc.A.dylib
__AUTH                     1e797d478-1e797e190 [    3352   3352   0K      0K] rw-/rw- SM=COW          /usr/lib/system/libsystem_c.dylib
__AUTH                     1e797e190-1e7980628 [    9K     9K     1576    0K] rw-/rw- SM=COW          /usr/lib/libc++.1.dylib
__AUTH                     1e7980628-1e7980670 [    72     72     72      0K] rw-/rw- SM=COW          /usr/lib/libc++abi.dylib
__AUTH                     1e7980670-1e79806b0 [    64     64     64      0K] rw-/rw- SM=COW          /usr/lib/system/libdyld.dylib
__AUTH                     1e79806b0-1e7980880 [    464    464    464     0K] rw-/rw- SM=COW          /usr/lib/system/libsystem_info.dylib
unused __AUTH              1e7980880-1e7982740 [    8K     8K     8K      0K] rw-/rw- SM=COW          ...y page  unused
/System/Library/Frameworks/CoreFoundation.framework/Versions/A/CoreFoundation
unused __AUTH              1e7982740-1e7984000 [    6K     6K     6K      0K] rw-/rw- SM=COW
...eServices.framework/Versions/A/Frameworks/LaunchServices.framework/Versions/A/LaunchServices
__AUTH                     1e7a0a640-1e7a0a660 [    32     32     0K      0K] rw-/rw- SM=COW          /usr/lib/system/libcommonCrypto.dylib
__AUTH                     1e7a0a660-1e7a0a668 [    8      8      0K      0K] rw-/rw- SM=COW          /usr/lib/libSystem.B.dylib
__OBJC_RW                  1e87f0000-1e8b08000 [  3168K  1616K    16K     0K] rw-/rw- SM=COW          /usr/lib/libobjc.A.dylib
MALLOC_NANO                600000000000-600008000000 [128.0M  144K   144K     0K] rw-/rwx SM=PRV     DefaultMallocZone_0x10466c000
MALLOC_NANO (empty)        600008000000-600010000000 [128.0M    0K     0K     0K] rw-/rwx SM=PRV
MALLOC_NANO (empty)        600010000000-600018000000 [128.0M    0K     0K     0K] rw-/rwx SM=PRV
MALLOC_NANO (empty)        600018000000-600020000000 [128.0M    0K     0K     0K] rw-/rwx SM=PRV


==== Legend
SM=sharing mode:
        COW=copy_on_write PRV=private NUL=empty ALI=aliased
        SHM=shared ZER=zero_filled S/A=shared_alias
PURGE=purgeable mode:
        V=volatile N=nonvolatile E=empty    otherwise is unpurgeable


==== Summary for process 89676
ReadOnly portion of Libraries: Total=582.2M resident=16.3M(3%) swapped_out_or_unallocated=565.8M(97%)
Writable regions: Total=540.8M written=464K(0%) resident=528K(0%) swapped_out=0K(0%) unallocated=540.3M(100%)


                            VIRTUAL RESIDENT   DIRTY  SWAPPED VOLATILE   NONVOL   EMPTY  REGION
REGION TYPE                    SIZE     SIZE    SIZE     SIZE     SIZE     SIZE    SIZE   COUNT (non-coalesced)
===========                 ======= ========   =====  ======= ========   ======  =====  =======
Kernel Alloc Once               32K      16K     16K      0K       0K       0K      0K       1
MALLOC guard page               96K       0K      0K      0K       0K       0K      0K       5
MALLOC metadata                176K     176K    176K      0K       0K       0K      0K       8
MALLOC_NANO                  128.0M     144K    144K      0K       0K       0K      0K       1     see MALLOC ZONE table below
MALLOC_NANO (empty)          384.0M       0K      0K      0K       0K       0K      0K       3     see MALLOC ZONE table below
MALLOC_SMALL                  16.0M      64K     64K      0K       0K       0K      0K       2     see MALLOC ZONE table below
MALLOC_TINY                   2048K      64K     64K      0K       0K       0K      0K       2     see MALLOC ZONE table below
STACK GUARD                   56.1M       0K      0K      0K       0K       0K      0K       6
Stack                         10.6M     112K    112K      0K       0K       0K      0K       6
__AUTH                          46K      46K    2176      0K       0K       0K      0K      11
__AUTH_CONST                    67K      67K      0K      0K       0K       0K      0K      38
__DATA                         173K     173K     77K      0K       0K       0K      0K      37
__DATA_CONST                   258K     162K     48K      0K       0K       0K      0K      40
__DATA_DIRTY                    73K      73K     73K      0K       0K       0K      0K      21
__LINKEDIT                    577.6M    11.9M     0K      0K       0K       0K      0K       3
__OBJC_CONST                    10K      10K      0K      0K       0K       0K      0K       5
__OBJC_RO                     83.0M     49.6M     0K      0K       0K       0K      0K       1
__OBJC_RW                     3168K    1616K     16K      0K       0K       0K      0K       1
__TEXT                        4708K    4500K      0K      0K       0K       0K      0K      43
dyld private memory          1024K      16K     16K      0K       0K       0K      0K       1
shared memory                  16K      16K     16K      0K       0K       0K      0K       1
unused but dirty shlib __DATA   72K      72K     72K      0K       0K       0K      0K      30
```

```
===========               ======= ========   ===== ======= ========   ======   ===== =======
TOTAL                        1.2G    68.6M     896K     0K      0K         0K      0K     266

                          VIRTUAL  RESIDENT    DIRTY  SWAPPED ALLOCATION        BYTES DIRTY+SWAP          REGION
MALLOC ZONE                  SIZE      SIZE     SIZE     SIZE      COUNT    ALLOCATED  FRAG SIZE  % FRAG    COUNT
===========               ======= =========  ======== ======== =========  ========= =========  ======  ======
DefaultMallocZone_0x10466c000 128.0M   144K     144K      0K        211         9K      135K     94%        1
MallocHelperZone_0x104630000   18.0M   128K     128K      0K          9         8K      120K     94%        4
===========               ======= =========  ======== ======== =========  ========= =========  ======  ======
TOTAL                       146.0M    272K     272K      0K        220        17K      255K     94%        5
```

88

Exercise X5

- **Goal:** Learn how to identify stack corruption

- **Patterns:** Truncated Stack Trace; Local Buffer Overflow; Execution Residue; Self-Diagnosis (User Mode)

- \AMCDA-Dumps\Exercise-X5.pdf

Exercise X5

Goal: Learn how to identify stack corruption.

Patterns: Truncated Stack Trace; Local Buffer Overflow; Execution Residue; Self-Diagnosis (User Mode).

1.   Identify the problem thread and application-specific diagnostic from the diagnostic report *App5-2022-12-02-192639.ips*:

```
-------------------------------------
Translated Report (Full Report Below)
-------------------------------------


Process:             App5 [90577]
Path:                /Users/USER/*/App5
Identifier:          App5
Version:             ???
Code Type:           ARM-64 (Native)
Parent Process:      zsh [73148]
Responsible:         Terminal [9503]
User ID:             501

Date/Time:           2022-12-02 19:26:38.9670 +0000
OS Version:          macOS 12.6 (21G115)
Report Version:      12
Anonymous UUID:      6F758133-2B79-4743-8B70-8B1D8C510718

Sleep/Wake UUID:     354190F1-428B-4DDE-A218-4CBF6ADB1827

Time Awake Since Boot: 150000 seconds
Time Since Wake:     207 seconds

System Integrity Protection: enabled

Crashed Thread:      1

Exception Type:      EXC_CRASH (SIGABRT)
Exception Codes:     0x0000000000000000, 0x0000000000000000
Exception Note:      EXC_CORPSE_NOTIFY

Application Specific Information:
stack buffer overflow


Thread 0::  Dispatch queue: com.apple.main-thread
0   libsystem_kernel.dylib             0x18e9ce06c __semwait_signal + 8
1   libsystem_c.dylib                  0x18e8d6fc8 nanosleep + 220
2   libsystem_c.dylib                  0x18e8e1b78 sleep + 52
3   libsystem_c.dylib                  0x18e8e1b90 sleep + 76
4   App5                               0x100ab7efc main + 164
5   dyld                               0x100c1508c start + 520

Thread 1 Crashed:
0   libsystem_kernel.dylib             0x18e9d2d98 __pthread_kill + 8
1   libsystem_pthread.dylib            0x18ea07ee0 pthread_kill + 288
2   libsystem_c.dylib                  0x18e9423cc __abort + 128
3   libsystem_c.dylib                  0x18e933d48 __stack_chk_fail + 96
4   App5                               0x100ab7cc0 procA + 92

Thread 2:
0   libsystem_kernel.dylib             0x18e9ce06c __semwait_signal + 8
1   libsystem_c.dylib                  0x18e8d6fc8 nanosleep + 220
2   libsystem_c.dylib                  0x18e8e1b78 sleep + 52
3   libsystem_c.dylib                  0x18e8e1b90 sleep + 76
4   App5                               0x100ab7d28 bar_two + 16
5   App5                               0x100ab7d3c foo_two + 12
6   App5                               0x100ab7d58 thread_two + 20
7   libsystem_pthread.dylib            0x18ea0826c _pthread_start + 148
8   libsystem_pthread.dylib            0x18ea0308c thread_start + 8
```

```
Thread 3:
0   libsystem_kernel.dylib              0x18e9ce06c __semwait_signal + 8
1   libsystem_c.dylib                   0x18e8d6fc8 nanosleep + 220
2   libsystem_c.dylib                   0x18e8e1b78 sleep + 52
3   libsystem_c.dylib                   0x18e8e1b90 sleep + 76
4   App5                                0x100ab7d78 bar_three + 16
5   App5                                0x100ab7d8c foo_three + 12
6   App5                                0x100ab7da8 thread_three + 20
7   libsystem_pthread.dylib             0x18ea0826c _pthread_start + 148
8   libsystem_pthread.dylib             0x18ea0308c thread_start + 8

Thread 4:
0   libsystem_kernel.dylib              0x18e9ce06c __semwait_signal + 8
1   libsystem_c.dylib                   0x18e8d6fc8 nanosleep + 220
2   libsystem_c.dylib                   0x18e8e1b78 sleep + 52
3   libsystem_c.dylib                   0x18e8e1b90 sleep + 76
4   App5                                0x100ab7dc8 bar_four + 16
5   App5                                0x100ab7ddc foo_four + 12
6   App5                                0x100ab7df8 thread_four + 20
7   libsystem_pthread.dylib             0x18ea0826c _pthread_start + 148
8   libsystem_pthread.dylib             0x18ea0308c thread_start + 8

Thread 5:
0   libsystem_kernel.dylib              0x18e9ce06c __semwait_signal + 8
1   libsystem_c.dylib                   0x18e8d6fc8 nanosleep + 220
2   libsystem_c.dylib                   0x18e8e1b78 sleep + 52
3   libsystem_c.dylib                   0x18e8e1b90 sleep + 76
4   App5                                0x100ab7e18 bar_five + 16
5   App5                                0x100ab7e2c foo_five + 12
6   App5                                0x100ab7e48 thread_five + 20
7   libsystem_pthread.dylib             0x18ea0826c _pthread_start + 148
8   libsystem_pthread.dylib             0x18ea0308c thread_start + 8


Thread 1 crashed with ARM Thread State (64-bit):
    x0: 0x0000000000000000   x1: 0x0000000000000000   x2: 0x0000000000000000   x3: 0x0000000000000000
    x4: 0x0000000000000000   x5: 0x0000000000000000   x6: 0x0000000000000000   x7: 0x000000018e9485fe
    x8: 0x6456705926032d4b   x9: 0x64567058493e1d4b  x10: 0x0000000000000000  x11: 0x0000000000000000
   x12: 0x0000000000000000  x13: 0x0000000000000000  x14: 0x0000000000000000  x15: 0x0000000000000000
   x16: 0x0000000000000148  x17: 0x00000001e8b2b680  x18: 0x0000000000000000  x19: 0x0000000000000006
   x20: 0x000000016f3d3000  x21: 0x0000000000001303  x22: 0x000000016f3d30e0  x23: 0x0000000000000000
   x24: 0x0000000000000000  x25: 0x0000000000000000  x26: 0x0000000000000000  x27: 0x0000000000000000
   x28: 0x0000000000000000   fp: 0x000000016f3d2ec0   lr: 0x000000018ea07ee0
    sp: 0x000000016f3d2ea0   pc: 0x000000018e9d2d98 cpsr: 0x40001000
   far: 0x0000000123636c18  esr: 0x56000080  Address size fault

Binary Images:
       0x18e9c9000 -        0x18ea00fff libsystem_kernel.dylib (*) <a9d87740-9c1d-3468-bf60-720a8d713cba>
/usr/lib/system/libsystem_kernel.dylib
       0x18e8c8000 -        0x18e949fff libsystem_c.dylib (*) <b25d2080-bb9e-38d6-8236-9cef4b2f11a3>
/usr/lib/system/libsystem_c.dylib
       0x100ab4000 -        0x100ab7fff App5 (*) <f8da6cdf-ca83-3678-969a-8bcf9519c8e9> /Users/USER/*/App5
       0x100c10000 -        0x100c6ffff dyld (*) <38ee9fe9-b66d-3066-8c5c-6ddf0d6944c6> /usr/lib/dyld
       0x18ea01000 -        0x18ea0dfff libsystem_pthread.dylib (*) <63c4eef9-69a5-38b1-996e-8d31b66a051d>
/usr/lib/system/libsystem_pthread.dylib

External Modification Summary:
  Calls made by other processes targeting this process:
    task_for_pid: 0
    thread_create: 0
    thread_set_state: 0
  Calls made by this process:
    task_for_pid: 0
    thread_create: 0
    thread_set_state: 0
  Calls made by all processes on this machine:
    task_for_pid: 0
    thread_create: 0
    thread_set_state: 0

VM Region Summary:
ReadOnly portion of Libraries: Total=582.2M resident=0K(0%) swapped_out_or_unallocated=582.2M(100%)
Writable regions: Total=531.8M written=0K(0%) resident=0K(0%) swapped_out=0K(0%) unallocated=531.8M(100%)
```

```
                              VIRTUAL  REGION
REGION TYPE                      SIZE   COUNT (non-coalesced)
===========                   =======  =======
Kernel Alloc Once                 32K        1
MALLOC                         137.3M       17
MALLOC_NANO (reserved)         384.0M        1    reserved VM address space (unallocated)
Stack                           10.7M       11
Stack (reserved)                56.0M        1    reserved VM address space (unallocated)
__AUTH                            46K       11
__AUTH_CONST                      67K       38
__DATA                           173K       37
__DATA_CONST                     258K       40
__DATA_DIRTY                      73K       21
__LINKEDIT                      577.6M       3
__OBJC_CONST                      10K        5
__OBJC_RO                       83.0M        1
__OBJC_RW                       3168K        1
__TEXT                          4708K       43
dyld private memory             1024K        1
shared memory                     16K        1
===========                   =======  =======
TOTAL                            1.2G      233
TOTAL, minus reserved VM space 817.9M      233
```

2.   Load a core dump *core.90577* and *App5* executable:

```
% lldb -c ~/AMCDA-Dumps/core.90577 -f ~/AMCDA-Dumps/Apps/App5/Build/Products/Release/App5
(lldb) target create "/Users/training/AMCDA-Dumps/Apps/App5/Build/Products/Release/App5" --
core "/Users/training/AMCDA-Dumps/core.90577"
Core file '/Users/training/AMCDA-Dumps/core.90577' (arm64) was loaded.
```

3.   Go to the identified problem core thread 1 (thread #2):

```
(lldb) thread select 2
* thread #2
    frame #0: 0x000000018e9d2d98 libsystem_kernel.dylib`__pthread_kill + 8
libsystem_kernel.dylib`:
->  0x18e9d2d98 <+8>:   b.lo   0x18e9d2db8              ; <+40>
    0x18e9d2d9c <+12>: pacibsp
    0x18e9d2da0 <+16>: stp    x29, x30, [sp, #-0x10]!
    0x18e9d2da4 <+20>: mov    x29, sp
```

```
(lldb) bt
* thread #2
  * frame #0: 0x000000018e9d2d98 libsystem_kernel.dylib`__pthread_kill + 8
    frame #1: 0x000000018ea07ee0 libsystem_pthread.dylib`pthread_kill + 288
    frame #2: 0x000000018e9423cc libsystem_c.dylib`__abort + 128
    frame #3: 0x000000018e933d48 libsystem_c.dylib`__stack_chk_fail + 96
    frame #4: 0x0000000100ab7cc0 App5`procA + 92
```

4.   We don't see expected beginning stack trace frames as on a normal thread:

```
(lldb) thread backtrace 3
  thread #3
    frame #0: 0x000000018e9ce06c libsystem_kernel.dylib`__semwait_signal + 8
    frame #1: 0x000000018e8d6fc8 libsystem_c.dylib`nanosleep + 220
    frame #2: 0x000000018e8e1b78 libsystem_c.dylib`sleep + 52
    frame #3: 0x000000018e8e1b90 libsystem_c.dylib`sleep + 76
    frame #4: 0x0000000100ab7d28 App5`bar_two + 16
    frame #5: 0x0000000100ab7d3c App5`foo_two + 12
    frame #6: 0x0000000100ab7d58 App5`thread_two + 20
    frame #7: 0x000000018ea0826c libsystem_pthread.dylib`_pthread_start + 148
```

5.   Dump raw stack data from the current stack pointer and find ASCII buffers around return addresses:

```
(lldb) x/100a $sp
0x16f3d2ea0: 0x0000000000000000
0x16f3d2ea8: 0x0000000000000000
0x16f3d2eb0: 0x0000000000000000
0x16f3d2eb8: 0x000000016f3d2ee8
0x16f3d2ec0: 0x000000016f3d2f00 ; x29
0x16f3d2ec8: 0xfd6700018e9423cc (0x000000018e9423cc) libsystem_c.dylib`__abort + 128
0x16f3d2ed0: 0x0000000000000000
0x16f3d2ed8: 0xffffffff00000000
0x16f3d2ee0: 0x0000000000000000
0x16f3d2ee8: 0x00000000ffffffdf
0x16f3d2ef0: 0x0000000000000000
0x16f3d2ef8: 0x000000018e9485fe "stack buffer overflow"
0x16f3d2f00: 0x000000016f3d2f50 ; x29
0x16f3d2f08: 0xc26300018e933d48 (0x000000018e933d48) libsystem_c.dylib`a64l ; x30
0x16f3d2f10: 0x6c61000035707041
0x16f3d2f18: 0x00000000006b7300
0x16f3d2f20: 0x0000000000000000
0x16f3d2f28: 0x0000000000000000
0x16f3d2f30: 0x0000000000000000
0x16f3d2f38: 0x0000000000000000
0x16f3d2f40: 0x0000000000000000
0x16f3d2f48: 0x000000016f3d3000
0x16f3d2f50: 0x000000016f3d2f80 ; x29
0x16f3d2f58: 0x0a18800100ab7cc0 (0x0000000100ab7cc0) App5`procA + 92 ; x30
0x16f3d2f60: 0x0000000000000000
0x16f3d2f68: 0x422077654e20794d
0x16f3d2f70: 0x7542207265676769
0x16f3d2f78: 0x0000000072656666
0x16f3d2f80: 0x0000000000000000 ; x29
0x16f3d2f88: 0x0000000000000000 ; x30
0x16f3d2f90: 0x0000000000000000
0x16f3d2f98: 0x0000000000000000
0x16f3d2fa0: 0x0000000000000000
0x16f3d2fa8: 0x0000000000000000
0x16f3d2fb0: 0x0000000000000000
0x16f3d2fb8: 0x0000000000000000
0x16f3d2fc0: 0x0000000000000000
0x16f3d2fc8: 0x0000000100000000
0x16f3d2fd0: 0x0000000000000000
0x16f3d2fd8: 0x0000000000000000
0x16f3d2fe0: 0x0000000000000000
0x16f3d2fe8: 0x823d80018ea0308c (0x000000018ea0308c) libsystem_pthread.dylib`thread_start + 8
0x16f3d2ff0: 0x0000000000000000
0x16f3d2ff8: 0x0000000000000000
0x16f3d3000: 0x6456705926032d4b
0x16f3d3008: 0x0000000000000000
0x16f3d3010: 0x000000016f45f000
0x16f3d3018: 0x0000000100c88590 dyld`_main_thread + 16
0x16f3d3020: 0x0000000000000000
0x16f3d3028: 0x0000000000000000
0x16f3d3030: 0x0000000000000101
0x16f3d3038: 0x0000000a0000001f
0x16f3d3040: 0x0000000000000000
0x16f3d3048: 0x0001000000000000
0x16f3d3050: 0x0000000000000000
0x16f3d3058: 0x0000000000000000
0x16f3d3060: 0x0000000000000000
0x16f3d3068: 0x0000000000000000
```

```
0x16f3d3070: 0x0000000000000000
0x16f3d3078: 0x0000000000000000
0x16f3d3080: 0x0000000000000000
0x16f3d3088: 0x0000000000000000
0x16f3d3090: 0x0000000100ab7cf4 App5`thread_one
0x16f3d3098: 0x0000000000000000
0x16f3d30a0: 0x0003000000000000
0x16f3d30a8: 0x0000000000000000
0x16f3d30b0: 0x000000016f3d3000
0x16f3d30b8: 0x000000016f350000
0x16f3d30c0: 0x000000016f34c000
0x16f3d30c8: 0x000000000008c000
0x16f3d30d0: 0x0000000000004000
0x16f3d30d8: 0x0000000000217fe1
0x16f3d30e0: 0x000000016f3d3000
0x16f3d30e8: 0x000000016f3d30ac
0x16f3d30f0: 0x0000000000000000
0x16f3d30f8: 0x0000000000001303
0x16f3d3100: 0x00000000000008ff
0x16f3d3108: 0x0000000000000000
0x16f3d3110: 0x0000000000000000
0x16f3d3118: 0x64567058493e1d4b
0x16f3d3120: 0x0000000000000000
0x16f3d3128: 0x0000000000000000
0x16f3d3130: 0x0000000000000000
0x16f3d3138: 0x0000000000000000
0x16f3d3140: 0x0000000000000000
0x16f3d3148: 0x0000000000000000
0x16f3d3150: 0x0000000000000000
0x16f3d3158: 0x0000000000000000
0x16f3d3160: 0x0000000000000000
0x16f3d3168: 0x0000000000000000
0x16f3d3170: 0x0000000000000000
0x16f3d3178: 0x0000000000000000
0x16f3d3180: 0x0000000000000000
0x16f3d3188: 0x0000000000000000
0x16f3d3190: 0x0000000000000000
0x16f3d3198: 0x0000000000000000
0x16f3d31a0: 0x0000000000000000
0x16f3d31a8: 0x0000000000000000
0x16f3d31b0: 0x0000000000000000
0x16f3d31b8: 0x0000000000000000
```

```
(lldb) x/s 0x16f3d2f68
0x16f3d2f68: "My New Bigger Buffer"
```

Note: We see the expected *thread_start* function on the raw stack so it could be the case of a local buffer overflow. We also see that the chain of saved x29 is broken, and overwritten by the ASCII buffer. The saved x30 register looks overwritten too.

Exercise X6

- **Goal:** Learn how to identify stack overflow, stack boundaries, reconstruct stack trace

- **Patterns:** Stack Overflow; Execution Residue

- \AMCDA-Dumps\Exercise-X6.pdf

Exercise X6

Goal: Learn how to identify stack overflow, stack boundaries, and reconstruct a stack trace.

Patterns: Stack Overflow; Execution Residue.

1.   Identify the problem thread and application-specific diagnostic from the diagnostic report *App6-2022-12-04-194532.ips*:

```
-------------------------------------
Translated Report (Full Report Below)
-------------------------------------

Process:             App6 [92493]
Path:                /Users/USER/*/App6
Identifier:          App6
Version:             ???
Code Type:           ARM-64 (Native)
Parent Process:      zsh [73148]
Responsible:         Terminal [9503]
User ID:             501

Date/Time:           2022-12-04 19:45:32.0270 +0000
OS Version:          macOS 12.6 (21G115)
Report Version:      12
Anonymous UUID:      6F758133-2B79-4743-8B70-8B1D8C510718

Sleep/Wake UUID:     0C497BA4-C21E-4C7D-929A-D764F724A2FA

Time Awake Since Boot: 160000 seconds
Time Since Wake:       1405 seconds

System Integrity Protection: enabled

Crashed Thread:      1

Exception Type:      EXC_BAD_ACCESS (SIGBUS)
Exception Codes:     KERN_PROTECTION_FAILURE at 0x000000016bb3bfe4
Exception Codes:     0x0000000000000002, 0x000000016bb3bfe4
Exception Note:      EXC_CORPSE_NOTIFY

Termination Reason:  Namespace SIGNAL, Code 10 Bus error: 10
Terminating Process: exc handler [92493]

VM Region Info: 0x16bb3bfe4 is in 0x16bb38000-0x16bb3c000;  bytes after start: 16356  bytes before end: 27
    REGION TYPE                START - END        [ VSIZE] PRT/MAX SHRMOD  REGION DETAIL
    Stack                  16b33c000-16bb38000    [ 8176K] rw-/rwx SM=PRV  thread 0
--->  Stack                  16bb38000-16bb3c000    [   16K] r--/rwx SM=PRV  thread 1
    Stack                  16bb3c000-16bbc4000    [  544K] rw-/rwx SM=PRV

Thread 0::  Dispatch queue: com.apple.main-thread
0   libsystem_kernel.dylib        0x18e9ce06c __semwait_signal + 8
1   libsystem_c.dylib             0x18e8d6fc8 nanosleep + 220
2   libsystem_c.dylib             0x18e8e1b78 sleep + 52
3   libsystem_c.dylib             0x18e8e1b90 sleep + 76
4   App6                          0x1042cbf70 main + 164
5   dyld                          0x1046c108c start + 520

Thread 1 Crashed:
0   App6                          0x1042cbca0 procF + 32
1   App6                          0x1042cbcd0 procF + 80
2   App6                          0x1042cbcd0 procF + 80
3   App6                          0x1042cbcd0 procF + 80
4   App6                          0x1042cbcd0 procF + 80
5   App6                          0x1042cbcd0 procF + 80
6   App6                          0x1042cbcd0 procF + 80
7   App6                          0x1042cbcd0 procF + 80
8   App6                          0x1042cbcd0 procF + 80
9   App6                          0x1042cbcd0 procF + 80
10  App6                          0x1042cbcd0 procF + 80
```

```
11   App6                         0x1042cbcd0 procF + 80
12   App6                         0x1042cbcd0 procF + 80
13   App6                         0x1042cbcd0 procF + 80
14   App6                         0x1042cbcd0 procF + 80
15   App6                         0x1042cbcd0 procF + 80
16   App6                         0x1042cbcd0 procF + 80
17   App6                         0x1042cbcd0 procF + 80
18   App6                         0x1042cbcd0 procF + 80
19   App6                         0x1042cbcd0 procF + 80
20   App6                         0x1042cbcd0 procF + 80
21   App6                         0x1042cbcd0 procF + 80
22   App6                         0x1042cbcd0 procF + 80
23   App6                         0x1042cbcd0 procF + 80
24   App6                         0x1042cbcd0 procF + 80
25   App6                         0x1042cbcd0 procF + 80
26   App6                         0x1042cbcd0 procF + 80
27   App6                         0x1042cbcd0 procF + 80
28   App6                         0x1042cbcd0 procF + 80
29   App6                         0x1042cbcd0 procF + 80
30   App6                         0x1042cbcd0 procF + 80
31   App6                         0x1042cbcd0 procF + 80
32   App6                         0x1042cbcd0 procF + 80
33   App6                         0x1042cbcd0 procF + 80
34   App6                         0x1042cbcd0 procF + 80
35   App6                         0x1042cbcd0 procF + 80
36   App6                         0x1042cbcd0 procF + 80
37   App6                         0x1042cbcd0 procF + 80
38   App6                         0x1042cbcd0 procF + 80
39   App6                         0x1042cbcd0 procF + 80
40   App6                         0x1042cbcd0 procF + 80
41   App6                         0x1042cbcd0 procF + 80
42   App6                         0x1042cbcd0 procF + 80
43   App6                         0x1042cbcd0 procF + 80
44   App6                         0x1042cbcd0 procF + 80
45   App6                         0x1042cbcd0 procF + 80
46   App6                         0x1042cbcd0 procF + 80
47   App6                         0x1042cbcd0 procF + 80
48   App6                         0x1042cbcd0 procF + 80
49   App6                         0x1042cbcd0 procF + 80
50   App6                         0x1042cbcd0 procF + 80
51   App6                         0x1042cbcd0 procF + 80
52   App6                         0x1042cbcd0 procF + 80
53   App6                         0x1042cbcd0 procF + 80
54   App6                         0x1042cbcd0 procF + 80
55   App6                         0x1042cbcd0 procF + 80
56   App6                         0x1042cbcd0 procF + 80
57   App6                         0x1042cbcd0 procF + 80
58   App6                         0x1042cbcd0 procF + 80
59   App6                         0x1042cbcd0 procF + 80
60   App6                         0x1042cbcd0 procF + 80
61   App6                         0x1042cbcd0 procF + 80
62   App6                         0x1042cbcd0 procF + 80
63   App6                         0x1042cbcd0 procF + 80
64   App6                         0x1042cbcd0 procF + 80
65   App6                         0x1042cbcd0 procF + 80
66   App6                         0x1042cbcd0 procF + 80
67   App6                         0x1042cbcd0 procF + 80
68   App6                         0x1042cbcd0 procF + 80
69   App6                         0x1042cbcd0 procF + 80
70   App6                         0x1042cbcd0 procF + 80
71   App6                         0x1042cbcd0 procF + 80
72   App6                         0x1042cbcd0 procF + 80
73   App6                         0x1042cbcd0 procF + 80
74   App6                         0x1042cbcd0 procF + 80
75   App6                         0x1042cbcd0 procF + 80
76   App6                         0x1042cbcd0 procF + 80
77   App6                         0x1042cbcd0 procF + 80
78   App6                         0x1042cbcd0 procF + 80
79   App6                         0x1042cbcd0 procF + 80
80   App6                         0x1042cbcd0 procF + 80
81   App6                         0x1042cbcd0 procF + 80
82   App6                         0x1042cbcd0 procF + 80
83   App6                         0x1042cbcd0 procF + 80
84   App6                         0x1042cbcd0 procF + 80
85   App6                         0x1042cbcd0 procF + 80
86   App6                         0x1042cbcd0 procF + 80
```

```
87  App6                         0x1042cbcd0 procF + 80
88  App6                         0x1042cbcd0 procF + 80
89  App6                         0x1042cbcd0 procF + 80
90  App6                         0x1042cbcd0 procF + 80
91  App6                         0x1042cbcd0 procF + 80
92  App6                         0x1042cbcd0 procF + 80
93  App6                         0x1042cbcd0 procF + 80
94  App6                         0x1042cbcd0 procF + 80
95  App6                         0x1042cbcd0 procF + 80
96  App6                         0x1042cbcd0 procF + 80
97  App6                         0x1042cbcd0 procF + 80
98  App6                         0x1042cbcd0 procF + 80
99  App6                         0x1042cbcd0 procF + 80
100 App6                         0x1042cbcd0 procF + 80
101 App6                         0x1042cbcd0 procF + 80
102 App6                         0x1042cbcd0 procF + 80
103 App6                         0x1042cbcd0 procF + 80
104 App6                         0x1042cbcd0 procF + 80
105 App6                         0x1042cbcd0 procF + 80
106 App6                         0x1042cbcd0 procF + 80
107 App6                         0x1042cbcd0 procF + 80
108 App6                         0x1042cbcd0 procF + 80
109 App6                         0x1042cbcd0 procF + 80
110 App6                         0x1042cbcd0 procF + 80
111 App6                         0x1042cbcd0 procF + 80
112 App6                         0x1042cbcd0 procF + 80
113 App6                         0x1042cbcd0 procF + 80
114 App6                         0x1042cbcd0 procF + 80
115 App6                         0x1042cbcd0 procF + 80
116 App6                         0x1042cbcd0 procF + 80
117 App6                         0x1042cbcd0 procF + 80
118 App6                         0x1042cbcd0 procF + 80
119 App6                         0x1042cbcd0 procF + 80
120 App6                         0x1042cbcd0 procF + 80
121 App6                         0x1042cbcd0 procF + 80
122 App6                         0x1042cbcd0 procF + 80
123 App6                         0x1042cbcd0 procF + 80
124 App6                         0x1042cbcd0 procF + 80
125 App6                         0x1042cbcd0 procF + 80
126 App6                         0x1042cbcd0 procF + 80
127 App6                         0x1042cbcd0 procF + 80
128 App6                         0x1042cbcd0 procF + 80
129 App6                         0x1042cbcd0 procF + 80
130 App6                         0x1042cbcd0 procF + 80
131 App6                         0x1042cbcd0 procF + 80
132 App6                         0x1042cbcd0 procF + 80
133 App6                         0x1042cbcd0 procF + 80
134 App6                         0x1042cbcd0 procF + 80
135 App6                         0x1042cbcd0 procF + 80
136 App6                         0x1042cbcd0 procF + 80
137 App6                         0x1042cbcd0 procF + 80
138 App6                         0x1042cbcd0 procF + 80
139 App6                         0x1042cbcd0 procF + 80
140 App6                         0x1042cbcd0 procF + 80
141 App6                         0x1042cbcd0 procF + 80
142 App6                         0x1042cbcd0 procF + 80
143 App6                         0x1042cbcd0 procF + 80
144 App6                         0x1042cbcd0 procF + 80
145 App6                         0x1042cbcd0 procF + 80
146 App6                         0x1042cbcd0 procF + 80
147 App6                         0x1042cbcd0 procF + 80
148 App6                         0x1042cbcd0 procF + 80
149 App6                         0x1042cbcd0 procF + 80
150 App6                         0x1042cbcd0 procF + 80
151 App6                         0x1042cbcd0 procF + 80
152 App6                         0x1042cbcd0 procF + 80
153 App6                         0x1042cbcd0 procF + 80
154 App6                         0x1042cbcd0 procF + 80
155 App6                         0x1042cbcd0 procF + 80
156 App6                         0x1042cbcd0 procF + 80
157 App6                         0x1042cbcd0 procF + 80
158 App6                         0x1042cbcd0 procF + 80
159 App6                         0x1042cbcd0 procF + 80
160 App6                         0x1042cbcd0 procF + 80
161 App6                         0x1042cbcd0 procF + 80
162 App6                         0x1042cbcd0 procF + 80
```

```
163  App6                              0x1042cbcd0 procF + 80
164  App6                              0x1042cbcd0 procF + 80
165  App6                              0x1042cbcd0 procF + 80
166  App6                              0x1042cbcd0 procF + 80
167  App6                              0x1042cbcd0 procF + 80
168  App6                              0x1042cbcd0 procF + 80
169  App6                              0x1042cbcd0 procF + 80
170  App6                              0x1042cbcd0 procF + 80
171  App6                              0x1042cbcd0 procF + 80
172  App6                              0x1042cbcd0 procF + 80
173  App6                              0x1042cbcd0 procF + 80
174  App6                              0x1042cbcd0 procF + 80
175  App6                              0x1042cbcd0 procF + 80
176  App6                              0x1042cbcd0 procF + 80
177  App6                              0x1042cbcd0 procF + 80
178  App6                              0x1042cbcd0 procF + 80
179  App6                              0x1042cbcd0 procF + 80
180  App6                              0x1042cbcd0 procF + 80
181  App6                              0x1042cbcd0 procF + 80
182  App6                              0x1042cbcd0 procF + 80
183  App6                              0x1042cbcd0 procF + 80
184  App6                              0x1042cbcd0 procF + 80
185  App6                              0x1042cbcd0 procF + 80
186  App6                              0x1042cbcd0 procF + 80
187  App6                              0x1042cbcd0 procF + 80
188  App6                              0x1042cbcd0 procF + 80
189  App6                              0x1042cbcd0 procF + 80
190  App6                              0x1042cbcd0 procF + 80
191  App6                              0x1042cbcd0 procF + 80
192  App6                              0x1042cbcd0 procF + 80
193  App6                              0x1042cbcd0 procF + 80
194  App6                              0x1042cbcd0 procF + 80
195  App6                              0x1042cbcd0 procF + 80
196  App6                              0x1042cbcd0 procF + 80
197  App6                              0x1042cbcd0 procF + 80
198  App6                              0x1042cbcd0 procF + 80
199  App6                              0x1042cbcd0 procF + 80
200  App6                              0x1042cbcd0 procF + 80
201  App6                              0x1042cbcd0 procF + 80
202  App6                              0x1042cbcd0 procF + 80
203  App6                              0x1042cbcd0 procF + 80
204  App6                              0x1042cbcd0 procF + 80
205  App6                              0x1042cbcd0 procF + 80
206  App6                              0x1042cbcd0 procF + 80
207  App6                              0x1042cbcd0 procF + 80
208  App6                              0x1042cbcd0 procF + 80
209  App6                              0x1042cbcd0 procF + 80
210  App6                              0x1042cbcd0 procF + 80
211  App6                              0x1042cbcd0 procF + 80
212  App6                              0x1042cbcd0 procF + 80
213  App6                              0x1042cbcd0 procF + 80
214  App6                              0x1042cbcd0 procF + 80
215  App6                              0x1042cbcd0 procF + 80
216  App6                              0x1042cbcd0 procF + 80
217  App6                              0x1042cbcd0 procF + 80
218  App6                              0x1042cbcd0 procF + 80
219  App6                              0x1042cbcd0 procF + 80
220  App6                              0x1042cbcd0 procF + 80
221  App6                              0x1042cbcd0 procF + 80
222  App6                              0x1042cbcd0 procF + 80
223  App6                              0x1042cbcd0 procF + 80
224  App6                              0x1042cbcd0 procF + 80
225  App6                              0x1042cbcd0 procF + 80
226  App6                              0x1042cbcd0 procF + 80
227  App6                              0x1042cbcd0 procF + 80
228  App6                              0x1042cbcd0 procF + 80
229  App6                              0x1042cbcd0 procF + 80
230  App6                              0x1042cbcd0 procF + 80
231  App6                              0x1042cbcd0 procF + 80
232  App6                              0x1042cbcd0 procF + 80
233  App6                              0x1042cbcd0 procF + 80
234  App6                              0x1042cbcd0 procF + 80
235  App6                              0x1042cbcd0 procF + 80
236  App6                              0x1042cbcd0 procF + 80
237  App6                              0x1042cbcd0 procF + 80
238  App6                              0x1042cbcd0 procF + 80
```

```
239 App6                    0x1042cbcd0 procF + 80
240 App6                    0x1042cbcd0 procF + 80
241 App6                    0x1042cbcd0 procF + 80
242 App6                    0x1042cbcd0 procF + 80
243 App6                    0x1042cbcd0 procF + 80
244 App6                    0x1042cbcd0 procF + 80
245 App6                    0x1042cbcd0 procF + 80
246 App6                    0x1042cbcd0 procF + 80
247 App6                    0x1042cbcd0 procF + 80
248 App6                    0x1042cbcd0 procF + 80
249 App6                    0x1042cbcd0 procF + 80
250 App6                    0x1042cbcd0 procF + 80
251 App6                    0x1042cbcd0 procF + 80
252 App6                    0x1042cbcd0 procF + 80
253 App6                    0x1042cbcd0 procF + 80
254 App6                    0x1042cbcd0 procF + 80
255 App6                    0x1042cbcd0 procF + 80
256 App6                    0x1042cbcd0 procF + 80
257 App6                    0x1042cbcd0 procF + 80
258 App6                    0x1042cbcd0 procF + 80
259 App6                    0x1042cbcd0 procF + 80
260 App6                    0x1042cbcd0 procF + 80
261 App6                    0x1042cbcd0 procF + 80
262 App6                    0x1042cbcd0 procF + 80
263 App6                    0x1042cbcd0 procF + 80
264 App6                    0x1042cbcd0 procF + 80
265 App6                    0x1042cbcd0 procF + 80
266 App6                    0x1042cbcd0 procF + 80
267 App6                    0x1042cbcd0 procF + 80
268 App6                    0x1042cbcd0 procF + 80
269 App6                    0x1042cbcd0 procF + 80
270 App6                    0x1042cbcd0 procF + 80
271 App6                    0x1042cbcd0 procF + 80
272 App6                    0x1042cbcd0 procF + 80
273 App6                    0x1042cbcd0 procF + 80
274 App6                    0x1042cbcd0 procF + 80
275 App6                    0x1042cbcd0 procF + 80
276 App6                    0x1042cbcd0 procF + 80
277 App6                    0x1042cbcd0 procF + 80
278 App6                    0x1042cbcd0 procF + 80
279 App6                    0x1042cbcd0 procF + 80
280 App6                    0x1042cbcd0 procF + 80
281 App6                    0x1042cbcd0 procF + 80
282 App6                    0x1042cbcd0 procF + 80
283 App6                    0x1042cbcd0 procF + 80
284 App6                    0x1042cbcd0 procF + 80
285 App6                    0x1042cbcd0 procF + 80
286 App6                    0x1042cbcd0 procF + 80
287 App6                    0x1042cbcd0 procF + 80
288 App6                    0x1042cbcd0 procF + 80
289 App6                    0x1042cbcd0 procF + 80
290 App6                    0x1042cbcd0 procF + 80
291 App6                    0x1042cbcd0 procF + 80
292 App6                    0x1042cbcd0 procF + 80
293 App6                    0x1042cbcd0 procF + 80
294 App6                    0x1042cbcd0 procF + 80
295 App6                    0x1042cbcd0 procF + 80
296 App6                    0x1042cbcd0 procF + 80
297 App6                    0x1042cbcd0 procF + 80
298 App6                    0x1042cbcd0 procF + 80
299 App6                    0x1042cbcd0 procF + 80
300 App6                    0x1042cbcd0 procF + 80
301 App6                    0x1042cbcd0 procF + 80
302 App6                    0x1042cbcd0 procF + 80
303 App6                    0x1042cbcd0 procF + 80
304 App6                    0x1042cbcd0 procF + 80
305 App6                    0x1042cbcd0 procF + 80
306 App6                    0x1042cbcd0 procF + 80
307 App6                    0x1042cbcd0 procF + 80
308 App6                    0x1042cbcd0 procF + 80
309 App6                    0x1042cbcd0 procF + 80
310 App6                    0x1042cbcd0 procF + 80
311 App6                    0x1042cbcd0 procF + 80
312 App6                    0x1042cbcd0 procF + 80
313 App6                    0x1042cbcd0 procF + 80
314 App6                    0x1042cbcd0 procF + 80
```

```
315 App6                          0x1042cbcd0 procF + 80
316 App6                          0x1042cbcd0 procF + 80
317 App6                          0x1042cbcd0 procF + 80
318 App6                          0x1042cbcd0 procF + 80
319 App6                          0x1042cbcd0 procF + 80
320 App6                          0x1042cbcd0 procF + 80
321 App6                          0x1042cbcd0 procF + 80
322 App6                          0x1042cbcd0 procF + 80
323 App6                          0x1042cbcd0 procF + 80
324 App6                          0x1042cbcd0 procF + 80
325 App6                          0x1042cbcd0 procF + 80
326 App6                          0x1042cbcd0 procF + 80
327 App6                          0x1042cbcd0 procF + 80
328 App6                          0x1042cbcd0 procF + 80
329 App6                          0x1042cbcd0 procF + 80
330 App6                          0x1042cbcd0 procF + 80
331 App6                          0x1042cbcd0 procF + 80
332 App6                          0x1042cbcd0 procF + 80
333 App6                          0x1042cbcd0 procF + 80
334 App6                          0x1042cbcd0 procF + 80
335 App6                          0x1042cbcd0 procF + 80
336 App6                          0x1042cbcd0 procF + 80
337 App6                          0x1042cbcd0 procF + 80
338 App6                          0x1042cbcd0 procF + 80
339 App6                          0x1042cbcd0 procF + 80
340 App6                          0x1042cbcd0 procF + 80
341 App6                          0x1042cbcd0 procF + 80
342 App6                          0x1042cbcd0 procF + 80
343 App6                          0x1042cbcd0 procF + 80
344 App6                          0x1042cbcd0 procF + 80
345 App6                          0x1042cbcd0 procF + 80
346 App6                          0x1042cbcd0 procF + 80
347 App6                          0x1042cbcd0 procF + 80
348 App6                          0x1042cbcd0 procF + 80
349 App6                          0x1042cbcd0 procF + 80
350 App6                          0x1042cbcd0 procF + 80
351 App6                          0x1042cbcd0 procF + 80
352 App6                          0x1042cbcd0 procF + 80
353 App6                          0x1042cbcd0 procF + 80
354 App6                          0x1042cbcd0 procF + 80
355 App6                          0x1042cbcd0 procF + 80
356 App6                          0x1042cbcd0 procF + 80
357 App6                          0x1042cbcd0 procF + 80
358 App6                          0x1042cbcd0 procF + 80
359 App6                          0x1042cbcd0 procF + 80
360 App6                          0x1042cbcd0 procF + 80
361 App6                          0x1042cbcd0 procF + 80
362 App6                          0x1042cbcd0 procF + 80
363 App6                          0x1042cbcd0 procF + 80
364 App6                          0x1042cbcd0 procF + 80
365 App6                          0x1042cbcd0 procF + 80
366 App6                          0x1042cbcd0 procF + 80
367 App6                          0x1042cbcd0 procF + 80
368 App6                          0x1042cbcd0 procF + 80
369 App6                          0x1042cbcd0 procF + 80
370 App6                          0x1042cbcd0 procF + 80
371 App6                          0x1042cbcd0 procF + 80
372 App6                          0x1042cbcd0 procF + 80
373 App6                          0x1042cbcd0 procF + 80
374 App6                          0x1042cbcd0 procF + 80
375 App6                          0x1042cbcd0 procF + 80
376 App6                          0x1042cbcd0 procF + 80
377 App6                          0x1042cbcd0 procF + 80
378 App6                          0x1042cbcd0 procF + 80
379 App6                          0x1042cbcd0 procF + 80
380 App6                          0x1042cbcd0 procF + 80
381 App6                          0x1042cbcd0 procF + 80
382 App6                          0x1042cbcd0 procF + 80
383 App6                          0x1042cbcd0 procF + 80
384 App6                          0x1042cbcd0 procF + 80
385 App6                          0x1042cbcd0 procF + 80
386 App6                          0x1042cbcd0 procF + 80
387 App6                          0x1042cbcd0 procF + 80
388 App6                          0x1042cbcd0 procF + 80
389 App6                          0x1042cbcd0 procF + 80
390 App6                          0x1042cbcd0 procF + 80
```

```
391  App6                                    0x1042cbcd0 procF + 80
392  App6                                    0x1042cbcd0 procF + 80
393  App6                                    0x1042cbcd0 procF + 80
394  App6                                    0x1042cbcd0 procF + 80
395  App6                                    0x1042cbcd0 procF + 80
396  App6                                    0x1042cbcd0 procF + 80
397  App6                                    0x1042cbcd0 procF + 80
398  App6                                    0x1042cbcd0 procF + 80
399  App6                                    0x1042cbcd0 procF + 80
400  App6                                    0x1042cbcd0 procF + 80
401  App6                                    0x1042cbcd0 procF + 80
402  App6                                    0x1042cbcd0 procF + 80
403  App6                                    0x1042cbcd0 procF + 80
404  App6                                    0x1042cbcd0 procF + 80
405  App6                                    0x1042cbcd0 procF + 80
406  App6                                    0x1042cbcd0 procF + 80
407  App6                                    0x1042cbcd0 procF + 80
408  App6                                    0x1042cbcd0 procF + 80
409  App6                                    0x1042cbcd0 procF + 80
410  App6                                    0x1042cbcd0 procF + 80
411  App6                                    0x1042cbcd0 procF + 80
412  App6                                    0x1042cbcd0 procF + 80
413  App6                                    0x1042cbcd0 procF + 80
414  App6                                    0x1042cbcd0 procF + 80
415  App6                                    0x1042cbcd0 procF + 80
416  App6                                    0x1042cbcd0 procF + 80
417  App6                                    0x1042cbcd0 procF + 80
418  App6                                    0x1042cbcd0 procF + 80
419  App6                                    0x1042cbcd0 procF + 80
420  App6                                    0x1042cbcd0 procF + 80
421  App6                                    0x1042cbcd0 procF + 80
422  App6                                    0x1042cbcd0 procF + 80
423  App6                                    0x1042cbcd0 procF + 80
424  App6                                    0x1042cbcd0 procF + 80
425  App6                                    0x1042cbcd0 procF + 80
426  App6                                    0x1042cbcd0 procF + 80
427  App6                                    0x1042cbcd0 procF + 80
428  App6                                    0x1042cbcd0 procF + 80
429  App6                                    0x1042cbcd0 procF + 80
430  App6                                    0x1042cbcd0 procF + 80
431  App6                                    0x1042cbcd0 procF + 80
432  App6                                    0x1042cbcd0 procF + 80
433  App6                                    0x1042cbcd0 procF + 80
434  App6                                    0x1042cbcd0 procF + 80
435  App6                                    0x1042cbcd0 procF + 80
436  App6                                    0x1042cbcd0 procF + 80
437  App6                                    0x1042cbcd0 procF + 80
438  App6                                    0x1042cbcd0 procF + 80
439  App6                                    0x1042cbcd0 procF + 80
440  App6                                    0x1042cbcd0 procF + 80
441  App6                                    0x1042cbcd0 procF + 80
442  App6                                    0x1042cbcd0 procF + 80
443  App6                                    0x1042cbcd0 procF + 80
444  App6                                    0x1042cbcd0 procF + 80
445  App6                                    0x1042cbcd0 procF + 80
446  App6                                    0x1042cbcd0 procF + 80
447  App6                                    0x1042cbcd0 procF + 80
448  App6                                    0x1042cbcd0 procF + 80
449  App6                                    0x1042cbcd0 procF + 80
450  App6                                    0x1042cbcd0 procF + 80
451  App6                                    0x1042cbcd0 procF + 80
452  App6                                    0x1042cbcd0 procF + 80
453  App6                                    0x1042cbcd0 procF + 80
454  App6                                    0x1042cbcd0 procF + 80
455  App6                                    0x1042cbcd0 procF + 80
456  App6                                    0x1042cbcd0 procF + 80
457  App6                                    0x1042cbcd0 procF + 80
458  App6                                    0x1042cbcd0 procF + 80
459  App6                                    0x1042cbcd0 procF + 80
460  App6                                    0x1042cbcd0 procF + 80
461  App6                                    0x1042cbcd0 procF + 80
462  App6                                    0x1042cbcd0 procF + 80
463  App6                                    0x1042cbcd0 procF + 80
464  App6                                    0x1042cbcd0 procF + 80
465  App6                                    0x1042cbcd0 procF + 80
466  App6                                    0x1042cbcd0 procF + 80
```

```
467  App6                                    0x1042cbcd0  procF + 80
468  App6                                    0x1042cbcd0  procF + 80
469  App6                                    0x1042cbcd0  procF + 80
470  App6                                    0x1042cbcd0  procF + 80
471  App6                                    0x1042cbcd0  procF + 80
472  App6                                    0x1042cbcd0  procF + 80
473  App6                                    0x1042cbcd0  procF + 80
474  App6                                    0x1042cbcd0  procF + 80
475  App6                                    0x1042cbcd0  procF + 80
476  App6                                    0x1042cbcd0  procF + 80
477  App6                                    0x1042cbcd0  procF + 80
478  App6                                    0x1042cbcd0  procF + 80
479  App6                                    0x1042cbcd0  procF + 80
480  App6                                    0x1042cbcd0  procF + 80
481  App6                                    0x1042cbcd0  procF + 80
482  App6                                    0x1042cbcd0  procF + 80
483  App6                                    0x1042cbcd0  procF + 80
484  App6                                    0x1042cbcd0  procF + 80
485  App6                                    0x1042cbcd0  procF + 80
486  App6                                    0x1042cbcd0  procF + 80
487  App6                                    0x1042cbcd0  procF + 80
488  App6                                    0x1042cbcd0  procF + 80
489  App6                                    0x1042cbcd0  procF + 80
490  App6                                    0x1042cbcd0  procF + 80
491  App6                                    0x1042cbcd0  procF + 80
492  App6                                    0x1042cbcd0  procF + 80
493  App6                                    0x1042cbcd0  procF + 80
494  App6                                    0x1042cbcd0  procF + 80
495  App6                                    0x1042cbcd0  procF + 80
496  App6                                    0x1042cbcd0  procF + 80
497  App6                                    0x1042cbcd0  procF + 80
498  App6                                    0x1042cbcd0  procF + 80
499  App6                                    0x1042cbcd0  procF + 80
500  App6                                    0x1042cbcd0  procF + 80
501  App6                                    0x1042cbcd0  procF + 80
502  App6                                    0x1042cbcd0  procF + 80
503  App6                                    0x1042cbcd0  procF + 80
504  App6                                    0x1042cbcd0  procF + 80
505  App6                                    0x1042cbcd0  procF + 80
506  App6                                    0x1042cbcd0  procF + 80
507  App6                                    0x1042cbcd0  procF + 80
508  App6                                    0x1042cbcd0  procF + 80
509  App6                                    0x1042cbcd0  procF + 80
510  App6                                    0x1042cbcd0  procF + 80

Thread 2:
0    libsystem_kernel.dylib                  0x18e9ce06c  __semwait_signal + 8
1    libsystem_c.dylib                       0x18e8d6fc8  nanosleep + 220
2    libsystem_c.dylib                       0x18e8e1b78  sleep + 52
3    libsystem_c.dylib                       0x18e8e1b90  sleep + 76
4    App6                                    0x1042cbd84  bar_two + 24
5    App6                                    0x1042cbd98  foo_two + 12
6    App6                                    0x1042cbdb4  thread_two + 20
7    libsystem_pthread.dylib                 0x18ea0826c  _pthread_start + 148
8    libsystem_pthread.dylib                 0x18ea0308c  thread_start + 8

Thread 3:
0    libsystem_kernel.dylib                  0x18e9ce06c  __semwait_signal + 8
1    libsystem_c.dylib                       0x18e8d6fc8  nanosleep + 220
2    libsystem_c.dylib                       0x18e8e1b78  sleep + 52
3    libsystem_c.dylib                       0x18e8e1b90  sleep + 76
4    App6                                    0x1042cbddc  bar_three + 24
5    App6                                    0x1042cbdf0  foo_three + 12
6    App6                                    0x1042cbe0c  thread_three + 20
7    libsystem_pthread.dylib                 0x18ea0826c  _pthread_start + 148
8    libsystem_pthread.dylib                 0x18ea0308c  thread_start + 8

Thread 4:
0    libsystem_kernel.dylib                  0x18e9ce06c  __semwait_signal + 8
1    libsystem_c.dylib                       0x18e8d6fc8  nanosleep + 220
2    libsystem_c.dylib                       0x18e8e1b78  sleep + 52
3    libsystem_c.dylib                       0x18e8e1b90  sleep + 76
4    App6                                    0x1042cbe34  bar_four + 24
5    App6                                    0x1042cbe48  foo_four + 12
6    App6                                    0x1042cbe64  thread_four + 20
7    libsystem_pthread.dylib                 0x18ea0826c  _pthread_start + 148
```

```
8    libsystem_pthread.dylib                    0x18ea0308c thread_start + 8

Thread 5:
0    libsystem_kernel.dylib                     0x18e9ce06c __semwait_signal + 8
1    libsystem_c.dylib                          0x18d6fc8 nanosleep + 220
2    libsystem_c.dylib                          0x18e8e1b78 sleep + 52
3    App6                                       0x1042cbe84 bar_five + 16
4    App6                                       0x1042cbea0 foo_five + 12
5    App6                                       0x1042cbebc thread_five + 20
6    libsystem_pthread.dylib                    0x18ea0826c _pthread_start + 148
7    libsystem_pthread.dylib                    0x18ea0308c thread_start + 8


Thread 1 crashed with ARM Thread State (64-bit):
    x0: 0x00000000000003be   x1: 0x0000000000000000   x2: 0xffffffffffffffd8   x3: 0x000000016bb3c3d8
    x4: 0x000000016bb3c280   x5: 0x0000000000000000   x6: 0x0000000000000000   x7: 0x0000000000000000
    x8: 0xc8ecebab51e8004e   x9: 0x00000000000003be  x10: 0x0000000000000011  x11: 0x0000000000000000
   x12: 0x0000000000000000  x13: 0x0000000000000000  x14: 0x0000000000000000  x15: 0x0000000000000000
   x16: 0x000000018ea1eda0  x17: 0x00000001e8b25968  x18: 0x0000000000000000  x19: 0x000000016bbbf000
   x20: 0x0000000000000000  x21: 0x0000000000000000  x22: 0x0000000000000000  x23: 0x0000000000000000
   x24: 0x0000000000000000  x25: 0x0000000000000000  x26: 0x0000000000000000  x27: 0x0000000000000000
   x28: 0x0000000000000000   fp: 0x000000016bb3c200   lr: 0x00000001042cbcd0
    sp: 0x000000016bb3bfe0   pc: 0x00000001042cbca0 cpsr: 0x80001000
   far: 0x000000016bb3bfe4  esr: 0x92000047 (Data Abort) byte write Translation fault

Binary Images:
      0x18e9c9000 -        0x18ea00fff libsystem_kernel.dylib (*) <a9d87740-9c1d-3468-bf60-720a8d713cba>
/usr/lib/system/libsystem_kernel.dylib
      0x18e8c8000 -        0x18e949fff libsystem_c.dylib (*) <b25d2080-bb9e-38d6-8236-9cef4b2f11a3>
/usr/lib/system/libsystem_c.dylib
      0x1042c8000 -        0x1042cbfff App6 (*) <f8047558-fc1a-3d6e-a2c1-f64414a67a2a> /Users/USER/*/App6
      0x1046bc000 -        0x10471bfff dyld (*) <38ee9fe9-b66d-3066-8c5c-6ddf0d6944c6> /usr/lib/dyld
      0x18ea01000 -        0x18ea0dfff libsystem_pthread.dylib (*) <63c4eef9-69a5-38b1-996e-8d31b66a051d>
/usr/lib/system/libsystem_pthread.dylib
            0x0 - 0xffffffffffffffff ??? (*) <00000000-0000-0000-0000-000000000000> ???

External Modification Summary:
  Calls made by other processes targeting this process:
    task_for_pid: 0
    thread_create: 0
    thread_set_state: 0
  Calls made by this process:
    task_for_pid: 0
    thread_create: 0
    thread_set_state: 0
  Calls made by all processes on this machine:
    task_for_pid: 0
    thread_create: 0
    thread_set_state: 0

VM Region Summary:
ReadOnly portion of Libraries: Total=582.2M resident=0K(0%) swapped_out_or_unallocated=582.2M(100%)
Writable regions: Total=531.8M written=0K(0%) resident=0K(0%) swapped_out=0K(0%) unallocated=531.8M(100%)
```

REGION TYPE	VIRTUAL SIZE	REGION COUNT (non-coalesced)	
===========	=======	=======	
Kernel Alloc Once	32K	1	
MALLOC	521.3M	20	
Stack	10.7M	11	
Stack (reserved)	56.0M	1	reserved VM address space (unallocated)
__AUTH	46K	11	
__AUTH_CONST	67K	38	
__DATA	173K	37	
__DATA_CONST	258K	40	
__DATA_DIRTY	73K	21	
__LINKEDIT	577.6M	3	
__OBJC_CONST	10K	5	
__OBJC_RO	83.0M	1	
__OBJC_RW	3168K	1	
__TEXT	4708K	43	
dyld private memory	1024K	1	
shared memory	16K	1	
===========	=======	=======	
TOTAL	1.2G	235	
TOTAL, minus reserved VM space	1.2G	235	

2.   Load a core dump *core.92493* and *App6* executable:

```
% lldb -c ~/AMCDA-Dumps/core.92493 -f ~/AMCDA-Dumps/Apps/App6/Build/Products/Release/App6
(lldb) target create "/Users/training/AMCDA-Dumps/Apps/App6/Build/Products/Release/App6" --
core "/Users/training/AMCDA-Dumps/core.92493"
Core file '/Users/training/AMCDA-Dumps/core.92493' (arm64) was loaded.
```

3.   Go to the identified problem core thread 1 (thread #2):

```
(lldb) thread select 2
* thread #2, stop reason = ESR_EC_DABORT_EL0 (fault address: 0x16bb3bfe4)
    frame #0: 0x00000001042cbca0 App6`procF + 32
App6`procF:
->  0x1042cbca0 <+32>: str     w0, [sp, #0x4]
    0x1042cbca4 <+36>: add     x0, sp, #0x8
    0x1042cbca8 <+40>: mov     x1, #0x200
    0x1042cbcac <+44>: bl      0x1042cbf8c                  ; symbol stub for: bzero


(lldb) bt
* thread #2, stop reason = ESR_EC_DABORT_EL0 (fault address: 0x16bb3bfe4)
  * frame #0: 0x00000001042cbca0 App6`procF + 32
    frame #1: 0x00000001042cbcd0 App6`procF + 80
    frame #2: 0x00000001042cbcd0 App6`procF + 80
    frame #3: 0x00000001042cbcd0 App6`procF + 80
    frame #4: 0x00000001042cbcd0 App6`procF + 80
    frame #5: 0x00000001042cbcd0 App6`procF + 80
    frame #6: 0x00000001042cbcd0 App6`procF + 80
    frame #7: 0x00000001042cbcd0 App6`procF + 80
    frame #8: 0x00000001042cbcd0 App6`procF + 80
    frame #9: 0x00000001042cbcd0 App6`procF + 80
    frame #10: 0x00000001042cbcd0 App6`procF + 80
    frame #11: 0x00000001042cbcd0 App6`procF + 80
    frame #12: 0x00000001042cbcd0 App6`procF + 80
    frame #13: 0x00000001042cbcd0 App6`procF + 80
    frame #14: 0x00000001042cbcd0 App6`procF + 80
    frame #15: 0x00000001042cbcd0 App6`procF + 80
    frame #16: 0x00000001042cbcd0 App6`procF + 80
    frame #17: 0x00000001042cbcd0 App6`procF + 80
    frame #18: 0x00000001042cbcd0 App6`procF + 80
    frame #19: 0x00000001042cbcd0 App6`procF + 80
    frame #20: 0x00000001042cbcd0 App6`procF + 80
    frame #21: 0x00000001042cbcd0 App6`procF + 80
    frame #22: 0x00000001042cbcd0 App6`procF + 80
    frame #23: 0x00000001042cbcd0 App6`procF + 80
    frame #24: 0x00000001042cbcd0 App6`procF + 80
    frame #25: 0x00000001042cbcd0 App6`procF + 80
    frame #26: 0x00000001042cbcd0 App6`procF + 80
    frame #27: 0x00000001042cbcd0 App6`procF + 80
    frame #28: 0x00000001042cbcd0 App6`procF + 80
    frame #29: 0x00000001042cbcd0 App6`procF + 80
    frame #30: 0x00000001042cbcd0 App6`procF + 80
    frame #31: 0x00000001042cbcd0 App6`procF + 80
    frame #32: 0x00000001042cbcd0 App6`procF + 80
[...]
    frame #952: 0x00000001042cbcd0 App6`procF + 80
    frame #953: 0x00000001042cbcd0 App6`procF + 80
    frame #954: 0x00000001042cbcd0 App6`procF + 80
    frame #955: 0x00000001042cbcd0 App6`procF + 80
    frame #956: 0x00000001042cbcd0 App6`procF + 80
```

```
    frame #957: 0x000000001042cbcd0 App6`procF + 80
    frame #958: 0x000000001042cbd10 App6`procE + 16
    frame #959: 0x000000001042cbd2c App6`bar_one + 20
    frame #960: 0x000000001042cbd40 App6`foo_one + 12
    frame #961: 0x000000001042cbd5c App6`thread_one + 20
    frame #962: 0x000000018ea0826c libsystem_pthread.dylib`_pthread_start + 148
```

Note: In the diagnostics report the stack trace was truncated at frame #510. The command **bt** output shows the full stack trace.

4.   Check if this is a stack overflow indeed. The stack region can be identified from the diagnostic report or *vmmap_92493.log* based on the thread number.

```
Process:        App6 [92493]
Path:           /Users/USER/*/App6
Load Address:   0x1042c8000
Identifier:     App6
Version:        ???
Code Type:      ARM64
Platform:       macOS
Parent Process: zsh [73148]

Date/Time:      2022-12-04 19:41:11.924 +0000
Launch Time:    2022-12-04 19:40:20.562 +0000
OS Version:     macOS 12.6 (21G115)
Report Version: 7
Analysis Tool:  /Applications/Xcode.app/Contents/Developer/usr/bin/vmmap
Analysis Tool Version:  Xcode 14.0.1 (14A400)
----

Virtual Memory Map of process 92493 (App6)
Output report format:  2.4  -- 64-bit process
VM page size:  16384 bytes

==== Non-writable regions for process 92493
REGION TYPE            START - END          [ VSIZE  RSDNT  DIRTY   SWAP] PRT/MAX SHRMOD PURGE   REGION DETAIL
__TEXT                 1042c8000-1042cc000  [   16K    16K     0K     0K] r-x/r-x SM=COW         /Users/USER/*/App6
__DATA_CONST           1042cc000-1042d0000  [   16K     0K     0K    16K] r--/rw- SM=COW         /Users/USER/*/App6
__LINKEDIT             1042d0000-1042d8000  [   32K    32K     0K     0K] r--/r-- SM=COW         /Users/USER/*/App6
dyld private memory    1042d8000-1043d8000  [ 1024K    16K    16K     0K] r--/rwx SM=PRV
shared memory          1043e0000-1043e4000  [   16K    16K    16K     0K] r--/r-- SM=SHM
MALLOC metadata        1043e4000-1043e8000  [   16K    16K    16K     0K] r--/rwx SM=ZER         MallocHelperZone_0x1043e4000 zone structure
MALLOC guard page      1043ec000-1043f0000  [   16K     0K     0K     0K] ---/rwx SM=ZER
MALLOC guard page      1043f8000-1043fc000  [   16K     0K     0K     0K] ---/rwx SM=ZER
MALLOC guard page      1043fc000-104400000  [   16K     0K     0K     0K] ---/rwx SM=NUL
MALLOC guard page      104408000-104410000  [   32K     0K     0K     0K] ---/rwx SM=NUL
MALLOC guard page      104418000-10441c000  [   16K     0K     0K     0K] ---/rwx SM=NUL
MALLOC metadata        10441c000-104420000  [   16K    16K    16K     0K] r--/rwx SM=PRV
MALLOC metadata        104420000-104424000  [   16K    16K    16K     0K] r--/rwx SM=ZER         DefaultMallocZone_0x104420000 zone structure
__TEXT                 1046bc000-10471c000  [  384K   384K     0K     0K] r-x/r-x SM=COW         /usr/lib/dyld
__DATA_CONST           10471c000-104734000  [   96K    16K    16K    16K] r--/rw- SM=COW         /usr/lib/dyld
__LINKEDIT             104738000-104770000  [  224K    80K     0K     0K] r--/r-- SM=COW         /usr/lib/dyld
STACK GUARD            167b38000-16b33c000  [ 56.0M     0K     0K     0K] ---/rwx SM=NUL         stack guard for thread 0
STACK GUARD            16bb38000-16bb3c000  [   16K     0K     0K     0K] ---/rwx SM=NUL         stack guard for thread 1
STACK GUARD            16bbc4000-16bbc8000  [   16K     0K     0K     0K] ---/rwx SM=NUL         stack guard for thread 2
STACK GUARD            16bc50000-16bc54000  [   16K     0K     0K     0K] ---/rwx SM=NUL         stack guard for thread 3
STACK GUARD            16bcdc000-16bce0000  [   16K     0K     0K     0K] ---/rwx SM=NUL         stack guard for thread 4
STACK GUARD            16bd68000-16bd6c000  [   16K     0K     0K     0K] ---/rwx SM=NUL         stack guard for thread 5
__TEXT                 18e72d000-18e72f000  [    8K     8K     0K     0K] r-x/r-x SM=COW         /usr/lib/system/libsystem_blocks.dylib
__TEXT                 18e72f000-18e771000  [  264K   264K     0K     0K] r-x/r-x SM=COW         /usr/lib/system/libxpc.dylib
__TEXT                 18e771000-18e78b000  [  104K   104K     0K     0K] r-x/r-x SM=COW         /usr/lib/system/libsystem_trace.dylib
__TEXT                 18e78b000-18e815000  [  552K   488K     0K     0K] r-x/r-x SM=COW         /usr/lib/system/libcorecrypto.dylib
__TEXT                 18e815000-18e840000  [  172K   172K     0K     0K] r-x/r-x SM=COW         /usr/lib/system/libsystem_malloc.dylib
__TEXT                 18e840000-18e887000  [  284K   284K     0K     0K] r-x/r-x SM=COW         /usr/lib/system/libdispatch.dylib
__TEXT                 18e887000-18e8c5000  [  248K   248K     0K     0K] r-x/r-x SM=COW         /usr/lib/libobjc.A.dylib
__TEXT                 18e8c5000-18e8c8000  [   12K    12K     0K     0K] r-x/r-x SM=COW         /usr/lib/system/libsystem_featureflags.dylib
__TEXT                 18e8c8000-18e94a000  [  520K   472K     0K     0K] r-x/r-x SM=COW         /usr/lib/system/libsystem_c.dylib
__TEXT                 18e94a000-18e9b1000  [  412K   380K     0K     0K] r-x/r-x SM=COW         /usr/lib/libc++.1.dylib
__TEXT                 18e9b1000-18e9c9000  [   96K    96K     0K     0K] r-x/r-x SM=COW         /usr/lib/libc++abi.dylib
__TEXT                 18e9c9000-18ea01000  [  224K   208K     0K     0K] r-x/r-x SM=COW         /usr/lib/system/libsystem_kernel.dylib
__TEXT                 18ea01000-18ea0e000  [   52K    52K     0K     0K] r-x/r-x SM=COW         /usr/lib/system/libsystem_pthread.dylib
__TEXT                 18ea0e000-18ea1b000  [   52K    52K     0K     0K] r-x/r-x SM=COW         /usr/lib/system/libdyld.dylib
__TEXT                 18ea1b000-18ea23000  [   32K    32K     0K     0K] r-x/r-x SM=COW         /usr/lib/system/libsystem_platform.dylib
__TEXT                 18ea23000-18ea50000  [  180K   164K     0K     0K] r-x/r-x SM=COW         /usr/lib/system/libsystem_info.dylib
__TEXT                 19113f000-19114a000  [   44K    44K     0K     0K] r-x/r-x SM=COW         /usr/lib/system/libsystem_darwin.dylib
__TEXT                 191598000-1915a8000  [   64K    64K     0K     0K] r-x/r-x SM=COW         /usr/lib/system/libsystem_notify.dylib
__TEXT                 193b14000-193b2d000  [  100K   100K     0K     0K] r-x/r-x SM=COW         /usr/lib/system/libsystem_networkextension.dylib
__TEXT                 193b86000-193b9e000  [   96K    96K     0K     0K] r-x/r-x SM=COW         /usr/lib/system/libsystem_asl.dylib
__TEXT                 1952ea000-1952f3000  [   36K    36K     0K     0K] r-x/r-x SM=COW         /usr/lib/system/libsystem_symptoms.dylib
__TEXT                 1972de000-1972fd000  [  124K   108K     0K     0K] r-x/r-x SM=COW         /usr/lib/system/libsystem_containermanager.dylib
__TEXT                 198085000-19808a000  [   20K    20K     0K     0K] r-x/r-x SM=COW         /usr/lib/system/libsystem_configuration.dylib
__TEXT                 19808a000-19808f000  [   20K    20K     0K     0K] r-x/r-x SM=COW         /usr/lib/system/libsystem_sandbox.dylib
__TEXT                 198bf0000-198bf3000  [   12K    12K     0K     0K] r-x/r-x SM=COW         /usr/lib/system/libquarantine.dylib
__TEXT                 19925d000-199263000  [   24K    24K     0K     0K] r-x/r-x SM=COW         /usr/lib/system/libsystem_coreservices.dylib
__TEXT                 1994c8000-1994ff000  [  220K   140K     0K     0K] r-x/r-x SM=COW         /usr/lib/system/libsystem_m.dylib
__TEXT                 199500000-199509000  [   36K    36K     0K     0K] r-x/r-x SM=COW         /usr/lib/system/libmacho.dylib
__TEXT                 199525000-199532000  [   52K    52K     0K     0K] r-x/r-x SM=COW         /usr/lib/system/libcommonCrypto.dylib
__TEXT                 199532000-19953d000  [   44K    44K     0K     0K] r-x/r-x SM=COW         /usr/lib/system/libunwind.dylib
__TEXT                 19953d000-199545000  [   32K    32K     0K     0K] r-x/r-x SM=COW         /usr/lib/liboah.dylib
__TEXT                 199545000-19954e000  [   36K    36K     0K     0K] r-x/r-x SM=COW         /usr/lib/system/libcopyfile.dylib
__TEXT                 19954e000-199552000  [   16K    16K     0K     0K] r-x/r-x SM=COW         /usr/lib/system/libcompiler_rt.dylib
```

```
  __TEXT                    199552000-199557000  [   20K    20K     0K     0K] r-x/r-x SM=COW   /usr/lib/system/libsystem_collections.dylib
  __TEXT                    199557000-19955a000  [   12K    12K     0K     0K] r-x/r-x SM=COW   /usr/lib/system/libsystem_secinit.dylib
  __TEXT                    19955a000-19955d000  [   12K    12K     0K     0K] r-x/r-x SM=COW   /usr/lib/system/libremovefile.dylib
  __TEXT                    19955d000-19955e000  [    4K     4K     0K     0K] r-x/r-x SM=COW   /usr/lib/system/libkeymgr.dylib
  __TEXT                    19955e000-199567000  [   36K    36K     0K     0K] r-x/r-x SM=COW   /usr/lib/system/libsystem_dnssd.dylib
  __TEXT                    199567000-19956d000  [   24K    24K     0K     0K] r-x/r-x SM=COW   /usr/lib/system/libcache.dylib
  __TEXT                    19956d000-19956f000  [    8K     8K     0K     0K] r-x/r-x SM=COW   /usr/lib/libSystem.B.dylib
  __TEXT                    19f8c1000-19f8c2000  [    4K     4K     0K     0K] r-x/r-x SM=COW   /usr/lib/system/libsystem_product_info_filter.dylib
  __OBJC_RO                 1d89c2000-1ddcc4000  [ 83.0M  47.8M     0K     0K] r-x/r-x SM=COW   /usr/lib/libobjc.A.dylib
  __DATA_CONST              1e0098000-1e0098130  [   304    304     0K     0K] r--/rw- SM=COW   /usr/lib/system/libsystem_blocks.dylib
  __DATA_CONST              1e0098130-1e00987d0  [  1696   1696     0K     0K] r--/rw- SM=COW   /usr/lib/system/libsystem_trace.dylib
  __DATA_CONST              1e00987d0-1e0098ef0  [  1824   1824     0K     0K] r--/rw- SM=COW   /usr/lib/system/libcorecrypto.dylib
  __DATA_CONST              1e0098ef0-1e0098f48  [    88     88     0K     0K] r--/rw- SM=COW   /usr/lib/system/libsystem_malloc.dylib
  __DATA_CONST              1e0098f50-1e0099b58  [  3080   3080     0K     0K] r--/rw- SM=COW   /usr/lib/libobjc.A.dylib
  __DATA_CONST              1e0099b58-1e0099b98  [    64     64     0K     0K] r--/rw- SM=COW   /usr/lib/system/libsystem_featureflags.dylib
  __DATA_CONST              1e0099b98-1e009b370  [    6K     6K     0K     0K] r--/rw- SM=COW   /usr/lib/system/libsystem_c.dylib
  __DATA_CONST              1e009b370-1e009bcd0  [  2400   2400     0K     0K] r--/rw- SM=COW   /usr/lib/libc++.1.dylib
  __DATA_CONST              1e009bcd0-1e009bda8  [   216    216     0K     0K] r--/rw- SM=COW   /usr/lib/libc++abi.dylib
  __DATA_CONST              1e009bda8-1e009e060  [    9K     9K     0K     0K] r--/rw- SM=COW   /usr/lib/system/libsystem_kernel.dylib
  __DATA_CONST              1e009e060-1e009e098  [    56     56     0K     0K] r--/rw- SM=COW   /usr/lib/system/libsystem_pthread.dylib
  __DATA_CONST              1e009e098-1e009e258  [   448    448     0K     0K] r--/rw- SM=COW   /usr/lib/system/libdyld.dylib
  __DATA_CONST              1e009e258-1e009e278  [    32     32     0K     0K] r--/rw- SM=COW   /usr/lib/system/libsystem_platform.dylib
  __DATA_CONST              1e009e278-1e009e790  [  1304   1304     0K     0K] r--/rw- SM=COW   /usr/lib/system/libsystem_info.dylib
  __DATA_CONST              1e0127148-1e0129ac0  [   10K    10K     0K     0K] r--/rw- SM=COW   /usr/lib/system/libsystem_darwin.dylib
  __DATA_CONST              1e0133dc0-1e0133f18  [   344    344     0K     0K] r--/rw- SM=COW   /usr/lib/system/libsystem_notify.dylib
  __DATA_CONST              1e02c9868-1e02c9d60  [  1272   1272     0K     0K] r--/rw- SM=COW   /usr/lib/system/libsystem_networkextension.dylib
  __DATA_CONST              1e02cac70-1e02cb290  [  1568   1568     0K     0K] r--/rw- SM=COW   /usr/lib/system/libsystem_asl.dylib
  __DATA_CONST              1e032ea80-1e032ec30  [   432    432     0K     0K] r--/rw- SM=COW   /usr/lib/system/libsystem_symptoms.dylib
  __DATA_CONST              1e05863b8-1e0586da0  [  2536   2536     0K     0K] r--/rw- SM=COW   /usr/lib/system/libsystem_containermanager.dylib
  __DATA_CONST              1e061d0e0-1e061d298  [   440    440     0K     0K] r--/rw- SM=COW   /usr/lib/system/libsystem_configuration.dylib
  __DATA_CONST              1e061d298-1e061d308  [   112    112     0K     0K] r--/rw- SM=COW   /usr/lib/system/libsystem_sandbox.dylib
  __DATA_CONST              1e064ac20-1e064ac70  [    80     80     0K     0K] r--/rw- SM=COW   /usr/lib/system/libquarantine.dylib
  __DATA_CONST              1e06d5660-1e06d5dc8  [  1896   1896     0K     0K] r--/rw- SM=COW   /usr/lib/system/libsystem_coreservices.dylib
  __DATA_CONST              1e06fd5a8-1e06fdcf0  [  1864   1864     0K     0K] r--/rw- SM=COW   /usr/lib/system/libmacho.dylib
  __DATA_CONST              1e06fdd00-1e06fe4a0  [  1952   1952     0K     0K] r--/rw- SM=COW   /usr/lib/system/libcommonCrypto.dylib
  __DATA_CONST              1e06fe4a0-1e06fe7c0  [   800    800     0K     0K] r--/rw- SM=COW   /usr/lib/system/libunwind.dylib
  __DATA_CONST              1e06fe7c0-1e06fe7d8  [    24     24     0K     0K] r--/rw- SM=COW   /usr/lib/liboah.dylib
  __DATA_CONST              1e06fe7d8-1e06fea98  [   704    704     0K     0K] r--/rw- SM=COW   /usr/lib/system/libcopyfile.dylib
  __DATA_CONST              1e06fea98-1e06feaa0  [     8      8     0K     0K] r--/rw- SM=COW   /usr/lib/system/libsystem_collections.dylib
  __DATA_CONST              1e06feaa0-1e06feb10  [   112    112     0K     0K] r--/rw- SM=COW   /usr/lib/system/libsystem_secinit.dylib
  __DATA_CONST              1e06feb10-1e06feb20  [    16     16     0K     0K] r--/rw- SM=COW   /usr/lib/system/libremovefile.dylib
  __DATA_CONST              1e06feb20-1e06feb30  [    16     16     0K     0K] r--/rw- SM=COW   /usr/lib/system/libkeymgr.dylib
  __DATA_CONST              1e06feb30-1e06feba8  [   120    120     0K     0K] r--/rw- SM=COW   /usr/lib/system/libsystem_dnssd.dylib
  __DATA_CONST              1e06feba8-1e06fec08  [    96     96     0K     0K] r--/rw- SM=COW   /usr/lib/system/libcache.dylib
  __DATA_CONST              1e06fec08-1e06fec18  [    16     16     0K     0K] r--/rw- SM=COW   /usr/lib/libSystem.B.dylib
  __AUTH_CONST              1e8b08000-1e8b08030  [    48     48     0K     0K] r--/rw- SM=COW   /usr/lib/system/libsystem_blocks.dylib
  __OBJC_CONST              1e8b08030-1e8b08390  [   864    864     0K     0K] r--/rw- SM=COW   /usr/lib/system/libsystem_blocks.dylib
  __DATA_CONST              1e8b08390-1e8b0ce20  [   19K    19K     0K     0K] r--/rw- SM=COW   /usr/lib/system/libxpc.dylib
  __OBJC_CONST              1e8b0ce20-1e8b0df90  [    4K     4K     0K     0K] r--/rw- SM=COW   /usr/lib/system/libxpc.dylib
  __AUTH_CONST              1e8b0df90-1e8b0ec90  [  3328   3328     0K     0K] r--/rw- SM=COW   /usr/lib/system/libsystem_trace.dylib
  __OBJC_CONST              1e8b0ec90-1e8b0ee40  [   432    432     0K     0K] r--/rw- SM=COW   /usr/lib/system/libsystem_trace.dylib
  __AUTH_CONST              1e8b0ee40-1e8b0ff10  [    4K     4K     0K     0K] r--/rw- SM=COW   /usr/lib/system/libcorecrypto.dylib
  __AUTH_CONST              1e8b0ff10-1e8b104e8  [  1496   1496     0K     0K] r--/rw- SM=COW   /usr/lib/system/libsystem_malloc.dylib
  __DATA_CONST              1e8b10500-1e8b238e8  [   77K    45K     0K     0K] r--/rw- SM=COW   /usr/lib/system/libdispatch.dylib
  __OBJC_CONST              1e8b238e8-1e8b24938  [    4K     4K     0K     0K] r--/rw- SM=COW   /usr/lib/system/libdispatch.dylib
  __AUTH_CONST              1e8b24940-1e8b253c8  [  2696   2696     0K     0K] r--/rw- SM=COW   /usr/lib/libobjc.A.dylib
  __OBJC_CONST              1e8b253c8-1e8b25698  [   720    720     0K     0K] r--/rw- SM=COW   /usr/lib/libobjc.A.dylib
  __AUTH_CONST              1e8b25698-1e8b25808  [   368    368     0K     0K] r--/rw- SM=COW   /usr/lib/system/libsystem_featureflags.dylib
  __AUTH_CONST              1e8b25808-1e8b26168  [  2400   2400     0K     0K] r--/rw- SM=COW   /usr/lib/system/libsystem_c.dylib
  __AUTH_CONST              1e8b26168-1e8b282a8  [    8K     8K     0K     0K] r--/rw- SM=COW   /usr/lib/libc++.1.dylib
  __AUTH_CONST              1e8b282a8-1e8b2b4b8  [   13K    13K     0K     0K] r--/rw- SM=COW   /usr/lib/libc++abi.dylib
  __AUTH_CONST              1e8b2b4b8-1e8b2b5e0  [   296    296     0K     0K] r--/rw- SM=COW   /usr/lib/system/libsystem_kernel.dylib
  __AUTH_CONST              1e8b2b5e0-1e8b2b810  [   560    560     0K     0K] r--/rw- SM=COW   /usr/lib/system/libsystem_pthread.dylib
  __AUTH_CONST              1e8b2b810-1e8b2bfc8  [  1976   1976     0K     0K] r--/rw- SM=COW   /usr/lib/system/libdyld.dylib
  __AUTH_CONST              1e8b2bfc8-1e8b2c250  [   648    648     0K     0K] r--/rw- SM=COW   /usr/lib/system/libsystem_platform.dylib
  __AUTH_CONST              1e8b2c250-1e8b2d3f0  [    4K     4K     0K     0K] r--/rw- SM=COW   /usr/lib/system/libsystem_info.dylib
  __AUTH_CONST              1e8c5bd48-1e8c5c1c8  [  1152   1152     0K     0K] r--/rw- SM=COW   /usr/lib/system/libsystem_darwin.dylib
  __AUTH_CONST              1e8c77a80-1e8c77e00  [   896    896     0K     0K] r--/rw- SM=COW   /usr/lib/system/libsystem_notify.dylib
  __AUTH_CONST              1e8dfea40-1e8dff608  [  3016   3016     0K     0K] r--/rw- SM=COW   /usr/lib/system/libsystem_networkextension.dylib
  __AUTH_CONST              1e8e4d718-1e8e4e160  [  2632   2632     0K     0K] r--/rw- SM=COW   /usr/lib/system/libsystem_asl.dylib
  __AUTH_CONST              1e8f17288-1e8f17560  [   728    728     0K     0K] r--/rw- SM=COW   /usr/lib/system/libsystem_symptoms.dylib
  __AUTH_CONST              1e904e480-1e904f8c0  [    5K     5K     0K     0K] r--/rw- SM=COW   /usr/lib/system/libsystem_containermanager.dylib
  __AUTH_CONST              1e915e250-1e915e560  [   784    784     0K     0K] r--/rw- SM=COW   /usr/lib/system/libsystem_configuration.dylib
  __AUTH_CONST              1e915e560-1e915e768  [   520    520     0K     0K] r--/rw- SM=COW   /usr/lib/system/libsystem_sandbox.dylib
  __AUTH_CONST              1e91a78b8-1e91a79c0  [   264    264     0K     0K] r--/rw- SM=COW   /usr/lib/system/libquarantine.dylib
  __AUTH_CONST              1e922eac0-1e922ed50  [   656    656     0K     0K] r--/rw- SM=COW   /usr/lib/system/libsystem_coreservices.dylib
  __AUTH_CONST              1e925ad88-1e925ada8  [    32     32     0K     0K] r--/rw- SM=COW   /usr/lib/system/libsystem_m.dylib
  __AUTH_CONST              1e925ae28-1e925ae98  [   112    112     0K     0K] r--/rw- SM=COW   /usr/lib/system/libmacho.dylib
  __AUTH_CONST              1e925afb0-1e925bd80  [  3536   3536     0K     0K] r--/rw- SM=COW   /usr/lib/system/libcommonCrypto.dylib
  __AUTH_CONST              1e925bd80-1e925be98  [   280    280     0K     0K] r--/rw- SM=COW   /usr/lib/system/libunwind.dylib
  __AUTH_CONST              1e925be98-1e925c168  [   720    720     0K     0K] r--/rw- SM=COW   /usr/lib/liboah.dylib
  __AUTH_CONST              1e925c168-1e925c5a0  [  1080   1080     0K     0K] r--/rw- SM=COW   /usr/lib/system/libcopyfile.dylib
  __AUTH_CONST              1e925c5a0-1e925c600  [    96     96     0K     0K] r--/rw- SM=COW   /usr/lib/system/libcompiler_rt.dylib
  __AUTH_CONST              1e925c600-1e925c750  [   336    336     0K     0K] r--/rw- SM=COW   /usr/lib/system/libsystem_collections.dylib
  __AUTH_CONST              1e925c750-1e925ca18  [   712    712     0K     0K] r--/rw- SM=COW   /usr/lib/system/libsystem_secinit.dylib
  __AUTH_CONST              1e925ca18-1e925cb78  [   352    352     0K     0K] r--/rw- SM=COW   /usr/lib/system/libremovefile.dylib
  __AUTH_CONST              1e925cb78-1e925cbf8  [   128    128     0K     0K] r--/rw- SM=COW   /usr/lib/system/libkeymgr.dylib
  __AUTH_CONST              1e925cbf8-1e925cdb0  [   440    440     0K     0K] r--/rw- SM=COW   /usr/lib/system/libsystem_dnssd.dylib
  __AUTH_CONST              1e925cdb0-1e925ce70  [   192    192     0K     0K] r--/rw- SM=COW   /usr/lib/system/libcache.dylib
  __AUTH_CONST              1e925ce70-1e925d120  [   688    688     0K     0K] r--/rw- SM=COW   /usr/lib/libSystem.B.dylib
  __LINKEDIT                222494000-2465e6000  [577.3M  11.8M     0K     0K] r--/r-- SM=COW   dyld shared cache combined __LINKEDIT

==== Writable regions for process 92493
REGION TYPE                    START - END       [ VSIZE  RSDNT  DIRTY   SWAP] PRT/MAX SHRMOD PURGE    REGION DETAIL
Kernel Alloc Once         1043d8000-1043e0000  [   32K     0K     0K    16K] rw-/rwx SM=PRV
MALLOC metadata           1043e8000-1043ec000  [   16K    16K    16K     0K] rw-/rwx SM=ZER
MALLOC metadata           1043f0000-1043f8000  [   32K    32K    32K     0K] rw-/rwx SM=ZER
MALLOC metadata           104400000-104408000  [   32K    32K    32K     0K] rw-/rwx SM=PRV
MALLOC metadata           104410000-104418000  [   32K     0K     0K    32K] rw-/rwx SM=PRV
MALLOC metadata           104424000-104428000  [   16K    16K    16K     0K] rw-/rwx SM=ZER
__DATA                    104734000-104738000  [   16K    16K    16K     0K] rw-/rw- SM=COW   /usr/lib/dyld
MALLOC_TINY               124e00000-124f00000  [ 1024K    16K    16K    16K] rw-/rwx SM=PRV   MallocHelperZone_0x1043e4000
```

```
MALLOC_SMALL            125000000-125800000     [ 8192K    16K    16K    16K] rw-/rwx SM=PRV        MallocHelperZone_0x1043e4000
Stack                   16b33c000-16bb38000     [ 8176K    16K    16K    16K] rw-/rwx SM=PRV        thread 0
Stack                   16bb3c000-16bbc4000     [  544K     0K     0K    16K] rw-/rwx SM=PRV        thread 1
Stack                   16bbc8000-16bc50000     [  544K     0K     0K    16K] rw-/rwx SM=PRV        thread 2
Stack                   16bc54000-16bcdc000     [  544K     0K     0K    16K] rw-/rwx SM=PRV        thread 3
Stack                   16bce0000-16bd68000     [  544K     0K     0K    16K] rw-/rwx SM=PRV        thread 4
Stack                   16bd6c000-16bdf4000     [  544K     0K     0K    16K] rw-/rwx SM=PRV        thread 5
__DATA                  1e4c04000-1e4c04060     [    96     0K     0K     96] rw-/rw- SM=COW        /usr/lib/system/libsystem_blocks.dylib
__DATA                  1e4c04060-1e4c04d18     [  3256     0K     0K   3256] rw-/rw- SM=COW        /usr/lib/system/libxpc.dylib
__DATA                  1e4c04d18-1e4c05050     [   824     0K     0K    824] rw-/rw- SM=COW        /usr/lib/system/libsystem_trace.dylib
__DATA                  1e4c05050-1e4c0c788     [   30K    16K     0K    14K] rw-/rw- SM=COW        /usr/lib/system/libcorecrypto.dylib
__DATA                  1e4c0c788-1e4c0ea24     [    9K     0K     0K     9K] rw-/rw- SM=COW        /usr/lib/system/libsystem_malloc.dylib
unused __DATA           1e4c0ea24-1e4c0ea40     [    28     0K     0K     28] rw-/rw- SM=COW        on dirty page  unused system shared lib __DATA
__DATA                  1e4c0ea40-1e4c120c0     [   14K     0K     0K    14K] rw-/rw- SM=COW        /usr/lib/libobjc.A.dylib
__DATA                  1e4c120c0-1e4c120f9     [    57     0K     0K     57] rw-/rw- SM=COW        /usr/lib/system/libsystem_featureflags.dylib
unused __DATA           1e4c120f9-1e4c12100     [     7     0K     0K      7] rw-/rw- SM=COW        on dirty page  unused system shared lib __DATA
__DATA                  1e4c12100-1e4c14270     [    8K     0K     0K     8K] rw-/rw- SM=COW        /usr/lib/system/libsystem_c.dylib
unused __DATA           1e4c14270-1e4c15000     [  3472     0K     0K   3472] rw-/rw- SM=COW        on dirty page  unused system shared lib __DATA
__DATA                  1e4c15000-1e4c1b720     [   26K    14K     0K    12K] rw-/rw- SM=COW        /usr/lib/libc++.1.dylib
__DATA                  1e4c1b720-1e4c1ba68     [   840    840     0K     0K] rw-/rw- SM=COW        /usr/lib/libc++abi.dylib
__DATA                  1e4c1ba68-1e4c1bcd9     [   625    625     0K     0K] rw-/rw- SM=COW        /usr/lib/system/libsystem_kernel.dylib
__DATA                  1e4c1c000-1e4c24000     [   32K    32K     0K     0K] rw-/rw- SM=COW        /usr/lib/system/libsystem_pthread.dylib
__DATA                  1e4c24000-1e4c28000     [   16K    16K     0K     0K] rw-/rw- SM=COW        /usr/lib/system/libsystem_pthread.dylib
__DATA                  1e4c28000-1e4c28048     [    72     72     0K     0K] rw-/rw- SM=COW        /usr/lib/system/libsystem_pthread.dylib
__DATA                  1e4c28048-1e4c28050     [     8      8     0K     0K] rw-/rw- SM=COW        /usr/lib/system/libdyld.dylib
__DATA                  1e4c28050-1e4c28090     [    64     64     0K     0K] rw-/rw- SM=COW        /usr/lib/system/libsystem_platform.dylib
__DATA                  1e4c28090-1e4c28be0     [  2896   2896     0K     0K] rw-/rw- SM=COW        /usr/lib/system/libsystem_info.dylib
__DATA                  1e4c96958-1e4c96968     [    16     16     0K     0K] rw-/rw- SM=COW        /usr/lib/system/libsystem_darwin.dylib
__DATA                  1e4c9de00-1e4c9de51     [    81     81     0K     0K] rw-/rw- SM=COW        /usr/lib/system/libsystem_notify.dylib
__DATA                  1e4d33600-1e4d33bd9     [  1497   1497     0K     0K] rw-/rw- SM=COW        /usr/lib/system/libsystem_networkextension.dylib
__DATA                  1e4d343b8-1e4d344c8     [   272    272     0K     0K] rw-/rw- SM=COW        /usr/lib/system/libsystem_asl.dylib
__DATA                  1e4d6a118-1e4d6a158     [    64     64     0K     0K] rw-/rw- SM=COW        /usr/lib/system/libsystem_symptoms.dylib
__DATA                  1e4deca18-1e4decb40     [   296    296     0K     0K] rw-/rw- SM=COW        /usr/lib/system/libsystem_containermanager.dylib
__DATA                  1e4e2d090-1e4e2d159     [   201    201     0K     0K] rw-/rw- SM=COW        /usr/lib/system/libsystem_configuration.dylib
__DATA                  1e4e2d160-1e4e2d188     [    40     40     0K     0K] rw-/rw- SM=COW        /usr/lib/system/libsystem_sandbox.dylib
__DATA                  1e4e4f280-1e4e4f290     [    16     16     0K     0K] rw-/rw- SM=COW        /usr/lib/system/libquarantine.dylib
__DATA                  1e4e61bb0-1e4e61c88     [   216    216     0K     0K] rw-/rw- SM=COW        /usr/lib/system/libsystem_coreservices.dylib
__DATA                  1e4e71a20-1e4e71a24     [     4      4     0K     0K] rw-/rw- SM=COW        /usr/lib/system/libsystem_m.dylib
__DATA                  1e4e71ae8-1e4e723d9     [  2289   2289     0K     0K] rw-/rw- SM=COW        /usr/lib/system/libunwind.dylib
__DATA                  1e4e723e0-1e4e723e8     [     8      8     0K     0K] rw-/rw- SM=COW        /usr/lib/liboah.dylib
__DATA                  1e4e723e8-1e4e723f8     [    16     16     0K     0K] rw-/rw- SM=COW        /usr/lib/system/libcopyfile.dylib
__DATA                  1e4e723f8-1e4e733f8     [    4K     4K     0K     0K] rw-/rw- SM=COW        /usr/lib/system/libcompiler_rt.dylib
__DATA                  1e4e733f8-1e4e73438     [    64     64     0K     0K] rw-/rw- SM=COW        /usr/lib/system/libsystem_secinit.dylib
__DATA                  1e4e73438-1e4e73468     [    48     48     0K     0K] rw-/rw- SM=COW        /usr/lib/system/libsystem_dnssd.dylib
__DATA                  1e4e73468-1e4e73470     [     8      8     0K     0K] rw-/rw- SM=COW        /usr/lib/libSystem.B.dylib
unused __DATA_DIRTY     1e7930000-1e7930120     [   288     0K     0K    288] rw-/rw- SM=COW        on dirty page  unused /usr/lib/libMobileGestalt.dylib
unused __DATA_DIRTY     1e7930120-1e7930170     [    80     0K     0K     80] rw-/rw- SM=COW        on dirty page  unused
/usr/lib/libUniversalAccess.dylib
unused __DATA_DIRTY     1e7930170-1e7930190     [    32     0K     0K     32] rw-/rw- SM=COW        on dirty page  unused
/usr/lib/libapp_launch_measurement.dylib
unused __DATA_DIRTY     1e7930190-1e7931010     [  3712     0K     0K   3712] rw-/rw- SM=COW        on dirty page  unused /usr/lib/libboringssl.dylib
__DATA_DIRTY            1e7931010-1e79321e0     [    4K     0K     0K     4K] rw-/rw- SM=COW        /usr/lib/libc++.1.dylib
__DATA_DIRTY            1e79321e0-1e7932208     [    40     0K     0K     40] rw-/rw- SM=COW        /usr/lib/libc++abi.dylib
unused __DATA_DIRTY     1e7932208-1e7934000     [    7K     0K     0K     7K] rw-/rw- SM=COW        on dirty page  unused /usr/lib/libcoreroutine.dylib
unused __DATA_DIRTY     1e7938000-1e793a1c8     [    8K     0K     0K     8K] rw-/rw- SM=COW        on dirty page  unused /usr/lib/libnetwork.dylib
unused __DATA           1e793a1c8-1e793a200     [    56     0K     0K     56] rw-/rw- SM=COW        on dirty page  unused system shared lib __DATA
__DATA_DIRTY            1e793a200-1e793d070     [   12K     0K     0K    12K] rw-/rw- SM=COW        /usr/lib/libobjc.A.dylib
unused __DATA_DIRTY     1e793d070-1e793d200     [   400     0K     0K    400] rw-/rw- SM=COW        on dirty page  unused
/usr/lib/libpartition2_dynamic.dylib
unused __DATA_DIRTY     1e793d200-1e793d299     [   153     0K     0K    153] rw-/rw- SM=COW        on dirty page  unused /usr/lib/libpmenergy.dylib
unused __DATA           1e793d299-1e793d2a0     [     7     0K     0K      7] rw-/rw- SM=COW        on dirty page  unused system shared lib __DATA
unused __DATA_DIRTY     1e793d2a0-1e793d3e8     [   328     0K     0K    328] rw-/rw- SM=COW        on dirty page  unused /usr/lib/libprequelite.dylib
unused __DATA_DIRTY     1e793d3e8-1e793d4f8     [   272     0K     0K    272] rw-/rw- SM=COW        on dirty page  unused /usr/lib/libquic.dylib
unused __DATA_DIRTY     1e793d4f8-1e793d530     [    56     0K     0K     56] rw-/rw- SM=COW        on dirty page  unused /usr/lib/libsandbox.1.dylib
unused __DATA           1e793d530-1e793d540     [    16     0K     0K     16] rw-/rw- SM=COW        on dirty page  unused system shared lib __DATA
unused __DATA_DIRTY     1e793d540-1e7940000     [   11K     0K     0K    11K] rw-/rw- SM=COW        on dirty page  unused /usr/lib/libsqlite3.dylib
unused __DATA_DIRTY     1e795c000-1e795e610     [   10K     0K     0K    10K] rw-/rw- SM=COW        on dirty page  unused
/usr/lib/swift/libswiftFoundation.dylib
unused __DATA_DIRTY     1e795e610-1e795e7a0     [   400     0K     0K    400] rw-/rw- SM=COW        on dirty page  unused
/usr/lib/swift/libswiftObjectiveC.dylib
unused __DATA_DIRTY     1e795e7a0-1e795e7b8     [    24     0K     0K     24] rw-/rw- SM=COW        on dirty page  unused /usr/lib/swift/libswiftos.dylib
__DATA_DIRTY            1e795e7b8-1e795ef10     [  1880     0K     0K   1880] rw-/rw- SM=COW        /usr/lib/system/libcorecrypto.dylib
unused __DATA           1e795ef10-1e795ef40     [    48     0K     0K     48] rw-/rw- SM=COW        on dirty page  unused system shared lib __DATA
__DATA_DIRTY            1e795ef40-1e79628e8     [   14K     0K     0K    14K] rw-/rw- SM=COW        /usr/lib/system/libdispatch.dylib
__DATA_DIRTY            1e79628e8-1e7962908     [    32     0K     0K     32] rw-/rw- SM=COW        /usr/lib/system/libdyld.dylib
unused __DATA           1e7962908-1e7962910     [     8     0K     0K      8] rw-/rw- SM=COW        on dirty page  unused system shared lib __DATA
__DATA_DIRTY            1e7962910-1e7962a6c     [   348     0K     0K    348] rw-/rw- SM=COW        /usr/lib/system/libsystem_asl.dylib
unused __DATA           1e7962a6c-1e7962a70     [     4     0K     0K      4] rw-/rw- SM=COW        on dirty page  unused system shared lib __DATA
__DATA_DIRTY            1e7962a70-1e7962c68     [   504     0K     0K    504] rw-/rw- SM=COW        /usr/lib/system/libsystem_blocks.dylib
__DATA_DIRTY            1e7962c68-1e79657f0     [   11K     6K     6K     5K] rw-/rw- SM=COW        /usr/lib/system/libsystem_c.dylib
__DATA_DIRTY            1e79657f0-1e7965820     [    48     48     48     0K] rw-/rw- SM=COW        /usr/lib/system/libsystem_darwin.dylib
__DATA_DIRTY            1e7965820-1e7965830     [    16     16     16     0K] rw-/rw- SM=COW        /usr/lib/system/libsystem_featureflags.dylib
__DATA_DIRTY            1e7965830-1e7965ac0     [   656    656    656     0K] rw-/rw- SM=COW        /usr/lib/system/libsystem_info.dylib
__DATA_DIRTY            1e7965ac0-1e7966184     [  1732   1732   1732     0K] rw-/rw- SM=COW        /usr/lib/system/libsystem_kernel.dylib
unused __DATA           1e7966184-1e7966188     [     4      4      4     0K] rw-/rw- SM=COW        on dirty page  unused system shared lib __DATA
__DATA_DIRTY            1e7966188-1e79663a0     [   536    536    536     0K] rw-/rw- SM=COW        /usr/lib/system/libsystem_malloc.dylib
__DATA_DIRTY            1e79663a0-1e79663e1     [    65     65     65     0K] rw-/rw- SM=COW        /usr/lib/system/libsystem_networkextension.dylib
unused __DATA           1e79663e1-1e79663e8     [     7      7      7     0K] rw-/rw- SM=COW        on dirty page  unused system shared lib __DATA
__DATA_DIRTY            1e79663e8-1e79663f0     [     8      8      8     0K] rw-/rw- SM=COW        /usr/lib/system/libsystem_notify.dylib
__DATA_DIRTY            1e79663f0-1e7966404     [    20     20     20     0K] rw-/rw- SM=COW        /usr/lib/system/libsystem_platform.dylib
unused __DATA           1e7966404-1e7968000     [    7K     7K     7K     0K] rw-/rw- SM=COW        on dirty page  unused system shared lib __DATA
__DATA_DIRTY            1e7968000-1e796d838     [   22K     0K     0K    22K] rw-/rw- SM=COW        /usr/lib/system/libsystem_pthread.dylib
__DATA_DIRTY            1e796d838-1e796d848     [    16     0K     0K     16] rw-/rw- SM=COW        /usr/lib/system/libsystem_symptoms.dylib
__DATA_DIRTY            1e796d848-1e796dcb8     [  1136     0K     0K   1136] rw-/rw- SM=COW        /usr/lib/system/libsystem_trace.dylib
__DATA_DIRTY            1e796dcb8-1e796e708     [  2640     0K     0K   2640] rw-/rw- SM=COW        /usr/lib/system/libxpc.dylib
unused __DATA           1e796e708-1e7970000     [    6K     0K     0K     6K] rw-/rw- SM=COW        on dirty page  unused system shared lib __DATA
__AUTH                  1e7970000-1e79701b8     [   440    440     0K     0K] rw-/rw- SM=COW        /usr/lib/system/libsystem_trace.dylib
__AUTH                  1e79701b8-1e7970218     [    96     96     0K     0K] rw-/rw- SM=COW        /usr/lib/system/libcorecrypto.dylib
__AUTH                  1e7974000-1e797c000     [   32K    32K     0K     0K] rw-/rw- SM=COW        /usr/lib/system/libsystem_malloc.dylib
__DATA                  1e797c000-1e797d400     [    5K     5K     0K     0K] rw-/rw- SM=COW        /usr/lib/system/libdispatch.dylib
__AUTH                  1e797d400-1e797d478     [   120    120     0K     0K] rw-/rw- SM=COW        /usr/lib/libobjc.A.dylib
__AUTH                  1e797d478-1e797e190     [  3352   3352     0K     0K] rw-/rw- SM=COW        /usr/lib/system/libsystem_c.dylib
```

```
__AUTH              1e797e190-1e7980628 [    9K     8K    0K  1576] rw-/rw- SM=COW          /usr/lib/libc++.1.dylib
__AUTH              1e7980628-1e7980670 [   72     0K    0K    72] rw-/rw- SM=COW          /usr/lib/libc++abi.dylib
__AUTH              1e7980670-1e79806b0 [   64     0K    0K    64] rw-/rw- SM=COW          /usr/lib/system/libdyld.dylib
__AUTH              1e79806b0-1e7980880 [  464     0K    0K   464] rw-/rw- SM=COW          /usr/lib/system/libsystem_info.dylib
unused __AUTH       1e7980880-1e7982740 [    8K     0K    0K     8K] rw-/rw- SM=COW          ...y page  unused
/System/Library/Frameworks/CoreFoundation.framework/Versions/A/CoreFoundation
unused __AUTH       1e7982740-1e7984000 [    6K     0K    0K     6K] rw-/rw- SM=COW
...eServices.framework/Versions/A/Frameworks/LaunchServices.framework/Versions/A/LaunchServices
__AUTH              1e7a0a640-1e7a0a660 [   32    32    0K    0K] rw-/rw- SM=COW          /usr/lib/system/libcommonCrypto.dylib
__AUTH              1e7a0a660-1e7a0a668 [    8     8    0K    0K] rw-/rw- SM=COW          /usr/lib/libSystem.B.dylib
__OBJC_RW           1e87f0000-1e8b08000 [ 3168K  1600K    0K    16K] rw-/rw- SM=COW          /usr/lib/libobjc.A.dylib
MALLOC_NANO         600000000000-600008000000 [128.0M   32K   32K   208K] rw-/rwx SM=PRV    DefaultMallocZone_0x104420000
MALLOC_NANO (empty) 600008000000-600020000000 [384.0M    0K    0K     0K] rw-/rwx SM=NUL


==== Legend
SM=sharing mode:
        COW=copy_on_write PRV=private NUL=empty ALI=aliased
        SHM=shared ZER=zero_filled S/A=shared_alias
PURGE=purgeable mode:
        V=volatile N=nonvolatile E=empty   otherwise is unpurgeable

==== Summary for process 92493
ReadOnly portion of Libraries: Total=582.2M resident=16.2M(3%) swapped_out_or_unallocated=565.9M(97%)
Writable regions: Total=531.8M written=496K(0%) resident=176K(0%) swapped_out=384K(0%) unallocated=531.2M(100%)

                            VIRTUAL RESIDENT   DIRTY SWAPPED VOLATILE  NONVOL  EMPTY  REGION
REGION TYPE                   SIZE    SIZE     SIZE   SIZE     SIZE     SIZE   SIZE  COUNT (non-coalesced)
===========                 ======= ========  =====  ======  ========  ======  =====  =======
Kernel Alloc Once              32K     0K       0K    16K      0K       0K     0K       1
MALLOC guard page              96K     0K       0K     0K      0K       0K     0K       5
MALLOC metadata               176K   144K     144K    32K      0K       0K     0K       8
MALLOC_NANO                  128.0M   32K      32K   208K      0K       0K     0K       1     see MALLOC ZONE table below
MALLOC_NANO (empty)          384.0M    0K       0K     0K      0K       0K     0K       1     see MALLOC ZONE table below
MALLOC_SMALL                  8192K   16K      16K    16K      0K       0K     0K       1     see MALLOC ZONE table below
MALLOC_TINY                   1024K   16K      16K    16K      0K       0K     0K       1     see MALLOC ZONE table below
STACK GUARD                   56.1M    0K       0K     0K      0K       0K     0K       6
Stack                         10.6M   16K      16K    96K      0K       0K     0K       6
__AUTH                          46K   44K       0K  2176       0K       0K     0K      11
__AUTH_CONST                    67K   67K       0K     0K      0K       0K     0K      38
__DATA                         173K  112K      16K    61K      0K       0K     0K      37
__DATA_CONST                   258K  130K      16K    32K      0K       0K     0K      40
__DATA_DIRTY                    73K    9K       9K    64K      0K       0K     0K      21
__LINKEDIT                    577.6M 11.9M      0K     0K      0K       0K     0K       3
__OBJC_CONST                    10K   10K       0K     0K      0K       0K     0K       5
__OBJC_RO                     83.0M  47.8M      0K     0K      0K       0K     0K       1
__OBJC_RW                     3168K 1600K       0K    16K      0K       0K     0K       1
__TEXT                        4708K 4436K       0K     0K      0K       0K     0K      43
dyld private memory           1024K   16K      16K     0K      0K       0K     0K       1
shared memory                   16K   16K      16K     0K      0K       0K     0K       1
unused but dirty shlib __DATA   72K    7K       7K    65K      0K       0K     0K      30
===============             ======= ========  =====  ======  ========  ======  =====  =======
TOTAL                          1.2G  66.2M    304K   624K      0K       0K     0K     262

                            VIRTUAL  RESIDENT    DIRTY  SWAPPED ALLOCATION      BYTES DIRTY+SWAP           REGION
MALLOC ZONE                    SIZE      SIZE     SIZE     SIZE      COUNT  ALLOCATED FRAG SIZE  % FRAG     COUNT
===========                 =======  ========  =======  ======= ========== ========= ========= ======     ======
DefaultMallocZone_0x104420000 128.0M    32K      32K    208K       211        9K      231K    97%         1
MallocHelperZone_0x1043e4000  9216K    32K      32K     32K         2      2064       62K    97%         2
===========                 =======  ========  =======  ======= ========== ========= ========= ======     ======
TOTAL                        137.0M    64K      64K    240K       213       11K      293K    97%         3
```

5.   We check that manually based on the stack pointer value (it can also be seen in the diagnostic report):

```
(lldb) x $sp
0x16bb3bfe0: 00 00 00 00 00 00 00 00 00 00 00 00 00 00 00 00  ................
0x16bb3bff0: 00 00 00 00 00 00 00 00 00 00 00 00 00 00 00 00  ................
```

Note: We see that the stack pointer is in the stack guard page range. We see contents because a non-read attribute is applied to code execution but memory contents were saved in this core dump.

```
(lldb) f 1
frame #1: 0x00000001042cbcd0 App6`procF + 80
App6`procF:
->  0x1042cbcd0 <+80>: ldur   x9, [x29, #-0x18]
    0x1042cbcd4 <+84>: adrp   x8, 1
    0x1042cbcd8 <+88>: ldr    x8, [x8, #0x8]
    0x1042cbcdc <+92>: ldr    x8, [x8]

(lldb) re r sp
     sp = 0x000000016bb3c210
```

```
(lldb) f 2
frame #2: 0x00000001042cbcd0 App6`procF + 80
App6`procF:
->  0x1042cbcd0 <+80>: ldur   x9, [x29, #-0x18]
    0x1042cbcd4 <+84>: adrp   x8, 1
    0x1042cbcd8 <+88>: ldr    x8, [x8, #0x8]
    0x1042cbcdc <+92>: ldr    x8, [x8]
```

```
(lldb) re r sp
      sp = 0x000000016bb3c440
```

Note: We see that in all other frames the stack pointer is in the range of stack pages.

6.   Dump the bottom of the raw stack to see execution residue such as thread startup code:

```
(lldb) x/1024a 0x16bbc0000-0x2000 --force
0x16bbbe000: 0x0000000000000000
0x16bbbe008: 0xc8ecebab51e8004e
0x16bbbe010: 0x0000000000000000
0x16bbbe018: 0x0000000000000000
0x16bbbe020: 0x000000016bbbe250
0x16bbbe028: 0x00000001042cbcd0 App6`procF + 80
0x16bbbe030: 0x0000000700000000
0x16bbbe038: 0x00000000ffffffff
0x16bbbe040: 0x0000000000000008
0x16bbbe048: 0x00000000ffffffff
0x16bbbe050: 0x0000000000000000
0x16bbbe058: 0x0000000000000000
0x16bbbe060: 0x0000000000000000
0x16bbbe068: 0x0000000000000000
0x16bbbe070: 0x0000000000000000
0x16bbbe078: 0x0000000000000000
0x16bbbe080: 0x0000000000000000
0x16bbbe088: 0x0000000000000000
0x16bbbe090: 0x0000000000000000
0x16bbbe098: 0x0000000000000000
0x16bbbe0a0: 0x0000000000000000
0x16bbbe0a8: 0x0000000000000000
0x16bbbe0b0: 0x0000000000000000
0x16bbbe0b8: 0x0000000000000000
0x16bbbe0c0: 0x0000000000000000
0x16bbbe0c8: 0x0000000000000000
0x16bbbe0d0: 0x0000000000000000
0x16bbbe0d8: 0x0000000000000000
0x16bbbe0e0: 0x0000000000000000
0x16bbbe0e8: 0x0000000000000000
0x16bbbe0f0: 0x0000000000000000
0x16bbbe0f8: 0x0000000000000000
0x16bbbe100: 0x0000000000000000
0x16bbbe108: 0x0000000000000000
0x16bbbe110: 0x0000000000000000
0x16bbbe118: 0x0000000000000000
0x16bbbe120: 0x0000000000000000
0x16bbbe128: 0x0000000000000000
0x16bbbe130: 0x0000000000000000
0x16bbbe138: 0x0000000000000000
0x16bbbe140: 0x0000000000000000
0x16bbbe148: 0x0000000000000000
0x16bbbe150: 0x0000000000000000
0x16bbbe158: 0x0000000000000000
0x16bbbe160: 0x0000000000000000
```

```
0x16bbbe168:  0x0000000000000000
0x16bbbe170:  0x0000000000000000
0x16bbbe178:  0x0000000000000000
0x16bbbe180:  0x0000000000000000
0x16bbbe188:  0x0000000000000000
0x16bbbe190:  0x0000000000000000
0x16bbbe198:  0x0000000000000000
0x16bbbe1a0:  0x0000000000000000
0x16bbbe1a8:  0x0000000000000000
0x16bbbe1b0:  0x0000000000000000
0x16bbbe1b8:  0x0000000000000000
0x16bbbe1c0:  0x0000000000000000
0x16bbbe1c8:  0x0000000000000000
0x16bbbe1d0:  0x0000000000000000
0x16bbbe1d8:  0x0000000000000000
0x16bbbe1e0:  0x0000000000000000
0x16bbbe1e8:  0x0000000000000000
0x16bbbe1f0:  0x0000000000000000
0x16bbbe1f8:  0x0000000000000000
0x16bbbe200:  0x0000000000000000
0x16bbbe208:  0x0000000000000000
0x16bbbe210:  0x0000000000000000
0x16bbbe218:  0x0000000000000000
0x16bbbe220:  0x0000000000000000
0x16bbbe228:  0x0000000000000000
0x16bbbe230:  0x0000000000000000
0x16bbbe238:  0xc8ecebab51e8004e
0x16bbbe240:  0x0000000000000000
0x16bbbe248:  0x0000000000000000
0x16bbbe250:  0x000000016bbbe480
0x16bbbe258:  0x00000001042cbcd0 App6`procF + 80
0x16bbbe260:  0x0000000600000000
0x16bbbe268:  0x00000000ffffffff
0x16bbbe270:  0x0000000000000007
0x16bbbe278:  0x00000000ffffffff
0x16bbbe280:  0x0000000000000000
0x16bbbe288:  0x0000000000000000
0x16bbbe290:  0x0000000000000000
0x16bbbe298:  0x0000000000000000
0x16bbbe2a0:  0x0000000000000000
0x16bbbe2a8:  0x0000000000000000
0x16bbbe2b0:  0x0000000000000000
0x16bbbe2b8:  0x0000000000000000
0x16bbbe2c0:  0x0000000000000000
0x16bbbe2c8:  0x0000000000000000
0x16bbbe2d0:  0x0000000000000000
0x16bbbe2d8:  0x0000000000000000
0x16bbbe2e0:  0x0000000000000000
0x16bbbe2e8:  0x0000000000000000
0x16bbbe2f0:  0x0000000000000000
0x16bbbe2f8:  0x0000000000000000
0x16bbbe300:  0x0000000000000000
0x16bbbe308:  0x0000000000000000
0x16bbbe310:  0x0000000000000000
0x16bbbe318:  0x0000000000000000
0x16bbbe320:  0x0000000000000000
0x16bbbe328:  0x0000000000000000
0x16bbbe330:  0x0000000000000000
0x16bbbe338:  0x0000000000000000
0x16bbbe340:  0x0000000000000000
0x16bbbe348:  0x0000000000000000
```

```
0x16bbbe350:  0x0000000000000000
0x16bbbe358:  0x0000000000000000
0x16bbbe360:  0x0000000000000000
0x16bbbe368:  0x0000000000000000
0x16bbbe370:  0x0000000000000000
0x16bbbe378:  0x0000000000000000
0x16bbbe380:  0x0000000000000000
0x16bbbe388:  0x0000000000000000
0x16bbbe390:  0x0000000000000000
0x16bbbe398:  0x0000000000000000
0x16bbbe3a0:  0x0000000000000000
0x16bbbe3a8:  0x0000000000000000
0x16bbbe3b0:  0x0000000000000000
0x16bbbe3b8:  0x0000000000000000
0x16bbbe3c0:  0x0000000000000000
0x16bbbe3c8:  0x0000000000000000
0x16bbbe3d0:  0x0000000000000000
0x16bbbe3d8:  0x0000000000000000
0x16bbbe3e0:  0x0000000000000000
0x16bbbe3e8:  0x0000000000000000
0x16bbbe3f0:  0x0000000000000000
0x16bbbe3f8:  0x0000000000000000
0x16bbbe400:  0x0000000000000000
0x16bbbe408:  0x0000000000000000
0x16bbbe410:  0x0000000000000000
0x16bbbe418:  0x0000000000000000
0x16bbbe420:  0x0000000000000000
0x16bbbe428:  0x0000000000000000
0x16bbbe430:  0x0000000000000000
0x16bbbe438:  0x0000000000000000
0x16bbbe440:  0x0000000000000000
0x16bbbe448:  0x0000000000000000
0x16bbbe450:  0x0000000000000000
0x16bbbe458:  0x0000000000000000
0x16bbbe460:  0x0000000000000000
0x16bbbe468:  0xc8ecebab51e8004e
0x16bbbe470:  0x0000000000000000
0x16bbbe478:  0x0000000000000000
0x16bbbe480:  0x000000016bbbe6b0
0x16bbbe488:  0x00000001042cbcd0 App6`procF + 80
0x16bbbe490:  0x0000000500000000
0x16bbbe498:  0x00000000ffffffff
0x16bbbe4a0:  0x0000000000000006
0x16bbbe4a8:  0x00000000ffffffff
0x16bbbe4b0:  0x0000000000000000
0x16bbbe4b8:  0x0000000000000000
0x16bbbe4c0:  0x0000000000000000
0x16bbbe4c8:  0x0000000000000000
0x16bbbe4d0:  0x0000000000000000
0x16bbbe4d8:  0x0000000000000000
0x16bbbe4e0:  0x0000000000000000
0x16bbbe4e8:  0x0000000000000000
0x16bbbe4f0:  0x0000000000000000
0x16bbbe4f8:  0x0000000000000000
0x16bbbe500:  0x0000000000000000
0x16bbbe508:  0x0000000000000000
0x16bbbe510:  0x0000000000000000
0x16bbbe518:  0x0000000000000000
0x16bbbe520:  0x0000000000000000
0x16bbbe528:  0x0000000000000000
0x16bbbe530:  0x0000000000000000
```

```
0x16bbbe538:  0x0000000000000000
0x16bbbe540:  0x0000000000000000
0x16bbbe548:  0x0000000000000000
0x16bbbe550:  0x0000000000000000
0x16bbbe558:  0x0000000000000000
0x16bbbe560:  0x0000000000000000
0x16bbbe568:  0x0000000000000000
0x16bbbe570:  0x0000000000000000
0x16bbbe578:  0x0000000000000000
0x16bbbe580:  0x0000000000000000
0x16bbbe588:  0x0000000000000000
0x16bbbe590:  0x0000000000000000
0x16bbbe598:  0x0000000000000000
0x16bbbe5a0:  0x0000000000000000
0x16bbbe5a8:  0x0000000000000000
0x16bbbe5b0:  0x0000000000000000
0x16bbbe5b8:  0x0000000000000000
0x16bbbe5c0:  0x0000000000000000
0x16bbbe5c8:  0x0000000000000000
0x16bbbe5d0:  0x0000000000000000
0x16bbbe5d8:  0x0000000000000000
0x16bbbe5e0:  0x0000000000000000
0x16bbbe5e8:  0x0000000000000000
0x16bbbe5f0:  0x0000000000000000
0x16bbbe5f8:  0x0000000000000000
0x16bbbe600:  0x0000000000000000
0x16bbbe608:  0x0000000000000000
0x16bbbe610:  0x0000000000000000
0x16bbbe618:  0x0000000000000000
0x16bbbe620:  0x0000000000000000
0x16bbbe628:  0x0000000000000000
0x16bbbe630:  0x0000000000000000
0x16bbbe638:  0x0000000000000000
0x16bbbe640:  0x0000000000000000
0x16bbbe648:  0x0000000000000000
0x16bbbe650:  0x0000000000000000
0x16bbbe658:  0x0000000000000000
0x16bbbe660:  0x0000000000000000
0x16bbbe668:  0x0000000000000000
0x16bbbe670:  0x0000000000000000
0x16bbbe678:  0x0000000000000000
0x16bbbe680:  0x0000000000000000
0x16bbbe688:  0x0000000000000000
0x16bbbe690:  0x0000000000000000
0x16bbbe698:  0xc8ecebab51e8004e
0x16bbbe6a0:  0x0000000000000000
0x16bbbe6a8:  0x0000000000000000
0x16bbbe6b0:  0x000000016bbbe8e0
0x16bbbe6b8:  0x00000001042cbcd0 App6`procF + 80
0x16bbbe6c0:  0x0000000400000000
0x16bbbe6c8:  0x00000000ffffffff
0x16bbbe6d0:  0x0000000000000005
0x16bbbe6d8:  0x00000000ffffffff
0x16bbbe6e0:  0x0000000000000000
0x16bbbe6e8:  0x0000000000000000
0x16bbbe6f0:  0x0000000000000000
0x16bbbe6f8:  0x0000000000000000
0x16bbbe700:  0x0000000000000000
0x16bbbe708:  0x0000000000000000
0x16bbbe710:  0x0000000000000000
0x16bbbe718:  0x0000000000000000
```

```
0x16bbbe720:  0x0000000000000000
0x16bbbe728:  0x0000000000000000
0x16bbbe730:  0x0000000000000000
0x16bbbe738:  0x0000000000000000
0x16bbbe740:  0x0000000000000000
0x16bbbe748:  0x0000000000000000
0x16bbbe750:  0x0000000000000000
0x16bbbe758:  0x0000000000000000
0x16bbbe760:  0x0000000000000000
0x16bbbe768:  0x0000000000000000
0x16bbbe770:  0x0000000000000000
0x16bbbe778:  0x0000000000000000
0x16bbbe780:  0x0000000000000000
0x16bbbe788:  0x0000000000000000
0x16bbbe790:  0x0000000000000000
0x16bbbe798:  0x0000000000000000
0x16bbbe7a0:  0x0000000000000000
0x16bbbe7a8:  0x0000000000000000
0x16bbbe7b0:  0x0000000000000000
0x16bbbe7b8:  0x0000000000000000
0x16bbbe7c0:  0x0000000000000000
0x16bbbe7c8:  0x0000000000000000
0x16bbbe7d0:  0x0000000000000000
0x16bbbe7d8:  0x0000000000000000
0x16bbbe7e0:  0x0000000000000000
0x16bbbe7e8:  0x0000000000000000
0x16bbbe7f0:  0x0000000000000000
0x16bbbe7f8:  0x0000000000000000
0x16bbbe800:  0x0000000000000000
0x16bbbe808:  0x0000000000000000
0x16bbbe810:  0x0000000000000000
0x16bbbe818:  0x0000000000000000
0x16bbbe820:  0x0000000000000000
0x16bbbe828:  0x0000000000000000
0x16bbbe830:  0x0000000000000000
0x16bbbe838:  0x0000000000000000
0x16bbbe840:  0x0000000000000000
0x16bbbe848:  0x0000000000000000
0x16bbbe850:  0x0000000000000000
0x16bbbe858:  0x0000000000000000
0x16bbbe860:  0x0000000000000000
0x16bbbe868:  0x0000000000000000
0x16bbbe870:  0x0000000000000000
0x16bbbe878:  0x0000000000000000
0x16bbbe880:  0x0000000000000000
0x16bbbe888:  0x0000000000000000
0x16bbbe890:  0x0000000000000000
0x16bbbe898:  0x0000000000000000
0x16bbbe8a0:  0x0000000000000000
0x16bbbe8a8:  0x0000000000000000
0x16bbbe8b0:  0x0000000000000000
0x16bbbe8b8:  0x0000000000000000
0x16bbbe8c0:  0x0000000000000000
0x16bbbe8c8:  0xc8ecebab51e8004e
0x16bbbe8d0:  0x0000000000000000
0x16bbbe8d8:  0x0000000000000000
0x16bbbe8e0:  0x000000016bbbeb10
0x16bbbe8e8:  0x00000001042cbcd0 App6`procF + 80
0x16bbbe8f0:  0x0000000300000000
0x16bbbe8f8:  0x00000000ffffffff
0x16bbbe900:  0x0000000000000004
```

```
0x16bbbe908:  0x00000000ffffffff
0x16bbbe910:  0x0000000000000000
0x16bbbe918:  0x0000000000000000
0x16bbbe920:  0x0000000000000000
0x16bbbe928:  0x0000000000000000
0x16bbbe930:  0x0000000000000000
0x16bbbe938:  0x0000000000000000
0x16bbbe940:  0x0000000000000000
0x16bbbe948:  0x0000000000000000
0x16bbbe950:  0x0000000000000000
0x16bbbe958:  0x0000000000000000
0x16bbbe960:  0x0000000000000000
0x16bbbe968:  0x0000000000000000
0x16bbbe970:  0x0000000000000000
0x16bbbe978:  0x0000000000000000
0x16bbbe980:  0x0000000000000000
0x16bbbe988:  0x0000000000000000
0x16bbbe990:  0x0000000000000000
0x16bbbe998:  0x0000000000000000
0x16bbbe9a0:  0x0000000000000000
0x16bbbe9a8:  0x0000000000000000
0x16bbbe9b0:  0x0000000000000000
0x16bbbe9b8:  0x0000000000000000
0x16bbbe9c0:  0x0000000000000000
0x16bbbe9c8:  0x0000000000000000
0x16bbbe9d0:  0x0000000000000000
0x16bbbe9d8:  0x0000000000000000
0x16bbbe9e0:  0x0000000000000000
0x16bbbe9e8:  0x0000000000000000
0x16bbbe9f0:  0x0000000000000000
0x16bbbe9f8:  0x0000000000000000
0x16bbbea00:  0x0000000000000000
0x16bbbea08:  0x0000000000000000
0x16bbbea10:  0x0000000000000000
0x16bbbea18:  0x0000000000000000
0x16bbbea20:  0x0000000000000000
0x16bbbea28:  0x0000000000000000
0x16bbbea30:  0x0000000000000000
0x16bbbea38:  0x0000000000000000
0x16bbbea40:  0x0000000000000000
0x16bbbea48:  0x0000000000000000
0x16bbbea50:  0x0000000000000000
0x16bbbea58:  0x0000000000000000
0x16bbbea60:  0x0000000000000000
0x16bbbea68:  0x0000000000000000
0x16bbbea70:  0x0000000000000000
0x16bbbea78:  0x0000000000000000
0x16bbbea80:  0x0000000000000000
0x16bbbea88:  0x0000000000000000
0x16bbbea90:  0x0000000000000000
0x16bbbea98:  0x0000000000000000
0x16bbbeaa0:  0x0000000000000000
0x16bbbeaa8:  0x0000000000000000
0x16bbbeab0:  0x0000000000000000
0x16bbbeab8:  0x0000000000000000
0x16bbbeac0:  0x0000000000000000
0x16bbbeac8:  0x0000000000000000
0x16bbbead0:  0x0000000000000000
0x16bbbead8:  0x0000000000000000
0x16bbbeae0:  0x0000000000000000
0x16bbbeae8:  0x0000000000000000
```

```
0x16bbbeaf0: 0x0000000000000000
0x16bbbeaf8: 0xc8ecebab51e8004e
0x16bbbeb00: 0x0000000000000000
0x16bbbeb08: 0x0000000000000000
0x16bbbeb10: 0x000000016bbbed40
0x16bbbeb18: 0x00000001042cbcd0 App6`procF + 80
0x16bbbeb20: 0x0000000200000000
0x16bbbeb28: 0x00000000ffffffff
0x16bbbeb30: 0x0000000000000003
0x16bbbeb38: 0x00000000ffffffff
0x16bbbeb40: 0x0000000000000000
0x16bbbeb48: 0x0000000000000000
0x16bbbeb50: 0x0000000000000000
0x16bbbeb58: 0x0000000000000000
0x16bbbeb60: 0x0000000000000000
0x16bbbeb68: 0x0000000000000000
0x16bbbeb70: 0x0000000000000000
0x16bbbeb78: 0x0000000000000000
0x16bbbeb80: 0x0000000000000000
0x16bbbeb88: 0x0000000000000000
0x16bbbeb90: 0x0000000000000000
0x16bbbeb98: 0x0000000000000000
0x16bbbeba0: 0x0000000000000000
0x16bbbeba8: 0x0000000000000000
0x16bbbebb0: 0x0000000000000000
0x16bbbebb8: 0x0000000000000000
0x16bbbebc0: 0x0000000000000000
0x16bbbebc8: 0x0000000000000000
0x16bbbebd0: 0x0000000000000000
0x16bbbebd8: 0x0000000000000000
0x16bbbebe0: 0x0000000000000000
0x16bbbebe8: 0x0000000000000000
0x16bbbebf0: 0x0000000000000000
0x16bbbebf8: 0x0000000000000000
0x16bbbec00: 0x0000000000000000
0x16bbbec08: 0x0000000000000000
0x16bbbec10: 0x0000000000000000
0x16bbbec18: 0x0000000000000000
0x16bbbec20: 0x0000000000000000
0x16bbbec28: 0x0000000000000000
0x16bbbec30: 0x0000000000000000
0x16bbbec38: 0x0000000000000000
0x16bbbec40: 0x0000000000000000
0x16bbbec48: 0x0000000000000000
0x16bbbec50: 0x0000000000000000
0x16bbbec58: 0x0000000000000000
0x16bbbec60: 0x0000000000000000
0x16bbbec68: 0x0000000000000000
0x16bbbec70: 0x0000000000000000
0x16bbbec78: 0x0000000000000000
0x16bbbec80: 0x0000000000000000
0x16bbbec88: 0x0000000000000000
0x16bbbec90: 0x0000000000000000
0x16bbbec98: 0x0000000000000000
0x16bbbeca0: 0x0000000000000000
0x16bbbeca8: 0x0000000000000000
0x16bbbecb0: 0x0000000000000000
0x16bbbecb8: 0x0000000000000000
0x16bbbecc0: 0x0000000000000000
0x16bbbecc8: 0x0000000000000000
0x16bbbecd0: 0x0000000000000000
```

```
0x16bbbecd8:  0x0000000000000000
0x16bbbece0:  0x0000000000000000
0x16bbbece8:  0x0000000000000000
0x16bbbecf0:  0x0000000000000000
0x16bbbecf8:  0x0000000000000000
0x16bbbed00:  0x0000000000000000
0x16bbbed08:  0x0000000000000000
0x16bbbed10:  0x0000000000000000
0x16bbbed18:  0x0000000000000000
0x16bbbed20:  0x0000000000000000
0x16bbbed28:  0xc8ecebab51e8004e
0x16bbbed30:  0x0000000000000000
0x16bbbed38:  0x0000000000000000
0x16bbbed40:  0x000000016bbbef70
0x16bbbed48:  0x00000001042cbcd0 App6`procF + 80
0x16bbbed50:  0x0000000100000000
0x16bbbed58:  0x00000000ffffffff
0x16bbbed60:  0x0000000000000002
0x16bbbed68:  0x00000000ffffffff
0x16bbbed70:  0x0000000000000000
0x16bbbed78:  0x0000000000000000
0x16bbbed80:  0x0000000000000000
0x16bbbed88:  0x0000000000000000
0x16bbbed90:  0x0000000000000000
0x16bbbed98:  0x0000000000000000
0x16bbbeda0:  0x0000000000000000
0x16bbbeda8:  0x0000000000000000
0x16bbbedb0:  0x0000000000000000
0x16bbbedb8:  0x0000000000000000
0x16bbbedc0:  0x0000000000000000
0x16bbbedc8:  0x0000000000000000
0x16bbbedd0:  0x0000000000000000
0x16bbbedd8:  0x0000000000000000
0x16bbbede0:  0x0000000000000000
0x16bbbede8:  0x0000000000000000
0x16bbbedf0:  0x0000000000000000
0x16bbbedf8:  0x0000000000000000
0x16bbbee00:  0x0000000000000000
0x16bbbee08:  0x0000000000000000
0x16bbbee10:  0x0000000000000000
0x16bbbee18:  0x0000000000000000
0x16bbbee20:  0x0000000000000000
0x16bbbee28:  0x0000000000000000
0x16bbbee30:  0x0000000000000000
0x16bbbee38:  0x0000000000000000
0x16bbbee40:  0x0000000000000000
0x16bbbee48:  0x0000000000000000
0x16bbbee50:  0x0000000000000000
0x16bbbee58:  0x0000000000000000
0x16bbbee60:  0x0000000000000000
0x16bbbee68:  0x0000000000000000
0x16bbbee70:  0x0000000000000000
0x16bbbee78:  0x0000000000000000
0x16bbbee80:  0x0000000000000000
0x16bbbee88:  0x0000000000000000
0x16bbbee90:  0x0000000000000000
0x16bbbee98:  0x0000000000000000
0x16bbbeea0:  0x0000000000000000
0x16bbbeea8:  0x0000000000000000
0x16bbbeeb0:  0x0000000000000000
0x16bbbeeb8:  0x0000000000000000
```

```
0x16bbbeec0:  0x0000000000000000
0x16bbbeec8:  0x0000000000000000
0x16bbbeed0:  0x0000000000000000
0x16bbbeed8:  0x0000000000000000
0x16bbbeee0:  0x0000000000000000
0x16bbbeee8:  0x0000000000000000
0x16bbbeef0:  0x0000000000000000
0x16bbbeef8:  0x0000000000000000
0x16bbbef00:  0x0000000000000000
0x16bbbef08:  0x0000000000000000
0x16bbbef10:  0x0000000000000000
0x16bbbef18:  0x0000000000000000
0x16bbbef20:  0x0000000000000000
0x16bbbef28:  0x0000000000000000
0x16bbbef30:  0x0000000000000000
0x16bbbef38:  0x0000000000000000
0x16bbbef40:  0x0000000000000000
0x16bbbef48:  0x0000000000000000
0x16bbbef50:  0x0000000000000000
0x16bbbef58:  0xc8ecebab51e8004e
0x16bbbef60:  0x0000000000000000
0x16bbbef68:  0x0000000000000000
0x16bbbef70:  0x000000016bbbef80
0x16bbbef78:  0x00000001042cbd10 App6`procE + 16
0x16bbbef80:  0x000000016bbbef90
0x16bbbef88:  0x00000001042cbd2c App6`bar_one + 20
0x16bbbef90:  0x000000016bbbefa0
0x16bbbef98:  0x00000001042cbd40 App6`foo_one + 12
0x16bbbefa0:  0x000000016bbbefc0
0x16bbbefa8:  0x00000001042cbd5c App6`thread_one + 20
0x16bbbefb0:  0x0000000000000000
0x16bbbefb8:  0x0000000000000000
0x16bbbefc0:  0x000000016bbbefe0
0x16bbbefc8:  0x000000018ea0826c libsystem_pthread.dylib`_pthread_start + 148
0x16bbbefd0:  0x0000000000000000
0x16bbbefd8:  0x0000000000000000
0x16bbbefe0:  0x0000000000000000
0x16bbbefe8:  0x0c7b80018ea0308c (0x000000018ea0308c) libsystem_pthread.dylib`thread_start + 8
0x16bbbeff0:  0x0000000000000000
0x16bbbeff8:  0x0000000000000000
0x16bbbf000:  0xd7a4cdcfe4493f6f
0x16bbbf008:  0x0000000000000000
0x16bbbf010:  0x000000016bc4b000
0x16bbbf018:  0x0000000104734590 dyld`_main_thread + 16
0x16bbbf020:  0x0000000000000000
0x16bbbf028:  0x0000000000000000
0x16bbbf030:  0x0000000000000101
0x16bbbf038:  0x0000000a0000001f
0x16bbbf040:  0x0000000000000000
0x16bbbf048:  0x0001000000000000
0x16bbbf050:  0x0000000000000000
0x16bbbf058:  0x0000000000000000
0x16bbbf060:  0x0000000000000000
0x16bbbf068:  0x0000000000000000
0x16bbbf070:  0x0000000000000000
0x16bbbf078:  0x0000000000000000
0x16bbbf080:  0x0000000000000000
0x16bbbf088:  0x0000000000000000
0x16bbbf090:  0x00000001042cbd48 App6`thread_one
0x16bbbf098:  0x0000000000000000
0x16bbbf0a0:  0x0003000000000000
```

```
0x16bbbf0a8:  0x0000003c00000000
0x16bbbf0b0:  0x000000016bbbf000
0x16bbbf0b8:  0x000000016bb3c000
0x16bbbf0c0:  0x000000016bb38000
0x16bbbf0c8:  0x000000000008c000
0x16bbbf0d0:  0x0000000000004000
0x16bbbf0d8:  0x000000000023933f
0x16bbbf0e0:  0x000000016bbbf000
0x16bbbf0e8:  0x000000016bbbf0ac
0x16bbbf0f0:  0x0000000000001103
0x16bbbf0f8:  0x0000000000001203
0x16bbbf100:  0x00000000000008ff
0x16bbbf108:  0x0000000000000000
0x16bbbf110:  0x0000000000000000
0x16bbbf118:  0xd7a4cdce8ff2cf6f
0x16bbbf120:  0x0000000000000000
0x16bbbf128:  0x0000000000000000
0x16bbbf130:  0x0000000000000000
0x16bbbf138:  0x0000000000000000
0x16bbbf140:  0x0000000000000000
0x16bbbf148:  0x0000000000000000
0x16bbbf150:  0x0000000000000000
0x16bbbf158:  0x0000000000000000
0x16bbbf160:  0x0000000000000000
0x16bbbf168:  0x0000000000000000
0x16bbbf170:  0x0000000000000000
0x16bbbf178:  0x0000000000000000
0x16bbbf180:  0x0000000000000000
0x16bbbf188:  0x0000000000000000
0x16bbbf190:  0x0000000000000000
0x16bbbf198:  0x0000000000000000
0x16bbbf1a0:  0x0000000000000000
0x16bbbf1a8:  0x0000000000000000
0x16bbbf1b0:  0x0000000000000000
0x16bbbf1b8:  0x0000000000000000
0x16bbbf1c0:  0x0000000000000000
0x16bbbf1c8:  0x0000000000000000
0x16bbbf1d0:  0x0000000000000000
0x16bbbf1d8:  0x0000000000000000
0x16bbbf1e0:  0x0000000000000000
0x16bbbf1e8:  0x0000000000000000
0x16bbbf1f0:  0x0000000000000000
0x16bbbf1f8:  0x0000000000000000
0x16bbbf200:  0x0000000000000000
0x16bbbf208:  0x0000000000000000
0x16bbbf210:  0x0000000000000000
0x16bbbf218:  0x0000000000000000
0x16bbbf220:  0x0000000000000000
0x16bbbf228:  0x0000000000000000
0x16bbbf230:  0x0000000000000000
0x16bbbf238:  0x0000000000000000
0x16bbbf240:  0x0000000000000000
0x16bbbf248:  0x0000000000000000
0x16bbbf250:  0x0000000000000000
0x16bbbf258:  0x0000000000000000
0x16bbbf260:  0x0000000000000000
0x16bbbf268:  0x0000000000000000
0x16bbbf270:  0x0000000000000000
0x16bbbf278:  0x0000000000000000
0x16bbbf280:  0x0000000000000000
0x16bbbf288:  0x0000000000000000
```

```
0x16bbbf290:  0x0000000000000000
0x16bbbf298:  0x0000000000000000
0x16bbbf2a0:  0x0000000000000000
0x16bbbf2a8:  0x0000000000000000
0x16bbbf2b0:  0x0000000000000000
0x16bbbf2b8:  0x0000000000000000
0x16bbbf2c0:  0x0000000000000000
0x16bbbf2c8:  0x0000000000000000
0x16bbbf2d0:  0x0000000000000000
0x16bbbf2d8:  0x0000000000000000
0x16bbbf2e0:  0x0000000000000000
0x16bbbf2e8:  0x0000000000000000
0x16bbbf2f0:  0x0000000000000000
0x16bbbf2f8:  0x0000000000000000
0x16bbbf300:  0x0000000000000000
0x16bbbf308:  0x0000000000000000
0x16bbbf310:  0x0000000000000000
0x16bbbf318:  0x0000000000000000
0x16bbbf320:  0x0000000000000000
0x16bbbf328:  0x0000000000000000
0x16bbbf330:  0x0000000000000000
0x16bbbf338:  0x0000000000000000
0x16bbbf340:  0x0000000000000000
0x16bbbf348:  0x0000000000000000
0x16bbbf350:  0x0000000000000000
0x16bbbf358:  0x0000000000000000
0x16bbbf360:  0x0000000000000000
0x16bbbf368:  0x0000000000000000
0x16bbbf370:  0x0000000000000000
0x16bbbf378:  0x0000000000000000
0x16bbbf380:  0x0000000000000000
0x16bbbf388:  0x0000000000000000
0x16bbbf390:  0x0000000000000000
0x16bbbf398:  0x0000000000000000
0x16bbbf3a0:  0x0000000000000000
0x16bbbf3a8:  0x0000000000000000
0x16bbbf3b0:  0x0000000000000000
0x16bbbf3b8:  0x0000000000000000
0x16bbbf3c0:  0x0000000000000000
0x16bbbf3c8:  0x0000000000000000
0x16bbbf3d0:  0x0000000000000000
0x16bbbf3d8:  0x0000000000000000
0x16bbbf3e0:  0x0000000000000000
0x16bbbf3e8:  0x0000000000000000
0x16bbbf3f0:  0x0000000000000000
0x16bbbf3f8:  0x0000000000000000
0x16bbbf400:  0x0000000000000000
0x16bbbf408:  0x0000000000000000
0x16bbbf410:  0x0000000000000000
0x16bbbf418:  0x0000000000000000
0x16bbbf420:  0x0000000000000000
0x16bbbf428:  0x0000000000000000
0x16bbbf430:  0x0000000000000000
0x16bbbf438:  0x0000000000000000
0x16bbbf440:  0x0000000000000000
0x16bbbf448:  0x0000000000000000
0x16bbbf450:  0x0000000000000000
0x16bbbf458:  0x0000000000000000
0x16bbbf460:  0x0000000000000000
0x16bbbf468:  0x0000000000000000
0x16bbbf470:  0x0000000000000000
```

```
0x16bbbf478:  0x0000000000000000
0x16bbbf480:  0x0000000000000000
0x16bbbf488:  0x0000000000000000
0x16bbbf490:  0x0000000000000000
0x16bbbf498:  0x0000000000000000
0x16bbbf4a0:  0x0000000000000000
0x16bbbf4a8:  0x0000000000000000
0x16bbbf4b0:  0x0000000000000000
0x16bbbf4b8:  0x0000000000000000
0x16bbbf4c0:  0x0000000000000000
0x16bbbf4c8:  0x0000000000000000
0x16bbbf4d0:  0x0000000000000000
0x16bbbf4d8:  0x0000000000000000
0x16bbbf4e0:  0x0000000000000000
0x16bbbf4e8:  0x0000000000000000
0x16bbbf4f0:  0x0000000000000000
0x16bbbf4f8:  0x0000000000000000
0x16bbbf500:  0x0000000000000000
0x16bbbf508:  0x0000000000000000
0x16bbbf510:  0x0000000000000000
0x16bbbf518:  0x0000000000000000
0x16bbbf520:  0x0000000000000000
0x16bbbf528:  0x0000000000000000
0x16bbbf530:  0x0000000000000000
0x16bbbf538:  0x0000000000000000
0x16bbbf540:  0x0000000000000000
0x16bbbf548:  0x0000000000000000
0x16bbbf550:  0x0000000000000000
0x16bbbf558:  0x0000000000000000
0x16bbbf560:  0x0000000000000000
0x16bbbf568:  0x0000000000000000
0x16bbbf570:  0x0000000000000000
0x16bbbf578:  0x0000000000000000
0x16bbbf580:  0x0000000000000000
0x16bbbf588:  0x0000000000000000
0x16bbbf590:  0x0000000000000000
0x16bbbf598:  0x0000000000000000
0x16bbbf5a0:  0x0000000000000000
0x16bbbf5a8:  0x0000000000000000
0x16bbbf5b0:  0x0000000000000000
0x16bbbf5b8:  0x0000000000000000
0x16bbbf5c0:  0x0000000000000000
0x16bbbf5c8:  0x0000000000000000
0x16bbbf5d0:  0x0000000000000000
0x16bbbf5d8:  0x0000000000000000
0x16bbbf5e0:  0x0000000000000000
0x16bbbf5e8:  0x0000000000000000
0x16bbbf5f0:  0x0000000000000000
0x16bbbf5f8:  0x0000000000000000
0x16bbbf600:  0x0000000000000000
0x16bbbf608:  0x0000000000000000
0x16bbbf610:  0x0000000000000000
0x16bbbf618:  0x0000000000000000
0x16bbbf620:  0x0000000000000000
0x16bbbf628:  0x0000000000000000
0x16bbbf630:  0x0000000000000000
0x16bbbf638:  0x0000000000000000
0x16bbbf640:  0x0000000000000000
0x16bbbf648:  0x0000000000000000
0x16bbbf650:  0x0000000000000000
0x16bbbf658:  0x0000000000000000
```

```
0x16bbbf660:  0x0000000000000000
0x16bbbf668:  0x0000000000000000
0x16bbbf670:  0x0000000000000000
0x16bbbf678:  0x0000000000000000
0x16bbbf680:  0x0000000000000000
0x16bbbf688:  0x0000000000000000
0x16bbbf690:  0x0000000000000000
0x16bbbf698:  0x0000000000000000
0x16bbbf6a0:  0x0000000000000000
0x16bbbf6a8:  0x0000000000000000
0x16bbbf6b0:  0x0000000000000000
0x16bbbf6b8:  0x0000000000000000
0x16bbbf6c0:  0x0000000000000000
0x16bbbf6c8:  0x0000000000000000
0x16bbbf6d0:  0x0000000000000000
0x16bbbf6d8:  0x0000000000000000
0x16bbbf6e0:  0x0000000000000000
0x16bbbf6e8:  0x0000000000000000
0x16bbbf6f0:  0x0000000000000000
0x16bbbf6f8:  0x0000000000000000
0x16bbbf700:  0x0000000000000000
0x16bbbf708:  0x0000000000000000
0x16bbbf710:  0x0000000000000000
0x16bbbf718:  0x0000000000000000
0x16bbbf720:  0x0000000000000000
0x16bbbf728:  0x0000000000000000
0x16bbbf730:  0x0000000000000000
0x16bbbf738:  0x0000000000000000
0x16bbbf740:  0x0000000000000000
0x16bbbf748:  0x0000000000000000
0x16bbbf750:  0x0000000000000000
0x16bbbf758:  0x0000000000000000
0x16bbbf760:  0x0000000000000000
0x16bbbf768:  0x0000000000000000
0x16bbbf770:  0x0000000000000000
0x16bbbf778:  0x0000000000000000
0x16bbbf780:  0x0000000000000000
0x16bbbf788:  0x0000000000000000
0x16bbbf790:  0x0000000000000000
0x16bbbf798:  0x0000000000000000
0x16bbbf7a0:  0x0000000000000000
0x16bbbf7a8:  0x0000000000000000
0x16bbbf7b0:  0x0000000000000000
0x16bbbf7b8:  0x0000000000000000
0x16bbbf7c0:  0x0000000000000000
0x16bbbf7c8:  0x0000000000000000
0x16bbbf7d0:  0x0000000000000000
0x16bbbf7d8:  0x0000000000000000
0x16bbbf7e0:  0x0000000000000000
0x16bbbf7e8:  0x0000000000000000
0x16bbbf7f0:  0x0000000000000000
0x16bbbf7f8:  0x0000000000000000
0x16bbbf800:  0x0000000000000000
0x16bbbf808:  0x0000000000000000
0x16bbbf810:  0x0000000000000000
0x16bbbf818:  0x0000000000000000
0x16bbbf820:  0x0000000000000000
0x16bbbf828:  0x0000000000000000
0x16bbbf830:  0x0000000000000000
0x16bbbf838:  0x0000000000000000
0x16bbbf840:  0x0000000000000000
```

```
0x16bbbf848:  0x0000000000000000
0x16bbbf850:  0x0000000000000000
0x16bbbf858:  0x0000000000000000
0x16bbbf860:  0x0000000000000000
0x16bbbf868:  0x0000000000000000
0x16bbbf870:  0x0000000000000000
0x16bbbf878:  0x0000000000000000
0x16bbbf880:  0x0000000000000000
0x16bbbf888:  0x0000000000000000
0x16bbbf890:  0x0000000000000000
0x16bbbf898:  0x0000000000000000
0x16bbbf8a0:  0x0000000000000000
0x16bbbf8a8:  0x0000000000000000
0x16bbbf8b0:  0x0000000000000000
0x16bbbf8b8:  0x0000000000000000
0x16bbbf8c0:  0x0000000000000000
0x16bbbf8c8:  0x0000000000000000
0x16bbbf8d0:  0x0000000000000000
0x16bbbf8d8:  0x0000000000000000
0x16bbbf8e0:  0x0000000000000000
0x16bbbf8e8:  0x0000000000000000
0x16bbbf8f0:  0x0000000000000000
0x16bbbf8f8:  0x0000000000000000
0x16bbbf900:  0x0000000000000000
0x16bbbf908:  0x0000000000000000
0x16bbbf910:  0x0000000000000000
0x16bbbf918:  0x0000000000000000
0x16bbbf920:  0x0000000000000000
0x16bbbf928:  0x0000000000000000
0x16bbbf930:  0x0000000000000000
0x16bbbf938:  0x0000000000000000
0x16bbbf940:  0x0000000000000000
0x16bbbf948:  0x0000000000000000
0x16bbbf950:  0x0000000000000000
0x16bbbf958:  0x0000000000000000
0x16bbbf960:  0x0000000000000000
0x16bbbf968:  0x0000000000000000
0x16bbbf970:  0x0000000000000000
0x16bbbf978:  0x0000000000000000
0x16bbbf980:  0x0000000000000000
0x16bbbf988:  0x0000000000000000
0x16bbbf990:  0x0000000000000000
0x16bbbf998:  0x0000000000000000
0x16bbbf9a0:  0x0000000000000000
0x16bbbf9a8:  0x0000000000000000
0x16bbbf9b0:  0x0000000000000000
0x16bbbf9b8:  0x0000000000000000
0x16bbbf9c0:  0x0000000000000000
0x16bbbf9c8:  0x0000000000000000
0x16bbbf9d0:  0x0000000000000000
0x16bbbf9d8:  0x0000000000000000
0x16bbbf9e0:  0x0000000000000000
0x16bbbf9e8:  0x0000000000000000
0x16bbbf9f0:  0x0000000000000000
0x16bbbf9f8:  0x0000000000000000
0x16bbbfa00:  0x0000000000000000
0x16bbbfa08:  0x0000000000000000
0x16bbbfa10:  0x0000000000000000
0x16bbbfa18:  0x0000000000000000
0x16bbbfa20:  0x0000000000000000
0x16bbbfa28:  0x0000000000000000
```

```
0x16bbbfa30:  0x0000000000000000
0x16bbbfa38:  0x0000000000000000
0x16bbbfa40:  0x0000000000000000
0x16bbbfa48:  0x0000000000000000
0x16bbbfa50:  0x0000000000000000
0x16bbbfa58:  0x0000000000000000
0x16bbbfa60:  0x0000000000000000
0x16bbbfa68:  0x0000000000000000
0x16bbbfa70:  0x0000000000000000
0x16bbbfa78:  0x0000000000000000
0x16bbbfa80:  0x0000000000000000
0x16bbbfa88:  0x0000000000000000
0x16bbbfa90:  0x0000000000000000
0x16bbbfa98:  0x0000000000000000
0x16bbbfaa0:  0x0000000000000000
0x16bbbfaa8:  0x0000000000000000
0x16bbbfab0:  0x0000000000000000
0x16bbbfab8:  0x0000000000000000
0x16bbbfac0:  0x0000000000000000
0x16bbbfac8:  0x0000000000000000
0x16bbbfad0:  0x0000000000000000
0x16bbbfad8:  0x0000000000000000
0x16bbbfae0:  0x0000000000000000
0x16bbbfae8:  0x0000000000000000
0x16bbbfaf0:  0x0000000000000000
0x16bbbfaf8:  0x0000000000000000
0x16bbbfb00:  0x0000000000000000
0x16bbbfb08:  0x0000000000000000
0x16bbbfb10:  0x0000000000000000
0x16bbbfb18:  0x0000000000000000
0x16bbbfb20:  0x0000000000000000
0x16bbbfb28:  0x0000000000000000
0x16bbbfb30:  0x0000000000000000
0x16bbbfb38:  0x0000000000000000
0x16bbbfb40:  0x0000000000000000
0x16bbbfb48:  0x0000000000000000
0x16bbbfb50:  0x0000000000000000
0x16bbbfb58:  0x0000000000000000
0x16bbbfb60:  0x0000000000000000
0x16bbbfb68:  0x0000000000000000
0x16bbbfb70:  0x0000000000000000
0x16bbbfb78:  0x0000000000000000
0x16bbbfb80:  0x0000000000000000
0x16bbbfb88:  0x0000000000000000
0x16bbbfb90:  0x0000000000000000
0x16bbbfb98:  0x0000000000000000
0x16bbbfba0:  0x0000000000000000
0x16bbbfba8:  0x0000000000000000
0x16bbbfbb0:  0x0000000000000000
0x16bbbfbb8:  0x0000000000000000
0x16bbbfbc0:  0x0000000000000000
0x16bbbfbc8:  0x0000000000000000
0x16bbbfbd0:  0x0000000000000000
0x16bbbfbd8:  0x0000000000000000
0x16bbbfbe0:  0x0000000000000000
0x16bbbfbe8:  0x0000000000000000
0x16bbbfbf0:  0x0000000000000000
0x16bbbfbf8:  0x0000000000000000
0x16bbbfc00:  0x0000000000000000
0x16bbbfc08:  0x0000000000000000
0x16bbbfc10:  0x0000000000000000
```

```
0x16bbbfc18:  0x0000000000000000
0x16bbbfc20:  0x0000000000000000
0x16bbbfc28:  0x0000000000000000
0x16bbbfc30:  0x0000000000000000
0x16bbbfc38:  0x0000000000000000
0x16bbbfc40:  0x0000000000000000
0x16bbbfc48:  0x0000000000000000
0x16bbbfc50:  0x0000000000000000
0x16bbbfc58:  0x0000000000000000
0x16bbbfc60:  0x0000000000000000
0x16bbbfc68:  0x0000000000000000
0x16bbbfc70:  0x0000000000000000
0x16bbbfc78:  0x0000000000000000
0x16bbbfc80:  0x0000000000000000
0x16bbbfc88:  0x0000000000000000
0x16bbbfc90:  0x0000000000000000
0x16bbbfc98:  0x0000000000000000
0x16bbbfca0:  0x0000000000000000
0x16bbbfca8:  0x0000000000000000
0x16bbbfcb0:  0x0000000000000000
0x16bbbfcb8:  0x0000000000000000
0x16bbbfcc0:  0x0000000000000000
0x16bbbfcc8:  0x0000000000000000
0x16bbbfcd0:  0x0000000000000000
0x16bbbfcd8:  0x0000000000000000
0x16bbbfce0:  0x0000000000000000
0x16bbbfce8:  0x0000000000000000
0x16bbbfcf0:  0x0000000000000000
0x16bbbfcf8:  0x0000000000000000
0x16bbbfd00:  0x0000000000000000
0x16bbbfd08:  0x0000000000000000
0x16bbbfd10:  0x0000000000000000
0x16bbbfd18:  0x0000000000000000
0x16bbbfd20:  0x0000000000000000
0x16bbbfd28:  0x0000000000000000
0x16bbbfd30:  0x0000000000000000
0x16bbbfd38:  0x0000000000000000
0x16bbbfd40:  0x0000000000000000
0x16bbbfd48:  0x0000000000000000
0x16bbbfd50:  0x0000000000000000
0x16bbbfd58:  0x0000000000000000
0x16bbbfd60:  0x0000000000000000
0x16bbbfd68:  0x0000000000000000
0x16bbbfd70:  0x0000000000000000
0x16bbbfd78:  0x0000000000000000
0x16bbbfd80:  0x0000000000000000
0x16bbbfd88:  0x0000000000000000
0x16bbbfd90:  0x0000000000000000
0x16bbbfd98:  0x0000000000000000
0x16bbbfda0:  0x0000000000000000
0x16bbbfda8:  0x0000000000000000
0x16bbbfdb0:  0x0000000000000000
0x16bbbfdb8:  0x0000000000000000
0x16bbbfdc0:  0x0000000000000000
0x16bbbfdc8:  0x0000000000000000
0x16bbbfdd0:  0x0000000000000000
0x16bbbfdd8:  0x0000000000000000
0x16bbbfde0:  0x0000000000000000
0x16bbbfde8:  0x0000000000000000
0x16bbbfdf0:  0x0000000000000000
0x16bbbfdf8:  0x0000000000000000
```

```
0x16bbbfe00:  0x0000000000000000
0x16bbbfe08:  0x0000000000000000
0x16bbbfe10:  0x0000000000000000
0x16bbbfe18:  0x0000000000000000
0x16bbbfe20:  0x0000000000000000
0x16bbbfe28:  0x0000000000000000
0x16bbbfe30:  0x0000000000000000
0x16bbbfe38:  0x0000000000000000
0x16bbbfe40:  0x0000000000000000
0x16bbbfe48:  0x0000000000000000
0x16bbbfe50:  0x0000000000000000
0x16bbbfe58:  0x0000000000000000
0x16bbbfe60:  0x0000000000000000
0x16bbbfe68:  0x0000000000000000
0x16bbbfe70:  0x0000000000000000
0x16bbbfe78:  0x0000000000000000
0x16bbbfe80:  0x0000000000000000
0x16bbbfe88:  0x0000000000000000
0x16bbbfe90:  0x0000000000000000
0x16bbbfe98:  0x0000000000000000
0x16bbbfea0:  0x0000000000000000
0x16bbbfea8:  0x0000000000000000
0x16bbbfeb0:  0x0000000000000000
0x16bbbfeb8:  0x0000000000000000
0x16bbbfec0:  0x0000000000000000
0x16bbbfec8:  0x0000000000000000
0x16bbbfed0:  0x0000000000000000
0x16bbbfed8:  0x0000000000000000
0x16bbbfee0:  0x0000000000000000
0x16bbbfee8:  0x0000000000000000
0x16bbbfef0:  0x0000000000000000
0x16bbbfef8:  0x0000000000000000
0x16bbbff00:  0x0000000000000000
0x16bbbff08:  0x0000000000000000
0x16bbbff10:  0x0000000000000000
0x16bbbff18:  0x0000000000000000
0x16bbbff20:  0x0000000000000000
0x16bbbff28:  0x0000000000000000
0x16bbbff30:  0x0000000000000000
0x16bbbff38:  0x0000000000000000
0x16bbbff40:  0x0000000000000000
0x16bbbff48:  0x0000000000000000
0x16bbbff50:  0x0000000000000000
0x16bbbff58:  0x0000000000000000
0x16bbbff60:  0x0000000000000000
0x16bbbff68:  0x0000000000000000
0x16bbbff70:  0x0000000000000000
0x16bbbff78:  0x0000000000000000
0x16bbbff80:  0x0000000000000000
0x16bbbff88:  0x0000000000000000
0x16bbbff90:  0x0000000000000000
0x16bbbff98:  0x0000000000000000
0x16bbbffa0:  0x0000000000000000
0x16bbbffa8:  0x0000000000000000
0x16bbbffb0:  0x0000000000000000
0x16bbbffb8:  0x0000000000000000
0x16bbbffc0:  0x0000000000000000
0x16bbbffc8:  0x0000000000000000
0x16bbbffd0:  0x0000000000000000
0x16bbbffd8:  0x0000000000000000
0x16bbbffe0:  0x0000000000000000
```

```
0x16bbbffe8: 0x0000000000000000
0x16bbbfff0: 0x0000000000000000
0x16bbbfff8: 0x0000000000000000
```

Note: We see that the reconstruction of the stack trace is possible because of the standard function prolog and epilog:

```
[...]
0x16bbbef60: 0x0000000000000000
0x16bbbef68: 0x0000000000000000
0x16bbbef70: 0x000000016bbbef80
0x16bbbef78: 0x00000001042cbd10 App6`procE + 16
0x16bbbef80: 0x000000016bbbef90
0x16bbbef88: 0x00000001042cbd2c App6`bar_one + 20
0x16bbbef90: 0x000000016bbbefa0
0x16bbbef98: 0x00000001042cbd40 App6`foo_one + 12
0x16bbbefa0: 0x000000016bbbefc0
0x16bbbefa8: 0x00000001042cbd5c App6`thread_one + 20
0x16bbbefb0: 0x0000000000000000
0x16bbbefb8: 0x0000000000000000
0x16bbbefc0: 0x000000016bbbefe0
0x16bbbefc8: 0x000000018ea0826c libsystem_pthread.dylib`_pthread_start + 148
0x16bbbefd0: 0x0000000000000000
0x16bbbefd8: 0x0000000000000000
0x16bbbefe0: 0x0000000000000000
0x16bbbefe8: 0x0c7b80018ea0308c (0x000000018ea0308c) libsystem_pthread.dylib`thread_start + 8
0x16bbbeff0: 0x0000000000000000
0x16bbbeff8: 0x0000000000000000
[...]
```

```
(lldb) di -n procF
App6`procF:
    0x1042cbc80 <+0>:    stp     x28, x27, [sp, #-0x20]!
    0x1042cbc84 <+4>:    stp     x29, x30, [sp, #0x10]
    0x1042cbc88 <+8>:    add     x29, sp, #0x10
    0x1042cbc8c <+12>:   sub     sp, sp, #0x210
    0x1042cbc90 <+16>:   adrp    x8, 1
    0x1042cbc94 <+20>:   ldr     x8, [x8, #0x8]
    0x1042cbc98 <+24>:   ldr     x8, [x8]
    0x1042cbc9c <+28>:   stur    x8, [x29, #-0x18]
->  0x1042cbca0 <+32>:   str     w0, [sp, #0x4]
    0x1042cbca4 <+36>:   add     x0, sp, #0x8
    0x1042cbca8 <+40>:   mov     x1, #0x200
    0x1042cbcac <+44>:   bl      0x1042cbf8c                ; symbol stub for: bzero
    0x1042cbcb0 <+48>:   mov     w8, #-0x1
    0x1042cbcb4 <+52>:   str     w8, [sp, #0x8]
    0x1042cbcb8 <+56>:   ldr     w9, [sp, #0x4]
    0x1042cbcbc <+60>:   add     w9, w9, #0x1
    0x1042cbcc0 <+64>:   str     w9, [sp, #0x10]
    0x1042cbcc4 <+68>:   str     w8, [sp, #0x18]
    0x1042cbcc8 <+72>:   ldr     w0, [sp, #0x10]
    0x1042cbccc <+76>:   bl      0x1042cbc80                ; <+0>
    0x1042cbcd0 <+80>:   ldur    x9, [x29, #-0x18]
    0x1042cbcd4 <+84>:   adrp    x8, 1
    0x1042cbcd8 <+88>:   ldr     x8, [x8, #0x8]
    0x1042cbcdc <+92>:   ldr     x8, [x8]
    0x1042cbce0 <+96>:   subs    x8, x8, x9
    0x1042cbce4 <+100>:  b.eq    0x1042cbcf0                ; <+112>
    0x1042cbce8 <+104>:  b       0x1042cbcec                ; <+108>
    0x1042cbcec <+108>:  bl      0x1042cbf80                ; symbol stub for: __stack_chk_fail
```

```
0x1042cbcf0 <+112>: add     sp, sp, #0x210
0x1042cbcf4 <+116>: ldp     x29, x30, [sp, #0x10]
0x1042cbcf8 <+120>: ldp     x28, x27, [sp], #0x20
0x1042cbcfc <+124>: ret
```

Exercise X7

- ◎ **Goal:** Learn how to identify active threads

- ◎ **Patterns:** Missing Thread; Active Thread; Near Exception

- ◎ \AMCDA-Dumps\Exercise-X7.pdf

Exercise X7

Goal: Learn how to identify active threads.

Patterns: Missing Thread; Active Thread; Near Exception.

1.   Identify the problem thread and application-specific diagnostic from the diagnostic report *App7-2022-12-07-183013.ips* (including non-waiting threads):

```
-------------------------------------
Translated Report (Full Report Below)
-------------------------------------

Process:             App7 [88726]
Path:                /Users/USER/*/App7
Identifier:          App7
Version:             ???
Code Type:           ARM-64 (Native)
Parent Process:      zsh [93565]
Responsible:         Terminal [9503]
User ID:             501

Date/Time:           2022-12-07 18:30:13.2920 +0000
OS Version:          macOS 12.6 (21G115)
Report Version:      12
Anonymous UUID:      6F758133-2B79-4743-8B70-8B1D8C510718

Sleep/Wake UUID:     A8996D95-6E2E-45B4-B8A2-A1D3FA12B8EF

Time Awake Since Boot: 200000 seconds
Time Since Wake:       544 seconds

System Integrity Protection: enabled

Crashed Thread:      1

Exception Type:      EXC_CRASH (SIGABRT)
Exception Codes:     0x0000000000000000, 0x0000000000000000
Exception Note:      EXC_CORPSE_NOTIFY

Application Specific Information:
stack buffer overflow


Thread 0::  Dispatch queue: com.apple.main-thread
0   libsystem_kernel.dylib              0x18e9ce06c __semwait_signal + 8
1   libsystem_c.dylib                   0x18e8d6fc8 nanosleep + 220
2   libsystem_c.dylib                   0x18e8e1b78 sleep + 52
3   libsystem_c.dylib                   0x18e8e1b90 sleep + 76
4   App7                                0x100ffbedc main + 164
5   dyld                                0x1013ad08c start + 520

Thread 1 Crashed:
0   libsystem_kernel.dylib              0x18e9d2d98 __pthread_kill + 8
1   libsystem_pthread.dylib             0x18ea07ee0 pthread_kill + 288
2   libsystem_c.dylib                   0x18e9423cc __abort + 128
3   libsystem_c.dylib                   0x18e933d48 __stack_chk_fail + 96
4   App7                                0x100ffbc80 procA + 92

Thread 2:
0   libsystem_kernel.dylib              0x18e9ce06c __semwait_signal + 8
1   libsystem_c.dylib                   0x18e8d6fc8 nanosleep + 220
2   libsystem_c.dylib                   0x18e8e1b78 sleep + 52
3   libsystem_c.dylib                   0x18e8e1b90 sleep + 76
4   App7                                0x100ffbcf8 bar_two + 24
5   App7                                0x100ffbd0c foo_two + 12
6   App7                                0x100ffbd28 thread_two + 20
7   libsystem_pthread.dylib             0x18ea0826c _pthread_start + 148
8   libsystem_pthread.dylib             0x18ea0308c thread_start + 8
```

```
Thread 3:
0    libsystem_kernel.dylib              0x18e9ce06c __semwait_signal + 8
1    libsystem_c.dylib                   0x18e8d6fc8 nanosleep + 220
2    libsystem_c.dylib                   0x18e8e1b78 sleep + 52
3    libsystem_c.dylib                   0x18e8e1b90 sleep + 76
4    App7                                0x100ffbda4 bar_four + 24
5    App7                                0x100ffbdb8 foo_four + 12
6    App7                                0x100ffbdd4 thread_four + 20
7    libsystem_pthread.dylib             0x18ea0826c _pthread_start + 148
8    libsystem_pthread.dylib             0x18ea0308c thread_start + 8

Thread 4:
0    App7                                0x100ffbaf0 procF + 52
1    App7                                0x100ffbad8 procF + 28
2    App7                                0x100ffbb20 procF + 100
3    App7                                0x100ffbb20 procF + 100
4    App7                                0x100ffbb20 procF + 100
5    App7                                0x100ffbb20 procF + 100
6    App7                                0x100ffbb20 procF + 100
7    App7                                0x100ffbb20 procF + 100
8    App7                                0x100ffbb20 procF + 100
9    App7                                0x100ffbb20 procF + 100
10   App7                                0x100ffbb20 procF + 100
11   App7                                0x100ffbb20 procF + 100
12   App7                                0x100ffbb20 procF + 100
13   App7                                0x100ffbb20 procF + 100
14   App7                                0x100ffbb20 procF + 100
15   App7                                0x100ffbb20 procF + 100
16   App7                                0x100ffbb20 procF + 100
17   App7                                0x100ffbb20 procF + 100
18   App7                                0x100ffbb20 procF + 100
19   App7                                0x100ffbb20 procF + 100
20   App7                                0x100ffbb20 procF + 100
21   App7                                0x100ffbb20 procF + 100
22   App7                                0x100ffbb20 procF + 100
23   App7                                0x100ffbb20 procF + 100
24   App7                                0x100ffbb20 procF + 100
25   App7                                0x100ffbb20 procF + 100
26   App7                                0x100ffbb20 procF + 100
27   App7                                0x100ffbb20 procF + 100
28   App7                                0x100ffbb20 procF + 100
29   App7                                0x100ffbb20 procF + 100
30   App7                                0x100ffbb20 procF + 100
31   App7                                0x100ffbb20 procF + 100
32   App7                                0x100ffbb20 procF + 100
33   App7                                0x100ffbb20 procF + 100
34   App7                                0x100ffbb20 procF + 100
35   App7                                0x100ffbb20 procF + 100
36   App7                                0x100ffbb20 procF + 100
37   App7                                0x100ffbb20 procF + 100
38   App7                                0x100ffbb20 procF + 100
39   App7                                0x100ffbb20 procF + 100
40   App7                                0x100ffbb20 procF + 100
41   App7                                0x100ffbb20 procF + 100
42   App7                                0x100ffbb20 procF + 100
43   App7                                0x100ffbb20 procF + 100
44   App7                                0x100ffbb20 procF + 100
45   App7                                0x100ffbb20 procF + 100
46   App7                                0x100ffbb20 procF + 100
47   App7                                0x100ffbb20 procF + 100
48   App7                                0x100ffbb20 procF + 100
49   App7                                0x100ffbb20 procF + 100
50   App7                                0x100ffbb20 procF + 100
51   App7                                0x100ffbb20 procF + 100
52   App7                                0x100ffbb20 procF + 100
53   App7                                0x100ffbb20 procF + 100
54   App7                                0x100ffbb20 procF + 100
55   App7                                0x100ffbb20 procF + 100
56   App7                                0x100ffbb20 procF + 100
57   App7                                0x100ffbb20 procF + 100
58   App7                                0x100ffbb20 procF + 100
59   App7                                0x100ffbb20 procF + 100
60   App7                                0x100ffbb20 procF + 100
61   App7                                0x100ffbb20 procF + 100
62   App7                                0x100ffbb20 procF + 100
63   App7                                0x100ffbb20 procF + 100
```

131

```
64   App7                                      0x100ffbb20 procF + 100
65   App7                                      0x100ffbb20 procF + 100
66   App7                                      0x100ffbb20 procF + 100
67   App7                                      0x100ffbb20 procF + 100
68   App7                                      0x100ffbb20 procF + 100
69   App7                                      0x100ffbb20 procF + 100
70   App7                                      0x100ffbb20 procF + 100
71   App7                                      0x100ffbb20 procF + 100
72   App7                                      0x100ffbb20 procF + 100
73   App7                                      0x100ffbb20 procF + 100
74   App7                                      0x100ffbb20 procF + 100
75   App7                                      0x100ffbb20 procF + 100
76   App7                                      0x100ffbb20 procF + 100
77   App7                                      0x100ffbb20 procF + 100
78   App7                                      0x100ffbb20 procF + 100
79   App7                                      0x100ffbb20 procF + 100
80   App7                                      0x100ffbb20 procF + 100
81   App7                                      0x100ffbb20 procF + 100
82   App7                                      0x100ffbb20 procF + 100
83   App7                                      0x100ffbb20 procF + 100
84   App7                                      0x100ffbb20 procF + 100
85   App7                                      0x100ffbb20 procF + 100
86   App7                                      0x100ffbb20 procF + 100
87   App7                                      0x100ffbb20 procF + 100
88   App7                                      0x100ffbb20 procF + 100
89   App7                                      0x100ffbb20 procF + 100
90   App7                                      0x100ffbb20 procF + 100
91   App7                                      0x100ffbb20 procF + 100
92   App7                                      0x100ffbb20 procF + 100
93   App7                                      0x100ffbb20 procF + 100
94   App7                                      0x100ffbb20 procF + 100
95   App7                                      0x100ffbb20 procF + 100
96   App7                                      0x100ffbb20 procF + 100
97   App7                                      0x100ffbb20 procF + 100
98   App7                                      0x100ffbb20 procF + 100
99   App7                                      0x100ffbb20 procF + 100
100  App7                                      0x100ffbb20 procF + 100
101  App7                                      0x100ffbb20 procF + 100
102  App7                                      0x100ffbb20 procF + 100
103  App7                                      0x100ffbb20 procF + 100
104  App7                                      0x100ffbb20 procF + 100
105  App7                                      0x100ffbb20 procF + 100
106  App7                                      0x100ffbb20 procF + 100
107  App7                                      0x100ffbb64 procE + 16
108  App7                                      0x100ffbdf8 bar_five + 20
109  App7                                      0x100ffbe0c foo_five + 12
110  App7                                      0x100ffbe28 thread_five + 20
111  libsystem_pthread.dylib                   0x18ea0826c _pthread_start + 148
112  libsystem_pthread.dylib                   0x18ea0308c thread_start + 8


Thread 1 crashed with ARM Thread State (64-bit):
    x0: 0x0000000000000000   x1: 0x0000000000000000   x2: 0x0000000000000000   x3: 0x0000000000000000
    x4: 0x0000000000000000   x5: 0x0000000000000000   x6: 0x0000000000000000   x7: 0x000000018e9485fe
    x8: 0x848ac2942cb074ac   x9: 0x848ac295425884ac  x10: 0x0000000000000011  x11: 0x0000000000000000
   x12: 0x0000000000000000  x13: 0x0000000000000000  x14: 0x0000000000000000  x15: 0x0000000000000000
   x16: 0x0000000000000148  x17: 0x00000001e8b2b680  x18: 0x0000000000000000  x19: 0x0000000000000006
   x20: 0x000000016ee8f000  x21: 0x0000000000000903  x22: 0x000000016ee8f0e0  x23: 0x0000000000000000
   x24: 0x0000000000000000  x25: 0x0000000000000000  x26: 0x0000000000000000  x27: 0x0000000000000000
   x28: 0x0000000000000000   fp: 0x000000016ee8eec0   lr: 0x000000018ea07ee0
    sp: 0x000000016ee8eea0   pc: 0x000000018e9d2d98 cpsr: 0x40001000
   far: 0x0000000101108028  esr: 0x56000080  Address size fault

Binary Images:
       0x18e9c9000 -        0x18ea00fff libsystem_kernel.dylib (*) <a9d87740-9c1d-3468-bf60-720a8d713cba>
/usr/lib/system/libsystem_kernel.dylib
       0x18e8c8000 -        0x18e949fff libsystem_c.dylib (*) <b25d2080-bb9e-38d6-8236-9cef4b2f11a3>
/usr/lib/system/libsystem_c.dylib
       0x100ff8000 -        0x100ffbfff App7 (*) <9f6200db-01ea-3f77-a8c2-7157bd91a7d2> /Users/USER/*/App7
       0x1013a8000 -        0x101407fff dyld (*) <38ee9fe9-b66d-3066-8c5c-6ddf0d6944c6> /usr/lib/dyld
       0x18ea01000 -        0x18ea0dfff libsystem_pthread.dylib (*) <63c4eef9-69a5-38b1-996e-8d31b66a051d>
/usr/lib/system/libsystem_pthread.dylib

External Modification Summary:
  Calls made by other processes targeting this process:
    task_for_pid: 0
```

```
      thread_create: 0
      thread_set_state: 0
  Calls made by this process:
      task_for_pid: 0
      thread_create: 0
      thread_set_state: 0
  Calls made by all processes on this machine:
      task_for_pid: 0
      thread_create: 0
      thread_set_state: 0


VM Region Summary:
ReadOnly portion of Libraries: Total=582.2M resident=0K(0%) swapped_out_or_unallocated=582.2M(100%)
Writable regions: Total=531.3M written=0K(0%) resident=0K(0%) swapped_out=0K(0%) unallocated=531.3M(100%)

                              VIRTUAL   REGION
REGION TYPE                      SIZE    COUNT (non-coalesced)
===========                   =======  =======
Kernel Alloc Once                32K        1
MALLOC                        521.3M       20
Stack                          10.2M       10
Stack (reserved)               56.0M        1         reserved VM address space (unallocated)
__AUTH                           46K       11
__AUTH_CONST                     67K       38
__DATA                          173K       37
__DATA_CONST                    258K       40
__DATA_DIRTY                     73K       21
__LINKEDIT                     577.6M       3
__OBJC_CONST                     10K        5
__OBJC_RO                      83.0M        1
__OBJC_RW                      3168K        1
__TEXT                         4708K       43
dyld private memory            1024K        1
shared memory                    16K        1
===========                   =======  =======
TOTAL                           1.2G      234
TOTAL, minus reserved VM space  1.2G      234
```

2.   Load a core dump *core.88726* and *App7* executable:

```
% lldb -c ~/AMCDA-Dumps/core.88726 -f ~/AMCDA-Dumps/Apps/App7/Build/Products/Release/App7
(lldb) target create "/Users/training/AMCDA-Dumps/Apps/App7/Build/Products/Release/App7" --
core "/Users/training/AMCDA-Dumps/core.88726"
Core file '/Users/training/AMCDA-Dumps/core.88726' (arm64) was loaded.
```

3.   Go to the problem core thread 1 (thread #2) that was reported as *crashed* and compare its stack trace with stack traces from the previous exercises:

```
(lldb) thread select 2
* thread #2
    frame #0: 0x000000018e9d2d98 libsystem_kernel.dylib`__pthread_kill + 8
libsystem_kernel.dylib`:
-> 0x18e9d2d98 <+8>:  b.lo   0x18e9d2db8               ; <+40>
   0x18e9d2d9c <+12>: pacibsp
   0x18e9d2da0 <+16>: stp    x29, x30, [sp, #-0x10]!
   0x18e9d2da4 <+20>: mov    x29, sp

(lldb) bt
* thread #2
  * frame #0: 0x000000018e9d2d98 libsystem_kernel.dylib`__pthread_kill + 8
    frame #1: 0x000000018ea07ee0 libsystem_pthread.dylib`pthread_kill + 288
    frame #2: 0x000000018e9423cc libsystem_c.dylib`__abort + 128
    frame #3: 0x000000018e933d48 libsystem_c.dylib`__stack_chk_fail + 96
    frame #4: 0x0000000102143c80 App7`procA + 92
```

Note: We see that the stack trace is the same as in Exercise X5.

133

4.   Check the currently executing instruction of identified non-waiting core thread 4 (thread #5) and compare stack pointer with stack region boundaries (we have recursive calls so potentially stack overflow):

```
(lldb) thread select 5
* thread #5, stop reason = ESR_EC_DABORT_EL0 (fault address: 0x16f053ba4)
    frame #0: 0x0000000100ffbaf0 App7`procF + 52
App7`procF:
-> 0x100ffbaf0 <+52>: str     w0, [sp, #0x4]
   0x100ffbaf4 <+56>: add     x0, sp, #0x8
   0x100ffbaf8 <+60>: mov     x1, #0x1000
   0x100ffbafc <+64>: bl      0x100ffbf04               ; symbol stub for: bzero
```

```
(lldb) re r sp
     sp = 0x000000016f053ba0
```

Note: We can see stack regions in *vmmap_88726.log*:

```
Process:        App7 [88726]
Path:           /Users/USER/*/App7
Load Address:   0x100ff8000
Identifier:     App7
Version:        ???
Code Type:      ARM64
Platform:       macOS
Parent Process: zsh [93565]

Date/Time:      2022-12-07 18:25:19.329 +0000
Launch Time:    2022-12-07 18:25:01.781 +0000
OS Version:     macOS 12.6 (21G115)
Report Version: 7
Analysis Tool:  /Applications/Xcode.app/Contents/Developer/usr/bin/vmmap
Analysis Tool Version: Xcode 14.0.1 (14A400)
----

Virtual Memory Map of process 88726 (App7)
Output report format:  2.4  -- 64-bit process
VM page size:  16384 bytes

==== Non-writable regions for process 88726
REGION TYPE            START - END         [ VSIZE  RSDNT  DIRTY   SWAP] PRT/MAX SHRMOD PURGE   REGION DETAIL
__TEXT                 100ff8000-100ffc000 [   16K    16K     0K     0K] r-x/r-x SM=COW         /Users/USER/*/App7
__DATA_CONST           100ffc000-101000000 [   16K    16K    16K     0K] r--/rw- SM=COW         /Users/USER/*/App7
__LINKEDIT             101000000-101008000 [   32K    16K     0K     0K] r--/r-- SM=COW         /Users/USER/*/App7
dyld private memory    101008000-101108000 [ 1024K    16K    16K     0K] r--/rwx SM=PRV
shared memory          101110000-101114000 [   16K    16K    16K     0K] r--/r-- SM=SHM
MALLOC metadata        101114000-101118000 [   16K    16K    16K     0K] r--/rwx SM=ZER        MallocHelperZone_0x101114000 zone structure
MALLOC guard page      10111c000-101120000 [   16K     0K     0K     0K] ---/rwx SM=ZER
MALLOC guard page      101128000-10112c000 [   16K     0K     0K     0K] ---/rwx SM=ZER
MALLOC guard page      10112c000-101130000 [   16K     0K     0K     0K] ---/rwx SM=NUL
MALLOC guard page      101138000-101140000 [   32K     0K     0K     0K] ---/rwx SM=NUL
MALLOC guard page      101148000-10114c000 [   16K     0K     0K     0K] ---/rwx SM=NUL
MALLOC metadata        10114c000-101150000 [   16K    16K     0K     0K] r--/rwx SM=PRV
MALLOC metadata        101150000-101154000 [   16K    16K    16K     0K] r--/rwx SM=ZER        DefaultMallocZone_0x101150000 zone structure
__TEXT                 1013a8000-101408000 [  384K   384K     0K     0K] r-x/r-x SM=COW         /usr/lib/dyld
__DATA_CONST           101408000-101420000 [   96K    32K    32K     0K] r--/rw- SM=COW         /usr/lib/dyld
__LINKEDIT             101424000-10145c000 [  224K   160K     0K     0K] r--/r-- SM=COW         /usr/lib/dyld
STACK GUARD            16ae08000-16e60c000 [ 56.0M     0K     0K     0K] ---/rwx SM=NUL         stack guard for thread 0
STACK GUARD            16ee08000-16ee0c000 [   16K     0K     0K     0K] ---/rwx SM=NUL         stack guard for thread 1
STACK GUARD            16ee94000-16ee98000 [   16K     0K     0K     0K] ---/rwx SM=NUL         stack guard for thread 2
STACK GUARD            16ef20000-16ef24000 [   16K     0K     0K     0K] ---/rwx SM=NUL         stack guard for thread 3
STACK GUARD            16efac000-16efb0000 [   16K     0K     0K     0K] ---/rwx SM=NUL         stack guard for thread 4
STACK GUARD            16f038000-16f03c000 [   16K     0K     0K     0K] ---/rwx SM=NUL         stack guard for thread 5
__TEXT                 18e72d000-18e72f000 [    8K     8K     0K     0K] r-x/r-x SM=COW         /usr/lib/system/libsystem_blocks.dylib
__TEXT                 18e72f000-18e771000 [  264K   264K     0K     0K] r-x/r-x SM=COW         /usr/lib/system/libxpc.dylib
__TEXT                 18e771000-18e78b000 [  104K   104K     0K     0K] r-x/r-x SM=COW         /usr/lib/system/libsystem_trace.dylib
__TEXT                 18e78b000-18e815000 [  552K   472K     0K     0K] r-x/r-x SM=COW         /usr/lib/system/libcorecrypto.dylib
__TEXT                 18e815000-18e840000 [  172K   172K     0K     0K] r-x/r-x SM=COW         /usr/lib/system/libsystem_malloc.dylib
__TEXT                 18e840000-18e887000 [  284K   284K     0K     0K] r-x/r-x SM=COW         /usr/lib/system/libdispatch.dylib
__TEXT                 18e887000-18e8c5000 [  248K   248K     0K     0K] r-x/r-x SM=COW         /usr/lib/libobjc.A.dylib
__TEXT                 18e8c5000-18e8c8000 [   12K    12K     0K     0K] r-x/r-x SM=COW         /usr/lib/system/libsystem_featureflags.dylib
__TEXT                 18e8c8000-18e94a000 [  520K   472K     0K     0K] r-x/r-x SM=COW         /usr/lib/system/libsystem_c.dylib
__TEXT                 18e94a000-18e9b1000 [  412K   396K     0K     0K] r-x/r-x SM=COW         /usr/lib/libc++.1.dylib
__TEXT                 18e9b1000-18e9c9000 [   96K    96K     0K     0K] r-x/r-x SM=COW         /usr/lib/libc++abi.dylib
__TEXT                 18e9c9000-18ea01000 [  224K   224K     0K     0K] r-x/r-x SM=COW         /usr/lib/system/libsystem_kernel.dylib
__TEXT                 18ea01000-18ea0e000 [   52K    52K     0K     0K] r-x/r-x SM=COW         /usr/lib/system/libsystem_pthread.dylib
__TEXT                 18ea0e000-18ea1b000 [   52K    52K     0K     0K] r-x/r-x SM=COW         /usr/lib/system/libdyld.dylib
__TEXT                 18ea1b000-18ea23000 [   32K    32K     0K     0K] r-x/r-x SM=COW         /usr/lib/system/libsystem_platform.dylib
__TEXT                 18ea23000-18ea50000 [  180K   164K     0K     0K] r-x/r-x SM=COW         /usr/lib/system/libsystem_info.dylib
__TEXT                 19113f000-19114a000 [   44K    44K     0K     0K] r-x/r-x SM=COW         /usr/lib/system/libsystem_darwin.dylib
__TEXT                 191598000-1915a8000 [   64K    64K     0K     0K] r-x/r-x SM=COW         /usr/lib/system/libsystem_notify.dylib
__TEXT                 193b14000-193b2d000 [  100K   100K     0K     0K] r-x/r-x SM=COW         /usr/lib/system/libsystem_networkextension.dylib
__TEXT                 193b86000-193b9e000 [   96K    96K     0K     0K] r-x/r-x SM=COW         /usr/lib/system/libsystem_asl.dylib
__TEXT                 1952ea000-1952f3000 [   36K    20K     0K     0K] r-x/r-x SM=COW         /usr/lib/system/libsystem_symptoms.dylib
__TEXT                 1972de000-1972fd000 [  124K   108K     0K     0K] r-x/r-x SM=COW         /usr/lib/system/libsystem_containermanager.dylib
__TEXT                 198085000-19808a000 [   20K    20K     0K     0K] r-x/r-x SM=COW         /usr/lib/system/libsystem_configuration.dylib
__TEXT                 19808a000-19808f000 [   20K    20K     0K     0K] r-x/r-x SM=COW         /usr/lib/system/libsystem_sandbox.dylib
__TEXT                 198bf0000-198bf3000 [   12K    12K     0K     0K] r-x/r-x SM=COW         /usr/lib/system/libquarantine.dylib
__TEXT                 19925d000-199263000 [   24K    24K     0K     0K] r-x/r-x SM=COW         /usr/lib/system/libsystem_coreservices.dylib
__TEXT                 1994c8000-1994ff000 [  220K   140K     0K     0K] r-x/r-x SM=COW         /usr/lib/system/libsystem_m.dylib
```

```
__TEXT                   199500000-199509000     [   36K   36K    0K    0K] r-x/r-x SM=COW    /usr/lib/system/libmacho.dylib
__TEXT                   199525000-199532000     [   52K   52K    0K    0K] r-x/r-x SM=COW    /usr/lib/system/libcommonCrypto.dylib
__TEXT                   199532000-19953d000     [   44K   44K    0K    0K] r-x/r-x SM=COW    /usr/lib/system/libunwind.dylib
__TEXT                   19953d000-199545000     [   32K   32K    0K    0K] r-x/r-x SM=COW    /usr/lib/liboah.dylib
__TEXT                   199545000-19954e000     [   36K   20K    0K    0K] r-x/r-x SM=COW    /usr/lib/system/libcopyfile.dylib
__TEXT                   19954e000-199552000     [   16K   16K    0K    0K] r-x/r-x SM=COW    /usr/lib/system/libcompiler_rt.dylib
__TEXT                   199552000-199557000     [   20K   20K    0K    0K] r-x/r-x SM=COW    /usr/lib/system/libsystem_collections.dylib
__TEXT                   199557000-19955a000     [   12K   12K    0K    0K] r-x/r-x SM=COW    /usr/lib/system/libsystem_secinit.dylib
__TEXT                   19955a000-19955d000     [   12K   12K    0K    0K] r-x/r-x SM=COW    /usr/lib/system/libremovefile.dylib
__TEXT                   19955d000-19955e000     [    4K    4K    0K    0K] r-x/r-x SM=COW    /usr/lib/system/libkeymgr.dylib
__TEXT                   19955e000-199567000     [   36K   36K    0K    0K] r-x/r-x SM=COW    /usr/lib/system/libsystem_dnssd.dylib
__TEXT                   199567000-19956d000     [   24K   24K    0K    0K] r-x/r-x SM=COW    /usr/lib/system/libcache.dylib
__TEXT                   19956d000-19956f000     [    8K    8K    0K    0K] r-x/r-x SM=COW    /usr/lib/libSystem.B.dylib
__TEXT                   19f8c1000-19f8c2000     [    4K    4K    0K    0K] r-x/r-x SM=COW    /usr/lib/system/libsystem_product_info_filter.dylib
__OBJC_RO                1d89c2000-1ddcc4000     [ 83.0M 67.6M    0K    0K] r-x/r-x SM=COW    /usr/lib/libobjc.A.dylib
__DATA_CONST             1e0098000-1e0098130     [   304   304    0K    0K] r--/rw- SM=COW    /usr/lib/system/libsystem_blocks.dylib
__DATA_CONST             1e0098130-1e00987d0     [  1696  1696    0K    0K] r--/rw- SM=COW    /usr/lib/system/libsystem_trace.dylib
__DATA_CONST             1e00987d0-1e0098ef0     [  1824  1824    0K    0K] r--/rw- SM=COW    /usr/lib/system/libcorecrypto.dylib
__DATA_CONST             1e0098ef0-1e0098f48     [    88    88    0K    0K] r--/rw- SM=COW    /usr/lib/system/libsystem_malloc.dylib
__DATA_CONST             1e0098f50-1e0099b58     [  3080  3080    0K    0K] r--/rw- SM=COW    /usr/lib/libobjc.A.dylib
__DATA_CONST             1e0099b58-1e0099b98     [    64    64    0K    0K] r--/rw- SM=COW    /usr/lib/system/libsystem_featureflags.dylib
__DATA_CONST             1e0099b98-1e009b370     [    6K    6K    0K    0K] r--/rw- SM=COW    /usr/lib/system/libsystem_c.dylib
__DATA_CONST             1e009b370-1e009bcd0     [  2400  2400    0K    0K] r--/rw- SM=COW    /usr/lib/libc++.1.dylib
__DATA_CONST             1e009bcd0-1e009bda8     [   216   216    0K    0K] r--/rw- SM=COW    /usr/lib/libc++abi.dylib
__DATA_CONST             1e009bda8-1e009e060     [    9K    9K    0K    0K] r--/rw- SM=COW    /usr/lib/system/libsystem_kernel.dylib
__DATA_CONST             1e009e060-1e009e098     [    56    56    0K    0K] r--/rw- SM=COW    /usr/lib/system/libsystem_pthread.dylib
__DATA_CONST             1e009e098-1e009e258     [   448   448    0K    0K] r--/rw- SM=COW    /usr/lib/system/libdyld.dylib
__DATA_CONST             1e009e258-1e009e278     [    32    32    0K    0K] r--/rw- SM=COW    /usr/lib/system/libsystem_platform.dylib
__DATA_CONST             1e009e278-1e009e790     [  1304  1304    0K    0K] r--/rw- SM=COW    /usr/lib/system/libsystem_info.dylib
__DATA_CONST             1e0127148-1e0129ac0     [   10K   10K    0K    0K] r--/rw- SM=COW    /usr/lib/system/libsystem_darwin.dylib
__DATA_CONST             1e0133dc0-1e0133f18     [   344   344    0K    0K] r--/rw- SM=COW    /usr/lib/system/libsystem_notify.dylib
__DATA_CONST             1e02c9868-1e02c9d60     [  1272  1272    0K    0K] r--/rw- SM=COW    /usr/lib/system/libsystem_networkextension.dylib
__DATA_CONST             1e02cac70-1e02cb290     [  1568  1568    0K    0K] r--/rw- SM=COW    /usr/lib/system/libsystem_asl.dylib
__DATA_CONST             1e032ea80-1e032ec30     [   432   432    0K    0K] r--/rw- SM=COW    /usr/lib/system/libsystem_symptoms.dylib
__DATA_CONST             1e05863b8-1e0586da0     [  2536  2536    0K    0K] r--/rw- SM=COW    /usr/lib/system/libsystem_containermanager.dylib
__DATA_CONST             1e061d0e0-1e061d298     [   440   440    0K    0K] r--/rw- SM=COW    /usr/lib/system/libsystem_configuration.dylib
__DATA_CONST             1e061d298-1e061d308     [   112   112    0K    0K] r--/rw- SM=COW    /usr/lib/system/libsystem_sandbox.dylib
__DATA_CONST             1e064ac20-1e064ac70     [    80    80    0K    0K] r--/rw- SM=COW    /usr/lib/system/libquarantine.dylib
__DATA_CONST             1e06d5660-1e06d5dc8     [  1896  1896    0K    0K] r--/rw- SM=COW    /usr/lib/system/libsystem_coreservices.dylib
__DATA_CONST             1e06fd5a8-1e06fdcf0     [  1864  1864    0K    0K] r--/rw- SM=COW    /usr/lib/system/libmacho.dylib
__DATA_CONST             1e06fdd00-1e06fe4a0     [  1952  1952    0K    0K] r--/rw- SM=COW    /usr/lib/system/libcommonCrypto.dylib
__DATA_CONST             1e06fe4a0-1e06fe7c0     [   800   800    0K    0K] r--/rw- SM=COW    /usr/lib/system/libunwind.dylib
__DATA_CONST             1e06fe7c0-1e06fe7d8     [    24    24    0K    0K] r--/rw- SM=COW    /usr/lib/liboah.dylib
__DATA_CONST             1e06fe7d8-1e06fea98     [   704   704    0K    0K] r--/rw- SM=COW    /usr/lib/system/libcopyfile.dylib
__DATA_CONST             1e06fea98-1e06feaa0     [     8     8    0K    0K] r--/rw- SM=COW    /usr/lib/system/libsystem_collections.dylib
__DATA_CONST             1e06feaa0-1e06feb10     [   112   112    0K    0K] r--/rw- SM=COW    /usr/lib/system/libsystem_secinit.dylib
__DATA_CONST             1e06feb10-1e06feb20     [    16    16    0K    0K] r--/rw- SM=COW    /usr/lib/system/libremovefile.dylib
__DATA_CONST             1e06feb20-1e06feb30     [    16    16    0K    0K] r--/rw- SM=COW    /usr/lib/system/libkeymgr.dylib
__DATA_CONST             1e06feb30-1e06feba8     [   120   120    0K    0K] r--/rw- SM=COW    /usr/lib/system/libsystem_dnssd.dylib
__DATA_CONST             1e06feba8-1e06fec08     [    96    96    0K    0K] r--/rw- SM=COW    /usr/lib/system/libcache.dylib
__DATA_CONST             1e06fec08-1e06fec18     [    16    16    0K    0K] r--/rw- SM=COW    /usr/lib/libSystem.B.dylib
__AUTH_CONST             1e8b08000-1e8b08030     [    48    48    0K    0K] r--/rw- SM=COW    /usr/lib/system/libsystem_blocks.dylib
__OBJC_CONST             1e8b08030-1e8b08390     [   864   864    0K    0K] r--/rw- SM=COW    /usr/lib/system/libsystem_blocks.dylib
__DATA_CONST             1e8b08390-1e8b0ce20     [   19K   19K    0K    0K] r--/rw- SM=COW    /usr/lib/system/libxpc.dylib
__OBJC_CONST             1e8b0ce20-1e8b0df90     [    4K    4K    0K    0K] r--/rw- SM=COW    /usr/lib/system/libxpc.dylib
__AUTH_CONST             1e8b0df90-1e8b0ec90     [  3328  3328    0K    0K] r--/rw- SM=COW    /usr/lib/system/libsystem_trace.dylib
__OBJC_CONST             1e8b0ec90-1e8b0ee40     [   432   432    0K    0K] r--/rw- SM=COW    /usr/lib/system/libsystem_trace.dylib
__AUTH_CONST             1e8b0ee40-1e8b0ff10     [    4K    4K    0K    0K] r--/rw- SM=COW    /usr/lib/system/libcorecrypto.dylib
__AUTH_CONST             1e8b0ff10-1e8b104e8     [  1496  1496    0K    0K] r--/rw- SM=COW    /usr/lib/system/libsystem_malloc.dylib
__DATA_CONST             1e8b10500-1e8b238e8     [   77K   77K    0K    0K] r--/rw- SM=COW    /usr/lib/system/libdispatch.dylib
__OBJC_CONST             1e8b238e8-1e8b24938     [    4K    4K    0K    0K] r--/rw- SM=COW    /usr/lib/system/libdispatch.dylib
__AUTH_CONST             1e8b24940-1e8b253c8     [  2696  2696    0K    0K] r--/rw- SM=COW    /usr/lib/libobjc.A.dylib
__OBJC_CONST             1e8b253c8-1e8b25698     [   720   720    0K    0K] r--/rw- SM=COW    /usr/lib/libobjc.A.dylib
__AUTH_CONST             1e8b25698-1e8b25808     [   368   368    0K    0K] r--/rw- SM=COW    /usr/lib/system/libsystem_featureflags.dylib
__AUTH_CONST             1e8b25808-1e8b26168     [  2400  2400    0K    0K] r--/rw- SM=COW    /usr/lib/system/libsystem_c.dylib
__AUTH_CONST             1e8b26168-1e8b282a8     [    8K    8K    0K    0K] r--/rw- SM=COW    /usr/lib/libc++.1.dylib
__AUTH_CONST             1e8b282a8-1e8b2b4b8     [   13K   13K    0K    0K] r--/rw- SM=COW    /usr/lib/libc++abi.dylib
__AUTH_CONST             1e8b2b4b8-1e8b2b5e0     [   296   296    0K    0K] r--/rw- SM=COW    /usr/lib/system/libsystem_kernel.dylib
__AUTH_CONST             1e8b2b5e0-1e8b2b810     [   560   560    0K    0K] r--/rw- SM=COW    /usr/lib/system/libsystem_pthread.dylib
__AUTH_CONST             1e8b2b810-1e8b2bfc8     [  1976  1976    0K    0K] r--/rw- SM=COW    /usr/lib/system/libdyld.dylib
__AUTH_CONST             1e8b2bfc8-1e8b2c250     [   648   648    0K    0K] r--/rw- SM=COW    /usr/lib/system/libsystem_platform.dylib
__AUTH_CONST             1e8b2c250-1e8b2d3f0     [    4K    4K    0K    0K] r--/rw- SM=COW    /usr/lib/system/libsystem_info.dylib
__AUTH_CONST             1e8c5bd48-1e8c5c1c8     [  1152  1152    0K    0K] r--/rw- SM=COW    /usr/lib/system/libsystem_darwin.dylib
__AUTH_CONST             1e8c77a80-1e8c77e00     [   896   896    0K    0K] r--/rw- SM=COW    /usr/lib/system/libsystem_notify.dylib
__AUTH_CONST             1e8dfea40-1e8dff608     [  3016  3016    0K    0K] r--/rw- SM=COW    /usr/lib/system/libsystem_networkextension.dylib
__AUTH_CONST             1e8e4d718-1e8e4e160     [  2632  2632    0K    0K] r--/rw- SM=COW    /usr/lib/system/libsystem_asl.dylib
__AUTH_CONST             1e8f17288-1e8f17560     [   728   728    0K    0K] r--/rw- SM=COW    /usr/lib/system/libsystem_symptoms.dylib
__AUTH_CONST             1e904e480-1e904f8c0     [    5K    0K    0K    0K] r--/rw- SM=COW    /usr/lib/system/libsystem_containermanager.dylib
__AUTH_CONST             1e915e250-1e915e560     [   784   784    0K    0K] r--/rw- SM=COW    /usr/lib/system/libsystem_configuration.dylib
__AUTH_CONST             1e915e560-1e915e768     [   520   520    0K    0K] r--/rw- SM=COW    /usr/lib/system/libsystem_sandbox.dylib
__AUTH_CONST             1e91a78b8-1e91a79c0     [   264   264    0K    0K] r--/rw- SM=COW    /usr/lib/system/libquarantine.dylib
__AUTH_CONST             1e922eac0-1e922ed50     [   656   656    0K    0K] r--/rw- SM=COW    /usr/lib/system/libsystem_coreservices.dylib
__AUTH_CONST             1e925ad88-1e925ada8     [    32    32    0K    0K] r--/rw- SM=COW    /usr/lib/system/libsystem_m.dylib
__AUTH_CONST             1e925ae28-1e925ae98     [   112   112    0K    0K] r--/rw- SM=COW    /usr/lib/system/libmacho.dylib
__AUTH_CONST             1e925afb0-1e925bd80     [  3536  3536    0K    0K] r--/rw- SM=COW    /usr/lib/system/libcommonCrypto.dylib
__AUTH_CONST             1e925bd80-1e925be98     [   280   280    0K    0K] r--/rw- SM=COW    /usr/lib/system/libunwind.dylib
__AUTH_CONST             1e925be98-1e925c168     [   720   720    0K    0K] r--/rw- SM=COW    /usr/lib/liboah.dylib
__AUTH_CONST             1e925c168-1e925c5a0     [  1080  1080    0K    0K] r--/rw- SM=COW    /usr/lib/system/libcopyfile.dylib
__AUTH_CONST             1e925c5a0-1e925c600     [    96    96    0K    0K] r--/rw- SM=COW    /usr/lib/system/libcompiler_rt.dylib
__AUTH_CONST             1e925c600-1e925c750     [   336   336    0K    0K] r--/rw- SM=COW    /usr/lib/system/libsystem_collections.dylib
__AUTH_CONST             1e925c750-1e925ca18     [   712   712    0K    0K] r--/rw- SM=COW    /usr/lib/system/libsystem_secinit.dylib
__AUTH_CONST             1e925ca18-1e925cb78     [   352   352    0K    0K] r--/rw- SM=COW    /usr/lib/system/libremovefile.dylib
__AUTH_CONST             1e925cb78-1e925cbf8     [   128   128    0K    0K] r--/rw- SM=COW    /usr/lib/system/libkeymgr.dylib
__AUTH_CONST             1e925cbf8-1e925cdb0     [   440   440    0K    0K] r--/rw- SM=COW    /usr/lib/system/libsystem_dnssd.dylib
__AUTH_CONST             1e925cdb0-1e925ce70     [   192   192    0K    0K] r--/rw- SM=COW    /usr/lib/system/libcache.dylib
__AUTH_CONST             1e925ce70-1e925d120     [   688   688    0K    0K] r--/rw- SM=COW    /usr/lib/libSystem.B.dylib
__LINKEDIT               222494000-2465e6000     [577.3M 71.2M    0K    0K] r--/r-- SM=COW    dyld shared cache combined __LINKEDIT

==== Writable regions for process 88726
REGION TYPE                 START - END          [ VSIZE  RSDNT  DIRTY   SWAP] PRT/MAX SHRMOD PURGE    REGION DETAIL
Kernel Alloc Once        101108000-101110000     [   32K   16K   16K    0K] rw-/rwx SM=PRV
MALLOC metadata          101118000-10111c000     [   16K   16K   16K    0K] rw-/rwx SM=ZER
```

```
MALLOC metadata          101120000-101128000    [   32K    32K    32K     0K] rw-/rwx SM=ZER
MALLOC metadata          101130000-101138000    [   32K    32K    32K     0K] rw-/rwx SM=PRV
MALLOC metadata          101140000-101148000    [   32K    32K    32K     0K] rw-/rwx SM=PRV
MALLOC metadata          101154000-101158000    [   16K    16K    16K     0K] rw-/rwx SM=ZER
__DATA                   101420000-101424000    [   16K    16K    16K     0K] rw-/rw- SM=COW      /usr/lib/dyld
MALLOC_TINY              153600000-153700000    [ 1024K    32K    32K     0K] rw-/rwx SM=PRV      MallocHelperZone_0x101114000
MALLOC_SMALL             153800000-154000000    [ 8192K    32K    32K     0K] rw-/rwx SM=PRV      MallocHelperZone_0x101114000
Stack                    16e60c000-16ee08000    [ 8176K    32K    32K     0K] rw-/rwx SM=PRV      thread 0
Stack                    16ee0c000-16ee94000    [  544K    16K    16K     0K] rw-/rwx SM=PRV      thread 1
Stack                    16ee98000-16ef20000    [  544K    16K    16K     0K] rw-/rwx SM=PRV      thread 2
Stack                    16ef24000-16efac000    [  544K    16K    16K     0K] rw-/rwx SM=PRV      thread 3
Stack                    16efb0000-16f038000    [  544K    16K    16K     0K] rw-/rwx SM=PRV      thread 4
Stack                    16f03c000-16f0c4000    [  544K    16K    16K     0K] rw-/rwx SM=PRV      thread 5
__DATA                   1e4c04000-1e4c04060    [    96     96     96     0K] rw-/rw- SM=COW      /usr/lib/system/libsystem_blocks.dylib
__DATA                   1e4c04060-1e4c04d18    [  3256   3256   3256     0K] rw-/rw- SM=COW      /usr/lib/system/libxpc.dylib
__DATA                   1e4c04d18-1e4c05050    [   824    824    824     0K] rw-/rw- SM=COW      /usr/lib/system/libsystem_trace.dylib
__DATA                   1e4c05050-1e4c0c788    [   30K    30K    14K     0K] rw-/rw- SM=COW      /usr/lib/system/libcorecrypto.dylib
__DATA                   1e4c0c788-1e4c0ea24    [    9K     9K     9K     0K] rw-/rw- SM=COW      /usr/lib/system/libsystem_malloc.dylib
unused __DATA            1e4c0ea24-1e4c0ea40    [    28     28     28     0K] rw-/rw- SM=COW      on dirty page  unused system shared lib __DATA
__DATA                   1e4c0ea40-1e4c120c0    [   14K    14K    14K     0K] rw-/rw- SM=COW      /usr/lib/libobjc.A.dylib
__DATA                   1e4c120c0-1e4c120f9    [    57     57     57     0K] rw-/rw- SM=COW      /usr/lib/system/libsystem_featureflags.dylib
unused __DATA            1e4c120f9-1e4c12100    [     7      7      7     0K] rw-/rw- SM=COW      on dirty page  unused system shared lib __DATA
__DATA                   1e4c12100-1e4c14270    [    8K     8K     8K     0K] rw-/rw- SM=COW      /usr/lib/system/libsystem_c.dylib
unused __DATA            1e4c14270-1e4c15000    [  3472   3472   3472     0K] rw-/rw- SM=COW      on dirty page  unused system shared lib __DATA
__DATA                   1e4c15000-1e4c1b720    [   26K    26K    12K     0K] rw-/rw- SM=COW      /usr/lib/libc++.1.dylib
__DATA                   1e4c1b720-1e4c1ba68    [   840    840     0K     0K] rw-/rw- SM=COW      /usr/lib/libc++abi.dylib
__DATA                   1e4c1ba68-1e4c1bcd9    [   625    625     0K     0K] rw-/rw- SM=COW      /usr/lib/system/libsystem_kernel.dylib
__DATA                   1e4c1c000-1e4c24000    [   32K    32K     0K     0K] rw-/rw- SM=COW      /usr/lib/system/libsystem_pthread.dylib
__DATA                   1e4c24000-1e4c28000    [   16K    16K     0K     0K] rw-/rw- SM=COW      /usr/lib/system/libsystem_pthread.dylib
__DATA                   1e4c28000-1e4c28048    [    72     72     0K     0K] rw-/rw- SM=COW      /usr/lib/system/libsystem_pthread.dylib
__DATA                   1e4c28048-1e4c28050    [     8      8     0K     0K] rw-/rw- SM=COW      /usr/lib/system/libdyld.dylib
__DATA                   1e4c28050-1e4c28090    [    64     64     0K     0K] rw-/rw- SM=COW      /usr/lib/system/libsystem_platform.dylib
__DATA                   1e4c28090-1e4c28be0    [  2896   2896     0K     0K] rw-/rw- SM=COW      /usr/lib/system/libsystem_info.dylib
__DATA                   1e4c96958-1e4c96968    [    16     16     0K     0K] rw-/rw- SM=COW      /usr/lib/system/libsystem_darwin.dylib
__DATA                   1e4c9de00-1e4c9de51    [    81     81     0K     0K] rw-/rw- SM=COW      /usr/lib/system/libsystem_notify.dylib
__DATA                   1e4d33600-1e4d33bd9    [  1497   1497     0K     0K] rw-/rw- SM=COW      /usr/lib/system/libsystem_networkextension.dylib
__DATA                   1e4d343b8-1e4d344c8    [   272    272     0K     0K] rw-/rw- SM=COW      /usr/lib/system/libsystem_asl.dylib
__DATA                   1e4d6a118-1e4d6a158    [    64     64     0K     0K] rw-/rw- SM=COW      /usr/lib/system/libsystem_symptoms.dylib
__DATA                   1e4deca18-1e4decb40    [   296    296     0K     0K] rw-/rw- SM=COW      /usr/lib/system/libsystem_containermanager.dylib
__DATA                   1e4e2d090-1e4e2d159    [   201    201     0K     0K] rw-/rw- SM=COW      /usr/lib/system/libsystem_configuration.dylib
__DATA                   1e4e2d160-1e4e2d188    [    40     40     0K     0K] rw-/rw- SM=COW      /usr/lib/system/libsystem_sandbox.dylib
__DATA                   1e4e4f280-1e4e4f290    [    16     16     0K     0K] rw-/rw- SM=COW      /usr/lib/system/libquarantine.dylib
__DATA                   1e4e61bb0-1e4e61c88    [   216    216     0K     0K] rw-/rw- SM=COW      /usr/lib/system/libsystem_coreservices.dylib
__DATA                   1e4e71a20-1e4e71a24    [     4      4     0K     0K] rw-/rw- SM=COW      /usr/lib/system/libsystem_m.dylib
__DATA                   1e4e71ae8-1e4e723d9    [  2289   2289     0K     0K] rw-/rw- SM=COW      /usr/lib/system/libunwind.dylib
__DATA                   1e4e723e0-1e4e723e8    [     8      8     0K     0K] rw-/rw- SM=COW      /usr/lib/liboah.dylib
__DATA                   1e4e723e8-1e4e723f8    [    16     16     0K     0K] rw-/rw- SM=COW      /usr/lib/system/libcopyfile.dylib
__DATA                   1e4e723f8-1e4e733f8    [    4K     4K     0K     0K] rw-/rw- SM=COW      /usr/lib/system/libcompiler_rt.dylib
__DATA                   1e4e733f8-1e4e73438    [    64     64     0K     0K] rw-/rw- SM=COW      /usr/lib/system/libsystem_secinit.dylib
__DATA                   1e4e73438-1e4e73468    [    48     48     0K     0K] rw-/rw- SM=COW      /usr/lib/system/libsystem_dnssd.dylib
__DATA                   1e4e73468-1e4e73470    [     8      8     0K     0K] rw-/rw- SM=COW      /usr/lib/libSystem.B.dylib
unused __DATA_DIRTY      1e7930000-1e7930120    [   288    288    288     0K] rw-/rw- SM=COW      on dirty page  unused /usr/lib/libMobileGestalt.dylib
unused __DATA_DIRTY      1e7930120-1e7930170    [    80     80     80     0K] rw-/rw- SM=COW      on dirty page  unused
/usr/lib/libUniversalAccess.dylib
unused __DATA_DIRTY      1e7930170-1e7930190    [    32     32     32     0K] rw-/rw- SM=COW      on dirty page  unused
/usr/lib/libapp_launch_measurement.dylib
unused __DATA_DIRTY      1e7930190-1e7931010    [  3712   3712   3712     0K] rw-/rw- SM=COW      on dirty page  unused /usr/lib/libboringssl.dylib
__DATA_DIRTY             1e7931010-1e79321e0    [    4K     4K     4K     0K] rw-/rw- SM=COW      /usr/lib/libc++.1.dylib
__DATA_DIRTY             1e79321e0-1e7932208    [    40     40     40     0K] rw-/rw- SM=COW      /usr/lib/libc++abi.dylib
unused __DATA_DIRTY      1e7932208-1e7934000    [    7K     7K     7K     0K] rw-/rw- SM=COW      on dirty page  unused /usr/lib/libcoreroutine.dylib
unused __DATA_DIRTY      1e7938000-1e793a1c8    [    8K     8K     8K     0K] rw-/rw- SM=COW      on dirty page  unused /usr/lib/libnetwork.dylib
unused __DATA            1e793a1c8-1e793a200    [    56     56     56     0K] rw-/rw- SM=COW      on dirty page  unused system shared lib __DATA
__DATA_DIRTY             1e793a200-1e793d070    [   12K    12K    12K     0K] rw-/rw- SM=COW      /usr/lib/libobjc.A.dylib
unused __DATA_DIRTY      1e793d070-1e793d200    [   400    400    400     0K] rw-/rw- SM=COW      on dirty page  unused
/usr/lib/libpartition2_dynamic.dylib
unused __DATA_DIRTY      1e793d200-1e793d299    [   153    153    153     0K] rw-/rw- SM=COW      on dirty page  unused /usr/lib/libpmenergy.dylib
unused __DATA            1e793d299-1e793d2a0    [     7      7      7     0K] rw-/rw- SM=COW      on dirty page  unused system shared lib __DATA
unused __DATA_DIRTY      1e793d2a0-1e793d3e8    [   328    328    328     0K] rw-/rw- SM=COW      on dirty page  unused /usr/lib/libprequelite.dylib
unused __DATA_DIRTY      1e793d3e8-1e793d4f8    [   272    272    272     0K] rw-/rw- SM=COW      on dirty page  unused /usr/lib/libquic.dylib
unused __DATA_DIRTY      1e793d4f8-1e793d530    [    56     56     56     0K] rw-/rw- SM=COW      on dirty page  unused /usr/lib/libsandbox.1.dylib
unused __DATA            1e793d530-1e793d540    [    16     16     16     0K] rw-/rw- SM=COW      on dirty page  unused system shared lib __DATA
unused __DATA_DIRTY      1e793d540-1e7940000    [   11K    11K    11K     0K] rw-/rw- SM=COW      on dirty page  unused /usr/lib/libsqlite3.dylib
unused __DATA_DIRTY      1e795c000-1e795e610    [   10K    10K    10K     0K] rw-/rw- SM=COW      on dirty page  unused
/usr/lib/swift/libswiftFoundation.dylib
unused __DATA_DIRTY      1e795e610-1e795e7a0    [   400    400    400     0K] rw-/rw- SM=COW      on dirty page  unused
/usr/lib/swift/libswiftObjectiveC.dylib
unused __DATA_DIRTY      1e795e7a0-1e795e7b8    [    24     24     24     0K] rw-/rw- SM=COW      on dirty page  unused /usr/lib/swift/libswiftos.dylib
__DATA_DIRTY             1e795e7b8-1e795ef10    [  1880   1880   1880     0K] rw-/rw- SM=COW      /usr/lib/system/libcorecrypto.dylib
unused __DATA            1e795ef10-1e795ef40    [    48     48     48     0K] rw-/rw- SM=COW      on dirty page  unused system shared lib __DATA
__DATA_DIRTY             1e795ef40-1e79628e8    [   14K    14K    14K     0K] rw-/rw- SM=COW      /usr/lib/system/libdispatch.dylib
__DATA_DIRTY             1e79628e8-1e7962908    [    32     32     32     0K] rw-/rw- SM=COW      /usr/lib/system/libdyld.dylib
unused __DATA            1e7962908-1e7962910    [     8      8      8     0K] rw-/rw- SM=COW      on dirty page  unused system shared lib __DATA
__DATA_DIRTY             1e7962910-1e7962a6c    [   348    348    348     0K] rw-/rw- SM=COW      /usr/lib/system/libsystem_asl.dylib
unused __DATA            1e7962a6c-1e7962a70    [     4      4      4     0K] rw-/rw- SM=COW      on dirty page  unused system shared lib __DATA
__DATA_DIRTY             1e7962a70-1e7962c68    [   504    504    504     0K] rw-/rw- SM=COW      /usr/lib/system/libsystem_blocks.dylib
__DATA_DIRTY             1e7962c68-1e79657f0    [   11K    11K    11K     0K] rw-/rw- SM=COW      /usr/lib/system/libsystem_c.dylib
__DATA_DIRTY             1e79657f0-1e7965820    [    48     48     48     0K] rw-/rw- SM=COW      /usr/lib/system/libsystem_darwin.dylib
__DATA_DIRTY             1e7965820-1e7965830    [    16     16     16     0K] rw-/rw- SM=COW      /usr/lib/system/libsystem_featureflags.dylib
__DATA_DIRTY             1e7965830-1e7965ac0    [   656    656    656     0K] rw-/rw- SM=COW      /usr/lib/system/libsystem_info.dylib
__DATA_DIRTY             1e7965ac0-1e7966184    [  1732   1732   1732     0K] rw-/rw- SM=COW      /usr/lib/system/libsystem_kernel.dylib
unused __DATA            1e7966184-1e7966188    [     4      4      4     0K] rw-/rw- SM=COW      on dirty page  unused system shared lib __DATA
__DATA_DIRTY             1e7966188-1e79663a0    [   536    536    536     0K] rw-/rw- SM=COW      /usr/lib/system/libsystem_malloc.dylib
__DATA_DIRTY             1e79663a0-1e79663e1    [    65     65     65     0K] rw-/rw- SM=COW      /usr/lib/system/libsystem_networkextension.dylib
unused __DATA            1e79663e1-1e79663e8    [     7      7      7     0K] rw-/rw- SM=COW      on dirty page  unused system shared lib __DATA
__DATA_DIRTY             1e79663e8-1e79663f0    [     8      8      8     0K] rw-/rw- SM=COW      /usr/lib/system/libsystem_notify.dylib
__DATA_DIRTY             1e79663f0-1e7966404    [    20     20     20     0K] rw-/rw- SM=COW      /usr/lib/system/libsystem_platform.dylib
unused __DATA            1e7966404-1e7968000    [    7K     7K     7K     0K] rw-/rw- SM=COW      on dirty page  unused system shared lib __DATA
__DATA_DIRTY             1e7968000-1e796d838    [   22K    22K    22K     0K] rw-/rw- SM=COW      /usr/lib/system/libsystem_pthread.dylib
__DATA_DIRTY             1e796d838-1e796d848    [    16     16     16     0K] rw-/rw- SM=COW      /usr/lib/system/libsystem_symptoms.dylib
__DATA_DIRTY             1e796d848-1e796dcb8    [  1136   1136   1136     0K] rw-/rw- SM=COW      /usr/lib/system/libsystem_trace.dylib
__DATA_DIRTY             1e796dcb8-1e796e708    [  2640   2640   2640     0K] rw-/rw- SM=COW      /usr/lib/system/libxpc.dylib
unused __DATA            1e796e708-1e7970000    [    6K     6K     6K     0K] rw-/rw- SM=COW      on dirty page  unused system shared lib __DATA
```

```
__AUTH          1e7970000-1e79701b8  [    440    440     0K     0K] rw-/rw- SM=COW          /usr/lib/system/libsystem_trace.dylib
__AUTH          1e79701b8-1e7970218  [     96     96     0K     0K] rw-/rw- SM=COW          /usr/lib/system/libcorecrypto.dylib
__AUTH          1e7974000-1e797c000  [    32K    32K     0K     0K] rw-/rw- SM=COW          /usr/lib/system/libsystem_malloc.dylib
__DATA          1e797c000-1e797d400  [     5K     5K     0K     0K] rw-/rw- SM=COW          /usr/lib/system/libdispatch.dylib
__AUTH          1e797d400-1e797d478  [    120    120     0K     0K] rw-/rw- SM=COW          /usr/lib/libobjc.A.dylib
__AUTH          1e797d478-1e797e190  [   3352   3352     0K     0K] rw-/rw- SM=COW          /usr/lib/system/libsystem_c.dylib
__AUTH          1e797e190-1e7980628  [     9K     9K   1576     0K] rw-/rw- SM=COW          /usr/lib/libc++.1.dylib
__AUTH          1e7980628-1e7980670  [     72     72     72     0K] rw-/rw- SM=COW          /usr/lib/libc++abi.dylib
__AUTH          1e7980670-1e79806b0  [     64     64     64     0K] rw-/rw- SM=COW          /usr/lib/system/libdyld.dylib
__AUTH          1e79806b0-1e7980880  [    464    464    464     0K] rw-/rw- SM=COW          /usr/lib/system/libsystem_info.dylib
unused __AUTH   1e7980880-1e7982740  [     8K     8K     8K     0K] rw-/rw- SM=COW          ...y page   unused
/System/Library/Frameworks/CoreFoundation.framework/Versions/A/CoreFoundation
unused __AUTH   1e7982740-1e7984000  [     6K     6K     6K     0K] rw-/rw- SM=COW
...eServices.framework/Versions/A/Frameworks/LaunchServices.framework/Versions/A/LaunchServices
__AUTH          1e7a0a640-1e7a0a660  [     32     0K     0K     0K] rw-/rw- SM=COW          /usr/lib/system/libcommonCrypto.dylib
__AUTH          1e7a0a660-1e7a0a668  [      8     0K     0K     0K] rw-/rw- SM=COW          /usr/lib/libSystem.B.dylib
__OBJC_RW       1e87f0000-1e8b08000  [  3168K   2960K    16K     0K] rw-/rw- SM=COW          /usr/lib/libobjc.A.dylib
MALLOC_NANO     600000000000-600008000000 [128.0M  144K   144K     0K] rw-/rwx SM=PRV          DefaultMallocZone_0x101150000
MALLOC_NANO (empty) 600008000000-600020000000 [384.0M   0K     0K     0K] rw-/rwx SM=NUL


==== Legend
SM=sharing mode:
        COW=copy_on_write PRV=private NUL=empty ALI=aliased
        SHM=shared ZER=zero_filled S/A=shared_alias
PURGE=purgeable mode:
        V=volatile N=nonvolatile E=empty    otherwise is unpurgeable


==== Summary for process 88726
ReadOnly portion of Libraries: Total=582.2M resident=75.7M(13%) swapped_out_or_unallocated=506.5M(87%)
Writable regions: Total=531.8M written=400K(0%) resident=464K(0%) swapped_out=0K(0%) unallocated=531.3M(100%)
```

REGION TYPE	VIRTUAL SIZE	RESIDENT SIZE	DIRTY SIZE	SWAPPED SIZE	VOLATILE SIZE	NONVOL SIZE	EMPTY SIZE	REGION COUNT (non-coalesced)	
Kernel Alloc Once	32K	16K	16K	0K	0K	0K	0K	1	
MALLOC guard page	96K	0K	0K	0K	0K	0K	0K	5	
MALLOC metadata	176K	176K	176K	0K	0K	0K	0K	8	
MALLOC_NANO	128.0M	144K	144K	0K	0K	0K	0K	1	see MALLOC ZONE table below
MALLOC_NANO (empty)	384.0M	0K	0K	0K	0K	0K	0K	1	see MALLOC ZONE table below
MALLOC_SMALL	8192K	32K	32K	0K	0K	0K	0K	1	see MALLOC ZONE table below
MALLOC_TINY	1024K	32K	32K	0K	0K	0K	0K	1	see MALLOC ZONE table below
STACK GUARD	56.1M	0K	0K	0K	0K	0K	0K	6	
Stack	10.6M	112K	112K	0K	0K	0K	0K	6	
__AUTH	46K	46K	2176	0K	0K	0K	0K	11	
__AUTH_CONST	67K	62K	0K	0K	0K	0K	0K	38	
__DATA	173K	173K	77K	0K	0K	0K	0K	37	
__DATA_CONST	258K	194K	48K	0K	0K	0K	0K	40	
__DATA_DIRTY	73K	73K	73K	0K	0K	0K	0K	21	
__LINKEDIT	577.6M	71.4M	0K	0K	0K	0K	0K	3	
__OBJC_CONST	10K	10K	0K	0K	0K	0K	0K	5	
__OBJC_RO	83.0M	67.6M	0K	0K	0K	0K	0K	1	
__OBJC_RW	3168K	2960K	16K	0K	0K	0K	0K	1	
__TEXT	4708K	4420K	0K	0K	0K	0K	0K	43	
dyld private memory	1024K	16K	16K	0K	0K	0K	0K	1	
shared memory	16K	16K	16K	0K	0K	0K	0K	1	
unused but dirty shlib __DATA	72K	72K	72K	0K	0K	0K	0K	30	
TOTAL	1.2G	147.3M	832K	0K	0K	0K	0K	262	

MALLOC ZONE	VIRTUAL SIZE	RESIDENT SIZE	DIRTY SIZE	SWAPPED SIZE	ALLOCATION COUNT	BYTES ALLOCATED	DIRTY+SWAP FRAG SIZE	% FRAG	REGION COUNT
DefaultMallocZone_0x101150000	128.0M	144K	144K	0K	211	9K	135K	94%	1
MallocHelperZone_0x101114000	9216K	64K	64K	0K	2	2064	62K	97%	2
TOTAL	137.0M	208K	208K	0K	213	11K	197K	95%	3

Note: We see that the value of **SP** is inside the stack region so **str** instruction would succeed (this is not a stack overflow case). Eventually, this would have hit the stack region boundary if we hadn't had an earlier local buffer overflow. However, thread numbers do not match, in the core dump it is core thread 4 and in the *vmmap* output, the stack region corresponds to thread 5 (both numberings start from 0).

5.   If we compare the number of threads in the core dump and the *spindump* output in *App7_sample.txt* (we could also save another core dump manually for comparison) we see that the latter has one more thread. Looking at stack traces we identify the missing thread:

```
Thread 0x2bad71    1001 samples (1-1001)    priority 31 (base 31)
1001  thread_start + 8 (libsystem_pthread.dylib + 8332) [0x18ea0308c]
  1001  _pthread_start + 148 (libsystem_pthread.dylib + 29292) [0x18ea0826c]
    1001  thread_three + 20 (App7 + 15740) [0x100ffbd7c]
      1001  foo_three + 12 (App7 + 15712) [0x100ffbd60]
        1001  bar_three + 16 (App7 + 15688) [0x100ffbd48]
          1001  sleep + 52 (libsystem_c.dylib + 105336) [0x18e8e1b78]
            1001  <patched truncated backtrace>
              1001  __semwait_signal + 8 (libsystem_kernel.dylib + 20588) [0x18e9ce06c]
```

Note: If we disassemble the *bar_three* function and follow the call path, we come to signed integer divide instruction that didn't generate the divide by zero exception as on the x64 platform so the thread exited normally.

```
(lldb) di -n bar_three
App7`bar_three:
    0x100ffbd38 <+0>:   stp    x29, x30, [sp, #-0x10]!
    0x100ffbd3c <+4>:   mov    x29, sp
    0x100ffbd40 <+8>:   mov    w0, #0x12c
    0x100ffbd44 <+12>:  bl     0x100ffbf28              ; symbol stub for: sleep
    0x100ffbd48 <+16>:  bl     0x100ffbb8c              ; procC
    0x100ffbd4c <+20>:  ldp    x29, x30, [sp], #0x10
    0x100ffbd50 <+24>:  ret
```

```
(lldb) di -n procC
App7`procC:
    0x100ffbb8c <+0>:   stp    x29, x30, [sp, #-0x10]!
    0x100ffbb90 <+4>:   mov    x29, sp
    0x100ffbb94 <+8>:   mov    w0, #0x1
    0x100ffbb98 <+12>:  mov    w1, #0x0
    0x100ffbb9c <+16>:  bl     0x100ffbb6c              ; procD
    0x100ffbba0 <+20>:  ldp    x29, x30, [sp], #0x10
    0x100ffbba4 <+24>:  ret
```

```
(lldb) di -n procD
App7`procD:
    0x100ffbb6c <+0>:   sub    sp, sp, #0x10
    0x100ffbb70 <+4>:   str    w0, [sp, #0xc]
    0x100ffbb74 <+8>:   str    w1, [sp, #0x8]
    0x100ffbb78 <+12>:  ldr    w8, [sp, #0xc]
    0x100ffbb7c <+16>:  ldr    w9, [sp, #0x8]
    0x100ffbb80 <+20>:  sdiv   w0, w8, w9
    0x100ffbb84 <+24>:  add    sp, sp, #0x10
    0x100ffbb88 <+28>:  ret
```

Exercise X8

- **Goal:** Learn how to identify runtime exceptions, past execution residue and stack traces, identify handled exceptions

- **Patterns:** C++ Exception; Execution Residue; Coincidental Symbolic Information; Handled Exception

- \AMCDA-Dumps\Exercise-X8.pdf

Exercise X8

Goal: Learn how to identify runtime exceptions, past execution residue and stack traces, and identify handled exceptions.

Patterns: C++ Exception; Execution Residue; Coincidental Symbolic Information; Handled Exception.

1.   Identify the problem thread and application-specific diagnostic from the diagnostic report *App8-2022-12-07-225601.ips*:

```
--------------------------------------
Translated Report (Full Report Below)
--------------------------------------

Process:             App8 [89800]
Path:                /Users/USER/*/App8
Identifier:          App8
Version:             ???
Code Type:           ARM-64 (Native)
Parent Process:      zsh [93565]
Responsible:         Terminal [9503]
User ID:             501

Date/Time:           2022-12-07 22:56:01.5953 +0000
OS Version:          macOS 12.6 (21G115)
Report Version:      12
Anonymous UUID:      6F758133-2B79-4743-8B70-8B1D8C510718

Sleep/Wake UUID:     .6B3BBC20-FE58-4C80-8D8C-DAEC78723A28

Time Awake Since Boot: 210000 seconds
Time Since Wake:       174 seconds

System Integrity Protection: enabled

Crashed Thread:      1

Exception Type:      EXC_CRASH (SIGABRT)
Exception Codes:     0x0000000000000000, 0x0000000000000000
Exception Note:      EXC_CORPSE_NOTIFY

Application Specific Information:
abort() called


Thread 0::  Dispatch queue: com.apple.main-thread
0   libsystem_kernel.dylib            0x18e9ce06c __semwait_signal + 8
1   libsystem_c.dylib                 0x18e8d6fc8 nanosleep + 220
2   libsystem_c.dylib                 0x18e8e1b78 sleep + 52
3   libsystem_c.dylib                 0x18e8e1b90 sleep + 76
4   App8                              0x102f4fbec main + 164
5   dyld                              0x102fcd08c start + 520

Thread 1 Crashed:
0   libsystem_kernel.dylib            0x18e9d2d98 __pthread_kill + 8
1   libsystem_pthread.dylib           0x18ea07ee0 pthread_kill + 288
2   libsystem_c.dylib                 0x18e942340 abort + 168
3   libc++abi.dylib                   0x18e9c2b08 abort_message + 132
4   libc++abi.dylib                   0x18e9b2950 demangling_terminate_handler() + 336
5   libobjc.A.dylib                   0x18e8a8330 _objc_terminate() + 160
6   libc++abi.dylib                   0x18e9c1ea4 std::__terminate(void (*)()) + 20
7   libc++abi.dylib                   0x18e9c4c1c __cxxabiv1::failed_throw(__cxxabiv1::__cxa_exception*) +
36
8   libc++abi.dylib                   0x18e9c4bc8 __cxa_throw + 140
9   App8                              0x102f4f7e8 procB() + 172
10  App8                              0x102f4f904 procA() + 12
11  App8                              0x102f4f9a8 procNH() + 20
12  App8                              0x102f4f9d8 bar_one() + 12
13  App8                              0x102f4f9ec foo_one() + 12
```

```
14  App8                                0x102f4fa08 thread_one(void*) + 20
15  libsystem_pthread.dylib             0x18ea0826c _pthread_start + 148
16  libsystem_pthread.dylib             0x18ea0308c thread_start + 8

Thread 2:
0   libsystem_kernel.dylib              0x18e9ce06c __semwait_signal + 8
1   libsystem_c.dylib                   0x18e8d6fc8 nanosleep + 220
2   libsystem_c.dylib                   0x18e8e1b78 sleep + 52
3   libsystem_c.dylib                   0x18e8e1b90 sleep + 76
4   App8                                0x102f4f9c4 procNE() + 20
5   App8                                0x102f4fa24 bar_two() + 12
6   App8                                0x102f4fa38 foo_two() + 12
7   App8                                0x102f4fa54 thread_two(void*) + 20
8   libsystem_pthread.dylib             0x18ea0826c _pthread_start + 148
9   libsystem_pthread.dylib             0x18ea0308c thread_start + 8

Thread 3:
0   libsystem_kernel.dylib              0x18e9ce06c __semwait_signal + 8
1   libsystem_c.dylib                   0x18e8d6fc8 nanosleep + 220
2   libsystem_c.dylib                   0x18e8e1b78 sleep + 52
3   libsystem_c.dylib                   0x18e8e1b90 sleep + 76
4   App8                                0x102f4f958 procH() + 56
5   App8                                0x102f4fa70 bar_three() + 12
6   App8                                0x102f4fa84 foo_three() + 12
7   App8                                0x102f4faa0 thread_three(void*) + 20
8   libsystem_pthread.dylib             0x18ea0826c _pthread_start + 148
9   libsystem_pthread.dylib             0x18ea0308c thread_start + 8

Thread 4:
0   libsystem_kernel.dylib              0x18e9ce06c __semwait_signal + 8
1   libsystem_c.dylib                   0x18e8d6fc8 nanosleep + 220
2   libsystem_c.dylib                   0x18e8e1b78 sleep + 52
3   libsystem_c.dylib                   0x18e8e1b90 sleep + 76
4   App8                                0x102f4f9c4 procNE() + 20
5   App8                                0x102f4fabc bar_four() + 12
6   App8                                0x102f4fad0 foo_four() + 12
7   App8                                0x102f4faec thread_four(void*) + 20
8   libsystem_pthread.dylib             0x18ea0826c _pthread_start + 148
9   libsystem_pthread.dylib             0x18ea0308c thread_start + 8

Thread 5:
0   libsystem_kernel.dylib              0x18e9ce06c __semwait_signal + 8
1   libsystem_c.dylib                   0x18e8d6fc8 nanosleep + 220
2   libsystem_c.dylib                   0x18e8e1b78 sleep + 52
3   libsystem_c.dylib                   0x18e8e1b90 sleep + 76
4   App8                                0x102f4f9c4 procNE() + 20
5   App8                                0x102f4fb08 bar_five() + 12
6   App8                                0x102f4fb1c foo_five() + 12
7   App8                                0x102f4fb38 thread_five(void*) + 20
8   libsystem_pthread.dylib             0x18ea0826c _pthread_start + 148
9   libsystem_pthread.dylib             0x18ea0308c thread_start + 8


Thread 1 crashed with ARM Thread State (64-bit):
   x0: 0x0000000000000000   x1: 0x0000000000000000   x2: 0x0000000000000000   x3: 0x0000000000000000
   x4: 0x000000018e9c60f5   x5: 0x000000016cf3aa20   x6: 0x000000000000002a   x7: 0x0000000000000001
   x8: 0xb60ce2c5aaa53405   x9: 0xb60ce2c4c6568405  x10: 0x0000000000000200  x11: 0x000000000000000a
  x12: 0x000000000000000a  x13: 0x000000016cf3aa44  x14: 0x000000018e9c611b  x15: 0x0000000000000014
  x16: 0x0000000000000148  x17: 0x000000001e8b2b680  x18: 0x0000000000000000  x19: 0x0000000000000006
  x20: 0x000000016cf3b000  x21: 0x0000000000001403  x22: 0x000000016cf3b0e0  x23: 0x000000014d704110
  x24: 0x0000000000000000  x25: 0x0000000000000000  x26: 0x0000000000000000  x27: 0x0000000000000000
  x28: 0x0000000000000000   fp: 0x000000016cf3a990   lr: 0x000000018ea07ee0
   sp: 0x000000016cf3a970   pc: 0x000000018e9d2d98 cpsr: 0x40001000
  far: 0x00000001e7968068  esr: 0x56000080  Address size fault

Binary Images:
     0x18e9c9000 -        0x18ea00fff libsystem_kernel.dylib (*) <a9d87740-9c1d-3468-bf60-720a8d713cba>
/usr/lib/system/libsystem_kernel.dylib
     0x18e8c8000 -        0x18e949fff libsystem_c.dylib (*) <b25d2080-bb9e-38d6-8236-9cef4b2f11a3>
/usr/lib/system/libsystem_c.dylib
     0x102f4c000 -        0x102f4ffff App8 (*) <f1f46b72-febf-3997-97ef-dabdf8e88f80> /Users/USER/*/App8
     0x102fc8000 -        0x103027fff dyld (*) <38ee9fe9-b66d-3066-8c5c-6ddf0d6944c6> /usr/lib/dyld
     0x18ea01000 -        0x18ea0dfff libsystem_pthread.dylib (*) <63c4eef9-69a5-38b1-996e-8d31b66a051d>
/usr/lib/system/libsystem_pthread.dylib
     0x18e9b1000 -        0x18e9c8fff libc++abi.dylib (*) <4e8d8a11-4217-3d56-9d41-5426f7cf307c> /usr/lib/libc+
+abi.dylib
```

```
        0x18e887000 -        0x18e8c4fff libobjc.A.dylib (*) <ec96f0fa-6341-3e1d-be54-49b544e17f7d>
/usr/lib/libobjc.A.dylib

External Modification Summary:
  Calls made by other processes targeting this process:
    task_for_pid: 0
    thread_create: 0
    thread_set_state: 0
  Calls made by this process:
    task_for_pid: 0
    thread_create: 0
    thread_set_state: 0
  Calls made by all processes on this machine:
    task_for_pid: 1
    thread_create: 0
    thread_set_state: 0

VM Region Summary:
ReadOnly portion of Libraries: Total=582.2M resident=0K(0%) swapped_out_or_unallocated=582.2M(100%)
Writable regions: Total=532.8M written=0K(0%) resident=0K(0%) swapped_out=0K(0%) unallocated=532.8M(100%)

                                VIRTUAL   REGION
REGION TYPE                        SIZE    COUNT (non-coalesced)
===========                     =======  =======
Kernel Alloc Once                   32K        1
MALLOC                           138.3M       18
MALLOC_NANO (reserved)           384.0M        1          reserved VM address space (unallocated)
Stack                             10.7M       11
Stack (reserved)                  56.0M        1          reserved VM address space (unallocated)
__AUTH                              46K       11
__AUTH_CONST                        67K       38
__DATA                             173K       37
__DATA_CONST                       258K       40
__DATA_DIRTY                        73K       21
__LINKEDIT                       577.6M        3
__OBJC_CONST                        10K        5
__OBJC_RO                         83.0M        1
__OBJC_RW                         3168K        1
__TEXT                            4708K       43
dyld private memory               1024K        1
shared memory                       16K        1
===========                     =======  =======
TOTAL                               1.2G      234
TOTAL, minus reserved VM space   818.9M      234
```

2.   Load a core dump *core.89800* and *App8* executable:

```
% lldb -c ~/AMCDA-Dumps/core.89800 -f ~/AMCDA-Dumps/Apps/App8/Build/Products/Release/App8
(lldb) target create "/Users/training/AMCDA-Dumps/Apps/App8/Build/Products/Release/App8" --
core "/Users/training/AMCDA-Dumps/core.89800"
Core file '/Users/training/AMCDA-Dumps/core.89800' (arm64) was loaded.
```

3.   Go to the normal core thread 2 (thread #3), identify execution residue of *work* functions and check their correctness:

```
(lldb) thread select 3
* thread #3
    frame #0: 0x000000018e9ce06c libsystem_kernel.dylib`__semwait_signal + 8
libsystem_kernel.dylib`:
->  0x18e9ce06c <+8>:  b.lo   0x18e9ce08c                    ; <+40>
    0x18e9ce070 <+12>: pacibsp
    0x18e9ce074 <+16>: stp    x29, x30, [sp, #-0x10]!
    0x18e9ce078 <+20>: mov    x29, sp
```

```
(lldb) bt
* thread #3
  * frame #0: 0x000000018e9ce06c libsystem_kernel.dylib`__semwait_signal + 8
    frame #1: 0x000000018e8d6fc8 libsystem_c.dylib`nanosleep + 220
    frame #2: 0x000000018e8e1b78 libsystem_c.dylib`sleep + 52
    frame #3: 0x000000018e8e1b90 libsystem_c.dylib`sleep + 76
    frame #4: 0x0000000102f4f9c4 App8`procNE() + 20
    frame #5: 0x0000000102f4fa24 App8`bar_two() + 12
    frame #6: 0x0000000102f4fa38 App8`foo_two() + 12
    frame #7: 0x0000000102f4fa54 App8`thread_two(void*) + 20
    frame #8: 0x000000018ea0826c libsystem_pthread.dylib`_pthread_start + 148

(lldb) x/600a $sp-0x1000 --force
0x16cfc5ec0: 0x0000000000000000
0x16cfc5ec8: 0x0000000000000000
0x16cfc5ed0: 0x0000000000000000
0x16cfc5ed8: 0x0000000000000000
0x16cfc5ee0: 0x0000000000000000
0x16cfc5ee8: 0x0000000000000000
0x16cfc5ef0: 0x0000000000000000
0x16cfc5ef8: 0x0000000000000000
0x16cfc5f00: 0x0000000000000000
0x16cfc5f08: 0x0000000000000000
0x16cfc5f10: 0x0000000000000000
0x16cfc5f18: 0x0000000000000000
0x16cfc5f20: 0x0000000000000000
0x16cfc5f28: 0x0000000000000000
0x16cfc5f30: 0x0000000000000000
0x16cfc5f38: 0x0000000000000000
0x16cfc5f40: 0x0000000000000000
0x16cfc5f48: 0x0000000000000000
0x16cfc5f50: 0x0000000000000000
0x16cfc5f58: 0x0000000000000000
0x16cfc5f60: 0x0000000000000000
0x16cfc5f68: 0x0000000000000000
0x16cfc5f70: 0x0000000000000000
0x16cfc5f78: 0x0000000000000000
0x16cfc5f80: 0x0000000000000000
0x16cfc5f88: 0x0000000000000000
0x16cfc5f90: 0x0000000000000000
0x16cfc5f98: 0x0000000000000000
0x16cfc5fa0: 0x0000000000000000
0x16cfc5fa8: 0x0000000000000000
0x16cfc5fb0: 0x0000000000000000
0x16cfc5fb8: 0x0000000000000000
0x16cfc5fc0: 0x0000000000000000
0x16cfc5fc8: 0x0000000000000000
0x16cfc5fd0: 0x0000000000000000
0x16cfc5fd8: 0x0000000000000000
0x16cfc5fe0: 0x0000000000000000
0x16cfc5fe8: 0x0000000000000000
0x16cfc5ff0: 0x0000000000000000
0x16cfc5ff8: 0x0000000000000000
0x16cfc6000: 0x0000000000000000
0x16cfc6008: 0x0000000000000000
0x16cfc6010: 0x0000000000000000
0x16cfc6018: 0x0000000000000000
0x16cfc6020: 0x0000000000000000
0x16cfc6028: 0x0000000000000000
0x16cfc6030: 0x0000000000000000
0x16cfc6038: 0x0000000000000000
```

```
0x16cfc6040:  0x0000000000000000
0x16cfc6048:  0x0000000000000000
0x16cfc6050:  0x0000000000000000
0x16cfc6058:  0x0000000000000000
0x16cfc6060:  0x0000000000000000
0x16cfc6068:  0x0000000000000000
0x16cfc6070:  0x0000000000000000
0x16cfc6078:  0x0000000000000000
0x16cfc6080:  0x0000000000000000
0x16cfc6088:  0x0000000000000000
0x16cfc6090:  0x0000000000000000
0x16cfc6098:  0x0000000000000000
0x16cfc60a0:  0x0000000000000000
0x16cfc60a8:  0x0000000000000000
0x16cfc60b0:  0x0000000000000000
0x16cfc60b8:  0x0000000000000000
0x16cfc60c0:  0x0000000000000000
0x16cfc60c8:  0x0000000000000000
0x16cfc60d0:  0x0000000000000000
0x16cfc60d8:  0x0000000000000000
0x16cfc60e0:  0x0000000000000000
0x16cfc60e8:  0x0000000000000000
0x16cfc60f0:  0x0000000000000000
0x16cfc60f8:  0x0000000000000000
0x16cfc6100:  0x0000000000000000
0x16cfc6108:  0x0000000000000000
0x16cfc6110:  0x0000000000000000
0x16cfc6118:  0x0000000000000000
0x16cfc6120:  0x0000000000000000
0x16cfc6128:  0x0000000000000000
0x16cfc6130:  0x0000000000000000
0x16cfc6138:  0x0000000000000000
0x16cfc6140:  0x0000000000000000
0x16cfc6148:  0x0000000000000000
0x16cfc6150:  0x0000000000000000
0x16cfc6158:  0x0000000000000000
0x16cfc6160:  0x0000000000000000
0x16cfc6168:  0x0000000000000000
0x16cfc6170:  0x0000000000000000
0x16cfc6178:  0x0000000000000000
0x16cfc6180:  0x0000000000000000
0x16cfc6188:  0x0000000000000000
0x16cfc6190:  0x0000000000000000
0x16cfc6198:  0x0000000000000000
0x16cfc61a0:  0x0000000000000000
0x16cfc61a8:  0x0000000000000000
0x16cfc61b0:  0x0000000000000000
0x16cfc61b8:  0x0000000000000000
0x16cfc61c0:  0x0000000000000000
0x16cfc61c8:  0x0000000000000000
0x16cfc61d0:  0x0000000000000000
0x16cfc61d8:  0x0000000000000000
0x16cfc61e0:  0x0000000000000000
0x16cfc61e8:  0x0000000000000000
0x16cfc61f0:  0x0000000000000000
0x16cfc61f8:  0x0000000000000000
0x16cfc6200:  0x0000000000000000
0x16cfc6208:  0x0000000000000000
0x16cfc6210:  0x0000000000000000
0x16cfc6218:  0x0000000000000000
0x16cfc6220:  0x0000000000000000
```

```
0x16cfc6228:  0x0000000000000000
0x16cfc6230:  0x0000000000000000
0x16cfc6238:  0x0000000000000000
0x16cfc6240:  0x0000000000000000
0x16cfc6248:  0x0000000000000000
0x16cfc6250:  0x0000000000000000
0x16cfc6258:  0x0000000000000000
0x16cfc6260:  0x0000000000000000
0x16cfc6268:  0x0000000000000000
0x16cfc6270:  0x0000000000000000
0x16cfc6278:  0x0000000000000000
0x16cfc6280:  0x0000000000000000
0x16cfc6288:  0x0000000000000000
0x16cfc6290:  0x0000000000000000
0x16cfc6298:  0x0000000000000000
0x16cfc62a0:  0x0000000000000000
0x16cfc62a8:  0x0000000000000000
0x16cfc62b0:  0x0000000000000000
0x16cfc62b8:  0x0000000000000000
0x16cfc62c0:  0x0000000000000000
0x16cfc62c8:  0x0000000000000000
0x16cfc62d0:  0x0000000000000000
0x16cfc62d8:  0x0000000000000000
0x16cfc62e0:  0x0000000000000000
0x16cfc62e8:  0x0000000000000000
0x16cfc62f0:  0x0000000000000000
0x16cfc62f8:  0x0000000000000000
0x16cfc6300:  0x0000000000000000
0x16cfc6308:  0x0000000000000000
0x16cfc6310:  0x0000000000000000
0x16cfc6318:  0x0000000000000000
0x16cfc6320:  0x0000000000000000
0x16cfc6328:  0x0000000000000000
0x16cfc6330:  0x0000000000000000
0x16cfc6338:  0x0000000000000000
0x16cfc6340:  0x0000000000000000
0x16cfc6348:  0x0000000000000000
0x16cfc6350:  0x0000000000000000
0x16cfc6358:  0x0000000000000000
0x16cfc6360:  0x0000000000000000
0x16cfc6368:  0x0000000000000000
0x16cfc6370:  0x0000000000000000
0x16cfc6378:  0x0000000000000000
0x16cfc6380:  0x0000000000000000
0x16cfc6388:  0x0000000000000000
0x16cfc6390:  0x0000000000000000
0x16cfc6398:  0x0000000000000000
0x16cfc63a0:  0x0000000000000000
0x16cfc63a8:  0x0000000000000000
0x16cfc63b0:  0x0000000000000000
0x16cfc63b8:  0x0000000000000000
0x16cfc63c0:  0x0000000000000000
0x16cfc63c8:  0x0000000000000000
0x16cfc63d0:  0x0000000000000000
0x16cfc63d8:  0x0000000000000000
0x16cfc63e0:  0x0000000000000000
0x16cfc63e8:  0x0000000000000000
0x16cfc63f0:  0x0000000000000000
0x16cfc63f8:  0x0000000000000000
0x16cfc6400:  0x0000000000000000
0x16cfc6408:  0x0000000000000000
```

```
0x16cfc6410:  0x0000000000000000
0x16cfc6418:  0x0000000000000000
0x16cfc6420:  0x0000000000000000
0x16cfc6428:  0x0000000000000000
0x16cfc6430:  0x0000000000000000
0x16cfc6438:  0x0000000000000000
0x16cfc6440:  0x0000000000000000
0x16cfc6448:  0x0000000000000000
0x16cfc6450:  0x0000000000000000
0x16cfc6458:  0x0000000000000000
0x16cfc6460:  0x0000000000000000
0x16cfc6468:  0x0000000000000000
0x16cfc6470:  0x0000000000000000
0x16cfc6478:  0x0000000000000000
0x16cfc6480:  0x0000000000000000
0x16cfc6488:  0x0000000000000000
0x16cfc6490:  0x0000000000000000
0x16cfc6498:  0x0000000000000000
0x16cfc64a0:  0x0000000000000000
0x16cfc64a8:  0x0000000000000000
0x16cfc64b0:  0x0000000000000000
0x16cfc64b8:  0x0000000000000000
0x16cfc64c0:  0x0000000000000000
0x16cfc64c8:  0x0000000000000000
0x16cfc64d0:  0x0000000000000000
0x16cfc64d8:  0x0000000000000000
0x16cfc64e0:  0x0000000000000000
0x16cfc64e8:  0x0000000000000000
0x16cfc64f0:  0x0000000000000000
0x16cfc64f8:  0x0000000000000000
0x16cfc6500:  0x0000000000000000
0x16cfc6508:  0x0000000000000000
0x16cfc6510:  0x0000000000000000
0x16cfc6518:  0x0000000000000000
0x16cfc6520:  0x0000000000000000
0x16cfc6528:  0x0000000000000000
0x16cfc6530:  0x0000000000000000
0x16cfc6538:  0x0000000000000000
0x16cfc6540:  0x0000000000000000
0x16cfc6548:  0x0000000000000000
0x16cfc6550:  0x0000000000000000
0x16cfc6558:  0x0000000000000000
0x16cfc6560:  0x0000000000000000
0x16cfc6568:  0x0000000000000000
0x16cfc6570:  0x0000000000000000
0x16cfc6578:  0x0000000000000000
0x16cfc6580:  0x0000000000000000
0x16cfc6588:  0x0000000000000000
0x16cfc6590:  0x0000000000000000
0x16cfc6598:  0x0000000000000000
0x16cfc65a0:  0x0000000000000000
0x16cfc65a8:  0x0000000000000000
0x16cfc65b0:  0x0000000000000000
0x16cfc65b8:  0x0000000000000000
0x16cfc65c0:  0x0000000000000000
0x16cfc65c8:  0x0000000000000000
0x16cfc65d0:  0x0000000000000000
0x16cfc65d8:  0x0000000000000000
0x16cfc65e0:  0x0000000000000000
0x16cfc65e8:  0x0000000000000000
0x16cfc65f0:  0x0000000000000000
```

```
0x16cfc65f8:  0x0000000000000000
0x16cfc6600:  0x0000000000000000
0x16cfc6608:  0x0000000000000000
0x16cfc6610:  0x0000000000000000
0x16cfc6618:  0x0000000000000000
0x16cfc6620:  0x0000000000000000
0x16cfc6628:  0x0000000000000000
0x16cfc6630:  0x0000000000000000
0x16cfc6638:  0x0000000000000000
0x16cfc6640:  0x0000000000000000
0x16cfc6648:  0x0000000000000000
0x16cfc6650:  0x0000000000000000
0x16cfc6658:  0x0000000000000000
0x16cfc6660:  0x0000000000000000
0x16cfc6668:  0x0000000000000000
0x16cfc6670:  0x0000000000000000
0x16cfc6678:  0x0000000000000000
0x16cfc6680:  0x0000000000000000
0x16cfc6688:  0x0000000000000000
0x16cfc6690:  0x0000000000000000
0x16cfc6698:  0x0000000000000000
0x16cfc66a0:  0x0000000000000000
0x16cfc66a8:  0x0000000000000000
0x16cfc66b0:  0x0000000000000000
0x16cfc66b8:  0x0000000000000000
0x16cfc66c0:  0x0000000000000000
0x16cfc66c8:  0x0000000000000000
0x16cfc66d0:  0x0000000000000000
0x16cfc66d8:  0x0000000000000000
0x16cfc66e0:  0x0000000000000000
0x16cfc66e8:  0x0000000000000000
0x16cfc66f0:  0x0000000000000000
0x16cfc66f8:  0x0000000000000000
0x16cfc6700:  0x0000000000000000
0x16cfc6708:  0x0000000000000000
0x16cfc6710:  0x0000000000000000
0x16cfc6718:  0x0000000000000000
0x16cfc6720:  0x0000000000000000
0x16cfc6728:  0x0000000000000000
0x16cfc6730:  0x0000000000000000
0x16cfc6738:  0x0000000000000000
0x16cfc6740:  0x0000000000000000
0x16cfc6748:  0x0000000000000000
0x16cfc6750:  0x0000000000000000
0x16cfc6758:  0x0000000000000000
0x16cfc6760:  0x0000000000000000
0x16cfc6768:  0x0000000000000000
0x16cfc6770:  0x0000000000000000
0x16cfc6778:  0x0000000000000000
0x16cfc6780:  0x0000000000000000
0x16cfc6788:  0x0000000000000000
0x16cfc6790:  0x0000000000000000
0x16cfc6798:  0x0000000000000000
0x16cfc67a0:  0x0000000000000000
0x16cfc67a8:  0x0000000000000000
0x16cfc67b0:  0x0000000000000000
0x16cfc67b8:  0x0000000000000000
0x16cfc67c0:  0x0000000000000000
0x16cfc67c8:  0x0000000000000000
0x16cfc67d0:  0x0000000000000000
0x16cfc67d8:  0x0000000000000000
```

```
0x16cfc67e0:  0x0000000000000000
0x16cfc67e8:  0x0000000000000000
0x16cfc67f0:  0x0000000000000000
0x16cfc67f8:  0x0000000000000000
0x16cfc6800:  0x0000000000000000
0x16cfc6808:  0x0000000000000000
0x16cfc6810:  0x0000000000000000
0x16cfc6818:  0x0000000000000000
0x16cfc6820:  0x0000000000000000
0x16cfc6828:  0x0000000000000000
0x16cfc6830:  0x0000000000000000
0x16cfc6838:  0x0000000000000000
0x16cfc6840:  0x0000000000000000
0x16cfc6848:  0x0000000000000000
0x16cfc6850:  0x0000000000000000
0x16cfc6858:  0x0000000000000000
0x16cfc6860:  0x0000000000000000
0x16cfc6868:  0x0000000000000000
0x16cfc6870:  0x0000000000000000
0x16cfc6878:  0x0000000000000000
0x16cfc6880:  0x0000000000000000
0x16cfc6888:  0x0000000000000000
0x16cfc6890:  0x0000000000000000
0x16cfc6898:  0x0000000000000000
0x16cfc68a0:  0x0000000000000000
0x16cfc68a8:  0x0000000000000000
0x16cfc68b0:  0x0000000000000000
0x16cfc68b8:  0x0000000000000000
0x16cfc68c0:  0x0000000000000000
0x16cfc68c8:  0x0000000000000000
0x16cfc68d0:  0x0000000000000000
0x16cfc68d8:  0x0000000000000000
0x16cfc68e0:  0x0000000000000000
0x16cfc68e8:  0x0000000000000000
0x16cfc68f0:  0x0000000000000000
0x16cfc68f8:  0x0000000000000000
0x16cfc6900:  0x0000000000000000
0x16cfc6908:  0x0000000000000000
0x16cfc6910:  0x0000000000000000
0x16cfc6918:  0x0000000000000000
0x16cfc6920:  0x0000000000000000
0x16cfc6928:  0x0000000000000000
0x16cfc6930:  0x0000000000000000
0x16cfc6938:  0x0000000000000000
0x16cfc6940:  0x0000000000000000
0x16cfc6948:  0x0000000000000000
0x16cfc6950:  0x0000000000000000
0x16cfc6958:  0x0000000000000000
0x16cfc6960:  0x0000000000000000
0x16cfc6968:  0x0000000000000000
0x16cfc6970:  0x0000000000000000
0x16cfc6978:  0x0000000000000000
0x16cfc6980:  0x0000000000000000
0x16cfc6988:  0x0000000000000000
0x16cfc6990:  0x0000000000000000
0x16cfc6998:  0x0000000000000000
0x16cfc69a0:  0x0000000000000000
0x16cfc69a8:  0x0000000000000000
0x16cfc69b0:  0x0000000000000000
0x16cfc69b8:  0x0000000000000000
0x16cfc69c0:  0x0000000000000000
```

```
0x16cfc69c8:  0x0000000000000000
0x16cfc69d0:  0x0000000000000000
0x16cfc69d8:  0x0000000000000000
0x16cfc69e0:  0x0000000000000000
0x16cfc69e8:  0x0000000000000000
0x16cfc69f0:  0x0000000000000000
0x16cfc69f8:  0x0000000000000000
0x16cfc6a00:  0x0000000000000000
0x16cfc6a08:  0x0000000000000000
0x16cfc6a10:  0x0000000000000000
0x16cfc6a18:  0x0000000000000000
0x16cfc6a20:  0x0000000000000000
0x16cfc6a28:  0x0000000000000000
0x16cfc6a30:  0x0000000000000000
0x16cfc6a38:  0x0000000000000000
0x16cfc6a40:  0x0000000000000000
0x16cfc6a48:  0x0000000000000000
0x16cfc6a50:  0x0000000000000000
0x16cfc6a58:  0x0000000000000000
0x16cfc6a60:  0x0000000000000000
0x16cfc6a68:  0x0000000000000000
0x16cfc6a70:  0x0000000000000000
0x16cfc6a78:  0x0000000000000000
0x16cfc6a80:  0x0000000000000000
0x16cfc6a88:  0x0000000000000000
0x16cfc6a90:  0x0000000000000000
0x16cfc6a98:  0x0000000000000000
0x16cfc6aa0:  0x0000000000000000
0x16cfc6aa8:  0x0000000000000000
0x16cfc6ab0:  0x000000016cfc6ac0
0x16cfc6ab8:  0x0000000102f4f664 App8`work_7() + 12
0x16cfc6ac0:  0x000000016cfc6ad0
0x16cfc6ac8:  0x0000000102f4f678 App8`work_6() + 12
0x16cfc6ad0:  0x000000016cfc6ae0
0x16cfc6ad8:  0x0000000102f4f68c App8`work_5() + 12
0x16cfc6ae0:  0x000000016cfc6af0
0x16cfc6ae8:  0x0000000102f4f6a0 App8`work_4() + 12
0x16cfc6af0:  0x000000016cfc6b00
0x16cfc6af8:  0x0000000102f4f6b4 App8`work_3() + 12
0x16cfc6b00:  0x000000016cfc6b10
0x16cfc6b08:  0x0000000102f4f6c8 App8`work_2() + 12
0x16cfc6b10:  0x000000016cfc6b20
0x16cfc6b18:  0x0000000102f4f6dc App8`work_1() + 12
0x16cfc6b20:  0x000000016cfc6f50
0x16cfc6b28:  0x0000000102f4f708 App8`work() + 36
0x16cfc6b30:  0x0000000000000000
0x16cfc6b38:  0x0000000000000000
0x16cfc6b40:  0x0000000000000000
0x16cfc6b48:  0x0000000000000000
0x16cfc6b50:  0x0000000000000000
0x16cfc6b58:  0x0000000000000000
0x16cfc6b60:  0x0000000000000000
0x16cfc6b68:  0x0000000000000000
0x16cfc6b70:  0x0000000000000000
0x16cfc6b78:  0x0000000000000000
0x16cfc6b80:  0x0000000000000000
0x16cfc6b88:  0x0000000000000000
0x16cfc6b90:  0x0000000000000000
0x16cfc6b98:  0x0000000000000000
0x16cfc6ba0:  0x0000000000000000
0x16cfc6ba8:  0x0000000000000000
```

```
0x16cfc6bb0:  0x0000000000000000
0x16cfc6bb8:  0x0000000000000000
0x16cfc6bc0:  0x0000000000000000
0x16cfc6bc8:  0x0000000000000000
0x16cfc6bd0:  0x0000000000000000
0x16cfc6bd8:  0x0000000000000000
0x16cfc6be0:  0x0000000000000000
0x16cfc6be8:  0x0000000000000000
0x16cfc6bf0:  0x0000000000000000
0x16cfc6bf8:  0x0000000000000000
0x16cfc6c00:  0x0000000000000000
0x16cfc6c08:  0x0000000000000000
0x16cfc6c10:  0x0000000000000000
0x16cfc6c18:  0x0000000000000000
0x16cfc6c20:  0x0000000000000000
0x16cfc6c28:  0x0000000000000000
0x16cfc6c30:  0x0000000000000000
0x16cfc6c38:  0x0000000000000000
0x16cfc6c40:  0x0000000000000000
0x16cfc6c48:  0x0000000000000000
0x16cfc6c50:  0x0000000000000000
0x16cfc6c58:  0x0000000000000000
0x16cfc6c60:  0x0000000000000000
0x16cfc6c68:  0x0000000000000000
0x16cfc6c70:  0x0000000000000000
0x16cfc6c78:  0x0000000000000000
0x16cfc6c80:  0x0000000000000000
0x16cfc6c88:  0x0000000000000000
0x16cfc6c90:  0x0000000000000000
0x16cfc6c98:  0x0000000000000000
0x16cfc6ca0:  0x0000000000000000
0x16cfc6ca8:  0x0000000000000000
0x16cfc6cb0:  0x0000000000000000
0x16cfc6cb8:  0x0000000000000000
0x16cfc6cc0:  0x0000000000000000
0x16cfc6cc8:  0x0000000000000000
0x16cfc6cd0:  0x0000000000000000
0x16cfc6cd8:  0x0000000000000000
0x16cfc6ce0:  0x0000000000000000
0x16cfc6ce8:  0x0000000000000000
0x16cfc6cf0:  0x0000000000000000
0x16cfc6cf8:  0x0000000000000000
0x16cfc6d00:  0x0000000000000000
0x16cfc6d08:  0x0000000000000000
0x16cfc6d10:  0x0000000000000000
0x16cfc6d18:  0x0000000000000000
0x16cfc6d20:  0x0000000000000000
0x16cfc6d28:  0x0000000000000000
0x16cfc6d30:  0x0000000000000000
0x16cfc6d38:  0x0000000000000000
0x16cfc6d40:  0x0000000000000000
0x16cfc6d48:  0x0000000000000000
0x16cfc6d50:  0x0000000000000000
0x16cfc6d58:  0x0000000000000000
0x16cfc6d60:  0x0000000000000000
0x16cfc6d68:  0x0000000000000000
0x16cfc6d70:  0x0000000000000000
0x16cfc6d78:  0x0000000000000000
0x16cfc6d80:  0x0000000000000000
0x16cfc6d88:  0x0000000000000000
0x16cfc6d90:  0x0000000000000000
```

```
0x16cfc6d98: 0x0000000000000000
0x16cfc6da0: 0x0000000000000000
0x16cfc6da8: 0x0000000000000000
0x16cfc6db0: 0x0000000000000000
0x16cfc6db8: 0x0000000000000000
0x16cfc6dc0: 0x0000000000000000
0x16cfc6dc8: 0x0000000000000000
0x16cfc6dd0: 0x0000000000000000
0x16cfc6dd8: 0x0000000000000000
0x16cfc6de0: 0x0000000000000000
0x16cfc6de8: 0x0000000000000000
0x16cfc6df0: 0x0000000000000000
0x16cfc6df8: 0x0000000000000000
0x16cfc6e00: 0x0000000000000000
0x16cfc6e08: 0x0000000000000000
0x16cfc6e10: 0x0000000000000000
0x16cfc6e18: 0x0000000000000000
0x16cfc6e20: 0x0000000000000000
0x16cfc6e28: 0x0000000000000000
0x16cfc6e30: 0x0000000000000000
0x16cfc6e38: 0x0000000000000000
0x16cfc6e40: 0x000000016cfc6f10
0x16cfc6e48: 0x000000016cfc6ed0
0x16cfc6e50: 0x000000016cfc6eb0
0x16cfc6e58: 0xdc3800018e9d02f8 (0x000000018e9d02f8) libsystem_kernel.dylib`clock_get_time +
100
0x16cfc6e60: 0x0000000000000000
0x16cfc6e68: 0x0000002c00001200
0x16cfc6e70: 0x0000120300000000
0x16cfc6e78: 0x0000044c00000000
0x16cfc6e80: 0x0000000100000000
0x16cfc6e88: 0x0003417e00000000
0x16cfc6e90: 0x0000000016a33d0e
0x16cfc6e98: 0x0000000000000008
0x16cfc6ea0: 0x000000016cfc6f10
0x16cfc6ea8: 0x000000016cfc6f00
0x16cfc6eb0: 0x000000016cfc6ef0
0x16cfc6eb8: 0x881280018e8d6f60 (0x000000018e8d6f60) libsystem_c.dylib`nanosleep + 116
0x16cfc6ec0: 0x0000000000000000
0x16cfc6ec8: 0x0000000000000000
0x16cfc6ed0: 0x16a33d0e0003417e
0x16cfc6ed8: 0x0000000000000000
0x16cfc6ee0: 0x0000000000000000
0x16cfc6ee8: 0x000000007fffffff
0x16cfc6ef0: 0x000000016cfc6f30
0x16cfc6ef8: 0xdb3000018e8e1b78 (0x000000018e8e1b78) libsystem_c.dylib`sleep + 52
0x16cfc6f00: 0x0000000000000000
0x16cfc6f08: 0x0000000000000000
0x16cfc6f10: 0x000000007fffffff
0x16cfc6f18: 0x0000000000000000
0x16cfc6f20: 0x0000000000000000
0x16cfc6f28: 0x00000000ffffffff
0x16cfc6f30: 0x000000016cfc6f70
0x16cfc6f38: 0xa90100018e8e1b90 (0x000000018e8e1b90) libsystem_c.dylib`sleep + 76
0x16cfc6f40: 0x0000000000000000
0x16cfc6f48: 0x0000000000000000
0x16cfc6f50: 0x000000016cfc6f60
0x16cfc6f58: 0x0000000102f4f8f0 App8`procNB() + 12
0x16cfc6f60: 0x0000000000000000
0x16cfc6f68: 0x000000016cfc7000
0x16cfc6f70: 0x000000016cfc6f80
```

```
0x16cfc6f78:  0x893e800102f4f9c4  (0x0000000102f4f9c4) App8`procNE() + 20
0x16cfc6f80:  0x000000016cfc6f90
0x16cfc6f88:  0x0000000102f4fa24  App8`bar_two() + 12
0x16cfc6f90:  0x000000016cfc6fa0
0x16cfc6f98:  0x0000000102f4fa38  App8`foo_two() + 12
0x16cfc6fa0:  0x000000016cfc6fc0
0x16cfc6fa8:  0x0000000102f4fa54  App8`thread_two(void*) + 20
0x16cfc6fb0:  0x0000000000000000
0x16cfc6fb8:  0x0000000000000000
0x16cfc6fc0:  0x000000016cfc6fe0
0x16cfc6fc8:  0x000000018ea0826c  libsystem_pthread.dylib`_pthread_start + 148
0x16cfc6fd0:  0x0000000000000000
0x16cfc6fd8:  0x0000000000000000
0x16cfc6fe0:  0x0000000000000000
0x16cfc6fe8:  0xf62280018ea0308c  (0x000000018ea0308c) libsystem_pthread.dylib`thread_start + 8
0x16cfc6ff0:  0x0000000000000000
0x16cfc6ff8:  0x0000000000000000
0x16cfc7000:  0xb60ce2c5aaaaf405
0x16cfc7008:  0x0000000000000000
0x16cfc7010:  0x000000016d053000
0x16cfc7018:  0x000000016cf3b010
0x16cfc7020:  0x0000000000000000
0x16cfc7028:  0x0000000000000000
0x16cfc7030:  0x0000000000000101
0x16cfc7038:  0x0000000a0000001f
0x16cfc7040:  0x0000000000000000
0x16cfc7048:  0x0001000000000000
0x16cfc7050:  0x0000000000000000
0x16cfc7058:  0x0000000000000000
0x16cfc7060:  0x0000000000000000
0x16cfc7068:  0x0000000000000000
0x16cfc7070:  0x0000000000000000
0x16cfc7078:  0x0000000000000000
0x16cfc7080:  0x0000000000000000
0x16cfc7088:  0x0000000000000000
0x16cfc7090:  0x0000000102f4fa40  App8`thread_two(void*)
0x16cfc7098:  0x0000000000000000
0x16cfc70a0:  0x0003000000000000
0x16cfc70a8:  0x0000000000000000
0x16cfc70b0:  0x000000016cfc7000
0x16cfc70b8:  0x000000016cf44000
0x16cfc70c0:  0x000000016cf40000
0x16cfc70c8:  0x000000000008c000
0x16cfc70d0:  0x0000000000004000
0x16cfc70d8:  0x00000000002c7418
0x16cfc70e0:  0x000000016cfc7000
0x16cfc70e8:  0x000000016cfc70ac
0x16cfc70f0:  0x0000000000001203
0x16cfc70f8:  0x0000000000001303
0x16cfc7100:  0x00000000000008ff
0x16cfc7108:  0x0000000000000000
0x16cfc7110:  0x0000000000000000
0x16cfc7118:  0xb60ce2c4c6568405
0x16cfc7120:  0x0000000000000000
0x16cfc7128:  0x0000000000000000
0x16cfc7130:  0x0000000000000000
0x16cfc7138:  0x0000000000000000
0x16cfc7140:  0x0000000000000000
0x16cfc7148:  0x0000000000000000
0x16cfc7150:  0x0000000000000000
0x16cfc7158:  0x0000000000000000
```

```
0x16cfc7160: 0x0000000000000000
0x16cfc7168: 0x0000000000000000
0x16cfc7170: 0x0000000000000000
0x16cfc7178: 0x0000000000000000
```

```
(lldb) di -a 0x0000000102f4f6b4
App8`work_3:
    0x102f4f6a8 <+0>:   stp    x29, x30, [sp, #-0x10]!
    0x102f4f6ac <+4>:   mov    x29, sp
    0x102f4f6b0 <+8>:   bl     0x102f4f694                ; work_4()
    0x102f4f6b4 <+12>:  ldp    x29, x30, [sp], #0x10
    0x102f4f6b8 <+16>:  ret
```

4.   Go to the core thread 3 (thread #4) and identify handled exception processing code:

```
(lldb) thread select 4
* thread #4
    frame #0: 0x000000018e9ce06c libsystem_kernel.dylib`__semwait_signal + 8
libsystem_kernel.dylib`:
->  0x18e9ce06c <+8>:   b.lo   0x18e9ce08c               ; <+40>
    0x18e9ce070 <+12>:  pacibsp
    0x18e9ce074 <+16>:  stp    x29, x30, [sp, #-0x10]!
    0x18e9ce078 <+20>:  mov    x29, sp
```

```
(lldb) bt
* thread #4
  * frame #0: 0x000000018e9ce06c libsystem_kernel.dylib`__semwait_signal + 8
    frame #1: 0x000000018e8d6fc8 libsystem_c.dylib`nanosleep + 220
    frame #2: 0x000000018e8e1b78 libsystem_c.dylib`sleep + 52
    frame #3: 0x000000018e8e1b90 libsystem_c.dylib`sleep + 76
    frame #4: 0x0000000102f4f958 App8`procH() + 56
    frame #5: 0x0000000102f4fa70 App8`bar_three() + 12
    frame #6: 0x0000000102f4fa84 App8`foo_three() + 12
    frame #7: 0x0000000102f4faa0 App8`thread_three(void*) + 20
    frame #8: 0x000000018ea0826c libsystem_pthread.dylib`_pthread_start + 148
```

```
(lldb) x/600a $sp-0x1000 --force
0x16d051eb0: 0x0000000000000002
0x16d051eb8: 0x0000000100000000
0x16d051ec0: 0x0000000102f4c5b0 App8`_mh_execute_header + 1456
0x16d051ec8: 0x0000000102f4c020 App8`_mh_execute_header + 32
0x16d051ed0: 0x0000000000000001
0x16d051ed8: 0x000000016d051f90 -> 0x0000000103040310 dyld`_NSConcreteStackBlock
0x16d051ee0: 0x0000000102f4c000 App8`_mh_execute_header
0x16d051ee8: 0x000000016d051ff8
0x16d051ef0: 0x000000016d051f80
0x16d051ef8: 0xee34000102fc9f98 (0x0000000102fc9f98) dyld`dyld3::MachOFile::forEachLoadCommand(Diagnostics&, void
(load_command const*, bool&) block_pointer) const + 168
0x16d051f00: 0x000000016d0521d0 -> 0x0000000103040310 dyld`_NSConcreteStackBlock
0x16d051f08: 0x000000000e6dc000
0x16d051f10: 0x000000016d051f90 -> 0x0000000103040310 dyld`_NSConcreteStackBlock
0x16d051f18: 0x0d6e800102fff970 (0x0000000102fff970) dyld`dyld3::MachOLoaded::getSlide() const + 184
0x16d051f20: 0x000000010307c060 -> 0x000000010302a400 dyld`vtable for dyld4::APIs + 16
0x16d051f28: 0x0000000103040310 dyld`_NSConcreteStackBlock
0x16d051f30: 0x0000000042000000
0x16d051f38: 0x0100000102fffda4 (0x0000000102fffda4) dyld`invocation function for block in
dyld3::MachOLoaded::getSlide() const
0x16d051f40: 0x434c4e47432b2b00
0x16d051f48: 0x0000000000000000
0x16d051f50: 0x0000000000000006
0x16d051f58: 0x0000000102f4c000 App8`_mh_execute_header
0x16d051f60: 0xd3a900016d052410
0x16d051f68: 0x000000010307c060 -> 0x000000010302a400 dyld`vtable for dyld4::APIs + 16
0x16d051f70: 0x0000000102f4c000 App8`_mh_execute_header
0x16d051f78: 0x000000016d052040 -> 0x0000000103040310 dyld`_NSConcreteStackBlock
0x16d051f80: 0x000000016d052030
```

```
0x16d051f88: 0x4743000102ffdc9c (0x0000000102ffdc9c) dyld`dyld3::MachOFile::forEachSection(void
(dyld3::MachOFile::SectionInfo const&, bool, bool&) block_pointer) const + 220
0x16d051f90: 0x0000000103040310 dyld`_NSConcreteStackBlock
0x16d051f98: 0x0000000042000000
0x16d051fa0: 0x0000000102ffdcc8 dyld`invocation function for block in dyld3::MachOFile::forEachSection(void
(dyld3::MachOFile::SectionInfo const&, bool, bool&) block_pointer) const
0x16d051fa8: 0x000000010302afd8 dyld`__block_descriptor_tmp.87
0x16d051fb0: 0x000000016d052040 -> 0x0000000103040310 dyld`_NSConcreteStackBlock
0x16d051fb8: 0x000000016d051fd8
0x16d051fc0: 0x0000000102f4c000 App8`_mh_execute_header
0x16d051fc8: 0x000000016d052004
0x16d051fd0: 0x000000016d052000
0x16d051fd8: 0x0000000000000000
0x16d051fe0: 0x000000016d051fd8
0x16d051fe8: 0x0000002000000000
0x16d051ff0: 0x0000000100000002
0x16d051ff8: 0x0000000000000000
0x16d052000: 0x63675f5f0000b000
0x16d052008: 0x7470656378655f63
0x16d052010: 0x000000006261745f
0x16d052018: 0x1f6f7b2200240021
0x16d052020: 0x0000000000000001
0x16d052028: 0x000000016d052120 -> 0x0000000102f4c000 App8`_mh_execute_header
0x16d052030: 0x000000016d0520c0
0x16d052038: 0x8158800103000380 (0x0000000103000380) dyld`dyld3::MachOLoaded::findSectionContent(char const*, char
const*, unsigned long long&, bool) const + 136
0x16d052040: 0x0000000103040310 dyld`_NSConcreteStackBlock
0x16d052048: 0x0000000042000000
0x16d052050: 0x00000001030003a8 dyld`invocation function for block in dyld3::MachOLoaded::findSectionContent(char
const*, char const*, unsigned long long&, bool) const
0x16d052058: 0x000000010302b2d8 dyld`__block_descriptor_tmp.59
0x16d052060: 0x000000016d052090
0x16d052068: 0x0000000102f4c000 App8`_mh_execute_header
0x16d052070: 0x000000010302100e "__unwind_info"
0x16d052078: 0x0000000103020ffc "__TEXT"
0x16d052080: 0x000000016d0520e0
0x16d052088: 0x0000000000000000
0x16d052090: 0x0000000000000000
0x16d052098: 0x000000016d052090
0x16d0520a0: 0x0000002000000000
0x16d0520a8: 0x0000000102f4ff14
0x16d0520b0: 0x0000000000000001
0x16d0520b8: 0x000000016d052120 -> 0x0000000102f4c000 App8`_mh_execute_header
0x16d0520c0: 0x000000016d052110
0x16d0520c8: 0xa707800102fefb98 (0x0000000102fefb98) dyld`dyld4::APIs::_dyld_find_unwind_sections(void*,
dyld_unwind_sections*) + 216
0x16d0520d0: 0x0000000000000000
0x16d0520d8: 0x0000000000000000
0x16d0520e0: 0x000000000000009c
0x16d0520e8: 0x0000000102f4c000 App8`_mh_execute_header
0x16d0520f0: 0xd3a900016d052410
0x16d0520f8: 0x000000016d052f70
0x16d052100: 0x0000000102f4f938 App8`procH() + 24
0x16d052108: 0x000000016d052410 -> 0x00000001e925bd90 libunwind.dylib`vtable for
libunwind::UnwindCursor<libunwind::LocalAddressSpace, libunwind::Registers_arm64> + 16
0x16d052110: 0x000000016d0521c0
0x16d052118: 0x5d7f000199536f24 (0x0000000199536f24)
libunwind.dylib`libunwind::UnwindCursor<libunwind::LocalAddressSpace,
libunwind::Registers_arm64>::setInfoBasedOnIPRegister(bool) + 120
0x16d052120: 0x0000000102f4c000 App8`_mh_execute_header
0x16d052128: 0x0000000102f4ffb0
0x16d052130: 0x0000000000000050
0x16d052138: 0x0000000102f4ff14
0x16d052140: 0x000000000000009c
0x16d052148: 0x000000016d052168
0x16d052150: 0x0000000199532000
0x16d052158: 0x000000016d052194
0x16d052160: 0x0000000000000000
0x16d052168: 0x0000000000000000
0x16d052170: 0x000000016d052168
0x16d052178: 0x0000002000000000
0x16d052180: 0x0000000000000001
0x16d052188: 0x0000000102f4c000 App8`_mh_execute_header
0x16d052190: 0x0000000102f4ffb0
0x16d052198: 0x0000000000000050
0x16d0521a0: 0x0000000102f4ff14
```

```
0x16d0521a8: 0x000000000000009c
0x16d0521b0: 0xca3a800102f4f938 (0x0000000102f4f938) App8`procH() + 24
0x16d0521b8: 0x000000016d052410 -> 0x00000001e925bd90 libunwind.dylib`vtable for
libunwind::UnwindCursor<libunwind::LocalAddressSpace, libunwind::Registers_arm64> + 16
0x16d0521c0: 0x000000016d052260
0x16d0521c8: 0xa87500019953ad74 (0x0000000019953ad74) libunwind.dylib`unw_set_reg + 452
0x16d0521d0: 0x0000000103040310 dyld`_NSConcreteStackBlock
0x16d0521d8: 0x0000000042000000
0x16d0521e0: 0x00000001030003a8 dyld`invocation function for block in dyld3::MachOLoaded::findSectionContent(char
const*, char const*, unsigned long long&, bool) const
0x16d0521e8: 0x0000000102f4f920 App8`procH()
0x16d0521f0: 0x0000000102f4f994 App8`procNH()
0x16d0521f8: 0x0000000102f4fec8 App8`GCC_except_table17
0x16d052200: 0x000000018e9c507c libc++abi.dylib`__gxx_personality_v0
0x16d052208: 0x0000000000000000
0x16d052210: 0x0000000000000001
0x16d052218: 0x0000000054000000
0x16d052220: 0x0000000000000000
0x16d052228: 0x0000000102f4c000 App8`_mh_execute_header
0x16d052230: 0x0000000000000006
0x16d052238: 0x0000000000000002
0x16d052240: 0x434c4e47432b2b00
0x16d052248: 0x0000000000000001
0x16d052250: 0x000000016d052410 -> 0x00000001e925bd90 libunwind.dylib`vtable for
libunwind::UnwindCursor<libunwind::LocalAddressSpace, libunwind::Registers_arm64> + 16
0x16d052258: 0x000000014d7040e0
0x16d052260: 0x000000016d052350
0x16d052268: 0x5a6b00018e9c5118 (0x000000018e9c5118) libc++abi.dylib`__gxx_personality_v0 + 156
0x16d052270: 0x000000000000014c
0x16d052278: 0x0000000102f4fe9c App8`GCC_except_table10
0x16d052280: 0x000000000000001e
0x16d052288: 0x434c4e47432b2b00
0x16d052290: 0x000000019953b770 libunwind.dylib`_Unwind_Resume + 228
0x16d052298: 0x0000000102f4f73c App8`procB()
0x16d0522a0: 0x0000000102f4fec8 App8`GCC_except_table17
0x16d0522a8: 0x0000009b99536f24
0x16d0522b0: 0x0000000000000001
0x16d0522b8: 0x0000000102f4fee5 App8`GCC_except_table17 + 29
0x16d0522c0: 0x0000000102f4fec8 App8`GCC_except_table17
0x16d0522c8: 0x0000000102f4f938 App8`procH() + 24
0x16d0522d0: 0x000000014d704100
0x16d0522d8: 0x0000000100000003
0x16d0522e0: 0x0000000102f4fe9c App8`GCC_except_table10
0x16d0522e8: 0x000000018e9c507c libc++abi.dylib`__gxx_personality_v0
0x16d0522f0: 0x0000000000000001
0x16d0522f8: 0x0000000000000000
0x16d052300: 0x0000000000000000
0x16d052308: 0x0000000000000000
0x16d052310: 0x0000000000000000
0x16d052318: 0x0000000000000000
0x16d052320: 0x0000000000000006
0x16d052328: 0x0000000000000002
0x16d052330: 0xd3a900016d052410
0x16d052338: 0x000000016d052f70
0x16d052340: 0x000000014d7040e0
0x16d052348: 0x000000016d052410 -> 0x00000001e925bd90 libunwind.dylib`vtable for
libunwind::UnwindCursor<libunwind::LocalAddressSpace, libunwind::Registers_arm64> + 16
0x16d052350: 0x000000016d0523f0
0x16d052358: 0xf02880019953b5f4 (0x000000019953b5f4) libunwind.dylib`unwind_phase2 + 468
0x16d052360: 0x0000000000000000
0x16d052368: 0x00000001e925bd90 libunwind.dylib`vtable for libunwind::UnwindCursor<libunwind::LocalAddressSpace,
libunwind::Registers_arm64> + 16
0x16d052370: 0x0000000102f4f920 App8`procH()
0x16d052378: 0x0000000102f4f994 App8`procNH()
0x16d052380: 0x0000000102f4fec8 App8`GCC_except_table17
0x16d052388: 0x000000018e9c507c libc++abi.dylib`__gxx_personality_v0
0x16d052390: 0x0000000000000000
0x16d052398: 0x0000000000000001
0x16d0523a0: 0x0000000054000000
0x16d0523a8: 0x0000000000000000
0x16d0523b0: 0x0000000102f4c000 App8`_mh_execute_header
0x16d0523b8: 0x0000000000000001
0x16d0523c0: 0x0000000000000000
0x16d0523c8: 0x0000000000000000
0x16d0523d0: 0x0000000000000000
0x16d0523d8: 0x0000000000000000
```

```
0x16d0523e0: 0x0000000000000000
0x16d0523e8: 0x000000014d7040e0
0x16d0523f0: 0x000000016d052f00
0x16d0523f8: 0x693900019953b788 (0x000000019953b788) libunwind.dylib`_Unwind_Resume + 252
0x16d052400: 0x00000001e8b2b390 (void *)0x000000019953b140: _Unwind_RaiseException
0x16d052408: 0x0000000000000000
0x16d052410: 0x00000001e925bd90 libunwind.dylib`vtable for libunwind::UnwindCursor<libunwind::LocalAddressSpace,
libunwind::Registers_arm64> + 16
0x16d052418: 0x00000001e4e71bd0 libunwind.dylib`libunwind::LocalAddressSpace::sThisAddressSpace
0x16d052420: 0x000000014d7040e0
0x16d052428: 0x0000000000000001
0x16d052430: 0x0000000000000000
0x16d052438: 0x0000600002244010
0x16d052440: 0x0000000000000000
0x16d052448: 0x000060000224d288
0x16d052450: 0x000000000000000a
0x16d052458: 0x0000000000000001
0x16d052460: 0x0000000000000000
0x16d052468: 0x000000016d0530e0
0x16d052470: 0xfffffffe7163e2bf
0x16d052478: 0x0000000000000001
0x16d052480: 0x00000000803ff7fb
0x16d052488: 0x00000000003ff000
0x16d052490: 0x0000000000200000
0x16d052498: 0x0000000000000014
0x16d0524a0: 0x000000019953b68c libunwind.dylib`_Unwind_Resume
0x16d0524a8: 0x9f020001e925bde0 (0x00000001e925bde0) libunwind.dylib`vtable for
libunwind::UnwindCursor<libunwind::LocalAddressSpace, libunwind::Registers_arm64> + 96
0x16d0524b0: 0x0000000000000000
0x16d0524b8: 0x000000016d053000
0x16d0524c0: 0x0000000000000000
0x16d0524c8: 0x0000000000000000
0x16d0524d0: 0x0000000000000000
0x16d0524d8: 0x0000000000000000
0x16d0524e0: 0x0000000000000000
0x16d0524e8: 0x0000000000000000
0x16d0524f0: 0x0000000000000000
0x16d0524f8: 0x0000000000000000
0x16d052500: 0x0000000000000000
0x16d052508: 0x000000016d052f80
0x16d052510: 0xf31580019953b770 (0x000000019953b770) libunwind.dylib`_Unwind_Resume + 228
0x16d052518: 0x000000016d052f70
0x16d052520: 0xea1d000102f4f938 (0x0000000102f4f938) App8`procH() + 24
0x16d052528: 0x0000000000000000
0x16d052530: 0x0000000000000000
0x16d052538: 0x0000000000000009
0x16d052540: 0x0706050403020100
0x16d052548: 0x0000000000000000
0x16d052550: 0x0000000000000000
0x16d052558: 0x0000000000000000
0x16d052560: 0x0000000000000000
0x16d052568: 0x0000000000000000
0x16d052570: 0x0000000000000000
0x16d052578: 0x0000000000000000
0x16d052580: 0x0000000000000000
0x16d052588: 0x0000000000000000
0x16d052590: 0x0000000000000000
0x16d052598: 0x0000000000000000
0x16d0525a0: 0x0000000000000000
0x16d0525a8: 0x0000000000000000
0x16d0525b0: 0x0000000000000000
0x16d0525b8: 0x0000000000000000
0x16d0525c0: 0x0000000000000000
0x16d0525c8: 0x0000000000000000
0x16d0525d0: 0x0000000000000000
0x16d0525d8: 0x0000000000000000
0x16d0525e0: 0x0000000000000000
0x16d0525e8: 0x0000000000000000
0x16d0525f0: 0x0000000000000000
0x16d0525f8: 0x0000000000000000
0x16d052600: 0x0000000000000000
0x16d052608: 0x0000000000000000
0x16d052610: 0x0000000000000000
0x16d052618: 0x0000000000000000
0x16d052620: 0x0000000000000000
0x16d052628: 0x0000000000000000
```

```
0x16d052630:  0x0000000102f4f920  App8`procH()
0x16d052638:  0x0000000102f4f994  App8`procNH()
0x16d052640:  0x0000000102f4fec8  App8`GCC_except_table17
0x16d052648:  0x000000018e9c507c  libc++abi.dylib`__gxx_personality_v0
0x16d052650:  0x0000000000000000
0x16d052658:  0x0000000000000001
0x16d052660:  0x0000000054000000
0x16d052668:  0x0000000000000000
0x16d052670:  0x0000000102f4c000  App8`_mh_execute_header
0x16d052678:  0x0000000000000000
0x16d052680:  0x0000000000000000
0x16d052688:  0x0000000000000000
0x16d052690:  0x0000000000000000
0x16d052698:  0x0000000000000000
0x16d0526a0:  0x0000000000000000
0x16d0526a8:  0x0000000000000000
0x16d0526b0:  0x0000000000000000
0x16d0526b8:  0x0000000000000000
0x16d0526c0:  0x0000000000000000
0x16d0526c8:  0x0000000000000000
0x16d0526d0:  0x0000000000000000
0x16d0526d8:  0x0000000000000000
0x16d0526e0:  0x0000000000000000
0x16d0526e8:  0x0000000000000000
0x16d0526f0:  0x0000000000000000
0x16d0526f8:  0x0000000000000000
0x16d052700:  0x0000000000000000
0x16d052708:  0x0000000000000000
0x16d052710:  0x0000000000000000
0x16d052718:  0x0000000000000000
0x16d052720:  0x0000000000000000
0x16d052728:  0x0000000000000000
0x16d052730:  0x0000000000000000
0x16d052738:  0x0000000000000000
0x16d052740:  0x0000000000000000
0x16d052748:  0x0000000000000000
0x16d052750:  0x0000000000000000
0x16d052758:  0x0000000000000000
0x16d052760:  0x0000000000000000
0x16d052768:  0x0000000000000000
0x16d052770:  0x0000000000000000
0x16d052778:  0x0000000000000000
0x16d052780:  0x0000000000000000
0x16d052788:  0x0000000000000000
0x16d052790:  0x0000000000000000
0x16d052798:  0x0000000000000000
0x16d0527a0:  0x0000000000000000
0x16d0527a8:  0x0000000000000000
0x16d0527b0:  0x0000000000000000
0x16d0527b8:  0x0000000000000000
0x16d0527c0:  0x0000000000000000
0x16d0527c8:  0x0000000000000000
0x16d0527d0:  0x0000000000000000
0x16d0527d8:  0x0000000000000000
0x16d0527e0:  0x0000000000000000
0x16d0527e8:  0x0000000000000000
0x16d0527f0:  0x0000000000000000
0x16d0527f8:  0x0000000000000000
0x16d052800:  0x0000000000000000
0x16d052808:  0x0000000000000000
0x16d052810:  0x0000000000000000
0x16d052818:  0x0000000000000000
0x16d052820:  0x0000000000000000
0x16d052828:  0x0000000000000000
0x16d052830:  0x0000000000000000
0x16d052838:  0x0000000000000000
0x16d052840:  0x0000000000000000
0x16d052848:  0x0000000000000000
0x16d052850:  0x0000000000000000
0x16d052858:  0x0000000000000000
0x16d052860:  0x0000000000000000
0x16d052868:  0x0000000000000000
0x16d052870:  0x0000000000000000
0x16d052878:  0x0000000000000000
0x16d052880:  0x0000000000000000
0x16d052888:  0x0000000000000000
```

```
0x16d052890: 0x0000000000000000
0x16d052898: 0x0000000000000000
0x16d0528a0: 0x0000000000000000
0x16d0528a8: 0x0000000000000000
0x16d0528b0: 0x0000000000000000
0x16d0528b8: 0x0000000000000000
0x16d0528c0: 0x0000000000000000
0x16d0528c8: 0x0000000000000000
0x16d0528d0: 0x0000000000000000
0x16d0528d8: 0x0000000000000000
0x16d0528e0: 0x0000000000000000
0x16d0528e8: 0x0000000000000000
0x16d0528f0: 0x0000000000000000
0x16d0528f8: 0x0000000000000000
0x16d052900: 0x000000016d052900
0x16d052908: 0x0000600002244000
0x16d052910: 0x0000000000000000
0x16d052918: 0x0000600002244010
0x16d052920: 0x0000000000000000
0x16d052928: 0x000060000224d288
0x16d052930: 0x000000000000000a
0x16d052938: 0x0000000000000001
0x16d052940: 0x0000000000000001
0x16d052948: 0x000000016d0530e0
0x16d052950: 0xfffffffe7163e2bf
0x16d052958: 0x0000000000000001
0x16d052960: 0x00000000803ff7fb
0x16d052968: 0x00000000003ff000
0x16d052970: 0x0000000000200000
0x16d052978: 0x0000000000000014
0x16d052980: 0x000000019953b140  libunwind.dylib`_Unwind_RaiseException
0x16d052988: 0x00000001e8b2b390 (void *)0x000000019953b140: _Unwind_RaiseException
0x16d052990: 0x0000000000000000
0x16d052998: 0x000000014d7040e0
0x16d0529a0: 0x000000016d052900
0x16d0529a8: 0x000000014d7040e0
0x16d0529b0: 0x000000016d0529b0
0x16d0529b8: 0x0000000000000000
0x16d0529c0: 0x0000000000000000
0x16d0529c8: 0x0000600002244010
0x16d0529d0: 0x0000000000000000
0x16d0529d8: 0x000060000224d288
0x16d0529e0: 0x000000000000000a
0x16d0529e8: 0x0000000000000001
0x16d0529f0: 0x0000000000000000
0x16d0529f8: 0x000000016d0530e0
0x16d052a00: 0xfffffffe7163e2bf
0x16d052a08: 0x0000000000000001
0x16d052a10: 0x00000000803ff7fb
0x16d052a18: 0x00000000003ff000
0x16d052a20: 0x0000000000200000
0x16d052a28: 0x0000000000000014
0x16d052a30: 0x000000019953b68c  libunwind.dylib`_Unwind_Resume
0x16d052a38: 0x9f020001e925bde0 (0x00000001e925bde0) libunwind.dylib`vtable for
libunwind::UnwindCursor<libunwind::LocalAddressSpace, libunwind::Registers_arm64> + 96
0x16d052a40: 0x0000000000000000
0x16d052a48: 0x000000014d7040e0
0x16d052a50: 0x0000000000000000
0x16d052a58: 0x0000000000000000
0x16d052a60: 0x0000000000000000
0x16d052a68: 0x0000000000000000
0x16d052a70: 0x0000000000000000
0x16d052a78: 0x0000000000000000
0x16d052a80: 0x0000000000000000
0x16d052a88: 0x0000000000000000
0x16d052a90: 0x0000000000000000
0x16d052a98: 0x000000016d052f00
0x16d052aa0: 0xf31580019953b770 (0x000000019953b770) libunwind.dylib`_Unwind_Resume + 228
0x16d052aa8: 0x000000016d052400 -> 0x00000001e8b2b390 (void *)0x000000019953b140: _Unwind_RaiseException
0x16d052ab0: 0xf31580019953b770 (0x000000019953b770) libunwind.dylib`_Unwind_Resume + 228
0x16d052ab8: 0x0000000000000000
0x16d052ac0: 0x0000000000000000
0x16d052ac8: 0x0000000000000009
0x16d052ad0: 0x0706050403020100
0x16d052ad8: 0x0000000000000000
0x16d052ae0: 0x0000000000000000
```

```
0x16d052ae8: 0x0000000000000000
0x16d052af0: 0x0000000000000000
0x16d052af8: 0x0000000000000000
0x16d052b00: 0x0000000000000000
0x16d052b08: 0x0000000000000000
0x16d052b10: 0x0000000000000000
0x16d052b18: 0x0000000000000000
0x16d052b20: 0x0000000000000000
0x16d052b28: 0x0000000000000000
0x16d052b30: 0x0000000000000000
0x16d052b38: 0x0000000000000000
0x16d052b40: 0x0000000000000000
0x16d052b48: 0x0000000000000000
0x16d052b50: 0x0000000000000000
0x16d052b58: 0x0000000000000000
0x16d052b60: 0x0000000000000000
0x16d052b68: 0x0000000000000000
0x16d052b70: 0x0000000000000000
0x16d052b78: 0x0000000000000000
0x16d052b80: 0x0000000000000000
0x16d052b88: 0x0000000000000000
0x16d052b90: 0x0000000000000000
0x16d052b98: 0x0000000000000000
0x16d052ba0: 0x0000000000000000
0x16d052ba8: 0x0000000000000000
0x16d052bb0: 0x0000000000000000
0x16d052bb8: 0x0000000000000000
0x16d052bc0: 0x0000000000000000
0x16d052bc8: 0x0000000000000000
0x16d052bd0: 0x0000000000000000
0x16d052bd8: 0x0000000000000000
0x16d052be0: 0x0000000000000000
0x16d052be8: 0x0000000000000000
0x16d052bf0: 0x0000000000000000
0x16d052bf8: 0x0000000000000000
0x16d052c00: 0x0000000000000000
0x16d052c08: 0x0000000000000000
0x16d052c10: 0x0000000000000000
0x16d052c18: 0x0000000000000000
0x16d052c20: 0x0000000000000000
0x16d052c28: 0x0000000000000000
0x16d052c30: 0x0000000000000000
0x16d052c38: 0x0000000000000000
0x16d052c40: 0x0000000000000000
0x16d052c48: 0x0000000000000000
0x16d052c50: 0x0000000000000000
0x16d052c58: 0x0000002030000000
0x16d052c60: 0x00000001e7965aec libsystem_kernel.dylib`mach_task_self_
0x16d052c68: 0x0000000102f74a04
0x16d052c70: 0x0000000700000003
0x16d052c78: 0x0000000007000001
0x16d052c80: 0x00000000000fffff
0x16d052c88: 0x0000000000000000
0x16d052c90: 0x0000000000000001
0x16d052c98: 0x0000000102fa4000
0x16d052ca0: 0x0000000000000000
0x16d052ca8: 0x00000000001ffffb
0x16d052cb0: 0x0000600000000000
0x16d052cb8: 0x000060000224d188
0x16d052cc0: 0x0000000000007010
0x16d052cc8: 0x0000000000000400
0x16d052cd0: 0x00000001e79661b8 libsystem_malloc.dylib`first_block_offset_by_size_class
0x16d052cd8: 0x0000000102fa4000
0x16d052ce0: 0x00000001e79661f8 libsystem_malloc.dylib`last_block_offset_by_size_class
0x16d052ce8: 0x00000001e4c0c7c0 nanov2_policy_config + 4
0x16d052cf0: 0x000000016d052db0
0x16d052cf8: 0x627300018e8167f0 (0x000000018e8167f0) libsystem_malloc.dylib`nanov2_find_block_and_allocate + 1160
0x16d052d00: 0x000000016d0530e0
0x16d052d08: 0x0000000102fa4000
0x16d052d10: 0x0000000102fab008
0x16d052d18: 0x0000000000000000
0x16d052d20: 0x0000000102fa8000
0x16d052d28: 0x000000010224d280
0x16d052d30: 0x0000000102fab034
0x16d052d38: 0x000000016d0530e0
0x16d052d40: 0x00000000e79661b8
```

```
0x16d052d48: 0x0000000102fab040
0x16d052d50: 0x0000600000000000
0x16d052d58: 0x0000600004000000
0x16d052d60: 0x000000016d0530e0
0x16d052d68: 0x0000000000000001
0x16d052d70: 0x0000000102fa8000
0x16d052d78: 0x0000000102faa000
0x16d052d80: 0x0000000000000000
0x16d052d88: 0x0000000102fab000
0x16d052d90: 0x0000000000000000
0x16d052d98: 0x0000000102fa4000
0x16d052da0: 0x0000000000000001
0x16d052da8: 0x0000000000000010
0x16d052db0: 0x000000016d052e10
0x16d052db8: 0xc93d80018e816280 (0x000000018e816280) libsystem_malloc.dylib`nanov2_allocate + 288
0x16d052dc0: 0x0000000000000000
0x16d052dc8: 0x0000000000000000
0x16d052dd0: 0x0000000000000000
0x16d052dd8: 0x0000000000000000
0x16d052de0: 0x0000000000000000
0x16d052de8: 0x0000000000000000
0x16d052df0: 0x0000000000000000
0x16d052df8: 0x0000000000000000
0x16d052e00: 0x0000000000000000
0x16d052e08: 0x0000000000000000
0x16d052e10: 0x0000000000000000
0x16d052e18: 0x0000000000000000
0x16d052e20: 0x0000000000000000
0x16d052e28: 0x0000000000000000
0x16d052e30: 0x000000016d052f00
0x16d052e38: 0x000000016d052ec0
0x16d052e40: 0x000000016d052ea0
0x16d052e48: 0xe31600018e9d02f8 (0x000000018e9d02f8) libsystem_kernel.dylib`clock_get_time + 100
0x16d052e50: 0x0000000102f4fec8 App8`GCC_except_table17
0x16d052e58: 0x0000002c00001200
0x16d052e60: 0x00000e0300000000
0x16d052e68: 0x0000044c00000000
0x16d052e70: 0x0000000100000000
0x16d052e78: 0x0003417e00000000
0x16d052e80: 0x0000000016a438d8
0x16d052e88: 0x0000000100000008
0x16d052e90: 0x000000016d052f00
0x16d052e98: 0x000000016d052ef0
0x16d052ea0: 0x000000016d052ee0
0x16d052ea8: 0xca7180018e8d6f60 (0x000000018e8d6f60) libsystem_c.dylib`nanosleep + 116
0x16d052eb0: 0x0000000102f500a0 App8`typeinfo for Exception*
0x16d052eb8: 0x0000000000000000
0x16d052ec0: 0x16a438d80003417e
0x16d052ec8: 0x0000000000000000
0x16d052ed0: 0x0000000000000000
0x16d052ed8: 0x000000007fffffff
0x16d052ee0: 0x000000016d052f20
0x16d052ee8: 0xd70d00018e8e1b78 (0x000000018e8e1b78) libsystem_c.dylib`sleep + 52
0x16d052ef0: 0x0000000000000000
0x16d052ef8: 0x0000000000000000
0x16d052f00: 0x000000007fffffff
0x16d052f08: 0x0000000000000000
0x16d052f10: 0x0000000000000000
0x16d052f18: 0x00000000ffffffff
0x16d052f20: 0x000000016d052f60
0x16d052f28: 0x141d00018e8e1b90 (0x000000018e8e1b90) libsystem_c.dylib`sleep + 76
0x16d052f30: 0x0000000000000000
0x16d052f38: 0x0000000000000000
0x16d052f40: 0x000000016d052f60
0x16d052f48: 0x653b80018e9c4c40 (0x000000018e9c4c40) libc++abi.dylib`__cxa_begin_catch + 28
0x16d052f50: 0x0000000000000000
0x16d052f58: 0x000000016d053000
0x16d052f60: 0x000000016d052f80
0x16d052f68: 0x0f5e800102f4f958 (0x0000000102f4f958) App8`procH() + 56
0x16d052f70: 0x0000000100000000
0x16d052f78: 0x000000014d7040e0
0x16d052f80: 0x000000016d052f90
0x16d052f88: 0x0000000102f4fa70 App8`bar_three() + 12
0x16d052f90: 0x000000016d052fa0
0x16d052f98: 0x0000000102f4fa84 App8`foo_three() + 12
0x16d052fa0: 0x000000016d052fc0
```

```
0x16d052fa8: 0x0000000102f4faa0 App8`thread_three(void*) + 20
0x16d052fb0: 0x0000000000000000
0x16d052fb8: 0x0000000000000000
0x16d052fc0: 0x000000016d052fe0
0x16d052fc8: 0x000000018ea0826c libsystem_pthread.dylib`_pthread_start + 148
0x16d052fd0: 0x0000000000000000
0x16d052fd8: 0x0000000000000000
0x16d052fe0: 0x0000000000000000
0x16d052fe8: 0x7a7e00018ea0308c (0x000000018ea0308c) libsystem_pthread.dylib`thread_start + 8
0x16d052ff0: 0x0000000000000000
0x16d052ff8: 0x0000000000000000
0x16d053000: 0xb60ce2c5ab53b405
0x16d053008: 0x0000000000000000
0x16d053010: 0x000000016d0df000
0x16d053018: 0x000000016cfc7010
0x16d053020: 0x0000000000000000
0x16d053028: 0x0000000000000000
0x16d053030: 0x0000000000000101
0x16d053038: 0x0000000a0000001f
0x16d053040: 0x0000000000000000
0x16d053048: 0x0001010200000000
0x16d053050: 0x0000000000000000
0x16d053058: 0x0000000000000000
0x16d053060: 0x0000000000000000
0x16d053068: 0x0000000000000000
0x16d053070: 0x0000000000000000
0x16d053078: 0x0000000000000000
0x16d053080: 0x0000000000000000
0x16d053088: 0x0000000000000000
0x16d053090: 0x0000000102f4fa8c App8`thread_three(void*)
0x16d053098: 0x0000000000000000
0x16d0530a0: 0x0003000000000000
0x16d0530a8: 0x0000000000000000
0x16d0530b0: 0x000000016d053000
0x16d0530b8: 0x000000016cfd0000
0x16d0530c0: 0x000000016cfcc000
0x16d0530c8: 0x000000000008c000
0x16d0530d0: 0x0000000000004000
0x16d0530d8: 0x00000000002c7419
0x16d0530e0: 0x000000016d053000
0x16d0530e8: 0x000000016d0530ac
0x16d0530f0: 0x0000000000000e03
0x16d0530f8: 0x0000000000001103
0x16d053100: 0x00000000000008ff
0x16d053108: 0x0000000000000000
0x16d053110: 0x0000000000000000
0x16d053118: 0xb60ce2c4c6568405
0x16d053120: 0x0000000000000000
0x16d053128: 0x0000000000000000
0x16d053130: 0x0000000000000000
0x16d053138: 0x0000000000000000
0x16d053140: 0x0000000000000000
0x16d053148: 0x0000000000000000
0x16d053150: 0x0000000000000000
0x16d053158: 0x0000000000000000
0x16d053160: 0x0000000000000000
0x16d053168: 0x0000000000000000
```

```
(lldb) di -a 0x000000019953b770
libunwind.dylib`:
    0x19953b68c <+0>:   pacibsp
    0x19953b690 <+4>:   stp    x20, x19, [sp, #-0x20]!
    0x19953b694 <+8>:   stp    x29, x30, [sp, #0x10]
    0x19953b698 <+12>:  add    x29, sp, #0x10
    0x19953b69c <+16>:  sub    sp, sp, #0xaf0
    0x19953b6a0 <+20>:  mov    x19, x0
    0x19953b6a4 <+24>:  movi.2d v0, #0000000000000000
    0x19953b6a8 <+28>:  str    q0, [sp, #0x7a0]
    0x19953b6ac <+32>:  str    q0, [sp, #0x790]
    0x19953b6b0 <+36>:  str    q0, [sp, #0x780]
    0x19953b6b4 <+40>:  str    q0, [sp, #0x770]
    0x19953b6b8 <+44>:  str    q0, [sp, #0x760]
    0x19953b6bc <+48>:  str    q0, [sp, #0x750]
```

```
0x19953b6c0 <+52>:   str    q0, [sp, #0x740]
0x19953b6c4 <+56>:   str    q0, [sp, #0x730]
0x19953b6c8 <+60>:   str    q0, [sp, #0x720]
0x19953b6cc <+64>:   str    q0, [sp, #0x710]
0x19953b6d0 <+68>:   str    q0, [sp, #0x700]
0x19953b6d4 <+72>:   str    q0, [sp, #0x6f0]
0x19953b6d8 <+76>:   str    q0, [sp, #0x6e0]
0x19953b6dc <+80>:   str    q0, [sp, #0x6d0]
0x19953b6e0 <+84>:   str    q0, [sp, #0x6c0]
0x19953b6e4 <+88>:   str    q0, [sp, #0x6b0]
0x19953b6e8 <+92>:   str    q0, [sp, #0x6a0]
0x19953b6ec <+96>:   str    q0, [sp, #0x690]
0x19953b6f0 <+100>:  str    q0, [sp, #0x680]
0x19953b6f4 <+104>:  str    q0, [sp, #0x670]
0x19953b6f8 <+108>:  str    q0, [sp, #0x660]
0x19953b6fc <+112>:  str    q0, [sp, #0x650]
0x19953b700 <+116>:  str    q0, [sp, #0x640]
0x19953b704 <+120>:  str    q0, [sp, #0x630]
0x19953b708 <+124>:  str    q0, [sp, #0x620]
0x19953b70c <+128>:  str    q0, [sp, #0x610]
0x19953b710 <+132>:  str    q0, [sp, #0x600]
0x19953b714 <+136>:  str    q0, [sp, #0x5f0]
0x19953b718 <+140>:  str    q0, [sp, #0x5e0]
0x19953b71c <+144>:  str    q0, [sp, #0x5d0]
0x19953b720 <+148>:  str    q0, [sp, #0x5c0]
0x19953b724 <+152>:  str    q0, [sp, #0x5b0]
0x19953b728 <+156>:  stp    q0, q0, [sp, #0x1f0]
0x19953b72c <+160>:  stp    q0, q0, [sp, #0x1d0]
0x19953b730 <+164>:  stp    q0, q0, [sp, #0x1b0]
0x19953b734 <+168>:  stp    q0, q0, [sp, #0x190]
0x19953b738 <+172>:  stp    q0, q0, [sp, #0x170]
0x19953b73c <+176>:  stp    q0, q0, [sp, #0x150]
0x19953b740 <+180>:  stp    q0, q0, [sp, #0x130]
0x19953b744 <+184>:  stp    q0, q0, [sp, #0x110]
0x19953b748 <+188>:  stp    q0, q0, [sp, #0xf0]
0x19953b74c <+192>:  stp    q0, q0, [sp, #0xd0]
0x19953b750 <+196>:  stp    q0, q0, [sp, #0xb0]
0x19953b754 <+200>:  stp    q0, q0, [sp, #0x90]
0x19953b758 <+204>:  stp    q0, q0, [sp, #0x70]
0x19953b75c <+208>:  stp    q0, q0, [sp, #0x50]
0x19953b760 <+212>:  stp    q0, q0, [sp, #0x30]
0x19953b764 <+216>:  stp    q0, q0, [sp, #0x10]
0x19953b768 <+220>:  add    x0, sp, #0x5b0
0x19953b76c <+224>:  bl     0x199536d34               ; unw_getcontext
0x19953b770 <+228>:  ldr    x3, [x19, #0x10]
0x19953b774 <+232>:  cbnz   x3, 0x19953b78c          ; <+256>
0x19953b778 <+236>:  add    x0, sp, #0x5b0
0x19953b77c <+240>:  add    x1, sp, #0x10
0x19953b780 <+244>:  mov    x2, x19
0x19953b784 <+248>:  bl     0x19953b420              ; unwind_phase2
0x19953b788 <+252>:  b      0x19953b7a0              ; <+276>
0x19953b78c <+256>:  ldr    x4, [x19, #0x18]
0x19953b790 <+260>:  add    x0, sp, #0x5b0
0x19953b794 <+264>:  add    x1, sp, #0x10
0x19953b798 <+268>:  mov    x2, x19
0x19953b79c <+272>:  bl     0x19953b7d8              ; unwind_phase2_forced
0x19953b7a0 <+276>:  adrp   x19, 291267
0x19953b7a4 <+280>:  ldr    x19, [x19, #0x4a8]
0x19953b7a8 <+284>:  ldr    x0, [x19]
0x19953b7ac <+288>:  adrp   x8, 1
0x19953b7b0 <+292>:  add    x8, x8, #0xd90           ; "_Unwind_Resume() can't return"
```

162

```
0x19953b7b4 <+296>: adrp    x9, 1
0x19953b7b8 <+300>: add     x9, x9, #0xd81          ; "_Unwind_Resume"
0x19953b7bc <+304>: stp     x9, x8, [sp]
0x19953b7c0 <+308>: adrp    x1, 1
0x19953b7c4 <+312>: add     x1, x1, #0xe1f          ; "libunwind: %s - %s\n"
0x19953b7c8 <+316>: bl      0x19953c48c            ; symbol stub for: fprintf
0x19953b7cc <+320>: ldr     x0, [x19]
0x19953b7d0 <+324>: bl      0x19953c47c            ; symbol stub for: fflush
0x19953b7d4 <+328>: bl      0x19953c43c            ; symbol stub for: abort
```

Exercise X9

- **Goal:** Learn how to identify heap leaks

- **Patterns:** Heap Leak; Execution Residue; Module Hint

- \AMCDA-Dumps\Exercise-X9.pdf

Exercise X9

Goal: Learn how to identify heap leaks.

Patterns: Heap Leak; Execution Residue; Module Hint.

1.   Identify increased heap memory consumption by comparing the *vmmap_92806_1.log, vmmap_92806_2.log,* and *vmmap_92806_3.log* reports taken at different times:

```
Process:       App9 [92806]
Path:          /Users/USER/*/App9
Load Address:  0x102874000
Identifier:    App9
Version:       ???
Code Type:     ARM64
Platform:      macOS
Parent Process: zsh [93724]

Date/Time:     2022-12-09 00:26:05.184 +0000
Launch Time:   2022-12-09 00:25:27.283 +0000
OS Version:    macOS 12.6 (21G115)
Report Version: 7
Analysis Tool: /Applications/Xcode.app/Contents/Developer/usr/bin/vmmap
Analysis Tool Version: Xcode 14.0.1 (14A400)
----

Virtual Memory Map of process 92806 (App9)
Output report format: 2.4  -- 64-bit process
VM page size:  16384 bytes

==== Non-writable regions for process 92806
REGION TYPE            START - END         [ VSIZE  RSDNT  DIRTY   SWAP] PRT/MAX SHRMOD PURGE   REGION DETAIL
__TEXT                 102874000-102878000 [   16K    16K    0K      0K] r-x/r-x SM=COW         /Users/USER/*/App9
__DATA_CONST           102878000-10287c000 [   16K    16K   16K      0K] r--/rw- SM=COW         /Users/USER/*/App9
__LINKEDIT             10287c000-102884000 [   32K    32K    0K      0K] r--/r-- SM=COW         /Users/USER/*/App9
dyld private memory    102884000-102984000 [ 1024K    16K   16K      0K] r--/rwx SM=PRV
shared memory          10298c000-102990000 [   16K    16K   16K      0K] r--/r-- SM=SHM
MALLOC metadata        102990000-102994000 [   16K    16K   16K      0K] r--/rwx SM=ZER         MallocHelperZone_0x102990000 zone structure
MALLOC guard page      102998000-10299c000 [   16K     0K    0K      0K] ---/rwx SM=ZER
MALLOC guard page      1029a4000-1029a8000 [   16K     0K    0K      0K] ---/rwx SM=ZER
MALLOC guard page      1029a8000-1029ac000 [   16K     0K    0K      0K] ---/rwx SM=NUL
MALLOC guard page      1029b4000-1029bc000 [   32K     0K    0K      0K] ---/rwx SM=NUL
MALLOC guard page      1029c4000-1029c8000 [   16K     0K    0K      0K] ---/rwx SM=NUL
MALLOC metadata        1029c8000-1029cc000 [   16K    16K   16K      0K] r--/rwx SM=PRV
MALLOC metadata        1029cc000-1029d0000 [   16K    16K   16K      0K] r--/rwx SM=ZER         DefaultMallocZone_0x1029cc000 zone structure
__TEXT                 102a48000-102aa8000 [  384K   384K    0K      0K] r-x/r-x SM=COW         /usr/lib/dyld
__DATA_CONST           102aa8000-102ac0000 [   96K    32K   32K      0K] r--/rw- SM=COW         /usr/lib/dyld
__LINKEDIT             102ac4000-102afc000 [  224K    80K    0K      0K] r--/r-- SM=COW         /usr/lib/dyld
STACK GUARD            16958c000-16cd90000 [ 56.0M     0K    0K      0K] ---/rwx SM=NUL         stack guard for thread 0
STACK GUARD            16d58c000-16d590000 [   16K     0K    0K      0K] ---/rwx SM=NUL         stack guard for thread 1
STACK GUARD            16d618000-16d61c000 [   16K     0K    0K      0K] ---/rwx SM=NUL         stack guard for thread 2
STACK GUARD            16d6a4000-16d6a8000 [   16K     0K    0K      0K] ---/rwx SM=NUL         stack guard for thread 3
STACK GUARD            16d730000-16d734000 [   16K     0K    0K      0K] ---/rwx SM=NUL         stack guard for thread 4
STACK GUARD            16d7bc000-16d7c0000 [   16K     0K    0K      0K] ---/rwx SM=NUL         stack guard for thread 5
__TEXT                 18e72d000-18e72f000 [    8K     8K    0K      0K] r-x/r-x SM=COW         /usr/lib/system/libsystem_blocks.dylib
__TEXT                 18e72f000-18e771000 [  264K   264K    0K      0K] r-x/r-x SM=COW         /usr/lib/system/libxpc.dylib
__TEXT                 18e771000-18e78b000 [  104K   104K    0K      0K] r-x/r-x SM=COW         /usr/lib/system/libsystem_trace.dylib
__TEXT                 18e78b000-18e815000 [  552K   504K    0K      0K] r-x/r-x SM=COW         /usr/lib/system/libcorecrypto.dylib
__TEXT                 18e815000-18e840000 [  172K   172K    0K      0K] r-x/r-x SM=COW         /usr/lib/system/libsystem_malloc.dylib
__TEXT                 18e840000-18e887000 [  284K   284K    0K      0K] r-x/r-x SM=COW         /usr/lib/system/libdispatch.dylib
__TEXT                 18e887000-18e8c5000 [  248K   248K    0K      0K] r-x/r-x SM=COW         /usr/lib/libobjc.A.dylib
__TEXT                 18e8c5000-18e8c8000 [   12K    12K    0K      0K] r-x/r-x SM=COW         /usr/lib/system/libsystem_featureflags.dylib
__TEXT                 18e8c8000-18e94a000 [  520K   472K    0K      0K] r-x/r-x SM=COW         /usr/lib/system/libsystem_c.dylib
__TEXT                 18e94a000-18e9b1000 [  412K   380K    0K      0K] r-x/r-x SM=COW         /usr/lib/libc++.1.dylib
__TEXT                 18e9b1000-18e9c9000 [   96K    96K    0K      0K] r-x/r-x SM=COW         /usr/lib/libc++abi.dylib
__TEXT                 18e9c9000-18ea01000 [  224K   208K    0K      0K] r-x/r-x SM=COW         /usr/lib/system/libsystem_kernel.dylib
__TEXT                 18ea01000-18ea0e000 [   52K    52K    0K      0K] r-x/r-x SM=COW         /usr/lib/system/libsystem_pthread.dylib
__TEXT                 18ea0e000-18ea1b000 [   52K    52K    0K      0K] r-x/r-x SM=COW         /usr/lib/system/libdyld.dylib
__TEXT                 18ea1b000-18ea23000 [   32K    32K    0K      0K] r-x/r-x SM=COW         /usr/lib/system/libsystem_platform.dylib
__TEXT                 18ea23000-18ea50000 [  180K   164K    0K      0K] r-x/r-x SM=COW         /usr/lib/system/libsystem_info.dylib
__TEXT                 19113f000-19114a000 [   44K    44K    0K      0K] r-x/r-x SM=COW         /usr/lib/system/libsystem_darwin.dylib
__TEXT                 191598000-1915a8000 [   64K    64K    0K      0K] r-x/r-x SM=COW         /usr/lib/system/libsystem_notify.dylib
__TEXT                 193b14000-193b2d000 [  100K   100K    0K      0K] r-x/r-x SM=COW         /usr/lib/system/libsystem_networkextension.dylib
__TEXT                 193b86000-193b9e000 [   96K    96K    0K      0K] r-x/r-x SM=COW         /usr/lib/system/libsystem_asl.dylib
__TEXT                 1952ea000-1952f3000 [   36K    20K    0K      0K] r-x/r-x SM=COW         /usr/lib/system/libsystem_symptoms.dylib
__TEXT                 1972de000-1972fd000 [  124K   124K    0K      0K] r-x/r-x SM=COW         /usr/lib/system/libsystem_containermanager.dylib
__TEXT                 198085000-19808a000 [   20K    20K    0K      0K] r-x/r-x SM=COW         /usr/lib/system/libsystem_configuration.dylib
__TEXT                 19808a000-19808f000 [   20K    20K    0K      0K] r-x/r-x SM=COW         /usr/lib/system/libsystem_sandbox.dylib
__TEXT                 198bf0000-198bf3000 [   12K    12K    0K      0K] r-x/r-x SM=COW         /usr/lib/system/libquarantine.dylib
__TEXT                 19925d000-199263000 [   24K    24K    0K      0K] r-x/r-x SM=COW         /usr/lib/system/libsystem_coreservices.dylib
__TEXT                 1994c8000-1994ff000 [  220K   156K    0K      0K] r-x/r-x SM=COW         /usr/lib/system/libsystem_m.dylib
__TEXT                 199500000-199509000 [   36K    36K    0K      0K] r-x/r-x SM=COW         /usr/lib/system/libmacho.dylib
__TEXT                 199525000-199532000 [   52K    52K    0K      0K] r-x/r-x SM=COW         /usr/lib/system/libcommonCrypto.dylib
__TEXT                 199532000-19953d000 [   44K    44K    0K      0K] r-x/r-x SM=COW         /usr/lib/system/libunwind.dylib
__TEXT                 19953d000-199545000 [   32K    32K    0K      0K] r-x/r-x SM=COW         /usr/lib/liboah.dylib
__TEXT                 199545000-19954e000 [   36K    36K    0K      0K] r-x/r-x SM=COW         /usr/lib/system/libcopyfile.dylib
__TEXT                 19954e000-199552000 [   16K    16K    0K      0K] r-x/r-x SM=COW         /usr/lib/system/libcompiler_rt.dylib
__TEXT                 199552000-199557000 [   20K    20K    0K      0K] r-x/r-x SM=COW         /usr/lib/system/libsystem_collections.dylib
__TEXT                 199557000-19955a000 [   12K    12K    0K      0K] r-x/r-x SM=COW         /usr/lib/system/libsystem_secinit.dylib
__TEXT                 19955a000-19955d000 [   12K    12K    0K      0K] r-x/r-x SM=COW         /usr/lib/system/libremovefile.dylib
```

```
__TEXT                      19955d000-19955e000    [    4K     4K     0K     0K] r-x/r-x SM=COW          /usr/lib/system/libkeymgr.dylib
__TEXT                      19955e000-199567000    [   36K    36K     0K     0K] r-x/r-x SM=COW          /usr/lib/system/libsystem_dnssd.dylib
__TEXT                      199567000-19956d000    [   24K    24K     0K     0K] r-x/r-x SM=COW          /usr/lib/system/libcache.dylib
__TEXT                      19956d000-19956f000    [    8K     8K     0K     0K] r-x/r-x SM=COW          /usr/lib/libSystem.B.dylib
__TEXT                      19f8c1000-19f8c2000    [    4K     4K     0K     0K] r-x/r-x SM=COW          /usr/lib/system/libsystem_product_info_filter.dylib
__OBJC_RO                   1d89c2000-1ddcc4000    [ 83.0M  51.4M     0K     0K] r-x/r-x SM=COW          /usr/lib/libobjc.A.dylib
__DATA_CONST                1e0098000-1e0098130    [   304    304     0K     0K] r--/rw- SM=COW          /usr/lib/system/libsystem_blocks.dylib
__DATA_CONST                1e0098130-1e00987d0    [  1696   1696     0K     0K] r--/rw- SM=COW          /usr/lib/system/libsystem_trace.dylib
__DATA_CONST                1e00987d0-1e0098ef0    [  1824   1824     0K     0K] r--/rw- SM=COW          /usr/lib/system/libcorecrypto.dylib
__DATA_CONST                1e0098ef0-1e0098f48    [    88     88     0K     0K] r--/rw- SM=COW          /usr/lib/system/libsystem_malloc.dylib
__DATA_CONST                1e0098f50-1e0099b58    [  3080   3080     0K     0K] r--/rw- SM=COW          /usr/lib/libobjc.A.dylib
__DATA_CONST                1e0099b58-1e0099b98    [    64     64     0K     0K] r--/rw- SM=COW          /usr/lib/system/libsystem_featureflags.dylib
__DATA_CONST                1e0099b98-1e009b370    [    6K     6K     0K     0K] r--/rw- SM=COW          /usr/lib/system/libsystem_c.dylib
__DATA_CONST                1e009b370-1e009bcd0    [  2400   2400     0K     0K] r--/rw- SM=COW          /usr/lib/libc++.1.dylib
__DATA_CONST                1e009bcd0-1e009bda8    [   216    216     0K     0K] r--/rw- SM=COW          /usr/lib/libc++abi.dylib
__DATA_CONST                1e009bda8-1e009e060    [    9K     9K     0K     0K] r--/rw- SM=COW          /usr/lib/system/libsystem_kernel.dylib
__DATA_CONST                1e009e060-1e009e098    [    56     56     0K     0K] r--/rw- SM=COW          /usr/lib/system/libsystem_pthread.dylib
__DATA_CONST                1e009e098-1e009e258    [   448    448     0K     0K] r--/rw- SM=COW          /usr/lib/system/libdyld.dylib
__DATA_CONST                1e009e258-1e009e278    [    32     32     0K     0K] r--/rw- SM=COW          /usr/lib/system/libsystem_platform.dylib
__DATA_CONST                1e009e278-1e009e790    [  1304   1304     0K     0K] r--/rw- SM=COW          /usr/lib/system/libsystem_info.dylib
__DATA_CONST                1e0127148-1e0129ac0    [   10K    10K     0K     0K] r--/rw- SM=COW          /usr/lib/system/libsystem_darwin.dylib
__DATA_CONST                1e0133dc0-1e0133f18    [   344    344     0K     0K] r--/rw- SM=COW          /usr/lib/system/libsystem_notify.dylib
__DATA_CONST                1e02c9868-1e02c9d60    [  1272   1272     0K     0K] r--/rw- SM=COW          /usr/lib/system/libsystem_networkextension.dylib
__DATA_CONST                1e02cac70-1e02cb290    [  1568   1568     0K     0K] r--/rw- SM=COW          /usr/lib/system/libsystem_asl.dylib
__DATA_CONST                1e032ea80-1e032ec30    [   432    432     0K     0K] r--/rw- SM=COW          /usr/lib/system/libsystem_symptoms.dylib
__DATA_CONST                1e05863b8-1e0586da0    [  2536   2536     0K     0K] r--/rw- SM=COW          /usr/lib/system/libsystem_containermanager.dylib
__DATA_CONST                1e061d0e0-1e061d298    [   440    440     0K     0K] r--/rw- SM=COW          /usr/lib/system/libsystem_configuration.dylib
__DATA_CONST                1e061d298-1e061d308    [   112    112     0K     0K] r--/rw- SM=COW          /usr/lib/system/libsystem_sandbox.dylib
__DATA_CONST                1e064ac20-1e064ac70    [    80     80     0K     0K] r--/rw- SM=COW          /usr/lib/system/libquarantine.dylib
__DATA_CONST                1e06d5660-1e06d5dc8    [  1896   1896     0K     0K] r--/rw- SM=COW          /usr/lib/system/libsystem_coreservices.dylib
__DATA_CONST                1e06fd5a8-1e06fdcf0    [  1864   1864     0K     0K] r--/rw- SM=COW          /usr/lib/system/libmacho.dylib
__DATA_CONST                1e06fdd00-1e06fe4a0    [  1952   1952     0K     0K] r--/rw- SM=COW          /usr/lib/system/libcommonCrypto.dylib
__DATA_CONST                1e06fe4a0-1e06fe7c0    [   800    800     0K     0K] r--/rw- SM=COW          /usr/lib/system/libunwind.dylib
__DATA_CONST                1e06fe7c0-1e06fe7d8    [    24     24     0K     0K] r--/rw- SM=COW          /usr/lib/liboah.dylib
__DATA_CONST                1e06fe7d8-1e06fea98    [   704    704     0K     0K] r--/rw- SM=COW          /usr/lib/system/libcopyfile.dylib
__DATA_CONST                1e06fea98-1e06feaa0    [     8      8     0K     0K] r--/rw- SM=COW          /usr/lib/system/libsystem_collections.dylib
__DATA_CONST                1e06feaa0-1e06feb10    [   112    112     0K     0K] r--/rw- SM=COW          /usr/lib/system/libsystem_secinit.dylib
__DATA_CONST                1e06feb10-1e06feb20    [    16     16     0K     0K] r--/rw- SM=COW          /usr/lib/system/libremovefile.dylib
__DATA_CONST                1e06feb20-1e06feb30    [    16     16     0K     0K] r--/rw- SM=COW          /usr/lib/system/libkeymgr.dylib
__DATA_CONST                1e06feb30-1e06feba8    [   120    120     0K     0K] r--/rw- SM=COW          /usr/lib/system/libsystem_dnssd.dylib
__DATA_CONST                1e06feba8-1e06fec08    [    96     96     0K     0K] r--/rw- SM=COW          /usr/lib/system/libcache.dylib
__DATA_CONST                1e06fec08-1e06fec18    [    16     16     0K     0K] r--/rw- SM=COW          /usr/lib/libSystem.B.dylib
__AUTH_CONST                1e8b08000-1e8b08030    [    48     48     0K     0K] r--/rw- SM=COW          /usr/lib/system/libsystem_blocks.dylib
__OBJC_CONST                1e8b08030-1e8b08390    [   864    864     0K     0K] r--/rw- SM=COW          /usr/lib/system/libsystem_blocks.dylib
__DATA_CONST                1e8b08390-1e8b0ce20    [   19K    19K     0K     0K] r--/rw- SM=COW          /usr/lib/system/libxpc.dylib
__OBJC_CONST                1e8b0ce20-1e8b0df90    [    4K     4K     0K     0K] r--/rw- SM=COW          /usr/lib/system/libxpc.dylib
__AUTH_CONST                1e8b0df90-1e8b0ec90    [  3328   3328     0K     0K] r--/rw- SM=COW          /usr/lib/system/libsystem_trace.dylib
__OBJC_CONST                1e8b0ec90-1e8b0ee40    [   432    432     0K     0K] r--/rw- SM=COW          /usr/lib/system/libsystem_trace.dylib
__AUTH_CONST                1e8b0ee40-1e8b0ff10    [    4K     4K     0K     0K] r--/rw- SM=COW          /usr/lib/system/libcorecrypto.dylib
__AUTH_CONST                1e8b0ff10-1e8b104e8    [  1496   1496     0K     0K] r--/rw- SM=COW          /usr/lib/system/libsystem_malloc.dylib
__DATA_CONST                1e8b10500-1e8b238e8    [   77K    45K     0K     0K] r--/rw- SM=COW          /usr/lib/system/libdispatch.dylib
__OBJC_CONST                1e8b238e8-1e8b24938    [    4K     4K     0K     0K] r--/rw- SM=COW          /usr/lib/system/libdispatch.dylib
__AUTH_CONST                1e8b24940-1e8b253c8    [  2696   2696     0K     0K] r--/rw- SM=COW          /usr/lib/libobjc.A.dylib
__OBJC_CONST                1e8b253c8-1e8b25698    [   720    720     0K     0K] r--/rw- SM=COW          /usr/lib/libobjc.A.dylib
__AUTH_CONST                1e8b25698-1e8b25808    [   368    368     0K     0K] r--/rw- SM=COW          /usr/lib/system/libsystem_featureflags.dylib
__AUTH_CONST                1e8b25808-1e8b26168    [  2400   2400     0K     0K] r--/rw- SM=COW          /usr/lib/system/libsystem_c.dylib
__AUTH_CONST                1e8b26168-1e8b282a8    [    8K     8K     0K     0K] r--/rw- SM=COW          /usr/lib/libc++.1.dylib
__AUTH_CONST                1e8b282a8-1e8b2b4b8    [   13K    13K     0K     0K] r--/rw- SM=COW          /usr/lib/libc++abi.dylib
__AUTH_CONST                1e8b2b4b8-1e8b2b5e0    [   296    296     0K     0K] r--/rw- SM=COW          /usr/lib/system/libsystem_kernel.dylib
__AUTH_CONST                1e8b2b5e0-1e8b2b810    [   560    560     0K     0K] r--/rw- SM=COW          /usr/lib/system/libsystem_pthread.dylib
__AUTH_CONST                1e8b2b810-1e8b2bfc8    [  1976   1976     0K     0K] r--/rw- SM=COW          /usr/lib/system/libdyld.dylib
__AUTH_CONST                1e8b2bfc8-1e8b2c250    [   648    648     0K     0K] r--/rw- SM=COW          /usr/lib/system/libsystem_platform.dylib
__AUTH_CONST                1e8b2c250-1e8b2d3f0    [    4K     4K     0K     0K] r--/rw- SM=COW          /usr/lib/system/libsystem_info.dylib
__AUTH_CONST                1e8c5bd48-1e8c5c1c8    [  1152   1152     0K     0K] r--/rw- SM=COW          /usr/lib/system/libsystem_darwin.dylib
__AUTH_CONST                1e8c77a80-1e8c77e00    [   896    896     0K     0K] r--/rw- SM=COW          /usr/lib/system/libsystem_notify.dylib
__AUTH_CONST                1e8dfea40-1e8dff608    [  3016   3016     0K     0K] r--/rw- SM=COW          /usr/lib/system/libsystem_networkextension.dylib
__AUTH_CONST                1e8e4d718-1e8e4e160    [  2632   2632     0K     0K] r--/rw- SM=COW          /usr/lib/system/libsystem_asl.dylib
__AUTH_CONST                1e8f17288-1e8f17560    [   728    728     0K     0K] r--/rw- SM=COW          /usr/lib/system/libsystem_symptoms.dylib
__AUTH_CONST                1e904e480-1e904f8c0    [    5K     5K     0K     0K] r--/rw- SM=COW          /usr/lib/system/libsystem_containermanager.dylib
__AUTH_CONST                1e915e250-1e915e560    [   784    784     0K     0K] r--/rw- SM=COW          /usr/lib/system/libsystem_configuration.dylib
__AUTH_CONST                1e915e560-1e915e768    [   520    520     0K     0K] r--/rw- SM=COW          /usr/lib/system/libsystem_sandbox.dylib
__AUTH_CONST                1e91a78b8-1e91a79c0    [   264    264     0K     0K] r--/rw- SM=COW          /usr/lib/system/libquarantine.dylib
__AUTH_CONST                1e922eac0-1e922ed50    [   656    656     0K     0K] r--/rw- SM=COW          /usr/lib/system/libsystem_coreservices.dylib
__AUTH_CONST                1e925ad88-1e925ada8    [    32     32     0K     0K] r--/rw- SM=COW          /usr/lib/system/libsystem_m.dylib
__AUTH_CONST                1e925ae28-1e925ae98    [   112    112     0K     0K] r--/rw- SM=COW          /usr/lib/system/libmacho.dylib
__AUTH_CONST                1e925afb0-1e925bd80    [  3536   3536     0K     0K] r--/rw- SM=COW          /usr/lib/system/libcommonCrypto.dylib
__AUTH_CONST                1e925bd80-1e925be98    [   280    280     0K     0K] r--/rw- SM=COW          /usr/lib/system/libunwind.dylib
__AUTH_CONST                1e925be98-1e925c168    [   720    720     0K     0K] r--/rw- SM=COW          /usr/lib/liboah.dylib
__AUTH_CONST                1e925c168-1e925c5a0    [  1080   1080     0K     0K] r--/rw- SM=COW          /usr/lib/system/libcopyfile.dylib
__AUTH_CONST                1e925c5a0-1e925c600    [    96     96     0K     0K] r--/rw- SM=COW          /usr/lib/system/libcompiler_rt.dylib
__AUTH_CONST                1e925c600-1e925c750    [   336    336     0K     0K] r--/rw- SM=COW          /usr/lib/system/libsystem_collections.dylib
__AUTH_CONST                1e925c750-1e925ca18    [   712    712     0K     0K] r--/rw- SM=COW          /usr/lib/system/libsystem_secinit.dylib
__AUTH_CONST                1e925ca18-1e925cb78    [   352    352     0K     0K] r--/rw- SM=COW          /usr/lib/system/libremovefile.dylib
__AUTH_CONST                1e925cb78-1e925cbf8    [   128    128     0K     0K] r--/rw- SM=COW          /usr/lib/system/libkeymgr.dylib
__AUTH_CONST                1e925cbf8-1e925cdb0    [   440    440     0K     0K] r--/rw- SM=COW          /usr/lib/system/libsystem_dnssd.dylib
__AUTH_CONST                1e925cdb0-1e925ce70    [   192    192     0K     0K] r--/rw- SM=COW          /usr/lib/system/libcache.dylib
__AUTH_CONST                1e925ce70-1e925d120    [   688    688     0K     0K] r--/rw- SM=COW          /usr/lib/libSystem.B.dylib
__LINKEDIT                  222494000-2465e6000    [577.3M  13.9M     0K     0K] r--/r-- SM=COW          dyld shared cache combined __LINKEDIT

==== Writable regions for process 92806
REGION TYPE                    START - END         [ VSIZE  RSDNT  DIRTY   SWAP] PRT/MAX SHRMOD PURGE    REGION DETAIL
Kernel Alloc Once           102984000-10298c000    [   32K    16K    16K     0K] rw-/rwx SM=PRV
MALLOC metadata             102994000-102998000    [   16K    16K    16K     0K] rw-/rwx SM=ZER
MALLOC metadata             10299c000-1029a4000    [   32K    32K    32K     0K] rw-/rwx SM=ZER
MALLOC metadata             1029ac000-1029b4000    [   32K    32K    32K     0K] rw-/rwx SM=PRV
MALLOC metadata             1029bc000-1029c4000    [   32K    32K    32K     0K] rw-/rwx SM=PRV
MALLOC metadata             1029d0000-1029d4000    [   16K    16K    16K     0K] rw-/rwx SM=ZER
__DATA                      102ac0000-102ac4000    [   16K    16K    16K     0K] rw-/rw- SM=COW          /usr/lib/dyld
MALLOC_TINY                 12b600000-12b700000    [ 1024K    32K    32K     0K] rw-/rwx SM=PRV          MallocHelperZone_0x102990000
MALLOC_SMALL                12b800000-12c000000    [ 8192K    32K    32K     0K] rw-/rwx SM=PRV          MallocHelperZone_0x102990000
MALLOC_SMALL                12c000000-12c800000    [ 8192K  2016K  2016K     0K] rw-/rwx SM=PRV          MallocHelperZone_0x102990000
Stack                       16cd90000-16d58c000    [ 8176K    32K    32K     0K] rw-/rwx SM=PRV          thread 0
```

```
Stack                    16d590000-16d618000    [  544K   16K   16K    0K] rw-/rwx SM=PRV          thread 1
Stack                    16d61c000-16d6a4000    [  544K   16K   16K    0K] rw-/rwx SM=PRV          thread 2
Stack                    16d6a8000-16d730000    [  544K   16K   16K    0K] rw-/rwx SM=PRV          thread 3
Stack                    16d734000-16d7bc000    [  544K   16K   16K    0K] rw-/rwx SM=PRV          thread 4
Stack                    16d7c0000-16d848000    [  544K   16K   16K    0K] rw-/rwx SM=PRV          thread 5
__DATA                   1e4c04000-1e4c04060    [    96    96    96    0K] rw-/rw- SM=COW          /usr/lib/system/libsystem_blocks.dylib
__DATA                   1e4c04060-1e4c04d18    [  3256  3256  3256    0K] rw-/rw- SM=COW          /usr/lib/system/libxpc.dylib
__DATA                   1e4c04d18-1e4c05050    [   824   824   824    0K] rw-/rw- SM=COW          /usr/lib/system/libsystem_trace.dylib
__DATA                   1e4c05050-1e4c0c788    [   30K   30K   14K    0K] rw-/rw- SM=COW          /usr/lib/system/libcorecrypto.dylib
__DATA                   1e4c0c788-1e4c0ea24    [    9K    9K    9K    0K] rw-/rw- SM=COW          /usr/lib/system/libsystem_malloc.dylib
unused __DATA            1e4c0ea24-1e4c0ea40    [    28    28    28    0K] rw-/rw- SM=COW          on dirty page  unused system shared lib __DATA
__DATA                   1e4c0ea40-1e4c120c0    [   14K   14K   14K    0K] rw-/rw- SM=COW          /usr/lib/libobjc.A.dylib
__DATA                   1e4c120c0-1e4c120f9    [    57    57    57    0K] rw-/rw- SM=COW          /usr/lib/system/libsystem_featureflags.dylib
unused __DATA            1e4c120f9-1e4c12100    [     7     7     7    0K] rw-/rw- SM=COW          on dirty page  unused system shared lib __DATA
__DATA                   1e4c12100-1e4c14270    [    8K    8K    8K    0K] rw-/rw- SM=COW          /usr/lib/system/libsystem_c.dylib
unused __DATA            1e4c14270-1e4c15000    [  3472  3472  3472    0K] rw-/rw- SM=COW          on dirty page  unused system shared lib __DATA
__DATA                   1e4c15000-1e4c1b720    [   26K   26K   12K    0K] rw-/rw- SM=COW          /usr/lib/libc++.1.dylib
__DATA                   1e4c1b720-1e4c1ba68    [   840   840    0K    0K] rw-/rw- SM=COW          /usr/lib/libc++abi.dylib
__DATA                   1e4c1ba68-1e4c1bcd9    [   625   625    0K    0K] rw-/rw- SM=COW          /usr/lib/system/libsystem_kernel.dylib
__DATA                   1e4c1c000-1e4c24000    [   32K   32K    0K    0K] rw-/rw- SM=COW          /usr/lib/system/libsystem_pthread.dylib
__DATA                   1e4c24000-1e4c28000    [   16K   16K    0K    0K] rw-/rw- SM=COW          /usr/lib/system/libsystem_pthread.dylib
__DATA                   1e4c28000-1e4c28048    [    72    72    0K    0K] rw-/rw- SM=COW          /usr/lib/system/libsystem_pthread.dylib
__DATA                   1e4c28048-1e4c28050    [     8     8    0K    0K] rw-/rw- SM=COW          /usr/lib/system/libdyld.dylib
__DATA                   1e4c28050-1e4c28090    [    64    64    0K    0K] rw-/rw- SM=COW          /usr/lib/system/libsystem_platform.dylib
__DATA                   1e4c28090-1e4c28be0    [  2896  2896    0K    0K] rw-/rw- SM=COW          /usr/lib/system/libsystem_info.dylib
__DATA                   1e4c96958-1e4c96968    [    16    16    0K    0K] rw-/rw- SM=COW          /usr/lib/system/libsystem_darwin.dylib
__DATA                   1e4c9de00-1e4c9de51    [    81    81    0K    0K] rw-/rw- SM=COW          /usr/lib/system/libsystem_notify.dylib
__DATA                   1e4d33600-1e4d33bd9    [  1497  1497    0K    0K] rw-/rw- SM=COW          /usr/lib/system/libsystem_networkextension.dylib
__DATA                   1e4d343b8-1e4d344c8    [   272   272    0K    0K] rw-/rw- SM=COW          /usr/lib/system/libsystem_asl.dylib
__DATA                   1e4d6a118-1e4d6a158    [    64    64    0K    0K] rw-/rw- SM=COW          /usr/lib/system/libsystem_symptoms.dylib
__DATA                   1e4deca18-1e4decb40    [   296   296    0K    0K] rw-/rw- SM=COW          /usr/lib/system/libsystem_containermanager.dylib
__DATA                   1e4e2d090-1e4e2d159    [   201    0K    0K    0K] rw-/rw- SM=COW          /usr/lib/system/libsystem_configuration.dylib
__DATA                   1e4e2d160-1e4e2d188    [    40    0K    0K    0K] rw-/rw- SM=COW          /usr/lib/system/libsystem_sandbox.dylib
__DATA                   1e4e4f280-1e4e4f290    [    16    16    0K    0K] rw-/rw- SM=COW          /usr/lib/system/libquarantine.dylib
__DATA                   1e4e61bb0-1e4e61c88    [   216   216    0K    0K] rw-/rw- SM=COW          /usr/lib/system/libsystem_coreservices.dylib
__DATA                   1e4e71a20-1e4e71a24    [     4     4    0K    0K] rw-/rw- SM=COW          /usr/lib/system/libsystem_m.dylib
__DATA                   1e4e71ae8-1e4e723d9    [  2289  2289    0K    0K] rw-/rw- SM=COW          /usr/lib/system/libunwind.dylib
__DATA                   1e4e723e0-1e4e723e8    [     8     8    0K    0K] rw-/rw- SM=COW          /usr/lib/liboah.dylib
__DATA                   1e4e723e8-1e4e723f8    [    16    16    0K    0K] rw-/rw- SM=COW          /usr/lib/system/libcopyfile.dylib
__DATA                   1e4e723f8-1e4e733f8    [    4K    4K    0K    0K] rw-/rw- SM=COW          /usr/lib/system/libcompiler_rt.dylib
__DATA                   1e4e733f8-1e4e73438    [    64    64    0K    0K] rw-/rw- SM=COW          /usr/lib/system/libsystem_secinit.dylib
__DATA                   1e4e73438-1e4e73468    [    48    48    0K    0K] rw-/rw- SM=COW          /usr/lib/system/libsystem_dnssd.dylib
__DATA                   1e4e73468-1e4e73470    [     8     8    0K    0K] rw-/rw- SM=COW          /usr/lib/libSystem.B.dylib
unused __DATA_DIRTY      1e7930000-1e7930120    [   288   288   288    0K] rw-/rw- SM=COW          on dirty page  unused /usr/lib/libMobileGestalt.dylib
unused __DATA_DIRTY      1e7930120-1e7930170    [    80    80    80    0K] rw-/rw- SM=COW          on dirty page  unused
/usr/lib/libUniversalAccess.dylib
unused __DATA_DIRTY      1e7930170-1e7930190    [    32    32    32    0K] rw-/rw- SM=COW          on dirty page  unused
/usr/lib/libapp_launch_measurement.dylib
unused __DATA_DIRTY      1e7930190-1e7931010    [  3712  3712  3712    0K] rw-/rw- SM=COW          on dirty page  unused /usr/lib/libboringssl.dylib
__DATA_DIRTY             1e7931010-1e79321e0    [    4K    4K    4K    0K] rw-/rw- SM=COW          /usr/lib/libc++.1.dylib
__DATA_DIRTY             1e79321e0-1e7932208    [    40    40    40    0K] rw-/rw- SM=COW          /usr/lib/libc++abi.dylib
unused __DATA_DIRTY      1e7932208-1e7934000    [    7K    7K    7K    0K] rw-/rw- SM=COW          on dirty page  unused /usr/lib/libcoreroutine.dylib
unused __DATA_DIRTY      1e7938000-1e793a1c8    [    8K    8K    8K    0K] rw-/rw- SM=COW          on dirty page  unused /usr/lib/libnetwork.dylib
unused __DATA            1e793a1c8-1e793a200    [    56    56    56    0K] rw-/rw- SM=COW          on dirty page  unused system shared lib __DATA
__DATA_DIRTY             1e793a200-1e793d070    [   12K   12K   12K    0K] rw-/rw- SM=COW          /usr/lib/libobjc.A.dylib
unused __DATA_DIRTY      1e793d070-1e793d200    [   400   400   400    0K] rw-/rw- SM=COW          on dirty page  unused
/usr/lib/libpartition2_dynamic.dylib
unused __DATA_DIRTY      1e793d200-1e793d299    [   153   153   153    0K] rw-/rw- SM=COW          on dirty page  unused /usr/lib/libpmenergy.dylib
unused __DATA            1e793d299-1e793d2a0    [     7     7     7    0K] rw-/rw- SM=COW          on dirty page  unused system shared lib __DATA
unused __DATA_DIRTY      1e793d2a0-1e793d3e8    [   328   328   328    0K] rw-/rw- SM=COW          on dirty page  unused /usr/lib/libprequelite.dylib
unused __DATA_DIRTY      1e793d3e8-1e793d4f8    [   272   272   272    0K] rw-/rw- SM=COW          on dirty page  unused /usr/lib/libquic.dylib
unused __DATA_DIRTY      1e793d4f8-1e793d530    [    56    56    56    0K] rw-/rw- SM=COW          on dirty page  unused /usr/lib/libsandbox.1.dylib
unused __DATA            1e793d530-1e793d540    [    16    16    16    0K] rw-/rw- SM=COW          on dirty page  unused system shared lib __DATA
unused __DATA_DIRTY      1e793d540-1e7940000    [   11K   11K   11K    0K] rw-/rw- SM=COW          on dirty page  unused /usr/lib/libsqlite3.dylib
unused __DATA_DIRTY      1e795c000-1e795e610    [   10K   10K   10K    0K] rw-/rw- SM=COW          on dirty page  unused
/usr/lib/swift/libswiftFoundation.dylib
unused __DATA_DIRTY      1e795e610-1e795e7a0    [   400   400   400    0K] rw-/rw- SM=COW          on dirty page  unused
/usr/lib/swift/libswiftObjectiveC.dylib
unused __DATA_DIRTY      1e795e7a0-1e795e7b8    [    24    24    24    0K] rw-/rw- SM=COW          on dirty page  unused /usr/lib/swift/libswiftos.dylib
__DATA_DIRTY             1e795e7b8-1e795ef10    [  1880  1880  1880    0K] rw-/rw- SM=COW          /usr/lib/system/libcorecrypto.dylib
unused __DATA            1e795ef10-1e795ef40    [    48    48    48    0K] rw-/rw- SM=COW          on dirty page  unused system shared lib __DATA
__DATA_DIRTY             1e795ef40-1e79628e8    [   14K   14K   14K    0K] rw-/rw- SM=COW          /usr/lib/system/libdispatch.dylib
__DATA_DIRTY             1e79628e8-1e7962908    [    32    32    32    0K] rw-/rw- SM=COW          /usr/lib/system/libdyld.dylib
unused __DATA            1e7962908-1e7962910    [     8     8     8    0K] rw-/rw- SM=COW          on dirty page  unused system shared lib __DATA
__DATA_DIRTY             1e7962910-1e7962a6c    [   348   348   348    0K] rw-/rw- SM=COW          /usr/lib/system/libsystem_asl.dylib
unused __DATA            1e7962a6c-1e7962a70    [     4     4     4    0K] rw-/rw- SM=COW          on dirty page  unused system shared lib __DATA
__DATA_DIRTY             1e7962a70-1e7962c68    [   504   504   504    0K] rw-/rw- SM=COW          /usr/lib/system/libsystem_blocks.dylib
__DATA_DIRTY             1e7962c68-1e79657f0    [   11K   11K   11K    0K] rw-/rw- SM=COW          /usr/lib/system/libsystem_c.dylib
__DATA_DIRTY             1e79657f0-1e7965820    [    48    48    48    0K] rw-/rw- SM=COW          /usr/lib/system/libsystem_darwin.dylib
__DATA_DIRTY             1e7965820-1e7965830    [    16    16    16    0K] rw-/rw- SM=COW          /usr/lib/system/libsystem_featureflags.dylib
__DATA_DIRTY             1e7965830-1e7965ac0    [   656   656   656    0K] rw-/rw- SM=COW          /usr/lib/system/libsystem_info.dylib
__DATA_DIRTY             1e7965ac0-1e7966184    [  1732  1732  1732    0K] rw-/rw- SM=COW          /usr/lib/system/libsystem_kernel.dylib
unused __DATA            1e7966184-1e7966188    [     4     4     4    0K] rw-/rw- SM=COW          on dirty page  unused system shared lib __DATA
__DATA_DIRTY             1e7966188-1e79663a0    [   536   536   536    0K] rw-/rw- SM=COW          /usr/lib/system/libsystem_malloc.dylib
__DATA_DIRTY             1e79663a0-1e79663e1    [    65    65    65    0K] rw-/rw- SM=COW          /usr/lib/system/libsystem_networkextension.dylib
unused __DATA            1e79663e1-1e79663e8    [     7     7     7    0K] rw-/rw- SM=COW          on dirty page  unused system shared lib __DATA
__DATA_DIRTY             1e79663e8-1e79663f0    [     8     8     8    0K] rw-/rw- SM=COW          /usr/lib/system/libsystem_notify.dylib
__DATA_DIRTY             1e79663f0-1e7966404    [    20    20    20    0K] rw-/rw- SM=COW          /usr/lib/system/libsystem_platform.dylib
unused __DATA            1e7966404-1e7968000    [    7K    7K    7K    0K] rw-/rw- SM=COW          on dirty page  unused system shared lib __DATA
__DATA_DIRTY             1e7968000-1e796d838    [   22K   22K   22K    0K] rw-/rw- SM=COW          /usr/lib/system/libsystem_pthread.dylib
__DATA_DIRTY             1e796d838-1e796d848    [    16    16    16    0K] rw-/rw- SM=COW          /usr/lib/system/libsystem_symptoms.dylib
__DATA_DIRTY             1e796d848-1e796dcb8    [  1136  1136  1136    0K] rw-/rw- SM=COW          /usr/lib/system/libsystem_trace.dylib
__DATA_DIRTY             1e796dcb8-1e796e708    [  2640  2640  2640    0K] rw-/rw- SM=COW          /usr/lib/system/libxpc.dylib
unused __DATA            1e796e708-1e7970000    [    6K    6K    6K    0K] rw-/rw- SM=COW          on dirty page  unused system shared lib __DATA
__AUTH                   1e7970000-1e79701b8    [   440   440    0K    0K] rw-/rw- SM=COW          /usr/lib/system/libsystem_trace.dylib
__AUTH                   1e79701b8-1e7970218    [    96    96    0K    0K] rw-/rw- SM=COW          /usr/lib/system/libcorecrypto.dylib
__AUTH                   1e7974000-1e797c000    [   32K   32K    0K    0K] rw-/rw- SM=COW          /usr/lib/system/libsystem_malloc.dylib
__DATA                   1e797c000-1e797d400    [    5K    5K    0K    0K] rw-/rw- SM=COW          /usr/lib/system/libdispatch.dylib
__AUTH                   1e797d400-1e797d478    [   120   120    0K    0K] rw-/rw- SM=COW          /usr/lib/libobjc.A.dylib
__AUTH                   1e797d478-1e797e190    [  3352  3352    0K    0K] rw-/rw- SM=COW          /usr/lib/system/libsystem_c.dylib
__AUTH                   1e797e190-1e7980628    [    9K    9K  1576    0K] rw-/rw- SM=COW          /usr/lib/libc++.1.dylib
__AUTH                   1e7980628-1e7980670    [    72    72    72    0K] rw-/rw- SM=COW          /usr/lib/libc++abi.dylib
```

```
__AUTH                  1e7980670-1e79806b0  [    64     64     64    0K] rw-/rw- SM=COW   /usr/lib/system/libdyld.dylib
__AUTH                  1e79806b0-1e7980880  [   464    464    464    0K] rw-/rw- SM=COW   /usr/lib/system/libsystem_info.dylib
unused __AUTH           1e7980880-1e7982740  [    8K     8K     8K    0K] rw-/rw- SM=COW   ...y page  unused
/System/Library/Frameworks/CoreFoundation.framework/Versions/A/CoreFoundation
unused __AUTH           1e7982740-1e7984000  [    6K     6K     6K    0K] rw-/rw- SM=COW
...eServices.framework/Versions/A/Frameworks/LaunchServices.framework/Versions/A/LaunchServices
__AUTH                  1e7a0a640-1e7a0a660  [    32     32      0K    0K] rw-/rw- SM=COW   /usr/lib/system/libcommonCrypto.dylib
__AUTH                  1e7a0a660-1e7a0a668  [     8      8      0K    0K] rw-/rw- SM=COW   /usr/lib/libSystem.B.dylib
__OBJC_RW               1e87f0000-1e8b08000  [ 3168K  1616K    16K    0K] rw-/rw- SM=COW   /usr/lib/libobjc.A.dylib
MALLOC_NANO             600000000000-600008000000 [128.0M  144K   144K    0K] rw-/rwx SM=PRV   DefaultMallocZone_0x1029cc000
MALLOC_NANO (empty)     600008000000-600020000000 [384.0M    0K     0K    0K] rw-/rwx SM=NUL


==== Legend
SM=sharing mode:
          COW=copy_on_write PRV=private NUL=empty ALI=aliased
          SHM=shared ZER=zero_filled S/A=shared_alias
PURGE=purgeable mode:
          V=volatile N=nonvolatile E=empty   otherwise is unpurgeable


==== Summary for process 92806
ReadOnly portion of Libraries: Total=582.2M resident=18.4M(3%) swapped_out_or_unallocated=563.8M(97%)
Writable regions: Total=539.8M written=2416K(0%) resident=2480K(0%) swapped_out=0K(0%) unallocated=537.4M(100%)
```

REGION TYPE	VIRTUAL SIZE	RESIDENT SIZE	DIRTY SIZE	SWAPPED SIZE	VOLATILE SIZE	NONVOL SIZE	EMPTY SIZE	REGION COUNT (non-coalesced)	
Kernel Alloc Once	32K	16K	16K	0K	0K	0K	0K	1	
MALLOC guard page	96K	0K	0K	0K	0K	0K	0K	5	
MALLOC metadata	176K	176K	176K	0K	0K	0K	0K	8	
MALLOC_NANO	128.0M	144K	144K	0K	0K	0K	0K	1	see MALLOC ZONE table below
MALLOC_NANO (empty)	384.0M	0K	0K	0K	0K	0K	0K	1	see MALLOC ZONE table below
MALLOC_SMALL	16.0M	2048K	2048K	0K	0K	0K	0K	2	see MALLOC ZONE table below
MALLOC_TINY	1024K	32K	32K	0K	0K	0K	0K	1	see MALLOC ZONE table below
STACK GUARD	56.1M	0K	0K	0K	0K	0K	0K	6	
Stack	10.6M	112K	112K	0K	0K	0K	0K	6	
__AUTH	46K	46K	2176	0K	0K	0K	0K	11	
__AUTH_CONST	67K	67K	0K	0K	0K	0K	0K	38	
__DATA	173K	173K	77K	0K	0K	0K	0K	37	
__DATA_CONST	258K	162K	48K	0K	0K	0K	0K	40	
__DATA_DIRTY	73K	73K	73K	0K	0K	0K	0K	21	
__LINKEDIT	577.6M	14.0M	0K	0K	0K	0K	0K	3	
__OBJC_CONST	10K	10K	0K	0K	0K	0K	0K	5	
__OBJC_RO	83.0M	51.4M	0K	0K	0K	0K	0K	1	
__OBJC_RW	3168K	1616K	16K	0K	0K	0K	0K	1	
__TEXT	4708K	4468K	0K	0K	0K	0K	0K	43	
dyld private memory	1024K	16K	16K	0K	0K	0K	0K	1	
shared memory	16K	16K	16K	0K	0K	0K	0K	1	
unused but dirty shlib __DATA	72K	72K	72K	0K	0K	0K	0K	30	
TOTAL	1.2G	74.4M	2848K	0K	0K	0K	0K	263	

MALLOC ZONE	VIRTUAL SIZE	RESIDENT SIZE	DIRTY SIZE	SWAPPED SIZE	ALLOCATION COUNT	BYTES ALLOCATED	DIRTY+SWAP FRAG SIZE	% FRAG	REGION COUNT
DefaultMallocZone_0x1029cc000	128.0M	144K	144K	0K	211	9K	135K	94%	1
MallocHelperZone_0x102990000	17.0M	2080K	2080K	0K	2002	2002K	78K	4%	3
TOTAL	145.0M	2224K	2224K	0K	2213	2011K	213K	10%	4

```
Process:          App9 [92806]
Path:             /Users/USER/*/App9
Load Address:     0x102874000
Identifier:       App9
Version:          ???
Code Type:        ARM64
Platform:         macOS
Parent Process:   zsh [93724]

Date/Time:        2022-12-09 00:31:10.602 +0000
Launch Time:      2022-12-09 00:25:27.283 +0000
OS Version:       macOS 12.6 (21G115)
Report Version:   7
Analysis Tool:    /Applications/Xcode.app/Contents/Developer/usr/bin/vmmap
Analysis Tool Version:  Xcode 14.0.1 (14A400)
----

Virtual Memory Map of process 92806 (App9)
Output report format:  2.4  -- 64-bit process
VM page size:  16384 bytes

==== Non-writable regions for process 92806
```

REGION TYPE	START - END	[VSIZE	RSDNT	DIRTY	SWAP]	PRT/MAX	SHRMOD	PURGE	REGION DETAIL
__TEXT	102874000-102878000	[16K	16K	0K	0K]	r-x/r-x	SM=COW		/Users/USER/*/App9
__DATA_CONST	102878000-10287c000	[16K	16K	16K	0K]	r--/rw-	SM=COW		/Users/USER/*/App9
__LINKEDIT	10287c000-102884000	[32K	32K	0K	0K]	r--/r--	SM=COW		/Users/USER/*/App9
dyld private memory	102884000-102984000	[1024K	16K	16K	0K]	r--/rwx	SM=PRV		
shared memory	10298c000-102990000	[16K	16K	16K	0K]	r--/r--	SM=SHM		
MALLOC metadata	102990000-102994000	[16K	16K	16K	0K]	r--/rwx	SM=COW		MallocHelperZone_0x102990000 zone structure
MALLOC guard page	102998000-10299c000	[16K	0K	0K	0K]	---/rwx	SM=ZER		
MALLOC guard page	1029a4000-1029a8000	[16K	0K	0K	0K]	---/rwx	SM=ZER		
MALLOC guard page	1029a8000-1029ac000	[16K	0K	0K	0K]	---/rwx	SM=NUL		
MALLOC guard page	1029b4000-1029bc000	[32K	0K	0K	0K]	---/rwx	SM=NUL		
MALLOC guard page	1029c4000-1029c8000	[16K	0K	0K	0K]	---/rwx	SM=NUL		
MALLOC metadata	1029c8000-1029cc000	[16K	16K	16K	0K]	r--/rwx	SM=PRV		
MALLOC metadata	1029cc000-1029d0000	[16K	16K	16K	0K]	r--/rwx	SM=COW		DefaultMallocZone_0x1029cc000 zone structure
__TEXT	102a48000-102aa8000	[384K	384K	0K	0K]	r-x/r-x	SM=COW		/usr/lib/dyld
__DATA_CONST	102aa8000-102ac0000	[96K	16K	16K	16K]	r--/rw-	SM=COW		/usr/lib/dyld
__LINKEDIT	102ac0000-102afc000	[224K	80K	0K	0K]	r--/r--	SM=COW		/usr/lib/dyld
STACK GUARD	16958c000-16cd90000	[56.0M	0K	0K	0K]	---/rwx	SM=NUL		stack guard for thread 0

```
STACK GUARD        16d58c000-16d590000   [   16K     0K     0K     0K] ---/rwx SM=NUL   stack guard for thread 1
STACK GUARD        16d618000-16d61c000   [   16K     0K     0K     0K] ---/rwx SM=NUL   stack guard for thread 2
STACK GUARD        16d6a4000-16d6a8000   [   16K     0K     0K     0K] ---/rwx SM=NUL   stack guard for thread 3
STACK GUARD        16d730000-16d734000   [   16K     0K     0K     0K] ---/rwx SM=NUL   stack guard for thread 4
STACK GUARD        16d7bc000-16d7c0000   [   16K     0K     0K     0K] ---/rwx SM=NUL   stack guard for thread 5
__TEXT             18e72d000-18e72f000   [    8K     8K     0K     0K] r-x/r-x SM=COW   /usr/lib/system/libsystem_blocks.dylib
__TEXT             18e72f000-18e771000   [  264K   264K     0K     0K] r-x/r-x SM=COW   /usr/lib/system/libxpc.dylib
__TEXT             18e771000-18e78b000   [  104K   104K     0K     0K] r-x/r-x SM=COW   /usr/lib/system/libsystem_trace.dylib
__TEXT             18e78b000-18e815000   [  552K   504K     0K     0K] r-x/r-x SM=COW   /usr/lib/system/libcorecrypto.dylib
__TEXT             18e815000-18e840000   [  172K   172K     0K     0K] r-x/r-x SM=COW   /usr/lib/system/libsystem_malloc.dylib
__TEXT             18e840000-18e887000   [  284K   284K     0K     0K] r-x/r-x SM=COW   /usr/lib/system/libdispatch.dylib
__TEXT             18e887000-18e8c5000   [  248K   248K     0K     0K] r-x/r-x SM=COW   /usr/lib/libobjc.A.dylib
__TEXT             18e8c5000-18e8c8000   [   12K    12K     0K     0K] r-x/r-x SM=COW   /usr/lib/system/libsystem_featureflags.dylib
__TEXT             18e8c8000-18e94a000   [  520K   472K     0K     0K] r-x/r-x SM=COW   /usr/lib/system/libsystem_c.dylib
__TEXT             18e94a000-18e9b1000   [  412K   380K     0K     0K] r-x/r-x SM=COW   /usr/lib/libc++.1.dylib
__TEXT             18e9b1000-18e9c9000   [   96K    96K     0K     0K] r-x/r-x SM=COW   /usr/lib/libc++abi.dylib
__TEXT             18e9c9000-18ea01000   [  224K   208K     0K     0K] r-x/r-x SM=COW   /usr/lib/system/libsystem_kernel.dylib
__TEXT             18ea01000-18ea0e000   [   52K    52K     0K     0K] r-x/r-x SM=COW   /usr/lib/system/libsystem_pthread.dylib
__TEXT             18ea0e000-18ea1b000   [   52K    52K     0K     0K] r-x/r-x SM=COW   /usr/lib/system/libdyld.dylib
__TEXT             18ea1b000-18ea23000   [   32K    32K     0K     0K] r-x/r-x SM=COW   /usr/lib/system/libsystem_platform.dylib
__TEXT             18ea23000-18ea50000   [  180K   164K     0K     0K] r-x/r-x SM=COW   /usr/lib/system/libsystem_info.dylib
__TEXT             19113f000-19114a000   [   44K    44K     0K     0K] r-x/r-x SM=COW   /usr/lib/system/libsystem_darwin.dylib
__TEXT             191598000-1915a8000   [   64K    64K     0K     0K] r-x/r-x SM=COW   /usr/lib/system/libsystem_notify.dylib
__TEXT             193b14000-193b2d000   [  100K   100K     0K     0K] r-x/r-x SM=COW   /usr/lib/system/libsystem_networkextension.dylib
__TEXT             193b86000-193b9e000   [   96K    96K     0K     0K] r-x/r-x SM=COW   /usr/lib/system/libsystem_asl.dylib
__TEXT             1952ea000-1952f3000   [   36K    20K     0K     0K] r-x/r-x SM=COW   /usr/lib/system/libsystem_symptoms.dylib
__TEXT             1972de000-1972fd000   [  124K   124K     0K     0K] r-x/r-x SM=COW   /usr/lib/system/libsystem_containermanager.dylib
__TEXT             198085000-19808a000   [   20K    20K     0K     0K] r-x/r-x SM=COW   /usr/lib/system/libsystem_configuration.dylib
__TEXT             19808a000-19808f000   [   20K    20K     0K     0K] r-x/r-x SM=COW   /usr/lib/system/libsystem_sandbox.dylib
__TEXT             198bf0000-198bf3000   [   12K    12K     0K     0K] r-x/r-x SM=COW   /usr/lib/system/libquarantine.dylib
__TEXT             19925d000-199263000   [   24K    24K     0K     0K] r-x/r-x SM=COW   /usr/lib/system/libsystem_coreservices.dylib
__TEXT             1994c8000-1994ff000   [  220K   156K     0K     0K] r-x/r-x SM=COW   /usr/lib/system/libsystem_m.dylib
__TEXT             199500000-199509000   [   36K    36K     0K     0K] r-x/r-x SM=COW   /usr/lib/system/libmacho.dylib
__TEXT             199525000-199532000   [   52K    52K     0K     0K] r-x/r-x SM=COW   /usr/lib/system/libcommonCrypto.dylib
__TEXT             199532000-19953d000   [   44K    44K     0K     0K] r-x/r-x SM=COW   /usr/lib/system/libunwind.dylib
__TEXT             19953d000-199545000   [   32K    32K     0K     0K] r-x/r-x SM=COW   /usr/lib/liboah.dylib
__TEXT             199545000-19954e000   [   36K    36K     0K     0K] r-x/r-x SM=COW   /usr/lib/system/libcopyfile.dylib
__TEXT             19954e000-199552000   [   16K    16K     0K     0K] r-x/r-x SM=COW   /usr/lib/system/libcompiler_rt.dylib
__TEXT             199552000-199557000   [   20K    20K     0K     0K] r-x/r-x SM=COW   /usr/lib/system/libsystem_collections.dylib
__TEXT             199557000-19955a000   [   12K    12K     0K     0K] r-x/r-x SM=COW   /usr/lib/system/libsystem_secinit.dylib
__TEXT             19955a000-19955d000   [   12K    12K     0K     0K] r-x/r-x SM=COW   /usr/lib/system/libremovefile.dylib
__TEXT             19955d000-19955e000   [    4K     4K     0K     0K] r-x/r-x SM=COW   /usr/lib/system/libkeymgr.dylib
__TEXT             19955e000-199567000   [   36K    36K     0K     0K] r-x/r-x SM=COW   /usr/lib/system/libsystem_dnssd.dylib
__TEXT             199567000-19956d000   [   24K    24K     0K     0K] r-x/r-x SM=COW   /usr/lib/system/libcache.dylib
__TEXT             19956d000-19956f000   [    8K     8K     0K     0K] r-x/r-x SM=COW   /usr/lib/libSystem.B.dylib
__TEXT             19f8c1000-19f8c2000   [    4K     4K     0K     0K] r-x/r-x SM=COW   /usr/lib/system/libsystem_product_info_filter.dylib
__OBJC_RO          1d89c2000-1ddcc4000   [ 83.0M  51.4M     0K     0K] r-x/r-x SM=COW   /usr/lib/libobjc.A.dylib
__DATA_CONST       1e0098000-1e0098130   [  304    304     0K     0K] r--/rw- SM=COW   /usr/lib/system/libsystem_blocks.dylib
__DATA_CONST       1e0098130-1e00987d0   [ 1696   1696     0K     0K] r--/rw- SM=COW   /usr/lib/system/libsystem_trace.dylib
__DATA_CONST       1e00987d0-1e0098ef0   [ 1824   1824     0K     0K] r--/rw- SM=COW   /usr/lib/system/libcorecrypto.dylib
__DATA_CONST       1e0098ef0-1e0098f48   [   88     88     0K     0K] r--/rw- SM=COW   /usr/lib/system/libsystem_malloc.dylib
__DATA_CONST       1e0098f50-1e0099b58   [ 3080   3080     0K     0K] r--/rw- SM=COW   /usr/lib/libobjc.A.dylib
__DATA_CONST       1e0099b58-1e0099b98   [   64     64     0K     0K] r--/rw- SM=COW   /usr/lib/system/libsystem_featureflags.dylib
__DATA_CONST       1e0099b98-1e009b370   [    6K     6K     0K     0K] r--/rw- SM=COW   /usr/lib/system/libsystem_c.dylib
__DATA_CONST       1e009b370-1e009bcd0   [ 2400   2400     0K     0K] r--/rw- SM=COW   /usr/lib/libc++.1.dylib
__DATA_CONST       1e009bcd0-1e009bda8   [  216    216     0K     0K] r--/rw- SM=COW   /usr/lib/libc++abi.dylib
__DATA_CONST       1e009bda8-1e009e060   [    9K     9K     0K     0K] r--/rw- SM=COW   /usr/lib/system/libsystem_kernel.dylib
__DATA_CONST       1e009e060-1e009e098   [   56     56     0K     0K] r--/rw- SM=COW   /usr/lib/system/libsystem_pthread.dylib
__DATA_CONST       1e009e098-1e009e258   [  448    448     0K     0K] r--/rw- SM=COW   /usr/lib/system/libdyld.dylib
__DATA_CONST       1e009e258-1e009e278   [   32     32     0K     0K] r--/rw- SM=COW   /usr/lib/system/libsystem_platform.dylib
__DATA_CONST       1e009e278-1e009e790   [ 1304   1304     0K     0K] r--/rw- SM=COW   /usr/lib/system/libsystem_info.dylib
__DATA_CONST       1e0127148-1e0129ac0   [   10K    10K     0K     0K] r--/rw- SM=COW   /usr/lib/system/libsystem_darwin.dylib
__DATA_CONST       1e0133dc0-1e0133f18   [  344    344     0K     0K] r--/rw- SM=COW   /usr/lib/system/libsystem_notify.dylib
__DATA_CONST       1e02c9868-1e02c9d60   [ 1272   1272     0K     0K] r--/rw- SM=COW   /usr/lib/system/libsystem_networkextension.dylib
__DATA_CONST       1e02cac70-1e02cb290   [ 1568   1568     0K     0K] r--/rw- SM=COW   /usr/lib/system/libsystem_asl.dylib
__DATA_CONST       1e032ea80-1e032ec30   [  432    432     0K     0K] r--/rw- SM=COW   /usr/lib/system/libsystem_symptoms.dylib
__DATA_CONST       1e05863b8-1e0586da0   [ 2536   2536     0K     0K] r--/rw- SM=COW   /usr/lib/system/libsystem_containermanager.dylib
__DATA_CONST       1e061d0e0-1e061d298   [  440    440     0K     0K] r--/rw- SM=COW   /usr/lib/system/libsystem_configuration.dylib
__DATA_CONST       1e061d298-1e061d308   [  112    112     0K     0K] r--/rw- SM=COW   /usr/lib/system/libsystem_sandbox.dylib
__DATA_CONST       1e064ac20-1e064ac70   [   80     80     0K     0K] r--/rw- SM=COW   /usr/lib/system/libquarantine.dylib
__DATA_CONST       1e06d5660-1e06d5dc8   [ 1896   1896     0K     0K] r--/rw- SM=COW   /usr/lib/system/libsystem_coreservices.dylib
__DATA_CONST       1e06fd5a8-1e06fdcf0   [ 1864   1864     0K     0K] r--/rw- SM=COW   /usr/lib/system/libmacho.dylib
__DATA_CONST       1e06fdd00-1e06fe4a0   [ 1952   1952     0K     0K] r--/rw- SM=COW   /usr/lib/system/libcommonCrypto.dylib
__DATA_CONST       1e06fe4a0-1e06fe7c0   [  800    800     0K     0K] r--/rw- SM=COW   /usr/lib/system/libunwind.dylib
__DATA_CONST       1e06fe7c0-1e06fe7d8   [   24     24     0K     0K] r--/rw- SM=COW   /usr/lib/liboah.dylib
__DATA_CONST       1e06fe7d8-1e06fea98   [  704    704     0K     0K] r--/rw- SM=COW   /usr/lib/system/libcopyfile.dylib
__DATA_CONST       1e06fea98-1e06feaa0   [    8      8     0K     0K] r--/rw- SM=COW   /usr/lib/system/libsystem_collections.dylib
__DATA_CONST       1e06feaa0-1e06feb10   [  112    112     0K     0K] r--/rw- SM=COW   /usr/lib/system/libsystem_secinit.dylib
__DATA_CONST       1e06feb10-1e06feb20   [   16     16     0K     0K] r--/rw- SM=COW   /usr/lib/system/libremovefile.dylib
__DATA_CONST       1e06feb20-1e06feb30   [   16     16     0K     0K] r--/rw- SM=COW   /usr/lib/system/libkeymgr.dylib
__DATA_CONST       1e06feb30-1e06feba8   [  120    120     0K     0K] r--/rw- SM=COW   /usr/lib/system/libsystem_dnssd.dylib
__DATA_CONST       1e06feba8-1e06fec08   [   96     96     0K     0K] r--/rw- SM=COW   /usr/lib/system/libcache.dylib
__DATA_CONST       1e06fec08-1e06fec18   [   16     16     0K     0K] r--/rw- SM=COW   /usr/lib/libSystem.B.dylib
__AUTH_CONST       1e8b08000-1e8b08030   [   48     48     0K     0K] r--/rw- SM=COW   /usr/lib/system/libsystem_blocks.dylib
__OBJC_CONST       1e8b08030-1e8b08390   [  864    864     0K     0K] r--/rw- SM=COW   /usr/lib/system/libsystem_blocks.dylib
__AUTH_CONST       1e8b08390-1e8b0ce20   [   19K    19K     0K     0K] r--/rw- SM=COW   /usr/lib/system/libxpc.dylib
__OBJC_CONST       1e8b0ce20-1e8b0df90   [    4K     4K     0K     0K] r--/rw- SM=COW   /usr/lib/system/libxpc.dylib
__AUTH_CONST       1e8b0df90-1e8b0ec90   [ 3328   3328     0K     0K] r--/rw- SM=COW   /usr/lib/system/libsystem_trace.dylib
__OBJC_CONST       1e8b0ec90-1e8b0ee40   [  432    432     0K     0K] r--/rw- SM=COW   /usr/lib/system/libsystem_trace.dylib
__AUTH_CONST       1e8b0ee40-1e8b0ff10   [    4K     4K     0K     0K] r--/rw- SM=COW   /usr/lib/system/libcorecrypto.dylib
__AUTH_CONST       1e8b0ff10-1e8b104e8   [ 1496   1496     0K     0K] r--/rw- SM=COW   /usr/lib/system/libsystem_malloc.dylib
__DATA_CONST       1e8b10500-1e8b238e8   [   77K    45K     0K     0K] r--/rw- SM=COW   /usr/lib/system/libdispatch.dylib
__OBJC_CONST       1e8b238e8-1e8b24938   [    4K     4K     0K     0K] r--/rw- SM=COW   /usr/lib/system/libdispatch.dylib
__AUTH_CONST       1e8b24940-1e8b253c8   [ 2696   2696     0K     0K] r--/rw- SM=COW   /usr/lib/libobjc.A.dylib
__OBJC_CONST       1e8b253c8-1e8b25698   [  720    720     0K     0K] r--/rw- SM=COW   /usr/lib/libobjc.A.dylib
__AUTH_CONST       1e8b25698-1e8b25808   [  368    368     0K     0K] r--/rw- SM=COW   /usr/lib/system/libsystem_featureflags.dylib
__AUTH_CONST       1e8b25808-1e8b26168   [ 2400   2400     0K     0K] r--/rw- SM=COW   /usr/lib/system/libsystem_c.dylib
__AUTH_CONST       1e8b26168-1e8b282a8   [    8K     8K     0K     0K] r--/rw- SM=COW   /usr/lib/libc++.1.dylib
__AUTH_CONST       1e8b282a8-1e8b2b4b8   [   13K    13K     0K     0K] r--/rw- SM=COW   /usr/lib/libc++abi.dylib
__AUTH_CONST       1e8b2b4b8-1e8b2b5e0   [  296    296     0K     0K] r--/rw- SM=COW   /usr/lib/system/libsystem_kernel.dylib
__AUTH_CONST       1e8b2b5e0-1e8b2b810   [  560    560     0K     0K] r--/rw- SM=COW   /usr/lib/system/libsystem_pthread.dylib
__AUTH_CONST       1e8b2b810-1e8b2bfc8   [ 1976   1976     0K     0K] r--/rw- SM=COW   /usr/lib/system/libdyld.dylib
```

```
__AUTH_CONST                 1e8b2bfc8-1e8b2c250    [  648   648    0K    0K] r--/rw- SM=COW          /usr/lib/system/libsystem_platform.dylib
__AUTH_CONST                 1e8b2c250-1e8b2d3f0    [   4K    4K    0K    0K] r--/rw- SM=COW          /usr/lib/system/libsystem_info.dylib
__AUTH_CONST                 1e8c5bd48-1e8c5c1c8    [ 1152  1152    0K    0K] r--/rw- SM=COW          /usr/lib/system/libsystem_darwin.dylib
__AUTH_CONST                 1e8c77a80-1e8c77e00    [  896   896    0K    0K] r--/rw- SM=COW          /usr/lib/system/libsystem_notify.dylib
__AUTH_CONST                 1e8dfea40-1e8dff608    [ 3016  3016    0K    0K] r--/rw- SM=COW          /usr/lib/system/libsystem_networkextension.dylib
__AUTH_CONST                 1e8e4d718-1e8e4e160    [ 2632  2632    0K    0K] r--/rw- SM=COW          /usr/lib/system/libsystem_asl.dylib
__AUTH_CONST                 1e8f17288-1e8f17560    [  728   728    0K    0K] r--/rw- SM=COW          /usr/lib/system/libsystem_symptoms.dylib
__AUTH_CONST                 1e904e480-1e904f8c0    [   5K    5K    0K    0K] r--/rw- SM=COW          /usr/lib/system/libsystem_containermanager.dylib
__AUTH_CONST                 1e915e250-1e915e560    [  784   784    0K    0K] r--/rw- SM=COW          /usr/lib/system/libsystem_configuration.dylib
__AUTH_CONST                 1e915e560-1e915e768    [  520   520    0K    0K] r--/rw- SM=COW          /usr/lib/system/libsystem_sandbox.dylib
__AUTH_CONST                 1e91a78b8-1e91a79c0    [  264   264    0K    0K] r--/rw- SM=COW          /usr/lib/system/libquarantine.dylib
__AUTH_CONST                 1e922eac0-1e922ed50    [  656   656    0K    0K] r--/rw- SM=COW          /usr/lib/system/libsystem_coreservices.dylib
__AUTH_CONST                 1e925ad88-1e925ada8    [   32    32    0K    0K] r--/rw- SM=COW          /usr/lib/system/libsystem_m.dylib
__AUTH_CONST                 1e925ae28-1e925ae98    [  112   112    0K    0K] r--/rw- SM=COW          /usr/lib/system/libmacho.dylib
__AUTH_CONST                 1e925afb0-1e925bd80    [ 3536  3536    0K    0K] r--/rw- SM=COW          /usr/lib/system/libcommonCrypto.dylib
__AUTH_CONST                 1e925bd80-1e925be98    [  280   280    0K    0K] r--/rw- SM=COW          /usr/lib/system/libunwind.dylib
__AUTH_CONST                 1e925be98-1e925c168    [  720   720    0K    0K] r--/rw- SM=COW          /usr/lib/liboah.dylib
__AUTH_CONST                 1e925c168-1e925c5a0    [ 1080  1080    0K    0K] r--/rw- SM=COW          /usr/lib/system/libcopyfile.dylib
__AUTH_CONST                 1e925c5a0-1e925c600    [   96    96    0K    0K] r--/rw- SM=COW          /usr/lib/system/libcompiler_rt.dylib
__AUTH_CONST                 1e925c600-1e925c750    [  336   336    0K    0K] r--/rw- SM=COW          /usr/lib/system/libsystem_collections.dylib
__AUTH_CONST                 1e925c750-1e925ca18    [  712   712    0K    0K] r--/rw- SM=COW          /usr/lib/system/libsystem_secinit.dylib
__AUTH_CONST                 1e925ca18-1e925cb78    [  352   352    0K    0K] r--/rw- SM=COW          /usr/lib/system/libremovefile.dylib
__AUTH_CONST                 1e925cb78-1e925cbf8    [  128   128    0K    0K] r--/rw- SM=COW          /usr/lib/system/libkeymgr.dylib
__AUTH_CONST                 1e925cbf8-1e925cdb0    [  440   440    0K    0K] r--/rw- SM=COW          /usr/lib/system/libsystem_dnssd.dylib
__AUTH_CONST                 1e925cdb0-1e925ce70    [  192   192    0K    0K] r--/rw- SM=COW          /usr/lib/system/libcache.dylib
__AUTH_CONST                 1e925ce70-1e925d120    [  688   688    0K    0K] r--/rw- SM=COW          /usr/lib/libSystem.B.dylib
__LINKEDIT                   222494000-2465e6000    [577.3M 13.9M    0K    0K] r--/r-- SM=COW          dyld shared cache combined __LINKEDIT

==== Writable regions for process 92806
REGION TYPE                     START - END         [ VSIZE  RSDNT  DIRTY   SWAP] PRT/MAX SHRMOD PURGE    REGION DETAIL
Kernel Alloc Once            102984000-10298c000    [   32K     0K     0K    16K] rw-/rwx SM=PRV
MALLOC metadata              102994000-102998000    [   16K    16K    16K     0K] rw-/rwx SM=PRV
MALLOC metadata              10299c000-1029a4000    [   32K    32K    32K     0K] rw-/rwx SM=COW
MALLOC metadata              1029ac000-1029b4000    [   32K    32K    32K     0K] rw-/rwx SM=PRV
MALLOC metadata              1029bc000-1029c4000    [   32K     0K     0K    32K] rw-/rwx SM=PRV
MALLOC metadata              1029d0000-1029d4000    [   16K    16K    16K     0K] rw-/rwx SM=COW
MALLOC metadata              1029d4000-1029dc000    [   32K    32K    32K     0K] rw-/rwx SM=PRV
__DATA                       102ac0000-102ac4000    [   16K    16K    16K     0K] rw-/rw- SM=COW          /usr/lib/dyld
MALLOC_SMALL                 10b800000-10c000000    [ 8192K  8192K  8192K     0K] rw-/rwx SM=PRV          MallocHelperZone_0x102990000
MALLOC_SMALL                 10c000000-10c800000    [ 8192K  8192K  8192K     0K] rw-/rwx SM=PRV          MallocHelperZone_0x102990000
MALLOC_SMALL                 10c800000-10d000000    [ 8192K  8192K  8192K     0K] rw-/rwx SM=PRV          MallocHelperZone_0x102990000
MALLOC_SMALL                 10d000000-10d800000    [ 8192K  8192K  8192K     0K] rw-/rwx SM=PRV          MallocHelperZone_0x102990000
MALLOC_SMALL                 10d800000-10e000000    [ 8192K  8192K  8192K     0K] rw-/rwx SM=PRV          MallocHelperZone_0x102990000
MALLOC_SMALL                 10e000000-10e800000    [ 8192K  8192K  8192K     0K] rw-/rwx SM=PRV          MallocHelperZone_0x102990000
MALLOC_SMALL                 10e800000-10f000000    [ 8192K  8192K  8192K     0K] rw-/rwx SM=PRV          MallocHelperZone_0x102990000
MALLOC_SMALL                 10f000000-10f800000    [ 8192K  8192K  8192K     0K] rw-/rwx SM=PRV          MallocHelperZone_0x102990000
MALLOC_SMALL                 10f800000-110000000    [ 8192K  8192K  8192K     0K] rw-/rwx SM=PRV          MallocHelperZone_0x102990000
MALLOC_SMALL                 110000000-110800000    [ 8192K  8192K  8192K     0K] rw-/rwx SM=PRV          MallocHelperZone_0x102990000
MALLOC_SMALL                 110800000-111000000    [ 8192K  8192K  8192K     0K] rw-/rwx SM=PRV          MallocHelperZone_0x102990000
MALLOC_SMALL                 111000000-111800000    [ 8192K  8192K  8192K     0K] rw-/rwx SM=PRV          MallocHelperZone_0x102990000
MALLOC_SMALL                 111800000-112000000    [ 8192K  8192K  8192K     0K] rw-/rwx SM=PRV          MallocHelperZone_0x102990000
MALLOC_SMALL                 112000000-112800000    [ 8192K  8192K  8192K     0K] rw-/rwx SM=PRV          MallocHelperZone_0x102990000
MALLOC_SMALL                 112800000-113000000    [ 8192K  4480K  4480K     0K] rw-/rwx SM=PRV          MallocHelperZone_0x102990000
MALLOC_SMALL                 11b800000-11c000000    [ 8192K  8192K  8192K     0K] rw-/rwx SM=PRV          MallocHelperZone_0x102990000
MALLOC_SMALL                 11c000000-11c800000    [ 8192K  8192K  8192K     0K] rw-/rwx SM=PRV          MallocHelperZone_0x102990000
MALLOC_SMALL                 11c800000-11d000000    [ 8192K  8192K  8192K     0K] rw-/rwx SM=PRV          MallocHelperZone_0x102990000
MALLOC_SMALL                 11d000000-11d800000    [ 8192K  8192K  8192K     0K] rw-/rwx SM=PRV          MallocHelperZone_0x102990000
MALLOC_SMALL                 11d800000-11e000000    [ 8192K  8192K  8192K     0K] rw-/rwx SM=PRV          MallocHelperZone_0x102990000
MALLOC_SMALL                 11e000000-11e800000    [ 8192K  8192K  8192K     0K] rw-/rwx SM=PRV          MallocHelperZone_0x102990000
MALLOC_SMALL                 11e800000-11f000000    [ 8192K  8192K  8192K     0K] rw-/rwx SM=PRV          MallocHelperZone_0x102990000
MALLOC_SMALL                 11f000000-11f800000    [ 8192K  8192K  8192K     0K] rw-/rwx SM=PRV          MallocHelperZone_0x102990000
MALLOC_SMALL                 11f800000-120000000    [ 8192K  8192K  8192K     0K] rw-/rwx SM=PRV          MallocHelperZone_0x102990000
MALLOC_SMALL                 120000000-120800000    [ 8192K  8192K  8192K     0K] rw-/rwx SM=PRV          MallocHelperZone_0x102990000
MALLOC_SMALL                 120800000-121000000    [ 8192K  8192K  8192K     0K] rw-/rwx SM=PRV          MallocHelperZone_0x102990000
MALLOC_SMALL                 121000000-121800000    [ 8192K  8192K  8192K     0K] rw-/rwx SM=PRV          MallocHelperZone_0x102990000
MALLOC_SMALL                 121800000-122000000    [ 8192K  8192K  8192K     0K] rw-/rwx SM=PRV          MallocHelperZone_0x102990000
MALLOC_SMALL                 122000000-122800000    [ 8192K  8192K  8192K     0K] rw-/rwx SM=PRV          MallocHelperZone_0x102990000
MALLOC_SMALL                 122800000-123000000    [ 8192K  8192K  8192K     0K] rw-/rwx SM=PRV          MallocHelperZone_0x102990000
MALLOC_SMALL                 123000000-123800000    [ 8192K  8192K  8192K     0K] rw-/rwx SM=PRV          MallocHelperZone_0x102990000
MALLOC_SMALL                 123800000-124000000    [ 8192K  8192K  8192K     0K] rw-/rwx SM=PRV          MallocHelperZone_0x102990000
MALLOC_SMALL                 124000000-124800000    [ 8192K  8192K  8192K     0K] rw-/rwx SM=PRV          MallocHelperZone_0x102990000
MALLOC_SMALL                 124800000-125000000    [ 8192K  8192K  8192K     0K] rw-/rwx SM=PRV          MallocHelperZone_0x102990000
MALLOC_SMALL                 125000000-125800000    [ 8192K  8192K  8192K     0K] rw-/rwx SM=PRV          MallocHelperZone_0x102990000
MALLOC_SMALL                 125800000-126000000    [ 8192K  8192K  8192K     0K] rw-/rwx SM=PRV          MallocHelperZone_0x102990000
MALLOC_SMALL                 126000000-126800000    [ 8192K    32K    32K     0K] rw-/rwx SM=PRV          MallocHelperZone_0x102990000
MALLOC_SMALL                 126800000-127000000    [ 8192K  8192K  8192K     0K] rw-/rwx SM=PRV          MallocHelperZone_0x102990000
MALLOC_SMALL                 127000000-127800000    [ 8192K  8192K  8192K     0K] rw-/rwx SM=PRV          MallocHelperZone_0x102990000
MALLOC_SMALL                 127800000-128000000    [ 8192K  8192K  8192K     0K] rw-/rwx SM=PRV          MallocHelperZone_0x102990000
MALLOC_SMALL                 128000000-128800000    [ 8192K  8192K  8192K     0K] rw-/rwx SM=PRV          MallocHelperZone_0x102990000
MALLOC_SMALL                 128800000-129000000    [ 8192K  8192K  8192K     0K] rw-/rwx SM=PRV          MallocHelperZone_0x102990000
MALLOC_SMALL                 129000000-129800000    [ 8192K  8192K  8192K     0K] rw-/rwx SM=PRV          MallocHelperZone_0x102990000
MALLOC_SMALL                 129800000-12a000000    [ 8192K  8192K  8192K     0K] rw-/rwx SM=PRV          MallocHelperZone_0x102990000
MALLOC_SMALL                 12a000000-12a800000    [ 8192K  8192K  8192K     0K] rw-/rwx SM=PRV          MallocHelperZone_0x102990000
MALLOC_SMALL                 12a800000-12b000000    [ 8192K  8192K  8192K     0K] rw-/rwx SM=PRV          MallocHelperZone_0x102990000
MALLOC_TINY                  12b600000-12b700000    [ 1024K    16K    16K    16K] rw-/rwx SM=PRV          MallocHelperZone_0x102990000
MALLOC_SMALL                 12b800000-12c000000    [ 8192K  1296K  1296K  3744K] rw-/rwx SM=PRV          MallocHelperZone_0x102990000
MALLOC_SMALL                 12c000000-12c800000    [ 8192K    64K    64K  8128K] rw-/rwx SM=PRV          MallocHelperZone_0x102990000
MALLOC_SMALL                 12c800000-12d000000    [ 8192K    48K    48K  8144K] rw-/rwx SM=PRV          MallocHelperZone_0x102990000
MALLOC_SMALL                 12d000000-12d800000    [ 8192K    48K    48K  8144K] rw-/rwx SM=PRV          MallocHelperZone_0x102990000
MALLOC_SMALL                 12d800000-12e000000    [ 8192K    48K    48K  8144K] rw-/rwx SM=PRV          MallocHelperZone_0x102990000
MALLOC_SMALL                 12e000000-12e800000    [ 8192K    96K    96K  8096K] rw-/rwx SM=PRV          MallocHelperZone_0x102990000
MALLOC_SMALL                 12e800000-12f000000    [ 8192K    80K    80K  8112K] rw-/rwx SM=PRV          MallocHelperZone_0x102990000
MALLOC_SMALL                 12f000000-12f800000    [ 8192K    64K    64K  8128K] rw-/rwx SM=PRV          MallocHelperZone_0x102990000
MALLOC_SMALL                 12f800000-130000000    [ 8192K    48K    48K  8144K] rw-/rwx SM=PRV          MallocHelperZone_0x102990000
MALLOC_SMALL                 130000000-130800000    [ 8192K    32K    32K  8160K] rw-/rwx SM=PRV          MallocHelperZone_0x102990000
MALLOC_SMALL                 130800000-131000000    [ 8192K   512K   512K  5216K] rw-/rwx SM=PRV          MallocHelperZone_0x102990000
MALLOC_SMALL                 131000000-131800000    [ 8192K    32K    32K  8160K] rw-/rwx SM=PRV          MallocHelperZone_0x102990000
MALLOC_SMALL                 131800000-132000000    [ 8192K   624K   624K  6016K] rw-/rwx SM=PRV          MallocHelperZone_0x102990000
MALLOC_SMALL                 132000000-132800000    [ 8192K    32K    32K  8160K] rw-/rwx SM=PRV          MallocHelperZone_0x102990000
MALLOC_SMALL                 132800000-133000000    [ 8192K    16K    16K  1008K] rw-/rwx SM=PRV          MallocHelperZone_0x102990000
MALLOC_SMALL                 133000000-133800000    [ 8192K    32K    32K  8160K] rw-/rwx SM=PRV          MallocHelperZone_0x102990000
MALLOC_SMALL                 133800000-134000000    [ 8192K    32K    32K  8160K] rw-/rwx SM=PRV          MallocHelperZone_0x102990000
```

```
MALLOC_SMALL                134000000-134800000    [ 8192K    32K    32K  8160K] rw-/rwx SM=PRV          MallocHelperZone_0x102990000
MALLOC_SMALL                134800000-135000000    [ 8192K  5520K  5520K  2672K] rw-/rwx SM=PRV          MallocHelperZone_0x102990000
MALLOC_SMALL                135000000-135800000    [ 8192K  8192K  8192K     0K] rw-/rwx SM=PRV          MallocHelperZone_0x102990000
MALLOC_SMALL                135800000-136000000    [ 8192K  8192K  8192K     0K] rw-/rwx SM=PRV          MallocHelperZone_0x102990000
MALLOC_SMALL                136000000-136800000    [ 8192K  8192K  8192K     0K] rw-/rwx SM=PRV          MallocHelperZone_0x102990000
MALLOC_SMALL                136800000-137000000    [ 8192K  8192K  8192K     0K] rw-/rwx SM=PRV          MallocHelperZone_0x102990000
MALLOC_SMALL                137000000-137800000    [ 8192K  8192K  8192K     0K] rw-/rwx SM=PRV          MallocHelperZone_0x102990000
MALLOC_SMALL                137800000-138000000    [ 8192K  8192K  8192K     0K] rw-/rwx SM=PRV          MallocHelperZone_0x102990000
MALLOC_SMALL                138000000-138800000    [ 8192K  8192K  8192K     0K] rw-/rwx SM=PRV          MallocHelperZone_0x102990000
MALLOC_SMALL                138800000-139000000    [ 8192K  8192K  8192K     0K] rw-/rwx SM=PRV          MallocHelperZone_0x102990000
MALLOC_SMALL                139000000-139800000    [ 8192K  8192K  8192K     0K] rw-/rwx SM=PRV          MallocHelperZone_0x102990000
MALLOC_SMALL                139800000-13a000000    [ 8192K  8192K  8192K     0K] rw-/rwx SM=PRV          MallocHelperZone_0x102990000
MALLOC_SMALL                13a000000-13a800000    [ 8192K  8192K  8192K     0K] rw-/rwx SM=PRV          MallocHelperZone_0x102990000
MALLOC_SMALL                13a800000-13b000000    [ 8192K  8192K  8192K     0K] rw-/rwx SM=PRV          MallocHelperZone_0x102990000
Stack                       16cd90000-16d58c000    [ 8176K    16K    16K    16K] rw-/rwx SM=PRV          thread 0
Stack                       16d590000-16d618000    [  544K     0K     0K    16K] rw-/rwx SM=PRV          thread 1
Stack                       16d61c000-16d6a4000    [  544K    16K    16K     0K] rw-/rwx SM=PRV          thread 2
Stack                       16d6a8000-16d730000    [  544K     0K     0K    16K] rw-/rwx SM=PRV          thread 3
Stack                       16d734000-16d7bc000    [  544K     0K     0K    16K] rw-/rwx SM=PRV          thread 4
Stack                       16d7c0000-16d848000    [  544K     0K     0K    16K] rw-/rwx SM=PRV          thread 5
__DATA                      1e4c04000-1e4c04060    [    96     0K     0K     96] rw-/rw- SM=COW          /usr/lib/system/libsystem_blocks.dylib
__DATA                      1e4c04060-1e4c04d18    [  3256     0K     0K   3256] rw-/rw- SM=COW          /usr/lib/system/libxpc.dylib
__DATA                      1e4c04d18-1e4c05050    [   824     0K     0K    824] rw-/rw- SM=COW          /usr/lib/system/libsystem_trace.dylib
__DATA                      1e4c05050-1e4c0c788    [   30K    18K   1928    12K] rw-/rw- SM=COW          /usr/lib/system/libcorecrypto.dylib
__DATA                      1e4c0c788-1e4c0ea24    [    9K     9K     9K     0K] rw-/rw- SM=COW          /usr/lib/system/libsystem_malloc.dylib
unused __DATA               1e4c0ea24-1e4c0ea40    [    28     28     28     0K] rw-/rw- SM=COW          on dirty page  unused system shared lib __DATA
__DATA                      1e4c0ea40-1e4c120c0    [   14K    14K    14K     0K] rw-/rw- SM=COW          /usr/lib/libobjc.A.dylib
__DATA                      1e4c120c0-1e4c120f9    [    57     57     57     0K] rw-/rw- SM=COW          /usr/lib/system/libsystem_featureflags.dylib
unused __DATA               1e4c120f9-1e4c12100    [     7      7      7     0K] rw-/rw- SM=COW          on dirty page  unused system shared lib __DATA
__DATA                      1e4c12100-1e4c14270    [    8K     8K     8K    624] rw-/rw- SM=COW          /usr/lib/system/libsystem_c.dylib
unused __DATA               1e4c14270-1e4c15000    [  3472     0K     0K   3472] rw-/rw- SM=COW          on dirty page  unused system shared lib __DATA
__DATA                      1e4c15000-1e4c1b720    [   26K    14K     0K    12K] rw-/rw- SM=COW          /usr/lib/libc++.1.dylib
__DATA                      1e4c1b720-1e4c1ba68    [   840    840     0K     0K] rw-/rw- SM=COW          /usr/lib/libc++abi.dylib
__DATA                      1e4c1ba68-1e4c1bcd9    [   625    625     0K     0K] rw-/rw- SM=COW          /usr/lib/system/libsystem_kernel.dylib
__DATA                      1e4c1c000-1e4c24000    [   32K    32K     0K     0K] rw-/rw- SM=COW          /usr/lib/system/libsystem_pthread.dylib
__DATA                      1e4c24000-1e4c28000    [   16K    16K     0K     0K] rw-/rw- SM=COW          /usr/lib/system/libsystem_pthread.dylib
__DATA                      1e4c28000-1e4c28048    [    72     72     0K     0K] rw-/rw- SM=COW          /usr/lib/system/libsystem_pthread.dylib
__DATA                      1e4c28048-1e4c28050    [     8      8     0K     0K] rw-/rw- SM=COW          /usr/lib/system/libdyld.dylib
__DATA                      1e4c28050-1e4c28090    [    64     64     0K     0K] rw-/rw- SM=COW          /usr/lib/system/libsystem_platform.dylib
__DATA                      1e4c28090-1e4c28be0    [  2896   2896     0K     0K] rw-/rw- SM=COW          /usr/lib/system/libsystem_info.dylib
__DATA                      1e4c96958-1e4c96968    [    16     16     0K     0K] rw-/rw- SM=COW          /usr/lib/system/libsystem_darwin.dylib
__DATA                      1e4c9de00-1e4c9de51    [    81     81     0K     0K] rw-/rw- SM=COW          /usr/lib/system/libsystem_notify.dylib
__DATA                      1e4d33600-1e4d33bd9    [  1497   1497     0K     0K] rw-/rw- SM=COW          /usr/lib/system/libsystem_networkextension.dylib
__DATA                      1e4d343b8-1e4d344c8    [   272    272     0K     0K] rw-/rw- SM=COW          /usr/lib/system/libsystem_asl.dylib
__DATA                      1e4d6a118-1e4d6a158    [    64     64     0K     0K] rw-/rw- SM=COW          /usr/lib/system/libsystem_symptoms.dylib
__DATA                      1e4deca18-1e4decb40    [   296    296     0K     0K] rw-/rw- SM=COW          /usr/lib/system/libsystem_containermanager.dylib
__DATA                      1e4e2d090-1e4e2d159    [   201    201     0K     0K] rw-/rw- SM=COW          /usr/lib/system/libsystem_configuration.dylib
__DATA                      1e4e2d160-1e4e2d188    [    40     40     0K     0K] rw-/rw- SM=COW          /usr/lib/system/libsystem_sandbox.dylib
__DATA                      1e4e4f280-1e4e4f290    [    16     16     0K     0K] rw-/rw- SM=COW          /usr/lib/system/libquarantine.dylib
__DATA                      1e4e61bb0-1e4e61c88    [   216    216     0K     0K] rw-/rw- SM=COW          /usr/lib/system/libsystem_coreservices.dylib
__DATA                      1e4e71a20-1e4e71a24    [     4      4     0K     0K] rw-/rw- SM=COW          /usr/lib/system/libsystem_m.dylib
__DATA                      1e4e71ae8-1e4e723d9    [  2289   2289     0K     0K] rw-/rw- SM=COW          /usr/lib/system/libunwind.dylib
__DATA                      1e4e723e0-1e4e723e8    [     8      8     0K     0K] rw-/rw- SM=COW          /usr/lib/liboah.dylib
__DATA                      1e4e723e8-1e4e723f8    [    16     16     0K     0K] rw-/rw- SM=COW          /usr/lib/system/libcopyfile.dylib
__DATA                      1e4e723f8-1e4e733f8    [    4K     4K     0K     0K] rw-/rw- SM=COW          /usr/lib/system/libcompiler_rt.dylib
__DATA                      1e4e733f8-1e4e73438    [    64     64     0K     0K] rw-/rw- SM=COW          /usr/lib/system/libsystem_secinit.dylib
__DATA                      1e4e73438-1e4e73468    [    48     48     0K     0K] rw-/rw- SM=COW          /usr/lib/system/libsystem_dnssd.dylib
__DATA                      1e4e73468-1e4e73470    [     8      8     0K     0K] rw-/rw- SM=COW          /usr/lib/libSystem.B.dylib
unused __DATA_DIRTY         1e7930000-1e7930120    [   288     0K     0K    288] rw-/rw- SM=COW          on dirty page  unused /usr/lib/libMobileGestalt.dylib
unused __DATA_DIRTY         1e7930120-1e7930170    [    80     0K     0K     80] rw-/rw- SM=COW          on dirty page  unused
/usr/lib/libUniversalAccess.dylib
unused __DATA_DIRTY         1e7930170-1e7930190    [    32     0K     0K     32] rw-/rw- SM=COW          on dirty page  unused
/usr/lib/libapp_launch_measurement.dylib
unused __DATA_DIRTY         1e7930190-1e7931010    [  3712     0K     0K   3712] rw-/rw- SM=COW          on dirty page  unused /usr/lib/libboringssl.dylib
__DATA_DIRTY                1e7931010-1e79321e0    [    4K     0K     0K     4K] rw-/rw- SM=COW          /usr/lib/libc++.1.dylib
__DATA_DIRTY                1e79321e0-1e7932208    [    40     0K     0K     40] rw-/rw- SM=COW          /usr/lib/libc++abi.dylib
unused __DATA_DIRTY         1e7932208-1e7934000    [    7K     0K     0K     7K] rw-/rw- SM=COW          on dirty page  unused /usr/lib/libcoreroutine.dylib
unused __DATA_DIRTY         1e7938000-1e793a1c8    [    8K     0K     0K     8K] rw-/rw- SM=COW          on dirty page  unused /usr/lib/libnetwork.dylib
unused __DATA               1e793a1c8-1e793a200    [    56     0K     0K     56] rw-/rw- SM=COW          on dirty page  unused system shared lib __DATA
__DATA_DIRTY                1e793a200-1e793d070    [   12K     0K     0K    12K] rw-/rw- SM=COW          /usr/lib/libobjc.A.dylib
unused __DATA_DIRTY         1e793d070-1e793d200    [   400     0K     0K    400] rw-/rw- SM=COW          on dirty page  unused
/usr/lib/libpartition2_dynamic.dylib
unused __DATA_DIRTY         1e793d200-1e793d299    [   153     0K     0K    153] rw-/rw- SM=COW          on dirty page  unused /usr/lib/libpmenergy.dylib
unused __DATA               1e793d299-1e793d2a0    [     7     0K     0K      7] rw-/rw- SM=COW          on dirty page  unused system shared lib __DATA
unused __DATA_DIRTY         1e793d2a0-1e793d3e8    [   328     0K     0K    328] rw-/rw- SM=COW          on dirty page  unused /usr/lib/libprequelite.dylib
unused __DATA_DIRTY         1e793d3e8-1e793d4f8    [   272     0K     0K    272] rw-/rw- SM=COW          on dirty page  unused /usr/lib/libquic.dylib
unused __DATA_DIRTY         1e793d4f8-1e793d530    [    56     0K     0K     56] rw-/rw- SM=COW          on dirty page  unused /usr/lib/libsandbox.1.dylib
unused __DATA               1e793d530-1e793d540    [    16     0K     0K     16] rw-/rw- SM=COW          on dirty page  unused system shared lib __DATA
unused __DATA_DIRTY         1e793d540-1e7940000    [   11K     0K     0K    11K] rw-/rw- SM=COW          on dirty page  unused /usr/lib/libsqlite3.dylib
unused __DATA_DIRTY         1e795c000-1e795e610    [   10K     0K     0K    10K] rw-/rw- SM=COW          on dirty page  unused
/usr/lib/swift/libswiftFoundation.dylib
unused __DATA_DIRTY         1e795e610-1e795e7a0    [   400     0K     0K    400] rw-/rw- SM=COW          on dirty page  unused
/usr/lib/swift/libswiftObjectiveC.dylib
unused __DATA_DIRTY         1e795e7a0-1e795e7b8    [    24     0K     0K     24] rw-/rw- SM=COW          on dirty page  unused /usr/lib/swift/libswiftos.dylib
__DATA_DIRTY                1e795e7b8-1e795ef10    [  1880     0K     0K   1880] rw-/rw- SM=COW          /usr/lib/system/libcorecrypto.dylib
unused __DATA               1e795ef10-1e795ef40    [    48     0K     0K     48] rw-/rw- SM=COW          on dirty page  unused system shared lib __DATA
__DATA_DIRTY                1e795ef40-1e79628e8    [   14K     0K     0K    14K] rw-/rw- SM=COW          /usr/lib/system/libdispatch.dylib
__DATA_DIRTY                1e79628e8-1e7962908    [    32     0K     0K     32] rw-/rw- SM=COW          /usr/lib/system/libdyld.dylib
unused __DATA               1e7962908-1e7962910    [     8     0K     0K      8] rw-/rw- SM=COW          on dirty page  unused system shared lib __DATA
__DATA_DIRTY                1e7962910-1e7962a6c    [   348     0K     0K    348] rw-/rw- SM=COW          /usr/lib/system/libsystem_asl.dylib
unused __DATA               1e7962a6c-1e7962a70    [     4     0K     0K      4] rw-/rw- SM=COW          on dirty page  unused system shared lib __DATA
__DATA_DIRTY                1e7962a70-1e7962c68    [   504     0K     0K    504] rw-/rw- SM=COW          /usr/lib/system/libsystem_blocks.dylib
__DATA_DIRTY                1e7962c68-1e79657f0    [   11K     6K     6K     5K] rw-/rw- SM=COW          /usr/lib/system/libsystem_c.dylib
__DATA_DIRTY                1e79657f0-1e7965820    [    48     48     48     0K] rw-/rw- SM=COW          /usr/lib/system/libsystem_darwin.dylib
__DATA_DIRTY                1e7965820-1e7965830    [    16     16     16     0K] rw-/rw- SM=COW          /usr/lib/system/libsystem_featureflags.dylib
__DATA_DIRTY                1e7965830-1e7965ac0    [   656    656    656     0K] rw-/rw- SM=COW          /usr/lib/system/libsystem_info.dylib
__DATA_DIRTY                1e7965ac0-1e7966184    [  1732   1732   1732     0K] rw-/rw- SM=COW          /usr/lib/system/libsystem_kernel.dylib
unused __DATA               1e7966184-1e7966188    [     4      4      4     0K] rw-/rw- SM=COW          on dirty page  unused system shared lib __DATA
__DATA_DIRTY                1e7966188-1e79663a0    [   536    536    536     0K] rw-/rw- SM=COW          /usr/lib/system/libsystem_malloc.dylib
__DATA_DIRTY                1e79663a0-1e79663e1    [    65     65     65     0K] rw-/rw- SM=COW          /usr/lib/system/libsystem_networkextension.dylib
unused __DATA               1e79663e1-1e79663e8    [     7      7      7     0K] rw-/rw- SM=COW          on dirty page  unused system shared lib __DATA
__DATA_DIRTY                1e79663e8-1e79663f0    [     8      8      8     0K] rw-/rw- SM=COW          /usr/lib/system/libsystem_notify.dylib
```

```
__DATA_DIRTY            1e79663f0-1e7966404  [    20     20     20      0K] rw-/rw- SM=COW  /usr/lib/system/libsystem_platform.dylib
unused __DATA           1e7966404-1e7968000  [    7K     7K     7K      0K] rw-/rw- SM=COW  on dirty page  unused system shared lib __DATA
__DATA_DIRTY            1e7968000-1e796d838  [   22K     0K     0K     22K] rw-/rw- SM=COW  /usr/lib/system/libsystem_pthread.dylib
__DATA_DIRTY            1e796d838-1e796d848  [    16     0K     0K     16] rw-/rw- SM=COW  /usr/lib/system/libsystem_symptoms.dylib
__DATA_DIRTY            1e796d848-1e796dcb8  [  1136     0K     0K   1136] rw-/rw- SM=COW  /usr/lib/system/libsystem_trace.dylib
__DATA_DIRTY            1e796dcb8-1e796e708  [  2640     0K     0K   2640] rw-/rw- SM=COW  /usr/lib/system/libxpc.dylib
unused __DATA           1e796e708-1e7970000  [    6K     0K     0K     6K] rw-/rw- SM=COW  on dirty page  unused system shared lib __DATA
__AUTH                  1e7970000-1e79701b8  [   440    440     0K      0K] rw-/rw- SM=COW  /usr/lib/system/libsystem_trace.dylib
__AUTH                  1e79701b8-1e7970218  [    96     96     0K      0K] rw-/rw- SM=COW  /usr/lib/system/libcorecrypto.dylib
__AUTH                  1e7974000-1e797c000  [   32K    32K     0K      0K] rw-/rw- SM=COW  /usr/lib/system/libsystem_malloc.dylib
__DATA                  1e797c000-1e797d400  [    5K     5K     0K      0K] rw-/rw- SM=COW  /usr/lib/system/libdispatch.dylib
__AUTH                  1e797d400-1e797d478  [   120    120     0K      0K] rw-/rw- SM=COW  /usr/lib/libobjc.A.dylib
__AUTH                  1e797d478-1e797e190  [  3352   3352     0K      0K] rw-/rw- SM=COW  /usr/lib/system/libsystem_c.dylib
__AUTH                  1e797e190-1e7980628  [    9K     8K     0K   1576] rw-/rw- SM=COW  /usr/lib/libc++.1.dylib
__AUTH                  1e7980628-1e7980670  [    72     0K     0K     72] rw-/rw- SM=COW  /usr/lib/libc++abi.dylib
__AUTH                  1e7980670-1e79806b0  [    64     0K     0K     64] rw-/rw- SM=COW  /usr/lib/system/libdyld.dylib
__AUTH                  1e79806b0-1e7980880  [   464     0K     0K    464] rw-/rw- SM=COW  /usr/lib/system/libsystem_info.dylib
unused __AUTH           1e7980880-1e7982740  [    8K     0K     0K     8K] rw-/rw- SM=COW  ...y page  unused
/System/Library/Frameworks/CoreFoundation.framework/Versions/A/CoreFoundation
unused __AUTH           1e7982740-1e7984000  [    6K     0K     0K     6K] rw-/rw- SM=COW
...eServices.framework/Versions/A/Frameworks/LaunchServices.framework/Versions/A/LaunchServices
__AUTH                  1e7a0a640-1e7a0a660  [    32     32     0K      0K] rw-/rw- SM=COW  /usr/lib/system/libcommonCrypto.dylib
__AUTH                  1e7a0a660-1e7a0a668  [     8      8     0K      0K] rw-/rw- SM=COW  /usr/lib/libSystem.B.dylib
__OBJC_RW               1e87f0000-1e8b08000  [ 3168K  1600K     0K     16K] rw-/rw- SM=COW  /usr/lib/libobjc.A.dylib
MALLOC_NANO             600000000000-600008000000 [128.0M  80K   80K    64K] rw-/rwx SM=PRV  DefaultMallocZone_0x1029cc000
MALLOC_NANO (empty)     600008000000-600010000000 [128.0M   0K    0K     0K] rw-/rwx SM=PRV
MALLOC_NANO (empty)     600010000000-600018000000 [128.0M   0K    0K     0K] rw-/rwx SM=PRV
MALLOC_NANO (empty)     600018000000-600020000000 [128.0M   0K    0K     0K] rw-/rwx SM=PRV
```

```
==== Legend
SM=sharing mode:
        COW=copy_on_write PRV=private NUL=empty ALI=aliased
        SHM=shared ZER=zero_filled S/A=shared_alias
PURGE=purgeable mode:
        V=volatile N=nonvolatile E=empty   otherwise is unpurgeable
```

```
==== Summary for process 92806
ReadOnly portion of Libraries: Total=582.2M resident=18.4M(3%) swapped_out_or_unallocated=563.8M(97%)
Writable regions: Total=1.1G written=590.8M(52%) resident=461.1M(40%) swapped_out=129.8M(11%) unallocated=549.0M(48%)
```

REGION TYPE	VIRTUAL SIZE	RESIDENT SIZE	DIRTY SIZE	SWAPPED SIZE	VOLATILE SIZE	NONVOL SIZE	EMPTY SIZE	REGION COUNT (non-coalesced)	
Kernel Alloc Once	32K	0K	0K	16K	0K	0K	0K	1	
MALLOC guard page	96K	0K	0K	0K	0K	0K	0K	5	
MALLOC metadata	208K	176K	176K	32K	0K	0K	0K	9	
MALLOC_NANO	128.0M	80K	80K	64K	0K	0K	0K	1	see MALLOC ZONE table below
MALLOC_NANO (empty)	384.0M	0K	0K	0K	0K	0K	0K	3	see MALLOC ZONE table below
MALLOC_SMALL	616.0M	460.9M	460.9M	129.5M	0K	0K	0K	77	see MALLOC ZONE table below
MALLOC_TINY	1024K	16K	16K	16K	0K	0K	0K	1	see MALLOC ZONE table below
STACK GUARD	56.1M	0K	0K	0K	0K	0K	0K	6	
Stack	10.6M	32K	32K	80K	0K	0K	0K	6	
__AUTH	46K	44K	0K	2176	0K	0K	0K	11	
__AUTH_CONST	67K	67K	0K	0K	0K	0K	0K	38	
__DATA	173K	144K	48K	29K	0K	0K	0K	37	
__DATA_CONST	258K	146K	32K	16K	0K	0K	0K	40	
__DATA_DIRTY	73K	9K	9K	64K	0K	0K	0K	21	
__LINKEDIT	577.6M	14.0M	0K	0K	0K	0K	0K	3	
__OBJC_CONST	10K	10K	0K	0K	0K	0K	0K	5	
__OBJC_RO	83.0M	51.4M	0K	0K	0K	0K	0K	1	
__OBJC_RW	3168K	1600K	0K	16K	0K	0K	0K	1	
__TEXT	4708K	4468K	0K	0K	0K	0K	0K	43	
dyld private memory	1024K	16K	16K	0K	0K	0K	0K	1	
shared memory	16K	16K	16K	0K	0K	0K	0K	1	
unused but dirty shlib __DATA	72K	7K	7K	65K	0K	0K	0K	30	
===========	======	======	======	======	======	=====	=====	======	
TOTAL	1.8G	532.9M	461.3M	129.9M	0K	0K	0K	341	

MALLOC ZONE	VIRTUAL SIZE	RESIDENT SIZE	DIRTY SIZE	SWAPPED SIZE	ALLOCATION COUNT	BYTES ALLOCATED	DIRTY+SWAP FRAG SIZE	% FRAG	REGION COUNT
MallocHelperZone_0x102990000	617.0M	460.9M	460.9M	129.6M	602002	587.9M	2606K	1%	78
DefaultMallocZone_0x1029cc000	128.0M	80K	80K	64K	211	9K	135K	94%	1
===========	======	=========	=========	=========	=========	=========	=========	======	======
TOTAL	745.0M	461.0M	461.0M	129.6M	602213	587.9M	2741K	1%	79

```
Process:         App9 [92806]
Path:            /Users/USER/*/App9
Load Address:    0x102874000
Identifier:      App9
Version:         ???
Code Type:       ARM64
Platform:        macOS
Parent Process:  zsh [93724]

Date/Time:       2022-12-09 00:35:41.263 +0000
Launch Time:     2022-12-09 00:25:27.283 +0000
OS Version:      macOS 12.6 (21G115)
Report Version:  7
Analysis Tool:   /Applications/Xcode.app/Contents/Developer/usr/bin/vmmap
Analysis Tool Version:  Xcode 14.0.1 (14A400)
----

Virtual Memory Map of process 92806 (App9)
Output report format: 2.4  -- 64-bit process
VM page size: 16384 bytes

==== Non-writable regions for process 92806
REGION TYPE            START - END          [ VSIZE RSDNT  DIRTY   SWAP] PRT/MAX SHRMOD PURGE    REGION DETAIL
```

```
__TEXT                     102874000-102878000    [   16K    16K     0K     0K] r-x/r-x SM=COW        /Users/USER/*/App9
__DATA_CONST               102878000-10287c000    [   16K    16K    16K     0K] r--/rw- SM=COW        /Users/USER/*/App9
__LINKEDIT                 10287c000-102884000    [   32K    32K     0K     0K] r--/r-- SM=COW        /Users/USER/*/App9
dyld private memory        102884000-102984000    [ 1024K    16K    16K     0K] r--/rwx SM=PRV
shared memory              10298c000-102990000    [   16K    16K    16K     0K] r--/r-- SM=SHM
MALLOC metadata            102990000-102994000    [   16K    16K    16K     0K] r--/rwx SM=COW        MallocHelperZone_0x102990000 zone structure
MALLOC guard page          102998000-10299c000    [   16K     0K     0K     0K] ---/rwx SM=ZER
MALLOC guard page          1029a4000-1029a8000    [   16K     0K     0K     0K] ---/rwx SM=ZER
MALLOC guard page          1029a8000-1029ac000    [   16K     0K     0K     0K] ---/rwx SM=NUL
MALLOC guard page          1029b4000-1029bc000    [   32K     0K     0K     0K] ---/rwx SM=NUL
MALLOC guard page          1029c4000-1029c8000    [   16K     0K     0K     0K] ---/rwx SM=NUL
MALLOC metadata            1029c8000-1029cc000    [   16K    16K    16K     0K] r--/rwx SM=PRV
MALLOC metadata            1029cc000-1029d0000    [   16K    16K    16K     0K] r--/rwx SM=COW        DefaultMallocZone_0x1029cc000 zone structure
__TEXT                     102a48000-102aa8000    [  384K   384K     0K     0K] r-x/r-x SM=COW        /usr/lib/dyld
__DATA_CONST               102aa8000-102ac0000    [   96K    16K    16K    16K] r--/rw- SM=COW        /usr/lib/dyld
__LINKEDIT                 102ac4000-102afc000    [  224K    80K     0K     0K] r--/r-- SM=COW        /usr/lib/dyld
STACK GUARD                16958c000-16cd90000    [ 56.0M     0K     0K     0K] ---/rwx SM=NUL        stack guard for thread 0
STACK GUARD                16d58c000-16d590000    [   16K     0K     0K     0K] ---/rwx SM=NUL        stack guard for thread 1
STACK GUARD                16d618000-16d61c000    [   16K     0K     0K     0K] ---/rwx SM=NUL        stack guard for thread 2
STACK GUARD                16d6a4000-16d6a8000    [   16K     0K     0K     0K] ---/rwx SM=NUL        stack guard for thread 3
STACK GUARD                16d730000-16d734000    [   16K     0K     0K     0K] ---/rwx SM=NUL        stack guard for thread 4
STACK GUARD                16d7bc000-16d7c0000    [   16K     0K     0K     0K] ---/rwx SM=NUL        stack guard for thread 5
__TEXT                     18e72d000-18e72f000    [    8K     8K     0K     0K] r-x/r-x SM=COW        /usr/lib/system/libsystem_blocks.dylib
__TEXT                     18e72f000-18e771000    [  264K   264K     0K     0K] r-x/r-x SM=COW        /usr/lib/system/libxpc.dylib
__TEXT                     18e771000-18e78b000    [  104K   104K     0K     0K] r-x/r-x SM=COW        /usr/lib/system/libsystem_trace.dylib
__TEXT                     18e78b000-18e815000    [  552K   504K     0K     0K] r-x/r-x SM=COW        /usr/lib/system/libcorecrypto.dylib
__TEXT                     18e815000-18e840000    [  172K   172K     0K     0K] r-x/r-x SM=COW        /usr/lib/system/libsystem_malloc.dylib
__TEXT                     18e840000-18e887000    [  284K   284K     0K     0K] r-x/r-x SM=COW        /usr/lib/system/libdispatch.dylib
__TEXT                     18e887000-18e8c5000    [  248K   248K     0K     0K] r-x/r-x SM=COW        /usr/lib/libobjc.A.dylib
__TEXT                     18e8c5000-18e8c8000    [   12K    12K     0K     0K] r-x/r-x SM=COW        /usr/lib/system/libsystem_featureflags.dylib
__TEXT                     18e8c8000-18e94a000    [  520K   472K     0K     0K] r-x/r-x SM=COW        /usr/lib/system/libsystem_c.dylib
__TEXT                     18e94a000-18e9b1000    [  412K   380K     0K     0K] r-x/r-x SM=COW        /usr/lib/libc++.1.dylib
__TEXT                     18e9b1000-18e9c9000    [   96K    96K     0K     0K] r-x/r-x SM=COW        /usr/lib/libc++abi.dylib
__TEXT                     18e9c9000-18ea01000    [  224K   208K     0K     0K] r-x/r-x SM=COW        /usr/lib/system/libsystem_kernel.dylib
__TEXT                     18ea01000-18ea0e000    [   52K    52K     0K     0K] r-x/r-x SM=COW        /usr/lib/system/libsystem_pthread.dylib
__TEXT                     18ea0e000-18ea1b000    [   52K    52K     0K     0K] r-x/r-x SM=COW        /usr/lib/system/libdyld.dylib
__TEXT                     18ea1b000-18ea23000    [   32K    32K     0K     0K] r-x/r-x SM=COW        /usr/lib/system/libsystem_platform.dylib
__TEXT                     18ea23000-18ea50000    [  180K   164K     0K     0K] r-x/r-x SM=COW        /usr/lib/system/libsystem_info.dylib
__TEXT                     19113f000-19114a000    [   44K    44K     0K     0K] r-x/r-x SM=COW        /usr/lib/system/libsystem_darwin.dylib
__TEXT                     191598000-1915a8000    [   64K    64K     0K     0K] r-x/r-x SM=COW        /usr/lib/system/libsystem_notify.dylib
__TEXT                     193b14000-193b2d000    [  100K   100K     0K     0K] r-x/r-x SM=COW        /usr/lib/system/libsystem_networkextension.dylib
__TEXT                     193b86000-193b9e000    [   96K    96K     0K     0K] r-x/r-x SM=COW        /usr/lib/system/libsystem_asl.dylib
__TEXT                     1952ea000-1952f3000    [   36K    20K     0K     0K] r-x/r-x SM=COW        /usr/lib/system/libsystem_symptoms.dylib
__TEXT                     1972de000-1972fd000    [  124K   124K     0K     0K] r-x/r-x SM=COW        /usr/lib/system/libsystem_containermanager.dylib
__TEXT                     198085000-19808a000    [   20K    20K     0K     0K] r-x/r-x SM=COW        /usr/lib/system/libsystem_configuration.dylib
__TEXT                     19808a000-19808f000    [   20K    20K     0K     0K] r-x/r-x SM=COW        /usr/lib/system/libsystem_sandbox.dylib
__TEXT                     198bf0000-198bf3000    [   12K    12K     0K     0K] r-x/r-x SM=COW        /usr/lib/system/libquarantine.dylib
__TEXT                     19925d000-199263000    [   24K    24K     0K     0K] r-x/r-x SM=COW        /usr/lib/system/libsystem_coreservices.dylib
__TEXT                     1994c8000-1994ff000    [  220K   156K     0K     0K] r-x/r-x SM=COW        /usr/lib/system/libsystem_m.dylib
__TEXT                     199500000-199509000    [   36K    36K     0K     0K] r-x/r-x SM=COW        /usr/lib/system/libmacho.dylib
__TEXT                     199525000-199532000    [   52K    52K     0K     0K] r-x/r-x SM=COW        /usr/lib/system/libcommonCrypto.dylib
__TEXT                     199532000-19953d000    [   44K    44K     0K     0K] r-x/r-x SM=COW        /usr/lib/system/libunwind.dylib
__TEXT                     19953d000-199545000    [   32K    32K     0K     0K] r-x/r-x SM=COW        /usr/lib/liboah.dylib
__TEXT                     199545000-19954e000    [   36K    36K     0K     0K] r-x/r-x SM=COW        /usr/lib/system/libcopyfile.dylib
__TEXT                     19954e000-199552000    [   16K    16K     0K     0K] r-x/r-x SM=COW        /usr/lib/system/libcompiler_rt.dylib
__TEXT                     199552000-199557000    [   20K    20K     0K     0K] r-x/r-x SM=COW        /usr/lib/system/libsystem_collections.dylib
__TEXT                     199557000-19955a000    [   12K    12K     0K     0K] r-x/r-x SM=COW        /usr/lib/system/libsystem_secinit.dylib
__TEXT                     19955a000-19955d000    [   12K    12K     0K     0K] r-x/r-x SM=COW        /usr/lib/system/libremovefile.dylib
__TEXT                     19955d000-19955e000    [    4K     4K     0K     0K] r-x/r-x SM=COW        /usr/lib/system/libkeymgr.dylib
__TEXT                     19955e000-199567000    [   36K    36K     0K     0K] r-x/r-x SM=COW        /usr/lib/system/libsystem_dnssd.dylib
__TEXT                     199567000-19956d000    [   24K    24K     0K     0K] r-x/r-x SM=COW        /usr/lib/system/libcache.dylib
__TEXT                     19956d000-19956f000    [    8K     8K     0K     0K] r-x/r-x SM=COW        /usr/lib/libSystem.B.dylib
__TEXT                     19f8c1000-19f8c2000    [    4K     4K     0K     0K] r-x/r-x SM=COW        /usr/lib/system/libsystem_product_info_filter.dylib
__OBJC_RO                  1d89c2000-1ddcc4000    [ 83.0M  51.4M     0K     0K] r-x/r-x SM=COW        /usr/lib/libobjc.A.dylib
__DATA_CONST               1e0098000-1e0098130    [   304    304     0K     0K] r--/rw- SM=COW        /usr/lib/system/libsystem_blocks.dylib
__DATA_CONST               1e0098130-1e00987d0    [  1696   1696     0K     0K] r--/rw- SM=COW        /usr/lib/system/libsystem_trace.dylib
__DATA_CONST               1e00987d0-1e0098ef0    [  1824   1824     0K     0K] r--/rw- SM=COW        /usr/lib/system/libcorecrypto.dylib
__DATA_CONST               1e0098ef0-1e0098f48    [    88     88     0K     0K] r--/rw- SM=COW        /usr/lib/system/libsystem_malloc.dylib
__DATA_CONST               1e0098f50-1e0099b58    [  3080   3080     0K     0K] r--/rw- SM=COW        /usr/lib/libobjc.A.dylib
__DATA_CONST               1e0099b58-1e0099b98    [    64     64     0K     0K] r--/rw- SM=COW        /usr/lib/system/libsystem_featureflags.dylib
__DATA_CONST               1e0099b98-1e009b370    [    6K     6K     0K     0K] r--/rw- SM=COW        /usr/lib/system/libsystem_c.dylib
__DATA_CONST               1e009b370-1e009bcd0    [  2400   2400     0K     0K] r--/rw- SM=COW        /usr/lib/libc++.1.dylib
__DATA_CONST               1e009bcd0-1e009bda8    [   216    216     0K     0K] r--/rw- SM=COW        /usr/lib/libc++abi.dylib
__DATA_CONST               1e009bda8-1e009e060    [    9K     9K     0K     0K] r--/rw- SM=COW        /usr/lib/system/libsystem_kernel.dylib
__DATA_CONST               1e009e060-1e009e098    [    56     56     0K     0K] r--/rw- SM=COW        /usr/lib/system/libsystem_pthread.dylib
__DATA_CONST               1e009e098-1e009e258    [   448    448     0K     0K] r--/rw- SM=COW        /usr/lib/system/libdyld.dylib
__DATA_CONST               1e009e258-1e009e278    [    32     32     0K     0K] r--/rw- SM=COW        /usr/lib/system/libsystem_platform.dylib
__DATA_CONST               1e009e278-1e009e790    [  1304   1304     0K     0K] r--/rw- SM=COW        /usr/lib/system/libsystem_info.dylib
__DATA_CONST               1e0127148-1e0129ac0    [   10K    10K     0K     0K] r--/rw- SM=COW        /usr/lib/system/libsystem_darwin.dylib
__DATA_CONST               1e0133dc0-1e0133f18    [   344    344     0K     0K] r--/rw- SM=COW        /usr/lib/system/libsystem_notify.dylib
__DATA_CONST               1e02c9868-1e02c9d60    [  1272   1272     0K     0K] r--/rw- SM=COW        /usr/lib/system/libsystem_networkextension.dylib
__DATA_CONST               1e02cac70-1e02cb290    [  1568   1568     0K     0K] r--/rw- SM=COW        /usr/lib/system/libsystem_asl.dylib
__DATA_CONST               1e032ea80-1e032ec30    [   432    432     0K     0K] r--/rw- SM=COW        /usr/lib/system/libsystem_symptoms.dylib
__DATA_CONST               1e05863b8-1e0586da0    [  2536   2536     0K     0K] r--/rw- SM=COW        /usr/lib/system/libsystem_containermanager.dylib
__DATA_CONST               1e061d0e0-1e061d298    [   440    440     0K     0K] r--/rw- SM=COW        /usr/lib/system/libsystem_configuration.dylib
__DATA_CONST               1e061d298-1e061d308    [   112    112     0K     0K] r--/rw- SM=COW        /usr/lib/system/libsystem_sandbox.dylib
__DATA_CONST               1e064ac20-1e064ac70    [    80     80     0K     0K] r--/rw- SM=COW        /usr/lib/system/libquarantine.dylib
__DATA_CONST               1e06d5660-1e06d5dc8    [  1896   1896     0K     0K] r--/rw- SM=COW        /usr/lib/system/libsystem_coreservices.dylib
__DATA_CONST               1e06fd5a8-1e06fdcf0    [  1864   1864     0K     0K] r--/rw- SM=COW        /usr/lib/system/libmacho.dylib
__DATA_CONST               1e06fdd00-1e06fe4a0    [  1952   1952     0K     0K] r--/rw- SM=COW        /usr/lib/system/libcommonCrypto.dylib
__DATA_CONST               1e06fe4a0-1e06fe7c0    [   800    800     0K     0K] r--/rw- SM=COW        /usr/lib/system/libunwind.dylib
__DATA_CONST               1e06fe7c0-1e06fe7d8    [    24     24     0K     0K] r--/rw- SM=COW        /usr/lib/liboah.dylib
__DATA_CONST               1e06fe7d8-1e06fea98    [   704    704     0K     0K] r--/rw- SM=COW        /usr/lib/system/libcopyfile.dylib
__DATA_CONST               1e06fea98-1e06feaa0    [     8      8     0K     0K] r--/rw- SM=COW        /usr/lib/system/libsystem_collections.dylib
__DATA_CONST               1e06feaa0-1e06feb10    [   112    112     0K     0K] r--/rw- SM=COW        /usr/lib/system/libsystem_secinit.dylib
__DATA_CONST               1e06feb10-1e06feb20    [    16     16     0K     0K] r--/rw- SM=COW        /usr/lib/system/libremovefile.dylib
__DATA_CONST               1e06feb20-1e06feb30    [    16     16     0K     0K] r--/rw- SM=COW        /usr/lib/system/libkeymgr.dylib
__DATA_CONST               1e06feb30-1e06feba8    [   120    120     0K     0K] r--/rw- SM=COW        /usr/lib/system/libsystem_dnssd.dylib
__DATA_CONST               1e06feba8-1e06fec08    [    96     96     0K     0K] r--/rw- SM=COW        /usr/lib/system/libcache.dylib
__DATA_CONST               1e06fec08-1e06fec18    [    16     16     0K     0K] r--/rw- SM=COW        /usr/lib/libSystem.B.dylib
__AUTH_CONST               1e8b08000-1e8b08030    [    48     48     0K     0K] r--/rw- SM=COW        /usr/lib/system/libsystem_blocks.dylib
__OBJC_CONST               1e8b08030-1e8b08390    [   864    864     0K     0K] r--/rw- SM=COW        /usr/lib/system/libsystem_blocks.dylib
```

```
__DATA_CONST           1e8b08390-1e8b0ce20     [   19K     19K      0K      0K] r--/rw- SM=COW          /usr/lib/system/libxpc.dylib
__OBJC_CONST           1e8b0ce20-1e8b0df90     [    4K      4K      0K      0K] r--/rw- SM=COW          /usr/lib/system/libxpc.dylib
__AUTH_CONST           1e8b0df90-1e8b0ec90     [  3328    3328      0K      0K] r--/rw- SM=COW          /usr/lib/system/libsystem_trace.dylib
__OBJC_CONST           1e8b0ec90-1e8b0ee40     [   432     432      0K      0K] r--/rw- SM=COW          /usr/lib/system/libsystem_trace.dylib
__AUTH_CONST           1e8b0ee40-1e8b0ff10     [    4K      4K      0K      0K] r--/rw- SM=COW          /usr/lib/system/libcorecrypto.dylib
__AUTH_CONST           1e8b0ff10-1e8b104e8     [  1496    1496      0K      0K] r--/rw- SM=COW          /usr/lib/system/libsystem_malloc.dylib
__DATA_CONST           1e8b10500-1e8b238e8     [   77K     45K      0K      0K] r--/rw- SM=COW          /usr/lib/system/libdispatch.dylib
__OBJC_CONST           1e8b238e8-1e8b24938     [    4K      4K      0K      0K] r--/rw- SM=COW          /usr/lib/system/libdispatch.dylib
__AUTH_CONST           1e8b24940-1e8b253c8     [  2696    2696      0K      0K] r--/rw- SM=COW          /usr/lib/libobjc.A.dylib
__OBJC_CONST           1e8b253c8-1e8b25698     [   720     720      0K      0K] r--/rw- SM=COW          /usr/lib/libobjc.A.dylib
__AUTH_CONST           1e8b25698-1e8b25808     [   368     368      0K      0K] r--/rw- SM=COW          /usr/lib/system/libsystem_featureflags.dylib
__AUTH_CONST           1e8b25808-1e8b26168     [  2400    2400      0K      0K] r--/rw- SM=COW          /usr/lib/system/libsystem_c.dylib
__AUTH_CONST           1e8b26168-1e8b282a8     [    8K      8K      0K      0K] r--/rw- SM=COW          /usr/lib/libc++.1.dylib
__AUTH_CONST           1e8b282a8-1e8b2b4b8     [   13K     13K      0K      0K] r--/rw- SM=COW          /usr/lib/libc++abi.dylib
__AUTH_CONST           1e8b2b4b8-1e8b2b5e0     [   296     296      0K      0K] r--/rw- SM=COW          /usr/lib/system/libsystem_kernel.dylib
__AUTH_CONST           1e8b2b5e0-1e8b2b810     [   560     560      0K      0K] r--/rw- SM=COW          /usr/lib/system/libsystem_pthread.dylib
__AUTH_CONST           1e8b2b810-1e8b2bfc8     [  1976    1976      0K      0K] r--/rw- SM=COW          /usr/lib/system/libdyld.dylib
__AUTH_CONST           1e8b2bfc8-1e8b2c250     [   648     648      0K      0K] r--/rw- SM=COW          /usr/lib/system/libsystem_platform.dylib
__AUTH_CONST           1e8b2c250-1e8b2d3f0     [    4K      4K      0K      0K] r--/rw- SM=COW          /usr/lib/system/libsystem_info.dylib
__AUTH_CONST           1e8c5bd48-1e8c5c1c8     [  1152    1152      0K      0K] r--/rw- SM=COW          /usr/lib/system/libsystem_darwin.dylib
__AUTH_CONST           1e8c77a80-1e8c77e00     [   896     896      0K      0K] r--/rw- SM=COW          /usr/lib/system/libsystem_notify.dylib
__AUTH_CONST           1e8dfea40-1e8dff608     [  3016    3016      0K      0K] r--/rw- SM=COW          /usr/lib/system/libsystem_networkextension.dylib
__AUTH_CONST           1e8e4d718-1e8e4e160     [  2632    2632      0K      0K] r--/rw- SM=COW          /usr/lib/system/libsystem_asl.dylib
__AUTH_CONST           1e8f17288-1e8f17560     [   728     728      0K      0K] r--/rw- SM=COW          /usr/lib/system/libsystem_symptoms.dylib
__AUTH_CONST           1e904e480-1e904f8c0     [    5K      5K      0K      0K] r--/rw- SM=COW          /usr/lib/system/libsystem_containermanager.dylib
__AUTH_CONST           1e915e250-1e915e560     [   784     784      0K      0K] r--/rw- SM=COW          /usr/lib/system/libsystem_configuration.dylib
__AUTH_CONST           1e915e560-1e915e768     [   520     520      0K      0K] r--/rw- SM=COW          /usr/lib/system/libsystem_sandbox.dylib
__AUTH_CONST           1e91a78b8-1e91a79c0     [   264     264      0K      0K] r--/rw- SM=COW          /usr/lib/system/libquarantine.dylib
__AUTH_CONST           1e922eac0-1e922ed50     [   656     656      0K      0K] r--/rw- SM=COW          /usr/lib/system/libsystem_coreservices.dylib
__AUTH_CONST           1e925ad88-1e925ada8     [    32      32      0K      0K] r--/rw- SM=COW          /usr/lib/system/libsystem_m.dylib
__AUTH_CONST           1e925ae28-1e925ae98     [   112     112      0K      0K] r--/rw- SM=COW          /usr/lib/system/libmacho.dylib
__AUTH_CONST           1e925afb0-1e925bd80     [  3536    3536      0K      0K] r--/rw- SM=COW          /usr/lib/system/libcommonCrypto.dylib
__AUTH_CONST           1e925bd80-1e925be98     [   280     280      0K      0K] r--/rw- SM=COW          /usr/lib/system/libunwind.dylib
__AUTH_CONST           1e925be98-1e925c168     [   720     720      0K      0K] r--/rw- SM=COW          /usr/lib/liboah.dylib
__AUTH_CONST           1e925c168-1e925c5a0     [  1080    1080      0K      0K] r--/rw- SM=COW          /usr/lib/system/libcopyfile.dylib
__AUTH_CONST           1e925c5a0-1e925c600     [    96      96      0K      0K] r--/rw- SM=COW          /usr/lib/system/libcompiler_rt.dylib
__AUTH_CONST           1e925c600-1e925c750     [   336     336      0K      0K] r--/rw- SM=COW          /usr/lib/system/libsystem_collections.dylib
__AUTH_CONST           1e925c750-1e925ca18     [   712     712      0K      0K] r--/rw- SM=COW          /usr/lib/system/libsystem_secinit.dylib
__AUTH_CONST           1e925ca18-1e925cb78     [   352     352      0K      0K] r--/rw- SM=COW          /usr/lib/system/libremovefile.dylib
__AUTH_CONST           1e925cb78-1e925cbf8     [   128     128      0K      0K] r--/rw- SM=COW          /usr/lib/system/libkeymgr.dylib
__AUTH_CONST           1e925cbf8-1e925cdb0     [   440     440      0K      0K] r--/rw- SM=COW          /usr/lib/system/libsystem_dnssd.dylib
__AUTH_CONST           1e925cdb0-1e925ce70     [   192     192      0K      0K] r--/rw- SM=COW          /usr/lib/system/libcache.dylib
__AUTH_CONST           1e925ce70-1e925d120     [   688     688      0K      0K] r--/rw- SM=COW          /usr/lib/libSystem.B.dylib
__LINKEDIT             222494000-2465e6000     [577.3M  13.9M      0K      0K] r--/r-- SM=COW          dyld shared cache combined __LINKEDIT

==== Writable regions for process 92806
REGION TYPE                  START - END       [ VSIZE  RSDNT   DIRTY    SWAP] PRT/MAX SHRMOD PURGE    REGION DETAIL
Kernel Alloc Once      102984000-10298c000     [   32K     0K      0K     16K] rw-/rwx SM=PRV
MALLOC metadata        102994000-102998000     [   16K    16K     16K      0K] rw-/rwx SM=PRV
MALLOC metadata        10299c000-1029a4000     [   32K    32K     32K      0K] rw-/rwx SM=COW
MALLOC metadata        1029ac000-1029b4000     [   32K    32K     32K      0K] rw-/rwx SM=PRV
MALLOC metadata        1029bc000-1029c4000     [   32K     0K      0K     32K] rw-/rwx SM=PRV
MALLOC metadata        1029d0000-1029d4000     [   16K    16K     16K      0K] rw-/rwx SM=COW
MALLOC metadata        1029d4000-1029dc000     [   32K    32K     32K      0K] rw-/rwx SM=PRV
MALLOC metadata        1029dc000-1029e0000     [   16K    16K     16K      0K] rw-/rwx SM=PRV
__DATA                 102ac0000-102ac4000     [   16K    16K     16K      0K] rw-/rw- SM=COW          /usr/lib/dyld
MALLOC_SMALL           103000000-103800000     [ 8192K  8192K   8192K      0K] rw-/rwx SM=PRV          MallocHelperZone_0x102990000
MALLOC_SMALL           103800000-104000000     [ 8192K  8192K   8192K      0K] rw-/rwx SM=PRV          MallocHelperZone_0x102990000
MALLOC_SMALL           104000000-104800000     [ 8192K  8192K   8192K      0K] rw-/rwx SM=PRV          MallocHelperZone_0x102990000
MALLOC_SMALL           104800000-105000000     [ 8192K  8192K   8192K      0K] rw-/rwx SM=PRV          MallocHelperZone_0x102990000
MALLOC_SMALL           105000000-105800000     [ 8192K  8192K   8192K      0K] rw-/rwx SM=PRV          MallocHelperZone_0x102990000
MALLOC_SMALL           105800000-106000000     [ 8192K  8192K   8192K      0K] rw-/rwx SM=PRV          MallocHelperZone_0x102990000
MALLOC_SMALL           106000000-106800000     [ 8192K  8192K   8192K      0K] rw-/rwx SM=PRV          MallocHelperZone_0x102990000
MALLOC_SMALL           106800000-107000000     [ 8192K  8192K   8192K      0K] rw-/rwx SM=PRV          MallocHelperZone_0x102990000
MALLOC_SMALL           107000000-107800000     [ 8192K  8192K   8192K      0K] rw-/rwx SM=PRV          MallocHelperZone_0x102990000
MALLOC_SMALL           107800000-108000000     [ 8192K  8192K   8192K      0K] rw-/rwx SM=PRV          MallocHelperZone_0x102990000
MALLOC_SMALL           108000000-108800000     [ 8192K  8192K   8192K      0K] rw-/rwx SM=PRV          MallocHelperZone_0x102990000
MALLOC_SMALL           108800000-109000000     [ 8192K  8192K   8192K      0K] rw-/rwx SM=PRV          MallocHelperZone_0x102990000
MALLOC_SMALL           109000000-109800000     [ 8192K  8192K   8192K      0K] rw-/rwx SM=PRV          MallocHelperZone_0x102990000
MALLOC_SMALL           109800000-10a000000     [ 8192K  8192K   8192K      0K] rw-/rwx SM=PRV          MallocHelperZone_0x102990000
MALLOC_SMALL           10a000000-10a800000     [ 8192K  8192K   8192K      0K] rw-/rwx SM=PRV          MallocHelperZone_0x102990000
MALLOC_SMALL           10a800000-10b000000     [ 8192K  8192K   8192K      0K] rw-/rwx SM=PRV          MallocHelperZone_0x102990000
MALLOC_SMALL           10b000000-10b800000     [ 8192K  8192K   8192K      0K] rw-/rwx SM=PRV          MallocHelperZone_0x102990000
MALLOC_SMALL           10b800000-10c000000     [ 8192K    48K     48K   8144K] rw-/rwx SM=PRV          MallocHelperZone_0x102990000
MALLOC_SMALL           10c000000-10c800000     [ 8192K    48K     48K   8144K] rw-/rwx SM=PRV          MallocHelperZone_0x102990000
MALLOC_SMALL           10c800000-10d000000     [ 8192K    48K     48K   8144K] rw-/rwx SM=PRV          MallocHelperZone_0x102990000
MALLOC_SMALL           10d000000-10d800000     [ 8192K    32K     32K   8160K] rw-/rwx SM=PRV          MallocHelperZone_0x102990000
MALLOC_SMALL           10d800000-10e000000     [ 8192K    48K     48K   8144K] rw-/rwx SM=PRV          MallocHelperZone_0x102990000
MALLOC_SMALL           10e000000-10e800000     [ 8192K    32K     32K   8160K] rw-/rwx SM=PRV          MallocHelperZone_0x102990000
MALLOC_SMALL           10e800000-10f000000     [ 8192K    48K     48K   8144K] rw-/rwx SM=PRV          MallocHelperZone_0x102990000
MALLOC_SMALL           10f000000-10f800000     [ 8192K    48K     48K   8144K] rw-/rwx SM=PRV          MallocHelperZone_0x102990000
MALLOC_SMALL           10f800000-110000000     [ 8192K    64K     64K   8128K] rw-/rwx SM=PRV          MallocHelperZone_0x102990000
MALLOC_SMALL           110000000-110800000     [ 8192K    32K     32K   8160K] rw-/rwx SM=PRV          MallocHelperZone_0x102990000
MALLOC_SMALL           110800000-111000000     [ 8192K    32K     32K   8160K] rw-/rwx SM=PRV          MallocHelperZone_0x102990000
MALLOC_SMALL           111000000-111800000     [ 8192K    32K     32K   8160K] rw-/rwx SM=PRV          MallocHelperZone_0x102990000
MALLOC_SMALL           111800000-112000000     [ 8192K    64K     64K   8128K] rw-/rwx SM=PRV          MallocHelperZone_0x102990000
MALLOC_SMALL           112000000-112800000     [ 8192K    48K     48K   8144K] rw-/rwx SM=PRV          MallocHelperZone_0x102990000
MALLOC_SMALL           112800000-113000000     [ 8192K  3776K   3776K   4416K] rw-/rwx SM=PRV          MallocHelperZone_0x102990000
MALLOC_SMALL           113000000-113800000     [ 8192K    32K     32K      0K] rw-/rwx SM=PRV          MallocHelperZone_0x102990000
MALLOC_SMALL           113800000-114000000     [ 8192K  8192K   8192K      0K] rw-/rwx SM=PRV          MallocHelperZone_0x102990000
MALLOC_SMALL           114000000-114800000     [ 8192K  8192K   8192K      0K] rw-/rwx SM=PRV          MallocHelperZone_0x102990000
MALLOC_SMALL           114800000-115000000     [ 8192K  8192K   8192K      0K] rw-/rwx SM=PRV          MallocHelperZone_0x102990000
MALLOC_SMALL           115000000-115800000     [ 8192K  8192K   8192K      0K] rw-/rwx SM=PRV          MallocHelperZone_0x102990000
MALLOC_SMALL           115800000-116000000     [ 8192K  8192K   8192K      0K] rw-/rwx SM=PRV          MallocHelperZone_0x102990000
MALLOC_SMALL           116000000-116800000     [ 8192K   400K    400K      0K] rw-/rwx SM=PRV          MallocHelperZone_0x102990000
MALLOC_SMALL           116800000-117000000     [ 8192K  8192K   8192K      0K] rw-/rwx SM=PRV          MallocHelperZone_0x102990000
MALLOC_SMALL           117000000-117800000     [ 8192K  8192K   8192K      0K] rw-/rwx SM=PRV          MallocHelperZone_0x102990000
MALLOC_SMALL           117800000-118000000     [ 8192K  3376K   3376K      0K] rw-/rwx SM=PRV          MallocHelperZone_0x102990000
MALLOC_SMALL           118000000-118800000     [ 8192K  8192K   8192K      0K] rw-/rwx SM=PRV          MallocHelperZone_0x102990000
MALLOC_SMALL           118800000-119000000     [ 8192K  8192K   8192K      0K] rw-/rwx SM=PRV          MallocHelperZone_0x102990000
MALLOC_SMALL           119000000-119800000     [ 8192K  8192K   8192K      0K] rw-/rwx SM=PRV          MallocHelperZone_0x102990000
MALLOC_SMALL           119800000-11a000000     [ 8192K  8192K   8192K      0K] rw-/rwx SM=PRV          MallocHelperZone_0x102990000
```

```
MALLOC_SMALL          11a000000-11a800000    [ 8192K  8192K  8192K     0K] rw-/rwx SM=PRV    MallocHelperZone_0x102990000
MALLOC_SMALL          11a800000-11b000000    [ 8192K  8192K  8192K     0K] rw-/rwx SM=PRV    MallocHelperZone_0x102990000
MALLOC_SMALL          11b000000-11b800000    [ 8192K  8192K  8192K     0K] rw-/rwx SM=PRV    MallocHelperZone_0x102990000
MALLOC_SMALL          11b800000-11c000000    [ 8192K    48K    48K  8144K] rw-/rwx SM=PRV    MallocHelperZone_0x102990000
MALLOC_SMALL          11c000000-11c800000    [ 8192K    64K    64K  8128K] rw-/rwx SM=PRV    MallocHelperZone_0x102990000
MALLOC_SMALL          11c800000-11d000000    [ 8192K    48K    48K  8144K] rw-/rwx SM=PRV    MallocHelperZone_0x102990000
MALLOC_SMALL          11d000000-11d800000    [ 8192K    48K    48K  8144K] rw-/rwx SM=PRV    MallocHelperZone_0x102990000
MALLOC_SMALL          11d800000-11e000000    [ 8192K    48K    48K  8144K] rw-/rwx SM=PRV    MallocHelperZone_0x102990000
MALLOC_SMALL          11e000000-11e800000    [ 8192K    32K    32K  8160K] rw-/rwx SM=PRV    MallocHelperZone_0x102990000
MALLOC_SMALL          11e800000-11f000000    [ 8192K    48K    48K  8144K] rw-/rwx SM=PRV    MallocHelperZone_0x102990000
MALLOC_SMALL          11f000000-11f800000    [ 8192K    32K    32K  8160K] rw-/rwx SM=PRV    MallocHelperZone_0x102990000
MALLOC_SMALL          11f800000-120000000    [ 8192K    48K    48K  8144K] rw-/rwx SM=PRV    MallocHelperZone_0x102990000
MALLOC_SMALL          120000000-120800000    [ 8192K    80K    80K  8112K] rw-/rwx SM=PRV    MallocHelperZone_0x102990000
MALLOC_SMALL          120800000-121000000    [ 8192K    48K    48K  8144K] rw-/rwx SM=PRV    MallocHelperZone_0x102990000
MALLOC_SMALL          121000000-121800000    [ 8192K    48K    48K  8144K] rw-/rwx SM=PRV    MallocHelperZone_0x102990000
MALLOC_SMALL          121800000-122000000    [ 8192K    48K    48K  8144K] rw-/rwx SM=PRV    MallocHelperZone_0x102990000
MALLOC_SMALL          122000000-122800000    [ 8192K    64K    64K  8128K] rw-/rwx SM=PRV    MallocHelperZone_0x102990000
MALLOC_SMALL          122800000-123000000    [ 8192K    48K    48K  8144K] rw-/rwx SM=PRV    MallocHelperZone_0x102990000
MALLOC_SMALL          123000000-123800000    [ 8192K    48K    48K  8144K] rw-/rwx SM=PRV    MallocHelperZone_0x102990000
MALLOC_SMALL          123800000-124000000    [ 8192K    48K    48K  8144K] rw-/rwx SM=PRV    MallocHelperZone_0x102990000
MALLOC_SMALL          124000000-124800000    [ 8192K    64K    64K  8128K] rw-/rwx SM=PRV    MallocHelperZone_0x102990000
MALLOC_SMALL          124800000-125000000    [ 8192K    32K    32K  8160K] rw-/rwx SM=PRV    MallocHelperZone_0x102990000
MALLOC_SMALL          125000000-125800000    [ 8192K    48K    48K  8144K] rw-/rwx SM=PRV    MallocHelperZone_0x102990000
MALLOC_SMALL          125800000-126000000    [ 8192K    48K    48K  8144K] rw-/rwx SM=PRV    MallocHelperZone_0x102990000
MALLOC_SMALL          126000000-126800000    [ 8192K  8192K  8192K     0K] rw-/rwx SM=PRV    MallocHelperZone_0x102990000
MALLOC_SMALL          126800000-127000000    [ 8192K    32K    32K  8160K] rw-/rwx SM=PRV    MallocHelperZone_0x102990000
MALLOC_SMALL          127000000-127800000    [ 8192K    48K    48K  8144K] rw-/rwx SM=PRV    MallocHelperZone_0x102990000
MALLOC_SMALL          127800000-128000000    [ 8192K    32K    32K  8160K] rw-/rwx SM=PRV    MallocHelperZone_0x102990000
MALLOC_SMALL          128000000-128800000    [ 8192K    32K    32K  8160K] rw-/rwx SM=PRV    MallocHelperZone_0x102990000
MALLOC_SMALL          128800000-129000000    [ 8192K    48K    48K  8144K] rw-/rwx SM=PRV    MallocHelperZone_0x102990000
MALLOC_SMALL          129000000-129800000    [ 8192K    32K    32K  8160K] rw-/rwx SM=PRV    MallocHelperZone_0x102990000
MALLOC_SMALL          129800000-12a000000    [ 8192K    32K    32K  8160K] rw-/rwx SM=PRV    MallocHelperZone_0x102990000
MALLOC_SMALL          12a000000-12a800000    [ 8192K    32K    32K  8160K] rw-/rwx SM=PRV    MallocHelperZone_0x102990000
MALLOC_SMALL          12a800000-12b000000    [ 8192K    32K    32K  8160K] rw-/rwx SM=PRV    MallocHelperZone_0x102990000
MALLOC_TINY           12b600000-12b700000    [ 1024K    16K    16K    16K] rw-/rwx SM=PRV    MallocHelperZone_0x102990000
MALLOC_SMALL          12b800000-12c000000    [ 8192K  3216K  3216K  4976K] rw-/rwx SM=PRV    MallocHelperZone_0x102990000
MALLOC_SMALL          12c000000-12c800000    [ 8192K    64K    64K  8128K] rw-/rwx SM=PRV    MallocHelperZone_0x102990000
MALLOC_SMALL          12c800000-12d000000    [ 8192K    48K    48K  8144K] rw-/rwx SM=PRV    MallocHelperZone_0x102990000
MALLOC_SMALL          12d000000-12d800000    [ 8192K    48K    48K  8144K] rw-/rwx SM=PRV    MallocHelperZone_0x102990000
MALLOC_SMALL          12d800000-12e000000    [ 8192K    48K    48K  8144K] rw-/rwx SM=PRV    MallocHelperZone_0x102990000
MALLOC_SMALL          12e000000-12e800000    [ 8192K    96K    96K  8096K] rw-/rwx SM=PRV    MallocHelperZone_0x102990000
MALLOC_SMALL          12e800000-12f000000    [ 8192K    80K    80K  8112K] rw-/rwx SM=PRV    MallocHelperZone_0x102990000
MALLOC_SMALL          12f000000-12f800000    [ 8192K    64K    64K  8128K] rw-/rwx SM=PRV    MallocHelperZone_0x102990000
MALLOC_SMALL          12f800000-130000000    [ 8192K    48K    48K  8144K] rw-/rwx SM=PRV    MallocHelperZone_0x102990000
MALLOC_SMALL          130000000-130800000    [ 8192K    32K    32K  8160K] rw-/rwx SM=PRV    MallocHelperZone_0x102990000
MALLOC_SMALL          130800000-131000000    [ 8192K  2512K  2512K  5664K] rw-/rwx SM=PRV    MallocHelperZone_0x102990000
MALLOC_SMALL          131000000-131800000    [ 8192K    48K    48K  8144K] rw-/rwx SM=PRV    MallocHelperZone_0x102990000
MALLOC_SMALL          131800000-132000000    [ 8192K  1632K  1632K  6560K] rw-/rwx SM=PRV    MallocHelperZone_0x102990000
MALLOC_SMALL          132000000-132800000    [ 8192K    48K    48K  8144K] rw-/rwx SM=PRV    MallocHelperZone_0x102990000
MALLOC_SMALL          132800000-133000000    [ 8192K  7216K  7216K   976K] rw-/rwx SM=PRV    MallocHelperZone_0x102990000
MALLOC_SMALL          133000000-133800000    [ 8192K    32K    32K  8160K] rw-/rwx SM=PRV    MallocHelperZone_0x102990000
MALLOC_SMALL          133800000-134000000    [ 8192K    32K    32K  8160K] rw-/rwx SM=PRV    MallocHelperZone_0x102990000
MALLOC_SMALL          134000000-134800000    [ 8192K    32K    32K  8160K] rw-/rwx SM=PRV    MallocHelperZone_0x102990000
MALLOC_SMALL          134800000-135000000    [ 8192K    48K    48K  8144K] rw-/rwx SM=PRV    MallocHelperZone_0x102990000
MALLOC_SMALL          135000000-135800000    [ 8192K    64K    64K  8128K] rw-/rwx SM=PRV    MallocHelperZone_0x102990000
MALLOC_SMALL          135800000-136000000    [ 8192K    48K    48K  8144K] rw-/rwx SM=PRV    MallocHelperZone_0x102990000
MALLOC_SMALL          136000000-136800000    [ 8192K    48K    48K  8144K] rw-/rwx SM=PRV    MallocHelperZone_0x102990000
MALLOC_SMALL          136800000-137000000    [ 8192K    48K    48K  8144K] rw-/rwx SM=PRV    MallocHelperZone_0x102990000
MALLOC_SMALL          137000000-137800000    [ 8192K    64K    64K  8128K] rw-/rwx SM=PRV    MallocHelperZone_0x102990000
MALLOC_SMALL          137800000-138000000    [ 8192K    32K    32K  8160K] rw-/rwx SM=PRV    MallocHelperZone_0x102990000
MALLOC_SMALL          138000000-138800000    [ 8192K    32K    32K  8160K] rw-/rwx SM=PRV    MallocHelperZone_0x102990000
MALLOC_SMALL          138800000-139000000    [ 8192K    48K    48K  8144K] rw-/rwx SM=PRV    MallocHelperZone_0x102990000
MALLOC_SMALL          139000000-139800000    [ 8192K    64K    64K  8128K] rw-/rwx SM=PRV    MallocHelperZone_0x102990000
MALLOC_SMALL          139800000-13a000000    [ 8192K    48K    48K  8144K] rw-/rwx SM=PRV    MallocHelperZone_0x102990000
MALLOC_SMALL          13a000000-13a800000    [ 8192K    80K    80K  8112K] rw-/rwx SM=PRV    MallocHelperZone_0x102990000
MALLOC_SMALL          13a800000-13b000000    [ 8192K    48K    48K  8144K] rw-/rwx SM=PRV    MallocHelperZone_0x102990000
MALLOC_SMALL          13b000000-13b800000    [ 8192K  8192K  8192K     0K] rw-/rwx SM=PRV    MallocHelperZone_0x102990000
MALLOC_SMALL          13b800000-13c000000    [ 8192K  8192K  8192K     0K] rw-/rwx SM=PRV    MallocHelperZone_0x102990000
MALLOC_SMALL          13c000000-13c800000    [ 8192K  8192K  8192K     0K] rw-/rwx SM=PRV    MallocHelperZone_0x102990000
MALLOC_SMALL          13c800000-13d000000    [ 8192K  8192K  8192K     0K] rw-/rwx SM=PRV    MallocHelperZone_0x102990000
MALLOC_SMALL          13d000000-13d800000    [ 8192K  8192K  8192K     0K] rw-/rwx SM=PRV    MallocHelperZone_0x102990000
MALLOC_SMALL          13d800000-13e000000    [ 8192K  8192K  8192K     0K] rw-/rwx SM=PRV    MallocHelperZone_0x102990000
MALLOC_SMALL          13e000000-13e800000    [ 8192K  8192K  8192K     0K] rw-/rwx SM=PRV    MallocHelperZone_0x102990000
MALLOC_SMALL          13e800000-13f000000    [ 8192K  8192K  8192K     0K] rw-/rwx SM=PRV    MallocHelperZone_0x102990000
MALLOC_SMALL          13f000000-13f800000    [ 8192K  8192K  8192K     0K] rw-/rwx SM=PRV    MallocHelperZone_0x102990000
MALLOC_SMALL          13f800000-140000000    [ 8192K  8192K  8192K     0K] rw-/rwx SM=PRV    MallocHelperZone_0x102990000
MALLOC_SMALL          140000000-140800000    [ 8192K  8192K  8192K     0K] rw-/rwx SM=PRV    MallocHelperZone_0x102990000
MALLOC_SMALL          140800000-141000000    [ 8192K  8192K  8192K     0K] rw-/rwx SM=PRV    MallocHelperZone_0x102990000
MALLOC_SMALL          141000000-141800000    [ 8192K  8192K  8192K     0K] rw-/rwx SM=PRV    MallocHelperZone_0x102990000
MALLOC_SMALL          141800000-142000000    [ 8192K  8192K  8192K     0K] rw-/rwx SM=PRV    MallocHelperZone_0x102990000
MALLOC_SMALL          142000000-142800000    [ 8192K  8192K  8192K     0K] rw-/rwx SM=PRV    MallocHelperZone_0x102990000
MALLOC_SMALL          142800000-143000000    [ 8192K  8192K  8192K     0K] rw-/rwx SM=PRV    MallocHelperZone_0x102990000
MALLOC_SMALL          143000000-143800000    [ 8192K  8192K  8192K     0K] rw-/rwx SM=PRV    MallocHelperZone_0x102990000
MALLOC_SMALL          143800000-144000000    [ 8192K  8192K  8192K     0K] rw-/rwx SM=PRV    MallocHelperZone_0x102990000
MALLOC_SMALL          144000000-144800000    [ 8192K  8192K  8192K     0K] rw-/rwx SM=PRV    MallocHelperZone_0x102990000
MALLOC_SMALL          144800000-145000000    [ 8192K  8192K  8192K     0K] rw-/rwx SM=PRV    MallocHelperZone_0x102990000
MALLOC_SMALL          145000000-145800000    [ 8192K  8192K  8192K     0K] rw-/rwx SM=PRV    MallocHelperZone_0x102990000
MALLOC_SMALL          145800000-146000000    [ 8192K  8192K  8192K     0K] rw-/rwx SM=PRV    MallocHelperZone_0x102990000
MALLOC_SMALL          146000000-146800000    [ 8192K  8192K  8192K     0K] rw-/rwx SM=PRV    MallocHelperZone_0x102990000
MALLOC_SMALL          146800000-147000000    [ 8192K  8192K  8192K     0K] rw-/rwx SM=PRV    MallocHelperZone_0x102990000
MALLOC_SMALL          147000000-147800000    [ 8192K  8192K  8192K     0K] rw-/rwx SM=PRV    MallocHelperZone_0x102990000
MALLOC_SMALL          147800000-148000000    [ 8192K  8192K  8192K     0K] rw-/rwx SM=PRV    MallocHelperZone_0x102990000
MALLOC_SMALL          148000000-148800000    [ 8192K  8192K  8192K     0K] rw-/rwx SM=PRV    MallocHelperZone_0x102990000
MALLOC_SMALL          148800000-149000000    [ 8192K  8192K  8192K     0K] rw-/rwx SM=PRV    MallocHelperZone_0x102990000
MALLOC_SMALL          149000000-149800000    [ 8192K  8192K  8192K     0K] rw-/rwx SM=PRV    MallocHelperZone_0x102990000
MALLOC_SMALL          149800000-14a000000    [ 8192K  8192K  8192K     0K] rw-/rwx SM=PRV    MallocHelperZone_0x102990000
MALLOC_SMALL          14a000000-14a800000    [ 8192K  8192K  8192K     0K] rw-/rwx SM=PRV    MallocHelperZone_0x102990000
MALLOC_SMALL          14a800000-14b000000    [ 8192K  8192K  8192K     0K] rw-/rwx SM=PRV    MallocHelperZone_0x102990000
MALLOC_SMALL          14b000000-14b800000    [ 8192K  8192K  8192K     0K] rw-/rwx SM=PRV    MallocHelperZone_0x102990000
MALLOC_SMALL          14b800000-14c000000    [ 8192K  8192K  8192K     0K] rw-/rwx SM=PRV    MallocHelperZone_0x102990000
MALLOC_SMALL          14c000000-14c800000    [ 8192K  8192K  8192K     0K] rw-/rwx SM=PRV    MallocHelperZone_0x102990000
MALLOC_SMALL          14c800000-14d000000    [ 8192K  8192K  8192K     0K] rw-/rwx SM=PRV    MallocHelperZone_0x102990000
```

Type	Address Range	Virtual	Resident	Dirty	Swapped	Perm SM	Detail
MALLOC_SMALL	14d000000-14d800000	[8192K	8192K	8192K	0K]	rw-/rwx SM=PRV	MallocHelperZone_0x102990000
MALLOC_SMALL	14d800000-14e000000	[8192K	8192K	8192K	0K]	rw-/rwx SM=PRV	MallocHelperZone_0x102990000
MALLOC_SMALL	14e000000-14e800000	[8192K	32K	32K	0K]	rw-/rwx SM=PRV	MallocHelperZone_0x102990000
MALLOC_SMALL	14e800000-14f000000	[8192K	7136K	7136K	0K]	rw-/rwx SM=PRV	MallocHelperZone_0x102990000
Stack	16cd90000-16d58c000	[8176K	16K	16K	16K]	rw-/rwx SM=PRV	thread 0
Stack	16d590000-16d618000	[544K	0K	0K	16K]	rw-/rwx SM=PRV	thread 1
Stack	16d61c000-16d6a4000	[544K	16K	16K	0K]	rw-/rwx SM=PRV	thread 2
Stack	16d6a8000-16d730000	[544K	0K	0K	16K]	rw-/rwx SM=PRV	thread 3
Stack	16d734000-16d7bc000	[544K	0K	0K	16K]	rw-/rwx SM=PRV	thread 4
Stack	16d7c0000-16d848000	[544K	0K	0K	16K]	rw-/rwx SM=PRV	thread 5
__DATA	1e4c04000-1e4c04060	[96	0K	0K	96]	rw-/rw- SM=COW	/usr/lib/system/libsystem_blocks.dylib
__DATA	1e4c04060-1e4c04d18	[3256	0K	0K	3256]	rw-/rw- SM=COW	/usr/lib/system/libxpc.dylib
__DATA	1e4c04d18-1e4c05050	[824	0K	0K	824]	rw-/rw- SM=COW	/usr/lib/system/libsystem_trace.dylib
__DATA	1e4c05050-1e4c0c788	[30K	18K	1928	12K]	rw-/rw- SM=COW	/usr/lib/system/libcorecrypto.dylib
__DATA	1e4c0c788-1e4c0ea24	[9K	9K	9K	0K]	rw-/rw- SM=COW	/usr/lib/system/libsystem_malloc.dylib
unused __DATA	1e4c0ea24-1e4c0ea40	[28	28	28	0K]	rw-/rw- SM=COW	on dirty page unused system shared lib __DATA
__DATA	1e4c0ea40-1e4c120c0	[14K	14K	14K	0K]	rw-/rw- SM=COW	/usr/lib/libobjc.A.dylib
__DATA	1e4c120c0-1e4c120f9	[57	57	57	0K]	rw-/rw- SM=COW	/usr/lib/system/libsystem_featureflags.dylib
unused __DATA	1e4c120f9-1e4c12100	[7	7	7	0K]	rw-/rw- SM=COW	on dirty page unused system shared lib __DATA
__DATA	1e4c12100-1e4c14270	[8K	8K	8K	624]	rw-/rw- SM=COW	/usr/lib/system/libsystem_c.dylib
unused __DATA	1e4c14270-1e4c15000	[3472	0K	0K	3472]	rw-/rw- SM=COW	on dirty page unused system shared lib __DATA
__DATA	1e4c15000-1e4c1b720	[26K	14K	0K	12K]	rw-/rw- SM=COW	/usr/lib/libc++.1.dylib
__DATA	1e4c1b720-1e4c1ba68	[840	840	0K	0K]	rw-/rw- SM=COW	/usr/lib/libc++abi.dylib
__DATA	1e4c1ba68-1e4c1bcd9	[625	625	0K	0K]	rw-/rw- SM=COW	/usr/lib/system/libsystem_kernel.dylib
__DATA	1e4c1c000-1e4c24000	[32K	32K	0K	0K]	rw-/rw- SM=COW	/usr/lib/system/libsystem_pthread.dylib
__DATA	1e4c24000-1e4c28000	[16K	16K	0K	0K]	rw-/rw- SM=COW	/usr/lib/system/libsystem_pthread.dylib
__DATA	1e4c28000-1e4c28048	[72	72	0K	0K]	rw-/rw- SM=COW	/usr/lib/system/libsystem_pthread.dylib
__DATA	1e4c28048-1e4c28050	[8	8	0K	0K]	rw-/rw- SM=COW	/usr/lib/system/libdyld.dylib
__DATA	1e4c28050-1e4c28090	[64	64	0K	0K]	rw-/rw- SM=COW	/usr/lib/system/libsystem_platform.dylib
__DATA	1e4c28090-1e4c28be0	[2896	2896	0K	0K]	rw-/rw- SM=COW	/usr/lib/system/libsystem_info.dylib
__DATA	1e4c96958-1e4c96968	[16	16	0K	0K]	rw-/rw- SM=COW	/usr/lib/system/libsystem_darwin.dylib
__DATA	1e4c9de00-1e4c9de51	[81	81	0K	0K]	rw-/rw- SM=COW	/usr/lib/system/libsystem_notify.dylib
__DATA	1e4d33600-1e4d33bd9	[1497	1497	0K	0K]	rw-/rw- SM=COW	/usr/lib/system/libsystem_networkextension.dylib
__DATA	1e4d343b8-1e4d344c8	[272	272	0K	0K]	rw-/rw- SM=COW	/usr/lib/system/libsystem_asl.dylib
__DATA	1e4d6a118-1e4d6a158	[64	64	0K	0K]	rw-/rw- SM=COW	/usr/lib/system/libsystem_symptoms.dylib
__DATA	1e4deca18-1e4decb40	[296	296	0K	0K]	rw-/rw- SM=COW	/usr/lib/system/libsystem_containermanager.dylib
__DATA	1e4e2d090-1e4e2d159	[201	201	0K	0K]	rw-/rw- SM=COW	/usr/lib/system/libsystem_configuration.dylib
__DATA	1e4e2d160-1e4e2d188	[40	40	0K	0K]	rw-/rw- SM=COW	/usr/lib/system/libsystem_sandbox.dylib
__DATA	1e4e4f280-1e4e4f290	[16	16	0K	0K]	rw-/rw- SM=COW	/usr/lib/system/libquarantine.dylib
__DATA	1e4e61bb0-1e4e61c88	[216	216	0K	0K]	rw-/rw- SM=COW	/usr/lib/system/libsystem_coreservices.dylib
__DATA	1e4e71a20-1e4e71a24	[4	4	0K	0K]	rw-/rw- SM=COW	/usr/lib/system/libsystem_m.dylib
__DATA	1e4e71ae8-1e4e723d9	[2289	2289	0K	0K]	rw-/rw- SM=COW	/usr/lib/system/libunwind.dylib
__DATA	1e4e723e0-1e4e723e8	[8	8	0K	0K]	rw-/rw- SM=COW	/usr/lib/liboah.dylib
__DATA	1e4e723e8-1e4e723f8	[16	16	0K	0K]	rw-/rw- SM=COW	/usr/lib/system/libcopyfile.dylib
__DATA	1e4e723f8-1e4e733f8	[4K	4K	0K	0K]	rw-/rw- SM=COW	/usr/lib/system/libcompiler_rt.dylib
__DATA	1e4e733f8-1e4e73438	[64	64	0K	0K]	rw-/rw- SM=COW	/usr/lib/system/libsystem_secinit.dylib
__DATA	1e4e73438-1e4e73468	[48	48	0K	0K]	rw-/rw- SM=COW	/usr/lib/system/libsystem_dnssd.dylib
__DATA	1e4e73468-1e4e73470	[8	8	0K	0K]	rw-/rw- SM=COW	/usr/lib/libSystem.B.dylib
unused __DATA_DIRTY	1e7930000-1e7930120	[288	0K	0K	288]	rw-/rw- SM=COW	on dirty page unused /usr/lib/libMobileGestalt.dylib
unused __DATA_DIRTY	1e7930120-1e7930170	[80	0K	0K	80]	rw-/rw- SM=COW	on dirty page unused /usr/lib/libUniversalAccess.dylib
unused __DATA_DIRTY	1e7930170-1e7930190	[32	0K	0K	32]	rw-/rw- SM=COW	on dirty page unused /usr/lib/libapp_launch_measurement.dylib
unused __DATA_DIRTY	1e7930190-1e7931010	[3712	0K	0K	3712]	rw-/rw- SM=COW	on dirty page unused /usr/lib/libboringssl.dylib
__DATA_DIRTY	1e7931010-1e79321e0	[4K	0K	0K	4K]	rw-/rw- SM=COW	/usr/lib/libc++.1.dylib
__DATA_DIRTY	1e79321e0-1e7932208	[40	0K	0K	40]	rw-/rw- SM=COW	/usr/lib/libc++abi.dylib
unused __DATA_DIRTY	1e7932208-1e7934000	[7K	0K	0K	7K]	rw-/rw- SM=COW	on dirty page unused /usr/lib/libcoroutine.dylib
unused __DATA_DIRTY	1e7938000-1e793a1c8	[8K	0K	0K	8K]	rw-/rw- SM=COW	on dirty page unused /usr/lib/libnetwork.dylib
unused __DATA	1e793a1c8-1e793a200	[56	0K	0K	56]	rw-/rw- SM=COW	on dirty page unused system shared lib __DATA
__DATA_DIRTY	1e793a200-1e793d070	[12K	0K	0K	12K]	rw-/rw- SM=COW	/usr/lib/libobjc.A.dylib
unused __DATA_DIRTY	1e793d070-1e793d200	[400	0K	0K	400]	rw-/rw- SM=COW	on dirty page unused /usr/lib/libpartition2_dynamic.dylib
unused __DATA_DIRTY	1e793d200-1e793d299	[153	0K	0K	153]	rw-/rw- SM=COW	on dirty page unused /usr/lib/libpmenergy.dylib
unused __DATA	1e793d299-1e793d2a0	[7	0K	0K	7]	rw-/rw- SM=COW	on dirty page unused system shared lib __DATA
unused __DATA_DIRTY	1e793d2a0-1e793d3e8	[328	0K	0K	328]	rw-/rw- SM=COW	on dirty page unused /usr/lib/libprequelite.dylib
unused __DATA_DIRTY	1e793d3e8-1e793d4f8	[272	0K	0K	272]	rw-/rw- SM=COW	on dirty page unused /usr/lib/libquic.dylib
unused __DATA_DIRTY	1e793d4f8-1e793d530	[56	0K	0K	56]	rw-/rw- SM=COW	on dirty page unused /usr/lib/libsandbox.1.dylib
unused __DATA	1e793d530-1e793d540	[16	0K	0K	16]	rw-/rw- SM=COW	on dirty page unused system shared lib __DATA
unused __DATA_DIRTY	1e793d540-1e7940000	[11K	0K	0K	11K]	rw-/rw- SM=COW	on dirty page unused /usr/lib/libsqlite3.dylib
unused __DATA_DIRTY	1e795c000-1e795e610	[10K	0K	0K	10K]	rw-/rw- SM=COW	on dirty page unused /usr/lib/swift/libswiftFoundation.dylib
unused __DATA_DIRTY	1e795e610-1e795e7a0	[400	0K	0K	400]	rw-/rw- SM=COW	on dirty page unused /usr/lib/swift/libswiftObjectiveC.dylib
unused __DATA_DIRTY	1e795e7a0-1e795e7b8	[24	0K	0K	24]	rw-/rw- SM=COW	on dirty page unused /usr/lib/swift/libswiftos.dylib
__DATA_DIRTY	1e795e7b8-1e795ef10	[1880	0K	0K	1880]	rw-/rw- SM=COW	/usr/lib/system/libcorecrypto.dylib
unused __DATA	1e795ef10-1e795ef40	[48	0K	0K	48]	rw-/rw- SM=COW	on dirty page unused system shared lib __DATA
__DATA_DIRTY	1e795ef40-1e79628e8	[14K	0K	0K	14K]	rw-/rw- SM=COW	/usr/lib/system/libdispatch.dylib
__DATA_DIRTY	1e79628e8-1e7962908	[32	0K	0K	32]	rw-/rw- SM=COW	/usr/lib/system/libdyld.dylib
unused __DATA	1e7962908-1e7962910	[8	0K	0K	8]	rw-/rw- SM=COW	on dirty page unused system shared lib __DATA
__DATA_DIRTY	1e7962910-1e7962a6c	[348	0K	0K	348]	rw-/rw- SM=COW	/usr/lib/system/libsystem_asl.dylib
unused __DATA	1e7962a6c-1e7962a70	[4	0K	0K	4]	rw-/rw- SM=COW	on dirty page unused system shared lib __DATA
__DATA_DIRTY	1e7962a70-1e7962c68	[504	0K	0K	504]	rw-/rw- SM=COW	/usr/lib/system/libsystem_blocks.dylib
__DATA_DIRTY	1e7962c68-1e79657f0	[11K	6K	6K	5K]	rw-/rw- SM=COW	/usr/lib/system/libsystem_c.dylib
__DATA_DIRTY	1e79657f0-1e7965820	[48	48	48	0K]	rw-/rw- SM=COW	/usr/lib/system/libsystem_darwin.dylib
__DATA_DIRTY	1e7965820-1e7965830	[16	16	16	0K]	rw-/rw- SM=COW	/usr/lib/system/libsystem_featureflags.dylib
__DATA_DIRTY	1e7965830-1e7965ac0	[656	656	656	0K]	rw-/rw- SM=COW	/usr/lib/system/libsystem_info.dylib
__DATA_DIRTY	1e7965ac0-1e7966184	[1732	1732	1732	0K]	rw-/rw- SM=COW	/usr/lib/system/libsystem_kernel.dylib
unused __DATA	1e7966184-1e7966188	[4	4	4	0K]	rw-/rw- SM=COW	on dirty page unused system shared lib __DATA
__DATA_DIRTY	1e7966188-1e79663a0	[536	536	536	0K]	rw-/rw- SM=COW	/usr/lib/system/libsystem_malloc.dylib
__DATA_DIRTY	1e79663a0-1e79663e1	[65	65	65	0K]	rw-/rw- SM=COW	/usr/lib/system/libsystem_networkextension.dylib
unused __DATA	1e79663e1-1e79663e8	[7	7	7	0K]	rw-/rw- SM=COW	on dirty page unused system shared lib __DATA
__DATA_DIRTY	1e79663e8-1e79663f0	[8	8	8	0K]	rw-/rw- SM=COW	/usr/lib/system/libsystem_notify.dylib
__DATA_DIRTY	1e79663f0-1e7966404	[20	20	20	0K]	rw-/rw- SM=COW	/usr/lib/system/libsystem_platform.dylib
unused __DATA	1e7966404-1e7968000	[7K	7K	7K	0K]	rw-/rw- SM=COW	on dirty page unused system shared lib __DATA
__DATA_DIRTY	1e7968000-1e796d838	[22K	0K	0K	22K]	rw-/rw- SM=COW	/usr/lib/system/libsystem_pthread.dylib
__DATA_DIRTY	1e796d838-1e796d848	[16	0K	0K	16]	rw-/rw- SM=COW	/usr/lib/system/libsystem_symptoms.dylib
__DATA_DIRTY	1e796d848-1e796dcb8	[1136	0K	0K	1136]	rw-/rw- SM=COW	/usr/lib/system/libsystem_trace.dylib
__DATA_DIRTY	1e796dcb8-1e796e708	[2640	0K	0K	2640]	rw-/rw- SM=COW	/usr/lib/system/libxpc.dylib
unused __DATA	1e796e708-1e7970000	[6K	0K	0K	6K]	rw-/rw- SM=COW	on dirty page unused system shared lib __DATA
__AUTH	1e7970008-1e79701b8	[440	440	0K	0K]	rw-/rw- SM=COW	/usr/lib/system/libsystem_trace.dylib
__AUTH	1e79701b8-1e7970218	[96	96	0K	0K]	rw-/rw- SM=COW	/usr/lib/system/libcorecrypto.dylib
__AUTH	1e7974000-1e797c000	[32K	32K	0K	0K]	rw-/rw- SM=COW	/usr/lib/system/libsystem_malloc.dylib

```
__DATA            1e797c000-1e797d400 [    5K    5K    0K    0K] rw-/rw- SM=COW    /usr/lib/system/libdispatch.dylib
__AUTH            1e797d400-1e797d478 [   120   120    0K    0K] rw-/rw- SM=COW    /usr/lib/libobjc.A.dylib
__AUTH            1e797d478-1e797e190 [  3352  3352    0K    0K] rw-/rw- SM=COW    /usr/lib/system/libsystem_c.dylib
__AUTH            1e797e190-1e7980628 [    9K    8K    0K  1576] rw-/rw- SM=COW    /usr/lib/libc++.1.dylib
__AUTH            1e7980628-1e7980670 [    72    0K    0K    72] rw-/rw- SM=COW    /usr/lib/libc++abi.dylib
__AUTH            1e7980670-1e79806b0 [    64    0K    0K    64] rw-/rw- SM=COW    /usr/lib/system/libdyld.dylib
__AUTH            1e79806b0-1e7980880 [   464    0K    0K   464] rw-/rw- SM=COW    /usr/lib/system/libsystem_info.dylib
unused __AUTH     1e7980880-1e7982740 [    8K    0K    0K    8K] rw-/rw- SM=COW    ...y page  unused
/System/Library/Frameworks/CoreFoundation.framework/Versions/A/CoreFoundation
unused __AUTH     1e7982740-1e7984000 [    6K    0K    0K    6K] rw-/rw- SM=COW
...eServices.framework/Versions/A/Frameworks/LaunchServices.framework/Versions/A/LaunchServices
__AUTH            1e7a0a640-1e7a0a660 [    32    32    0K    0K] rw-/rw- SM=COW    /usr/lib/system/libcommonCrypto.dylib
__AUTH            1e7a0a660-1e7a0a668 [     8     8    0K    0K] rw-/rw- SM=COW    /usr/lib/libSystem.B.dylib
__OBJC_RW         1e87f0000-1e8b08000 [  3168K 1600K    0K   16K] rw-/rw- SM=COW    /usr/lib/libobjc.A.dylib
MALLOC_NANO       600000000000-600008000000 [128.0M   80K   80K   64K] rw-/rwx SM=PRV    DefaultMallocZone_0x1029cc000
MALLOC_NANO (empty) 600008000000-600010000000 [128.0M    0K    0K    0K] rw-/rwx SM=PRV
MALLOC_NANO (empty) 600010000000-600018000000 [128.0M    0K    0K    0K] rw-/rwx SM=PRV
MALLOC_NANO (empty) 600018000000-600020000000 [128.0M    0K    0K    0K] rw-/rwx SM=PRV

==== Legend
SM=sharing mode:
        COW=copy_on_write PRV=private NUL=empty ALI=aliased
        SHM=shared ZER=zero_filled S/A=shared_alias
PURGE=purgeable mode:
        V=volatile N=nonvolatile E=empty    otherwise is unpurgeable

==== Summary for process 92806
ReadOnly portion of Libraries: Total=582.2M resident=18.4M(3%) swapped_out_or_unallocated=563.8M(97%)
Writable regions: Total=1.7G written=1.2G(68%) resident=592.2M(34%) swapped_out=587.0M(34%) unallocated=552.7M(32%)
```

	VIRTUAL	RESIDENT	DIRTY	SWAPPED	VOLATILE	NONVOL	EMPTY	REGION	
REGION TYPE	SIZE	SIZE	SIZE	SIZE	SIZE	SIZE	SIZE	COUNT (non-coalesced)
===========	=======	========	=====	=======	========	======	=====	=======	
Kernel Alloc Once	32K	0K	0K	16K	0K	0K	0K	1	
MALLOC guard page	96K	0K	0K	0K	0K	0K	0K	5	
MALLOC metadata	224K	192K	192K	32K	0K	0K	0K	10	
MALLOC_NANO	128.0M	80K	80K	64K	0K	0K	0K	1	see MALLOC ZONE table below
MALLOC_NANO (empty)	384.0M	0K	0K	0K	0K	0K	0K	3	see MALLOC ZONE table below
MALLOC_SMALL	1.2G	591.9M	591.9M	586.8M	0K	0K	0K	151	see MALLOC ZONE table below
MALLOC_TINY	1024K	16K	16K	16K	0K	0K	0K	1	see MALLOC ZONE table below
STACK GUARD	56.1M	0K	0K	0K	0K	0K	0K	6	
Stack	10.6M	32K	32K	80K	0K	0K	0K	6	
__AUTH	46K	44K	0K	2176	0K	0K	0K	11	
__AUTH_CONST	67K	67K	0K	0K	0K	0K	0K	38	
__DATA	173K	144K	48K	29K	0K	0K	0K	37	
__DATA_CONST	258K	146K	32K	16K	0K	0K	0K	40	
__DATA_DIRTY	73K	9K	9K	64K	0K	0K	0K	21	
__LINKEDIT	577.6M	14.0M	0K	0K	0K	0K	0K	3	
__OBJC_CONST	10K	10K	0K	0K	0K	0K	0K	5	
__OBJC_RO	83.0M	51.4M	0K	0K	0K	0K	0K	1	
__OBJC_RW	3168K	1600K	0K	16K	0K	0K	0K	1	
__TEXT	4708K	4468K	0K	0K	0K	0K	0K	43	
dyld private memory	1024K	16K	16K	0K	0K	0K	0K	1	
shared memory	16K	16K	16K	0K	0K	0K	0K	1	
unused but dirty shlib __DATA	72K	7K	7K	65K	0K	0K	0K	30	
===========	=======	========	=====	=======	========	======	=====	=======	
TOTAL	2.4G	664.0M	592.4M	587.2M	0K	0K	0K	416	

	VIRTUAL	RESIDENT	DIRTY	SWAPPED	ALLOCATION	BYTES	DIRTY+SWAP		REGION
MALLOC ZONE	SIZE	SIZE	SIZE	SIZE	COUNT	ALLOCATED	FRAG SIZE	% FRAG	COUNT
===========	=======	=========	=========	=========	=========	=========	=========	======	======	
MallocHelperZone_0x102990000	1.2G	592.0M	592.0M	586.8M	1202002	1.1G	5022K	1%	152
DefaultMallocZone_0x1029cc000	128.0M	80K	80K	'64K	211	9K	135K	94%	1
===========	=======	=========	=========	=========	=========	=========	=========	======	======	
TOTAL	1.3G	592.0M	592.0M	586.8M	1202213	1.1G	5157K	1%	153

Note: The saved core dump includes all reserved virtual memory, not only committed memory. As a result, for sparse small-size heap allocations, the size of a memory dump may be very large far exceeding the memory size shown in Activity Monitor.

2.   Load a core dump *App9-92806-20221209T003559Z* and *App9* executable:

```
% lldb -c ~/AMCDA-Dumps/App9-92806-20221209T003559Z -f
~/AMCDA-Dumps/Apps/App9/Build/Products/Release/App9
(lldb) target create "/Users/training/AMCDA-Dumps/Apps/App9/Build/Products/Release/App9" --
core "/Users/training/AMCDA-Dumps/App9-92806-20221209T003559Z"
Core file '/Users/training/AMCDA-Dumps/App9-92806-20221209T003559Z' (arm64) was loaded.
```

3. Identify the "section stream":

```
(lldb) image dump sections App9-92806-20221209T003559Z
Sections for '/Users/training/AMCDA-Dumps/App9-92806-20221209T003559Z' (arm64):
  SectID     Type             Load Address                             Perm File Off.  File Size  Flags      Section Name
  ---------- ---------------- ---------------------------------------  ---- ---------- ---------- ---------- ----------------------------
  0x00000100 container        [0x0000000102874000-0x0000000102878000)* r-x  0x00004000 0x00004000 0x00000000 App9-92806-20221209T003559Z.
  0x00000200 container        [0x0000000102878000-0x000000010287c000)* r--  0x00008000 0x00004000 0x00000000 App9-92806-20221209T003559Z.
  0x00000300 container        [0x000000010287c000-0x0000000102884000)* r--  0x0000c000 0x00008000 0x00000000 App9-92806-20221209T003559Z.
  0x00000400 container        [0x0000000102884000-0x0000000102984000)* r--  0x00014000 0x00100000 0x00000000 App9-92806-20221209T003559Z.
  0x00000500 container        [0x0000000102984000-0x000000010298c000)* rw-  0x00114000 0x00008000 0x00000000 App9-92806-20221209T003559Z.
  0x00000600 container        [0x000000010298c000-0x0000000102990000)* r--  0x0011c000 0x00004000 0x00000000 App9-92806-20221209T003559Z.
  0x00000700 container        [0x0000000102990000-0x0000000102994000)* r--  0x00120000 0x00004000 0x00000000 App9-92806-20221209T003559Z.
  0x00000800 container        [0x0000000102994000-0x0000000102998000)* rw-  0x00124000 0x00004000 0x00000000 App9-92806-20221209T003559Z.
  0x00000900 container        [0x000000010299c000-0x00000001029a4000)* rw-  0x00128000 0x00008000 0x00000000 App9-92806-20221209T003559Z.
  0x00000a00 container        [0x00000001029ac000-0x00000001029b4000)* rw-  0x00130000 0x00008000 0x00000000 App9-92806-20221209T003559Z.
  0x00000b00 container        [0x00000001029bc000-0x00000001029c4000)* rw-  0x00138000 0x00008000 0x00000000 App9-92806-20221209T003559Z.
  0x00000c00 container        [0x00000001029c8000-0x00000001029cc000)* r--  0x00140000 0x00004000 0x00000000 App9-92806-20221209T003559Z.
  0x00000d00 container        [0x00000001029cc000-0x00000001029d0000)* r--  0x00144000 0x00004000 0x00000000 App9-92806-20221209T003559Z.
  0x00000e00 container        [0x00000001029d0000-0x00000001029d4000)* rw-  0x00148000 0x00004000 0x00000000 App9-92806-20221209T003559Z.
  0x00000f00 container        [0x00000001029d4000-0x00000001029dc000)* rw-  0x0014c000 0x00008000 0x00000000 App9-92806-20221209T003559Z.
  0x00001000 container        [0x00000001029dc000-0x00000001029e0000)* rw-  0x00154000 0x00004000 0x00000000 App9-92806-20221209T003559Z.
  0x00001100 container        [0x0000000102a48000-0x0000000102aa8000)* r-x  0x00158000 0x00060000 0x00000000 App9-92806-20221209T003559Z.
  0x00001200 container        [0x0000000102aa8000-0x0000000102ac0000)* r--  0x001b8000 0x00018000 0x00000000 App9-92806-20221209T003559Z.
  0x00001300 container        [0x0000000102ac0000-0x0000000102ac4000)* rw-  0x001d0000 0x00004000 0x00000000 App9-92806-20221209T003559Z.
  0x00001400 container        [0x0000000102ac4000-0x0000000102afc000)* r--  0x001d4000 0x00038000 0x00000000 App9-92806-20221209T003559Z.
  0x00001500 container        [0x0000000103000000-0x0000000103800000)* rw-  0x0020c000 0x00800000 0x00000000 App9-92806-20221209T003559Z.
  0x00001600 container        [0x0000000103800000-0x0000000104000000)* rw-  0x00a0c000 0x00800000 0x00000000 App9-92806-20221209T003559Z.
  0x00001700 container        [0x0000000104000000-0x0000000104800000)* rw-  0x0120c000 0x00800000 0x00000000 App9-92806-20221209T003559Z.
  0x00001800 container        [0x0000000104800000-0x0000000105000000)* rw-  0x01a0c000 0x00800000 0x00000000 App9-92806-20221209T003559Z.
  0x00001900 container        [0x0000000105000000-0x0000000105800000)* rw-  0x0220c000 0x00800000 0x00000000 App9-92806-20221209T003559Z.
  0x00001a00 container        [0x0000000105800000-0x0000000106000000)* rw-  0x02a0c000 0x00800000 0x00000000 App9-92806-20221209T003559Z.
  0x00001b00 container        [0x0000000106000000-0x0000000106800000)* rw-  0x0320c000 0x00800000 0x00000000 App9-92806-20221209T003559Z.
  0x00001c00 container        [0x0000000106800000-0x0000000107000000)* rw-  0x03a0c000 0x00800000 0x00000000 App9-92806-20221209T003559Z.
  0x00001d00 container        [0x0000000107000000-0x0000000107800000)* rw-  0x0420c000 0x00800000 0x00000000 App9-92806-20221209T003559Z.
  0x00001e00 container        [0x0000000107800000-0x0000000108000000)* rw-  0x04a0c000 0x00800000 0x00000000 App9-92806-20221209T003559Z.
  0x00001f00 container        [0x0000000108000000-0x0000000108800000)* rw-  0x0520c000 0x00800000 0x00000000 App9-92806-20221209T003559Z.
  0x00002000 container        [0x0000000108800000-0x0000000109000000)* rw-  0x05a0c000 0x00800000 0x00000000 App9-92806-20221209T003559Z.
  0x00002100 container        [0x0000000109000000-0x0000000109800000)* rw-  0x0620c000 0x00800000 0x00000000 App9-92806-20221209T003559Z.
  0x00002200 container        [0x0000000109800000-0x000000010a000000)* rw-  0x06a0c000 0x00800000 0x00000000 App9-92806-20221209T003559Z.
  0x00002300 container        [0x000000010a000000-0x000000010a800000)* rw-  0x0720c000 0x00800000 0x00000000 App9-92806-20221209T003559Z.
  0x00002400 container        [0x000000010a800000-0x000000010b000000)* rw-  0x07a0c000 0x00800000 0x00000000 App9-92806-20221209T003559Z.
  0x00002500 container        [0x000000010b000000-0x000000010b800000)* rw-  0x0820c000 0x00800000 0x00000000 App9-92806-20221209T003559Z.
  0x00002600 container        [0x000000010b800000-0x000000010c000000)* rw-  0x08a0c000 0x00800000 0x00000000 App9-92806-20221209T003559Z.
  0x00002700 container        [0x000000010c000000-0x000000010c800000)* rw-  0x0920c000 0x00800000 0x00000000 App9-92806-20221209T003559Z.
  0x00002800 container        [0x000000010c800000-0x000000010d000000)* rw-  0x09a0c000 0x00800000 0x00000000 App9-92806-20221209T003559Z.
  0x00002900 container        [0x000000010d000000-0x000000010d800000)* rw-  0x0a20c000 0x00800000 0x00000000 App9-92806-20221209T003559Z.
  0x00002a00 container        [0x000000010d800000-0x000000010e000000)* rw-  0x0aa0c000 0x00800000 0x00000000 App9-92806-20221209T003559Z.
  0x00002b00 container        [0x000000010e000000-0x000000010e800000)* rw-  0x0b20c000 0x00800000 0x00000000 App9-92806-20221209T003559Z.
  0x00002c00 container        [0x000000010e800000-0x000000010f000000)* rw-  0x0ba0c000 0x00800000 0x00000000 App9-92806-20221209T003559Z.
  0x00002d00 container        [0x000000010f000000-0x000000010f800000)* rw-  0x0c20c000 0x00800000 0x00000000 App9-92806-20221209T003559Z.
  0x00002e00 container        [0x000000010f800000-0x0000000110000000)* rw-  0x0ca0c000 0x00800000 0x00000000 App9-92806-20221209T003559Z.
  0x00002f00 container        [0x0000000110000000-0x0000000110800000)* rw-  0x0d20c000 0x00800000 0x00000000 App9-92806-20221209T003559Z.
  0x00003000 container        [0x0000000110800000-0x0000000111000000)* rw-  0x0da0c000 0x00800000 0x00000000 App9-92806-20221209T003559Z.
  0x00003100 container        [0x0000000111000000-0x0000000111800000)* rw-  0x0e20c000 0x00800000 0x00000000 App9-92806-20221209T003559Z.
  0x00003200 container        [0x0000000111800000-0x0000000112000000)* rw-  0x0ea0c000 0x00800000 0x00000000 App9-92806-20221209T003559Z.
  0x00003300 container        [0x0000000112000000-0x0000000112800000)* rw-  0x0f20c000 0x00800000 0x00000000 App9-92806-20221209T003559Z.
  0x00003400 container        [0x0000000112800000-0x0000000113000000)* rw-  0x0fa0c000 0x00800000 0x00000000 App9-92806-20221209T003559Z.
  0x00003500 container        [0x0000000113000000-0x0000000113800000)* rw-  0x1020c000 0x00800000 0x00000000 App9-92806-20221209T003559Z.
  0x00003600 container        [0x0000000113800000-0x0000000114000000)* rw-  0x10a0c000 0x00800000 0x00000000 App9-92806-20221209T003559Z.
  0x00003700 container        [0x0000000114000000-0x0000000114800000)* rw-  0x1120c000 0x00800000 0x00000000 App9-92806-20221209T003559Z.
  0x00003800 container        [0x0000000114800000-0x0000000115000000)* rw-  0x11a0c000 0x00800000 0x00000000 App9-92806-20221209T003559Z.
  0x00003900 container        [0x0000000115000000-0x0000000115800000)* rw-  0x1220c000 0x00800000 0x00000000 App9-92806-20221209T003559Z.
  0x00003a00 container        [0x0000000115800000-0x0000000116000000)* rw-  0x12a0c000 0x00800000 0x00000000 App9-92806-20221209T003559Z.
  0x00003b00 container        [0x0000000116000000-0x0000000116800000)* rw-  0x1320c000 0x00800000 0x00000000 App9-92806-20221209T003559Z.
  0x00003c00 container        [0x0000000116800000-0x0000000117000000)* rw-  0x13a0c000 0x00800000 0x00000000 App9-92806-20221209T003559Z.
  0x00003d00 container        [0x0000000117000000-0x0000000117800000)* rw-  0x1420c000 0x00800000 0x00000000 App9-92806-20221209T003559Z.
  0x00003e00 container        [0x0000000117800000-0x0000000118000000)* rw-  0x14a0c000 0x00800000 0x00000000 App9-92806-20221209T003559Z.
  0x00003f00 container        [0x0000000118000000-0x0000000118800000)* rw-  0x1520c000 0x00800000 0x00000000 App9-92806-20221209T003559Z.
  0x00004000 container        [0x0000000118800000-0x0000000119000000)* rw-  0x15a0c000 0x00800000 0x00000000 App9-92806-20221209T003559Z.
  0x00004100 container        [0x0000000119000000-0x0000000119800000)* rw-  0x1620c000 0x00800000 0x00000000 App9-92806-20221209T003559Z.
  0x00004200 container        [0x0000000119800000-0x000000011a000000)* rw-  0x16a0c000 0x00800000 0x00000000 App9-92806-20221209T003559Z.
  0x00004300 container        [0x000000011a000000-0x000000011a800000)* rw-  0x1720c000 0x00800000 0x00000000 App9-92806-20221209T003559Z.
  0x00004400 container        [0x000000011a800000-0x000000011b000000)* rw-  0x17a0c000 0x00800000 0x00000000 App9-92806-20221209T003559Z.
  0x00004500 container        [0x000000011b000000-0x000000011b800000)* rw-  0x1820c000 0x00800000 0x00000000 App9-92806-20221209T003559Z.
  0x00004600 container        [0x000000011b800000-0x000000011c000000)* rw-  0x18a0c000 0x00800000 0x00000000 App9-92806-20221209T003559Z.
  0x00004700 container        [0x000000011c000000-0x000000011c800000)* rw-  0x1920c000 0x00800000 0x00000000 App9-92806-20221209T003559Z.
  0x00004800 container        [0x000000011c800000-0x000000011d000000)* rw-  0x19a0c000 0x00800000 0x00000000 App9-92806-20221209T003559Z.
  0x00004900 container        [0x000000011d000000-0x000000011d800000)* rw-  0x1a20c000 0x00800000 0x00000000 App9-92806-20221209T003559Z.
  0x00004a00 container        [0x000000011d800000-0x000000011e000000)* rw-  0x1aa0c000 0x00800000 0x00000000 App9-92806-20221209T003559Z.
  0x00004b00 container        [0x000000011e000000-0x000000011e800000)* rw-  0x1b20c000 0x00800000 0x00000000 App9-92806-20221209T003559Z.
  0x00004c00 container        [0x000000011e800000-0x000000011f000000)* rw-  0x1ba0c000 0x00800000 0x00000000 App9-92806-20221209T003559Z.
  0x00004d00 container        [0x000000011f000000-0x000000011f800000)* rw-  0x1c20c000 0x00800000 0x00000000 App9-92806-20221209T003559Z.
  0x00004e00 container        [0x000000011f800000-0x0000000120000000)* rw-  0x1ca0c000 0x00800000 0x00000000 App9-92806-20221209T003559Z.
  0x00004f00 container        [0x0000000120000000-0x0000000120800000)* rw-  0x1d20c000 0x00800000 0x00000000 App9-92806-20221209T003559Z.
  0x00005000 container        [0x0000000120800000-0x0000000121000000)* rw-  0x1da0c000 0x00800000 0x00000000 App9-92806-20221209T003559Z.
  0x00005100 container        [0x0000000121000000-0x0000000121800000)* rw-  0x1e20c000 0x00800000 0x00000000 App9-92806-20221209T003559Z.
  0x00005200 container        [0x0000000121800000-0x0000000122000000)* rw-  0x1ea0c000 0x00800000 0x00000000 App9-92806-20221209T003559Z.
  0x00005300 container        [0x0000000122000000-0x0000000122800000)* rw-  0x1f20c000 0x00800000 0x00000000 App9-92806-20221209T003559Z.
  0x00005400 container        [0x0000000122800000-0x0000000123000000)* rw-  0x1fa0c000 0x00800000 0x00000000 App9-92806-20221209T003559Z.
  0x00005500 container        [0x0000000123000000-0x0000000123800000)* rw-  0x2020c000 0x00800000 0x00000000 App9-92806-20221209T003559Z.
  0x00005600 container        [0x0000000123800000-0x0000000124000000)* rw-  0x20a0c000 0x00800000 0x00000000 App9-92806-20221209T003559Z.
  0x00005700 container        [0x0000000124000000-0x0000000124800000)* rw-  0x2120c000 0x00800000 0x00000000 App9-92806-20221209T003559Z.
  0x00005800 container        [0x0000000124800000-0x0000000125000000)* rw-  0x21a0c000 0x00800000 0x00000000 App9-92806-20221209T003559Z.
  0x00005900 container        [0x0000000125000000-0x0000000125800000)* rw-  0x2220c000 0x00800000 0x00000000 App9-92806-20221209T003559Z.
  0x00005a00 container        [0x0000000125800000-0x0000000126000000)* rw-  0x22a0c000 0x00800000 0x00000000 App9-92806-20221209T003559Z.
  0x00005b00 container        [0x0000000126000000-0x0000000126800000)* rw-  0x2320c000 0x00800000 0x00000000 App9-92806-20221209T003559Z.
  0x00005c00 container        [0x0000000126800000-0x0000000127000000)* rw-  0x23a0c000 0x00800000 0x00000000 App9-92806-20221209T003559Z.
  0x00005d00 container        [0x0000000127000000-0x0000000127800000)* rw-  0x2420c000 0x00800000 0x00000000 App9-92806-20221209T003559Z.
```

```
0x00005e00 container     [0x0000000127800000-0x0000000128000000)* rw-  0x24a0c000 0x00800000 0x00000000 App9-92806-20221209T003559Z.
0x00005f00 container     [0x0000000128000000-0x0000000128800000)* rw-  0x2520c000 0x00800000 0x00000000 App9-92806-20221209T003559Z.
0x00006000 container     [0x0000000128800000-0x0000000129000000)* rw-  0x25a0c000 0x00800000 0x00000000 App9-92806-20221209T003559Z.
0x00006100 container     [0x0000000129000000-0x0000000129800000)* rw-  0x2620c000 0x00800000 0x00000000 App9-92806-20221209T003559Z.
0x00006200 container     [0x0000000129800000-0x000000012a000000)* rw-  0x26a0c000 0x00800000 0x00000000 App9-92806-20221209T003559Z.
0x00006300 container     [0x000000012a000000-0x000000012a800000)* rw-  0x2720c000 0x00800000 0x00000000 App9-92806-20221209T003559Z.
0x00006400 container     [0x000000012a800000-0x000000012b000000)* rw-  0x27a0c000 0x00800000 0x00000000 App9-92806-20221209T003559Z.
0x00006500 container     [0x000000012b600000-0x000000012b700000)* rw-  0x2820c000 0x00100000 0x00000000 App9-92806-20221209T003559Z.
0x00006600 container     [0x000000012b800000-0x000000012c000000)* rw-  0x2830c000 0x00800000 0x00000000 App9-92806-20221209T003559Z.
0x00006700 container     [0x000000012c000000-0x000000012c800000)* rw-  0x28b0c000 0x00800000 0x00000000 App9-92806-20221209T003559Z.
0x00006800 container     [0x000000012c800000-0x000000012d000000)* rw-  0x2930c000 0x00800000 0x00000000 App9-92806-20221209T003559Z.
0x00006900 container     [0x000000012d000000-0x000000012d800000)* rw-  0x29b0c000 0x00800000 0x00000000 App9-92806-20221209T003559Z.
0x00006a00 container     [0x000000012d800000-0x000000012e000000)* rw-  0x2a30c000 0x00800000 0x00000000 App9-92806-20221209T003559Z.
0x00006b00 container     [0x000000012e000000-0x000000012e800000)* rw-  0x2ab0c000 0x00800000 0x00000000 App9-92806-20221209T003559Z.
0x00006c00 container     [0x000000012e800000-0x000000012f000000)* rw-  0x2b30c000 0x00800000 0x00000000 App9-92806-20221209T003559Z.
0x00006d00 container     [0x000000012f000000-0x000000012f800000)* rw-  0x2bb0c000 0x00800000 0x00000000 App9-92806-20221209T003559Z.
0x00006e00 container     [0x000000012f800000-0x0000000130000000)* rw-  0x2c30c000 0x00800000 0x00000000 App9-92806-20221209T003559Z.
0x00006f00 container     [0x0000000130000000-0x0000000130800000)* rw-  0x2cb0c000 0x00800000 0x00000000 App9-92806-20221209T003559Z.
0x00007000 container     [0x0000000130800000-0x0000000131000000)* rw-  0x2d30c000 0x00800000 0x00000000 App9-92806-20221209T003559Z.
0x00007100 container     [0x0000000131000000-0x0000000131800000)* rw-  0x2db0c000 0x00800000 0x00000000 App9-92806-20221209T003559Z.
0x00007200 container     [0x0000000131800000-0x0000000132000000)* rw-  0x2e30c000 0x00800000 0x00000000 App9-92806-20221209T003559Z.
0x00007300 container     [0x0000000132000000-0x0000000132800000)* rw-  0x2eb0c000 0x00800000 0x00000000 App9-92806-20221209T003559Z.
0x00007400 container     [0x0000000132800000-0x0000000133000000)* rw-  0x2f30c000 0x00800000 0x00000000 App9-92806-20221209T003559Z.
0x00007500 container     [0x0000000133000000-0x0000000133800000)* rw-  0x2fb0c000 0x00800000 0x00000000 App9-92806-20221209T003559Z.
0x00007600 container     [0x0000000133800000-0x0000000134000000)* rw-  0x3030c000 0x00800000 0x00000000 App9-92806-20221209T003559Z.
0x00007700 container     [0x0000000134000000-0x0000000134800000)* rw-  0x30b0c000 0x00800000 0x00000000 App9-92806-20221209T003559Z.
0x00007800 container     [0x0000000134800000-0x0000000135000000)* rw-  0x3130c000 0x00800000 0x00000000 App9-92806-20221209T003559Z.
0x00007900 container     [0x0000000135000000-0x0000000135800000)* rw-  0x31b0c000 0x00800000 0x00000000 App9-92806-20221209T003559Z.
0x00007a00 container     [0x0000000135800000-0x0000000136000000)* rw-  0x3230c000 0x00800000 0x00000000 App9-92806-20221209T003559Z.
0x00007b00 container     [0x0000000136000000-0x0000000136800000)* rw-  0x32b0c000 0x00800000 0x00000000 App9-92806-20221209T003559Z.
0x00007c00 container     [0x0000000136800000-0x0000000137000000)* rw-  0x3330c000 0x00800000 0x00000000 App9-92806-20221209T003559Z.
0x00007d00 container     [0x0000000137000000-0x0000000137800000)* rw-  0x33b0c000 0x00800000 0x00000000 App9-92806-20221209T003559Z.
0x00007e00 container     [0x0000000137800000-0x0000000138000000)* rw-  0x3430c000 0x00800000 0x00000000 App9-92806-20221209T003559Z.
0x00007f00 container     [0x0000000138000000-0x0000000138800000)* rw-  0x34b0c000 0x00800000 0x00000000 App9-92806-20221209T003559Z.
0x00008000 container     [0x0000000138800000-0x0000000139000000)* rw-  0x3530c000 0x00800000 0x00000000 App9-92806-20221209T003559Z.
0x00008100 container     [0x0000000139000000-0x0000000139800000)* rw-  0x35b0c000 0x00800000 0x00000000 App9-92806-20221209T003559Z.
0x00008200 container     [0x0000000139800000-0x000000013a000000)* rw-  0x3630c000 0x00800000 0x00000000 App9-92806-20221209T003559Z.
0x00008300 container     [0x000000013a000000-0x000000013a800000)* rw-  0x36b0c000 0x00800000 0x00000000 App9-92806-20221209T003559Z.
0x00008400 container     [0x000000013a800000-0x000000013b000000)* rw-  0x3730c000 0x00800000 0x00000000 App9-92806-20221209T003559Z.
0x00008500 container     [0x000000013b000000-0x000000013b800000)* rw-  0x37b0c000 0x00800000 0x00000000 App9-92806-20221209T003559Z.
0x00008600 container     [0x000000013b800000-0x000000013c000000)* rw-  0x3830c000 0x00800000 0x00000000 App9-92806-20221209T003559Z.
0x00008700 container     [0x000000013c000000-0x000000013c800000)* rw-  0x38b0c000 0x00800000 0x00000000 App9-92806-20221209T003559Z.
0x00008800 container     [0x000000013c800000-0x000000013d000000)* rw-  0x3930c000 0x00800000 0x00000000 App9-92806-20221209T003559Z.
0x00008900 container     [0x000000013d000000-0x000000013d800000)* rw-  0x39b0c000 0x00800000 0x00000000 App9-92806-20221209T003559Z.
0x00008a00 container     [0x000000013d800000-0x000000013e000000)* rw-  0x3a30c000 0x00800000 0x00000000 App9-92806-20221209T003559Z.
0x00008b00 container     [0x000000013e000000-0x000000013e800000)* rw-  0x3ab0c000 0x00800000 0x00000000 App9-92806-20221209T003559Z.
0x00008c00 container     [0x000000013e800000-0x000000013f000000)* rw-  0x3b30c000 0x00800000 0x00000000 App9-92806-20221209T003559Z.
0x00008d00 container     [0x000000013f000000-0x000000013f800000)* rw-  0x3bb0c000 0x00800000 0x00000000 App9-92806-20221209T003559Z.
0x00008e00 container     [0x000000013f800000-0x0000000140000000)* rw-  0x3c30c000 0x00800000 0x00000000 App9-92806-20221209T003559Z.
0x00008f00 container     [0x0000000140000000-0x0000000140800000)* rw-  0x3cb0c000 0x00800000 0x00000000 App9-92806-20221209T003559Z.
0x00009000 container     [0x0000000140800000-0x0000000141000000)* rw-  0x3d30c000 0x00800000 0x00000000 App9-92806-20221209T003559Z.
0x00009100 container     [0x0000000141000000-0x0000000141800000)* rw-  0x3db0c000 0x00800000 0x00000000 App9-92806-20221209T003559Z.
0x00009200 container     [0x0000000141800000-0x0000000142000000)* rw-  0x3e30c000 0x00800000 0x00000000 App9-92806-20221209T003559Z.
0x00009300 container     [0x0000000142000000-0x0000000142800000)* rw-  0x3eb0c000 0x00800000 0x00000000 App9-92806-20221209T003559Z.
0x00009400 container     [0x0000000142800000-0x0000000143000000)* rw-  0x3f30c000 0x00800000 0x00000000 App9-92806-20221209T003559Z.
0x00009500 container     [0x0000000143000000-0x0000000143800000)* rw-  0x3fb0c000 0x00800000 0x00000000 App9-92806-20221209T003559Z.
0x00009600 container     [0x0000000143800000-0x0000000144000000)* rw-  0x4030c000 0x00800000 0x00000000 App9-92806-20221209T003559Z.
0x00009700 container     [0x0000000144000000-0x0000000144800000)* rw-  0x40b0c000 0x00800000 0x00000000 App9-92806-20221209T003559Z.
0x00009800 container     [0x0000000144800000-0x0000000145000000)* rw-  0x4130c000 0x00800000 0x00000000 App9-92806-20221209T003559Z.
0x00009900 container     [0x0000000145000000-0x0000000145800000)* rw-  0x41b0c000 0x00800000 0x00000000 App9-92806-20221209T003559Z.
0x00009a00 container     [0x0000000145800000-0x0000000146000000)* rw-  0x4230c000 0x00800000 0x00000000 App9-92806-20221209T003559Z.
0x00009b00 container     [0x0000000146000000-0x0000000146800000)* rw-  0x42b0c000 0x00800000 0x00000000 App9-92806-20221209T003559Z.
0x00009c00 container     [0x0000000146800000-0x0000000147000000)* rw-  0x4330c000 0x00800000 0x00000000 App9-92806-20221209T003559Z.
0x00009d00 container     [0x0000000147000000-0x0000000147800000)* rw-  0x43b0c000 0x00800000 0x00000000 App9-92806-20221209T003559Z.
0x00009e00 container     [0x0000000147800000-0x0000000148000000)* rw-  0x4430c000 0x00800000 0x00000000 App9-92806-20221209T003559Z.
0x00009f00 container     [0x0000000148000000-0x0000000148800000)* rw-  0x44b0c000 0x00800000 0x00000000 App9-92806-20221209T003559Z.
0x0000a000 container     [0x0000000148800000-0x0000000149000000)* rw-  0x4530c000 0x00800000 0x00000000 App9-92806-20221209T003559Z.
0x0000a100 container     [0x0000000149000000-0x0000000149800000)* rw-  0x45b0c000 0x00800000 0x00000000 App9-92806-20221209T003559Z.
0x0000a200 container     [0x0000000149800000-0x000000014a000000)* rw-  0x4630c000 0x00800000 0x00000000 App9-92806-20221209T003559Z.
0x0000a300 container     [0x000000014a000000-0x000000014a800000)* rw-  0x46b0c000 0x00800000 0x00000000 App9-92806-20221209T003559Z.
0x0000a400 container     [0x000000014a800000-0x000000014b000000)* rw-  0x4730c000 0x00800000 0x00000000 App9-92806-20221209T003559Z.
0x0000a500 container     [0x000000014b000000-0x000000014b800000)* rw-  0x47b0c000 0x00800000 0x00000000 App9-92806-20221209T003559Z.
0x0000a600 container     [0x000000014b800000-0x000000014c000000)* rw-  0x4830c000 0x00800000 0x00000000 App9-92806-20221209T003559Z.
0x0000a700 container     [0x000000014c000000-0x000000014c800000)* rw-  0x48b0c000 0x00800000 0x00000000 App9-92806-20221209T003559Z.
0x0000a800 container     [0x000000014c800000-0x000000014d000000)* rw-  0x4930c000 0x00800000 0x00000000 App9-92806-20221209T003559Z.
0x0000a900 container     [0x000000014d000000-0x000000014d800000)* rw-  0x49b0c000 0x00800000 0x00000000 App9-92806-20221209T003559Z.
0x0000aa00 container     [0x000000014d800000-0x000000014e000000)* rw-  0x4a30c000 0x00800000 0x00000000 App9-92806-20221209T003559Z.
0x0000ab00 container     [0x000000014e000000-0x000000014e800000)* rw-  0x4ab0c000 0x00800000 0x00000000 App9-92806-20221209T003559Z.
0x0000ac00 container     [0x000000014e800000-0x000000014f000000)* rw-  0x4b30c000 0x00800000 0x00000000 App9-92806-20221209T003559Z.
0x0000ad00 container     [0x000000016cd90000-0x000000016d58c000)* rw-  0x4bb0c000 0x007fc000 0x00000000 App9-92806-20221209T003559Z.
0x0000ae00 container     [0x000000016d590000-0x000000016d618000)* rw-  0x4c308000 0x00088000 0x00000000 App9-92806-20221209T003559Z.
0x0000af00 container     [0x000000016d61c000-0x000000016d6a4000)* rw-  0x4c390000 0x00088000 0x00000000 App9-92806-20221209T003559Z.
0x0000b000 container     [0x000000016d6a8000-0x000000016d730000)* rw-  0x4c418000 0x00088000 0x00000000 App9-92806-20221209T003559Z.
0x0000b100 container     [0x000000016d734000-0x000000016d7bc000)* rw-  0x4c4a0000 0x00088000 0x00000000 App9-92806-20221209T003559Z.
0x0000b200 container     [0x000000016d7c0000-0x000000016d848000)* rw-  0x4c528000 0x00088000 0x00000000 App9-92806-20221209T003559Z.
0x0000b300 container     [0x000000018e6dc000-0x00000001de098000)* r-x  0x4c5b0000 0x4f9bc000 0x00000000 App9-92806-20221209T003559Z.
0x0000b400 container     [0x00000001e0098000-0x00000001e2c04000)* r--  0x9bf6c000 0x02b6c000 0x00000000 App9-92806-20221209T003559Z.
0x0000b500 container     [0x00000001e4c04000-0x00000001e4c24000)* rw-  0x9ead8000 0x00020000 0x00000000 App9-92806-20221209T003559Z.
0x0000b600 container     [0x00000001e4c24000-0x00000001e4c28000)* rw-  0x9eaf8000 0x00004000 0x00000000 App9-92806-20221209T003559Z.
0x0000b700 container     [0x00000001e4c28000-0x00000001e6000000)* rw-  0x9eafc000 0x013d8000 0x00000000 App9-92806-20221209T003559Z.
0x0000b800 container     [0x00000001e6000000-0x00000001e7414000)* rw-  0x9fed4000 0x01414000 0x00000000 App9-92806-20221209T003559Z.
0x0000b900 container     [0x00000001e7414000-0x00000001e8b08000)* rw-  0xa12e8000 0x016f4000 0x00000000 App9-92806-20221209T003559Z.
0x0000ba00 container     [0x00000001e8b08000-0x00000001ebe90000)* r--  0xa29dc000 0x03388000 0x00000000 App9-92806-20221209T003559Z.
0x0000bb00 container     [0x00000001ede90000-0x00000001edebc000)* r--  0xa5d64000 0x0002c000 0x00000000 App9-92806-20221209T003559Z.
0x0000bc00 container     [0x00000001edebc000-0x00000002164f8000)* r-x  0xa5d90000 0x2863c000 0x00000000 App9-92806-20221209T003559Z.
0x0000bd00 container     [0x00000002184f8000-0x00000002193a0000)* r--  0xce3cc000 0x00ea8000 0x00000000 App9-92806-20221209T003559Z.
0x0000be00 container     [0x000000021b3a0000-0x000000021c000000)* rw-  0xcf274000 0x00c60000 0x00000000 App9-92806-20221209T003559Z.
0x0000bf00 container     [0x000000021c000000-0x000000021dc40000)* rw-  0xcfed4000 0x01c40000 0x00000000 App9-92806-20221209T003559Z.
0x0000c000 container     [0x000000021dc40000-0x000000021ea24000)* rw-  0xd1b14000 0x00de4000 0x00000000 App9-92806-20221209T003559Z.
0x0000c100 container     [0x000000021ea24000-0x000000021fcf0000)* r--  0xd28f8000 0x012cc000 0x00000000 App9-92806-20221209T003559Z.
0x0000c200 container     [0x0000000221cf0000-0x0000000249dec000)* r--  0xd3bc4000 0x280fc000 0x00000000 App9-92806-20221209T003559Z.
0x0000c300 container     [0x0000600000000000-0x0000600008000000)* rw-  0xfbcc0000 0x08000000 0x00000000 App9-92806-20221209T003559Z.
```

```
0x0000c400 container     [0x0000600008000000-0x0000600010000000)* rw-  0x103cc0000 0x08000000 0x00000000 App9-92806-20221209T003559Z.
0x0000c500 container     [0x0000600010000000-0x0000600018000000)* rw-  0x10bcc0000 0x08000000 0x00000000 App9-92806-20221209T003559Z.
0x0000c600 container     [0x0000600018000000-0x0000600020000000)* rw-  0x113cc0000 0x08000000 0x00000000 App9-92806-20221209T003559Z.
```

4.   Calculate the size of the segment 0x0000000140000000-0x0000000140800000 in pointers:

```
(lldb) print (0x0000000140800000 - 0x0000000140000000)/8
(long) $0 = 1048576
```

5.   Examine the segment contents for any execution residue and hints:

```
(lldb) x/1048576a 0x0000000140000000 --force
0x140000000:  0x000000013f800000
0x140000008:  0x0000000142800000
0x140000010:  0x00000000007f7c00
0x140000018:  0x0000000000000005
0x140000020:  0x0000000000000000
0x140000028:  0x0000000200000002
0x140000030:  0x0000000200000002
0x140000038:  0x0000000200000002
0x140000040:  0x0000000200000002
[...]
0x140007f30:  0x0000000200000002
0x140007f38:  0x0000000200000002
0x140007f40:  0x0000000200000002
0x140007f48:  0x0000000200000002
0x140007f50:  0x0000000200000002
0x140007f58:  0x0000000200000002
0x140007f60:  0x0000000200000002
0x140007f68:  0x0000000200000002
0x140007f70:  0x0000000200000002
0x140007f78:  0x0000000200000002
0x140007f80:  0x0000000200000002
0x140007f88:  0x0000000200000002
0x140007f90:  0x0000000200000002
0x140007f98:  0x0000000200000002
0x140007fa0:  0x0000800100000002
0x140007fa8:  0x0000000000000000
0x140007fb0:  0x0000000000000000
0x140007fb8:  0x0000000000000000
0x140007fc0:  0x0000000000000000
0x140007fc8:  0x0000000000000000
0x140007fd0:  0x0000000000000000
0x140007fd8:  0x0000000000000000
0x140007fe0:  0x0000000000000000
0x140007fe8:  0x0000000000000000
0x140007ff0:  0x0000000000000000
0x140007ff8:  0x0000000000000000
0x140008000:  0x0000000000000000
0x140008008:  0x0000000000000000
0x140008010:  0x0000000000000000
0x140008018:  0x0000000000000000
0x140008020:  0x0000000000000000
0x140008028:  0x0000000000000000
0x140008030:  0x0000000000000000
0x140008038:  0x0000000000000000
0x140008040:  0x0000000000000000
0x140008048:  0x0000000000000000
0x140008050:  0x0000000000000000
0x140008058:  0x0000000000000000
0x140008060:  0x0000000000000000
```

```
0x140008068:  0x0000000000000000
0x140008070:  0x0000000000000000
0x140008078:  0x0000000000000000
0x140008080:  0x0000000000000000
0x140008088:  0x0000000000000000
0x140008090:  0x0000000000000000
0x140008098:  0x0000000000000000
0x1400080a0:  0x0000000000000000
0x1400080a8:  0x0000000000000000
0x1400080b0:  0x0000000000000000
0x1400080b8:  0x0000000000000000
0x1400080c0:  0x0000000000000000
0x1400080c8:  0x0000000000000000
0x1400080d0:  0x0000000000000000
0x1400080d8:  0x0000000000000000
0x1400080e0:  0x0000000000000000
0x1400080e8:  0x0000000000000000
0x1400080f0:  0x0000000000000000
0x1400080f8:  0x0000000000000000
0x140008100:  0x0000000000000000
0x140008108:  0x0000000000000000
0x140008110:  0x0000000000000000
0x140008118:  0x0000000000000000
0x140008120:  0x0000000000000000
0x140008128:  0x0000000000000000
0x140008130:  0x0000000000000000
0x140008138:  0x0000000000000000
0x140008140:  0x0000000000000000
0x140008148:  0x0000000000000000
0x140008150:  0x0000000000000000
0x140008158:  0x0000000000000000
0x140008160:  0x0000000000000000
0x140008168:  0x0000000000000000
0x140008170:  0x0000000000000000
0x140008178:  0x0000000000000000
0x140008180:  0x0000000000000000
0x140008188:  0x0000000000000000
0x140008190:  0x0000000000000000
0x140008198:  0x0000000000000000
0x1400081a0:  0x0000000000000000
0x1400081a8:  0x0000000000000000
0x1400081b0:  0x0000000000000000
0x1400081b8:  0x0000000000000000
0x1400081c0:  0x0000000000000000
0x1400081c8:  0x0000000000000000
0x1400081d0:  0x0000000000000000
0x1400081d8:  0x0000000000000000
0x1400081e0:  0x0000000000000000
0x1400081e8:  0x0000000000000000
0x1400081f0:  0x0000000000000000
0x1400081f8:  0x0000746600000000
0x140008200:  0x657461636f6c6c61
0x140008208:  0x79726f6d656d2064
0x140008210:  0x0000000000000000
0x140008218:  0x0000000000000000
0x140008220:  0x0000000102877c48  App9`procD
0x140008228:  0x0000000000000000
0x140008230:  0x0000000000000000
0x140008238:  0x0000000000000000
0x140008240:  0x0000000000000000
0x140008248:  0x0000000000000000
```

```
0x140008250:  0x0000000000000000
0x140008258:  0x0000000000000000
0x140008260:  0x0000000000000000
0x140008268:  0x0000000000000000
0x140008270:  0x0000000000000000
0x140008278:  0x0000000000000000
0x140008280:  0x0000000000000000
0x140008288:  0x0000000000000000
0x140008290:  0x0000000000000000
0x140008298:  0x0000000000000000
0x1400082a0:  0x0000000000000000
0x1400082a8:  0x0000000000000000
0x1400082b0:  0x0000000000000000
0x1400082b8:  0x0000000000000000
0x1400082c0:  0x0000000000000000
0x1400082c8:  0x0000000000000000
0x1400082d0:  0x0000000000000000
0x1400082d8:  0x0000000000000000
0x1400082e0:  0x0000000000000000
0x1400082e8:  0x0000000000000000
0x1400082f0:  0x0000000000000000
0x1400082f8:  0x0000000000000000
0x140008300:  0x0000000000000000
0x140008308:  0x0000000000000000
0x140008310:  0x0000000000000000
0x140008318:  0x0000000000000000
0x140008320:  0x0000000000000000
0x140008328:  0x0000000000000000
0x140008330:  0x0000000000000000
0x140008338:  0x0000000000000000
0x140008340:  0x0000000000000000
0x140008348:  0x0000000000000000
0x140008350:  0x0000000000000000
0x140008358:  0x0000000000000000
0x140008360:  0x0000000000000000
0x140008368:  0x0000000000000000
0x140008370:  0x0000000000000000
0x140008378:  0x0000000000000000
0x140008380:  0x0000000000000000
0x140008388:  0x0000000000000000
0x140008390:  0x0000000000000000
0x140008398:  0x0000000000000000
0x1400083a0:  0x0000000000000000
0x1400083a8:  0x0000000000000000
0x1400083b0:  0x0000000000000000
0x1400083b8:  0x0000000000000000
0x1400083c0:  0x0000000000000000
0x1400083c8:  0x0000000000000000
0x1400083d0:  0x0000000000000000
0x1400083d8:  0x0000000000000000
0x1400083e0:  0x0000000000000000
0x1400083e8:  0x0000000000000000
0x1400083f0:  0x0000000000000000
0x1400083f8:  0x0000000000000000
0x140008400:  0x0000000000000000
0x140008408:  0x0000000000000000
0x140008410:  0x0000000000000000
0x140008418:  0x0000000000000000
0x140008420:  0x0000000000000000
0x140008428:  0x0000000000000000
0x140008430:  0x0000000000000000
```

```
0x140008438:  0x0000000000000000
0x140008440:  0x0000000000000000
0x140008448:  0x0000000000000000
0x140008450:  0x0000000000000000
0x140008458:  0x0000000000000000
0x140008460:  0x0000000000000000
0x140008468:  0x0000000000000000
0x140008470:  0x0000000000000000
0x140008478:  0x0000000000000000
0x140008480:  0x0000000000000000
0x140008488:  0x0000000000000000
0x140008490:  0x0000000000000000
0x140008498:  0x0000000000000000
0x1400084a0:  0x0000000000000000
0x1400084a8:  0x0000000000000000
0x1400084b0:  0x0000000000000000
0x1400084b8:  0x0000000000000000
0x1400084c0:  0x0000000000000000
0x1400084c8:  0x0000000000000000
0x1400084d0:  0x0000000000000000
0x1400084d8:  0x0000000000000000
0x1400084e0:  0x0000000000000000
0x1400084e8:  0x0000000000000000
0x1400084f0:  0x0000000000000000
0x1400084f8:  0x0000000000000000
0x140008500:  0x0000000000000000
0x140008508:  0x0000000000000000
0x140008510:  0x0000000000000000
0x140008518:  0x0000000000000000
0x140008520:  0x0000000000000000
0x140008528:  0x0000000000000000
0x140008530:  0x0000000000000000
0x140008538:  0x0000000000000000
0x140008540:  0x0000000000000000
0x140008548:  0x0000000000000000
0x140008550:  0x0000000000000000
0x140008558:  0x0000000000000000
0x140008560:  0x0000000000000000
0x140008568:  0x0000000000000000
0x140008570:  0x0000000000000000
0x140008578:  0x0000000000000000
0x140008580:  0x0000000000000000
0x140008588:  0x0000000000000000
0x140008590:  0x0000000000000000
0x140008598:  0x0000000000000000
0x1400085a0:  0x0000000000000000
0x1400085a8:  0x0000000000000000
0x1400085b0:  0x0000000000000000
0x1400085b8:  0x0000000000000000
0x1400085c0:  0x0000000000000000
0x1400085c8:  0x0000000000000000
0x1400085d0:  0x0000000000000000
0x1400085d8:  0x0000000000000000
0x1400085e0:  0x0000000000000000
0x1400085e8:  0x0000000000000000
0x1400085f0:  0x0000000000000000
0x1400085f8:  0x0000000000000000
0x140008600:  0x657461636f6c6c61
0x140008608:  0x79726f6d656d2064
0x140008610:  0x0000000000000000
0x140008618:  0x0000000000000000
```

```
0x140008620: 0x0000000102877c48 App9`procD
0x140008628: 0x0000000000000000
0x140008630: 0x0000000000000000
0x140008638: 0x0000000000000000
0x140008640: 0x0000000000000000
0x140008648: 0x0000000000000000
0x140008650: 0x0000000000000000
0x140008658: 0x0000000000000000
0x140008660: 0x0000000000000000
0x140008668: 0x0000000000000000
0x140008670: 0x0000000000000000
0x140008678: 0x0000000000000000
0x140008680: 0x0000000000000000
0x140008688: 0x0000000000000000
0x140008690: 0x0000000000000000
0x140008698: 0x0000000000000000
0x1400086a0: 0x0000000000000000
0x1400086a8: 0x0000000000000000
0x1400086b0: 0x0000000000000000
0x1400086b8: 0x0000000000000000
0x1400086c0: 0x0000000000000000
0x1400086c8: 0x0000000000000000
0x1400086d0: 0x0000000000000000
0x1400086d8: 0x0000000000000000
0x1400086e0: 0x0000000000000000
0x1400086e8: 0x0000000000000000
0x1400086f0: 0x0000000000000000
0x1400086f8: 0x0000000000000000
0x140008700: 0x0000000000000000
0x140008708: 0x0000000000000000
0x140008710: 0x0000000000000000
0x140008718: 0x0000000000000000
0x140008720: 0x0000000000000000
0x140008728: 0x0000000000000000
0x140008730: 0x0000000000000000
0x140008738: 0x0000000000000000
0x140008740: 0x0000000000000000
0x140008748: 0x0000000000000000
0x140008750: 0x0000000000000000
0x140008758: 0x0000000000000000
0x140008760: 0x0000000000000000
0x140008768: 0x0000000000000000
0x140008770: 0x0000000000000000
0x140008778: 0x0000000000000000
0x140008780: 0x0000000000000000
0x140008788: 0x0000000000000000
0x140008790: 0x0000000000000000
0x140008798: 0x0000000000000000
0x1400087a0: 0x0000000000000000
0x1400087a8: 0x0000000000000000
0x1400087b0: 0x0000000000000000
0x1400087b8: 0x0000000000000000
0x1400087c0: 0x0000000000000000
0x1400087c8: 0x0000000000000000
0x1400087d0: 0x0000000000000000
0x1400087d8: 0x0000000000000000
0x1400087e0: 0x0000000000000000
0x1400087e8: 0x0000000000000000
0x1400087f0: 0x0000000000000000
0x1400087f8: 0x0000000000000000
0x140008800: 0x0000000000000000
```

```
0x140008808:  0x0000000000000000
0x140008810:  0x0000000000000000
0x140008818:  0x0000000000000000
0x140008820:  0x0000000000000000
0x140008828:  0x0000000000000000
0x140008830:  0x0000000000000000
0x140008838:  0x0000000000000000
0x140008840:  0x0000000000000000
0x140008848:  0x0000000000000000
0x140008850:  0x0000000000000000
0x140008858:  0x0000000000000000
0x140008860:  0x0000000000000000
0x140008868:  0x0000000000000000
0x140008870:  0x0000000000000000
0x140008878:  0x0000000000000000
0x140008880:  0x0000000000000000
0x140008888:  0x0000000000000000
0x140008890:  0x0000000000000000
0x140008898:  0x0000000000000000
0x1400088a0:  0x0000000000000000
0x1400088a8:  0x0000000000000000
0x1400088b0:  0x0000000000000000
0x1400088b8:  0x0000000000000000
0x1400088c0:  0x0000000000000000
0x1400088c8:  0x0000000000000000
0x1400088d0:  0x0000000000000000
0x1400088d8:  0x0000000000000000
0x1400088e0:  0x0000000000000000
0x1400088e8:  0x0000000000000000
0x1400088f0:  0x0000000000000000
0x1400088f8:  0x0000000000000000
0x140008900:  0x0000000000000000
0x140008908:  0x0000000000000000
0x140008910:  0x0000000000000000
0x140008918:  0x0000000000000000
0x140008920:  0x0000000000000000
0x140008928:  0x0000000000000000
0x140008930:  0x0000000000000000
0x140008938:  0x0000000000000000
0x140008940:  0x0000000000000000
0x140008948:  0x0000000000000000
0x140008950:  0x0000000000000000
0x140008958:  0x0000000000000000
0x140008960:  0x0000000000000000
0x140008968:  0x0000000000000000
0x140008970:  0x0000000000000000
0x140008978:  0x0000000000000000
0x140008980:  0x0000000000000000
0x140008988:  0x0000000000000000
0x140008990:  0x0000000000000000
0x140008998:  0x0000000000000000
0x1400089a0:  0x0000000000000000
0x1400089a8:  0x0000000000000000
0x1400089b0:  0x0000000000000000
0x1400089b8:  0x0000000000000000
0x1400089c0:  0x0000000000000000
0x1400089c8:  0x0000000000000000
0x1400089d0:  0x0000000000000000
0x1400089d8:  0x0000000000000000
0x1400089e0:  0x0000000000000000
0x1400089e8:  0x0000000000000000
```

```
0x1400089f0:  0x0000000000000000
0x1400089f8:  0x0000000000000000
0x140008a00:  0x657461636f6c6c61
0x140008a08:  0x79726f6d656d2064
0x140008a10:  0x0000000000000000
0x140008a18:  0x0000000000000000
0x140008a20:  0x0000000102877c48  App9`procD
0x140008a28:  0x0000000000000000
0x140008a30:  0x0000000000000000
0x140008a38:  0x0000000000000000
0x140008a40:  0x0000000000000000
0x140008a48:  0x0000000000000000
0x140008a50:  0x0000000000000000
0x140008a58:  0x0000000000000000
0x140008a60:  0x0000000000000000
0x140008a68:  0x0000000000000000
0x140008a70:  0x0000000000000000
0x140008a78:  0x0000000000000000
0x140008a80:  0x0000000000000000
0x140008a88:  0x0000000000000000
0x140008a90:  0x0000000000000000
0x140008a98:  0x0000000000000000
0x140008aa0:  0x0000000000000000
0x140008aa8:  0x0000000000000000
0x140008ab0:  0x0000000000000000
0x140008ab8:  0x0000000000000000
0x140008ac0:  0x0000000000000000
0x140008ac8:  0x0000000000000000
0x140008ad0:  0x0000000000000000
0x140008ad8:  0x0000000000000000
0x140008ae0:  0x0000000000000000
0x140008ae8:  0x0000000000000000
0x140008af0:  0x0000000000000000
0x140008af8:  0x0000000000000000
0x140008b00:  0x0000000000000000
0x140008b08:  0x0000000000000000
0x140008b10:  0x0000000000000000
0x140008b18:  0x0000000000000000
0x140008b20:  0x0000000000000000
0x140008b28:  0x0000000000000000
0x140008b30:  0x0000000000000000
0x140008b38:  0x0000000000000000
0x140008b40:  0x0000000000000000
0x140008b48:  0x0000000000000000
0x140008b50:  0x0000000000000000
0x140008b58:  0x0000000000000000
0x140008b60:  0x0000000000000000
0x140008b68:  0x0000000000000000
0x140008b70:  0x0000000000000000
0x140008b78:  0x0000000000000000
0x140008b80:  0x0000000000000000
0x140008b88:  0x0000000000000000
0x140008b90:  0x0000000000000000
0x140008b98:  0x0000000000000000
0x140008ba0:  0x0000000000000000
0x140008ba8:  0x0000000000000000
0x140008bb0:  0x0000000000000000
0x140008bb8:  0x0000000000000000
0x140008bc0:  0x0000000000000000
0x140008bc8:  0x0000000000000000
0x140008bd0:  0x0000000000000000
```

```
0x140008bd8:  0x0000000000000000
0x140008be0:  0x0000000000000000
0x140008be8:  0x0000000000000000
0x140008bf0:  0x0000000000000000
0x140008bf8:  0x0000000000000000
0x140008c00:  0x0000000000000000
0x140008c08:  0x0000000000000000
0x140008c10:  0x0000000000000000
0x140008c18:  0x0000000000000000
0x140008c20:  0x0000000000000000
0x140008c28:  0x0000000000000000
0x140008c30:  0x0000000000000000
0x140008c38:  0x0000000000000000
0x140008c40:  0x0000000000000000
0x140008c48:  0x0000000000000000
0x140008c50:  0x0000000000000000
0x140008c58:  0x0000000000000000
0x140008c60:  0x0000000000000000
0x140008c68:  0x0000000000000000
0x140008c70:  0x0000000000000000
0x140008c78:  0x0000000000000000
0x140008c80:  0x0000000000000000
0x140008c88:  0x0000000000000000
0x140008c90:  0x0000000000000000
0x140008c98:  0x0000000000000000
0x140008ca0:  0x0000000000000000
0x140008ca8:  0x0000000000000000
0x140008cb0:  0x0000000000000000
0x140008cb8:  0x0000000000000000
0x140008cc0:  0x0000000000000000
0x140008cc8:  0x0000000000000000
0x140008cd0:  0x0000000000000000
0x140008cd8:  0x0000000000000000
0x140008ce0:  0x0000000000000000
0x140008ce8:  0x0000000000000000
0x140008cf0:  0x0000000000000000
0x140008cf8:  0x0000000000000000
0x140008d00:  0x0000000000000000
0x140008d08:  0x0000000000000000
0x140008d10:  0x0000000000000000
0x140008d18:  0x0000000000000000
0x140008d20:  0x0000000000000000
0x140008d28:  0x0000000000000000
0x140008d30:  0x0000000000000000
0x140008d38:  0x0000000000000000
0x140008d40:  0x0000000000000000
0x140008d48:  0x0000000000000000
0x140008d50:  0x0000000000000000
0x140008d58:  0x0000000000000000
0x140008d60:  0x0000000000000000
0x140008d68:  0x0000000000000000
0x140008d70:  0x0000000000000000
0x140008d78:  0x0000000000000000
0x140008d80:  0x0000000000000000
0x140008d88:  0x0000000000000000
0x140008d90:  0x0000000000000000
0x140008d98:  0x0000000000000000
0x140008da0:  0x0000000000000000
0x140008da8:  0x0000000000000000
0x140008db0:  0x0000000000000000
0x140008db8:  0x0000000000000000
```

```
0x140008dc0:  0x0000000000000000
0x140008dc8:  0x0000000000000000
0x140008dd0:  0x0000000000000000
0x140008dd8:  0x0000000000000000
0x140008de0:  0x0000000000000000
0x140008de8:  0x0000000000000000
0x140008df0:  0x0000000000000000
0x140008df8:  0x0000000000000000
0x140008e00:  0x657461636f6c6c61
0x140008e08:  0x79726f6d656d2064
0x140008e10:  0x0000000000000000
0x140008e18:  0x0000000000000000
0x140008e20:  0x0000000102877c48 App9`procD
0x140008e28:  0x0000000000000000
0x140008e30:  0x0000000000000000
0x140008e38:  0x0000000000000000
0x140008e40:  0x0000000000000000
0x140008e48:  0x0000000000000000
0x140008e50:  0x0000000000000000
[...]
0x1407ff600:  0x657461636f6c6c61
0x1407ff608:  0x79726f6d656d2064
0x1407ff610:  0x0000000000000000
0x1407ff618:  0x0000000000000000
0x1407ff620:  0x0000000102877c48 App9`procD
0x1407ff628:  0x0000000000000000
0x1407ff630:  0x0000000000000000
0x1407ff638:  0x0000000000000000
0x1407ff640:  0x0000000000000000
0x1407ff648:  0x0000000000000000
0x1407ff650:  0x0000000000000000
0x1407ff658:  0x0000000000000000
0x1407ff660:  0x0000000000000000
0x1407ff668:  0x0000000000000000
0x1407ff670:  0x0000000000000000
0x1407ff678:  0x0000000000000000
0x1407ff680:  0x0000000000000000
0x1407ff688:  0x0000000000000000
0x1407ff690:  0x0000000000000000
0x1407ff698:  0x0000000000000000
0x1407ff6a0:  0x0000000000000000
0x1407ff6a8:  0x0000000000000000
0x1407ff6b0:  0x0000000000000000
0x1407ff6b8:  0x0000000000000000
0x1407ff6c0:  0x0000000000000000
0x1407ff6c8:  0x0000000000000000
0x1407ff6d0:  0x0000000000000000
0x1407ff6d8:  0x0000000000000000
0x1407ff6e0:  0x0000000000000000
0x1407ff6e8:  0x0000000000000000
0x1407ff6f0:  0x0000000000000000
0x1407ff6f8:  0x0000000000000000
0x1407ff700:  0x0000000000000000
0x1407ff708:  0x0000000000000000
0x1407ff710:  0x0000000000000000
0x1407ff718:  0x0000000000000000
0x1407ff720:  0x0000000000000000
0x1407ff728:  0x0000000000000000
0x1407ff730:  0x0000000000000000
0x1407ff738:  0x0000000000000000
0x1407ff740:  0x0000000000000000
```

```
0x1407ff748:  0x0000000000000000
0x1407ff750:  0x0000000000000000
0x1407ff758:  0x0000000000000000
0x1407ff760:  0x0000000000000000
0x1407ff768:  0x0000000000000000
0x1407ff770:  0x0000000000000000
0x1407ff778:  0x0000000000000000
0x1407ff780:  0x0000000000000000
0x1407ff788:  0x0000000000000000
0x1407ff790:  0x0000000000000000
0x1407ff798:  0x0000000000000000
0x1407ff7a0:  0x0000000000000000
0x1407ff7a8:  0x0000000000000000
0x1407ff7b0:  0x0000000000000000
0x1407ff7b8:  0x0000000000000000
0x1407ff7c0:  0x0000000000000000
0x1407ff7c8:  0x0000000000000000
0x1407ff7d0:  0x0000000000000000
0x1407ff7d8:  0x0000000000000000
0x1407ff7e0:  0x0000000000000000
0x1407ff7e8:  0x0000000000000000
0x1407ff7f0:  0x0000000000000000
0x1407ff7f8:  0x0000000000000000
0x1407ff800:  0x0000000000000000
0x1407ff808:  0x0000000000000000
0x1407ff810:  0x0000000000000000
0x1407ff818:  0x0000000000000000
0x1407ff820:  0x0000000000000000
0x1407ff828:  0x0000000000000000
0x1407ff830:  0x0000000000000000
0x1407ff838:  0x0000000000000000
0x1407ff840:  0x0000000000000000
0x1407ff848:  0x0000000000000000
0x1407ff850:  0x0000000000000000
0x1407ff858:  0x0000000000000000
0x1407ff860:  0x0000000000000000
0x1407ff868:  0x0000000000000000
0x1407ff870:  0x0000000000000000
0x1407ff878:  0x0000000000000000
0x1407ff880:  0x0000000000000000
0x1407ff888:  0x0000000000000000
0x1407ff890:  0x0000000000000000
0x1407ff898:  0x0000000000000000
0x1407ff8a0:  0x0000000000000000
0x1407ff8a8:  0x0000000000000000
0x1407ff8b0:  0x0000000000000000
0x1407ff8b8:  0x0000000000000000
0x1407ff8c0:  0x0000000000000000
0x1407ff8c8:  0x0000000000000000
0x1407ff8d0:  0x0000000000000000
0x1407ff8d8:  0x0000000000000000
0x1407ff8e0:  0x0000000000000000
0x1407ff8e8:  0x0000000000000000
0x1407ff8f0:  0x0000000000000000
0x1407ff8f8:  0x0000000000000000
0x1407ff900:  0x0000000000000000
0x1407ff908:  0x0000000000000000
0x1407ff910:  0x0000000000000000
0x1407ff918:  0x0000000000000000
0x1407ff920:  0x0000000000000000
0x1407ff928:  0x0000000000000000
```

```
0x1407ff930:  0x0000000000000000
0x1407ff938:  0x0000000000000000
0x1407ff940:  0x0000000000000000
0x1407ff948:  0x0000000000000000
0x1407ff950:  0x0000000000000000
0x1407ff958:  0x0000000000000000
0x1407ff960:  0x0000000000000000
0x1407ff968:  0x0000000000000000
0x1407ff970:  0x0000000000000000
0x1407ff978:  0x0000000000000000
0x1407ff980:  0x0000000000000000
0x1407ff988:  0x0000000000000000
0x1407ff990:  0x0000000000000000
0x1407ff998:  0x0000000000000000
0x1407ff9a0:  0x0000000000000000
0x1407ff9a8:  0x0000000000000000
0x1407ff9b0:  0x0000000000000000
0x1407ff9b8:  0x0000000000000000
0x1407ff9c0:  0x0000000000000000
0x1407ff9c8:  0x0000000000000000
0x1407ff9d0:  0x0000000000000000
0x1407ff9d8:  0x0000000000000000
0x1407ff9e0:  0x0000000000000000
0x1407ff9e8:  0x0000000000000000
0x1407ff9f0:  0x0000000000000000
0x1407ff9f8:  0x0000000000000000
0x1407ffa00:  0x657461636f6c6c61
0x1407ffa08:  0x79726f6d656d2064
0x1407ffa10:  0x0000000000000000
0x1407ffa18:  0x0000000000000000
0x1407ffa20:  0x0000000102877c48  App9`procD
0x1407ffa28:  0x0000000000000000
0x1407ffa30:  0x0000000000000000
0x1407ffa38:  0x0000000000000000
0x1407ffa40:  0x0000000000000000
0x1407ffa48:  0x0000000000000000
0x1407ffa50:  0x0000000000000000
0x1407ffa58:  0x0000000000000000
0x1407ffa60:  0x0000000000000000
0x1407ffa68:  0x0000000000000000
0x1407ffa70:  0x0000000000000000
0x1407ffa78:  0x0000000000000000
0x1407ffa80:  0x0000000000000000
0x1407ffa88:  0x0000000000000000
0x1407ffa90:  0x0000000000000000
0x1407ffa98:  0x0000000000000000
0x1407ffaa0:  0x0000000000000000
0x1407ffaa8:  0x0000000000000000
0x1407ffab0:  0x0000000000000000
0x1407ffab8:  0x0000000000000000
0x1407ffac0:  0x0000000000000000
0x1407ffac8:  0x0000000000000000
0x1407ffad0:  0x0000000000000000
0x1407ffad8:  0x0000000000000000
0x1407ffae0:  0x0000000000000000
0x1407ffae8:  0x0000000000000000
0x1407ffaf0:  0x0000000000000000
0x1407ffaf8:  0x0000000000000000
0x1407ffb00:  0x0000000000000000
0x1407ffb08:  0x0000000000000000
0x1407ffb10:  0x0000000000000000
```

```
0x1407ffb18:  0x0000000000000000
0x1407ffb20:  0x0000000000000000
0x1407ffb28:  0x0000000000000000
0x1407ffb30:  0x0000000000000000
0x1407ffb38:  0x0000000000000000
0x1407ffb40:  0x0000000000000000
0x1407ffb48:  0x0000000000000000
0x1407ffb50:  0x0000000000000000
0x1407ffb58:  0x0000000000000000
0x1407ffb60:  0x0000000000000000
0x1407ffb68:  0x0000000000000000
0x1407ffb70:  0x0000000000000000
0x1407ffb78:  0x0000000000000000
0x1407ffb80:  0x0000000000000000
0x1407ffb88:  0x0000000000000000
0x1407ffb90:  0x0000000000000000
0x1407ffb98:  0x0000000000000000
0x1407ffba0:  0x0000000000000000
0x1407ffba8:  0x0000000000000000
0x1407ffbb0:  0x0000000000000000
0x1407ffbb8:  0x0000000000000000
0x1407ffbc0:  0x0000000000000000
0x1407ffbc8:  0x0000000000000000
0x1407ffbd0:  0x0000000000000000
0x1407ffbd8:  0x0000000000000000
0x1407ffbe0:  0x0000000000000000
0x1407ffbe8:  0x0000000000000000
0x1407ffbf0:  0x0000000000000000
0x1407ffbf8:  0x0000000000000000
0x1407ffc00:  0x0000000000000000
0x1407ffc08:  0x0000000000000000
0x1407ffc10:  0x0000000000000000
0x1407ffc18:  0x0000000000000000
0x1407ffc20:  0x0000000000000000
0x1407ffc28:  0x0000000000000000
0x1407ffc30:  0x0000000000000000
0x1407ffc38:  0x0000000000000000
0x1407ffc40:  0x0000000000000000
0x1407ffc48:  0x0000000000000000
0x1407ffc50:  0x0000000000000000
0x1407ffc58:  0x0000000000000000
0x1407ffc60:  0x0000000000000000
0x1407ffc68:  0x0000000000000000
0x1407ffc70:  0x0000000000000000
0x1407ffc78:  0x0000000000000000
0x1407ffc80:  0x0000000000000000
0x1407ffc88:  0x0000000000000000
0x1407ffc90:  0x0000000000000000
0x1407ffc98:  0x0000000000000000
0x1407ffca0:  0x0000000000000000
0x1407ffca8:  0x0000000000000000
0x1407ffcb0:  0x0000000000000000
0x1407ffcb8:  0x0000000000000000
0x1407ffcc0:  0x0000000000000000
0x1407ffcc8:  0x0000000000000000
0x1407ffcd0:  0x0000000000000000
0x1407ffcd8:  0x0000000000000000
0x1407ffce0:  0x0000000000000000
0x1407ffce8:  0x0000000000000000
0x1407ffcf0:  0x0000000000000000
0x1407ffcf8:  0x0000000000000000
```

```
0x1407ffd00:  0x0000000000000000
0x1407ffd08:  0x0000000000000000
0x1407ffd10:  0x0000000000000000
0x1407ffd18:  0x0000000000000000
0x1407ffd20:  0x0000000000000000
0x1407ffd28:  0x0000000000000000
0x1407ffd30:  0x0000000000000000
0x1407ffd38:  0x0000000000000000
0x1407ffd40:  0x0000000000000000
0x1407ffd48:  0x0000000000000000
0x1407ffd50:  0x0000000000000000
0x1407ffd58:  0x0000000000000000
0x1407ffd60:  0x0000000000000000
0x1407ffd68:  0x0000000000000000
0x1407ffd70:  0x0000000000000000
0x1407ffd78:  0x0000000000000000
0x1407ffd80:  0x0000000000000000
0x1407ffd88:  0x0000000000000000
0x1407ffd90:  0x0000000000000000
0x1407ffd98:  0x0000000000000000
0x1407ffda0:  0x0000000000000000
0x1407ffda8:  0x0000000000000000
0x1407ffdb0:  0x0000000000000000
0x1407ffdb8:  0x0000000000000000
0x1407ffdc0:  0x0000000000000000
0x1407ffdc8:  0x0000000000000000
0x1407ffdd0:  0x0000000000000000
0x1407ffdd8:  0x0000000000000000
0x1407ffde0:  0x0000000000000000
0x1407ffde8:  0x0000000000000000
0x1407ffdf0:  0x0000000000000000
0x1407ffdf8:  0x0000000000000000
0x1407ffe00:  0x0000000142fffe00
0x1407ffe08:  0x0000000000000044
0x1407ffe10:  0x000000013ffffe00
0x1407ffe18:  0x000000000000005f
0x1407ffe20:  0x0000000000000000
0x1407ffe28:  0x0000000000000000
0x1407ffe30:  0x0000000000000000
0x1407ffe38:  0x0000000000000000
0x1407ffe40:  0x0000000000000000
0x1407ffe48:  0x0000000000000000
0x1407ffe50:  0x0000000000000000
0x1407ffe58:  0x0000000000000000
0x1407ffe60:  0x0000000000000000
0x1407ffe68:  0x0000000000000000
0x1407ffe70:  0x0000000000000000
0x1407ffe78:  0x0000000000000000
0x1407ffe80:  0x0000000000000000
0x1407ffe88:  0x0000000000000000
0x1407ffe90:  0x0000000000000000
0x1407ffe98:  0x0000000000000000
0x1407ffea0:  0x0000000000000000
0x1407ffea8:  0x0000000000000000
0x1407ffeb0:  0x0000000000000000
0x1407ffeb8:  0x0000000000000000
0x1407ffec0:  0x0000000000000000
0x1407ffec8:  0x0000000000000000
0x1407ffed0:  0x0000000000000000
0x1407ffed8:  0x0000000000000000
0x1407ffee0:  0x0000000000000000
```

```
0x1407ffee8: 0x0000000000000000
0x1407ffef0: 0x0000000000000000
0x1407ffef8: 0x0000000000000000
0x1407fff00: 0x0000000000000000
0x1407fff08: 0x0000000000000000
0x1407fff10: 0x0000000000000000
0x1407fff18: 0x0000000000000000
0x1407fff20: 0x0000000000000000
0x1407fff28: 0x0000000000000000
0x1407fff30: 0x0000000000000000
0x1407fff38: 0x0000000000000000
0x1407fff40: 0x0000000000000000
0x1407fff48: 0x0000000000000000
0x1407fff50: 0x0000000000000000
0x1407fff58: 0x0000000000000000
0x1407fff60: 0x0000000000000000
0x1407fff68: 0x0000000000000000
0x1407fff70: 0x0000000000000000
0x1407fff78: 0x0000000000000000
0x1407fff80: 0x0000000000000000
0x1407fff88: 0x0000000000000000
0x1407fff90: 0x0000000000000000
0x1407fff98: 0x0000000000000000
0x1407fffa0: 0x0000000000000000
0x1407fffa8: 0x0000000000000000
0x1407fffb0: 0x0000000000000000
0x1407fffb8: 0x0000000000000000
0x1407fffc0: 0x0000000000000000
0x1407fffc8: 0x0000000000000000
0x1407fffd0: 0x0000000000000000
0x1407fffd8: 0x0000000000000000
0x1407fffe0: 0x0000000000000000
0x1407fffe8: 0x0000000000000000
0x1407ffff0: 0x0000000000000000
0x1407ffff8: 0x0000000000000000
```

Note: After 2 pages of possible allocation metadata, the rest is filled with uniform allocations showing possible origin in *procD*. We also examine ASCII-like data:

```
(lldb) x/s 0x1407ffa00
0x1407ffa00: "allocated memory"
```

Exercise X10

- **Goal:** Learn how to identify contention wait chains, synchronization issues, advanced disassembly, dump arrays

- **Patterns:** Double Free; High Contention; Wait Chain; Critical Region; Self-Diagnosis

- \AMCDA-Dumps\Exercise-X10.pdf

Exercise X10

Goal: Learn how to identify contention wait chains, synchronization issues, advanced disassembly, and dump arrays.

Patterns: Double Free; High Contention; Wait Chain; Critical Region; Self-Diagnostics.

1.   Identify heap problem and log contention from the diagnostic report *App10-2022-12-09-182325.ips*:

```
-------------------------------------
Translated Report (Full Report Below)
-------------------------------------


Process:              App10 [93314]
Path:                 /Users/USER/*/App10
Identifier:           App10
Version:              ???
Code Type:            ARM-64 (Native)
Parent Process:       zsh [93724]
Responsible:          Terminal [9503]
User ID:              501

Date/Time:            2022-12-09 18:23:25.1475 +0000
OS Version:           macOS 12.6 (21G115)
Report Version:       12
Anonymous UUID:       6F758133-2B79-4743-8B70-8B1D8C510718

Sleep/Wake UUID:      ECFA53CB-4E47-48DB-90DB-6393DB591F0B

Time Awake Since Boot: 240000 seconds
Time Since Wake:       456 seconds

System Integrity Protection: enabled

Crashed Thread:       3

Exception Type:       EXC_CRASH (SIGABRT)
Exception Codes:      0x0000000000000000, 0x0000000000000000
Exception Note:       EXC_CORPSE_NOTIFY

Application Specific Information:
abort() called


Thread 0::  Dispatch queue: com.apple.main-thread
0   libsystem_kernel.dylib           0x18e9ce06c __semwait_signal + 8
1   libsystem_c.dylib                0x18e8d6fc8 nanosleep + 220
2   libsystem_c.dylib                0x18e8e1b78 sleep + 52
3   libsystem_c.dylib                0x18e8e1b90 sleep + 76
4   App10                            0x104777f6c main + 164
5   dyld                             0x1047d508c start + 520

Thread 1:
0   libsystem_kernel.dylib           0x18e9cc834 __ulock_wait + 8
1   libsystem_platform.dylib         0x18ea1e82c _os_once_gate_wait + 144
2   libsystem_platform.dylib         0x18ea21064 _simple_asl_get_fd + 148
3   libsystem_platform.dylib         0x18ea20b18 _os_log_simple_send + 40
4   libsystem_platform.dylib         0x18ea20ad8 __os_log_simple_offset + 260
5   libsystem_malloc.dylib           0x18e824790 malloc_vreport + 248
6   libsystem_malloc.dylib           0x18e839c84 malloc_zone_error + 100
7   libsystem_malloc.dylib           0x18e82da3c free_small_botch + 40
8   App10                            0x104777d1c proc + 116
9   App10                            0x104777d58 bar_one + 12
10  App10                            0x104777d6c foo_one + 12
11  App10                            0x104777d88 thread_one + 20
12  libsystem_pthread.dylib          0x18ea0826c _pthread_start + 148
13  libsystem_pthread.dylib          0x18ea0308c thread_start + 8

Thread 2:
0   libsystem_malloc.dylib           0x18e81c550 small_free_list_add_ptr + 280
1   libsystem_malloc.dylib           0x18e81a0d4 free_small + 884
2   App10                            0x104777d1c proc + 116
```

```
3    App10                         0x104777da4 bar_two + 12
4    App10                         0x104777db8 foo_two + 12
5    App10                         0x104777dd4 thread_two + 20
6    libsystem_pthread.dylib       0x18ea0826c _pthread_start + 148
7    libsystem_pthread.dylib       0x18ea0308c thread_start + 8

Thread 3 Crashed:
0    libsystem_kernel.dylib        0x18e9d2d98 __pthread_kill + 8
1    libsystem_pthread.dylib       0x18ea07ee0 pthread_kill + 288
2    libsystem_c.dylib             0x18e942340 abort + 168
3    libsystem_malloc.dylib        0x18e8248c0 malloc_vreport + 552
4    libsystem_malloc.dylib        0x18e827f34 malloc_report + 64
5    libsystem_malloc.dylib        0x18e816cf4 free + 300
6    App10                         0x104777d1c proc + 116
7    App10                         0x104777df0 bar_three + 12
8    App10                         0x104777e04 foo_three + 12
9    App10                         0x104777e20 thread_three + 20
10   libsystem_pthread.dylib       0x18ea0826c _pthread_start + 148
11   libsystem_pthread.dylib       0x18ea0308c thread_start + 8

Thread 4:
0    libsystem_kernel.dylib        0x18e9cf100 __connect + 8
1    libsystem_platform.dylib      0x18ea1e438 _simple_asl_connect_once + 164
2    libsystem_platform.dylib      0x18ea1c940 _os_once_callout + 32
3    libsystem_platform.dylib      0x18ea21064 _simple_asl_get_fd + 148
4    libsystem_platform.dylib      0x18ea20b18 _os_log_simple_send + 40
5    libsystem_platform.dylib      0x18ea20ad8 __os_log_simple_offset + 260
6    libsystem_malloc.dylib        0x18e824790 malloc_vreport + 248
7    libsystem_malloc.dylib        0x18e839c84 malloc_zone_error + 100
8    libsystem_malloc.dylib        0x18e82da3c free_small_botch + 40
9    App10                         0x104777d1c proc + 116
10   App10                         0x104777e3c bar_four + 12
11   App10                         0x104777e50 foo_four + 12
12   App10                         0x104777e6c thread_four + 20
13   libsystem_pthread.dylib       0x18ea0826c _pthread_start + 148
14   libsystem_pthread.dylib       0x18ea0308c thread_start + 8

Thread 5:
0    libsystem_kernel.dylib        0x18e9cbe68 __proc_info + 8
1    libsystem_kernel.dylib        0x18e9cbe50 proc_pidinfo + 40
2    libsystem_platform.dylib      0x18ea20a4c __os_log_simple_offset + 120
3    libsystem_malloc.dylib        0x18e824790 malloc_vreport + 248
4    libsystem_malloc.dylib        0x18e839c84 malloc_zone_error + 100
5    libsystem_malloc.dylib        0x18e82da3c free_small_botch + 40
6    App10                         0x104777d1c proc + 116
7    App10                         0x104777e88 bar_five + 12
8    App10                         0x104777e9c foo_five + 12
9    App10                         0x104777eb8 thread_five + 20
10   libsystem_pthread.dylib       0x18ea0826c _pthread_start + 148
11   libsystem_pthread.dylib       0x18ea0308c thread_start + 8


Thread 3 crashed with ARM Thread State (64-bit):
    x0: 0x0000000000000000   x1: 0x0000000000000000   x2: 0x0000000000000000   x3: 0x0000000000000000
    x4: 0x0000000000000000   x5: 0x0000000000000000   x6: 0x0000000000000001   x7: 0x0000000000000001
    x8: 0x9480577608ce0eee   x9: 0x94805777634cbeee  x10: 0xcccccccccccccccd  x11: 0x000000000000000a
   x12: 0x0000000000000000  x13: 0x0000000000000039  x14: 0x0000000000200000  x15: 0x0000000000000014
   x16: 0x0000000000000148  x17: 0x00000001e8b2b680  x18: 0x0000000000000000  x19: 0x0000000000000006
   x20: 0x000000016b82b000  x21: 0x0000000000001203  x22: 0x000000016b82b0e0  x23: 0x00000001049a4000
   x24: 0x0000000000000000  x25: 0x0000000000000000  x26: 0x0000000104834256  x27: 0x000000016b82b000
   x28: 0x0000000000000000   fp: 0x000000016b82ae10   lr: 0x000000018ea07ee0
    sp: 0x000000016b82adf0   pc: 0x000000018e9d2d98 cpsr: 0x40001000
   far: 0x00000001049a8000  esr: 0x56000080  Address size fault

Binary Images:
       0x18e9c9000 -        0x18ea00fff libsystem_kernel.dylib (*) <a9d87740-9c1d-3468-bf60-720a8d713cba>
/usr/lib/system/libsystem_kernel.dylib
       0x18e8c8000 -        0x18e949fff libsystem_c.dylib (*) <b25d2080-bb9e-38d6-8236-9cef4b2f11a3>
/usr/lib/system/libsystem_c.dylib
       0x104774000 -        0x104777fff App10 (*) <890afbf8-f400-3bf5-8167-279ca08548a3> /Users/USER/*/App10
       0x1047d0000 -        0x10482ffff dyld (*) <38ee9fe9-b66d-3066-8c5c-6ddf0d6944c6> /usr/lib/dyld
       0x18ea1b000 -        0x18ea22fff libsystem_platform.dylib (*) <a57fe7fb-9ff8-30ce-97a2-625d6da20d00>
/usr/lib/system/libsystem_platform.dylib
       0x18e815000 -        0x18e83ffff libsystem_malloc.dylib (*) <427675c6-c4bf-390a-af93-b28dac36876a>
/usr/lib/system/libsystem_malloc.dylib
```

```
    0x18ea01000 -        0x18ea0dfff libsystem_pthread.dylib (*) <63c4eef9-69a5-38b1-996e-8d31b66a051d>
/usr/lib/system/libsystem_pthread.dylib

External Modification Summary:
  Calls made by other processes targeting this process:
    task_for_pid: 0
    thread_create: 0
    thread_set_state: 0
  Calls made by this process:
    task_for_pid: 0
    thread_create: 0
    thread_set_state: 0
  Calls made by all processes on this machine:
    task_for_pid: 1
    thread_create: 0
    thread_set_state: 0

VM Region Summary:
ReadOnly portion of Libraries: Total=582.2M resident=0K(0%) swapped_out_or_unallocated=582.2M(100%)
Writable regions: Total=558.9M written=0K(0%) resident=0K(0%) swapped_out=0K(0%) unallocated=558.9M(100%)

                         VIRTUAL   REGION
REGION TYPE                 SIZE    COUNT (non-coalesced)
===========              =======  =======
Kernel Alloc Once           32K        1
MALLOC                    164.3M       23
MALLOC_NANO (reserved)    384.0M        1          reserved VM address space (unallocated)
Stack                      10.7M       11
Stack (reserved)           56.0M        1          reserved VM address space (unallocated)
VM_ALLOCATE                 64K         1
__AUTH                      46K        11
__AUTH_CONST                67K        38
__DATA                     253K        38
__DATA_CONST               258K        40
__DATA_DIRTY                73K        21
__LINKEDIT                577.6M        3
__OBJC_CONST                10K         5
__OBJC_RO                  83.0M        1
__OBJC_RW                 3168K         1
__TEXT                    4708K        43
dyld private memory       1024K         1
shared memory               16K         1
===========              =======  =======
TOTAL                       1.3G      241
TOTAL, minus reserved VM space 845.1M  241
```

Note: We see that core threads #2, #4, and #5 were running through some malloc reporting and not waiting, core thread #1 was blocked in a lock when doing malloc reporting, and core thread #3 crashed after freeing memory and malloc reporting. On the terminal we had this output:

```
App10(93314,0x16b713000) malloc: double free for ptr 0x11e872e00
App10(93314,0x16b8b7000) malloc: double free for ptr 0x120009c00
App10(93314,0x16b82b000) malloc: *** error for object 0x120057400: pointer being freed was not allocated
App10(93314,0x16b82b000) malloc: *** set a breakpoint in malloc_error_break to debug
App10(93314,0x16b943000) malloc: double free for ptr 0x11e8f7208
```

2.   Load a core dump *core.93314* and *App10* executable:

```
% lldb -c ~/AMCDA-Dumps/core.93314 -f ~/AMCDA-Dumps/Apps/App10/Build/Products/Release/App10
(lldb) target create "/Users/training/AMCDA-Dumps/Apps/App10/Build/Products/Release/App10" --
core "/Users/training/AMCDA-Dumps/core.93314"
Core file '/Users/training/AMCDA-Dumps/core.93314' (arm64) was loaded.
```

3.   Check thread 2 (core thread #1) and find where it was being executed:

```
(lldb) thread select 2
* thread #2
    frame #0: 0x000000018e9cc834 libsystem_kernel.dylib`__ulock_wait + 8
libsystem_kernel.dylib`:
->  0x18e9cc834 <+8>:  b.lo    0x18e9cc854                  ; <+40>
    0x18e9cc838 <+12>: pacibsp
    0x18e9cc83c <+16>: stp     x29, x30, [sp, #-0x10]!
    0x18e9cc840 <+20>: mov     x29, sp
```

```
(lldb) bt
* thread #2
  * frame #0: 0x000000018e9cc834 libsystem_kernel.dylib`__ulock_wait + 8
    frame #1: 0x000000018ea1e82c libsystem_platform.dylib`_os_once_gate_wait + 144
    frame #2: 0x000000018ea21064 libsystem_platform.dylib`_simple_asl_get_fd + 148
    frame #3: 0x000000018ea20b18 libsystem_platform.dylib`_os_log_simple_send + 40
    frame #4: 0x000000018ea20ad8 libsystem_platform.dylib`__os_log_simple_offset + 260
    frame #5: 0x000000018e824790 libsystem_malloc.dylib`malloc_vreport + 248
    frame #6: 0x000000018e839c84 libsystem_malloc.dylib`malloc_zone_error + 100
    frame #7: 0x000000018e82da3c libsystem_malloc.dylib`free_small_botch + 40
    frame #8: 0x0000000104777d1c App10`proc + 116
    frame #9: 0x0000000104777d58 App10`bar_one + 12
    frame #10: 0x0000000104777d6c App10`foo_one + 12
    frame #11: 0x0000000104777d88 App10`thread_one + 20
    frame #12: 0x000000018ea0826c libsystem_pthread.dylib`_pthread_start + 148
```

Note: It is probably waiting for its turn to write to a log compared to the stack trace from thread 5 (core thread #4):

```
(lldb) thread backtrace 5
* thread #5
    frame #0: 0x000000018e9cf100 libsystem_kernel.dylib`__connect + 8
    frame #1: 0x000000018ea1e438 libsystem_platform.dylib`_simple_asl_connect_once + 164
    frame #2: 0x000000018ea1c940 libsystem_platform.dylib`_os_once_callout + 32
    frame #3: 0x000000018ea21064 libsystem_platform.dylib`_simple_asl_get_fd + 148
    frame #4: 0x000000018ea20b18 libsystem_platform.dylib`_os_log_simple_send + 40
    frame #5: 0x000000018ea20ad8 libsystem_platform.dylib`__os_log_simple_offset + 260
    frame #6: 0x000000018e824790 libsystem_malloc.dylib`malloc_vreport + 248
    frame #7: 0x000000018e839c84 libsystem_malloc.dylib`malloc_zone_error + 100
    frame #8: 0x000000018e82da3c libsystem_malloc.dylib`free_small_botch + 40
  * frame #9: 0x0000000104777d1c App10`proc + 116
    frame #10: 0x0000000104777e3c App10`bar_four + 12
    frame #11: 0x0000000104777e50 App10`foo_four + 12
    frame #12: 0x0000000104777e6c App10`thread_four + 20
    frame #13: 0x000000018ea0826c libsystem_pthread.dylib`_pthread_start + 148
```

4.   Check thread 3 (core thread #2) and find where it was being executed:

```
(lldb) thread select 3
* thread #3, stop reason = ESR_EC_DABORT_EL0 (fault address: 0x11e8f7208)
    frame #0: 0x000000018e81c550 libsystem_malloc.dylib`small_free_list_add_ptr + 280
libsystem_malloc.dylib`small_free_list_add_ptr:
->  0x18e81c550 <+280>: strb    w13, [x2, #0x8]
    0x18e81c554 <+284>: str     xzr, [x2]
    0x18e81c558 <+288>: eor     x13, x9, x0
    0x18e81c55c <+292>: eor     x12, x13, x12
```

```
(lldb) bt
* thread #3, stop reason = ESR_EC_DABORT_EL0 (fault address: 0x11e8f7208)
  * frame #0: 0x000000018e81c550 libsystem_malloc.dylib`small_free_list_add_ptr + 280
    frame #1: 0x000000018e81a0d4 libsystem_malloc.dylib`free_small + 884
    frame #2: 0x0000000104777d1c App10`proc + 116
    frame #3: 0x0000000104777da4 App10`bar_two + 12
    frame #4: 0x0000000104777db8 App10`foo_two + 12
    frame #5: 0x0000000104777dd4 App10`thread_two + 20
    frame #6: 0x000000018ea0826c libsystem_pthread.dylib`_pthread_start + 148

(lldb) di -n proc
App10`proc:
    0x104777ca8 <+0>:    sub    sp, sp, #0x30
    0x104777cac <+4>:    stp    x29, x30, [sp, #0x20]
    0x104777cb0 <+8>:    add    x29, sp, #0x20
    0x104777cb4 <+12>:   b      0x104777cb8               ; <+16>
    0x104777cb8 <+16>:   bl     0x104777fa0               ; symbol stub for: rand
    0x104777cbc <+20>:   mov    w9, #0x2710
    0x104777cc0 <+24>:   stur   w9, [x29, #-0xc]
    0x104777cc4 <+28>:   sdiv   w8, w0, w9
    0x104777cc8 <+32>:   mul    w8, w8, w9
    0x104777ccc <+36>:   subs   w8, w0, w8
    0x104777cd0 <+40>:   stur   w8, [x29, #-0x4]
    0x104777cd4 <+44>:   bl     0x104777fa0               ; symbol stub for: rand
    0x104777cd8 <+48>:   ldur   w9, [x29, #-0xc]
    0x104777cdc <+52>:   sdiv   w8, w0, w9
    0x104777ce0 <+56>:   mul    w8, w8, w9
    0x104777ce4 <+60>:   subs   w8, w0, w8
    0x104777ce8 <+64>:   stur   w8, [x29, #-0x8]
    0x104777cec <+68>:   ldursw x9, [x29, #-0x4]
    0x104777cf0 <+72>:   adrp   x8, 5
    0x104777cf4 <+76>:   add    x8, x8, #0x0              ; pAllocBuf
    0x104777cf8 <+80>:   ldr    x8, [x8, x9, lsl #3]
    0x104777cfc <+84>:   cbz    x8, 0x104777d30          ; <+136>
    0x104777d00 <+88>:   b      0x104777d04               ; <+92>
    0x104777d04 <+92>:   ldursw x9, [x29, #-0x4]
    0x104777d08 <+96>:   adrp   x8, 5
    0x104777d0c <+100>:  add    x8, x8, #0x0              ; pAllocBuf
    0x104777d10 <+104>:  str    x8, [sp, #0x8]
    0x104777d14 <+108>:  ldr    x0, [x8, x9, lsl #3]
    0x104777d18 <+112>:  bl     0x104777f7c               ; symbol stub for: free
    0x104777d1c <+116>:  ldr    x9, [sp, #0x8]
    0x104777d20 <+120>:  ldursw x10, [x29, #-0x4]
    0x104777d24 <+124>:  mov    x8, #0x0
    0x104777d28 <+128>:  str    x8, [x9, x10, lsl #3]
    0x104777d2c <+132>:  b      0x104777d30               ; <+136>
    0x104777d30 <+136>:  ldursw x0, [x29, #-0x8]
    0x104777d34 <+140>:  bl     0x104777f88               ; symbol stub for: malloc
    0x104777d38 <+144>:  ldursw x9, [x29, #-0x4]
    0x104777d3c <+148>:  adrp   x8, 5
    0x104777d40 <+152>:  add    x8, x8, #0x0              ; pAllocBuf
    0x104777d44 <+156>:  str    x0, [x8, x9, lsl #3]
    0x104777d48 <+160>:  b      0x104777cb8               ; <+16>
```

5.   Check thread 6 (core thread #5) and find a diagnostic message:

```
(lldb) thread list
Process 0 stopped
  thread #1: tid = 0x0000, 0x000000018e9ce06c libsystem_kernel.dylib`__semwait_signal + 8
  thread #2: tid = 0x0001, 0x000000018e9cc834 libsystem_kernel.dylib`__ulock_wait + 8
* thread #3: tid = 0x0002, 0x000000018e81c550 libsystem_malloc.dylib`small_free_list_add_ptr + 280, stop reason =
ESR_EC_DABORT_EL0 (fault address: 0x11e8f7208)
  thread #4: tid = 0x0003, 0x000000018e9d2d98 libsystem_kernel.dylib`__pthread_kill + 8
  thread #5: tid = 0x0004, 0x000000018e9cf100 libsystem_kernel.dylib`__connect + 8
  thread #6: tid = 0x0005, 0x000000018e9cbe68 libsystem_kernel.dylib`__proc_info + 8
```

```
(lldb) thread select 6
* thread #6
    frame #0: 0x000000018e9cbe68 libsystem_kernel.dylib`__proc_info + 8
libsystem_kernel.dylib`:
->  0x18e9cbe68 <+8>:  b.lo    0x18e9cbe88               ; <+40>
    0x18e9cbe6c <+12>: pacibsp
    0x18e9cbe70 <+16>: stp     x29, x30, [sp, #-0x10]!
    0x18e9cbe74 <+20>: mov     x29, sp
```

```
(lldb) bt
* thread #6
  * frame #0: 0x000000018e9cbe68 libsystem_kernel.dylib`__proc_info + 8
    frame #1: 0x000000018e9cbe50 libsystem_kernel.dylib`proc_pidinfo + 40
    frame #2: 0x000000018ea20a4c libsystem_platform.dylib`__os_log_simple_offset + 120
    frame #3: 0x000000018e824790 libsystem_malloc.dylib`malloc_vreport + 248
    frame #4: 0x000000018e839c84 libsystem_malloc.dylib`malloc_zone_error + 100
    frame #5: 0x000000018e82da3c libsystem_malloc.dylib`free_small_botch + 40
    frame #6: 0x0000000104777d1c App10`proc + 116
    frame #7: 0x0000000104777e88 App10`bar_five + 12
    frame #8: 0x0000000104777e9c App10`foo_five + 12
    frame #9: 0x0000000104777eb8 App10`thread_five + 20
    frame #10: 0x000000018ea0826c libsystem_pthread.dylib`_pthread_start + 148
```

```
(lldb) di -a 0x000000018e82da3c
libsystem_malloc.dylib`free_small_botch:
    0x18e82da14 <+0>:  pacibsp
    0x18e82da18 <+4>:  sub     sp, sp, #0x20
    0x18e82da1c <+8>:  stp     x29, x30, [sp, #0x10]
    0x18e82da20 <+12>: add     x29, sp, #0x10
    0x18e82da24 <+16>: ldr     w0, [x0, #0x26c]
    0x18e82da28 <+20>: str     x1, [sp]
    0x18e82da2c <+24>: adrp    x2, 14
    0x18e82da30 <+28>: add     x2, x2, #0xe2b           ; "double free for ptr %p\n"
    0x18e82da34 <+32>: mov     w1, #0x1
    0x18e82da38 <+36>: bl      0x18e839c20              ; malloc_zone_error
    0x18e82da3c <+40>: ldp     x29, x30, [sp, #0x10]
    0x18e82da40 <+44>: add     sp, sp, #0x20
    0x18e82da44 <+48>: retab
```

```
(lldb) x/s 0x18e82d000+0x1000*14+0xe2b
0x18e83be2b: "double free for ptr %p\n"
```

6.   Check the address of being freed:

```
(lldb) bt
* thread #6
  * frame #0: 0x000000018e9cbe68 libsystem_kernel.dylib`__proc_info + 8
    frame #1: 0x000000018e9cbe50 libsystem_kernel.dylib`proc_pidinfo + 40
    frame #2: 0x000000018ea20a4c libsystem_platform.dylib`__os_log_simple_offset + 120
    frame #3: 0x000000018e824790 libsystem_malloc.dylib`malloc_vreport + 248
    frame #4: 0x000000018e839c84 libsystem_malloc.dylib`malloc_zone_error + 100
    frame #5: 0x000000018e82da3c libsystem_malloc.dylib`free_small_botch + 40
    frame #6: 0x0000000104777d1c App10`proc + 116
    frame #7: 0x0000000104777e88 App10`bar_five + 12
    frame #8: 0x0000000104777e9c App10`foo_five + 12
    frame #9: 0x0000000104777eb8 App10`thread_five + 20
    frame #10: 0x000000018ea0826c libsystem_pthread.dylib`_pthread_start + 148
```

```
(lldb) di -n proc
App10`proc:
    0x104777ca8 <+0>:    sub     sp, sp, #0x30
    0x104777cac <+4>:    stp     x29, x30, [sp, #0x20]
    0x104777cb0 <+8>:    add     x29, sp, #0x20
    0x104777cb4 <+12>:   b       0x104777cb8               ; <+16>
    0x104777cb8 <+16>:   bl      0x104777fa0               ; symbol stub for: rand
    0x104777cbc <+20>:   mov     w9, #0x2710
    0x104777cc0 <+24>:   stur    w9, [x29, #-0xc]
    0x104777cc4 <+28>:   sdiv    w8, w0, w9
    0x104777cc8 <+32>:   mul     w8, w8, w9
    0x104777ccc <+36>:   subs    w8, w0, w8
    0x104777cd0 <+40>:   stur    w8, [x29, #-0x4]
    0x104777cd4 <+44>:   bl      0x104777fa0               ; symbol stub for: rand
    0x104777cd8 <+48>:   ldur    w9, [x29, #-0xc]
    0x104777cdc <+52>:   sdiv    w8, w0, w9
    0x104777ce0 <+56>:   mul     w8, w8, w9
    0x104777ce4 <+60>:   subs    w8, w0, w8
    0x104777ce8 <+64>:   stur    w8, [x29, #-0x8]
    0x104777cec <+68>:   ldursw  x9, [x29, #-0x4]
    0x104777cf0 <+72>:   adrp    x8, 5
    0x104777cf4 <+76>:   add     x8, x8, #0x0             ; pAllocBuf
    0x104777cf8 <+80>:   ldr     x8, [x8, x9, lsl #3]
    0x104777cfc <+84>:   cbz     x8, 0x104777d30          ; <+136>
    0x104777d00 <+88>:   b       0x104777d04               ; <+92>
    0x104777d04 <+92>:   ldursw  x9, [x29, #-0x4]
    0x104777d08 <+96>:   adrp    x8, 5
    0x104777d0c <+100>:  add     x8, x8, #0x0             ; pAllocBuf
    0x104777d10 <+104>:  str     x8, [sp, #0x8]
    0x104777d14 <+108>:  ldr     x0, [x8, x9, lsl #3]
    0x104777d18 <+112>:  bl      0x104777f7c               ; symbol stub for: free
    0x104777d1c <+116>:  ldr     x9, [sp, #0x8]
    0x104777d20 <+120>:  ldursw  x10, [x29, #-0x4]
    0x104777d24 <+124>:  mov     x8, #0x0
    0x104777d28 <+128>:  str     x8, [x9, x10, lsl #3]
    0x104777d2c <+132>:  b       0x104777d30               ; <+136>
    0x104777d30 <+136>:  ldursw  x0, [x29, #-0x8]
    0x104777d34 <+140>:  bl      0x104777f88               ; symbol stub for: malloc
    0x104777d38 <+144>:  ldursw  x9, [x29, #-0x4]
    0x104777d3c <+148>:  adrp    x8, 5
    0x104777d40 <+152>:  add     x8, x8, #0x0             ; pAllocBuf
    0x104777d44 <+156>:  str     x0, [x8, x9, lsl #3]
    0x104777d48 <+160>:  b       0x104777cb8               ; <+16>
```

Note: Some calculations were going on before the *free* call. The parameter passed was in X0 and the calculation of that value involved X8, X9, and +8 offset. The latter value looks like the size of a pointer value; X9 is probably used as an index into the base address from X8. Let's examine these registers.

```
(lldb) f 6
frame #6: 0x0000000104777d1c App10`proc + 116
App10`proc:
->  0x104777d1c <+116>: ldr    x9, [sp, #0x8]
    0x104777d20 <+120>: ldursw x10, [x29, #-0x4]
    0x104777d24 <+124>: mov    x8, #0x0
    0x104777d28 <+128>: str    x8, [x9, x10, lsl #3]

(lldb) x/wd $x29-4
0x16b942f7c: 2192

(lldb) p/x 0x104777000+0x1000*5+0
(long) $1 = 0x000000010477c000

(lldb) p/x &pAllocBuf
(void **) $2 = 0x000000010477c000

(lldb) x/gx 0x000000010477c000+2192*8
0x104780480: 0x000000011f228600
```

7.   Dump the first 1000 elements of the array (`0x000000010477c000`) found in the *proc* function disassembly and identify a few addresses at the beginning:

```
(lldb) x/1000gx 0x000000010477c000 --force
0x10477c000: 0x000000011f08e400 0x0000000000000000
0x10477c010: 0x0000000000000000 0x0000000000000000
0x10477c020: 0x0000000000000000 0x0000000000000000
0x10477c030: 0x0000000000000000 0x0000000000000000
0x10477c040: 0x0000000000000000 0x0000000000000000
0x10477c050: 0x0000000000000000 0x0000000000000000
0x10477c060: 0x0000000000000000 0x0000000000000000
0x10477c070: 0x0000000000000000 0x0000000000000000
0x10477c080: 0x0000000000000000 0x0000000000000000
0x10477c090: 0x0000000000000000 0x0000000000000000
0x10477c0a0: 0x0000000000000000 0x0000000000000000
0x10477c0b0: 0x0000000000000000 0x0000000000000000
0x10477c0c0: 0x0000000000000000 0x0000000000000000
0x10477c0d0: 0x0000000000000000 0x0000000000000000
0x10477c0e0: 0x0000000000000000 0x0000000000000000
0x10477c0f0: 0x0000000000000000 0x0000000000000000
0x10477c100: 0x0000000000000000 0x0000000000000000
0x10477c110: 0x0000000000000000 0x0000000000000000
0x10477c120: 0x0000000000000000 0x0000000000000000
0x10477c130: 0x0000000000000000 0x0000000000000000
0x10477c140: 0x0000000000000000 0x0000000000000000
0x10477c150: 0x0000000000000000 0x0000000000000000
0x10477c160: 0x0000000000000000 0x0000000000000000
0x10477c170: 0x0000000000000000 0x0000000000000000
0x10477c180: 0x0000000000000000 0x0000000000000000
0x10477c190: 0x0000000000000000 0x0000000000000000
0x10477c1a0: 0x0000000000000000 0x000000011f075000
0x10477c1b0: 0x0000000000000000 0x0000000000000000
0x10477c1c0: 0x0000000000000000 0x0000000000000000
0x10477c1d0: 0x0000000000000000 0x0000000000000000
0x10477c1e0: 0x0000000000000000 0x0000000000000000
0x10477c1f0: 0x0000000000000000 0x0000000000000000
```

```
0x10477c200:  0x0000000000000000  0x0000000000000000
0x10477c210:  0x0000000000000000  0x0000000000000000
0x10477c220:  0x0000000000000000  0x0000000000000000
0x10477c230:  0x0000000000000000  0x0000000000000000
0x10477c240:  0x0000000000000000  0x000000011f008200
0x10477c250:  0x0000000000000000  0x0000000000000000
0x10477c260:  0x0000000000000000  0x0000000000000000
0x10477c270:  0x0000000000000000  0x0000000000000000
0x10477c280:  0x0000000000000000  0x0000000000000000
0x10477c290:  0x0000000000000000  0x0000000000000000
0x10477c2a0:  0x0000000000000000  0x0000000000000000
0x10477c2b0:  0x0000000000000000  0x0000000000000000
0x10477c2c0:  0x0000000000000000  0x0000000000000000
0x10477c2d0:  0x0000000000000000  0x0000000000000000
0x10477c2e0:  0x0000000000000000  0x000000011f1fa600
0x10477c2f0:  0x000000011f04e800  0x0000000000000000
0x10477c300:  0x0000000000000000  0x0000000000000000
0x10477c310:  0x0000000000000000  0x0000000000000000
0x10477c320:  0x0000000000000000  0x0000000120086c00
0x10477c330:  0x0000000000000000  0x0000000000000000
0x10477c340:  0x0000000000000000  0x000000011f804430
0x10477c350:  0x0000000000000000  0x0000000000000000
0x10477c360:  0x0000000000000000  0x0000000000000000
0x10477c370:  0x0000000000000000  0x0000000000000000
0x10477c380:  0x0000000000000000  0x0000000000000000
0x10477c390:  0x0000000000000000  0x0000000000000000
0x10477c3a0:  0x0000000000000000  0x0000000000000000
0x10477c3b0:  0x0000000000000000  0x0000000000000000
0x10477c3c0:  0x0000000000000000  0x0000000000000000
0x10477c3d0:  0x0000000000000000  0x0000000000000000
0x10477c3e0:  0x0000000000000000  0x0000000000000000
0x10477c3f0:  0x0000000000000000  0x0000000000000000
0x10477c400:  0x0000000000000000  0x0000000000000000
0x10477c410:  0x0000000000000000  0x0000000000000000
0x10477c420:  0x0000000000000000  0x0000000000000000
0x10477c430:  0x0000000000000000  0x0000000000000000
0x10477c440:  0x0000000000000000  0x0000000000000000
0x10477c450:  0x0000000000000000  0x0000000000000000
0x10477c460:  0x0000000000000000  0x0000000000000000
0x10477c470:  0x0000000000000000  0x0000000000000000
0x10477c480:  0x0000000000000000  0x0000000000000000
0x10477c490:  0x0000000000000000  0x0000000000000000
0x10477c4a0:  0x0000000000000000  0x0000000000000000
0x10477c4b0:  0x0000000000000000  0x0000000000000000
0x10477c4c0:  0x0000000000000000  0x0000000000000000
0x10477c4d0:  0x0000000000000000  0x0000000000000000
0x10477c4e0:  0x0000000000000000  0x0000000000000000
0x10477c4f0:  0x0000000000000000  0x0000000000000000
0x10477c500:  0x0000000000000000  0x0000000000000000
0x10477c510:  0x0000000000000000  0x0000000000000000
0x10477c520:  0x0000000000000000  0x0000000000000000
0x10477c530:  0x0000000000000000  0x0000000000000000
0x10477c540:  0x0000000000000000  0x0000000000000000
0x10477c550:  0x0000000000000000  0x000000011f0bb600
0x10477c560:  0x0000000000000000  0x0000000000000000
[...]
```

Exercise X11

- **Goal:** Learn how to identify synchronization wait chains, deadlocks, hidden and handled exceptions

- **Patterns:** Wait Chains; Deadlock; Execution Residue; Handled Exception

- \AMCDA-Dumps\Exercise-X11.pdf

Exercise X11

Goal: Learn how to identify synchronization wait chains, deadlocks, hidden and handled exceptions.

Patterns: Wait Chains; Deadlock; Execution Residue; Handled Exception.

1.   Identify possible wait chain and deadlock in the process sample report *App11_sample.txt* which was generated after the process appeared hanging:

```
Sampling process 95061 for 3 seconds with 1 millisecond of run time between samples
Sampling completed, processing symbols...
Analysis of sampling App11 (pid 95061) every 1 millisecond
Process:         App11 [95061]
Path:            /Users/USER/*/App11
Load Address:    0x10493c000
Identifier:      App11
Version:         0
Code Type:       ARM64
Platform:        macOS
Parent Process:  zsh [93724]

Date/Time:       2022-12-10 11:48:43.519 +0000
Launch Time:     2022-12-10 11:29:44.648 +0000
OS Version:      macOS 12.6 (21G115)
Report Version:  7
Analysis Tool:   /usr/bin/sample

Physical footprint:        1089K
Physical footprint (peak): 1089K
----

Call graph:
    2554 Thread_3253936   DispatchQueue_1: com.apple.main-thread  (serial)
    + 2554 start  (in dyld) + 520  [0x1049c908c]
    +   2554 main  (in App11) + 204  [0x10493ff10]
    +     2554 sleep  (in libsystem_c.dylib) + 76  [0x18e8e1b90]
    +       2554 sleep  (in libsystem_c.dylib) + 52  [0x18e8e1b78]
    +         2554 nanosleep  (in libsystem_c.dylib) + 220  [0x18e8d6fc8]
    +           2554 __semwait_signal  (in libsystem_kernel.dylib) + 8  [0x18e9ce06c]
    2554 Thread_3253937
    + 2554 thread_start  (in libsystem_pthread.dylib) + 8  [0x18ea0308c]
    +   2554 _pthread_start  (in libsystem_pthread.dylib) + 148  [0x18ea0826c]
    +     2554 thread_one(void*)  (in App11) + 20  [0x10493fcfc]
    +       2554 foo_one()  (in App11) + 12  [0x10493fce0]
    +         2554 bar_one()  (in App11) + 16  [0x10493fccc]
    +           2554 sleep  (in libsystem_c.dylib) + 76  [0x18e8e1b90]
    +             2554 sleep  (in libsystem_c.dylib) + 52  [0x18e8e1b78]
    +               2554 nanosleep  (in libsystem_c.dylib) + 220  [0x18e8d6fc8]
    +                 2554 __semwait_signal  (in libsystem_kernel.dylib) + 8  [0x18e9ce06c]
    2554 Thread_3253938
    + 2554 thread_start  (in libsystem_pthread.dylib) + 8  [0x18ea0308c]
    +   2554 _pthread_start  (in libsystem_pthread.dylib) + 148  [0x18ea0826c]
    +     2554 thread_two(void*)  (in App11) + 20  [0x10493fd48]
    +       2554 foo_two()  (in App11) + 12  [0x10493fd2c]
    +         2554 bar_two()  (in App11) + 12  [0x10493fd18]
    +           2554 procA()  (in App11) + 112  [0x10493fc58]
    +             2554 _pthread_mutex_firstfit_lock_slow  (in libsystem_pthread.dylib) + 248  [0x18ea02cf8]
    +               2554 _pthread_mutex_firstfit_lock_wait  (in libsystem_pthread.dylib) + 84  [0x18ea05384]
    +                 2554 __psynch_mutexwait  (in libsystem_kernel.dylib) + 8  [0x18e9cd738]
    2554 Thread_3253987
    + 2554 thread_start  (in libsystem_pthread.dylib) + 8  [0x18ea0308c]
    +   2554 _pthread_start  (in libsystem_pthread.dylib) + 148  [0x18ea0826c]
    +     2554 thread_three(void*)  (in App11) + 20  [0x10493fd98]
    +       2554 foo_three()  (in App11) + 12  [0x10493fd7c]
    +         2554 bar_three()  (in App11) + 16  [0x10493fd68]
    +           2554 sleep  (in libsystem_c.dylib) + 76  [0x18e8e1b90]
    +             2554 sleep  (in libsystem_c.dylib) + 52  [0x18e8e1b78]
    +               2554 nanosleep  (in libsystem_c.dylib) + 220  [0x18e8d6fc8]
    +                 2554 __semwait_signal  (in libsystem_kernel.dylib) + 8  [0x18e9ce06c]
    2554 Thread_3253988
    + 2554 thread_start  (in libsystem_pthread.dylib) + 8  [0x18ea0308c]
    +   2554 _pthread_start  (in libsystem_pthread.dylib) + 148  [0x18ea0826c]
    +     2554 thread_four(void*)  (in App11) + 20  [0x10493fde4]
    +       2554 foo_four()  (in App11) + 12  [0x10493fdc8]
    +         2554 bar_four()  (in App11) + 12  [0x10493fdb4]
    +           2554 procB()  (in App11) + 44  [0x10493fc98]
    +             2554 _pthread_mutex_firstfit_lock_slow  (in libsystem_pthread.dylib) + 248  [0x18ea02cf8]
    +               2554 _pthread_mutex_firstfit_lock_wait  (in libsystem_pthread.dylib) + 84  [0x18ea05384]
    +                 2554 __psynch_mutexwait  (in libsystem_kernel.dylib) + 8  [0x18e9cd738]
    2554 Thread_3253989
      2554 thread_start  (in libsystem_pthread.dylib) + 8  [0x18ea0308c]
        2554 _pthread_start  (in libsystem_pthread.dylib) + 148  [0x18ea0826c]
          2554 thread_five(void*)  (in App11) + 20  [0x10493fe34]
            2554 foo_five()  (in App11) + 12  [0x10493fe18]
              2554 bar_five()  (in App11) + 16  [0x10493fe04]
                2554 sleep  (in libsystem_c.dylib) + 76  [0x18e8e1b90]
                  2554 sleep  (in libsystem_c.dylib) + 52  [0x18e8e1b78]
                    2554 nanosleep  (in libsystem_c.dylib) + 220  [0x18e8d6fc8]
                      2554 __semwait_signal  (in libsystem_kernel.dylib) + 8  [0x18e9ce06c]
```

```
Total number in stack (recursive counted multiple, when >=5):
    5       _pthread_start  (in libsystem_pthread.dylib) + 148  [0x18ea0826c]
    5       thread_start  (in libsystem_pthread.dylib) + 8  [0x18ea0308c]

Sort by top of stack, same collapsed (when >= 5):
    __semwait_signal  (in libsystem_kernel.dylib)       10216
    __psynch_mutexwait  (in libsystem_kernel.dylib)      5108

Binary Images:
    0x10493c000 -      0x10493ffff +App11 (0) <759D22A7-7E47-3ADD-8E48-A4867F24E04E> /Users/*/App11
    0x1049c4000 -      0x104a2174b  dyld (960) <38EE9FE9-B66D-3066-8C5C-6DDF0D6944C6> /usr/lib/dyld
    0x18e72d000 -      0x18e72effe  libsystem_blocks.dylib (79.1) <96462BD5-6BB4-3B69-89C9-2C70FA8852E7> /usr/lib/system/libsystem_blocks.dylib
    0x18e72f000 -      0x18e770ff3  libxpc.dylib (2236.140.2) <21D05A8B-D782-3FA7-9A9D-55A45E6E6621> /usr/lib/system/libxpc.dylib
    0x18e771000 -      0x18e78affe  libsystem_trace.dylib (1375.140.2) <B5524014-1A7F-3D07-8855-5E75A55E4A11> /usr/lib/system/libsystem_trace.dylib
    0x18e78b000 -      0x18e814fef  libcorecrypto.dylib (1218.120.10) <2D00FEEC-7984-342B-9516-5D49C5D98204> /usr/lib/system/libcorecrypto.dylib
    0x18e815000 -      0x18e83fffb  libsystem_malloc.dylib (374.120.1) <427675C6-C4BF-390A-AF93-B28DAC36876A> /usr/lib/system/libsystem_malloc.dylib
    0x18e840000 -      0x18e886ff7  libdispatch.dylib (1325.120.2) <B3C7A004-1069-3171-B630-2C386A8B399C> /usr/lib/system/libdispatch.dylib
    0x18e887000 -      0x18e8c4fee  libobjc.A.dylib (841.13) <EC96F0FA-6341-3E1D-BE54-49B544E17F7D> /usr/lib/libobjc.A.dylib
    0x18e8c5000 -      0x18e8c7fff  libsystem_featureflags.dylib (56) <5B14B45B-A15B-31AD-93FB-BAC43C001A23> /usr/lib/system/libsystem_featureflags.dylib
    0x18e8c8000 -      0x18e949fff  libsystem_c.dylib (1507.100.9) <B25D2080-BB9E-38D6-8236-9CEF4B2F11A3> /usr/lib/system/libsystem_c.dylib
    0x18e94a000 -      0x18e9b0ffb  libc++.1.dylib (1300.25) <3D1E6031-901D-3DF1-9E9A-F85FF1C2E803> /usr/lib/libc++.1.dylib
    0x18e9b1000 -      0x18e9c8ffb  libc++abi.dylib (1300.25) <4E8D8A11-4217-3D56-9D41-5426F7CF307C> /usr/lib/libc++abi.dylib
    0x18e9c9000 -      0x18ea00ffb  libsystem_kernel.dylib (8020.140.49) <A9D87740-9C1D-3468-BF60-720A8D713CBA> /usr/lib/system/libsystem_kernel.dylib
    0x18ea01000 -      0x18ea0dff3  libsystem_pthread.dylib (486.100.11) <63C4EEF9-69A5-38B1-996E-8D31B66A051D> /usr/lib/system/libsystem_pthread.dylib
    0x18ea0e000 -      0x18ea1afff  libdyld.dylib (960) <F298A03D-5BC7-3BCA-8880-B956E52EAD01> /usr/lib/system/libdyld.dylib
    0x18ea1b000 -      0x18ea22feb  libsystem_platform.dylib (273.100.5) <A57FE7FB-9FF8-30CE-97A2-625D6DA20D00> /usr/lib/system/libsystem_platform.dylib
    0x18ea23000 -      0x18ea4ffff  libsystem_info.dylib (554.120.2) <413C2A97-5D32-317D-8E32-4258B8E728CE> /usr/lib/system/libsystem_info.dylib
    0x19113f000 -      0x191149ff3  libsystem_darwin.dylib (1507.100.9) <5D456083-E21E-319D-9BA0-57702B3FB09B> /usr/lib/system/libsystem_darwin.dylib
    0x191598000 -      0x1915a7fff  libsystem_notify.dylib (301) <12A2A8B6-80B4-36CA-8245-830EBEDEF1C4> /usr/lib/system/libsystem_notify.dylib
    0x193b14000 -      0x193b2cf7  libsystem_networkextension.dylib (1471.141.2) <4C9F32FA-D88C-3966-A2F0-7030841C8093>
/usr/lib/system/libsystem_networkextension.dylib
    0x193b86000 -      0x193b9dff7  libsystem_asl.dylib (392.100.2) <EC04DA81-C3B5-3AC5-9042-7F07DF48B42A> /usr/lib/system/libsystem_asl.dylib
    0x1952ea000 -      0x1952fcfff  libsystem_symptoms.dylib (1617.140.3) <2906E453-3254-32EA-880E-14AEEF5D7ECD> /usr/lib/system/libsystem_symptoms.dylib
    0x1972de000 -      0x1972fcfff  libsystem_containermanager.dylib (383.120.2) <D38210EF-8F23-380B-8B43-BB06A7305F67>
/usr/lib/system/libsystem_containermanager.dylib
    0x198085000 -      0x198089fff  libsystem_configuration.dylib (1163.140.3) <3977B29D-624D-3DEE-94EF-95D29FB25252>
/usr/lib/system/libsystem_configuration.dylib
    0x19808a000 -      0x19808efff  libsystem_sandbox.dylib (1657.140.5) <2A2EB0A4-9822-36D1-999B-181D1BB964B5> /usr/lib/system/libsystem_sandbox.dylib
    0x198bf0000 -      0x198bf2fff  libquarantine.dylib (133.120.2) <B887350E-B17A-386C-B5EB-26F08C7C0152> /usr/lib/system/libquarantine.dylib
    0x19925d000 -      0x199262fff  libsystem_coreservices.dylib (133) <D5F19732-3AA0-3B93-9F25-318A27DE5AC5>
/usr/lib/system/libsystem_coreservices.dylib
    0x1994c8000 -      0x1994feffb  libsystem_m.dylib (3204.80.2) <31A9DAE0-FB1F-3CB8-8AB6-CA5A1192DFD8> /usr/lib/system/libsystem_m.dylib
    0x199500000 -      0x199508ff3  libmacho.dylib (994) <ED4EE8AE-EA60-33B7-9676-E6119B7449E3> /usr/lib/system/libmacho.dylib
    0x199525000 -      0x199531ffb  libcommonCrypto.dylib (60191.100.1) <FB7DF5AC-35DB-3B80-B2F6-BC69375390AE> /usr/lib/system/libcommonCrypto.dylib
    0x199532000 -      0x19953cfff  libunwind.dylib (202.2) <D9CA1CE3-6B1A-3E2B-BBAD-9D9B1DB00F92> /usr/lib/system/libunwind.dylib
    0x19953d000 -      0x199544ffb  liboah.dylib (254.25) <7E53021F-FDCE-3EC9-8B4C-97AD3B21D02E> /usr/lib/liboah.dylib
    0x199545000 -      0x19954dff7  libcopyfile.dylib (180.100.3) <654D0DA0-8277-361D-88DC-1430504B5436> /usr/lib/system/libcopyfile.dylib
    0x19954e000 -      0x199551ffb  libcompiler_rt.dylib (103.1) <68788078-BF1D-3C01-91A7-4C59FD78FB75> /usr/lib/system/libcompiler_rt.dylib
    0x199552000 -      0x199556fff  libsystem_collections.dylib (1507.100.9) <4928F3C4-D438-354F-BA1C-0BD79F6475F3>
/usr/lib/system/libsystem_collections.dylib
    0x199557000 -      0x19959ffb  libsystem_secinit.dylib (107.100.5) <18F251D3-8C66-3B8B-817A-C124498478F4> /usr/lib/system/libsystem_secinit.dylib
    0x19955a000 -      0x19955cfff  libremovefile.dylib (60) <157C8E50-D4A5-3DFC-8E0B-756E03E2082B> /usr/lib/system/libremovefile.dylib
    0x19955d000 -      0x19955dfff  libkeymgr.dylib (31) <49D72074-0C58-317C-9B8B-762C13C0C084> /usr/lib/system/libkeymgr.dylib
    0x19955e000 -      0x199566fff  libsystem_dnssd.dylib (1557.140.5.0.1) <10A4374A-D15A-31C8-AC6F-2DCC10D06444> /usr/lib/system/libsystem_dnssd.dylib
    0x199567000 -      0x19956cff7  libcache.dylib (85) <7E9E684F-57B6-3196-8AEC-908B46DEEBD4> /usr/lib/system/libcache.dylib
    0x19956d000 -      0x19956efff  libSystem.B.dylib (1311.120.1) <9232C168-6ECA-3B7D-B081-E7C46B379836> /usr/lib/libSystem.B.dylib
    0x19f8c1000 -      0x19f8c1fff  libsystem_product_info_filter.dylib (10) <E49E2F05-0E01-352E-8CB7-276F8EF8E6D6>
/usr/lib/system/libsystem_product_info_filter.dylib
Sample analysis of process 95061 written to file /dev/stdout
```

Note: We see core threads #2 and #4 blocked waiting for a mutex lock.

2.   Load a core dump *App11-95061-20221210T114941Z, App11* executable and list all threads:

```
% lldb -c ~/AMCDA-Dumps/App11-95061-20221210T114941Z -f
~/AMCDA-Dumps/Apps/App11/Build/Products/Release/App11
(lldb) target create "/Users/training/AMCDA-Dumps/Apps/App11/Build/Products/Release/App11" --
core "/Users/training/AMCDA-Dumps/App11-95061-20221210T114941Z"
Core file '/Users/training/AMCDA-Dumps/App11-95061-20221210T114941Z' (arm64) was loaded.
```

```
(lldb) thread backtrace all
* thread #1
  * frame #0: 0x000000018e9ce06c libsystem_kernel.dylib`__semwait_signal + 8
    frame #1: 0x000000018e8d6fc8 libsystem_c.dylib`nanosleep + 220
    frame #2: 0x000000018e8e1b78 libsystem_c.dylib`sleep + 52
    frame #3: 0x000000018e8e1b90 libsystem_c.dylib`sleep + 76
    frame #4: 0x000000010493ff10 App11`main + 204
    frame #5: 0x000000001049c908c dyld`start + 520
  thread #2
    frame #0: 0x000000018e9ce06c libsystem_kernel.dylib`__semwait_signal + 8
    frame #1: 0x000000018e8d6fc8 libsystem_c.dylib`nanosleep + 220
    frame #2: 0x000000018e8e1b78 libsystem_c.dylib`sleep + 52
    frame #3: 0x000000018e8e1b90 libsystem_c.dylib`sleep + 76
    frame #4: 0x000000010493fccc App11`bar_one() + 16
    frame #5: 0x000000010493fce0 App11`foo_one() + 12
```

```
      frame #6: 0x000000010493fcfc App11`thread_one(void*) + 20
      frame #7: 0x000000018ea0826c libsystem_pthread.dylib`_pthread_start + 148
  thread #3
    frame #0: 0x000000018e9cd738 libsystem_kernel.dylib`__psynch_mutexwait + 8
      frame #1: 0x000000018ea05384 libsystem_pthread.dylib`_pthread_mutex_firstfit_lock_wait + 84
      frame #2: 0x000000018ea02cf8 libsystem_pthread.dylib`_pthread_mutex_firstfit_lock_slow + 248
      frame #3: 0x000000010493fc58 App11`procA() + 112
      frame #4: 0x000000010493fd18 App11`bar_two() + 12
      frame #5: 0x000000010493fd2c App11`foo_two() + 12
      frame #6: 0x000000010493fd48 App11`thread_two(void*) + 20
      frame #7: 0x000000018ea0826c libsystem_pthread.dylib`_pthread_start + 148
  thread #4
      frame #0: 0x000000018e9ce06c libsystem_kernel.dylib`__semwait_signal + 8
      frame #1: 0x000000018e8d6fc8 libsystem_c.dylib`nanosleep + 220
      frame #2: 0x000000018e8e1b78 libsystem_c.dylib`sleep + 52
      frame #3: 0x000000018e8e1b90 libsystem_c.dylib`sleep + 76
      frame #4: 0x000000010493fd68 App11`bar_three() + 16
      frame #5: 0x000000010493fd7c App11`foo_three() + 12
      frame #6: 0x000000010493fd98 App11`thread_three(void*) + 20
      frame #7: 0x000000018ea0826c libsystem_pthread.dylib`_pthread_start + 148
  thread #5
    frame #0: 0x000000018e9cd738 libsystem_kernel.dylib`__psynch_mutexwait + 8
      frame #1: 0x000000018ea05384 libsystem_pthread.dylib`_pthread_mutex_firstfit_lock_wait + 84
      frame #2: 0x000000018ea02cf8 libsystem_pthread.dylib`_pthread_mutex_firstfit_lock_slow + 248
      frame #3: 0x000000010493fc98 App11`procB() + 44
      frame #4: 0x000000010493fdb4 App11`bar_four() + 12
      frame #5: 0x000000010493fdc8 App11`foo_four() + 12
      frame #6: 0x000000010493fde4 App11`thread_four(void*) + 20
      frame #7: 0x000000018ea0826c libsystem_pthread.dylib`_pthread_start + 148
  thread #6
      frame #0: 0x000000018e9ce06c libsystem_kernel.dylib`__semwait_signal + 8
      frame #1: 0x000000018e8d6fc8 libsystem_c.dylib`nanosleep + 220
      frame #2: 0x000000018e8e1b78 libsystem_c.dylib`sleep + 52
      frame #3: 0x000000018e8e1b90 libsystem_c.dylib`sleep + 76
      frame #4: 0x000000010493fe04 App11`bar_five() + 16
      frame #5: 0x000000010493fe18 App11`foo_five() + 12
      frame #6: 0x000000010493fe34 App11`thread_five(void*) + 20
      frame #7: 0x000000018ea0826c libsystem_pthread.dylib`_pthread_start + 148
```

2.   Check thread 5 (core thread #4) and its waiting code:

```
(lldb) thread select 5
* thread #5
    frame #0: 0x000000018e9cd738 libsystem_kernel.dylib`__psynch_mutexwait + 8
libsystem_kernel.dylib`:
->  0x18e9cd738 <+8>:  b.lo    0x18e9cd758               ; <+40>
    0x18e9cd73c <+12>: pacibsp
    0x18e9cd740 <+16>: stp     x29, x30, [sp, #-0x10]!
    0x18e9cd744 <+20>: mov     x29, sp


(lldb) bt
* thread #5
  * frame #0: 0x000000018e9cd738 libsystem_kernel.dylib`__psynch_mutexwait + 8
    frame #1: 0x000000018ea05384 libsystem_pthread.dylib`_pthread_mutex_firstfit_lock_wait + 84
    frame #2: 0x000000018ea02cf8 libsystem_pthread.dylib`_pthread_mutex_firstfit_lock_slow + 248
    frame #3: 0x000000010493fc98 App11`procB() + 44
    frame #4: 0x000000010493fdb4 App11`bar_four() + 12
    frame #5: 0x000000010493fdc8 App11`foo_four() + 12
    frame #6: 0x000000010493fde4 App11`thread_four(void*) + 20
    frame #7: 0x000000018ea0826c libsystem_pthread.dylib`_pthread_start + 148
```

```
(lldb) di -n procB
App11`procB:
    0x10493fc6c <+0>:  sub     sp, sp, #0x20
    0x10493fc70 <+4>:  stp     x29, x30, [sp, #0x10]
    0x10493fc74 <+8>:  add     x29, sp, #0x10
    0x10493fc78 <+12>: adrp    x0, 5
    0x10493fc7c <+16>: add     x0, x0, #0x40           ; mutexB
    0x10493fc80 <+20>: str     x0, [sp, #0x8]
    0x10493fc84 <+24>: bl      0x10493ff68             ; symbol stub for: pthread_mutex_lock
    0x10493fc88 <+28>: adrp    x0, 5
    0x10493fc8c <+32>: add     x0, x0, #0x0            ; mutexA
    0x10493fc90 <+36>: str     x0, [sp]
    0x10493fc94 <+40>: bl      0x10493ff68             ; symbol stub for: pthread_mutex_lock
    0x10493fc98 <+44>: mov     w0, #0x1e
    0x10493fc9c <+48>: bl      0x10493ff80             ; symbol stub for: sleep
    0x10493fca0 <+52>: ldr     x0, [sp]
    0x10493fca4 <+56>: bl      0x10493ff68             ; symbol stub for: pthread_mutex_lock
    0x10493fca8 <+60>: ldr     x0, [sp, #0x8]
    0x10493fcac <+64>: bl      0x10493ff68             ; symbol stub for: pthread_mutex_lock
    0x10493fcb0 <+68>: ldp     x29, x30, [sp, #0x10]
    0x10493fcb4 <+72>: add     sp, sp, #0x20
    0x10493fcb8 <+76>: ret
```

Note: We see that mutexA was passed to the second mutex lock call. We see the thread owns mutexB but is waiting for mutexA.

3.   Check thread 3 (core thread #2) and its waiting code:

```
(lldb) thread select 3
* thread #3
    frame #0: 0x000000018e9cd738 libsystem_kernel.dylib`__psynch_mutexwait + 8
libsystem_kernel.dylib`:
->  0x18e9cd738 <+8>:  b.lo    0x18e9cd758             ; <+40>
    0x18e9cd73c <+12>: pacibsp
    0x18e9cd740 <+16>: stp     x29, x30, [sp, #-0x10]!
    0x18e9cd744 <+20>: mov     x29, sp
```

```
(lldb) bt
* thread #3
  * frame #0: 0x000000018e9cd738 libsystem_kernel.dylib`__psynch_mutexwait + 8
    frame #1: 0x000000018ea05384 libsystem_pthread.dylib`_pthread_mutex_firstfit_lock_wait + 84
    frame #2: 0x000000018ea02cf8 libsystem_pthread.dylib`_pthread_mutex_firstfit_lock_slow + 248
    frame #3: 0x000000010493fc58 App11`procA() + 112
    frame #4: 0x000000010493fd18 App11`bar_two() + 12
    frame #5: 0x000000010493fd2c App11`foo_two() + 12
    frame #6: 0x000000010493fd48 App11`thread_two(void*) + 20
    frame #7: 0x000000018ea0826c libsystem_pthread.dylib`_pthread_start + 148
```

```
(lldb) di -n procA
App11`procA:
    0x10493fbe8 <+0>:  sub     sp, sp, #0x30
    0x10493fbec <+4>:  stp     x29, x30, [sp, #0x20]
    0x10493fbf0 <+8>:  add     x29, sp, #0x20
    0x10493fbf4 <+12>: adrp    x0, 5
    0x10493fbf8 <+16>: add     x0, x0, #0x0            ; mutexA
    0x10493fbfc <+20>: bl      0x10493ff68             ; symbol stub for: pthread_mutex_lock
    0x10493fc00 <+24>: b       0x10493fc04            ; <+28>
    0x10493fc04 <+28>: bl      0x10493fbc4            ; procC()
    0x10493fc08 <+32>: b       0x10493fc0c            ; <+36>
    0x10493fc0c <+36>: adrp    x0, 5
    0x10493fc10 <+40>: add     x0, x0, #0x0            ; mutexA
    0x10493fc14 <+44>: bl      0x10493ff74             ; symbol stub for: pthread_mutex_unlock
```

```
0x10493fc18 <+48>:  b     0x10493fc1c              ; <+52>
0x10493fc1c <+52>:  b     0x10493fc40              ; <+88>
0x10493fc20 <+56>:  mov   x8, x1
0x10493fc24 <+60>:  stur  x0, [x29, #-0x8]
0x10493fc28 <+64>:  stur  w8, [x29, #-0xc]
0x10493fc2c <+68>:  b     0x10493fc30              ; <+72>
0x10493fc30 <+72>:  ldur  x0, [x29, #-0x8]
0x10493fc34 <+76>:  bl    0x10493ff2c              ; symbol stub for: __cxa_begin_catch
0x10493fc38 <+80>:  bl    0x10493ff38              ; symbol stub for: __cxa_end_catch
0x10493fc3c <+84>:  b     0x10493fc40              ; <+88>
0x10493fc40 <+88>:  mov   w0, #0x14
0x10493fc44 <+92>:  bl    0x10493ff80              ; symbol stub for: sleep
0x10493fc48 <+96>:  adrp  x0, 5
0x10493fc4c <+100>: add   x0, x0, #0x40            ; mutexB
0x10493fc50 <+104>: str   x0, [sp, #0x8]
0x10493fc54 <+108>: bl    0x10493ff68              ; symbol stub for: pthread_mutex_lock
0x10493fc58 <+112>: ldr   x0, [sp, #0x8]
0x10493fc5c <+116>: bl    0x10493ff74              ; symbol stub for: pthread_mutex_unlock
0x10493fc60 <+120>: ldp   x29, x30, [sp, #0x20]
0x10493fc64 <+124>: add   sp, sp, #0x30
0x10493fc68 <+128>: ret
```

Note: We see that the thread is waiting for mutexB and possibly owns mutexA. Summarizing: one thread running through procB owns mutexB and is waiting for mutexA. The other thread running through procA owns mutexA (not released because of some exceptions) and is waiting for mutexB. We have an example of a deadlock here.

4.   We notice catch function calls, determine the start of the exception processing block, and check if there was any past exception processing and the block start address references (execution residue):

```
(lldb) x/512a $sp-0x1000 --force
0x16b5d5f00: 0xd3a900016b5d63a8
0x16b5d5f08: 0x0000000104a78060 -> 0x0000000104a26400 dyld`vtable for dyld4::APIs + 16
0x16b5d5f10: 0x000000010493c000 App11`_mh_execute_header
0x16b5d5f18: 0x000000016b5d5fe0 -> 0x0000000104a3c310 dyld`_NSConcreteStackBlock
0x16b5d5f20: 0x000000016b5d5fd0
0x16b5d5f28: 0xc1010001049f9c9c (0x00000001049f9c9c) dyld`dyld3::MachOFile::forEachSection(void
(dyld3::MachOFile::SectionInfo const&, bool, bool&) block_pointer) const + 220
0x16b5d5f30: 0x0000000104a3c310 dyld`_NSConcreteStackBlock
0x16b5d5f38: 0x0000000042000000
0x16b5d5f40: 0x00000001049f9cc8 dyld`invocation function for block in dyld3::MachOFile::forEachSection(void
(dyld3::MachOFile::SectionInfo const&, bool, bool&) block_pointer) const
0x16b5d5f48: 0x0000000104a26fd8 dyld`__block_descriptor_tmp.87
0x16b5d5f50: 0x000000016b5d5fe0 -> 0x0000000104a3c310 dyld`_NSConcreteStackBlock
0x16b5d5f58: 0x000000016b5d5f78
0x16b5d5f60: 0x000000010493c000 App11`_mh_execute_header
0x16b5d5f68: 0x000000016b5d5fa4
0x16b5d5f70: 0x000000016b5d6000
0x16b5d5f78: 0x0000000000000000
0x16b5d5f80: 0x000000016b5d5f78
0x16b5d5f88: 0x0000000200000000
0x16b5d5f90: 0x0000000100000002
0x16b5d5f98: 0x0000000000000000
0x16b5d5fa0: 0x63675f5f0000b000
0x16b5d5fa8: 0x7470656378655f63
0x16b5d5fb0: 0x000000006261745f
0x16b5d5fb8: 0xd239cff916f50002
0x16b5d5fc0: 0x0000000000000001
0x16b5d5fc8: 0x000000016b5d60c0 -> 0x000000010493c000 App11`_mh_execute_header
0x16b5d5fd0: 0x000000016b5d6060
0x16b5d5fd8: 0x272e0001049fc380 (0x00000001049fc380) dyld`dyld3::MachOLoaded::findSectionContent(char const*, char
const*, unsigned long long&, bool) const + 136
0x16b5d5fe0: 0x0000000104a3c310 dyld`_NSConcreteStackBlock
0x16b5d5fe8: 0x0000000042000000
0x16b5d5ff0: 0x00000001049fc3a8 dyld`invocation function for block in dyld3::MachOLoaded::findSectionContent(char
const*, char const*, unsigned long long&, bool) const
0x16b5d5ff8: 0x0000000104a272d8 dyld`__block_descriptor_tmp.59
0x16b5d6000: 0x000000016b5d6030
0x16b5d6008: 0x000000010493c000 App11`_mh_execute_header
0x16b5d6010: 0x0000000104a1d00e "__unwind_info"
```

```
0x16b5d6018: 0x0000000104a1cffc "__TEXT"
0x16b5d6020: 0x000000016b5d6080
0x16b5d6028: 0x0000000000000000
0x16b5d6030: 0x0000000000000000
0x16b5d6038: 0x000000016b5d6030
0x16b5d6040: 0x0000002000000000
0x16b5d6048: 0x000000010493ffa0
0x16b5d6050: 0x0000000000000001
0x16b5d6058: 0x000000016b5d60c0 -> 0x000000010493c000 App11`_mh_execute_header
0x16b5d6060: 0x000000016b5d60b0
0x16b5d6068: 0x1c798001049ebb98 (0x00000001049ebb98) dyld`dyld4::APIs::_dyld_find_unwind_sections(void*,
dyld_unwind_sections*) + 216
0x16b5d6070: 0x0000000000000000
0x16b5d6078: 0x0000000000000000
0x16b5d6080: 0x0000000000000060
0x16b5d6088: 0x000000010493c000 App11`_mh_execute_header
0x16b5d6090: 0xd3a900016b5d63a8
0x16b5d6098: 0x000000016b5d6f60
0x16b5d60a0: 0x000000010493fc20 App11`procA() + 56
0x16b5d60a8: 0x000000016b5d63a8 -> 0x00000001e925bd90 libunwind.dylib`vtable for
libunwind::UnwindCursor<libunwind::LocalAddressSpace, libunwind::Registers_arm64> + 16
0x16b5d60b0: 0x000000016b5d6160
0x16b5d60b8: 0xdb4a000199536f24 (0x0000000199536f24)
libunwind.dylib`libunwind::UnwindCursor<libunwind::LocalAddressSpace,
libunwind::Registers_arm64>::setInfoBasedOnIPRegister(bool) + 120
0x16b5d60c0: 0x000000010493c000 App11`_mh_execute_header
0x16b5d60c8: 0x0000000000000000
0x16b5d60d0: 0x0000000000000000
0x16b5d60d8: 0x000000010493ffa0
0x16b5d60e0: 0x0000000000000060
0x16b5d60e8: 0x000000016b5d6108
0x16b5d60f0: 0x0000000199532000
0x16b5d60f8: 0x000000016b5d6134
0x16b5d6100: 0x0000000000000000
0x16b5d6108: 0x0000000000000000
0x16b5d6110: 0x000000016b5d6108
0x16b5d6118: 0x0000002000000000
0x16b5d6120: 0x0000000000000001
0x16b5d6128: 0x000000010493c000 App11`_mh_execute_header
0x16b5d6130: 0x0000000000000000
0x16b5d6138: 0x0000000000000000
0x16b5d6140: 0x000000010493ffa0
0x16b5d6148: 0x0000000000000060
0x16b5d6150: 0xa11780010493fc20 (0x000000010493fc20) App11`procA() + 56
0x16b5d6158: 0x000000016b5d63a8 -> 0x00000001e925bd90 libunwind.dylib`vtable for
libunwind::UnwindCursor<libunwind::LocalAddressSpace, libunwind::Registers_arm64> + 16
0x16b5d6160: 0x000000016b5d6200
0x16b5d6168: 0x240e00019953ad74 (0x000000019953ad74) libunwind.dylib`unw_set_reg + 452
0x16b5d6170: 0x0000000104a3c310 dyld`_NSConcreteStackBlock
0x16b5d6178: 0x0000000042000000
0x16b5d6180: 0x00000001049fc3a8 dyld`invocation function for block in dyld3::MachOLoaded::findSectionContent(char
const*, char const*, unsigned long long&, bool) const
0x16b5d6188: 0x000000010493fbe8 App11`procA()
0x16b5d6190: 0x000000010493fc6c App11`procB()
0x16b5d6198: 0x000000010493ff8c App11`GCC_except_table1
0x16b5d61a0: 0x000000018e9c507c libc++abi.dylib`__gxx_personality_v0
0x16b5d61a8: 0x0000000000000000
0x16b5d61b0: 0x0000000000000001
0x16b5d61b8: 0x0000000054000000
0x16b5d61c0: 0x0000000000000000
0x16b5d61c8: 0x000000010493c000 App11`_mh_execute_header
0x16b5d61d0: 0x0000000000000006
0x16b5d61d8: 0x0000000000000002
0x16b5d61e0: 0x434c4e47432b2b00
0x16b5d61e8: 0x0000000000000001
0x16b5d61f0: 0x000000016b5d63a8 -> 0x00000001e925bd90 libunwind.dylib`vtable for
libunwind::UnwindCursor<libunwind::LocalAddressSpace, libunwind::Registers_arm64> + 16
0x16b5d61f8: 0x000000013ef040e0
0x16b5d6200: 0x000000016b5d62f0
0x16b5d6208: 0x574b80018e9c5118 (0x000000018e9c5118) libc++abi.dylib`__gxx_personality_v0 + 156
0x16b5d6210: 0x000000000000014c
0x16b5d6218: 0x0000000199532000
0x16b5d6220: 0xd3a900016b5d63a8
0x16b5d6228: 0x000000016b5d6940
0x16b5d6230: 0x0000000199953b1b0 libunwind.dylib`_Unwind_RaiseException + 112
```

```
0x16b5d6238: 0x000000016b5d63a8 -> 0x00000001e925bd90 libunwind.dylib`vtable for
libunwind::UnwindCursor<libunwind::LocalAddressSpace, libunwind::Registers_arm64> + 16
0x16b5d6240: 0x000000016b5d62f0
0x16b5d6248: 0xda32800199536f24 (0x0000000199536f24)
libunwind.dylib`libunwind::UnwindCursor<libunwind::LocalAddressSpace,
libunwind::Registers_arm64>::setInfoBasedOnIPRegister(bool) + 120
0x16b5d6250: 0x0000000000000001
0x16b5d6258: 0x000000010493ff99 App11`GCC_except_table1 + 13
0x16b5d6260: 0x000000010493ff8c App11`GCC_except_table1
0x16b5d6268: 0x000000010493fc20 App11`procA() + 56
0x16b5d6270: 0x000000013ef04100
0x16b5d6278: 0x0000000000000001
0x16b5d6280: 0x000000016b5d62a0
0x16b5d6288: 0x385080018e9c5b7c (0x0000000018e9c5b7c) libc++abi.dylib`__cxxabiv1::get_shim_type_info(unsigned long
long, unsigned char const*, unsigned char, bool, _Unwind_Exception*, unsigned long) + 80
0x16b5d6290: 0x0000000000000001
0x16b5d6298: 0x0000000000000000
0x16b5d62a0: 0x0000000000000000
0x16b5d62a8: 0x0000000000000000
0x16b5d62b0: 0x0000000000000000
0x16b5d62b8: 0x0000000000000000
0x16b5d62c0: 0x0000000000000006
0x16b5d62c8: 0x0000000000000002
0x16b5d62d0: 0xd3a900016b5d63a8
0x16b5d62d8: 0x000000016b5d6f60
0x16b5d62e0: 0x000000013ef040e0
0x16b5d62e8: 0x000000016b5d63a8 -> 0x00000001e925bd90 libunwind.dylib`vtable for
libunwind::UnwindCursor<libunwind::LocalAddressSpace, libunwind::Registers_arm64> + 16
0x16b5d62f0: 0x000000016b5d6390
0x16b5d62f8: 0x211000019953b5f4 (0x000000019953b5f4) libunwind.dylib`unwind_phase2 + 468
0x16b5d6300: 0x000000010493ff8c App11`GCC_except_table1
0x16b5d6308: 0x000000010493fc20 App11`procA() + 56
0x16b5d6310: 0x000000010493fbe8 App11`procA()
0x16b5d6318: 0x000000010493fc6c App11`procB()
0x16b5d6320: 0x000000010493ff8c App11`GCC_except_table1
0x16b5d6328: 0x000000018e9c507c libc++abi.dylib`__gxx_personality_v0
0x16b5d6330: 0x0000000000000000
0x16b5d6338: 0x0000000000000001
0x16b5d6340: 0x0000000054000000
0x16b5d6348: 0x0000000000000000
0x16b5d6350: 0x000000010493c000 App11`_mh_execute_header
0x16b5d6358: 0x0000000000000000
0x16b5d6360: 0x0000000000000000
0x16b5d6368: 0x000000013ef04080
0x16b5d6370: 0x000000016b5d63a8 -> 0x00000001e925bd90 libunwind.dylib`vtable for
libunwind::UnwindCursor<libunwind::LocalAddressSpace, libunwind::Registers_arm64> + 16
0x16b5d6378: 0xd3a900016b5d63a8
0x16b5d6380: 0x000000016b5d6940
0x16b5d6388: 0x000000013ef040e0
0x16b5d6390: 0x000000016b5d6f00
0x16b5d6398: 0x201500019953b408 (0x000000019953b408) libunwind.dylib`_Unwind_RaiseException + 712
0x16b5d63a0: 0x0000000000000000
0x16b5d63a8: 0x00000001e925bd90 libunwind.dylib`vtable for libunwind::UnwindCursor<libunwind::LocalAddressSpace,
libunwind::Registers_arm64> + 16
0x16b5d63b0: 0x00000001e4e71bd0 libunwind.dylib`libunwind::LocalAddressSpace::sThisAddressSpace
0x16b5d63b8: 0x000000013ef040e0
0x16b5d63c0: 0x0000000000000001
0x16b5d63c8: 0x0000000000000000
0x16b5d63d0: 0x0000600003dc8010
0x16b5d63d8: 0x0000000000000000
0x16b5d63e0: 0x0000600003dc31f4
0x16b5d63e8: 0x000000000000000a
0x16b5d63f0: 0x0000000000000001
0x16b5d63f8: 0x0000000000000001
0x16b5d6400: 0x000000016b5d70e0
0x16b5d6408: 0xfffffffe7163e2bf
0x16b5d6410: 0x0000000000000001
0x16b5d6418: 0x00000000803ff7fb
0x16b5d6420: 0x00000000003ff000
0x16b5d6428: 0x0000000000200000
0x16b5d6430: 0x0000000000000014
0x16b5d6438: 0x000000019953b140 libunwind.dylib`_Unwind_RaiseException
0x16b5d6440: 0x00000001e8b2b390 (void *)0x000000019953b140: _Unwind_RaiseException
0x16b5d6448: 0x0000000000000000
0x16b5d6450: 0x000000016b5d7000
0x16b5d6458: 0x0000000000000000
```

```
0x16b5d6460: 0x0000000000000000
0x16b5d6468: 0x0000000000000000
0x16b5d6470: 0x0000000000000000
0x16b5d6478: 0x0000000000000000
0x16b5d6480: 0x0000000000000000
0x16b5d6488: 0x0000000000000000
0x16b5d6490: 0x0000000000000000
0x16b5d6498: 0x0000000000000000
0x16b5d64a0: 0x000000016b5d6f80
0x16b5d64a8: 0x0e6880019953b1b0  (0x000000019953b1b0) libunwind.dylib`_Unwind_RaiseException + 112
0x16b5d64b0: 0x000000016b5d6f60
0x16b5d64b8: 0x435000010493fc20  (0x000000010493fc20) App11`procA() + 56
0x16b5d64c0: 0x0000000000000000
0x16b5d64c8: 0x0000000000000000
0x16b5d64d0: 0x0000020000000200
0x16b5d64d8: 0x0000000000000000
0x16b5d64e0: 0x0000000000000000
0x16b5d64e8: 0x0000000000000000
0x16b5d64f0: 0x0000000000000000
0x16b5d64f8: 0x0000000000000000
0x16b5d6500: 0x0000000000000000
0x16b5d6508: 0x0000000000000000
0x16b5d6510: 0x0000000000000000
0x16b5d6518: 0x0000000000000000
0x16b5d6520: 0x0000000000000000
0x16b5d6528: 0x0000000000000000
0x16b5d6530: 0x0000000000000000
0x16b5d6538: 0x0000000000000000
0x16b5d6540: 0x0000000000000000
0x16b5d6548: 0x0000000000000000
0x16b5d6550: 0x0000000000000000
0x16b5d6558: 0x0000000000000000
0x16b5d6560: 0x0000000000000000
0x16b5d6568: 0x0000000000000000
0x16b5d6570: 0x0000000000000000
0x16b5d6578: 0x0000000000000000
0x16b5d6580: 0x0000000000000000
0x16b5d6588: 0x0000000000000000
0x16b5d6590: 0x0000000000000000
0x16b5d6598: 0x0000000000000000
0x16b5d65a0: 0x0000000000000000
0x16b5d65a8: 0x0000000000000000
0x16b5d65b0: 0x0000000000000000
0x16b5d65b8: 0x0000000000000000
0x16b5d65c0: 0x0000000000000000
0x16b5d65c8: 0x000000010493fbe8  App11`procA()
0x16b5d65d0: 0x000000010493fc6c  App11`procB()
0x16b5d65d8: 0x000000010493ff8c  App11`GCC_except_table1
0x16b5d65e0: 0x000000018e9c507c  libc++abi.dylib`__gxx_personality_v0
0x16b5d65e8: 0x0000000000000000
0x16b5d65f0: 0x0000000000000001
0x16b5d65f8: 0x0000000054000000
0x16b5d6600: 0x0000000000000000
0x16b5d6608: 0x000000010493c000  App11`_mh_execute_header
0x16b5d6610: 0x0000000000000000
0x16b5d6618: 0x0000000000000000
0x16b5d6620: 0x0000000000000000
0x16b5d6628: 0x0000000000000000
0x16b5d6630: 0x0000000000000000
0x16b5d6638: 0x0000000000000000
0x16b5d6640: 0x0000000000000000
0x16b5d6648: 0x0000000000000000
0x16b5d6650: 0x0000000000000000
0x16b5d6658: 0x0000000000000000
0x16b5d6660: 0x0000000000000000
0x16b5d6668: 0x0000000000000000
0x16b5d6670: 0x0000000000000000
0x16b5d6678: 0x0000000000000000
0x16b5d6680: 0x0000000000000000
0x16b5d6688: 0x0000000000000000
0x16b5d6690: 0x0000000000000000
0x16b5d6698: 0x0000000000000000
0x16b5d66a0: 0x0000000000000000
0x16b5d66a8: 0x0000000000000000
0x16b5d66b0: 0x0000000000000000
0x16b5d66b8: 0x0000000000000000
```

```
0x16b5d66c0:  0x0000000000000000
0x16b5d66c8:  0x0000000000000000
0x16b5d66d0:  0x0000000000000000
0x16b5d66d8:  0x0000000000000000
0x16b5d66e0:  0x0000000000000000
0x16b5d66e8:  0x0000000000000000
0x16b5d66f0:  0x0000000000000000
0x16b5d66f8:  0x0000000000000000
0x16b5d6700:  0x0000000000000000
0x16b5d6708:  0x0000000000000000
0x16b5d6710:  0x0000000000000000
0x16b5d6718:  0x0000000000000000
0x16b5d6720:  0x0000000000000000
0x16b5d6728:  0x0000000000000000
0x16b5d6730:  0x0000000000000000
0x16b5d6738:  0x0000000000000000
0x16b5d6740:  0x0000000000000000
0x16b5d6748:  0x0000000000000000
0x16b5d6750:  0x0000000000000000
0x16b5d6758:  0x0000000000000000
0x16b5d6760:  0x0000000000000000
0x16b5d6768:  0x0000000000000000
0x16b5d6770:  0x0000000000000000
0x16b5d6778:  0x0000000000000000
0x16b5d6780:  0x0000000000000000
0x16b5d6788:  0x0000000000000000
0x16b5d6790:  0x0000000000000000
0x16b5d6798:  0x0000000000000000
0x16b5d67a0:  0x0000000000000000
0x16b5d67a8:  0x0000000000000000
0x16b5d67b0:  0x0000000000000000
0x16b5d67b8:  0x0000000000000000
0x16b5d67c0:  0x0000000000000000
0x16b5d67c8:  0x0000000000000000
0x16b5d67d0:  0x0000000000000000
0x16b5d67d8:  0x0000000000000000
0x16b5d67e0:  0x0000000000000000
0x16b5d67e8:  0x0000000000000000
0x16b5d67f0:  0x0000000000000000
0x16b5d67f8:  0x0000000000000000
0x16b5d6800:  0x0000000000000000
0x16b5d6808:  0x0000000000000000
0x16b5d6810:  0x0000000000000000
0x16b5d6818:  0x0000000000000000
0x16b5d6820:  0x0000000000000000
0x16b5d6828:  0x0000000000000000
0x16b5d6830:  0x0000000000000000
0x16b5d6838:  0x0000000000000000
0x16b5d6840:  0x0000000000000000
0x16b5d6848:  0x0000000000000000
0x16b5d6850:  0x0000000000000000
0x16b5d6858:  0x0000000000000000
0x16b5d6860:  0x0000000000000000
0x16b5d6868:  0x0000000000000000
0x16b5d6870:  0x0000000000000000
0x16b5d6878:  0x0000000000000000
0x16b5d6880:  0x0000000000000000
0x16b5d6888:  0x0000000000000000
0x16b5d6890:  0x0000000000000000
0x16b5d6898:  0x0000000000000000
0x16b5d68a0:  0x0000000000000000
0x16b5d68a8:  0x0000000000000000
0x16b5d68b0:  0x0000000000000000
0x16b5d68b8:  0x0000000000000000
0x16b5d68c0:  0x0000000000000000
0x16b5d68c8:  0x0000000000000000
0x16b5d68d0:  0x0000000000000000
0x16b5d68d8:  0x0000000000000000
0x16b5d68e0:  0x0000000000000000
0x16b5d68e8:  0x0000000000000000
0x16b5d68f0:  0x0000000000000000
0x16b5d68f8:  0x0000000000000000
0x16b5d6900:  0x0000000000000000
0x16b5d6908:  0x0000000000000000
0x16b5d6910:  0x0000000000000000
0x16b5d6918:  0x0000000000000000
```

```
0x16b5d6920: 0x0000000000000000
0x16b5d6928: 0x0000000000000000
0x16b5d6930: 0x0000000000000000
0x16b5d6938: 0x0000000000000000
0x16b5d6940: 0x000000016b5d6940
0x16b5d6948: 0x0000600003dc8000
0x16b5d6950: 0x0000000000000000
0x16b5d6958: 0x0000600003dc8010
0x16b5d6960: 0x0000000000000000
0x16b5d6968: 0x0000600003dc31f4
0x16b5d6970: 0x000000000000000a
0x16b5d6978: 0x0000000000000001
0x16b5d6980: 0x0000000000000001
0x16b5d6988: 0x000000016b5d70e0
0x16b5d6990: 0xffffffffe7163e2bf
0x16b5d6998: 0x0000000000000001
0x16b5d69a0: 0x00000000803ff7fb
0x16b5d69a8: 0x00000000003ff000
0x16b5d69b0: 0x0000000000200000
0x16b5d69b8: 0x0000000000000014
0x16b5d69c0: 0x000000019953b140  libunwind.dylib`_Unwind_RaiseException
0x16b5d69c8: 0x00000001e8b2b390  (void *)0x000000019953b140: _Unwind_RaiseException
0x16b5d69d0: 0x0000000000000000
0x16b5d69d8: 0x000000013ef040e0
0x16b5d69e0: 0x000000016b5d6940
0x16b5d69e8: 0x000000013ef040e0
0x16b5d69f0: 0x0000600003dc8000
0x16b5d69f8: 0x000000013ef04080
0x16b5d6a00: 0x0000000000000000
0x16b5d6a08: 0x0000000000000000
0x16b5d6a10: 0x0000000000000000
0x16b5d6a18: 0x0000000000000000
0x16b5d6a20: 0x0000000000000000
0x16b5d6a28: 0x000000016b5d6f00
0x16b5d6a30: 0x0e6880019953b1b0  (0x000000019953b1b0) libunwind.dylib`_Unwind_RaiseException + 112
0x16b5d6a38: 0x000000016b5d63a0
0x16b5d6a40: 0x0e6880019953b1b0  (0x000000019953b1b0) libunwind.dylib`_Unwind_RaiseException + 112
0x16b5d6a48: 0x0000000000000000
0x16b5d6a50: 0x0000000000000000
0x16b5d6a58: 0x0000020000000200
0x16b5d6a60: 0x0000000000000000
0x16b5d6a68: 0x0000000000000000
0x16b5d6a70: 0x0000000000000000
0x16b5d6a78: 0x0000000000000000
0x16b5d6a80: 0x0000000000000000
0x16b5d6a88: 0x0000000000000000
0x16b5d6a90: 0x0000000000000000
0x16b5d6a98: 0x0000000000000000
0x16b5d6aa0: 0x0000000000000000
0x16b5d6aa8: 0x0000000000000000
0x16b5d6ab0: 0x0000000000000000
0x16b5d6ab8: 0x0000000000000000
0x16b5d6ac0: 0x0000000000000000
0x16b5d6ac8: 0x0000000000000000
0x16b5d6ad0: 0x0000000000000000
0x16b5d6ad8: 0x0000000000000000
0x16b5d6ae0: 0x0000000000000000
0x16b5d6ae8: 0x0000000000000000
0x16b5d6af0: 0x0000000000000000
0x16b5d6af8: 0x0000000000000000
0x16b5d6b00: 0x0000000000000000
0x16b5d6b08: 0x0000000000000000
0x16b5d6b10: 0x0000000000000000
0x16b5d6b18: 0x0000000000000000
0x16b5d6b20: 0x0000000000000000
0x16b5d6b28: 0x0000000000000000
0x16b5d6b30: 0x0000000000000000
0x16b5d6b38: 0x0000000000000000
0x16b5d6b40: 0x0000000000000000
0x16b5d6b48: 0x0000000000000000
0x16b5d6b50: 0x0000000000000000
0x16b5d6b58: 0x0000000000000000
0x16b5d6b60: 0x0000000000000000
0x16b5d6b68: 0x0000000000000000
0x16b5d6b70: 0x0000000000000000
0x16b5d6b78: 0x0000000000000000
```

```
0x16b5d6b80:  0x0000000000000000
0x16b5d6b88:  0x0000000000000000
0x16b5d6b90:  0x0000000000000000
0x16b5d6b98:  0x0000000000000000
0x16b5d6ba0:  0x0000000000000000
0x16b5d6ba8:  0x0000000000000000
0x16b5d6bb0:  0x0000000000000000
0x16b5d6bb8:  0x0000000000000000
0x16b5d6bc0:  0x0000000000000000
0x16b5d6bc8:  0x0000000000000000
0x16b5d6bd0:  0x0000000000000000
0x16b5d6bd8:  0x0000000000000000
0x16b5d6be0:  0x0000000000000000
0x16b5d6be8:  0x0000000000000000
0x16b5d6bf0:  0x0000000000000000
0x16b5d6bf8:  0x0000000000000000
0x16b5d6c00:  0x0000000000000000
0x16b5d6c08:  0x0000000000000000
0x16b5d6c10:  0x0000000000000000
0x16b5d6c18:  0x0000000000000000
0x16b5d6c20:  0x0000000000000000
0x16b5d6c28:  0x0000000000000000
0x16b5d6c30:  0x0000000000000000
0x16b5d6c38:  0x0000000000000000
0x16b5d6c40:  0x0000000000000000
0x16b5d6c48:  0x0000000000000000
0x16b5d6c50:  0x0000000000000000
0x16b5d6c58:  0x0000000000000000
0x16b5d6c60:  0x0000000000000000
0x16b5d6c68:  0x0000000000000000
0x16b5d6c70:  0x0000000000000000
0x16b5d6c78:  0x0000000000000000
0x16b5d6c80:  0x0000000000000000
0x16b5d6c88:  0x0000000000000000
0x16b5d6c90:  0x0000000000000000
0x16b5d6c98:  0x0000020300000000
0x16b5d6ca0:  0x00000001e7965aec libsystem_kernel.dylib`mach_task_self_
0x16b5d6ca8:  0x0000000104969404
0x16b5d6cb0:  0x0000000700000003
0x16b5d6cb8:  0x0000000007000001
0x16b5d6cc0:  0x00000000000fffff
0x16b5d6cc8:  0x0000000000000000
0x16b5d6cd0:  0x0000000000000001
0x16b5d6cd8:  0x0000000104998000
0x16b5d6ce0:  0x0000000000000000
0x16b5d6ce8:  0x00000000001ffffb
0x16b5d6cf0:  0x0000600000000000
0x16b5d6cf8:  0x0000600003dc32f4
0x16b5d6d00:  0x0000000000007010
0x16b5d6d08:  0x0000000000000400
0x16b5d6d10:  0x00000001e79661b8 libsystem_malloc.dylib`first_block_offset_by_size_class
0x16b5d6d18:  0x0000000104998000
0x16b5d6d20:  0x00000001e79661f8 libsystem_malloc.dylib`last_block_offset_by_size_class
0x16b5d6d28:  0x00000001e4c0c7c0 nanov2_policy_config + 4
0x16b5d6d30:  0x000000016b5d6df0
0x16b5d6d38:  0x347b00018e8167f0 (0x000000018e8167f0) libsystem_malloc.dylib`nanov2_find_block_and_allocate + 1160
0x16b5d6d40:  0x000000016b5d70e0
0x16b5d6d48:  0x0000000104969404
0x16b5d6d50:  0x000000010499f008
0x16b5d6d58:  0x0000000000000000
0x16b5d6d60:  0x000000010499c008
0x16b5d6d68:  0x0000000104968a00
0x16b5d6d70:  0x000000010499f034
0x16b5d6d78:  0x000000016b5d70e0
0x16b5d6d80:  0x0000000000000009
0x16b5d6d88:  0x000000010499f040
0x16b5d6d90:  0x0000600000000000
0x16b5d6d98:  0x0000600004000000
0x16b5d6da0:  0x000000016b5d70e0
0x16b5d6da8:  0x0000000000000001
0x16b5d6db0:  0x000000010499c008
0x16b5d6db8:  0x000000010499e004
0x16b5d6dc0:  0x0000000000000000
0x16b5d6dc8:  0x000000010499f000
0x16b5d6dd0:  0x0000000000000000
0x16b5d6dd8:  0x0000000104998000
```

```
0x16b5d6de0: 0x0000000000000001
0x16b5d6de8: 0x0000000000000010
0x16b5d6df0: 0x000000016b5d6e50
0x16b5d6df8: 0xac3b80018e816280 (0x000000018e816280) libsystem_malloc.dylib`nanov2_allocate + 288
0x16b5d6e00: 0x0000000000000000
0x16b5d6e08: 0x0000000000000000
0x16b5d6e10: 0x0000000000000000
0x16b5d6e18: 0x0000000000000000
0x16b5d6e20: 0x0000000000000000
0x16b5d6e28: 0x0000000000000000
0x16b5d6e30: 0x0000000000000000
0x16b5d6e38: 0x0000000000000000
0x16b5d6e40: 0x0000000000000000
0x16b5d6e48: 0x0000000000000000
0x16b5d6e50: 0x0000000000000000
0x16b5d6e58: 0x0000000000000000
0x16b5d6e60: 0x000000016b5d6f30
0x16b5d6e68: 0x000000016b5d6ef0
0x16b5d6e70: 0x000000016b5d6ed0
0x16b5d6e78: 0xb35100018e9d02f8 (0x000000018e9d02f8) libsystem_kernel.dylib`clock_get_time + 100
0x16b5d6e80: 0x000000010493fbe8 App11`procA()
0x16b5d6e88: 0x0000002c00001200
0x16b5d6e90: 0x000000016b5d6f30
0x16b5d6e98: 0x000000000000003c
0x16b5d6ea0: 0x000000016b5d6ec0
0x16b5d6ea8: 0x9b2380018e9cc340 (0x000000018e9cc340) libsystem_kernel.dylib`cerror + 24
0x16b5d6eb0: 0x000000016b5d6f30
0x16b5d6eb8: 0x000000016b5d6f20
0x16b5d6ec0: 0x000000016b5d6ed0
0x16b5d6ec8: 0xb93f80018e9ce080 (0x000000018e9ce080) libsystem_kernel.dylib`__semwait_signal + 28
0x16b5d6ed0: 0x000000016b5d6f10
0x16b5d6ed8: 0xc13480018e8d6fc8 (0x000000018e8d6fc8) libsystem_c.dylib`nanosleep + 220
0x16b5d6ee0: 0x0000000000000000
0x16b5d6ee8: 0x0000000000000000
0x16b5d6ef0: 0x076f851b0003f0be
0x16b5d6ef8: 0x0000000000000000
```

Exercise X12

- **Goal:** Learn how to dump memory for post-processing, get the list of functions and module variables, load symbols, inspect arguments and local variables, list symbols, inspect types, search memory

- **Patterns:** Module Variable

- \AMCDA-Dumps\Exercise-X12.pdf

Exercise X12

Goal: Learn how to dump memory for post-processing, get the list of functions and module variables, load symbols, inspect arguments and local variables, list symbols, inspect types, and search memory.

Patterns: Module Variable.

1.   Load a core dump *App11-95061-20221210T114941Z* and *App11* executable:

```
% lldb -c ~/AMCDA-Dumps/App11-95061-20221210T114941Z -f
~/AMCDA-Dumps/Apps/App11/Build/Products/Release/App11
(lldb) target create "/Users/training/AMCDA-Dumps/Apps/App11/Build/Products/Release/App11" --
core "/Users/training/AMCDA-Dumps/App11-95061-20221210T114941Z"
Core file '/Users/training/AMCDA-Dumps/App11-95061-20221210T114941Z' (arm64) was loaded.
```

2.   Check the current thread stack trace:

```
(lldb) bt
* thread #1
  * frame #0: 0x000000018e9ce06c libsystem_kernel.dylib`__semwait_signal + 8
    frame #1: 0x000000018e8d6fc8 libsystem_c.dylib`nanosleep + 220
    frame #2: 0x000000018e8e1b78 libsystem_c.dylib`sleep + 52
    frame #3: 0x000000018e8e1b90 libsystem_c.dylib`sleep + 76
    frame #4: 0x000000010493ff10 App11`main + 204
    frame #5: 0x00000001049c908c dyld`start + 520
```

3.   Open *Symbols.zip* in Finder (it should automatically unzip itself) and then load a symbol file for *App11*:

```
(lldb) target symbol add ~/AMCDA-Dumps/Symbols/App11.dSYM/Contents/Resources/DWARF/App11
symbol file '/Users/training/AMCDA-Dumps/Symbols/App11.dSYM/Contents/Resources/DWARF/App11'
has been added to '/Users/training/AMCDA-Dumps/Apps/App11/Build/Products/Release/App11'
```

4.   List all thread stack traces:

```
(lldb) thread backtrace all
* thread #1
  * frame #0: 0x000000018e9ce06c libsystem_kernel.dylib`__semwait_signal + 8
    frame #1: 0x000000018e8d6fc8 libsystem_c.dylib`nanosleep + 220
    frame #2: 0x000000018e8e1b78 libsystem_c.dylib`sleep + 52
    frame #3: 0x000000018e8e1b90 libsystem_c.dylib`sleep + 76
    frame #4: 0x000000010493ff10 App11`main(argc=1, argv=0x000000016b4c3a88) at main.cpp:85:5
    frame #5: 0x00000001049c908c dyld`start + 520
  thread #2
    frame #0: 0x000000018e9ce06c libsystem_kernel.dylib`__semwait_signal + 8
    frame #1: 0x000000018e8d6fc8 libsystem_c.dylib`nanosleep + 220
    frame #2: 0x000000018e8e1b78 libsystem_c.dylib`sleep + 52
    frame #3: 0x000000018e8e1b90 libsystem_c.dylib`sleep + 76
    frame #4: 0x000000010493fccc App11`bar_one() at main.cpp:65:1
    frame #5: 0x000000010493fce0 App11`foo_one() at main.cpp:65:1
    frame #6: 0x000000010493fcfc App11`thread_one(arg=0x0000000000000000) at main.cpp:65:1
    frame #7: 0x000000018ea0826c libsystem_pthread.dylib`_pthread_start + 148
  thread #3
    frame #0: 0x000000018e9cd738 libsystem_kernel.dylib`__psynch_mutexwait + 8
    frame #1: 0x000000018ea05384 libsystem_pthread.dylib`_pthread_mutex_firstfit_lock_wait + 84
    frame #2: 0x000000018ea02cf8 libsystem_pthread.dylib`_pthread_mutex_firstfit_lock_slow + 248
    frame #3: 0x000000010493fc58 App11`procA() at main.cpp:35:5
    frame #4: 0x000000010493fd18 App11`bar_two() at main.cpp:66:1
    frame #5: 0x000000010493fd2c App11`foo_two() at main.cpp:66:1
    frame #6: 0x000000010493fd48 App11`thread_two(arg=0x0000000000000000) at main.cpp:66:1
```

```
        frame #7: 0x000000018ea0826c libsystem_pthread.dylib`_pthread_start + 148
    thread #4
        frame #0: 0x000000018e9ce06c libsystem_kernel.dylib`__semwait_signal + 8
        frame #1: 0x000000018e8d6fc8 libsystem_c.dylib`nanosleep + 220
        frame #2: 0x000000018e8e1b78 libsystem_c.dylib`sleep + 52
        frame #3: 0x000000018e8e1b90 libsystem_c.dylib`sleep + 76
        frame #4: 0x000000010493fd68 App11`bar_three() at main.cpp:67:1
        frame #5: 0x000000010493fd7c App11`foo_three() at main.cpp:67:1
        frame #6: 0x000000010493fd98 App11`thread_three(arg=0x0000000000000000) at main.cpp:67:1
        frame #7: 0x000000018ea0826c libsystem_pthread.dylib`_pthread_start + 148
    thread #5
        frame #0: 0x000000018e9cd738 libsystem_kernel.dylib`__psynch_mutexwait + 8
        frame #1: 0x000000018ea05384 libsystem_pthread.dylib`_pthread_mutex_firstfit_lock_wait + 84
        frame #2: 0x000000018ea02cf8 libsystem_pthread.dylib`_pthread_mutex_firstfit_lock_slow + 248
        frame #3: 0x000000010493fc98 App11`procB() at main.cpp:42:5
        frame #4: 0x000000010493fdb4 App11`bar_four() at main.cpp:68:1
        frame #5: 0x000000010493fdc8 App11`foo_four() at main.cpp:68:1
        frame #6: 0x000000010493fde4 App11`thread_four(arg=0x0000000000000000) at main.cpp:68:1
        frame #7: 0x000000018ea0826c libsystem_pthread.dylib`_pthread_start + 148
    thread #6
        frame #0: 0x000000018e9ce06c libsystem_kernel.dylib`__semwait_signal + 8
        frame #1: 0x000000018e8d6fc8 libsystem_c.dylib`nanosleep + 220
        frame #2: 0x000000018e8e1b78 libsystem_c.dylib`sleep + 52
        frame #3: 0x000000018e8e1b90 libsystem_c.dylib`sleep + 76
        frame #4: 0x000000010493fe04 App11`bar_five() at main.cpp:69:1
        frame #5: 0x000000010493fe18 App11`foo_five() at main.cpp:69:1
        frame #6: 0x000000010493fe34 App11`thread_five(arg=0x0000000000000000) at main.cpp:69:1
        frame #7: 0x000000018ea0826c libsystem_pthread.dylib`_pthread_start + 148
```

5.   Switch to frame 4 of the current thread and list arguments and locals:

```
(lldb) f 4
frame #4: 0x000000010493ff10 App11`main(argc=1, argv=0x000000016b4c3a88) at main.cpp:85:5
```

```
(lldb) frame variable --no-locals
(int) argc = 1
(const char **) argv = 0x000000016b4c3a88
```

```
(lldb) print argv[0]
warning: could not execute support code to read Objective-C class data in the process. This
may reduce the quality of type information available.
```

```
(const char *) $0 = 0x000000016b4c3bb8 "./App11"
```

```
(lldb) frame variable --no-args
```

6.   Dump region the current code region to a binary file:

```
(lldb) re r pc
     pc = 0x000000010493ff10  App11`main + 204 at main.cpp:85:5
```

```
(lldb) memory region 0x000000010493ff10
[0x000000010493c000-0x0000000104940000) r-x __TEXT
```

```
(lldb) memory read -o ~/AMCDA-Dumps/mem.raw -b 0x000000010493c000 0x0000000104940000 --force
16384 bytes written to '/Users/training/AMCDA-Dumps/mem.raw'
```

7. Check in Finder and use your favorite application to open it. I use Photoshop to interpret it as a picture:

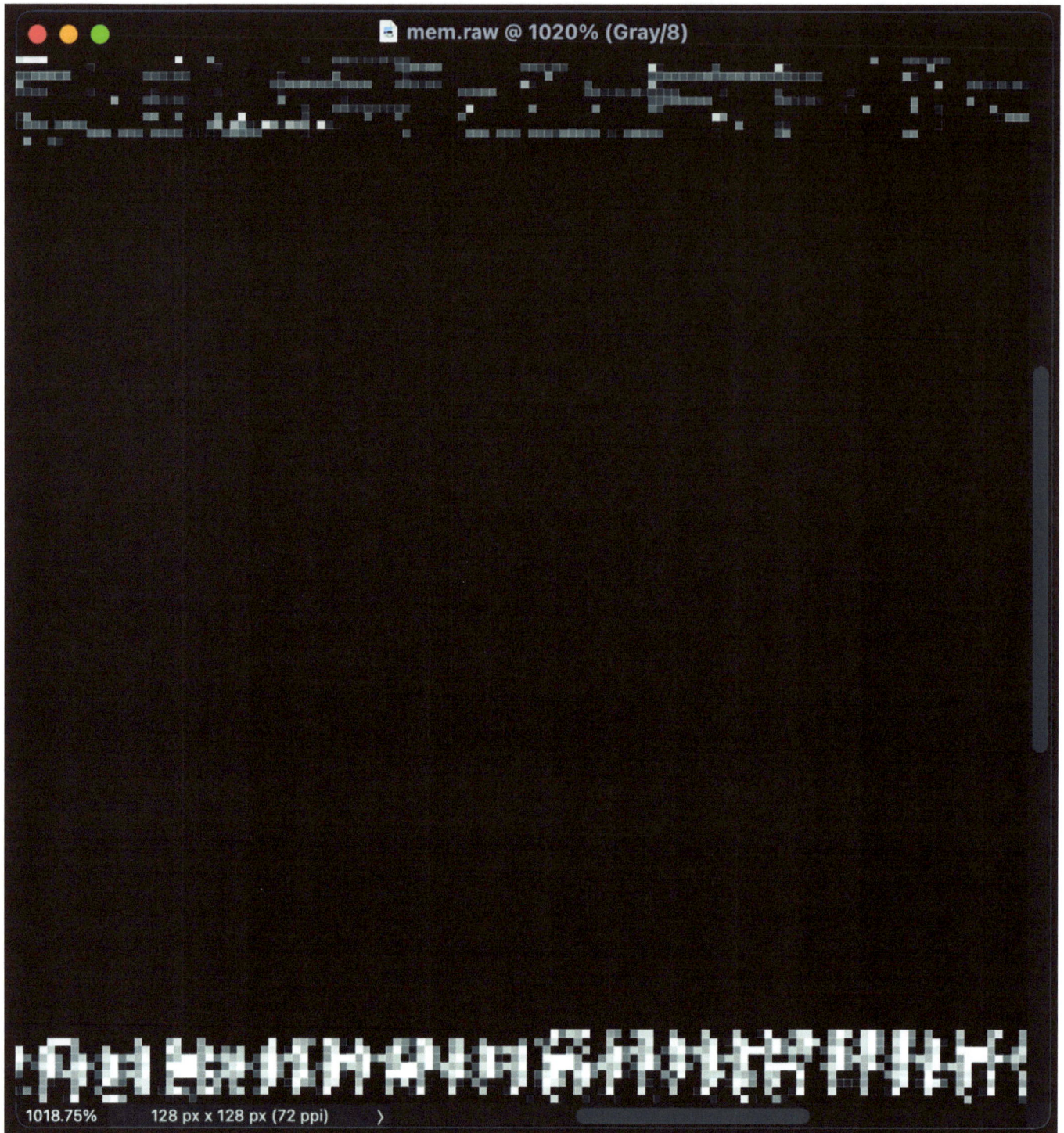

8. List *bar* functions:

```
(lldb) image lookup -r -s bar_
```
5 symbols match the regular expression 'bar_' in /Users/training/AMCDA-Dumps/Apps/App11/Build/Products/Release/App11:
        Address: App11[0x0000000100003cbc] (App11.__TEXT.__text + 248)
        Summary: App11`bar_one() at main.cpp:65   Address: App11[0x0000000100003d0c] (App11.__TEXT.__text + 328)
        Summary: App11`bar_two() at main.cpp:66   Address: App11[0x0000000100003d58] (App11.__TEXT.__text + 404)
        Summary: App11`bar_three() at main.cpp:67   Address: App11[0x0000000100003da8] (App11.__TEXT.__text + 484)
        Summary: App11`bar_four() at main.cpp:68   Address: App11[0x0000000100003df4] (App11.__TEXT.__text + 560)
        Summary: App11`bar_five() at main.cpp:69

9.   List *mutexA* and *mutexB* variables:

```
(lldb) image lookup -r -s mutex[A|B]
2 symbols match the regular expression 'mutex[A|B]' in
/Users/training/AMCDA-Dumps/Apps/App11/Build/Products/Release/App11:
        Address: App11[0x0000000100008000] (App11.__DATA.__common + 0)
        Summary: App11`mutexA        Address: App11[0x0000000100008040] (App11.__DATA.__common + 64)
        Summary: App11`mutexB
```

10.   List modules:

```
(lldb) image list
[  0] 759D22A7-7E47-3ADD-8E48-A4867F24E04E 0x000000010493c000
/Users/training/AMCDA-Dumps/Apps/App11/Build/Products/Release/App11
        /Users/training/AMCDA-Dumps/Symbols/App11.dSYM/Contents/Resources/DWARF/App11
[  1] 38EE9FE9-B66D-3066-8C5C-6DDF0D6944C6 0x00000001049c4000 /usr/lib/dyld
[  2] 3D1E6031-901D-3DF1-9E9A-F85FF1C2E803 0x000000018e94a000 /usr/lib/libc++.1.dylib
[  3] 9232C168-6ECA-3B7D-B081-E7C46B379836 0x000000019956d000 /usr/lib/libSystem.B.dylib
[  4] 4E8D8A11-4217-3D56-9D41-5426F7CF307C 0x000000018e9b1000 /usr/lib/libc++abi.dylib
[  5] 7E9E684F-57B6-3196-8AEC-908B46DEEBD4 0x0000000199567000 /usr/lib/system/libcache.dylib
[  6] FB7DF5AC-35DB-3B80-B2F6-BC69375390AE 0x0000000199525000 /usr/lib/system/libcommonCrypto.dylib
[  7] 68788078-BF1D-3CD1-91A7-4C59FD78FB75 0x000000019954e000 /usr/lib/system/libcompiler_rt.dylib
[  8] 654D0DA0-8277-361D-88DC-1430504B5436 0x0000000199545000 /usr/lib/system/libcopyfile.dylib
[  9] 2D00FEEC-7984-342B-9516-5D49C5D98204 0x000000018e78b000 /usr/lib/system/libcorecrypto.dylib
[ 10] B3C7A004-1069-3171-B630-2C386A8B399C 0x000000018e840000 /usr/lib/system/libdispatch.dylib
[ 11] F298A03D-5BC7-3BCA-8880-B956E52EAD01 0x000000018ea0e000 /usr/lib/system/libdyld.dylib
[ 12] 49D72074-0C58-317C-9B8B-762C13C0C084 0x000000019955d000 /usr/lib/system/libkeymgr.dylib
[ 13] ED4EE8AE-EA60-33B7-9676-E6119B7449E3 0x0000000199500000 /usr/lib/system/libmacho.dylib
[ 14] B887350E-B1C9-386C-B5EB-26F08C7C0152 0x00000001980f0000 /usr/lib/system/libquarantine.dylib
[ 15] 157C8E50-D4A5-3DFC-8E0B-756E03E2082B 0x000000019955a000 /usr/lib/system/libremovefile.dylib
[ 16] EC04DA81-C3B5-3AC5-9042-7F07DF48B42A 0x00000001935b86000 /usr/lib/system/libsystem_asl.dylib
[ 17] 96462BD5-6BB4-3B69-89C9-2C70FA8852E7 0x000000018e72d000 /usr/lib/system/libsystem_blocks.dylib
[ 18] B25D2080-BB9E-38D6-8236-9CEF4B2F11A3 0x000000018e8c8000 /usr/lib/system/libsystem_c.dylib
[ 19] 4928F3C4-D438-354F-BA1C-0BD79F6475F3 0x0000000199552000 /usr/lib/system/libsystem_collections.dylib
[ 20] 3977B29D-624D-3DEE-94EF-95D29FB25252 0x0000000198085000 /usr/lib/system/libsystem_configuration.dylib
[ 21] D38210EF-8F23-380B-8B43-BB06A7305F67 0x00000001972de000 /usr/lib/system/libsystem_containermanager.dylib
[ 22] D5F19732-3AA0-3B93-9F25-318A27DE5AC5 0x000000019925d000 /usr/lib/system/libsystem_coreservices.dylib
[ 23] 5D456083-E21E-319D-9BA0-57702B3FB09B 0x000000019113f000 /usr/lib/system/libsystem_darwin.dylib
[ 24] 10A4374A-D15A-31C8-AC6F-2DCC10D06444 0x000000019955e000 /usr/lib/system/libsystem_dnssd.dylib
[ 25] 5B14B45B-A15B-31AD-93FB-BAC43C001A23 0x000000018e8c5000 /usr/lib/system/libsystem_featureflags.dylib
[ 26] 413C2A97-5D32-317D-8E32-4258B8E728CE 0x000000018ea23000 /usr/lib/system/libsystem_info.dylib
[ 27] 31A9DAE0-FB1F-3CB8-8AB6-CA5A1192DFD8 0x000000019984c000 /usr/lib/system/libsystem_m.dylib
[ 28] 427675C6-C4BF-390A-AF93-B28DAC36876A 0x000000018e815000 /usr/lib/system/libsystem_malloc.dylib
[ 29] 4C9F32FA-D88C-3966-A2F0-7030841C8093 0x00000001935b14000 /usr/lib/system/libsystem_networkextension.dylib
[ 30] 12A2A8B6-80B4-36CA-8245-830EBEDEF1C4 0x0000000191598000 /usr/lib/system/libsystem_notify.dylib
[ 31] E49E2F05-0E01-352E-8CB7-276F8EF8E6D6 0x000000019f8c1000 /usr/lib/system/libsystem_product_info_filter.dylib
[ 32] 2A2EB0A4-9822-36D1-999B-181D1BB964B5 0x000000019808a000 /usr/lib/system/libsystem_sandbox.dylib
[ 33] 18F251D3-8C66-3B8B-817A-C124498478F4 0x0000000199557000 /usr/lib/system/libsystem_secinit.dylib
[ 34] A9D87740-9C1D-3468-BF60-720A8D713CBA 0x000000018e9c9000 /usr/lib/system/libsystem_kernel.dylib
[ 35] A57FE7FB-9FF8-30CE-97A2-625D6DA20D00 0x000000018ea1b000 /usr/lib/system/libsystem_platform.dylib
[ 36] 63C4EEF9-69A5-38B1-996E-8D31B66A051D 0x000000018ea01000 /usr/lib/system/libsystem_pthread.dylib
[ 37] 2906E453-3254-32EA-880E-14AEEF5D7ECD 0x00000001952ea000 /usr/lib/system/libsystem_symptoms.dylib
[ 38] B5524014-1A7F-3D07-8855-5E75A55E4A11 0x000000018e771000 /usr/lib/system/libsystem_trace.dylib
[ 39] D9CA1CE3-6B1A-3E2B-BBAD-9D9B1DB00F92 0x0000000199532000 /usr/lib/system/libunwind.dylib
[ 40] 21D05A8B-D782-3FA7-9A9D-55A45E6E6621 0x000000018e72f000 /usr/lib/system/libxpc.dylib
[ 41] EC96F0FA-6341-3E1D-BE54-49B544E17F7D 0x000000018e887000 /usr/lib/libobjc.A.dylib
[ 42] 7E53021F-FDCE-3EC9-8B4C-97AD3B21D02E 0x000000019953d000 /usr/lib/liboah.dylib
```

11.   List memory regions for the *App11* module:

```
(lldb) image dump sections App11
Sections for '/Users/training/AMCDA-Dumps/Apps/App11/Build/Products/Release/App11' (arm64):
  SectID     Type            Load Address                                       Perm File Off.  File Size  Flags       Section Name
  ---------- --------------- -------------------------------------------------- ---- ---------- ---------- ----------  -------------------------
  0x00000100 container       [0x0000000000000000-0x0000000100000000)*          ---  0x00000000 0x00000000 0x00000000  App11.__PAGEZERO
  0x00000200 container       [0x000000010493c000-0x0000000104940000)           r-x  0x00000000 0x00004000 0x00000000  App11.__TEXT
  0x00000001 code           [0x0000000104933bc4-0x000000010493ff20)           r-x  0x00003bc4 0x0000035c 0x80000400  App11.__TEXT.__text
  0x00000002 code           [0x000000010493ff20-0x000000010493ff8c)           r-x  0x00003f20 0x0000006c 0x80000408  App11.__TEXT.__stubs
  0x00000003 regular         [0x000000010493ff8c-0x000000010493ffa0)           r-x  0x00003f8c 0x00000014 0x00000000  App11.__TEXT.__gcc_except_tab
  0x00000004 compact-unwind  [0x000000010493ffa0-0x0000000104940000)           r-x  0x00003fa0 0x00000060 0x00000000  App11.__TEXT.__unwind_info
  0x00000300 container       [0x0000000104940000-0x0000000104944000)           rw-  0x00004000 0x00004000 0x00000010  App11.__DATA_CONST
  0x00000005 data-ptrs       [0x0000000104940000-0x0000000104940058)           rw-  0x00004000 0x00000058 0x00000006  App11.__DATA_CONST.__got
  0x00000400 container       [0x0000000104944000-0x0000000104948000)           rw-  0x00008000 0x00000000 0x00000000  App11.__DATA
  0x00000006 zero-fill       [0x0000000104944000-0x0000000104944080)           rw-  0x00000000 0x00000000 0x00000001  App11.__DATA.__common
  0x00000500 container       [0x0000000104948000-0x0000000104950000)           r--  0x00008000 0x00005770 0x00000000  App11.__LINKEDIT
  0x00000200 container       [0x000000010000d000-0x000000010000f000)*          rw-  0x00002000 0x000011c7 0x00000000  App11.__DWARF
```

```
0x00000001 dwarf-line          [0x000000010000d000-0x000000010000d249)* rw-   0x00002000 0x00000249 0x00000000 App11.__DWARF.__debug_line
0x00000002 dwarf-aranges       [0x000000010000d249-0x000000010000d279)* rw-   0x00002249 0x00000030 0x00000000 App11.__DWARF.__debug_aranges
0x00000003 dwarf-info          [0x000000010000d279-0x000000010000d6bf)* rw-   0x00002279 0x00000446 0x00000000 App11.__DWARF.__debug_info
0x00000004 dwarf-abbrev        [0x000000010000d6bf-0x000000010000d7da)* rw-   0x000026bf 0x0000011b 0x00000000 App11.__DWARF.__debug_abbrev
0x00000005 dwarf-str           [0x000000010000d7da-0x000000010000dbbe)* rw-   0x000027da 0x000003e4 0x00000000 App11.__DWARF.__debug_str
0x00000006 apple-names         [0x000000010000dbbe-0x000000010000dfd2)* rw-   0x00002bbe 0x00000414 0x00000000 App11.__DWARF.__apple_names
0x00000007 apple-namespaces    [0x000000010000dfd2-0x000000010000dff6)* rw-   0x00002fd2 0x00000024 0x00000000 App11.__DWARF.__apple_namespac
0x00000008 apple-types         [0x000000010000dff6-0x000000010000e1a3)* rw-   0x00002ff6 0x000001ad 0x00000000 App11.__DWARF.__apple_types
0x00000009 apple-objc          [0x000000010000e1a3-0x000000010000e1c7)* rw-   0x000031a3 0x00000024 0x00000000 App11.__DWARF.__apple_objc
```

11. Dump all symbols from the *App11* module:

```
(lldb) image dump symtab App11
Symtab, file = /Users/training/AMCDA-Dumps/Apps/App11/Build/Products/Release/App11, num_symbols = 36:
               Debug symbol
               |Synthetic symbol
               ||Externally Visible
               |||
Index   UserID DSX Type             File Address/Value Load Address         Size               Flags       Name
------- ------ --- ---------------- ------------------ ------------------   ------------------ ----------
------------------------------------
[    0]     23 D   SourceFile       0x0000000000000000                      Sibling -> [  24] 0x00640000
/Users/training/AMCDA-Old/Apps/App11/App11/main.cpp
[    1]     25 D   ObjectFile       0x000000006394689b                      0x0000000000000000 0x00660001
/Users/training/AMCDA-Old/Apps/App11/Build/Intermediates.noindex/App11.build/Release/App11.build/Objects-normal/arm64/main.o
[    2]     27 D   Code             0x0000000100003bc4 0x000000010493fbc4   0x0000000000000024 0x001e0000  procC()
[    3]     31 D   Code             0x0000000100003be8 0x000000010493fbe8   0x0000000000000084 0x001e0000  procA()
[    4]     35 D   Code             0x0000000100003c6c 0x000000010493fc6c   0x0000000000000050 0x001e0000  procB()
[    5]     39 D   Code             0x0000000100003cbc 0x000000010493fcbc   0x0000000000000018 0x001e0000  bar_one()
[    6]     43 D   Code             0x0000000100003cd4 0x000000010493fcd4   0x0000000000000014 0x001e0000  foo_one()
[    7]     47 D   Code             0x0000000100003ce8 0x000000010493fce8   0x0000000000000024 0x001e0000  thread_one(void*)
[    8]     51 D   Code             0x0000000100003d0c 0x000000010493fd0c   0x0000000000000014 0x001e0000  bar_two()
[    9]     55 D   Code             0x0000000100003d20 0x000000010493fd20   0x0000000000000014 0x001e0000  foo_two()
[   10]     59 D   Code             0x0000000100003d34 0x000000010493fd34   0x0000000000000024 0x001e0000  thread_two(void*)
[   11]     63 D   Code             0x0000000100003d58 0x000000010493fd58   0x0000000000000018 0x001e0000  bar_three()
[   12]     67 D   Code             0x0000000100003d70 0x000000010493fd70   0x0000000000000014 0x001e0000  foo_three()
[   13]     71 D   Code             0x0000000100003d84 0x000000010493fd84   0x0000000000000024 0x001e0000  thread_three(void*)
[   14]     75 D   Code             0x0000000100003da8 0x000000010493fda8   0x0000000000000014 0x001e0000  bar_four()
[   15]     79 D   Code             0x0000000100003dbc 0x000000010493fdbc   0x0000000000000014 0x001e0000  foo_four()
[   16]     83 D   Code             0x0000000100003dd0 0x000000010493fdd0   0x0000000000000024 0x001e0000  thread_four(void*)
[   17]     87 D   Code             0x0000000100003df4 0x000000010493fdf4   0x0000000000000018 0x001e0000  bar_five()
[   18]     91 D   Code             0x0000000100003e0c 0x000000010493fe0c   0x0000000000000014 0x001e0000  foo_five()
[   19]     95 D   Code             0x0000000100003e20 0x000000010493fe20   0x0000000000000024 0x001e0000  thread_five(void*)
[   20]     99 D   Code             0x0000000100003e44 0x000000010493fe44   0x00000000000000dc 0x001e0000  main
[   21]    102 D   Data             0x0000000100003f8c 0x000000010493ff8c   0x0000000000000014 0x000e0000  GCC_except_table1
[   22]    103 D X Data             0x0000000100008000 0x0000000104944000   0x0000000000000040 0x001e0000  mutexA
[   23]    104 D X Data             0x0000000100008040 0x0000000104944040   0x0000000000000040 0x001e0000  mutexB
[   24]    106   X Data             0x0000000000000000 0x000000010493c000   0x00000000000003bc4 0x000f0010 _mh_execute_header
[   25]    107   X Undefined        0x0000000000000000                      0x0000000000000000 0x00010100  typeinfo for int
[   26]    108     Trampoline       0x0000000100003f20 0x000000010493ff20   0x000000000000000c 0x00010100  __cxa_allocate_exception
[   27]    109     Trampoline       0x0000000100003f2c 0x000000010493ff2c   0x000000000000000c 0x00010100  __cxa_begin_catch
[   28]    110     Trampoline       0x0000000100003f38 0x000000010493ff38   0x000000000000000c 0x00010100  __cxa_end_catch
[   29]    111     Trampoline       0x0000000100003f44 0x000000010493ff44   0x000000000000000c 0x00010100  __cxa_throw
[   30]    112   X Undefined        0x0000000000000000                      0x0000000000000000 0x00010100  __gxx_personality_v0
[   31]    113     Trampoline       0x0000000100003f50 0x000000010493ff50   0x000000000000000c 0x00010200  pthread_create
[   32]    114     Trampoline       0x0000000100003f5c 0x000000010493ff5c   0x000000000000000c 0x00010200  pthread_mutex_init
[   33]    115     Trampoline       0x0000000100003f68 0x000000010493ff68   0x000000000000000c 0x00010200  pthread_mutex_lock
[   34]    116     Trampoline       0x0000000100003f74 0x000000010493ff74   0x000000000000000c 0x00010200  pthread_mutex_unlock
[   35]    117     Trampoline       0x0000000100003f80 0x000000010493ff80   0x000000000000000c 0x00010200  sleep
```

12. Inspect *pthread_mutex_t* type:

```
(lldb) image lookup --type pthread_mutex_t
Best match found in /Users/training/AMCDA-Dumps/Apps/App11/Build/Products/Release/App11:
id = {0x00000047}, name = "pthread_mutex_t", byte-size = 64, decl = _pthread_mutex_t.h:31, compiler_type = "typedef pthread_mutex_t"
     typedef 'pthread_mutex_t': id = {0x00000052}, name = "__darwin_pthread_mutex_t", byte-size = 64, decl = _pthread_types.h:113, compiler_type = "typedef
__darwin_pthread_mutex_t"
     typedef '__darwin_pthread_mutex_t': id = {0x0000005d}, name = "_opaque_pthread_mutex_t", byte-size = 64, decl = _pthread_types.h:78, compiler_type =
"struct _opaque_pthread_mutex_t {
    long __sig;
    char __opaque[56];
}"
```

12. Search for "PATH" string in environment:

```
(lldb) memory region environ
[0x000000016acc8000-0x000000016b4c4000) rw-
```

```
(lldb) memory find -s "PATH" 0x000000016acc8000 0x000000016b4c4000
data found at location: 0x16b4c3d45
0x16b4c3d45: 50 41 54 48 3d 2f 75 73 72 2f 6c 6f 63 61 6c 2f  PATH=/usr/local/
0x16b4c3d55: 62 69 6e 3a 2f 75 73 72 2f 62 69 6e 3a 2f 62 69  bin:/usr/bin:/bi
```

Resources

- DumpAnalysis.org / SoftwareDiagnostics.Institute / PatternDiagnostics.com
- Debugging.TV / YouTube.com/DebuggingTV / YouTube.com/PatternDiagnostics
- Accelerated Linux Core Dump Analysis, Second Edition (ARM64, WinDbg)
- Accelerated Linux Core Dump Analysis, Third Edition (ARM64, GDB)
- Accelerated Linux Disassembly, Reconstruction and Reversing (ARM64, GDB)
- The LLDB Debugger
- A64 Instruction Set Architecture
- A64 Base Instructions
- GDB to LLDB Command Map
- WinDbg and LLDB Commands
- LLDB Cheat Sheet
- Enable core dumps on Mac OS X Monterey M1 Pro
- PAC it up: Towards Pointer Integrity using ARM Pointer Authentication
- iOS Crash Dump Analysis, Second Edition
- Advanced Apple Debugging & Reverse Engineering: Exploring Apple code through LLDB, Python, and DTrace, Third Edition
- Foundations of ARM64 Linux Debugging, Disassembling, Reversing (Apress)
- Practical Foundations of macOS Debugging, Disassembling, Reversing (forthcoming)

© 2022 Software Diagnostics Services

Software Diagnostics Institute:

https://www.dumpanalysis.org/

Software Diagnostics Services:

https://www.patterndiagnostics.com
https://www.youtube.com/PatternDiagnostics

Debugging TV:

http://www.debugging.tv/
https://www.youtube.com/DebuggingTV

Accelerated Linux Core Dump Analysis, Second Edition (ARM64, WinDbg)
Accelerated Linux Core Dump Analysis, Third Edition (ARM64, GDB)

https://www.patterndiagnostics.com/accelerated-linux-core-dump-analysis-book

Accelerated Linux Disassembly, Reconstruction and Reversing (ARM64, GDB)

https://www.patterndiagnostics.com/accelerated-linux-disassembly-reconstruction-reversing-book

The LLDB Debugger

https://lldb.llvm.org/

A64 Instruction Set Architecture

https://developer.arm.com/documentation/102374/latest/

A64 Base Instructions

https://developer.arm.com/documentation/ddi0596/2021-12/Base-Instructions?lang=en

GDB to LLDB Command Map

https://lldb.llvm.org/use/map.html

WinDbg and LLDB Commands

https://gist.github.com/rafaelldi/b22efe030510eb63a71b983b27764ccf

LLDB Cheat Sheet

https://www.nesono.com/sites/default/files/lldb%20cheat%20sheet.pdf

Enable core dumps on Mac OS X Monterey M1 Pro

https://developer.apple.com/forums/thread/694233

PAC it up: Towards Pointer Integrity using ARM Pointer Authentication

https://www.usenix.org/conference/usenixsecurity19/presentation/liljestrand

App Source Code

App0

```c
//
//  main.c
//  App0 - Exercise 0 - Testing Xcode GDB
//
//  Copyright (c) 2012 - 2022 Software Diagnostics Services. All rights reserved.
//

#include <stdlib.h>

void bar()
{
    abort();
}

void foo()
{
    bar();
}

int main(int argc, const char * argv[])
{
    foo();
    return 0;
}
```

App1

```c
//
//  main.c
//  App1 - Normal application with multiple threads
//
//  Copyright (c) 2012 - 2022 Software Diagnostics Services. All rights reserved.
//

#include <stdio.h>
#include <pthread.h>
#include <unistd.h>
#include <string.h>
#include <stdlib.h>

#define THREAD_DECLARE(num) void bar_##num()\
{\
    sleep(-1);\
}\
\
void foo_##num()\
{\
    bar_##num();\
}\
\
void * thread_##num (void *arg)\
{\
    foo_##num();\
\
    return 0;\
}

THREAD_DECLARE(one)
THREAD_DECLARE(two)
THREAD_DECLARE(three)
THREAD_DECLARE(four)
THREAD_DECLARE(five)

#define THREAD_CREATE(num) {pthread_t threadID_##num; pthread_create (&threadID_##num, NULL,
thread_##num, NULL);}

int main(int argc, const char * argv[])
{
    THREAD_CREATE(one)
    THREAD_CREATE(two)
    THREAD_CREATE(three)
    THREAD_CREATE(four)
    THREAD_CREATE(five)

    sleep(-1);
    return 0;
}
```

App2

```c
//
//  main.c
//  App2 - Shows multiple exceptions: NULL data and NULL code pointers
//
//  Copyright (c) 2012 - 2022 Software Diagnostics Services. All rights reserved.
//

#include <stdio.h>
#include <pthread.h>
#include <unistd.h>
#include <string.h>
#include <stdlib.h>

void procA()
{
    int *p = NULL;
    *p = 1;
}

void procB()
{
    void (*pf)() = NULL;

    pf();
}

#define THREAD_DECLARE(num,func) void bar_##num()\
{\
func;\
}\
\
void foo_##num()\
{\
bar_##num();\
}\
\
void * thread_##num (void *arg)\
{\
foo_##num();\
\
return 0;\
}

THREAD_DECLARE(one,sleep(-1))
THREAD_DECLARE(two,procA())
THREAD_DECLARE(three,sleep(-1))
THREAD_DECLARE(four,procB())
THREAD_DECLARE(five,sleep(-1))

#define THREAD_CREATE(num) {pthread_t threadID_##num; pthread_create (&threadID_##num, NULL,
thread_##num, NULL);}
```

```
int main(int argc, const char * argv[])
{
    THREAD_CREATE(one)
    THREAD_CREATE(two)
    THREAD_CREATE(three)
    THREAD_CREATE(four)
    THREAD_CREATE(five)

    sleep(3);
    return 0;
}
```

```
//
//  main.c
//  App3 - Spiking Thread pattern
//
//  Copyright (c) 2012 - 2022 Software Diagnostics Services. All rights reserved.
//

#include <stdio.h>
#include <pthread.h>
#include <unistd.h>
#include <string.h>
#include <stdlib.h>
#include <math.h>

void procA()
{
    while (1)
    {
        sleep(1);
    }
}

void procB()
{
    double d = 1.0/3.0;
    while (1)
    {
        d = sqrt(d);
    }
}

#define THREAD_DECLARE(num,func) void bar_##num()\
{\
func;\
}\
\
void foo_##num()\
{\
bar_##num();\
}\
\
void * thread_##num (void *arg)\
{\
foo_##num();\
\
return 0;\
}

THREAD_DECLARE(one,sleep(-1))
THREAD_DECLARE(two,sleep(-1))
THREAD_DECLARE(three,procA())
THREAD_DECLARE(four,sleep(-1))
THREAD_DECLARE(five,procB())

#define THREAD_CREATE(num) {pthread_t threadID_##num; pthread_create (&threadID_##num, NULL,
thread_##num, NULL);}
```

```c
int main(int argc, const char * argv[])
{
    THREAD_CREATE(one)
    THREAD_CREATE(two)
    THREAD_CREATE(three)
    THREAD_CREATE(four)
    THREAD_CREATE(five)

    sleep(-1);
    return 0;
}
```

```
//
//  main.c
//  App4 - Heap Corruption pattern
//
//  Copyright (c) 2012 - 2022 Software Diagnostics Services. All rights reserved.
//

#include <stdio.h>
#include <pthread.h>
#include <unistd.h>
#include <string.h>
#include <stdlib.h>

void proc()
{
    char *p1 = (char *) malloc (1024);
    char *p2 = (char *) malloc (1024);
    char *p3 = (char *) malloc (1024);
    char *p4 = (char *) malloc (1024);
    char *p5 = (char *) malloc (1024);
    char *p6 = (char *) malloc (1024);
    char *p7 = (char *) malloc (1024);

    free(p6);
    free(p4);
    free(p2);

    strcpy(p2, "Hello Crash!");
    strcpy(p4, "Hello Crash!");
    strcpy(p6, "Hello Crash!");

    p2 = (char *) malloc (512);
    p4 = (char *) malloc (1024);
    p6 = (char *) malloc (512);

    sleep(300);

    free (p7);
    free (p6);
    free (p5);
    free (p4);
    free (p3);
    free (p2);
    free (p1);

    sleep(-1);
}

#define THREAD_DECLARE(num,func) void bar_##num()\
{\
func;\
}\
\
void foo_##num()\
{\
bar_##num();\
```

```c
}\
\
void * thread_##num (void *arg)\
{\
foo_##num();\
\
return 0;\
}

THREAD_DECLARE(one,sleep(-1))
THREAD_DECLARE(two,sleep(-1))
THREAD_DECLARE(three,proc())
THREAD_DECLARE(four,sleep(-1))
THREAD_DECLARE(five,sleep(-1))

#define THREAD_CREATE(num) {pthread_t threadID_##num; pthread_create (&threadID_##num, NULL,
thread_##num, NULL);}

int main(int argc, const char * argv[])
{
    THREAD_CREATE(one)
    THREAD_CREATE(two)
    THREAD_CREATE(three)
    THREAD_CREATE(four)
    THREAD_CREATE(five)

    sleep(-1);
    return 0;
}
```

App5

```c
//
//  main.c
//  App5 - Local Buffer Overflow
//
//  Copyright (c) 2012 - 2022 Software Diagnostics Services. All rights reserved.
//

#include <stdio.h>
#include <pthread.h>
#include <unistd.h>
#include <string.h>
#include <stdlib.h>

void procB(char *buffer)
{
    char data[100] = "My New Bigger Buffer";
    memcpy (buffer, data, sizeof(data));
}

void procA()
{
    char data[10] = "My Buffer";
    procB(data);
}

#define THREAD_DECLARE(num,func) void bar_##num()\
{\
func;\
}\
\
void foo_##num()\
{\
bar_##num();\
}\
\
void * thread_##num (void *arg)\
{\
foo_##num();\
\
return 0;\
}

THREAD_DECLARE(one,procA())
THREAD_DECLARE(two,sleep(-1))
THREAD_DECLARE(three,sleep(-1))
THREAD_DECLARE(four,sleep(-1))
THREAD_DECLARE(five,sleep(-1))

#define THREAD_CREATE(num) {pthread_t threadID_##num; pthread_create (&threadID_##num, NULL,
thread_##num, NULL);}
```

```c
int main(int argc, const char * argv[])
{
    THREAD_CREATE(one)
    THREAD_CREATE(two)
    THREAD_CREATE(three)
    THREAD_CREATE(four)
    THREAD_CREATE(five)

    sleep(-1);
    return 0;
}
```

```c
//
//  main.c
//  App6 - Stack Overflow
//
//  Copyright (c) 2012 - 2022 Software Diagnostics Services. All rights reserved.
//

#include <stdio.h>
#include <pthread.h>
#include <unistd.h>
#include <string.h>
#include <stdlib.h>

void procF(int i)
{
    int buffer[128] = {-1, 0, i+1, 0, -1};

    procF(buffer[2]);
}

void procE()
{
    procF(1);
}

#define THREAD_DECLARE(num,func) void bar_##num()\
{\
sleep(300);\
func;\
}\
\
void foo_##num()\
{\
bar_##num();\
}\
\
void * thread_##num (void *arg)\
{\
foo_##num();\
\
return 0;\
}

THREAD_DECLARE(one,procE())
THREAD_DECLARE(two,sleep(-1))
THREAD_DECLARE(three,sleep(-1))
THREAD_DECLARE(four,sleep(-1))
THREAD_DECLARE(five,sleep(-1))

#define THREAD_CREATE(num) {pthread_t threadID_##num; pthread_create (&threadID_##num, NULL, thread_##num, NULL);}
```

```
int main(int argc, const char * argv[])
{
    THREAD_CREATE(one)
    THREAD_CREATE(two)
    THREAD_CREATE(three)
    THREAD_CREATE(four)
    THREAD_CREATE(five)

    sleep(-1);
    return 0;
}
```

```c
//
//  main.c
//  App7 - Divide by Zero and Active Threads
//
//  Copyright (c) 2012 - 2022 Software Diagnostics Services. All rights reserved.
//

#include <stdio.h>
#include <pthread.h>
#include <unistd.h>
#include <string.h>
#include <stdlib.h>

void procF(int i)
{
    int buffer[1024] = {-1, 0, i+1, 0, -1};

    procF(buffer[2]);
}

void procE()
{
    procF(1);
}

int procD(int a, int b)
{
    return a/b;
}

int procC()
{
    return procD(1,0);
}

void procB(char *buffer)
{
    char data[100] = "My New Bigger Buffer";
    memcpy (buffer, data, sizeof(data));
}

void procA()
{
    char data[10] = "My Buffer";
    procB(data);
}

#define THREAD_DECLARE(num,func) void bar_##num()\
{\
sleep(300);\
func;\
}\
\
void foo_##num()\
{\
bar_##num();\
```

```
}\
\
void * thread_##num (void *arg)\
{\
foo_##num();\
\
return 0;\
}

THREAD_DECLARE(one,procA())
THREAD_DECLARE(two,sleep(-1))
THREAD_DECLARE(three,procC())
THREAD_DECLARE(four,sleep(-1))
THREAD_DECLARE(five,procE())

#define THREAD_CREATE(num) {pthread_t threadID_##num; pthread_create (&threadID_##num, NULL,
thread_##num, NULL);}

int main(int argc, const char * argv[])
{
    THREAD_CREATE(one)
    THREAD_CREATE(two)
    THREAD_CREATE(three)
    THREAD_CREATE(four)
    THREAD_CREATE(five)

    sleep(-1);
    return 0;
}
```

```cpp
//
//  main.cpp
//  App8 - C++ Exception, Execution Residue, Handled Exception
//
//  Copyright (c) 2012 - 2022 Software Diagnostics Services. All rights reserved.
//

#include <unistd.h>
#include <string>

#define def_call(name,x,y) void name##_##x() { name##_##y(); }
#define def_final(name,x) void name##_##x() { }
#define def_init(name,y,size) void name() { int arr[size]; name##_##y(); *arr=0; }

def_final(work,9)
def_call(work,8,9)
def_call(work,7,8)
def_call(work,6,7)
def_call(work,5,6)
def_call(work,4,5)
def_call(work,3,4)
def_call(work,2,3)
def_call(work,1,2)
def_init(work,1,256)

class Exception
{
    int code;
    std::string description;

public:
    Exception(int _code, std::string _desc) : code(_code), description(_desc) {}
};

void procB()
{
    throw new Exception(5, "Access Denied");
}

void procNB()
{
    work();
}

void procA()
{
    procB();
}

void procNA()
{
    procNB();
}
```

```
void procH()
{
    try {
        procA();
    } catch (...) {
        sleep(-1);
    }
}

void procNH()
{
    sleep(300);
    procA();
}

void procNE()
{
    try {
        procNA();
    }
    catch (...)
    {
    }
    sleep(-1);
}

#define THREAD_DECLARE(num,func) void bar_##num()\
{\
func;\
}\
\
void foo_##num()\
{\
bar_##num();\
}\
\
void * thread_##num (void *arg)\
{\
foo_##num();\
\
return 0;\
}

THREAD_DECLARE(one,procNH())
THREAD_DECLARE(two,procNE())
THREAD_DECLARE(three,procH())
THREAD_DECLARE(four,procNE())
THREAD_DECLARE(five,procNE())

#define THREAD_CREATE(num) {pthread_t threadID_##num; pthread_create (&threadID_##num, NULL,
thread_##num, NULL);}
```

```
int main(int argc, const char * argv[])
{
    THREAD_CREATE(one)
    THREAD_CREATE(two)
    THREAD_CREATE(three)
    THREAD_CREATE(four)
    THREAD_CREATE(five)

    sleep(-1);
    return 0;
}
```

```c
//
//  main.c
//  App9 - Heap Leak pattern
//
//  Copyright (c) 2012 - 2022 Software Diagnostics Services. All rights reserved.
//

#include <stdio.h>
#include <pthread.h>
#include <unistd.h>
#include <string.h>
#include <stdlib.h>

void procD()
{
}

typedef void (**PFUNC)();

void procC(int iter)
{
    for (int i = 0; i < iter; ++i)
    {
        char *p = malloc(1024);
        strcpy(p, "allocated memory");

        *(PFUNC)(p + 32) = &procD;
    }
}

void procB()
{
    procC(600000);
    sleep(300);
    procC(600000);
    sleep(-1);
}

void procA()
{
    procC(2000);
    sleep(300);
    procB();
}

#define THREAD_DECLARE(num,func) void bar_##num()\
{\
func;\
}\
\
void foo_##num()\
{\
bar_##num();\
}\
\
```

```
void * thread_##num (void *arg)\
{\
foo_##num();\
\
return 0;\
}

THREAD_DECLARE(one,sleep(-1))
THREAD_DECLARE(two,procA())
THREAD_DECLARE(three,sleep(-1))
THREAD_DECLARE(four,sleep(-1))
THREAD_DECLARE(five,sleep(-1))

#define THREAD_CREATE(num) {pthread_t threadID_##num; pthread_create (&threadID_##num, NULL,
thread_##num, NULL);}

int main(int argc, const char * argv[])
{
    THREAD_CREATE(one)
    THREAD_CREATE(two)
    THREAD_CREATE(three)
    THREAD_CREATE(four)
    THREAD_CREATE(five)

    sleep(-1);
    return 0;
}
```

```c
//
//  main.c
//  App10 - Heap Corruption, Heap Contention, Critical Region, Wait Chains, Self-Diagnostics
patterns
//
//  Copyright (c) 2012 - 2022 Software Diagnostics Services. All rights reserved.
//

#include <stdio.h>
#include <pthread.h>
#include <unistd.h>
#include <string.h>
#include <stdlib.h>

#define ARR_SIZE 10000

char *pAllocBuf [ARR_SIZE] = {0};

void proc()
{
    while (1)
    {
        int idx = rand()%ARR_SIZE;
        int malloc_size = rand()%ARR_SIZE;

        if (pAllocBuf[idx])
        {
            free(pAllocBuf[idx]);
            pAllocBuf[idx] = 0;
        }

        pAllocBuf[idx] = malloc(malloc_size);
    }
}

#define THREAD_DECLARE(num,func) void bar_##num()\
{\
func;\
}\
\
void foo_##num()\
{\
bar_##num();\
}\
\
void * thread_##num (void *arg)\
{\
foo_##num();\
\
return 0;\
}

THREAD_DECLARE(one,proc())
THREAD_DECLARE(two,proc())
THREAD_DECLARE(three,proc())
THREAD_DECLARE(four,proc())
```

```
THREAD_DECLARE(five,proc())

#define THREAD_CREATE(num) {pthread_t threadID_##num; pthread_create (&threadID_##num, NULL,
thread_##num, NULL);}

int main(int argc, const char * argv[])
{
    THREAD_CREATE(one)
    THREAD_CREATE(two)
    THREAD_CREATE(three)
    THREAD_CREATE(four)
    THREAD_CREATE(five)

    sleep(-1);
    return 0;
}
```

```
//
//  main.c
//  App11 - Wait Chains, Deadlock, Handled Exception patterns
//
//  Copyright (c) 2012 - 2022 Software Diagnostics Services. All rights reserved.
//

#include <stdio.h>
#include <pthread.h>
#include <unistd.h>
#include <string.h>
#include <stdlib.h>

pthread_mutex_t mutexA, mutexB;

void procC()
{
    throw 0;
}

void procA()
{
    try
    {
        pthread_mutex_lock(&mutexA);
        procC();
        pthread_mutex_unlock(&mutexA);
    }
    catch(...)
    {

    }

    sleep(20);
    pthread_mutex_lock(&mutexB);
    pthread_mutex_unlock(&mutexB);
}

void procB()
{
    pthread_mutex_lock(&mutexB);
    pthread_mutex_lock(&mutexA);
    sleep(30);
    pthread_mutex_lock(&mutexA);
    pthread_mutex_lock(&mutexB);
}

#define THREAD_DECLARE(num,func) void bar_##num()\
{\
func;\
}\
\
void foo_##num()\
{\
bar_##num();\
}\
```

```
\
void * thread_##num (void *arg)\
{\
foo_##num();\
\
return 0;\
}

THREAD_DECLARE(one,sleep(-1))
THREAD_DECLARE(two,procA())
THREAD_DECLARE(three,sleep(-1))
THREAD_DECLARE(four,procB())
THREAD_DECLARE(five,sleep(-1))

#define THREAD_CREATE(num) {pthread_t threadID_##num; pthread_create (&threadID_##num, NULL,
thread_##num, NULL);}

int main(int argc, const char * argv[])
{
    pthread_mutex_init(&mutexA, NULL);
    pthread_mutex_init(&mutexB, NULL);

    THREAD_CREATE(one)
    THREAD_CREATE(two)
    sleep(10);
    THREAD_CREATE(three)
    THREAD_CREATE(four)
    THREAD_CREATE(five)

    sleep(-1);
    return 0;
}
```

www.ingramcontent.com/pod-product-compliance
Lightning Source LLC
Chambersburg PA
CBHW041726210326

41598CB00008B/788